George R. Bliss

Commentary on the Gospel of Luke

Volume 2

George R. Bliss

Commentary on the Gospel of Luke
Volume 2

ISBN/EAN: 9783337285579

Printed in Europe, USA, Canada, Australia, Japan

Cover: Foto ©Lupo / pixelio.de

More available books at **www.hansebooks.com**

ON THE

GOSPEL OF LUKE.

BY
GEORGE R. BLISS, D. D.

PHILADELPHIA:
AMERICAN BAPTIST PUBLICATION SOCIETY,
1420 Chestnut Street.

Entered, according to Act of Congress, in the year 1884, by the
AMERICAN BAPTIST PUBLICATION SOCIETY,
In the Office of the Librarian of Congress, at Washington, D. C.

PREFACE.

The work of a commentary, so far as exposition is concerned, is superseded, to a considerable extent, by an adequate translation. The volumes in the series to which this belongs proceed on the basis of our Common Version (C. V.). This requires amendment in many places, and the attempt is often made in this work to effect the necessary modification, in citing the portion of the text to be commented on. Changes are placed in parentheses, or are separated from the general text by the use of the dash, and substitutions are printed in Italics. These are generally taken from the Revised Version (R. V.), which also stands at the head of the page. A commentary on the familiar version thus improved may become practically a commentary on the Revised Version. The different renderings afforded us from that source, are by no means always absolutely the best, especially as the ground-work of an interpretation; but their relation to the context can be conveniently seen, and they carry with them the authority of that very able body of scholars by whom the recent revision was effected. However far their work may seem to have fallen below perfection, regarded as a substitute for the Testament of King James' Revisers, the present writer, at least, is confirmed in the opinion that it very seldom deviates from the latter without more adequately conveying the sense of the text which it adopts. This is assuredly one prime excellence of a translation.

As regards the Greek Text here followed,[1] the author has made constant reference to the critical editions of Lachmann, Tregelles, Tischendorf, Westcott and Hort, and occasionally, to the beautiful pages of Griesbach. (4 Parts in 2 Vols. fol.: Leipzig, 1803–1807). He has also had easy access, in cases where it seemed important, to the magnificient fac-simile editions of the Codices ℵ and B, the former by Tischendorf, the latter by Vercellone and several coadjutors; to Cowper's edition of Codex A; to Kipling's fac-simile, and Scrivener's better edition in common type, of Cod. D. These are largely superseded for practical use by the critical editions of Tischendorf and Tregelles. Very convenient for comparison of manuscript readings is E. H. Hansell's *Novum Testamentum Græce*, in 4 volumes, 8vo, showing in parallel columns the texts of A B C D, with a separate collation of readings of the Sinaitic manuscript.

The full use of these manuscript materials presupposes, beside a rare natural gift for such work, an amount of special devotion to their study, to which the

---

[1] See the General Introduction to the Complete Commentary, by the General Editor, pp. xxxiv.-xliii., preceding Rev. Dr. W. N. Clark's Commentary on Mark.

writer makes no pretension. One may find them helpful sometimes, in weighing the diverse opinions of the great experts above named, to whom Scrivener, on account of his abundant work in aid of textual criticism, should by all means be added. He contends bravely and ably to guide and check the tendency which, since Griesbach began, a hundred years ago, has moved steadily toward the substitution, in place of the truly hap-hazard form of the New Testament which was first published in print in A. D. 1516, and, with no material change, again and again, until it became in 1624 the Received Text—toward the substitution for this of a text established on the earliest attainable authority of manuscript, confirmed by the earliest versions and testimony of the Christian Fathers. The recent edition of Westcott and Hort shows the issue of this tendency, in a Greek New Testament which restores, indeed, some words and phrases omitted by previous editions, but more often shocks our feeling of attachment to passages familiar and edifying to us, by proving them the work of mistaken or officious copyists of later times. Protracted familiarity with this work, however, seems to us calculated to give one the impression of a peculiar homogeneity and intrinsic consistency, so that one becomes almost ready to think it could not be expanded by many additions without manifest deterioration. As a contribution to Textual Criticism of the New Testament, their work, as explained in the Introduction and Appendix, has the virtue of proposing objective, tangible, and apparently scientific reasons why a very few early uncial manuscripts should outweigh in authority a multitude of later ones, whether uncial or cursive. In particular, they present a view of the character of the two earliest manuscripts, ℵ and B, which can be deliberately tested, and their judgment that "readings common to ℵ and B are virtually readings of a lost manuscript above two centuries earlier" (as early therefore as the last years of Polycarp), offers a definite, and most important, topic of argument. A decisive discussion of this point, and of some other characteristic views of Westcott and Hort is now naturally to be expected, and, if it can be conducted thoroughly on the other side by Scrivener and men like him, is much to be desired. It may either confirm the principles on which all progress in criticism has been made, and on which, as at last stated, a Text may solidly stand, or (*absit omen*) will leave us still under the necessity of counting the manuscripts, pro and con, on each verse, and of choosing, after all, which reading *we like best*. Men competent to do this work are notoriously few, and, considering the native character, the irksome training, and, we may add, the divine grace required for its effectual accomplishment, are not likely ever to be numerous. Dr. John Brown McClellan, in his learned work, *The New Testament, a New Translation*, etc., Vol. I.: London, 1875, pp. xxi.–xxxvii., and *passim*, evinces much attention to the Text, and zeal for its purity, but also a passionate perturbation of judgment, almost as if his devotion to the Internal Evidence had carried him into a belief in himself as an original source of revelation. Still more truly is the great learning of the Quarterly Reviewer[1] lost on men of deliberation, through the frantic

[1] *Quarterly Review*, Oct. 1881. The Revised New Testament: the New Greek Text.

outbursts of what seem personal griefs and hostilities in which it abounds. It is evidence which is needed, not personal feelings; evidence mainly external, documentary; but at all events evidence which carries light, dry light, to the understanding of those who are interested to know what is the word of God.

In this Commentary, where the writer's judgment in regard to the text agrees with that of the Anglo-American Revisers, he has often followed that without remark. The deliberate conclusions of such a body of scholars, including within their number the names of Tregelles (too soon removed from earthly work), Scrivener, Westcott, Hort, Bishops Ellicott and Lightfoot, and, in the American section, that of Dr. Ezra Abbot, certainly, carry with them a very strong presumption in their favor. Did we not know that, under the Rules which governed their action, any number of the names above mentioned might be in the minority upon each question decided concerning the Text, it would seem presumptuous to question its validity. As it is, good reasons may justify any one in forming a different judgment.

The commentary on the text in this volume aims simply to aid the reader to understand the Gospel as one of its first readers would supposably do. This involves, besides correctness of the translation, and the due grammatical explanation of clauses and sentences, special care in tracing the continuous train of thought, and the needed historical, local, and archæological information, something of which even the first readers of the Gospel may have required. Through and beyond all this the purpose has been to make plain Luke's own conception of the person, the life, the character, and the achievements of Him who was the glorious and beloved theme of this most beautiful record. Did any one ever attempt such a task without being made ashamed of his failure to accomplish it aright?

Greek words have been quoted only where it seemed necessary; but the original text has been constantly regarded as the ultimate source of the sense.

To hit the proper medium of copiousness in annotation, where a wide variety of readers is in view, is difficult; and here will be occasion for charity of judgment on the part of those who would prefer less, or more.

On a few points of Biblico-theological importance the author has indulged in somewhat extended remarks, but generally little has been attempted of practical or homiletical comment. It has seemed best to stop with trying to help each reader to a position where he can make his own comments.

Only occasional and partial attention has been given to the harmonizing of Luke's narrative with those of the other evangelists. This, which is conceived to be a matter of real importance, as it would be where there is a plurality of testimonies about any matter of history, requires, in the more perplexing cases, an exhibition of fundamental principles, as well as of the details proper to an independent work, and need not intervene to hinder our distinct apprehension of the view of each sacred author.

The prescribed limits of the volume, and the varied circles of readers contemplated, alike forbade the full discussion of particular expositions. The writer has carefully considered, on all points of doubt, the views of many authorities, for and against, and has set down his own conclusions. Indeed, the exegetical apparatus furnished in the Bucknell Library of this Seminary, reaching from Origen to Plumptre and B. Weiss, almost of the present year, warrants the writer in saying with fullest confidence, that he has uttered no thought that has not for substance been said before him; and that something to the contrary has been said by somebody on every point. His most useful helpers, after all, have been, naturally, among the more recent. Van Oosterzee, in Lange's Commentary, has produced a very valuable work, especially in his Doctrinal Ethical additions. His exegesis is able, and occasionally suggests the hand of a systematic theologian rather than of a strict interpreter. Meyer and Godet are the two great lights on this Gospel, but each needing complement and correction from the other. The former, with great depth of intellectual discernment, and exactness of exposition, often betrays a disbelief of the full credibility of the evangelist, and a lack of spiritual appreciation of the truth which he discloses to us; the latter shows cordial reverence and love for the inspired word, which, however, leaves him occasionally to attempt real *tours de force* in gaining a desired, possibly a novel and fanciful, sense. Together they have done so well that where they are both at hand, no *scholar* will suffer for lack of Commentaries on Luke. Farrar's Commentary, in the Cambridge Bible for Schools, is interesting, of course, applying to this use much matter condensed from his Life of Christ, and in various respects has been useful here, in the final revision of what had been written.

The writer cannot put the finishing touch to his present work without emotion. For several years, in fragments of the time, and in vacation periods, through solid weeks of continuous application, it has been before his mind and on his heart. No man can see so clearly as he how much more perfect the result ought to have been. But he thanks the Supreme Author of the Gospel for having been enabled even thus to bring it to a close, and devoutly prays that it may be made the means of some good. He can say with Bishop Horne, in the Preface to his Commentary on the Book of Psalms: "Could the author flatter himself that any one would take half the pleasure in reading the following exposition which he hath taken in writing it, he would not fear the loss of his labor." He might add, slightly changing the Bishop's words: "Happier hours than those which have been spent on these meditations upon the Gospel of the Son of man, he never expects to see in this world. Very pleasantly did they pass, and moved smoothly and swiftly along; for when thus engaged, he counted no time. They are gone, but have left a relish and a fragrance on the mind, and the remembrance of them is sweet."

GEORGE R. BLISS.

CROZER THEOLOGICAL SEMINARY, *Jan. 10, 1884.*

INTRODUCTION TO THE GOSPEL OF LUKE.

THE AUTHOR.

The name Luke occurs three times in the Epistles of Paul—Col. 4 : 14; Philem 24 ; 2 Tim. 4 : 11. In all these it represents some faithful and highly esteemed fellow-laborer of the apostle, in the gospel. In the first passage the latter associates him with himself in the salutations to the Church at Colosse : "Luke, the beloved physician, and Demas, salute you." Here we learn that he was by profession a physician, to whom the apostle was tenderly attached ; and, from the description of those named with him, that he was engaged in the furtherance of the gospel. It is also extremely probable, in fact almost certain, from the way in which Paul, in verse 11, distinguishes those previously mentioned as "of the circumcision," that Luke, with Epaphras and Demas, was of Gentile birth. This perfectly agrees with all the other indications concerning him. The reference shows that he was with the apostle in Rome at the date of the letter to the Colossians, A. D. 63 or 64. The mention of him in Philemon 24 only adds evidence that he was in Rome about that time, as a fellow-laborer with Paul, with Mark also, and Aristarchus. That he is *not* mentioned in the salutations of the letter to the Philippians, written also from Rome during that imprisonment, renders it probable that he was not with the apostle, although it cannot show whether this was earlier or later. Second Timothy 4 : 11, was written three or four years later, and proves Luke to have been in the same place, as the only helper present with Paul, in his second imprisonment, and at the last stage of his life.

This Luke has been recognized, from the earliest times, and still is, by a great majority even of the most unrestrained Biblical critics, as the author of our third Gospel.

While he is not named elsewhere in the New Testament, he presents himself freely in those parts of the Acts of the Apostles, where the writer speaks in the first person plural ("we came," etc.) 16 : 11–17 ; 20 : 5, and *passim*. We see plainly, from such passages, that the author of the Acts traveled with the apostle on his second missionary journey, from Troas to Philippi. There he appears to have tarried until Paul, after six or seven years, returned from Achaia through Philippi, on his last visit to Jerusalem. After that we find him in company with Paul as far as to Jerusalem. At the close of the two years' imprisonment in Cesarea, the author again appears as one of the company of Paul, ready to sail for Rome. Although it is not distinctly stated, we may well suppose him to have been in the neighborhood of his teacher during the whole two years ; the more readily as we are told that Paul's friends had free access to him all the time, and as Luke's profession would, if he were dependent on it, in any town secure him the means of subsistence. Thenceforth he was with the apostle on the long and eventful voyage to the capital, and through the first two years of his captivity, as we have seen, and again in a probable second imprisonment.

Those, indeed, who assume that the writer of the whole work has only incorporated into it the passages containing "we," from the travels of some companion of Paul, escape the conclusion that the actual author was such a companion. But the assumption involves an impeachment of his literary skill, entirely gratuitous and inconsistent with his manner in general, or a slander on his honesty, which, considering the spirit of the writing, is little creditable to the morality of such critics themselves. Few deny any longer that the obvious and long received interpretation of these passages is the correct one.

The interest to us of this information lies in the fact that the writer of the Acts (1 : 1) represents himself as being, and is universally admitted to have been, the author of the Gospel bearing the name of Luke. We thus gain some incidental knowledge of him beyond, and strikingly congruous with, the import of Paul's allusions before cited. This renders us morally certain that the writer of our Gospel accompanied the great apostle, or acted in co-operation with him, for the promotion of the gospel, during ten or twelve years of his life. The relation between them was affectionate, and so close and confidential as to give Luke a most favorable opportunity to acquire whatever knowledge his teacher could impart, concerning the earthly history of our Lord. We may be sure, also, that from his intimacy with the apostle to the Gentiles, as well as from his own personal and professional character, he enjoyed special advantages, in their long journeyings together, at Antioch, Corinth, Cesarea, Jerusalem, Rome, to meet eye-witnesses of the Saviour's work, who could give him exact knowledge of the facts of the Gospel.

Of the life of Luke prior to the time when he joined Paul, at Troas, nothing is certain ; and it is scarcely possible to repeat the conjectures embodied in early traditions, still less to hazard new ones, without danger of leading many minds to ascribe greater probability to them than they at all warrant. That he was of Greek origin, is supported not only by the natural interpretation of Col. 4 : 11, and by his name, but by the purity of his Greek style, free from Hebraisms, except where he is apparently handling Aramæan reports, which he may have needed to have translated by others. Of his family, we do not know that there is even any tradition. Some later stories located his birth at Antioch, others, in southern Italy. Both suppositions are backed up with about equal force by modern writers, when they respectively urge the evidence from his special acquaintance with places in and near Italy, Acts. 28 : 11 ff, on the one part, and with the affairs of the Church at Antioch, on the other, as indicated in Acts 11 : 19, and the chapters following. We think these latter passages might justify the hypothesis that he had resided at Antioch, and there become acquainted with Paul, whom he afterward met, by design or otherwise, at Troas. His name cannot be identified with that of Lucius of Cyrene, Acts 13 : 1, by any legitimate process of transmutation. That he was converted to Christianity through Paul, is extremely probable, and that he must have sympathized with the latter in his distinguishing views of the gospel, is not only practically certain from what we have already seen, but is put beyond question by the character of the Gospel before us. So clearly was this seen, at an early day, that Eusebius, and Origen before him, assumes that when Paul used the phrase "my gospel," he meant the Gospel according to Luke, as expressing his particular view. This, however, was mere fancy. That Luke was "the brother whose praise is in the gospel throughout all the churches" (2 Cor. 8 : 18), is a supposition, plausible at least, considering that Paul was probably writing from Macedonia, during the time that Luke seems to have tarried in Philippi, and that we hear of no other one in that region likely to have merited that description. As a physician, he would naturally have had an education above that which was common. We cannot, however, hence infer any superiority of birth, since trained freedmen, or even slaves, sometimes practiced medicine. His company in this character might be a special help and comfort to the apostle, who suffered much with bodily infirmity, the pain of which was to him sometimes as "a thorn," or, more properly, "a sharp stake," "to the flesh."

Of the fortunes of the evangelist, after the date of Paul's second letter to Timothy, we can with certainty say nothing, nothing at all, of the time, place, or manner of his death.*

OCCASION AND DESIGN.

The occasion was, primarily, the religious need of a convert to Christianity, of the name of Theophilus, whose name (repeated by Luke, 1: 3; Acts 1: 1), is all that we know concerning the man. Of this, and of his apparent station and character, as we may infer from the prologue of the Gospel, we have spoken in the Notes on 1: 3. It is commonly assumed that he had embraced the gospel as presented by Paul and those who sympathized with him; a doctrine, namely, of perfectly free, gratuitous, and complete salvation, on the ground of faith in Jesus, the Son of God, as crucified for sin and raised again from the dead. At all events, within the sphere of Paul's evangelical labors, any thoughtful man would be exposed to the disturbing influence of Judaizing legalists, who would tell him that he ought to be circumcised also, and to keep the Mosaic law. Heathen skepticism also, the current philosophy, habits of early thinking, might, if he were of Gentile origin, as his name of Theophilus slightly intimates, suggest doubts and perplexities in his new faith. These, in the absence of documentary information as to the origin and history of the Christian doctrine, when, moreover, the testimony of apostles, or other eye-witnesses, was for him a rare and transient privilege, might become a serious temptation. Whatever the reason of his necessity, whether external or from within, from Jewish bigotry or from heathen associations and prejudices, our author addresses him as needing to have his faith clarified and confirmed in those teachings on which he had rested his eternal hope. He may have requested the assistance of Luke, as a friend and well known teacher, toward this end. The latter indicates (1 : 1-4) that he thought a good way to supply the want of Theophilus would be to set forth, first, in a narrative, well ordered, chronologically, and according to rational sequence of the facts, those teachings, works, sufferings of the Founder of Christianity which the apostles were wont to present to men, as best suited to prove him the fulfillment of prophecy and the Author of salvation for the world.

We need not suppose that Luke was moved to this work simply to do a favor to Theophilus. He had probably, from what he says, been long engaged in researches for something of this kind, and dedicated his work to his respected friend, not as a private letter, but with the expectation that an extensive section of the church, in the same necessity as he, would share the same help. He intended to give not only a truthful, full, consistent view, but also a somewhat different view from what others had attempted in writing, of the history of Jesus and, ultimately, of the Christian cause.

Such being the occasion, as we confidently infer, *the design*, as plainly stated by Luke

---

* It may be worth the space here to append some of the things reported, anciently, without any tangible ground of credibility, respecting Luke. Among them are, besides those just mentioned concerning the place of his birth, etc., that he was one of the seventy disciples; the companion of Cleopas on the way to Emmaus; that he labored in the gospel in Dalmatia, Italy, Gaul, Africa; that he was a painter, and painted pictures of the virgin Mary and others named; that he died when eighty-four years old, in Constantinople, in Achaia, in Bithynia; that his remains were taken to Constantinople by the Emperor Constantine, and buried in the Church of the Apostles; that he suffered martyrdom, by decapitation, by crucifixion, etc., etc. Of course, there may have been a grain of truth in some of these legends—in some of them there could not be; but without any contemporary evidence to distinguish between the true and the fictitious, we most safely leave it all in the region of fables.

in his Preface, was simply involved in that His object in writing at all, and in writing as he did, was that Theophilus might thereby "know the certainty," the "unshakable truth," (ἀσφάλεια), concerning the words in which he had been instructed. Of course, he designed that the same benefit should accrue to as many as possible, to whom, through Theophilus, the knowledge of his Gospel should come. The full accomplishment of his purpose would require the carrying forward of the work begun by Jesus, through the Book of the Acts. This, we think, was distinctly in his mind from the first, but not so as to hinder the Gospel, as introduced by its Preface, from being intended as a separate work.

THE GOSPEL.

This, on a particular examination, seems admirably suited to accomplish such a design, and lends powerful support to the views already expressed, by its perfect consistency with the supposition of such an author writing to such a friend. We note—

(1) Special familiarity with the Greek language. The first sentence of the Gospel presents us a finished period, worthy of any classical writer of the time, and such as can hardly be thought of from the hand of any other New Testament writer, unless it be the author of the Epistle to the Hebrews. This quality appears, as might be expected, more commonly in the Acts, in those parts, as the journey to Rome, where there was least of Jewish fact or discourse. In the Gospel, the subjects were so exclusively Palestinian and Hebraistic; the records of them, and the oral accounts, were so entirely in Aramæan, or in Aramaic Greek, that the faithful delivery of them to his readers, whether through his own translations or those furnished by others, would leave little room for his own unhampered style. Still, the general character and literary spirit of the Gospel may strike the mind even through a translation, as more free and flowing than that of either of the other evangelists. The narrative frequently bespeaks an intellectual as well as a doctrinal catholicity, born of the liberty of Greek thought and utterance, rather than of the stereotyped and meagre formality of Aramæan, or the rigorous inflexibility of Roman speech.

(2) The influence of Luke's profession, as a physician, on the literary character of his Gospel, is less obvious from special traits than is the case with the Book of Acts. In that, several observations occur which are very likely to have been suggested by his medical experience. The judgment of Jerome that his education for his calling contributed to the superiority of his Greek style, is very probable. And scholars have noticed the coincidence of his mention of "a great fever" in the case of Peter's mother-in-law (4: 38) with the language of Galen, Hippocrates, and Celsus, in distinguishing fevers and other diseases. See the citations in Wetstein on the passage. The mention of the "sweat like clots of blood" (22: 44) has been thought to evince the intelligence of a physician, in selecting the particulars of Christ's agony in the garden. Yet he does not hesitate, in the account of the woman with the issue of blood (8: 43), to tell us that the physicians had not been able to help her, though he does not add, like Mark, that, besides spending her fortune in vain, she had grown worse.

It is more in the general tone of his writing, the wide interest which he betrays in people of every quality, of both sexes, and of all ages and conditions, that we seem to see the spirit of a physician, experienced, genial, and kind, according to the epithet "beloved." (Col. 4: 14). It was, to be sure, Christ's own universality of concern for all humanity which Luke is faithfully relating; but it is because he also thinks nothing human foreign to himself that he, pre-eminently, is led to bring forward these traits of the Saviour's ministry and life. He must, probably, have obtained from Mary, or other members of the family of our Lord, the particulars of the birth, infancy, and boyhood of Jesus, and of John the Baptist, which he gives as additional to those presented by Matthew. In his case, too, it is not from a necessity to show the fulfillment of prophecy, and the evidence of a divine origin, so much as to satisfy a human interest in the complete history of the Son of man. He, too, preserves the language of Jesus which shows him attentive to the sports of children, (7 : 31 ff). He alone mentions that when Jesus commended the example of a child to his disciples (9 : 47), "he took the little child and set him by his side." In Luke alone (10 : 38-41), we have treasured for us that gem of the Gospel, the fireside scene with Jesus in the midst, at the house of Martha and Mary. He also tells, what we should not otherwise know, of the ministry of certain faithful women, who cared for the comfort of Jesus and his disciples in their journeys, following him even to Jerusalem, to the cross, to the tomb, (8 : 1 ff ; 23 : 49, 55). These and other women, as Luke informs us, Jesus addressed—"daughters of Jerusalem"—while on the way to Calvary, although his lips were sealed toward every one besides, (23 : 28). His social quality appears in the easy affability of some of the parables and instructions of the Saviour, as reported by him, (7 : 40 ff ; 14 : 7-14 ; 18 : 2-6). The gentleness of Christ, his consideration for the deficiencies and failures of men in their imperfect piety, his charity, in short, toward such as others would condemn, appears in several peculiar traits of Luke's narrative, and reflects its light on the disposition of the compiler. See 5 : 39 ; 9 : 54-56 ; 12 : 48 ; 15 : 28-32 ; 22 : 24-30 ; 23 : 34 ; comp. Acts 3 : 17.

(3) The indications of intimate companionship and co-operation with Paul. It is not strange that some of the Fathers, as was said, suspected that the apostle referred to Luke's writing, when he said "my gospel." The character and training of Luke led him, in providing for the satisfaction of the inquiries of Theophilus, to produce just such an account of Jesus Christ as is pre-supposed in all the Pauline doctrine of salvation. The indispensableness to all men of God's righteousness through faith in Jesus ; the provision of salvation for all ; and the free offer of it to all,—appear as distinctly in our Gospel as in the Epistle to the Romans. It is not, as has been sometimes represented, a Gospel specifically adapted to the Gentiles—Marcion had to mutilate it to render it such— still less, perhaps, is it for the Jews, although dwelling much on the teachings and institutions of the Old Testament. It refers to "the law" more frequently than Matthew ; Mark does not once name it. Particular expressions in unusual number might suit the views of a Gentile, but others would please a Jew, even a Pharisee. As a whole, the writing was for neither. but for both. It was for and against Jew ; for and against Gentile ; because it was for the human race.

Not only as between Jew and Gentile, but between the various classes, grades of society, and temporal conditions within those two comprehensive sections of humanity, the Christ of Luke maintains the most complete impartiality of good will. To high and low, to master and slave, to rich and poor, to Pharisee and publican, to man and woman, to parent and child, the offer of sympathy, instruction, physical cure, and soul salvation, is held forth with absolute freeness and benevolence of desire. In this respect the Gospel is fully in the spirit of Paul. Christ's blessing is here "unto all and upon all them that believe." There is also to be seen in Luke something of the Pauline qualification, "to the Jew first"; but yet this does not in the least impair the sufficiency and accessibleness of salvation to men of every sort. Nay, we easily trace the peculiar warmth of our author's interest in the welfare of the least favored of human beings, the least happy, the least good. The grace of God "which bringeth salvation to all men" is celebrated by him in its beneficient bearing on the most deeply lost—even on the corrupt and benighted heathen. Our Gospel welcomes every one to the rich provision of eternal life, but goes forth most intensely toward the needy, helpless, diseased, and outcast of the earth, rejoicing, with the angels in heaven, over one sinner that repenteth, more than over ninety and nine righteous, who have no need of repentance.

This Pauline universality of the theory of salvation, with a preponderance of personal interest in the classes and individuals who seemed most to need the gospel, determines to some perceptible extent the selection and distribution of material throughout Luke's narrative. This opens with an account of the birth of our Lord's forerunner, of a priestly stock, in connection with the national temple, yet far removed in character and station from the Sadducaic magnates, or the religious nobility of the time. Jesus himself is born of a humble maiden, in circumstances below those of ordinary poverty; and angels celebrate the fact as one of supreme joyfulness to heaven and earth, in the presence of humble shepherds. The Genealogy traces back his line, beyond the beginning of the Hebrew stock in Abraham, through the whole course of humanity, and thence to God, whom it binds, through Jesus, to all mankind. Zacharias had dimly seen (1 : 79) that his coming was to "give light to them that sit in darkness and in the shadow of death," and Simeon, with the infant in his arms, thanked God for him as "a light (Revision) for revelation to the Gentiles, and the glory of thy people Israel." The infancy, childhood, and early maturity of Jesus were spent, as Luke causes us to see, in the retirement of domestic village life. His first reported discourse, 4 : 16–27, revealed him as the Messiah promised in the prophecy, and implied, at its close, that God might send the salvation which he had announced to their dull, though wondering ears, to heathen sinners as well as to them. The Sermon on the Mount (ch. 6) omits all that concerned the law (comp. Matt. 5 : 17–43). In the house of a Pharisee he receives the adoration of a repenting woman "which was in the city, a sinner" (7 : 36–50), and shows the proud and self-righteous, how her faith and love won blessings unattainable for them. In the instructions to the twelve apostles (9 : 1–6), no prohibitions against crossing the boundaries of the Jews are recorded; and the mission of the seventy (10 : 1–11), at a time when access to the fields which he had so faithfully striven to occupy in Galilee seemed to be cut off, might indicate that their rejection of his salvation (10 : 12–16), was preparing for the wider diffusion of the blessing in other lands. He had no scruple against entering the territory of the Samaritans, in the course of his journeys (9 : 52); and when he would picture brotherly love such as the law required (10 : 25–37), he presents it in the conduct of a worse than heathen—a Samaritan. By the parable of the barren fig-tree (13 : 6–9), he warned the Jewish nation that the mercy which yearned over them would soon turn to condemnation; and solemnly predicts their sorrow and dismay when they find themselves shut out of the banquet of his kingdom, where men from every quarter of the earth will be the guests. The lesson of the great supper (14 : 15–24), should have impressed the truth that the privileges which they had scorned and forfeited, would be given to people whom they despised. The three beautiful parables in chapter 15, although they do not directly celebrate the joy of God in the conversion of heathen men, yet refer directly to men who were worse than heathen in the view of Pharisees, and indirectly might well suggest the widest application to all mankind. Of the ten lepers who desired cleansing (17 : 12–17), Jew and Samaritan shared alike in the physical blessing, but the Samaritan alone is shown to have received spiritual cure. The parable of the vineyard (20: 9-17), reveals in startling terms that the theocracy, which had been entrusted to the unwilling Jews, was about to be taken from them and given to others—but to whom? The ominous word "Gentiles," in the solemn prophecy uttered on the Mount of Olives, that same day at evening, showed to whom: "and Jerusalem shall be trodden down of the Gentiles, until the times of the Gentiles be fulfilled" (21 : 24). In his parting charge (24 : 47), the risen Master orders that "repentance and remission of sins should be preached among all nations." We need not quote evidence that Jesus in this Gospel offered salvation to the seed of Abraham of every class. None of the Gospels could prove this more plainly. The above passages, additional, for the most part, to what it has in common with the rest, may serve to show the peculiar sympathy of the writer with the sentiment of Paul, that the blessing was provided and sent to the Jew first, indeed, but also and unstintedly to the Greek.

SOURCES OF KNOWLEDGE.

Our author himself has happily given the needed explanation on this point, in his opening sentence. That is discussed in the Commentary. A few remarks may here be allowable, to show how the present writer conceives of the circumstances attending the origin of this Gospel. Luke probably knew nothing of the writing of Matthew, or of Mark, (of course not of John's). As a Greek (in the wide application of that name), he would feel none of those scruples, and be liable to none of those hindrances which naturally kept the original apostles from early attempting written memoirs of their glorified Lord. Some interested hearers of the apostles (Mark was such toward Peter), probably first put in writing what they heard told of the works and words of Jesus. The apostles, laboring together, principally in Jerusalem, for several years, had, in the absence of written records, fixed upon such parts of the boundless subject of Christ's mission as experience had proved most useful in bringing men to believe in him as their Saviour. His most striking words would be repeated with literal exactness, and his language, generally, would be more nearly stereotyped in a common form, than the accounts of facts. The discourses would, some of them, be illustrated by connection with the related events in Christ's life. Thus groups of associated facts and discourses would become crystallized in combinations such as we may see in our Synoptic Gospels, substanstantially the same with all, yet not precluding liberty in the individual relators, according to their several recollections of the subject matter. The foundation of all this, to a great extent the execution of all, was the work of the apostles. Its use was not intended as a history of Christ's life, or a biography, in any proper sense, but for practical instruction—"preaching," or the relation of such truth from and about Jesus, as would on each occasion be best suited to produce faith and conversion. Such was for many years the preached "gospel." When it came to be written, each recorder would take down more or less of it, from the lips now of one, now of another apostle, and his work might grow to be of considerable length. Before any one of the original apostles had accomplished the writing of a complete narrative (it was early believed that Matthew did this first, in the Aramæan tongue), "many" had, according to Luke (1: 1), done something of this preliminary work, whose attempts, though only partially satisfactory, were known to him. In regard to these, he had opportunity during his travels through the scenes of Christ's life to learn how far they presented the apostolic teaching. He saw, doubtless, different apostles personally, and other eye-witnesses, as Mary the mother of Jesus, and his brothers, with whom he could compare and complete the accounts which he was gathering. These included some not communicated to us in other Gospels, but specially suited to his purpose, and interesting to his turn of mind. Finally, let us recall what we have seen of his close association with the Apostle Paul, and we may be at no loss as to how Luke, though not an apostle, or one directly acquainted with Jesus, acquired the rich store of truth which has rendered his charming narrative a treasure of the Christian world. His account of the Lord's Supper, compared with 1 Cor. 11: 24-26, shows an identity of view, as does his mention (24: 34) of the Lord's appearance to Peter after the resurrection (comp. 1 Cor. 15: 5). It is doubtful whether Paul ever saw a complete Gospel in writing, but we cannot doubt that if he had read that of "the beloved physician," it would have answered to the conception of his own heart.

DATE.

The limit below which this cannot fall, is indicated by Luke himself. It must have been earlier than the composition of the Acts (see Acts 1 : 1), and the Acts may have been completed about A. D. 64 (see Hackett, *Commentary on the Acts*, Intro. p. 19). However the Gospel could not have been written later than about A. D. 70, when Jerusalem was captured and the temple destroyed. This appears from the eschatological discourse in 21 : 20 ff. In the other Synoptics Jesus appears to associate directly the destruction of Jerusalem with his second advent for the full, eternal redemption of his followers, so that the latter shall follow "immediately" upon the other. In Luke, the report of the discourse, differing in other respects from Mark, and still more from Matthew, makes a period of the subjugation of Jerusalem by Gentiles (v. 24) to intervene after its capture, before the redemption shall draw nigh. But that Luke does not understand this to mean any long period, is evident, since he also gives, in ver. 32, the declaration: "This generation shall not pass away, till all things be accomplished" (Revision). Compare for a like understanding of what naturally seems to be a long period, 2 Thess. 2: 3-8, with 1 Thess. 4: 15, 17. We might suppose, in consistency with this, that Luke wrote a short time *after* A. D. 70; but the general identity, in matter and form, of his work with that of the other Synoptics, its contrast with that of John, which *was* written later; the fact that neither in the Gospel, nor even in the Acts, does he make allusion to anything of later date than Paul's first captivity; that he was ignorant of Matthew's Gospel, in its present form, and of Mark's, so far as appears; lastly, that his representation of the state, organization, and officers of the church in his day, is so widely different from what we find existing in the second half of the second century, all render it decidedly more likely that the Gospel was written not later than the destruction of Jerusalem. As to the place of the writing, conjecture has ranged from Cesarea, through Asia Minor and Greece, to Rome.

GENUINENESS.

There was never any question of the authorship of this Gospel, until within about the last one hundred years. The skeptical disposition which has so largely prevailed in Biblical criticism during this period, has taken offence at the miraculous account of the origin and of the apostolic history of Christianity, and both writings of Luke, like the rest of the Bible, have been subjected to violence. Some have labored to show that this Gospel was only an adaptation of that which the heretic Marcion fabricated toward the middle of the second century. Others have supposed that as late as that, or later, some entirely unknown person, desiring to appease an assumed belligerency between a strong Jewish and Pauline party in the early church, had palmed himself off as a companion of Paul while the latter was alive, and had made up a narrative concerning Jesus and his first followers, pretending that they taught essentially in the spirit of Paul, when, in reality, it was far otherwise. The view underwent many modifications, being refuted at every new turn, as one may see in Fisher's *Beginnings of Christianity*, or Güder, Art. *Lukas*, in Herzog and Plitt's *Real Encyclopädie*. The latter writer, after stating the chief suppositions of recent criticism on the subject, reverent and irreverent, concludes with the judgment that the reasons for the authorship of the Acts, and so of the Gospel also, by Luke, are incomparably stronger than for any other supposition which has been advanced; and even that the very working out of these suppositions, tends ever still to confirm the hereditary view of Christendom. That view began to find distinct and formal expression soon after the middle of the second century, when the Muratorian Canon plainly refers the third Gospel to Luke, a companion of Paul. Justin Martyr had still earlier quoted from the Gospel in passages conveniently copied by S. Davidson in his *Introduction to the New Testament* (2 : 19-22), and had been used by Marcion, as we have already seen, probably Basilides also (about A. D. 125). See Sanday, *Gospels in the Second Century*, p. 382. Before this time it had been translated into the Old Latin, and in the earliest Syrian version of the New Testament. The Muratorian Canon is rightly supposed to have expressed the judgment of the Church at Rome, and its extensive dependencies, as the Syrian did that of the Eastern Church, and the Old Latin that of all Northern Africa. A little later, Irenæus names Luke as the author (*Adv. Hæres*, 1. 14. Euseb. E. H. 5. 8), see Davidson *Ibid* p. 24. "Clement of Alexandria adopts the same opinion, and the Fathers generally follow it." *Ibid*. When Davidson adds: "It (the Gospel) does not appear to have been known much out of Rome in their time ; nor was it preferred by them to an extra-canonical gospel or gospels which they employed along with it," he probably does not intend to place it on any other footing than our other Synoptical Gospels, and has no authority for denying that it was already, as in the Muratorian Canon, separated from all books of other than apostolical authority. Enough that before the middle of the second century, while Christian teachers were yet living who had conversed with the apostles and their associates, and were deeply interested in whatever was of importance to the cause of Christ, the Gospel of Luke was familiarly known and ascribed to Luke as its author. As such it has been used by the whole church ever since. It has been often said, and will bear repetition, that for no writing of classical antiquity have we anything like the same proof of its genuineness as we have for the Gospel of Luke. On the basis of the New Testament itself, Godet, in chapter 3, sect. 3, of his *Conclusion*, makes out a convincing argument for *Luke's* authorship, from a comparison of the proem to the Gospel with other information from the Gospel, the Acts, and the Epistles of Paul. In that *Conclusion* will be found also a very full, able, and generally satisfactory discussion of most of the questions pertaining to an Introduction to the writings of Luke.

PLAN.

That Luke followed a distinct aim in the arrangement of his material, is indicated beforehand, by the "in order" (καθεξῆς), of his Preface, and a plan was obviously necessary to reach that aim, in giving immovable certainty to Theophilus. The aim was to be reached by showing the divine origin of Jesus the Christ; his manifestation in humanity, as a babe, a boy, a young man (conversant with all these experiences of men); his external inauguration to his public office by his baptism; the intrinsic, personal inauguration by his triumph over Satan in the great temptation. This portion of the Gospel we have, in the Commentary, treated as Part First (1 : 5—4 : 13). Then follows his ministry in Galilee, Part Second (4 : 14—9 : 50), by which he gave the people abundant proofs of his Messiahship, and desire to save them; was believed on temporarily by multitudes without a true appreciation of his real character; but was distrusted, by degrees hated and persecuted by the ruling classes, and abandoned by the deluded masses, only a few of whom remained faithful. In Part Third (9 : 51—19 : 11), the author has gathered a mass of most valuable material, from a source or sources not used by the other evangelists, without apparent chronological or geographical sequence; but treated as pertaining to a slow journey toward Jerusalem, on which Jesus had resolved (9 : 59), that he might, through his sufferings, be raised to the position of a universal and an eternal Saviour.

The present incorrigibleness of the Jews, as a body, has now become hopelessly manifest; but he is, if possible, still more abundant and earnest in endeavors to save some. He takes care for an increase of laborers in the field from which he is about to be removed, and rejoices that through the ministry of such, the reign of Satan over men is in effect broken. He teaches his servants much about the work before them, the dangers and pains to which they are appointed; but assures them of ever present, effectual help from on high, of a success that shall fill the world, and of a glorious recognition by himself when he shall return (as he will) in royal majesty, for the full and eternal blessedness of his kingdom, and the separation from it of those who would not have this man to reign over them.

Part Fourth relates his triumphant entrance into Jerusalem as acknowledged Lord of the Temple; his victorious contests with the ruling sects and authorities; his clear testimonies to the truth; his provision for the fellowship of his followers in remembrance of him; his propitiatory death; accompanied with fresh and amazing proofs of his divine mission; his resurrection from the grave; his charge that the gospel should be proclaimed in his name among all the nations; and his ascension to glory (19 : 12; 24 : 53).

The evangelist thus leaves the Author of Christianity where, through the very unbelief and murderous cruelty of the Jews, he can, without respect of persons, save all alike who call upon him, and carry forward to the ends of the world that glad announcement, which has already reached as far as Rome. What could be better suited to give Theophilus that "certainty" in regard to the elementary teachings of the Gospel which he desired?

THE
GOSPEL ACCORDING TO LUKE.

CHAPTER I.

FORASMUCH as many have taken in hand to set forth in order a declaration of those things which are most surely believed among us,

1 FORASMUCH as many have taken in hand to draw up a narrative concerning those matters which have

Ch. 1: 1-4. PREFACE.

1. Forasmuch as. A conjunction of the same force as "since, indeed," it serves to connect the main verb of the sentence, "it seemed good," ver. 3, with the clauses which here follow, as in some sense its ground, or condition. In explaining why he has set out to write his Gospel, the author says he does it **forasmuch as** others have done the same, or a similar, thing.—**Many have taken in hand**—more exactly, *took in hand*. The tense, is a preterit, or indefinite past. "To take in hand" is "to undertake," "to attempt"; but the familiar phrase is more nearly true to the etymology of the original verb, "to lay hand to." It might be used equally of a right or of a reprehensible attempt, denoting a certain amount of resolution, and of itself suggests no disparagement of the effort, or intimation that it has failed of intended success. That the attempts had not resulted in such a **declaration** as Luke thought suitable for his time and purpose is all that we need suppose. That he refers to them in a past tense may possibly indicate that he thought of them as obsolete, or no longer serviceable, even in the degrees in which they might once have been so. The "many" were Christian men unknown to us; almost certainly not including either of the authors of our Canonical Gospels. John and Matthew are out of the question, for other reasons and because they were themselves among the "eye-witnesses" as afterwards spoken of, whose testimony constituted the rule according to which the "many" attempted to compose their narrations. He could not have had our Mark in mind, because, as we suppose him to have used out of those earlier "declarations" what was germane to his plan, we should find in his Gospel more of, and more like, Mark.—**To set forth in order a declaration,** etc. The Revised Version is preferable here, in several points. "*To draw up*," or "*to arrange,*" is better than **to set forth in order. A declaration** should be understood as "a narration," or "historical revelation."[1]—**Those things which are most surely believed among us,** should be, *concerning the things which have been fully accomplished among us.* The Greek verb means primarily "to bring full," then "to make full," "to complete." This is spoken of things, (2 Tim. 4:5, 17). "Make full proof of (*fully perform*) thy ministry;" "that by me the preaching (*proclamation*) might be fully known (*fully accomplished*)." In the Bible, and in later Christian writers, it was used to signify specially "to cause full belief," so that in the passive it is rightly translated "to be fully persuaded," "let every man be fully persuaded," (Rom. 14:5; comp. 4:21). But for this, manifestly, a person must be the subject. Of things, it is only said that they "are completely done." Whether in our passage it is employed in the sense of a cognate Greek verb, "to fulfill," as if Luke had in mind the fulfillment of prophecy in the **things,** facts, or topics treated of in the Gospel, or matters of which he speaks, is uncertain. So the Revised Version seems to view it. **Those things**—as appears from what follows, are the facts concerning Christ's life, words, works, sufferings, humiliation, death, resurrection, and ascension to glory; all, in short, which constituted the theme of the original preaching. These had, before the time of Luke's writing, and before that of the previous attempts, fully come to pass, or been accomplished. **Among us**—as Christians, whom Luke identifies as being

---

[1] It has been doubted even whether their "declaration," which must of course be understood distributively—the declaration of each—was a written or an oral account. The fact that Luke in proposing to "write" (ver. 3), supports himself by their example, would seem to settle the question.

2 ᵃ Even as they delivered them unto us, which ᵇ from the beginning were eyewitnesses, and ministers of the word;
3 ᶜ It seemed good to me also, having had perfect understanding of all things from the very first, to write unto thee ᵈ in order, ᵉ most excellent Theophilus,

2 been ¹fulfilled among us, even as they delivered them unto us, who from the beginning were eye-
3 witnesses and ministers of the word, it seemed good to me also, having traced the course of all things accurately from the first, to write unto thee in order,

a Heb. 2:3; 1 Pet. 5:1; 2 Pet. 1:16; 1 John 1:1....*b* Mark 1:1; John 15:27....*c* Acts 15:19, 25, 28; 1 Cor. 7:40....*d* Acts 11:4 ....*e* Acts 1:1.—¹ Or, *fully established.*

all one body, from the time of the first disciples. The **many** who had previously written are included.

2. Even as they delivered them unto us which from the beginning, etc. The persons here referred to were the companions and servants of Jesus. If the authority of the apostles exclusively had been appealed to, they would certainly have been named as such; but now we are referred to them and other disciples of the Lord, including, probably, "the seventy," and many others like Barsabas, and those referred to by Peter as possible apostles, (Acts 1:23, 21). They authoritatively **delivered** (*handed down*) information concerning Christ. This information furnished the standard, as to the substance and manner, of the narratives which the "many" had composed. This is denoted by, **even as**. They undertook each one to draw up a narrative concerning "those things" according to what, and **even as** those personally intimate with Jesus had instructed them.—The same persons **were eyewitnesses** (of the facts) **from the beginning,** (i. e., of the public work), **and** [*became*] **ministers of the word**; namely, the gospel of Christ's kingdom. This word they dispensed, "ministered," as the servants of Jesus, in the office of apostles and of other witnesses for him. But while private Christians, like Mary, the mother of Jesus, or Lazarus and his sisters, are excluded from any share in determining the substance and form of the gospel proclamation, we are not hindered from thinking that a subsequent investigator, like Luke, might derive light as to details and minute points from such sources. Especially does this apply to matters like the Nativity, which lay outside of the earliest contents of the oral gospel.

3. It seemed good to me also. This is the apodosis, and principal clause of the sentence, as we have said, to which all the foregoing is introductory and subordinate. Forasmuch as they did that, it seemed good to me also to do this. If others had not, it might seem presumptuous in me to attempt such a thing. **It seemed good to me** is nearly equivalent to "I resolved" to, "I thought I would."—**Having had perfect understanding of all things from the very first.** The Revision is nearer to the original. The participle signifies properly "to follow along with," either a person, so as to become intimate and well acquainted with him, or a subject of investigation, so as to have mastered it, have followed it through. Of this process, the Common Version gives substantially the result: "to have clear and full understanding," overlooking the process. A question arises as to the relation of time between this participle and the author's determination to write. It might be equivalent to "because I already had understanding," or to "after I should come to have." Examples of the former use need not be repeated. The latter would be like Acts 15:22, where the Greek is: "Then it seemed good to the apostles, . . . having chosen men, . . . to send them to Antioch," rightly translated, "to choose men and send them." So Luke 9:59, Greek, "suffer me first, having gone, to bury," meaning, "suffer me first to go and bury"; comp. Matt. 8:21, where it is so expressed in the Greek. (Comp. also the Greek of ver. 9 in this chapter). After this analogy, which we think most appropriate here, our passage would mean, "I resolved to acquire a full and exact understanding of all things, and write."—**From the very first. Very** might be omitted, and still leave us to gather that Luke determined to extend his investigation beyond the ordinary beginning of the evangelical proclamation, the preaching of John the Baptist, (Mark 1:1 ff; Acts 1:21, 22). He is going back to the birth of John, and of the Lord Jesus.—**To write unto thee in order, most excellent Theophilus.** Who this Theophilus was, is entirely unknown, although a variety of uncertain traditions was afterwards hatched to supply the place of knowledge. They may be read in the Bible Dictionaries, great care being taken to

4 *That thou mightest know the certainty of those things, wherein thou hast been instructed.

4 most excellent Theophilus; that thou mightest know the certainty concerning the ¹ things ² wherein thou wast instructed.

a John 20: 31.——1 Gr. *words*....2 Or, *which thou wast taught by word of mouth.*

scrutinize the alleged authorities. The name signifies "dear to God," or "friend of God." That a real person was intended, and not a mere imaginary representative of Christian piety, is much more probable, both from the nature of the case, in introducing a real history, repeated again in the second section of Luke's work (Acts 1:1), and from the commonness of the name in that day, which would make it less suitable for an allegorical effect. The name, being Greek, affords some probability that its bearer was of Gentile origin, and in this respect falls in with the whole impression made by all other circumstances connected with the book. The epithet, **most excellent**, has encouraged the speculation that he was of high rank, or stood in high official position, especially as it is applied to Felix and Festus. (Acts 23: 26; 24: 3; 26: 25). That use of it shows that it *might* be employed to ascribe excellence, however falsely, to potentates; but it is not likely that we should be left to so slender evidence, if there had been at that time a convert to Christianity, within the knowledge of Luke, of any such standing. It is enough to accept it as denoting intelligence and moral excellence becoming to an influential Christian man. The evangelist writes to him, not simply for his personal satisfaction and behoof, but as a good medium through whom to communicate, to a certain circle of believers, the full and exact truth concerning Christ and the beginnings of his religion. This was a common mode of making public their writings by ancient authors, to dedicate them to some friend, or eminent man whose name would give them credit with other readers. To Theophilus, Luke proposes to write **in order,** *i. e.,* in an orderly way. It would most naturally be understood of a chronological order, and indeed it is hard to see what order could have been intended not including that; but as Luke, on a comparison with the other evangelists, sometimes appears to fail of the more probable succession of events in time, we may perhaps interpret his word more generally, as denoting a consistent series according to a *logical* principle; such an arrangement of topics as shall best conduce to the object at which he aims. The argument in favor of this latitude of signification of the adverb (καθεξῆς), is well put by Dr. J. B. McClellan (*New Translation of the New Testament,* I., 424-26); only he perhaps too confidently assumes that Luke was distinctly aware that he followed an order not chronological. This object, at which Luke aims, he gives in the next words.

4. That thou mightest know the certainty of (*concerning*) **those things wherein thou hast been** (*wast*) **instructed.** The terseness of the original it is hard to express idiomatically in English with equal vigor: "That thou mightest know clearly, concerning what words thou wast taught, the solid truth." **Know** here represents a compound word, sometimes "recognize," but more generally, "know definitely," accurately, clearly. For the Greek noun here (λόγων), literally, *words*, Versions and many other authorities give "things," as the term is often used metaphorically for the subject matter of the words. But here there seems to be no sufficient reason for thinking of anything else than the "words," that is, discourses, accounts, reports, of Christ, his deeds, and his doctrine, which Theophilus had been taught. This teaching (κατηχήθης) had been oral, as the special word here used most naturally signifies. It is that from which, through the practice of the early Greek Christians, our word "catechize" and its cognates come, although that practice was only gradually developed from the simple plan of communicating the truths of the gospel, publicly and privately, by word of mouth, which is called "preaching" in the New Testament. These words Theophilus had already believed; but, lest he should be hesitating between variant statements, Luke assumes that for him to have the whole narrative of the origin of Christianity presented in writing, with accuracy, in an orderly consecution of facts, would give certainty and firmness to his faith.

REMARK.—This short Preface is of special interest to a student of the New Testament in several respects. There is nothing elsewhere in Scripture in any degree like it, except the mere address to the same Theophilus in the first verse of Acts. It throws important light—

1. On the author. He was thoroughly at home in the Greek language; which was not the case with most of the New Testament writers. By a single sentence he sets forth the reasons which encouraged him to write, the sources of his matter, the competency which he had sought for the task, and the precise aim of his effort. He does it clearly, simply, tersely, and with a grammatical skill in the development of his thought which results in a period scarcely to be excelled in the Greek of that age, and which even Demosthenes need not have despised. A like quality of style appears elsewhere, occasionally, in his writing, especially in the Acts, by comparison of which passages we may infer that he more commonly translates out of Hebrew (Aramæan) sources, preserving something of their foreign quality, or copies documents of such origin. A noble modesty breathes through his language He makes no claim to original authorship, but only to the collection of facts which others had given, and the arrangement of them in an appropriate narrative, suited to serve a very important purpose. Intelligence, honesty, and care in all the processes of his work are unmistakably evinced. He does not stop short of the authentic, and, when it was necessary, the divinely accredited sources of knowledge, which he studies patiently, perseveringly, thoroughly, sparing no labor by which he may assure certainty on the most important subjects to his readers. We are thus prepared to expect in his narrative consistency with all other known truthful accounts of the same matters; and, uniformly finding this, we reasonably accept his historical statements in cases, such as "the enrollment" by order of Augustus, under Cyrenius as governor of Syria (2:1, 2), the Tetrarchy of Lysanias in Abilene (3:1), where we lack the express confirmation of other writers.

2. On the origin of our Canonical, particularly of the Synoptic, Gospels. In solving the very interesting problem here presented, to account at once for the remarkable similarity of those writings, amounting in occasional passages to complete identity, while explaining at the same time the striking differences, amounting sometimes almost to contradiction, the view most prevalent, though with endless modifications, has latterly been, that they, the first three Gospels, are so many forms in which was preserved the *spoken* gospel of the apostolic preaching. This had fastened itself on a comparatively scant selection of facts, out of the Saviour's life and discourses, and especially his passion. They were chosen because of their fitness to represent his whole work and teaching, chiefly to show on the one hand that he was the Messiah of the Jews, and on the other that he was the Saviour of the whole world. These would be elaborated with care that they might truly report the facts, would naturally express in substance the view common to the apostles, who remained some years together in Jerusalem, and, when giving Christ's more important sayings, would nearly or exactly coincide. Thus, "those who were eye-witnesses and became ministers of the word," delivered to their contemporaries and successors the things that had been accomplished among them.

But not in writing, until a considerable number of years had passed. Even the Gospel according to Matthew, as we now have it, dates from thirty-five or more years after Christ's death, and John, still a good deal later. When, therefore, Luke, as is revealed in his Preface, desired a complete, self-consistent, and reasoned account of the themes of the original preaching, for the benefit of believers who, like Theophilus, had received the word, as the spoken testimony of men that knew their truth, and felt their power, he could find no such account. He knew of several faithful attempts at something more or less approaching what he wished for, and, as a Greek, would feel none of that scruple against writing down divine truths, which would hamper an ordinary Hebrew of that day. He had close association with the Apostle Paul, who, although, like himself, at the second remove from Christ, had enjoyed special revelations of the gospel, besides unusual opportunities for the natural acquisition of knowledge about the Lord; he could avail himself of the work of those many previous writers; and finally he could still have access in his researches to some now well advanced in years,

THERE was *in the days of Herod, the king of Judea, a certain priest named Zacharias, *b* of the course of Abia: and his wife *was* of the daughters of Aaron, and her name *was* Elisabeth.

6 And they were both *c* righteous before God, walking in all the commandments and ordinances of the Lord blameless.

5 THERE was in the days of Herod, king of Judæa, a certain priest named Zacharias, of the course of Abijah; and he had a wife of the daughters of Aaron, and her name was Elisabeth. And they were both righteous before God, walking in all the commandments and ordinances of the Lord blameless.

a Matt. 2: 1....*b* 1 Chron. 24: 10, 19; Neh. 12: 4, 17,....*c* Gen. 7: 1; 17: 1; 1 Kings 9: 4; 2 Kings 20: 3; Job 1: 1; Acts 23: 1; 24: 16; Phil. 3: 6.

who could supply deficiencies in his accounts from their own memory, and perhaps furnish documents of highest authority not generally known. From all indications concerning Luke, and from his known intimacy with the Apostle Paul, we may well suppose that he would welcome those accounts, especially, of Christ's teaching and conduct, which most clearly bespoke his catholic and universal interest in the salvation of the men of every nation, and of every grade.

The view of the origin of the Gospels above intimated, is ably maintained, with a criticism of counter views which have been held, by B. F. Westcott, in his *Introduction to the Study of the Gospels*, chap. 3.

The scholar will find the interpretation and significance of this Preface well discussed in the same work, pp. 196-198, Am. Edition; in G. Fisher, *Beginnings of Christianity;* C. F. Nösgen, in the *Studien und Kritiken*, 1876, pp. 265-275; and above all, C. L. W. Grimm (the lexicographer), in the *Jahrbücher für deutsche Theologie*, B. 16, 1871, pp. 33-78.

PART I. **Ch. 1: 5-4: 13.** PRELIMINARY TO THE PUBLIC MINISTRY OF JESUS. This part is plainly divided into three sections by the careful indications of date. (Ch. 1:5; 2:1; 3:1 ff).

Sect. 1, ch. 1: 5 80, presents (1) the annunciation of the birth of John the Baptist as our Lord's forerunner; (2) the annunciation of the birth of Jesus; (3) the birth of John—with the attendant circumstances of each event.

1: 5-23. ANNUNCIATION OF THE BIRTH OF JOHN.

5. There was in the days of Herod, the king of Judea. It is better, with the Revision, to omit the article before **king.** Herod I., surnamed the Great, son of Antipater, an Idumæan, came, through the favor of the Romans, to reign over Judea, from A. U. C. 714, and afterward over Samaria and other districts also, until A. U. C. 750, when he died. **The days of Herod,** therefore, covered about thirty-six years, and what is here recorded took place very late in that period.—**A certain priest named Zacharias, of the course of Abia.** As a priest, he would at that time be reckoned of the nobility of the Jews. (See Josephus' *Life*, ¾ 1.) There might be thought some significance in his name, which in Hebrew meant "Jehovah remembers." **Abia** is properly given in the Revision as *Abijah*, on the principle that the names of Old Testament personages should be in the New Testament the same as in the Old. This would require that **Zacharias** should be changed to Zachariah, or Zechariah, if the person here intended had been mentioned in the Old Testament. Abijah was the head of one of the twenty-four "courses" or divisions (1 Chron. 24: 1, 10) into which David distributed the priests of his day, for the more orderly performance of their duties. Abijah stood first in the eighth of them, and as the date of the destruction of the temple (A. D. 70) is known, and the course of the priests (that of Joarib) then officiating is known, it has been supposed that something definite could be concluded by reckoning backward from that date, as to the week here intended, then, as to the time of John's birth, then, as to the year, the month, the week, and even the day, of the birth of Jesus. How precarious such inferences must be is obvious. Any opinion even as to whether the order of the courses was the same now as when they began is, for one thing, so uncertain as scarcely to deserve the credit of slight probability, whatever that opinion may be.—**And his wife was (***he had a wife***) of the daughters of Aaron, and her name was Elisabeth.** Both parents of John were thus of the priestly class. Their character was that of the highest type of Old Testament religion.

6. They were both righteous before God. Under a system of legal requirements "righteousness" is the natural description of piety. That would apply to a person as he most fully met those requirements, and con-

7 And they had no child, because that Elisabeth was barren, and they both were *now* well stricken in years.
8 And it came to pass, that while he executed the priest's office before God *a* in the order of his course,
9 According to the custom of the priest's office, his lot was *b* to burn incense when he went into the temple of the Lord.

7 less. And they had no child, because that Elisabeth was barren, and they both were *now*[1] well stricken in years.
8 Now it came to pass, while he executed the priest's
9 office before God in the order of his course, according to the custom of the priest's office, his lot was to enter into the [1] temple of the Lord and burn incense.

a 1 Chron. 24 : 19; 2 Chron. 8 : 14; 31 : 2....*b* Ex. 30; 7, 8; 1 Sam. 2 : 28; 1 Chron. 23 : 13; 2 Chron. 29 : 11.—1 Gr. *advanced in their days*....2 Or, *sanctuary*.

formed his disposition and conduct to the standard of the law. He would so be right, *i. e.*, righteous, and this quality of his character would be called righteousness. **Before God,** not in their own view, or in that of their neighbors, merely, but as seen by God. Yet it was a legal righteousness, as appears from the description following.—**Walking** is a Hebrew metaphor for "living," "conducting oneself," in the various relations of men to each other and to God.—**The commandments** are particular precepts.—**Ordinances** may be, more generally, the appointments of God, his statutes or decisions of any form, indicative of his will concerning his people.—**Blameless,** as Paul speaks (Phil. 3 : 6) of his own character as having been, according to the law, and no more exclusive of the need of justification by faith, or implying absolute perfection on the part of Zacharias and Elisabeth. It was the righteousness of supreme reverence for Jehovah's will and sincere endeavor to comply with it, often claimed by pious men under the old covenant (comp. Ps 18 : 20-24; 7 : 8), and ascribed to them in a multitude of places.

7. And they had no child, because that Elisabeth was barren. The one great trouble, apparently, of their lives, and especially severe in the estimation of a married pair among the Jews, where childlessness was esteemed almost a curse.—**And they both were now well stricken in years,** literally, *were advanced in their days,* and so, doubtless feeling that there was less and less reason to hope for offspring. Still, there is nothing to indicate the natural impossibility that they might yet be so blessed, or to forbid their prayers.

8-23. THE ANNUNCIATION. Ver. 8-12 give the occasion and mode; ver. 13-17 the annunciation itself; and ver. 18-23 the token by which Zachariah should know that it was to come true.

8-12. 8. Executed the priest's office, (*discharged the duties of a priest*) **before**

God. A different expression in the Greek from that in ver. 6, "in God's presence, as manifested in the temple," "as unto God."—**In the order of his course,** *i. e.*, on some day of that week in which, twice in the year, the course of Abijah would be on duty at the temple. The twenty-four courses would have to take their turn at least twice every year.

9. According to the custom of the priest's office. This custom, as Jewish authorities declare (see Winer, *Real-Wörterbuch,* 2, 323, n. 3, 2 ed.), was for the "course" to distribute themselves into six sections, one of which had charge of the temple duties for each secular day, while on the Sabbath the whole course joined in the services. It is natural to suppose that each section would then divide by lot the several functions necessary to be performed each day. Thus it was that on the particular day in question **his lot was** (*he obtained by lot*) **to burn incense,** etc. The Revision renders rightly. (See on ver. 3). The purpose of his entering into the temple was to offer incense. This function was regarded as of special privilege and solemnity, both from the signification of the act (Rev. 5 : 8), and because it brought the priest officiating into near proximity to God's seat. For "the temple" here is the sacred edifice itself, into which none but the priests might enter, in the outer chamber of which stood the altar of incense, separated by nothing but the second vail from that mysterious gloom of "the holy of holies," where the Shekinah and the cherubim over the ark had once betokened the special presence of Jehovah (Ex. 30 : 1, 6), and where he was still thought to receive the odors of the incense as an acceptable symbol of the prayers of the people. Much more commonly in our English Bible, the word "temple" stands for another Greek word, denoting the whole congeries of sacred buildings (Mark 13 : 1) and courts, which surrounded the temple edifice proper, and does not really

10 *And the whole multitude of the people were praying without at the time of incense.
11 And there appeared unto him an angel of the Lord standing on the right side of *the altar of incense.
12 And when Zacharias saw *him*, *he was troubled, and fear fell upon him.
13 But the angel said unto him Fear not, Zacharias: for thy prayer is heard; and thy wife Elisabeth shall bear thee a son, and *thou shalt call his name John.
14 And thou shalt have joy and gladness: and *many shall rejoice at his birth.

10 And the whole multitude of the people were praying without at the hour of incense. And there appeared unto him an angel of the Lord standing on the right
12 side of the altar of incense. And Zacharias was troubled when he saw *him*, and fear fell upon him.
13 But the angel said unto him, Fear not, Zacharias: because thy supplication is heard, and thy wife Elisabeth shall bear thee a son, and thou shalt call
14 his name John. And thou shalt have joy and glad-

a Lev. 16:17; Rev. 8:3, 4.... *b* Ex. 30:1.... *c* Judg. 6:22; 13:22; Dan. 10:8; ver. 29; ch. 2:9; Acts 10:4; Rev. 1:17.... *d* ver. 60, 63.... *e* ver. 58.

apply to that at all. It is a pity that the Revision has not indicated the distinction by using for the latter word referred to, "temple courts," "temple buildings," or some suitably distinctive term, as Dr. McClellan has done.

10. The whole multitude. Whether greater than the ordinary attendance of worshipers, as if it were some festival day, we have no intimation.—**Were praying without.** Simultaneously with the offering of the incense, (comp. Rev. 8:3, 4).—**At the time [hour] of incense.** There were two hours of incense daily—one in the morning, when the lamps were trimmed, after the night's use, the other at evening, when they were lighted (Ex. 30:7, 8); but which this was we can only conjecture. Meyer is scarcely warranted in deciding for the morning, on the ground that "the casting of the lots has just preceded."

11. An angel of the Lord. Ver. 19 shows that among the numerous host of super-earthly messengers who did the bidding of God in heaven, and on earth when the interests of his kingdom here required, the one now sent was Gabriel, who had already long before appeared to Daniel (Dan. 8:16; 9:21), to enlighten and comfort him. His coming now was indicative of another crisis in the history of redemption, where supernatural tokens from above were most natural.—**Standing on the right side of the altar.** The altar of incense stood near the curtain which vailed the most holy place, centrally, in front of the sacred ark behind the vail. The right side might have been so named with reference to the altar, which would be at the left hand of the priest as he entered, an honorable position in relation to the divine presence represented by the altar; but quite as probably the angel stood at the right side with reference to Zacharias facing the altar, in which case the fact was mentioned as of good omen to the servant of God.

12. He (Zacharias) was troubled, and fear fell upon him. His trouble and fear was not so much alarm or dread of danger, as the holy awe which naturally rises in the heart of one conscious of sin before any unusual, especially a sudden, manifestation of the near presence of God.

13-17. Fear not, Zacharias; for thy prayer (*supplication*) **is heard** (*was heard*). Not harm, but rather blessing to him is portended. Not the usual word for prayer is employed, but one more specific in its import, and implying earnestness; and it probably points to the entreaties which Zacharias had urged before God for a son. If we knew that public prayer on his part attended the burning of the incense, we might suppose (although the special word supplication is not so suitable to this view) that he had been asking for the advent of the Messiah, and that the granting of this request was assured to him in the announcement of the birth of the forerunner. But it is too much of hypothesis to assume that there was some prayer, and then that it was this particular prayer. There was rather a revelation of a domestic blessing, primarily, which grows to be of great public influence also.—**Thy wife Elisabeth shall bear thee a son.** Not merely a child, but a son, who may continue the paternal name among the families of Israel, and more than remove that stain which was felt to attach to childlessness. From the view which we have taken of ver. 7, it is not necessary to understand a miracle, as in the case of Abraham and Sarah, but only a remarkable interposition of the divine favor.—**And thou shalt call his name John**, (*Jehovah is gracious*). The name was well suited to confirm hope.

14. And thou shalt have joy and gladness (*exultation*); **and many shall rejoice at his birth.** The rejoicing predicted for Zacharias and his friends, at the birth of a son to him in his old age, is historically

15 For he shall be great in the sight of the Lord, and *a* shall drink neither wine nor strong drink; and he shall be filled with the Holy Ghost, *b* even from his mother's womb.
16 *c* And many of the children of Israel shall he turn to the Lord their God.

15 ness; and many shall rejoice at his birth. For he shall be great in the sight of the Lord, and he shall drink no wine nor ¹ strong drink; and he shall be filled with the Holy Spirit, even from his mother's
16 womb. And many of the children of Israel shall he

a Num. 6 : 3 ; Judg. 13 : 4 ; ch. 7 : 33....*b* Jer. 1 : 5 ; Gal. 1 : 15....*c* Mal. 4 : 5, 6.——1 Gr. *sikera*.

realized in ver. 64-66 [comp. ver. 58], and it there runs into religious delight in the character and work of the future herald. Such a high destination is indicated here by the **for** in ver. 15.

15. For he shall (*will*) **be great in the sight of the Lord.** Of him, that is, "who looketh on the heart"; truly, inwardly great, —great in character, as well as in work.— **Strong drink.** That of the Hebrews was a liquor produced by fermentation from the juice of other fruits than grapes; from honey, and from decoctions of various grains. The use of this and of wine was absolutely forbidden to the Nazarites of the Old Testament, whose obligations seem to have been now revived and laid on the expected offspring of the priest. They were men who consecrated themselves specially to Jehovah, as his possession, for his service only, either for a definite period, or for the whole of life, as the case might be. Sometimes, as with Samuel (1 Sam. 1 : 11), the vow of consecration was made for one by another (comp. Judges 13 : 5); thus in effect constituting him a Nazarite, though he is not expressly so called. The law of the Nazarite is laid down in Num. 6 : 1-21, and its requirements of abstinence from strong drink, and wine, and everything pertaining to the grape, as well as that no razor should ever touch the hair or beard, were partly ascetic, to cultivate a character and habit of life able to bear hardships and privations, and partly symbolical of the peculiar separation from everything else to God, which was the burden of his vow. This was all very appropriate to one who was to stand in a peculiar nearness to the coming Lord, Messiah, and especially as he was to follow in the line of the heroes of the nation, of whom Samuel was an example.—**And he shall** (*will*) **be filled with the Holy Ghost,** (*Spirit*) **even from his mother's womb.**

The Holy Spirit is here mentioned in the Old Testament sense, as that divine force which imparted to men high and special qualification for the service of God, in works of the hand, the understanding, the heart. Its power should influence John from his birth. This is what is meant by **even from his mother's womb.** We see no need of going, as do even Meyer and Godet, beyond the statement of the sacred writer and make him mean "in" his mother's womb, when he says "from." The latter is a strongly hyperbolical expression of the truth that, whereas most men became the agents of the Holy Spirit at a more advanced stage of life, John should be an organ of his operations from his earliest rational consciousness. The other view supposes either an immaculate conception of the forerunner, in which case there *might*, doubtless, have been a hypostatic union between the embryo human spirit and the divine, but surely not even then involving intelligence, in any sense apprehensible to us, or, a purely local presence of the Divine Spirit, in effect disunited from the human, and not apparently of any rational use. If the Scripture told us plainly of such a fact, we might accept it without question; but to put it into the narrative of Scripture on so shadowy a ground as that of the particle **even** (ἔτι), is another thing. The support for it drawn from ver. 41, 44, we will consider at that place. We add only that "from the mother's womb" is so frequently and so exclusively used in the Old and New Testaments to signify "from the time of birth," that one wishing to express a different idea, as, for example, that of being filled with the Spirit before birth, would naturally avoid that phrase, or so modify it as to prevent misunderstanding.¹

16. His work described in reference to its effects.—**And many of the children**

---

¹ The Greek adverb (ἔτι), meaning commonly "yet," "still," which has been supposed to imply that being *still* so he must have been so before, is rather used here with a transfer of position, like that in Rom. 5 : 6 (in most texts), in the modified sense of "already." So Grimm's *Clavis s. v.*, rightly, where examples are cited from Plutarch, *Consol*, p. 104; (ἔτι ἀπ' ἀρχῆς), "already from the beginning," and from the *Anthol.*, 9, 567 (ἔτι ἐκ βρέφους), already from a babe. Kypke *in loc*, has accumulated passages from classic authors, several of which fairly sustain the view here adopted.

17 ᵃAnd he shall go before him in the spirit and power of Elias, to turn the hearts of the fathers to the children, and the disobedient to the wisdom of the just; to make ready a people prepared for the Lord.

17 turn unto the Lord their God. And he shall ¹go before his face in the spirit and power of Elijah, to turn the hearts of the fathers to the children, and the disobedient *to walk* in the wisdom of the just: to make ready for the Lord a people prepared *for him*.

a Mal. 4:5; Matt. 11:14; Mark 9:12. —1 Some ancient authorities read, *come nigh before his face*.

(sons) of Israel shall he turn to the Lord their God. The Hebrew and the Hebraistic Greek almost always says "sons" in naming offspring, or descendants, quite regardless whether daughters also are intended. "Sons of Israel" are all descendants of Jacob. (Compare for the sense Matt. 3:5 ff; 21:26; Mark 1:5; 11:32; Luke 3:7 ff; 20:6; John 5:35). It is an application to John of the prophecy in Malachi 4:6, and shows that this man, "greater than a prophet," shall effect such a change in the views and purposes of many of his countrymen concerning God and their duty to him (which is repentance), as would lead them to more humble and spiritual lives, and so prepare them for a place in the Messiah's kingdom when he should appear. This is conversion; and the verb turn here used is that which is often translated "convert" or "be converted." How truly this was fulfilled, the citations above show.

17. And he shall go before him. He is strongly emphatic, nearly equivalent to "he himself," as distinguished from "many of the sons." By him is intended "the Lord their God," mentioned in the preceding verse; not directly, therefore, Jesus the Christ, but indirectly, as from the prophetic point of view. In that view the opening of the Messianic age was a glorious and fearful manifestation of Jehovah himself—"a day of Jehovah." That we know Jesus of Nazareth to be intended as the representative and equivalent of Jehovah, proves plainly, as Godet says, that "in the view of the Old as well as of the New Testament, the coming of the Messiah is the supreme Theophany." **Shall go before,** namely, as a courier, a forerunner, to lead the way, and in the eye of him that follows. The mode and particular objects are specified in the following clauses.—**In the spirit and power of Elias.** In a spirit imparted by God, and with a power resulting from the possession of that spirit, of which the spirit and power operative in Elijah was the type. This was the sense of the prediction in Mal. 4:5. From this language it is not strange that the Jews should have drawn the inference that Elijah was literally to return to life and make himself known as the precursor of the Messiah. (John 1:21; Matt. 17:9). But the Saviour afterward showed (Matt. 17:10-12; Mark 9:12, 13), that they should have understood it typically of one *like* Elijah, and that such a one had appeared in the Baptist. Like Elijah, John was to be a stern reformer of the morals and religious practice of his age; and like him he should be fitted for the task by a proved superiority to the fashions and indulgences of his age.—The first aim of his precursorship is **To turn the hearts of the fathers to the children,** or, more correctly, omitting the article, "of fathers to children." This obscure passage was probably intended by Malachi to denote one of the most important features of a great moral reformation, looked at from the midst of such a disordered condition of domestic and social life, as he intimates (ch. 2) in consequence of the scandalous license of divorce. Its application to the state of the people at the time of Christ's advent, after ages of belligerent partisanship and of civil and foreign wars, would be still more significant of a radical social amendment. This idea was completed in the prophecy by showing the change reciprocated, "and the heart of children to their fathers" (Hebrew); but the angel finishes his prediction independently, by a general mention of the conversion of sinners.—**And the disobedient to the wisdom of the just.** The article here again in connection with the persons is strictly unwarranted. "Wisdom" is specifically practical wisdom, "prudence," which eminently characterizes those who make their peace with God and walk in his fear. The preposition rendered *to* is properly *in*, and looks back to "shall turn." By a common abbreviation of the Greek phrase it notes the state *into* which the disobedient shall turn and *in* which they shall remain: "and disobedient men into the prudence of just, [or, *righteous*] men." Disobedient persons were those who refused to hear the

18 And Zacharias said unto the angel, *Whereby shall I know this? for I am an old man, and my wife well stricken in years.
19 And the angel answering said unto him, I am *Gabriel, that stand in the presence of God; and am sent to speak unto thee, and to shew thee these glad tidings.
20 And, behold, *thou shalt be dumb, and not able to speak, until the day that these things shall be performed, because thou believest not my words, which shall be fulfilled in their season.
21 And the people waited for Zacharias, and marvelled that he tarried so long in the temple.

18 And Zacharias said unto the angel, Whereby know this? for I am an old man, and my wife ¹ well stricken in years. And the angel answering said 19 unto him, I am Gabriel, that stand in the presence of God; and I was sent to speak unto thee, and to 20 bring thee these good tidings. And behold, thou shalt be silent and not able to speak, until the day that these things shall come to pass, because thou believedst not my words, which shall be fulfilled in 21 their season. And the people were waiting for Zacharias, and they marvelled ² while he tarried in

a Gen. 17: 17....*b* Dan. 8: 16; 9: 21, 22, 23; Matt. 18: 10; Heb. 1: 14....*c* Ezek. 3: 26; 24: 27.—1 Gr. *advanced in her days*.....
² Or, *at his tarrying*.

Lord's call to repentance and a righteous life; and the prudence of the just was celebrated especially in the Proverbs, in Job also, and was exemplified in Zacharias and Elisabeth, in Martha and Mary, and in all their kind. Godet's very ingenious view of the passage is quite abstruse, and is set aside by the absence of the article with "fathers" and "children" in both the Hebrew and Greek.¹— **To make ready a people prepared for the Lord.** The Revision is right in placing "for the Lord" after "ready." This is a further purpose of John's going before the Messiah. To bring about such a character and state of mind among the whole people, completed the ideal function of the great herald. They would thus be made ready for the Lord, as intellectually and morally prepared to welcome the glad news of the kingdom at hand.

18. And Zacharias said unto the angel, Whereby shall I know this? His question appears at first sight very natural and blameless, especially in view of the age of himself and wife, which he alleges as a reason for desiring a sign whereby, or a criterion according to which, he might be assured that what was predicted would indeed come to pass.

19. The answer shows that the evidence afforded in the very appearance of the messenger must have been so clear and strong as to make the priest in some degree culpable for even questioning the certainty of the promise.—**I am Gabriel, that stand in the presence of God.** The name is evidently symbolical—"God's hero"—and accommodated to our need of having some designation, if we would identify a particular heavenly being through his various manifestations (Compare Michael, i. e., Who is like God? Dan. 10:13-21; Jude 9). Gabriel also had been named in Dan. 8: 16; 9: 20.—**That stand in the presence of God**—a position of exalted dignity, implying capacity for the most important services, and readiness to overtake them whenever required. "They also serve who only stand and wait." The manner of his appearance, and probably something quite superhuman in his very look, awe-inspiring to the beholder (see ver. 12), should have prevented the need of special confirmation of the **glad tidings,** which he was sent to show. Something of the gospel (εὐαγγελίσασθαι) is involved in this initial promise. It is a favorite word with Luke.

20. And, behold, thou shalt be dumb (*silent*), etc., **until the day that these things shall be performed** (*come to pass*). This might have seemed merely a sign appointed by God in his pleasure, if the following clause—**because thou believest not my words**—had not distinctly made it a penalty. —**Which shall be fulfilled in their season.** The day of the performance of the things is thus shown to be the **season,** the fit and proper time, when the words of the prediction shall be fulfilled. It means that Zacharias must remain dumb, till the birth and naming of the child.

21. And the people waited (*were waiting*) **for Zacharias.** From this it would appear

¹ He thinks that "The true sense of these words may be gathered from other prophetic passages, such as these: Isaiah 29: 22; 'Jacob shall not be ashamed, neither shall his face wax pale when he seeth his children become the work of my hands'; 63: 16; 'Doubtless thou art our Father, though Abraham be ignorant of us, and Israel acknowledge us not; thou, O Lord, art our Father, our Redeemer!' Abraham and Jacob, in the place of their rest, had blushed at the sight of their guilty descendants, and turned away their faces from them; but now they would turn again towards them with satisfaction, in consequence of the change produced by the ministry of John." . . . "With this meaning, the modification introduced into the second member of the phrase is easily explained. The children who will turn towards their fathers (Malachi), are the Jews of the time of the Messiah, *the children of the obedient,* who return to the *wisdom of the pious patriarchs* (Luke)."

22 And when he came out, he could not speak unto them: and they perceived that he had seen a vision in the temple: for he beckoned unto them, and remained speechless.
23 And it came to pass, that, as soon as ᵃ the days of his ministration were accomplished, he departed to his own house.
24 And after those days his wife Elisabeth conceived, and hid herself five months, saying,
25 Thus hath the Lord dealt with me in the days wherein he looked on *me*, to ᵇ take away my reproach among men.

22 the ¹ temple. And when he came out, he could not speak unto them: and they perceived that he had seen a vision in the ¹ temple: and he continued
23 making signs unto them, and remained dumb. And it came to pass, when the days of his ministration were fulfilled, he departed unto his house.
24 And after these days Elisabeth his wife conceived;
25 and she hid herself five months, saying, Thus hath the Lord done unto me in the days wherein he looked upon *me*, to take away my reproach among men.

a See 2 Kings 11 : 5 ; 1 Chron. 9 : 25.... *b* Gen. 30 : 23 ; Isa. 4 : 1 ; 54 : 1, 4.——1 Or, *sanctuary*.

that custom required them to remain until the priest came out, perhaps to dismiss them with some formality.— **And marvelled that (*while*) he tarried so long in the temple.** Jewish tradition tells us that the priests were accustomed to hasten from the holy place as soon as possible, fearing the fatal consequences of any irregularity, as intimated in Lev. 16: 13. The wonder of the people was not lessened when, on coming out, they noted his manner.

22. He could not speak unto them.— They perceived that he had seen a vision. This is accounted for by the fact that the strange effect had been wrought within the holy place, where a supernatural manifestation might be thought most likely, and partly also by his signs and gestures, intended to convey that knowledge. We are not, however, to understand that **he beckoned** (was nodding or making signs) **to them,** to convey this special information (Meyer). In this clause **he** is emphatic, equivalent to "*he himself*," "he on his part," "as for him, he"; and the strongly imperfect form of the Greek verb, "was beckoning" goes with **remained speechless** [*dumb*], to show that his dumbness was permanent, and that this was his habit through the period "foretold by the angel."—For is utterly without support in the Greek. That has "*and* the angel."

23. The days of his ministration were the week through which his "course" would have to perform the services of the sanctuary —from one Sabbath evening to the morning of the next.—**He departed to his own house.** We may suppose that his functions as priest would end altogether until so serious a bodily infirmity as had been put upon him should cease. Thus it is with reason supposed that at the next half-yearly term of service, he was absent from his "course," and that there was a symbolic import in his deprivation of speech. While John and Jesus were to come

in the line of the Mosaic economy, represented eminently in the priesthood, the latter would terminate with the glorification of the Great High Priest, and it was now shown to be ready to vanish away. Bengel well says: "It was the prelude to the abolition of the ceremonial law at the coming of Christ." **His own house** was in the hill country of Judea (ver. 39); but whether at Hebron, or in some neighboring priest-city, or whether, necessarily at this time in a priest-city at all, is quite unknown.

24, 25. The Fulfillment.

24. And after those days his wife Elisabeth conceived. How long after is mere matter of guess-work; so that all attempts to make out of the fact related an element in the calculations concerning the precise date of the Saviour's birth, are utterly frustrated by the vagueness of this statement.—**And hid herself five months.** Why she **hid herself,** and why for **five months,** has been variously conjectured by those who have chosen rather to guess than to note the reason given by Elisabeth herself.

25. Thus hath the Lord dealt with me (*done unto me*). Here emphasis lies in **the Lord.** We need not insert "because" before **thus** (Meyer); the logical sequence lies in the order of the clauses. Her argument seems to be: "In a special way, the Lord has brought about this state of things. I will, in quiet seclusion, await the further development of *his* will, and let him reveal the fact." It may be intended in ver. 58 that her kindred and friends even were not acquainted with her condition until the birth of her son. At all events, the evangelist almost certainly connects the five months of her complete retirement with the date of the annunciation to Mary, in the sixth month (ver. 26), when God did reveal for Elisabeth the true state of the case.—**He looked on me.** Nearly the same as the Hebrew expression, "*He visited*

26 And in the sixth month the angel Gabriel was sent from God unto a city of Galilee, named Nazareth,
27 To a virgin *espoused to a man whose name was Joseph, of the house of David; and the virgin's name was Mary.

26 Now in the sixth month the angel Gabriel was sent from God unto a city of Galilee, named Nazareth, to a virgin betrothed to a man whose name was Joseph, of the house of David; and the virgin's

a Matt. 1: 18; ch. 2: 4, 5.

me" (i. e., in a friendly sense). It is of God's blessing that she has hope of offspring.—**To take away my reproach among men.** The reproach of childlessness (Gen. 30: 23; 1 Sam. 1: 68). The language touchingly implies that she had been taunted with her barrenness by her acquaintances. The taking this away was, in effect, accomplished by the communication to Mary (ver. 36).

On the foregoing passage, it is proper to remark how the opening of the gospel record is illustrated by the extraordinary interposition of God in the affairs of man. Centuries had elapsed since the occurrence of divinely reported or well authenticated facts of the special revelation of God to his people. All had gone on according to the course of ordinary history, of government and anarchy, of peace and war, of victory and defeat, independence, oppression, prosperity, and misery. Now, again, the vail is parted between the visible and the unseen world; and the greatness of the crisis is intimated by the angelic declaration of God's plan. Such unusual deviation from the familiar course of things is not at all improbable in a series of developments which was to culminate in the presence among us of God Incarnate—Emanuel. At those points in that series which it was most important to authenticate, and to impress on the thoughts of men, supernatural events were most natural. Nothing could be so difficult to accept as the one supreme miracle of Christ, if it stood absolutely alone. Further, that the miraculous phenomena should be of a nature and style best adapted to the social and religious state of those whom they were intended to impress, lay in the very conception of a historical revelation.

Again, the temple and the priesthood are the passage-way between the Old Testament and the New. Christianity is a growth out of the soil of Hebraism.

John's ministry was a *necessary* link between the sacred activity of the two Dispensations. While he arose on the ground of Jewish prophecy, and there remained, his agency was indispensable, and efficacious to prepare the way for the Messiah of the world. We may see, in some measure, as we proceed, *how* he served "to prepare the way of the Lord," and how inaccessible even God's chosen people would have been to the gospel, without the work of John.

26-38. ANNOUNCEMENT TO MARY OF THE BIRTH OF JESUS.

APPEARANCE TO HER OF THE ANGEL GABRIEL, 26-29.

26. And in the sixth month—reckoning from the starting point of the five months in ver. 24. **Gabriel,** as the messenger of cheer and comfort (ver. 19).—**Galilee,** at the opposite extremity of the land of Palestine, northward. It embraced most of the territory assigned by Joshua to the tribes of Issachar, Zebulon, and Naphthali, and had the Sea of Galilee and the River Jordan north and south of it for its eastern border. Of great fertility and flourishing traffic, at the period now before us, it had a numerous population, inhabiting two hundred and forty towns and villages, each containing not less than 15,000 inhabitants, if we may trust Josephus. (See his *Life,* 45; *Jew. Wars,* 3. 3, 1. 2.) It became the scene of our Saviour's early life, and of the greater part of his recorded ministry.—**Nazareth,** a town near the southern border of Galilee, not mentioned in the Old Testament, but henceforth, as the home of the parents of Jesus, and "place where he was brought up," to be forever remembered with tender interest by the countless multitudes to whom he shall have been found "the chiefest among ten thousand, and the one altogether lovely."

27. A virgin espoused (*betrothed,* or *plighted*). Betrothal, in Jewish custom, was equivalent to marriage in its power to bind the parties to each other. In reference to the Romish dogma of the perpetual virginity of Mary, and of the superior sanctity of the unwedded state, it is worthy of notice that their almost divine pattern of saintship was, in an ordinary way, plighted in marriage to another saint (Joseph), and without the appearance of any objection on either side.—**Joseph, of**

LUKE. [Сн. I.

28 And the angel came in unto her, and said, "Hail, thou that art highly favoured, the Lord is with thee: blessed art thou among women.
29 And when she saw him, she was troubled at his saying, and cast in her mind what manner of salutation this should be.
30 And the angel said unto her, Fear not, Mary: for thou hast found favour with God.
31 And, behold, thou shalt conceive in thy womb, and bring forth a son, and shalt call his name JESUS.
32 He shall be great, and shall be called the Son of the Highest: and the Lord God shall give unto him the throne of his father David:

28 name was Mary. And he came in unto her, and said, Hail, thou that art highly favoured, the Lord
29 is with thee. But she was greatly troubled at the saying, and cast in her mind what manner of salutation
30 this might be. And the angel said unto her, Fear not, Mary: for thou hast found favour
31 with God. And behold, thou shalt conceive in thy womb, and bring forth a son, and shalt call his name
32 JESUS. He shall be great, and shall be called the Son of the Most High: and the Lord God shall give

a Dan. 9 : 23; 10 : 19....b Judg. 6 : 12....c ver. 12....d Isa. 7 : 14; Matt. 1 : 21....e ch. 2 : 21..../ Mark 5 : 7....g 2 Sam. 7 : 11, 12; Ps. 132 : 11; Isa. 9 : 6, 7; 16 : 5; Jer. 23 : 5; Rev. 3 : 7.—1 Or, endured with grace....2 Many authorities add, blessed art thou among women. See ver. 42....3 Or, grace.

the **house of David**, *i. e.*, one of David's descendants (Matt. 1 : 6-16), as it had been abundantly intimated that the Messiah should be. This assigned him, ostensibly on Joseph's part, and actually on Mary's part, if she was, as we hold probable, of the line of David, to the tribe of Judah, and to the royal family of that tribe.—**Mary**—in the Aramæan Greek Mariam—another pronunciation of Miriam, which we first find applied (Ex. 16 : 20) to the sister of Moses. It signifies bitterness, trouble, sorrow.

28. Came in unto her. What the manner of his apparition was we can only guess. We naturally think of him as taking the human form, and may reject all accessories of wings and other appurtenances with which the fancy of poets and painters has teemed.—**Hail,** (*joy to thee*). A common salutation of that time, but here appropriately significant.—**Highly favoured.** One who hast been regarded with favor, *i. e.*, by God. This the messenger from God is able to affirm, and in consistency with it he adds, **The Lord is with thee.** With thee to bless thee, and to confer that distinction which will rank thee above the daughters of Israel.—**Blessed art thou among women**—is left out of the text with good reason by the Revision. The words rightly stand in ver. 42.

29. She was troubled (*disturbed in mind*) **at his** (*the*) **saying.** The word of blessing which he spoke.—**When she saw him** has been inserted by a later hand, probably to make a correspondence with ver. 12.—**Cast in her mind.** Deliberated, or reasoned.—**What manner of salutation this should be.** How it was to be classed in her thinking; what it meant; how it was to be accounted for. It was so extraordinary in its source, the abruptness of its manner, the singularity of its apparent purport, that she was very naturally at a loss. Not only perplexity, but an anxiety amounting to fear, must have appeared in her countenance.

30. And the angel said unto her, Fear not, Mary. My appearance portends no harm to thee, (as was the case with Zacharias, ver. 13). Here, as there, the reason for confidence and cheerfulness is introduced by **for.—For thou hast found favour with God**—more exactly, *didst find*. **Favour** is the same as is often rendered "grace"; so also in ver. 28.

31. And—in consequence of that favor—**behold**—it is a fact deserving particular attention. How noteworthy must it have seemed to her as one after another the items were enumerated. She should **bring forth a son**—a special blessing—**and shalt call his name JESUS**—as significant of the high office to which he is destined—"because he shall save his people from their sins" (Matt. 1 : 21). **Jesus** was the equivalent, in the Alexandrine Greek, of Joshua, in the Hebrew, originally, "Jehoshua," meaning "Jehovah is salvation." This already involved his Messiahship, which is more clearly brought to view in what follows.

32. He shall be great—great in holiness and all excellence of character, great in the works which he will perform, and in the dignity of his relations—**and shall be called the Son of the Highest,** *i. e.*, Son of God, as that was one of the recognized designations of the coming Messiah, (Matt. 26 : 63; John 1 : 49); yet the designation did not yet convey the metaphysical and Trinitarian idea which we now attach to it. That was brought out in the New Testament itself. Mary may have thought only of some extraordinary and mysterious relationship between the being now promised as a son and the God of Israel. His extraordinary emi-

33 a And he shall reign over the house of Jacob for ever; and of his kingdom there shall be no end.
34 Then said Mary unto the angel, How shall this be, seeing I know not a man?
35 And the angel answered and said unto her, b The Holy Ghost shall come upon thee, and the power of the Highest shall overshadow thee: therefore also that holy thing which shall be born of thee shall be called c the Son of God.

33 unto him the throne of his father David: and he shall reign over the house of Jacob 1 for ever; and 34 of his kingdom there shall be no end. And Mary said unto the angel, How shall this be, seeing I know 35 not a man? And the angel answered and said unto her, The Holy Spirit shall come upon thee, and the power of the Most High shall overshadow thee: wherefore also 2 the holy thing that is begotten shall

a Dan. 2:44; 7:14, 27; Obad. 21; Micah 4:7; John 12:34; Heb. 1:8....b Matt. 1:20....c Matt. 14:33; 26:63, 64; Mark 1:11; John 1:34; 20:31; Acts 8:37; Rom. 1:4.—1 Gr. *unto the ages*....2 Or, *that which is to be born shall be called holy, the Son of God*. Some ancient authorities insert, *of thee*.

nence is farther indicated in the function predicted of him—a function consonant with all those attributes of majesty.—**The Lord God shall give unto him the throne of his father David.**

33. And he shall reign over the house of Jacob forever; and of his kingdom there shall be no end. The thought and the language are thoroughly in the strain of Old Testament prophecy. "The throne of David" is in the prophecies the seat of the Messianic rule over a people chosen out of the Jewish nation, and of those who should join them, of whom that nation was a type—as David was of the Christ—and not a type merely, but, in the divine plan, the substance. When they should have been purified from their dross in the fires of chastening, and should turn unto Jehovah from all their rebellion and unrighteousness, the Spirit of God would be poured out upon them, they would receive a new heart, and serve the Lord in inward obedience and holiness; then "the King's Son," "the sprout out of the root of Jesse," should sway over them the peaceful sceptre of his beneficent reign. Their unbelief balked this plan, indeed, so far as the body of the nation was concerned; but we are here in the age of anticipation and hope of the ideal kingdom; and the New Testament will show how God brought about the substantial accomplishment of the old oracles, through the medium, but not in the experience, of his ancient people.

The house of Jacob—as explained by the facts, is the company of those, whether Jew or Gentile, who, under the Messiah's rule, stand toward God in the relation of faith and obedience, in which Jacob stood, in the typical theocracy.—"He shall reign over the house of Jacob forever," etc. His kingdom, having been witnessed by the fleeting types and shadows of the earlier time, is itself permanent, and shall continue without end. The promise would commonly be understood, then, of an endless duration of the earthly reign, over the actual but converted Israel.

34. Then [*and*] **said Mary unto the angel, How shall this be, seeing I know not a man?** Her question does not, like that of Zacharias, demand proof of the fact announced, but only desires to know how this is consistent with her conscious virginity. It is evident that she thinks of the promised birth as taking place soon, before her marriage. Her assertion of her virginity is of a present fact and not of any vow, or future state, as Romanists have sometimes claimed. That would be strangely inconsistent with the fact of her espousal to a future husband.

35. In the answer of the angel, Mary's doubt is resolved.—**The Holy Ghost (***Spirit***) shall come upon thee, and the power of the Highest shall overshadow thee.** It has been often noticed how the sublime statement clothes itself in the peculiar form—parallelism of the clauses—of Hebrew poetry. **Holy Spirit, Power of the Highest,** and **come upon** (*overshadow*), in the two members repeat, and at the same time, diversify the leading thoughts. The idea of coming upon, and of overshadowing, is probably drawn from the fact of the Shekinah, or mysterious symbol of Jehovah's presence over the ark, between the cherubim in the tabernacle, whither he went and when he settled down (Ex. 25:22). The purport of the whole account is that the origination of that extraordinary life of which Mary was to be the mother, would, in the entire absence of the ordinary, human, conditions, be effected by the direct agency of God himself—she being still, and remaining, so far as this birth was concerned, an unsullied virgin. This may possibly aid us to understand how the human germ, impregnated without any particle of human passion, by God's own power, should come to be a man without blemish or spot, and able to live without sin. Such a person would evidently be, as never

36 And, behold, thy cousin Elisabeth, she hath also conceived a son in her old age; and this is the sixth month with her, who was called barren.
37 For *with God nothing shall be impossible.
38 And Mary said, Behold the handmaid of the Lord; be it unto me according to thy word. And the angel departed from her.
39 And Mary arose in those days, and went into the hill country with haste, *b* into a city of Judah;
40 And entered into the house of Zacharias, and saluted Elisabeth.

36 be called the Son of God. And behold, Elisabeth thy kinswoman, she also hath conceived a son in her old age: and this is the sixth month with her 37 that ¹ was called barren. For no word from God 38 shall be void of power. And Mary said, Behold, the ² bondmaid of the Lord; be it unto me according to thy word. And the angel departed from her.
39 And Mary arose in these days and went into the 40 hill country with haste, into a city of Judah; and entered into the house of Zacharias and saluted

a Gen. 18: 14; Jer. 32: 17; Zech. 8: 6; Matt. 19: 26; Mark 10: 27; ch. 18: 27; Rom. 4: 21....b Josh. 21: 9, 10, 11.——1 Or, is....
2 Gr. bondmaid.

was another of woman born, fitted to be the partner and vehicle of the Divine Person, the Eternal Word, in his becoming flesh.—**Therefore also**—seeing that God himself is here the father—**the holy thing which shall be born of thee**—the pure embryo—**shall**—when born—**be called the Son of God. Shall be called** is equivalent to *shall be*, and thus the proper metaphysical Sonship, growing out of identity of nature with God, is asserted of Jesus. To remove, in a measure, the natural improbability of such a thing, the angel voluntarily gives to Mary a sort of sign by which her trustful mind might be altogether assured.

36. And, behold—another very remarkable fact—**thy cousin Elisabeth** (*Elisabeth thy kinswoman*), **she hath also conceived a son in her old age.** What the degree of relationship between the two women was, is not intimated by the Greek word, and cannot be more definitely known. Elisabeth was of the tribe of Levi; and Mary's father, of the tribe of Judah, had probably married into that tribe, so as to bring her into relationship to Elisabeth. That the latter had conceived **in her old age,** was a thing so much out of the natural way as to constitute an instance calculated to confirm Mary's confidence. "Behold an example in thy own family!" (Grotius, cited by Meyer.)—**Who was called barren.** Called so in the way of reproach and taunt. This throws light on the joy of Zacharias promised in ver. 14, above.

37. For with God nothing shall be impossible. This is more accurately given in the Revision.—*For no word from God shall be void of power.* This explains how so strange a thing could have taken place with Elisabeth. God promised, and was able to fulfill; and, at the same time, guarantees that the prediction to Mary shall be accomplished. Every word which he has spoken will have power from God.

38. Behold the handmaid [*bondmaid*] **of the Lord; be it unto me according to thy word.** There was no more struggle of mind or hesitation; but, at the same time, there was no forwardness. She has come, in some measure, to understand what is foretold, and doubtless feels a corresponding humility, as well as a sense of the honor. She is the Lord's servant, and let it be, however amazing to her, as to him seems best.

39-45. MARY'S VISIT TO ELISABETH.

39. In those days—almost immediately, or, at least, within a month after what was just related, as would appear from considering the dates (ver. 36, 56, 57).—**The hill country**—or *mountain country*, is a natural, though uncommon, designation of the tract of high land surrounding Jerusalem for a considerable distance, especially northward and southward, rising in many places nearly three thousand feet above the level of the Mediterranean, and much more than that above the Jordan and the Dead Sea. So strikingly was this the case, that in approaching Jerusalem from any direction but the south, they were in strict propriety said to "go up." Most of the territory of Ephraim, Benjamin, and Judah lay on this long mountain ridge.—**With haste**—indicates the eagerness with which Mary sought, as soon as possible, an interview with the aged relative who shared with her the special favor of God. **A city of Judah** (*Judea*). Luke seems not to have known what city, and we know not. It is doubtful whether at this time the priests lived, as a matter of course, in the priest-cities anciently allotted to them. Hebron was such a city, near Jerusalem, and may have been the one intended, the more probably since it is described in Joshua 21: 11, as in the mountain (hill country) of Judah.

40. And entered into the house of Zacharias, and saluted Elisabeth. The enumeration of particulars marks the eager-

C

41 And it came to pass, that, when Elisabeth heard the salutation of Mary, the babe leaped in her womb; and Elisabeth was filled with the Holy Ghost:

42 And she spake out with a loud voice, and said, a Blessed *art* thou among women, and blessed *is* the fruit of thy womb.

43 And whence *is* this to me, that the mother of my Lord should come to me?

44 For, lo, as soon as the voice of thy salutation sounded in mine ears, the babe leaped in my womb for joy.

45 And blessed *is* she that believed: for there shall be a performance of those things which were told her from the Lord.

41 Elisabeth. And it came to pass, when Elisabeth heard the salutation of Mary, the babe leaped in her womb; and Elisabeth was filled with the Holy

42 Spirit; and she lifted up her voice with a loud cry, and said, Blessed *art* thou among women, and blessed

43 *is* the fruit of thy womb. And whence is this to me, that the mother of my Lord should come unto me?

44 For behold, when the voice of thy salutation came into mine ears, the babe leaped in my womb for joy.

45 And blessed *is* she that 1 believed; for there shall be a fulfilment of the things which have been spoken

a ver. 28; Judg. 5:24.——1 Or. *believed that there shall be.*

---

ness with which Mary, weary and foot-sore, hastened to the object of her journey.

41. When Elisabeth heard the salutation of Mary, the babe leaped in her womb. The salutation was more, certainly, than a mere "Hail," or "Peace to thee." It must have indicated who the visitor was, and probably may have been the first announcement to Elisabeth from any woman that her condition was known. Thus God had himself dealt with her, in his own strange way, to terminate her reproach among men. The movement of the babe has generally been treated as the proof to Elisabeth that the mother of her Lord was present. It was rather an incident of the discovery. Elisabeth's excitement of mind under all these circumstances may quite naturally account for the phenomenon (although it may well have contributed to Mary's exultation) which she interpreted as a distinct experience of the unconcious babe (ver. 44). "The emotion which possesses her is communicated to the child, whose life is as yet one with her own; and at the sudden leaping of this being, who she knows is compassed about by special blessing, the veil is rent." (Godet). Meagre support can rationally be got from this occurrence for the opinion of those who find, in ver. 15, that John was filled with the Holy Spirit before he was born. Just as little does it warrant the old figment of desperate advocates of infant baptism, that unconscious babes can exercise gospel faith.—**Elisabeth was filled with the Holy Ghost** (*Spirit*). She was miraculously confirmed in the supposition that Mary was the mother of the Messiah, and qualified to pour forth, like an ancient prophet, God's truth concerning the virgin, her son, and his work.

42. Thus she spake out (*exclaimed*) **with a loud voice** (*or shout*)—showing the overmastering strength of the prophetic impulse which urged her—**Blessed art thou among women**—peculiarly favored by God, over all other women, as selected to be the mother of the Christ—**blessed is the fruit of thy womb**. Elisabeth is enlightened as to the fact of the conception foretold in ver. 35. This fact is to be referred to a point of time between ver. 38 and 39.

43. And whence is this to me—from what source have I the privilege? The lowly wonder of her soul desires explanation.—**That the mother of my Lord should come to me?** That equivalent nearly to "in order that," depends on the preceding **this** in such a way as to make the latter include the reason for, quite as much as the fact of, Mary's coming. **The mother of my Lord.**—Elisabeth recognizes in the future son of Mary, whom her own son was to precede and assist (ver. 17) her own Lord (ver. 16), whom she already accepts in the person of his mother.

44. For. The womanly heart finds in this experience a confirmation, or reason, of that knowledge of the dignity of the embryo son of Mary, which was due to the prophetic inspiration mentioned in ver. 41.

45. And blessed is she that believed: for there shall be a performance (*accomplishment*) **of those things,** etc. The alternative rendering of the Revision—"believed that there will be"—seems decidedly preferable, not only because the main thing promised Mary is, in effect, already accomplished (Meyer), but because it is too palpable a truism to say that one is happy because such great promises are to be fulfilled, while the real happiness is in having cherished such a faith as did not doubt, when Mary might have doubted, like Zacharias, that such things could be, and so have lost the blessing.

46-55. MARY'S HYMN OF PRAISE TO GOD.

46 And Mary said, *My soul doth magnify the Lord,
47 And my spirit hath rejoiced in God my Saviour.

46 to her from the Lord. And Mary said,
   My soul doth magnify the Lord,
47 And my spirit hath rejoiced in God my Saviour

*1 Sam. 2 : 1 ; Ps. 34 : 2, 3 ; 35 : 9 ; Hab. 3 : 18.

46. And Mary said. Note the calm simplicity of style, as compared with the almost tumultuous vehemence of Elisabeth. Her whole effusion is an echo of the lyrical poetry of the Old Testament, especially of the song of praise of Hannah, the mother of Samuel, (1 Sam. ch. 2). (Meyer). Of analogous aim, but immeasurably lower in tone, is the laud ascribed to Judith in the fiction of the Apochrypha, (Judith 16 : 1-17). It is rightly printed in poetic *stichoi*, or lines, and displays that rhythm of thoughts, leading to a variant repetition or parallelism of members, which appears so conspicuous in many of the Psalms, in the Proverbs, and the prophetic poetry of the Old Testament. A loosely strophical character of the piece may be discerned, according to which Mary utters her sentiments of joyous praise to God for his personal favors to her; and celebrates the far-reaching influences of this visitation on society, in its various grades, and on the nation of Israel. (Compare Godet, p. 100 f).

46, 47. My soul. Distinguished from "spirit," in the next member, as the middle element of the human constitution between the body on one hand and the spirit on the other. It may be regarded, generally, as the seat of the sensations, perceptions, understanding, emotions, and will of the individual man. [For another view of the terms "soul" (ψυχή), and "spirit" (πνεῦμα), in the New Testament, see a brief article by Prof. D. R. Goodwin, D. D., in the "Journal of the Society of Biblical Literature and Exegesis," June and December, 1881. He reaches the following conclusions: "(1) The words soul and spirit are generally employed in the Scriptures in an indiscriminate way, each as denoting the whole mind or inner man. (2) In some few cases *spirit* may be used to denote especially the higher faculties or functions of the mind or soul, but even then not in direct contrast with the soul itself. (3) In some cases *spirit* is used for what does not at all belong to man in his natural state; but, for a certain temper, disposition, and direction of the heart, imparted by the Divine Spirit in the life of Christ, by virtue of which Christians are called spiritual (or *pneumatic*) men. But (4) there is no ground in the Scripture use of the words soul and spirit for the trichomistic doctrine of a sharp and radical distinction between the two, as co-ordinate facts of man's nature—much less as distinct substances in his constitution."—A. H]. **Doth magnify** = make great, exalt, and celebrate with praises. The verb represents the word which comes first in the sentence of the Latin Vulgate—*magnificat*—from which the whole hymn received that title in the musical service of the early churches, and has retained it ever since.—**My spirit**—the highest and specifically human element of man, among earthly creatures, by virtue of which he has knowledge of realities above the objects of sense, forms ideas far transcending the bounds of the understanding, and is capable of sentiments akin to those of angels and of God. It is the subject of faith; the meeting-place where all the faculties and experiences of our being may come into intercourse with God. It is not always used thus in Scripture, as sharply discriminated from soul and body, but is frequently so used, and especially when, as here, one or both the other terms are used in connexion with it. Nothing in this, and nothing in Scripture, warrants us in affirming that the human soul and spirit are distinct entities, or separable elements of the mental constitution. When Bishop Ellicott, in his note on 1 Thess. 5: 23, (*Commentaries*, p. 90), and still more elaborately in Sermon V. on the *Destiny of the Creature* (p. 99 ff.), solemnly argues that the mention of "body, soul, and spirit," binds us to believe that they are really different essences composing the human being, he seems to urge a claim, not only groundless, but perilous to faith. He is in danger of branding the whole science of psychology as antichristian. We think of the distinction intended by the terms here in question as analogous to that between the understanding and reason; or, between either of these and sense; or, between mind and heart. See again Dr. Hovey's comment, above.—**Hath rejoiced** (rather, *did exult*) **in God my**

48 For *he hath regarded the low estate of his handmaiden; for, behold, from henceforth *all generations shall call me blessed.
49 For he that is mighty *hath done to me great things; and *holy *is* his name.
50 And *his mercy *is* on them that fear him from generation to generation.
51 *He hath shewed strength with his arm: *he hath scattered the proud in the imagination of their hearts.
52 *He hath put down the mighty from *their* seats, and exalted them of low degree.
53 *He hath filled the hungry with good things; and the rich he hath sent empty away.
54 He hath holpen his servant Israel, *in remembrance of *his* mercy;
55 *As he spake to our fathers, to Abraham, and to his seed for ever.

48 For he hath looked upon the low estate of his ¹handmaiden:
For behold, from henceforth all generations shall call me blessed.
49 For he that is mighty hath done to me great things;
And holy is his name.
50 And his mercy is unto generations and generations
On them that fear him.
51 He hath shewed strength with his arm;
He hath scattered the proud ² in the imagination of their heart.
52 He hath put down princes from *their* thrones,
And hath exalted them of low degree.
53 The hungry he hath filled with good things;
And the rich he hath sent empty away.
54 He hath holpen Israel his servant,
That he might remember mercy
55 (As he spake unto our fathers)
Toward Abraham and his seed for ever.

a 1 Sam. 1: 11; Ps. 138: 6....b Mal. 3: 12; ch. 11: 27....c Ps. 71: 19; 126: 2, 3,....d Ps. 111: 9....e Gen. 17: 7; Ex. 20: 6; Ps. 103: 17, 18....f Ps. 99: 1; 115: 15; Isa. 40: 10; 51: 9; 52: 10,....g Ps. 33: 10; 1 Pet. 5: 5... h 1 Sam. 2: 6, etc.; Job 5: 11; Ps. 113: 6.... i 1 Sam. 2: 5; Ps. 34: 10....k Ps 98: 3; Jer. 31: 3, 20....l Gen. 17: 19; Ps. 132: 11; Rom. 11: 28; Gal. 3: 16.——1 Gr. *bond-maiden.* ....2 Or. *by.*

Saviour. Mary's present extolling of God as Lord, is an expression of her understanding and heart through her vocal organs, and is rooted in a former experience, recorded in ver. 36-38, where her spirit was entranced in a revelation of him as now her Saviour, and in what sense a Saviour, is explained by reference to a definite act.

48. For he hath regarded (rather, *has looked upon*, preterit again) **the low estate** (*the humiliation*) **of his handmaiden.** Though he is high, yet had he respect unto the lowly. Upon her in her common lot, of poor parents, as would seem, and betrothed to a man of a class despised by the high and religiously influential among the people, has he bestowed the greatest distinction ever conferred on a mortal. This is confirmed by the wonderful truth that follows.—**Behold, from henceforth all generations shall call me blessed.** Surely he has taken her out of her humiliation, and placed her on high. Elisabeth, in declaring her "blessed among women," has but anticipated the judgment of all who shall hear truly concerning her to the end of time. Mary's humility of spirit in all her adoring gratitude for God's great favor, is the best proof how she would have revolted at the thought of being herself deified in subsequent ages, and made to stand between the millions of worshipers and God her Saviour.

49. She ascribes it all to him **that is mighty**—thus bringing forward the power of him who has done these great things (comp. 2: 35), "power of the Highest," according to the promise in ver. 35 above. **And holy is his name.** This designation, "The Mighty One," reflecting one phase of his character, is to be associated in our minds with the idea of holiness (Ps. 89: 19; 111: 9; Rev. 15: 4).

50. And his mercy is on them that fear him from generation to generation. *And his mercy is unto generations and generations.* Revision (comp. Ps. 89: 1, 4; Gen. 17: 9; Ex. 20). This appears to be a general truth to which Mary is led by a consideration of God's gracious dealing with her.

51-53. These verses are specially like the strain of Hannah (1 Sam. 2: 4 ff.), and may be viewed as Mary's prophetic history of the blessings to be experienced through the reign of her Son. The verbs are all, as far as ver. 55, in the aorist (preterit) tense, and represent the Hebrew perfect, as expressive of general truths, or of future events, regarded in prophecy as having already taken place. They anticipate the beatitudes of the Sermon on the Mount, especially as given by Luke, where the promises are directly of temporal gifts to them that are physically needy and wretched; but to them, doubtless, as being therefore prepared in spirit for the gifts which the spiritual nature craves. **The proud, the mighty,** and **the rich,** in these verses, are the leading class of the Jewish nation represented, in their haughtiness, arrogance, and tyranny, by the scribes and Pharisees and chief priests of that age.—Those of **low degree** and **the hungry**—are such as Zacharias, Simeon, Anna, Lazarus, and his sisters, and the common people who heard Jesus gladly, yet were despised by the self-righteous rulers.

54, 55. In all this Mary finds the fulfill-

CH. I.]　　　　　　　　　　　　LUKE.　　　　　　　　　　　　　37

56 And Mary abode with her about three months, and returned to her own house.
57 Now Elisabeth's full time came that she should be delivered; and she brought forth a son.
58 And her neighbours and her cousins heard how the Lord had shewed great mercy upon her; and ᵃ they rejoiced with her.
59 And it came to pass, that ᵇ on the eighth day they came to circumcise the child; and they called him Zacharias, after the name of his father.
60 And his mother answered and said, ᶜ Not *so;* but he shall be called John.
61 And they said unto her, There is none of thy kindred that is called by this name.
62 And they made signs to his father, how he would have him called.
63 And he asked for a writing table, and wrote, saying, ᵈ His name is John. And they marvelled all.

56 And Mary abode with her about three months, and returned unto her house.
57 Now Elisabeth's time was fulfilled that she should 58 be delivered; and she brought forth a son. And her neighbours and her kinsfolk heard that the Lord had magnified his mercy towards her; and they 59 rejoiced with her. And it came to pass on the eighth day, that they came to circumcise the child; and they would have called him Zacharias, after the 60 name of his father. And his mother answered and 61 said, Not so; but he shall be called John. And they said unto her, There is none of thy kindred that is 62 called by this name. And they made signs to his 63 father, what he would have him called. And he asked for a writing tablet, and wrote, saying, His

a ver. 14....*b* Gen. 17: 12; Lev. 12: 3....*c* ver. 13....*d* ver. 13.

ment of the ancient promises of help to Israel through the reign of the Messiah. The Revision is a decided improvement, although strict fidelity requires all these narrative verbs to be expressed in the preterit tense.

56. MARY'S RETURN. The three months brought her near to the birth of John. To some it will seem strange that she should leave before Elisabeth had passed her trial; and it has been supposed by some that this statement is placed by anticipation before its true order. But had it been true that Mary had staid so long, it could hardly fail to have been related distinctly.

57-66. BIRTH OF JOHN THE BAPTIST.

58. **And her neighbours and her cousins** (kinsfolk), family connections of all degrees, **heard how** (that) **the Lord had shewed great mercy** (rather, *was magnifying his mercy*) **upon her.** The blessing is not mentioned as though it had been an instantaneous thing, already past, but it was permanent in the presence and preservation of the child, so remarkable a boon to its aged parents. We have nothing said to intimate that they knew anything as yet to distinguish the birth from any other in extraordinary circumstances, where offspring had been greatly desired.

59. **On the eighth day**—the regularly appointed time (Gen 17:12; Phil. 3:5). The parents walked here in the ordinances of the Lord blameless (ver. 6). Only by circumcision did the son of a Jewish family become a citizen, a member of the nation, and so, indirectly, a sharer in important religious privileges of that people. That the rite was directly of civil significance only, suits with its exclusive applicability to the male sex. It was performed by the parents, or one appointed by them, and

the occasion was regarded as a domestic festival. **And they called him Zacharias**—("would have called," Revised Version, "were for calling," Davidson); literally, "*were in the act of calling.*" They may have used the word, but before it had been formally applied to the child, the mother interposed, and prevented its being done. The naming took place in connection with the circumcision, as Abraham received his full name (as also did Sarah) at the time of his circumcision.

60. **And his mother answered**—to their proposal of the name Zacharias—**and said, Not so; but he shall be called John.** Some have thought this mention of John implied a supernatural, prophetic, coincidence with the name given by the angel (ver. 13); but it seems not at all unlikely that during the subsequent months Zacharias had communicated to his wife what occurred with him in the temple, including the name. He could do this by writing, as we see just below.

61. Early in the Jewish history, names were applied to their children almost always with direct reference to the appellative significance of the words used, and without any regard to the names of parent or ancestors. Now, the neighbors of Elisabeth took it for granted that she would use for her child his father's name, or that of some relative. Nor would they desist from their intention until they had applied to the father for his wish in the matter.

62. **And they made signs.** That they consulted him by making **signs**, literally, by "*nodding to*" him, appears to indicate that he had become deaf as well as speechless. Yet it is not a decisive proof.

63. **On a writing table** (*tablet*), he very positively confirms the direction of the angel. —**His name is John,** which heaven had de-

38 LUKE. [Ch. I.

64 ^a And his mouth was opened immediately, and his tongue loosed, and he spake, and praised God.
65 And fear came on all that dwelt round about them; and all these ^bsayings were noised abroad throughout all ^cthe hill country of Judea.
66 And all they that heard them, ^dlaid them up in their hearts, saying, What manner of child shall this be! And ^ethe hand of the Lord was with him.
67 And his father Zacharias ^f was filled with the Holy Ghost, and prophesied, saying,
68 ^g Blessed be the Lord God of Israel; for ^h he hath visited and redeemed his people,

61 name is John. And they marvelled all. And his mouth was opened immediately, and his tongue
65 loosed, and he spake, blessing God. And fear came on all that dwelt round about them: and all these sayings were noised abroad throughout all the hill
66 country of Judea. And all that heard them laid them up in their heart, saying, What then shall this child be? For the hand of the Lord was with him.
67 And his father Zacharias was filled with the Holy Spirit, and prophesied, saying,
68 Blessed be the Lord, the God of Israel;
For he hath visited and wrought redemption for his people,

a ver. 20....b Or, things....c ver. 39....d ch. 2: 19, 51....e Gen. 39: 2; Ps. 80: 17; 89: 21; Acts 11: 21....f Joel 2: 28....g 1 Kings 1: 48; Ps. 41: 13; 72: 18; 106: 48....h Ex. 3: 16; 4: 31; Ps. 111: 9; ch. 7: 16.

clared that it should be.—**And they marvelled all,** because of this inexplicable agreement between the parents in a purpose so singular. Now had the day come (ver. 20) in which the things promised to the priest, in the holy place, were accomplished, so that his penalty of dumbness might be remitted.

64. And his mouth was opened immediately, and his tongue was loosed. The divine power which had inflicted on him that silence for a definite period, now that the period was precisely complete, released him from all restraint on his speech.—**And he spake, and praised God.** Doubtless even the penalty which he had endured, seen now in its connection with all God's working in the matter of his Son, would seem a proper theme of praise, and his whole soul would go out in thoughtful adoration (*praising or blessing*) in his recovered utterance.

65, 66. These verses describe the natural effects of such an interposition of God's hand, in an age of lively expectation of Messianic events; effects which immediately began to be experienced, and are here summarily related, as extending through a considerable period of time.—We may note in the brief record how widely the report spread, so that the natural fear extended not only to all the neighboring people, but in the whole mountain land of Judea **all these sayings were noised abroad** (*talked over and over* διελαλεῖτο); while among those who had heard them the heart-wonder deepened as they pondered, and they asked, **What manner of child shall this be?** See Revised Version. Surely such a birth imports an exalted destiny. Thus was the way preparing for that reception which John should meet, when he came forth at last with his call to repentance and preparation for the kingdom of God.

67-79. Prophetic Hymn of Zacharias.

67. And his father Zacharias was filled with the Holy Ghost (*Spirit*), **and prophesied.** The latter statement again defines and explains the former; he was filled with the Holy Spirit so as to qualify him for the prophetic utterances which follow, and in which his inspiration appears. The time of this is probably that of the circumcision and naming, and may be part in the discourse which then he spake, *blessing God.* Luke's frequent manner of introducing proleptically historical facts led him first to follow out the impression made by what had so far occurred (ver. 65, 66), and now he resumes the psalm of Zacharias. This suits better with the necessity of assuming *some* special occasion for the discourse, and with the address (ver. 76 ff.) to the "little child," as present.

68. Saying, Blessed be the Lord (*the*) **God of Israel,** etc. In this noble psalm Zacharias celebrates, first (ver. 68-70), the fulfillment of God's ancient promises, through the gift of the Messiah, whose coming and its consequences are present to him as an accomplished fact; next (ver. 71-75), the blessings that follow from it to Israel; then (ver. 76, 77), the connection of his own Son with this epiphany and its blessed results; and, finally (ver. 78, 79), he traces all back to God's mercy, and forward to the enlightenment of them that sit in darkness (including, though perhaps not consciously, the heathen world), and the attainment of the path of peace. The form of the expressions, the character of the imagery, the quality of the salvation, all are, as we should expect, still Hebraistic, as is true of the utterances of all participants, human and celestial, in this prelude to the gospel. Everything is conceived as would be natural to a pious son of Abraham, to whom "the things which God has prepared for them that love him" were only partially revealed by his Spirit. (Comp. 1 Cor. 2: 9, 10). We are still in

Cн. I.] LUKE. 39

69	^a And hath raised up an horn of salvation for us in the house of his servant David;	69	And hath raised up a horn of salvation for us in the house of his servant David
70	^b As he spake by the mouth of his holy prophets, which have been since the world began:	70	(As he spake by the mouth of his holy prophets that have been of old),
71	That we should be saved from our enemies, and from the hand of all that hate us;	71	Salvation from our enemies, and from the hand of all that hate us;
72	^c To perform the mercy *promised* to our fathers, and to remember his holy covenant;	72	To shew mercy towards our fathers, And to remember his holy covenant;
73	^d The oath which he sware to our father Abraham,	73	The oath which he sware unto Abraham our father,
74	That he would grant unto us, that we being delivered out of the hands of our enemies might *serve* him without fear,	74	To grant unto us that we being delivered out of the hand of our enemies

a Ps. 132: 17.... b Jer. 23: 5, 6; 30: 10; Dan. 9: 24; Acts 3: 21; Rom 1: 2.... c Lev. 26: 42; Ps. 98: 3; 105. 8, 9, 106: 14, Ezek. 16: 60; ver. 54....d Gen. 12: 3; 17: 4; 22: 16, 17; Heb. 6: 13, 17 ...e Rom. 6: 18, 22; Heb. 9: 14.

---

the twilight, amid the shadows of a preparatory era. The tenses of verbs are in the preterit of Hebrew prophecy. Things future are seen as already realized. The translation of this passage, as used in the Latin and other liturgies, is called, from the Latin of the first word, the *Benedictus*.—**Visited and redeemed his people**—rather, *wrought redemption for* (Revised Version), or, *made a ransom.*

69. An horn of salvation—a designation of the Messiah—**horn** in the Old Testament, being a familiar symbol of strength and victory. **Of salvation,** as affording salvation. This appears in the house of David, i. e., as one of the family of David. Zacharias would appear to have thought of the posterity of David.

70. As he spake, etc. This great boon is thus characterized as the fulfillment of the prophecies in all the Old Testament, from the beginning of human history.

71. That we should be saved (literally, *salvation*) **from our enemies,** in loose apposition with "horn of salvation," ver. 69, the intervening verse being parenthetical. The provision for salvation has passed into the idea of salvation experienced. It is conceived of as a national blessing, as was natural to a Hebrew, and its character is evolved in the following verses to 75 inclusive. That rescue from external enemies (see also ver. 74), appears so prominent in the description of "salvation," is thoroughly consistent with a multitude of expressions in the Old Testament, and most natural in the mouth of a pious Israelite, living in the distressed circumstances of his people, oppressed and degraded under a Pagan rule, at the time of John's birth.

72. To perform the mercy promised to our fathers. This is involved in that salvation, and is now spoken of as divinely intended in the gift. The literal translation would be: "*to do mercy with our fathers*"; but it is not obvious *how* affording salvation to this late age was doing "mercy with the fathers." The thought may possibly be that the fathers are ever present in their children, mercy shown to whom, in fulfillment of promises in which the former trusted, is mercy to them. But Isa. 29: 22, 23, ascribes shame to Jacob and paleness of face, (on account of the unrighteousness of his posterity), which will be removed when they repent and sanctify their father's God. (Comp. Mic. 7: 20, and Lange's note on the place.) In the New Testament, also, Abraham rejoices to see the day of Christ (John 8: 56); is represented as conversant with the fortunes of men on the earth (Luke 16: 25 ff.); and all the fathers live unto God (20: 38). In conformity with this view, which might be much enlarged by references to the Apocryphal literature of the Jews, we may, perhaps, best understand the language before us as practically meaning, that the procurement of the Messianic salvation is literally showing mercy to the fathers, who are waiting for it, "to Abraham and his seed" (ver. 55, Revised Version).—**And to remember his holy covenant**—a parallel, in which nearly the same thought is brought out in other terms. The covenant always involved promises, if it did not really consist in them (Gen. 15: 18; 17: 2 ff., Ex. 24. 7, 8). The promises, hitherto unfulfilled, God now remembers so as to accomplish.

73. The oath which he sware, etc., is only another designation of the same engagement of the Lord, made pointedly specific by reference to Abraham (Gen. 12: 1-3; 17: 4; 22: 16 f. Comp. Heb. 6: 13, 17).

74. That he would grant unto us, that we being delivered, etc. This also is a part of the salvation (ver. 71). Being in the participal form, it views the deliverance from

75 *In holiness and righteousness before him, all the days of our life.
76 And thou, child, shalt be called the prophet of the Highest: for *thou shalt go before the face of the Lord to prepare his ways;
77 To give knowledge of salvation unto his people *d by the remission of their sins,
78 Through the *tender mercy of our God; whereby the *dayspring from on high hath visited us,

75 Should serve him without fear,
In holiness and righteousness before him all our days.
76 Yea and thou, child, shalt be called the prophet of the Most High:
For thou shalt go before the face of the Lord to make ready his ways;
77 To give knowledge of salvation unto his people In the remission of their sins,
78 Because of the *tender mercy of our God,
*Whereby the dayspring from on high *shall visit us,

a Jer. 32: 39, 40; Eph. 4: 24; 2 Thess. 2: 13; 2 Tim. 1: 9. Tit. 2: 12; 1 Pet. 1: 15; 2 Pet. 1: 4.. .b Isa. 40: 3; Mal. 3: 1; 4: 5; Matt. 11: 10; ver. 17....c Mark 1: 4; ch. 3: 3,...d Or. for....e Or, bowels of the mercy....f Or, sun-rising, or, branch, Num. 21: 17; Isa. 11: 1; Zech. 3: 8; 6, 12, Mal. 4: 2.—1 Or, heart of mercy... 2 Or, Wherein.. .3 Many ancient authorities read, hath visited us.

human foes as a condition of the higher blessings next mentioned. It is not grammatically dependent on "the oath," etc.; but is parallel to "to perform," and "to remember" (ver. 72). **That we might [***should***] serve him without fear**—fear of unsympathizing, worldly, sometimes hostile and intensely cruel rulers, such as had so often afflicted the nation for generations past.

75. In holiness—not the ordinary word for holiness, nearly equivalent to purity—**and righteousness**, such as that ascribed to Zacharias and Elisabeth (ver. 6). This immaculate religiousness of service the prophet sees destined for the Messianic worshipers as a perpetual distinction, not, as heretofore, an occasional, transient, partial quality, which faded away as the early dew.—**Before him all the days of our life**. As long as the nation continues. *All our days*, omitting "of our life," is the correct text.

76. And thou [*also***], child, shalt be called the prophet of the Highest.** He has celebrated the Messiah and his benefits, first, but is not allowed to omit a notice of the preparatory part which his son is to play in this great fulfillment of eternal plans. "And thou, *also*, child," (the Revised Version would give the force of *also* by the preceding "Yea"), implies that his announcement *is not complete* without adding something concerning him. **Child**, my offspring, child, though thou art. **Shalt be called**, equivalent to *shall be*, as in ver. 35. "The prophet" is, primarily, the spokesman for God, who, uttering the divine counsels generally, incidentally *foretells* some things.—**For thou shalt go before the face of the Lord.** The *for* explains and confirms the designation of **prophet**. **To go before the face** is, as in ver 17, to precede in time, and to go in the view, under the eye, on the errand, of another. **The Lord** here is, probably, to Zacharias the same person as "the Highest" in the preceding sentence, and yet the event shows him to be the Messiah.—**To prepare his ways**, viz., to make ready for his coming, by teaching the people the true nature and necessary conditions of the salvation which he will bring; for the very idea of evangelical salvation had died out of the minds of the proud and work-righteous seed of Abraham, as a mass. How indispensable such a preparation was appears from the fact that neither Zacharias himself, nor Mary, nor Elisabeth, has *distinctly* noticed, in these inspired utterances, the subject of repentance, the new heart, the spiritual transformation, in which the blessings promised by them would really be found. The "salvation" of which they catch a glimpse, is national, mainly external, and its conditions are expressed in terms of Old Testament prophecy. They scarcely see these things so clearly now as, in occasional visions, did Daniel, Isaiah, Jeremiah, Micah, Ezekiel. "It is darkest just before day."

77. To give knowledge of salvation ... by (*in***) the remission of their sins.** Here is the nearest approach to an essentially gospel view. This was John's first aim, "preaching a baptism of repentance for the remission of sins." He should teach that salvation involved pardon; that pardon was required because of sins, and could be received through a new view, a new heart, new purposes, a new life before God. Even those who were to prove "his people," were ignorant of these things now.

78. Through the tender mercy of our God. God already appears more in his special relation to the heart of his worshipers, as **our God**. **Tender mercy** is literally, "the bowels of mercy," as in Phil. 2: 1. The "**bowels**," like our word "heart," denotes,

79 *a* To give light to them that sit in darkness and in the shadow of death, to guide our feet into the way of peace.
80 And *b* the child grew, and waxed strong in spirit, and *c* was in the deserts till the day of his shewing unto Israel.

79 To shine upon them that sit in darkness and the shadow of death;
To guide our feet into the way of peace.
80 And the child grew, and waxed strong in spirit, and was in the deserts till the day of his shewing unto Israel.

a Mark 1:4; ch. 3:3, *b* Isa. 9:2; 42:7; 49:9; Matt. 4:16; Acts 26:18....*b* ch. 2:40....*c* Matt. 3:1; 11:1.

metaphorically, in Hebrew, the seat of affections, emotions, strong, especially tender, feeling. It is this tender compassion of God *through*, literally, "on account of," which, all these provisions of blessing are furnished us.—**Whereby**—("*wherein*," in the exercise of which feelings of mercy)—**the dayspring from on high hath visited us.**—Rather, "a dayspring," literally, "a rising," as of the sun, or, possibly, of a bright star. The word also means sometimes an upspringing, viz., of the shoot of a plant; then "the dawn," as occasioned by the approaching rise of the sun. It is here plainly a figure for the Messiah; (compare Malachi 4:2—"shall the Sun of Righteousness arise").. It might, indeed, have been used in the sense of "the branch" (Zech. 3:8; 6:12); "the rod out of the stem of Jesse" (Isa. 11:1); but here all the adjuncts **visited**, literally "looked upon," and—**from on high**, favor the sense of "dawn" or "sunrise." What metaphor could be more expressive of the joyfulness of the promised salvation? The preterit tense of the verb, **hath visited**, properly, *visited*, is in precise accordance with the usage through this whole psalm, and has strongly the support of the internal evidence. On the other hand, the best manuscripts favor the reading followed in the Revised Version, "will visit us"; and unless other light arises on the passage, that will probably be accepted by-and-by.

79. To give light to (*to shine forth upon*) **them that sit in darkness.** The infinitive marks the result of the day-spring visiting us. **Darkness** is the symbol of ignorance, moral corruption, and consequent misery.—**The shadow of death** is a Hebrew expression for the deepest gloom (Ps. 23:4)—such gloom as the imagination associates with the idea of death.—**To guide our feet into the way of peace.** Peace was to the Hebrew a summary designation of complete welfare. **This way of peace** was in the Old Testament the way of wisdom, or the pious conformity of all one's spirit and conduct to the requirements of Jehovah (Prov. 3:13-17); in the New Testament it will be found in wearing the yoke of Jesus (Matt. 11:32; comp. John 14:27; 16:33). Toward this the shining of that light would **guide** (literally, *direct*) our feet. Zacharias includes himself among those who needed this direction.

80. And the child grew, and waxed strong (*was strengthened*) **in spirit.** This verse contains all that we are permitted to know further concerning the private life of John; and these words give the whole account of his domestic development. He grew normally, in body, and mentally and morally he became strong. The clause, **in spirit**, here expresses the whole complement of the body in making up the man—soul being included. Strength is the quality which seems to have attracted attention in his character from the first, and this agrees with the sternness and severity of his public function. Not a word of *grace* or *favor*, either as a trait of his disposition, or existing in the regard had for him by God or man. The other quality was the conspicuous one, remembered in the narratives of his home life, which were preserved. Compare and contrast the two somewhat analogous cases of Samuel (1 Sam. 2:18, 19, 26) and Jesus (Luke 2:40-52).—**And was in the deserts till the day of his shewing unto Israel.** This was all that could be told of his life from the time when he left the shelter of his home. That home, considering the age of his parents, may have been broken up while he was yet young, and his seclusion from the world may have continued a number of years, before he began, at the age of thirty, to preach and baptize. His natural disposition would, it seems, make such seclusion congenial; but he probably adopted it in part from a desire to cultivate a religious life, and to prepare himself, like Elijah and other early prophets, for that office which he recognized a call to perform. Nobody of any consequence now pretends to connect John with the Essenes, or any other known ascetic and recluse school or sect of men; but we perceive a degree of individual asceticism, such as has been popularly associated in all ages with the conception of eminent piety.

CHAPTER II.

AND it came to pass in those days, that there went out a decree from Cæsar Augustus, that all the world should be ᵃ taxed.

1 Now it came to pass in those days, there went out a decree from Cæsar Augustus, that all ¹ the world

a Or, enrolled.—1 Gr. the inhabited earth.

The deserts here referred to were parts of the "wilderness of Judea" (Matt. 3:1; Luke 3:2, "the wilderness"). It lay southeast of Jerusalem, within the borders of Judah, and since John was baptizing in the Jordan "in the wilderness," the term would seem to have embraced a certain portion of the desert country bordering that river from its mouth northward. It was not a desert like Sahara, but an arid, barren country, much of it mountainous, with treeless, rocky slopes and summits, broken through by deep chasms worn by the waters of occasional rains, uncheered by verdure, except for a short time in the spring, and at other seasons along the beds of streams that might still trickle down the ravines, or around the much-prized springs, and rare perennial brooks. In a very narrow strip, close on the banks of the Jordan, vegetation flourished, bordered by the parched desert. Many natural caves and hollows of the rocks afforded shelter for hermits, whether cenobites or solitaries. Somewhere in this quarter dwelt the strange sect of the Essenes, a monkish community of the Jews, who in that period had retired thither from the world, to avoid its contamination, and to cultivate a more religious life. All attempts, however, to identify John with them, in principles or practice, have so utterly failed, that they are only remembered as things of the past. John would find the rough and uninviting solitudes of the wilderness suitable for abundant communion with God; and its privations would train him to that sturdiness and independence which were needed in facing the worldly and self-indulgent ways of a stiff-necked and gainsaying people. Whether he returned at all to his birthplace, during the years before **his shewing** to the people; whether he took part in feasts and fasts, or any solemn rites of his nation, we cannot tell. There he abode mainly, at least, **till the day of his shewing unto Israel.** It was God that showed him, or pointed him out, "when the word of God came unto" him, and sent him forth among the people (2:2, 3).

PART I. SECT. II. Ch. 2: 1-52. BIRTH AND PRIVATE LIFE OF JESUS. This section of the Gospel treats (1) of the birth of Jesus (ver 1-7); (2) the announcement of the fact to shepherds, and joy of the angels thereupon (8-14); (3) visit of the shepherds to the babe and his mother in Bethlehem (15-20); (4) the circumcision (21); (5) the presentation in the temple, and the prophetic recognition of the Messiah by Simeon and Anna (22-38); (6) the private life of Jesus through childhood and youth (39-52).

1-7. THE BIRTH OF JESUS. In those days. A loose designation of the period within which the birth of John the Baptist fell—overlooking the brief statements in ver. 80 of the preceding chapter.—**There went out a decree.** What the decree ordered was an enrollment, or registration of all the population of the empire—**the whole world.** Literally "*the inhabited world,*" which, so far as definitely known, was then mostly included within the Roman Empire. This enrollment was not properly a "taxing," as we now understand that term; but might have been only to secure such an enumeration of persons, with their age, their occupation, standing, and property—a census, in short—as would afford a basis for taxation, for enlistment into the army, and other measures. The credibility of Luke's statement that such a census was then ordered, has been impugned on the ground that profane history gives no account of it, and that if there had been one, it could not have taken place in Judea, which was not yet made a province, but was governed by Herod as an "associate" king. In reply to the last objection, it may be remarked that Tacitus expressly names (Annal. 1:11) kingdoms (*regna*) as well as provinces, among the subjects included in the great Domesday Book of the whole empire, which Augustus had drawn up with his own hands. And certainly Herod, who was the mere creature of the emperor, would not be spared the necessity, as he would not lack the willingness, to contribute to the revenues by which,

2 (*And* this taxing was first made when Cyrenius was governor of Syria.) | 2 should be enrolled. This was the first enrollment

a Acts 5: 37.

in effect, his own government would be sustained. As to the manner of it, the emperor would naturally allow Herod to conduct the enrollment in conformity with Jewish customs, and the latter would probably be able to show that it was not made with reference to any tax immediately to be levied. That Augustus required such a census to be taken about that time is supported by the authority of Luke himself, a historian as trustworthy, for all that appears, as any of his age. His testimony cannot be cancelled by the mere silence of others, considering how scanty details we have of the transactions of that period. But we are not left without other evidence. The Roman historians mention an enrollment as occurring in the year of Rome 746. Now it is not at all likely that this would be effected simultaneously throughout the vast empire; and in the uncertainty as to the precise year of the Saviour's birth, that one may have been yet unfinished in Palestine at our present point of time.

To this may be added that the Christian apologists, in the second century, appeal to census lists as existing, taken in Palestine by Quirinius, which all persons could examine for themselves, and none of their acute and learned opponents disputed them on this point.

2. And this taxing was first made. Omit the *and*, and read, *This enrollment, first*—or, *as a first one*—*took place*—**when Cyrenius was governor of Syria.** The translation will vary as we receive or reject, according to different texts, the article, *the first*, or *a first*. There seems to be a plain reference to another enrollment made, as a second, under the governorship of Cyrenius over Syria in A. D. 6, about ten years after this, when Judas the Galilean raised an insurrection (Acts 5: 37). To the accuracy of this statement it is objected that Cyrenius (in Latin, *Quirinus* or *Quirinius*) was governor (*proconsul*) of Syria in and after A. D. 6. It is assumed then that Luke has mistaken the governor of the time. Surely not of necessity, unless we know that Cyrenius was somewhere else at the time when Christ was born, or that somebody else was then in that office.

Assuming that he could not have held it twice, a great variety of violent grammatical expedients have been hazarded to obviate the discrepancy. These have been treated in Godet (who unfortunately adds one of his own), and other extended commentaries; and it is hardly worth while to discuss them here. If Godet were right in saying (I., p. 123), "history proves that Quirinius did not become governor until the year 4," in any sense of the word governor, we should have simply to admit that, in the scarcity of information as to the actual circumstances of that province at the time in question, we must fall back on the authority of Luke, and not try to explain how the fact here asserted by him consists with the other fact, that Quirinius is known to have been governor there ten years afterward (Acts. 6:37), "in the days of the taxing." Comp. Joseph., *Jew. Antiq.* 18: 1. 1 f.). But since the arguments of A. W. Zumpt on this subject (*Commentatio Epigraphica de Syria Romanorum provincia*. etc., V. 2, Berlin, 1854, it is thought by many not at all improbable, that Quir'nius was first governor of Syria *about* the time of Christ's birth, say, from some time in the year 750, U. C. So probable is this, that if it were not that Matthew informs us that the nativity occurred while Herod was yet alive, little difficulty would be felt. (See a synopsis of Zumpt's reasoning in Smith's *Dict. of Biography*, p. 625 f.) But President Woolsey, in his candid consideration of the matter in that Article, shows clearly that however nearly he has made out what we should be glad to have proved, his result does not relieve us, because we seem to see in Josephus that Quintilius Varus was president of Syria during the last years of Herod, and until after his death. But we may still suppose that Quirinius, being in that part of the empire, was employed as a special commissioner to superintend the enrollment, he having proved himself a vigorous and efficient officer, which Varus was not. We should then have to suppose further that Luke had employed the Greek word (ἡγεμών), which may designate any leadership, in a more loose sense than he is in the habit of

44 LUKE. [Ch. II.

3 And all went to be taxed, every one into his own city.
4 And Joseph also went up from Galilee, out of the city of Nazareth, into Judea, unto ᵃthe city of David, which is called Bethlehem; (ᵇ because he was of the house and lineage of David;)
5 To be taxed with Mary ᶜ his espoused wife, being great with child.

3 made when Quirinius was governor of Syria. And all went to enrol themselves, every one to his own 4 city. And Joseph also went up from Galilee, out of the city of Nazareth, into Judea, to the city of David, which is called Bethlehem, because he was of 5 the house and family of David; to enrol himself with Mary, who was betrothed to him, being great

a 1 Sam. 16 : 1, 4 ; John 7 : 42....b Matt. 1 : 16 ; ch. 1 : 27....c Matt. 1 : 18 ; ch. 1 : 27.

doing. This view is regarded with favor by Farrar (*Com. on Luke* in the *Cambridge Bible for Schools*, p. 64); and Meyer, who has no objection to finding Luke, or any other Biblical writer, out of harmony with facts, admits and maintains that it is probably correct. It may be added that to Luke's own authority (compare remark, p. 43), may be added the

4. And Joseph also went up . . . On went up, see on 1 : 39.—**Out of the city of Nazareth,** see on 1 : 26.—**Into Judea,** from the northern to the southern district of the Holy Land.—**City of David,** where David was born, or at least where his father, Jesse, lived (1 Sam. 16:1), and from which David came forth to the public view.—**Unto Bethlehem,**

NAZARETH.

testimony of some of the earliest Church Fathers, who appeal to evidence as existing in their day, of the historical accuracy of our passage (Justin Martyr, *Apol.* 1, 34, 46 ; Tertul. *Adv. Marcion*, 4, 7. Cited by McClellan, *Translation of the New Testament*, I. 395 f., where the whole question is copiously discussed).

3. And all went to be taxed (*enrolled*), **every one into his own city,** viz., the city of his ancestors, where the family records were kept. This was according to the Jewish custom, which, as we have seen, the emperor would be likely to respect.

about six miles south of Jerusalem. It was on even higher ground than the capital city, was hallowed from very early times as the burial place of Rachel, and the scene of many interesting events.—**Because he was of the house and lineage** (*family*) **of David. The house** was the immediate family and descendants of David; **the lineage** (πατριά) was the clan, family in a wider sense, that sprang from one of the immediate sons of Judah.

5. To be taxed (*to enroll himself*) **with Mary his espoused wife** (*who was betrothed to him*), **being great with child.** Omit

6 And so it was, that, while they were there, the days were accomplished that she should be delivered.
7 And *she brought forth her firstborn son, and wrapped him in swaddling clothes, and laid him in a manger; because there was no room for them in the inn.

6 with child. And it came to pass, while they were there, the days were fulfilled that she should be delivered.
7 And she brought forth her firstborn son; and she wrapped him in swaddling clothes, and laid him in a manger, because there was no room for them in the inn.

a Matt. 1 : 25.

---

great. Mary may have gone with him simply from unwillingness to be separated from her espoused, or, possibly, that she might be in the place (Bethlehem, Mic. 5: 1) foretold in prophecy; but we can only conjecture. Their journey, from all that we know of their circumstances, must have been on foot; but this would not then be regarded as a special hardship.

6. While they were there, etc. How long a time they had spent there, we cannot tell. If they were dependent on the meagre accommodations of an **inn**, we could hardly suppose them to have tarried very long. But the word translated **inn** is very different from that employed in ch. 10: 34. It is that which is rendered "guest chamber" (22: 11); so that it is as likely, perhaps, to mean the room allotted to visitors in a private house. Whether so or not, privacy at the critical moment could be afforded to the expectant mother only in a place which was probably common in use to the family and to domestic animals. Such were often found or prepared in the natural or artificial hollows of the rock, of which the hills about Bethlehem consisted. We are in no case to think of a house of entertainment, such as our word now suggests; but, at the most, of a simple structure furnished by the hospitality of the neighborhood, in which travelers might shelter themselves and their beasts, supplying themselves, for the most part, with bedding and food.

7. And she brought forth her first-born son. Plainly implying, and proving, unless some reason can be shown for taking the adjective in a sense different from the obvious one, that she afterward bore other sons, or another, in reference to whom this was the first. These appear often in the gospel history as sons of Joseph and Mary.—**And wrapped him in swaddling clothes.** This early suggested to some expositors that Mary passed through her trial without the pains and infirmity of ordinary child-birth, that she should be able to act as her own nurse, and the child's.—**And laid him in a manger.**

Manger cannot mean stable, here, as some have supposed; it is what we commonly understand by the word, the feeding trough for the cattle; but it implies that the scene was a place which partook of the character of a stable. This was, in its circumstances, a lowly entrance upon life, as became one whose home was to be lowly, and whose friends would be the poor and despised, chiefly; and whose earthly end, a thousand times more pitiable than his birth. As we have already intimated, it would not seem so squalid to the people of that time, and of the condition of Joseph's family, as to us; yet few who have at any time since experienced the hardships of poverty, loneliness, and neglect, could think of the birth of the Saviour without feeling that he could sympathize with all their griefs. It is not related here as any notable privation or distress, but is calmly explained by the statement that **there was no room for them in the inn,** or lodging place. Was ever an event of literally infinite consequence told in words so unambitious and plain?

The date of this event has occasioned discussion enough to fill a library, if the record of it could be got together in books; but with no proper definiteness of result. The year assumed in making Christ's birth the epoch of the Christian Era, is *very* generally agreed now to be too late by at least four years (Herod having died in the spring of 750 U. C., and not in 753), and possibly by five or seven. If we arrive at the exact date of Herod's death, we have not a particle of testimony as to how long before that was the Nativity, and every point from which men would, by long and intricate inferences, reach the day, or month, or year, is itself unstable, so that no certainty results. It is sad to think that so much learning, historical, mathematical, astronomical, has failed of the desired result in the treatises of Ideler, Browne, Wieseler, Zumpt, McClellan, Greswell, and others. But each one generally aims to destroy the conclusions of his predecessor, and effectually

8 And there were in the same country shepherds abiding in the field, keeping ᵃ watch over their flock by night.
9 And, lo, the angel of the Lord came upon them, and the glory of the Lord shone round about them: ᵇ and they were sore afraid.
10 And the angel said unto them, Fear not: for, behold, I bring you good tidings of great joy, ᶜ which shall be to all people.

8 And there were shepherds in the same country abiding in the field, and keeping ¹ watch by night
9 over their flock. And an angel of the Lord stood by them, and the glory of the Lord shone round about
10 them: and they were sore afraid. And the angel said unto them, Be not afraid; for, behold, I bring you good tidings of great joy which shall be to all the

a Or, the night watches.... b ch. 1:12.... c Gen. 12:3; Matt. 28:19; Mark 1:15; ver. 31, 32; ch. 24:47; Col. 1:23.—1 Or, night watches.

does it; while a critical examination shows his own process to be an enumeration of *probabilities* to his mind, ending in a verdict which might fairly be interpreted: "I guess that this opinion is a demonstrated truth." Does he think that by increasing the weight and number of links, he can strengthen the chain while yet every link, where the strain comes, is as weak as the first that was ever tried? One thing has now, perhaps, been sufficiently proved—that God has not been pleased to allow us a certain knowledge of the day or the hour of the first advent of his Son, any more than of that which is yet to take place. Hence we may infer with *practical* assurance, that it is of no serious consequence that we should have such knowledge. It could hardly have been a matter of care to Luke, or his researches would have brought him to a statement clear and unquestionable; for almost certainly the truth would have been within the knowledge of any of those who personally associated with Christ.

8-14. ANGELIC ANNOUNCEMENT OF THE BIRTH TO THE SHEPHERDS.

8. And there were in the same country shepherds abiding in the field. The narrative concerns not itself about kings or princes, or the great and rich of the earth, in palaces, which angels had seldom visited, except on errands of retribution; but with **shepherds,** men of the people, of such grade as were most intently expecting the promised salvation, and would be found most ready to welcome it.—**Abiding in the field** (*living in the open air*). **In the same country,** *i. e.,* Judea, where Abraham had ranged with his family, and his flocks and herds, and where David had for years tended his father's sheep; for the region about Bethlehem, for some distance, seems to have been adapted to nothing so well as nomadic pasturage.—**Keeping watch . . . . by night.** This statement would not, indeed, prove that it was not now mid-winter; for shepherds may have had to be in the fields, sometimes in the most inclement weather. But when we consider that the night air made a charcoal fire necessary to those who were standing out in a palatial court, in the heart of Jerusalem, on an April night (John 18:18), it is certainly very hard to think of shepherds exposed to the rigors of mid-winter, on the lofty mountains of Judea. The number of the shepherds may have been considerable, although there was but one flock; for the flocks were often very large.

9. And the (*an*) **angel of the Lord came upon them.** This better expresses the notion of some suddenness and surprise attending the visit, which the Greek verb often insinuates (10:40; 24:4; Acts 4:1; 1 Thess. 5:3), than the Revision. All at once there was present to them an angel. Lo seems not to have been in the original text.—**And the glory of the Lord shone round about them.** The glory was probably a brightness, a radiant glow, such as others had been conscious of, who had been allowed special visitations of the divine presence, such as we may imagine as constituting the light of heaven, where there is no light of the sun, neither of the moon.—**And they were sore afraid.** It was again that awe which smites the mind in the more sensible nearness of God, or of anything plainly supernatural.

10. And the angel said unto them, Fear not. The real design of the revelations of God in the Bible, particularly the New Testament, is to remove fear from the human heart. It aims rather to kindle a love which casts out fear, by not only showing God reconciled, but bringing us to reconciliation.—**For, behold**—it is an important announcement—**I bring you good tidings.** In the form of a verb (εὐαγγελίζομαι), the Greek announces that "good news"—the gospel—which was henceforth to constitute the burden of revelation unto the end, the news of salvation for sinners, amply provided, freely

CH. II.] LUKE. 47

11 ᵃ For unto you is born this day in the city of David ᵇ a Saviour, ᶜ which is Christ the Lord.
12 And this *shall be* a sign unto you; Ye shall find the babe wrapped in swaddling clothes, lying in a manger.
13 ᵈ And suddenly there was with the angel a multitude of the heavenly host praising God, and saying,
14 ᵉ Glory to God in the highest, and on earth ᶠ peace, ᵍ good will toward men.

11 people: for there is born to you this day in the city
12 of David a Saviour, who is ¹ Christ the Lord. And this *is* the sign unto you; Ye shall find a babe wrapped in swaddling clothes, and lying in a manger.
13 And suddenly there was with the angel a multitude of the heavenly host praising God, and saying,
14   Glory to God in the highest,
     And on earth ² peace among ³ men in whom he is well pleased.

ᵃ Isa. 9:6....ᵇ Matt. 1:21....ᶜ Matt. 1:16; 16:16; 1:43; Acts 2:36; 10:36; Phil. 2:11....ᵈ Gen. 28:12; 32:1, 2; 105:20, Ps. 21; 148:2; Dan. 7:10; Heb. 1:11; Rev. 5:11....ᵉ ch. 19:38; Ephes. 1:6; 3:10, 21; Rev. 5:13..../ Isa. 57:11; ch. 1:79; Rom. 5:1; Ephes. 2:17; Col. 1:20....ᵍ John 3:16; Ephes. 2:4, 7; 2 Thess. 2, 16; 1 John 4:9, 10.— ¹ *Or, Anointed Lord*....
² Many ancient authorities read, *peace, good pleasure among men*....3 Gr. *men of good pleasure*.

offered, and available for all, without distinction of nationality, rank, or condition. This is fully brought out in the following clauses.—**Of great joy,** *i. e.*, suited to occasion great joy.—**Which** (*great joy*) **shall be to all** (*the*) **people,** *i. e.*, the Jewish nation. Such it was fit to be in its intrinsic nature and in the design of its Author; such it became transiently to the mass of that people (John 6:15), and eternally to a prepared few (John 1:12,13); and such it is to be, finally and permanently, to the nation as a whole (Rom. 11:26,31).

11. **For unto you is born,** etc.,—properly, "*was born.*" The promise long deferred and waited for has been fulfilled. The birth is stated first (as in the Revision) as nearest to the heart.—**This day,** since the sunset which closed yesterday. **In the city of David,** as the ancient prophecies foretold (Mic. 5:2; compare Matt. 2:6; John 7:42). This sentence stands last in the original, being reserved until what was more important had been told.—**A Saviour**—a Greek word is used, equivalent to Jesus, the Grecized Hebrew, as in ch. 1:31; Matt. 1:21.—**Which** (*who*) **is Christ the Lord.**—**Christ** is equivalent to *anointed*. This may accordingly be taken as *anointed Lord*, which view Westcott and Hort indicate in their form of the Greek text, though the sense before given is probably correct. Either way, the Saviour born is declared to be the Messiah, and divine. The angelic ken discerns as already realized that which the Apostle Paul long after celebrates as the result of the incarnation, death, and ascension of the Saviour, "that every knee should bow, and every tongue confess that Jesus Christ is Lord, to the glory of God the Father."

12. **And this shall be** (*is*) **a sign unto you;** *i. e.*, the statement which I will now make is a token by which you can test the verity of my announcement.—**Ye shall find**

the (*a*) **babe wrapped,** etc. The extraordinary fact of a babe just born lying in a manger, swathed in bands wrapped round and round, in lack of more comfortable clothing, would prove to them that the angel had spoken with superhuman knowledge.

13, 14. **And suddenly there was with the angel.** The language gives the impression of a marvelous apparition. In an instant, without an intimation of how, or whence, in place of a single angel amid the vacant night, there came to be **a multitude of the heavenly host,** or army. With reference to the number of his angels, Jehovah is named the Lord God of Sabaoth. They are called a host, as a convenient way of indicating a vast number—not a confused throng—but in ordered ranks, and, perhaps, with leadership of well-adjusted grades. While earth slept, not dreaming even of the change initiated in its moral situation and eternal prospects, all heaven is seen astir and thrilling with unwonted interest.—**Praising God, and saying, Glory to God,** etc. Verse 14, is to be regarded as a declaration by the angels that glory is rendered to God in heaven on account of the birth of Jesus.—**Glory to God** is adoring honor, the expressed recognition of those excellencies which God has displayed in this gift of a Saviour, as being worthy of universal worship. This was manifested **in the highest,** viz., "*places,*" the loftiest heavens in which he resides (Job 16:19; Ps. 148:1; Matt. 21:9; Eph. 1:3).—**And on earth**—as opposed to the highest—**peace,** viz., "*is prepared.*" Such had been promised to be the fact in the Messianic times (Isa. 9:6,7; 52:7,10; Mic. 5:2-5). The predictions would have led us to expect a cessation of war and conflicts among men, as one fruit of the advent of Christ. We may still hope that the expectation shall some time be fulfilled, although blood still flows in rivers, and hearts still break, by myriads, through the atrocities of war. But it was peace in a higher sense that was chiefly intended—the cessation of conflict with God through sin, and of his anger toward the sinner in Christ (Rom. 1:7; 5:1; Eph. 2:14-17). To Jews, familiar with the comprehensive significance of the Hebrew word *Shalom*, Greek (εἰρήνη), "peace" would still more broadly suggest all welfare and blessing, even all of salvation. Jesus himself seemed so little to expect it in the other sense, as a speedy result of his influence, that he rather spoke of himself as come to send a sword. Yet his peace, once generally established in human souls, is the sure and only hope of all peace.—**Good will** (rather, *good pleasure*) **toward** (or, *among*) **men.** The "good pleasure" is God's gracious regard for men as manifested in the gift of salvation to them in their lost and wretched condition. Compare 12:32; Phil. 2:13, where salvation, in another aspect, is the fruit of God's good pleasure. Such is the apparent sense of this brief and comprehensive song, according to the familiar form of the text, in its last clause. Some prefer to understand the expressions in an optative or hortatory sense: "Let there be glory—peace—good will.". But as it is all said "praising God" (ver. 13); as the glory is in "the highest" places unto God, and as "the good will" to men is hardly now a matter of prayer, it seems better to regard the whole as a declaration of what *is* in heaven, and is portended on the earth. But it will be noticed that the Revised Version gives quite another rendering of the last clause. This depends on the addition of a letter, in excellent authorities for the Greek text, to the word translated "good pleasure," turning it into a possessive case, "of good pleasure." Then the strict translation becomes, "*and on earth peace in men of good pleasure.*" This sounds strangely to our ears, but the evidence in its favor is so weighty that most of the greatest critics of the age have been constrained to accept it as what was actually written. Indeed, if this sentence had been familiar to us, and seen to be consistent with the context, the reasons in favor of the old reading would be easily answered. In this form, too, the parallel between the two members of the hymn is more satisfactory —*on earth* answering to *in the highest; peace,*

BETHLEHEM.

Ch. II.] LUKE. 49

15 And it came to pass, as the angels were gone away from them into heaven, *the shepherds said one to another, Let us now go even unto Bethlehem, and see this thing which is come to pass, which the Lord hath made known unto us.
16 And they came with haste, and found Mary, and Joseph, and the babe lying in a manger.
17 And when they had seen it, they made known abroad the saying which was told them concerning this child.
18 And all they that heard it wondered at those things which were told them by the shepherds.
19 ᵇBut Mary kept all these things, and pondered them in her heart.
20 And the shepherds returned, glorifying and praising God for all the things that they had heard and seen, as it was told unto them.
21 ᶜAnd when eight days were accomplished for the circumcising of the child, his name was called ᵈJESUS, which was so named of the angel before he was conceived in the womb.

15 And it came to pass, when the angels went away from them into heaven, the shepherds said one to another, Let us now go even unto Bethlehem, and see this ¹ thing that is come to pass, which the Lord hath made known unto us.
16 And they came with haste, and found both Mary and Joseph, and the babe lying in the manger.
17 And when they saw it, they made known concerning the saying which was spoken to them about this child.
18 And all that heard it wondered at the things which were spoken unto them by the shepherds. But Mary kept all these
20 ² sayings, pondering them in her heart. And the shepherds returned, glorifying and praising God for all the things that they had heard and seen, even as it was spoken unto them.
21 And when eight days were fulfilled for circumcising him, his name was called JESUS, which was so called by the angel before he was conceived in the womb.

a Gr. *the men, the shepherds*....*b* Gen. 37 ; 11 ; ch. 1 : 66 ; ver. 51.....*c* Gen. 17 : 12 ; Lev. 12 : 3 ; ch. 1 : 59....*d* Matt. 1 ; 21, 25 : ch. 1 : 31.—1 Or, *saying*....² Or, *things*.

to glory; in men, to to God. The clause *men of good pleasure* is certainly singular and obscure. Yet to the Hebrew mind it would naturally convey the idea of "men whose good pleasure it was," viz., to receive the peace provided in Christ, or, as the connection might require, "men who were the objects of good pleasure," viz., God's, described above. This is much the more probable sense, and is given more idiomatically by the Revision, as "men in whom he is well pleased." It does not refer to particular men in distinction from others, but to all men, regarded now as objects of God's good pleasure, in that he has sent them a Saviour. Meyer substantially adopts the other view. Neither of the two texts is so unquestionably certain as to nullify the other, and we have thought it right to comment on both, while we strongly incline, as a matter of documentary evidence, with the light now afforded, to accept as genuine the reading, "men of good pleasure."

15-20. VISIT OF THE SHEPHERDS.

15. Such an announcement must be followed up, especially as the departure of the angels, now distinctly visible, through the upper regions of the atmosphere, **into heaven, gave it** additional solemnity.—**Let us now go even unto Bethlehem**—a way of speaking which implies that it was a considerable journey for them to undertake. They would not stop short of the very spot.—**And see this thing** —strictly, "*this saying*"—interpreted by the last clause of the verse—**which the Lord**, etc.

16. And found—discovered, after search— **Mary, and Joseph, and the babe lying in a (*the*) manger.** Insert *both* before **Mary.** The sign (ver. 12) was thus literally realized, and they saw what God had made known to them. That they should be permitted to intrude on the privacy of such a scene, may have been partly owing to the simple manners of the time; but more to the unavoidable freedom of the place—whether a stable in our sense, or the broad, open court of the inn, or a cave for the shelter of beasts; and somewhat, perhaps, to a preliminary intimation of the reason of their visit.

17. And—they made known abroad— to those who were present, not **abroad.** The word *abroad* is better omitted.—**The saying—concerning the child.** The Revision is better: "*Concerning the saying which was spoken to them about this child.*"

18. Until this intelligence from the shepherds, we have no reason to suppose that any person there, except Joseph and Mary, knew that anything out of the way of nature had taken place.

19. But Mary kept all these things (*sayings*) **and pondered** (or, *pondering*) **them in her heart.** Her mother-heart, not comprehending clearly yet what it was to have borne the Messiah, suffered not a word that could afford light to fall; "pondering," strictly, "putting together," "comparing" them all to see what conclusion they would warrant. The process was carried on **in her heart.**

20. The complete correspondence of what the shepherds heard and saw at the manger, with what was said to them by the angel, cleared their knowledge, confirmed their faith, and filled them with a livelier spirit of thanksgiving and praise.

21. THE CIRCUMCISION OF JESUS. And

D

50 LUKE. [Ch. II.

22 And *a* when the days of her purification according to the law of Moses were accomplished, they brought him to Jerusalem, to present *him* to the Lord;
23 (As it is written in the law of the Lord, *b* Every male that openeth the womb shall be called holy to the Lord;)
24 And to offer a sacrifice according to *c* that which is said in the law of the Lord, A pair of turtledoves, or two young pigeons.
25 And, behold, there was a man in Jerusalem, whose name *was* Simeon; and the same man *was* just and devout, *d* waiting for the consolation of Israel: and the Holy Ghost was upon him.

22 And when the days of their purification according to the law of Moses were fulfilled, they brought him 23 up to Jerusalem, to present him to the Lord (as it is written in the law of the Lord, Every male that openeth the womb shall be called holy to the Lord), 24 and to offer a sacrifice according to that which is said in the law of the Lord, A pair of turtledoves, or two 25 young pigeons. And behold, there was a man in Jerusalem, whose name was Simeon; and this man was righteous and devout, looking for the consolation of Israel: and the Holy Spirit was upon him.

a Lev. 12: 2, 3, 4, 6....b Ex. 13: 2; 22: 29; 34·19; Num. 3: 13; 8: 17; 18: 15....c Lev. 12: 2, 6, 8....Is. 40: 1; Mark 15: 43; ver. 38.

when eight days were accomplished (*fulfilled*) for the circumcising of the child (*of him*), his name was called Jesus. It will be noticed that the fact of his being circumcised is simply assumed, and that everything about it claims little attention, compared with the case of John (1:59 f). This has led some to surmise less subserviency to the ritual law; but is it not rather from the overwhelming interest in that name, JESUS, Saviour, which, however common previously, as an appellation of men, was thenceforth to be holy as "the name above every name" in heaven and on earth, for time and for eternity? Yet our Lord, "being made of a woman, made under the law," must be circumcised, that he might in every sense fulfill the law.

22-24. THE PURIFICATION IN THE TEMPLE.

22. And when the days of her (*their*) purification were accomplished (*fulfilled*). The law of Moses regarded the woman who had given birth to a child as ceremonially unclean, in the case of a son, for forty days; after which certain purifying rites, involving a sacrifice, were to be performed, before she could be regarded as ritually clean. Purification was not required of the child; but as another ceremony was appointed for the first-born son on such an occasion, both mother and child are associated here in the pronoun "their" of the correct text. The law for the mother, may be read in Lev. 12: 2-4; for the child, in Ex. 13: 2; 22: 29; 34: 20; Num. 3: 13.—They brought him to Jerusalem. Circumcision might be performed in private; but the purification and presentation must take place at the sanctuary, through the priest.—To present him to the Lord, as it is written, etc. (See Ex. 13: 2.) This presentation was in order to the ceremonial redemption, by which every first-born son must be bought off by his parents. The ground of this necessity is, with much probability, supposed to have been that, before the limitation of the priesthood to the family of Aaron, the Lord had claimed every first-born son for a priest. After that institution, the claim was not enforced, but was kept in remembrance by requiring that such son, at the age of a month, should appear at the sanctuary, and be "redeemed" by paying five shekels to the sacred treasury, for the priests who took his place (Num. 18: 15, 16). If the claim of five shekels (more than three dollars in silver), still held, it must have been a heavy tax on those who, like Joseph and Mary, had to avail themselves of the concession in the law (Ex. 13: 8), which allowed those who could not afford a lamb for the purification sacrifice, or even the **pair of turtle doves,** to present what was still cheaper and more easy to procure, two **young** (unfledged) **pigeons.** The offering required, for the redemption of their Son from the ritual priesthood, that he might become the High Priest of God for all mankind, may well have forbidden the expense of a lamb for the mother (Lev. 12: 6).

25-38. PROPHECIES OF SIMEON AND ANNA.

1. OF SIMEON, 25-35.

25. And behold—calls attention to a remarkable coincidence.—There was a man in Jerusalem, apparently residing there, and well known for his piety and his great age.—And the same (*this*) man was just (*righteous*) and devout, belonging to the same class of worshipers as Zacharias and Elisabeth (1: 5, 6), and Joseph of Arimathea (Mark 15: 43). Righteous in the same sense as in the passage cited, while devout corresponds to "walking in the commandments and ordinances of the Lord blameless."—Waiting for the consolation of Israel, *i. e.*, for the great relief to Israel from their

26 And it was revealed unto him by the Holy Ghost, that he should not *see death, before he had seen the Lord's Christ.
27 And he came ᵇby the Spirit into the temple: and when the parents brought in the child Jesus, to do for him after the custom of the law,
28 Then took he him up in his arms, and blessed God, and said,
29 Lord, ᶜnow lettest thou thy servant depart in peace, according to thy word:
30 For mine eyes ᵈhave seen thy salvation,
31 Which thou hast prepared before the face of all people;
32 ᵉA light to lighten the Gentiles, and the glory of thy people Israel.
33 And Joseph and his mother marvelled at those things which were spoken of him.

26 And it had been revealed unto him by the Holy Spirit, that he should not see death, before he had
27 seen the Lord's Christ. And he came in the Spirit into the temple: and when the parents brought in the child Jesus, that they might do concerning him
28 after the custom of the law, then he received him into his arms, and blessed God, and said,
29 Now lettest thou thy ¹servant depart, O ² Lord, According to thy word, in peace;
30 For mine eyes have seen thy salvation,
31 Which thou hast prepared before the face of all peoples;
32 A light for ³ revelation to the Gentiles, And the glory of thy people Israel.
33 And his father and his mother were marvelling at

<small>a Ps. 89:48; Heb. 11:5....b Matt. 4:1....c Gen. 46:30; Phil. 1:23....d Isa. 52:10; ch. 3:6....e Isa. 9:2; 42:6; 49:6; 60:1, 2, 3; Matt. 4:16; Acts 13:47; 28:28.——1 Gr. bondservant....2 Master....3 Or. the unveiling of the Gentiles.</small>

prostration, ungodliness, and suffering. (Compare Gen. 49:18; Isa. 40:1; 49:23), which he looked for as coming through the Messiah.—**And the Holy Ghost** (*Spirit*) **was upon him.** This seems to be stated as if it were habitually qualifying him for the revelation next spoken of, and for the special discernment which he now displayed.

26. And it was (*had been*) **revealed unto him that he should not see death, etc.**—and with the addition, as we may judge from ver. 29, that when he *had* seen **the Lord's Christ** he would die

27-29. And he came by (*in*) **the Spirit into the temple**—not of his own personal impulse, therefore, but moved by the Spirit of God to visit the temple just at that time.—**And when the parents**—as they were both taken to be—**brought in the child Jesus to do for him after the custom of the law;** namely, to redeem as described, on ver. 22, 23, **then took he him up** (*received him*—strictly, *it*—) **in his arms; received** as though it had been offered to him for his blessing; **into his arms,** with affectionate tenderness.—**And blessed God;** returning thanks with praise.—**Now, Lord, lettest thou thy servant depart in peace, according to thy word.** The order of the words is correctly represented in the Revision. The Greek for **Lord** (δεσπότης), is not the one ordinarily used, but one which names the master in relation to the servant. It recurs often in Luke. **Lettest thou thy servant depart** (*thou dost dismiss, or set him free*). **Thy word** is the saying in which the revelation of ver. 26 had been expressed. The whole verse is thus a joyful and adoring recognition of the fact that the term of his detention on the earth is fulfilled, and that

with the appearance of the infant Messiah his release is beginning. Now—after so long a time—art thou at last setting thy bondservant free, O Master, as thy long cherished promise foretold, in blessed peace. He is divinely assured that this infant is the promised Saviour, and finds in the fact a proof that he may now go to his rest.

30. For mine eyes have seen thy salvation. Thy salvation is more nearly, "*thy provision for salvation,*" the Greek word (σωτήριον) being different from that which ordinarily expresses the idea (σωτηρία).

31. Which thou hast prepared (*preparedst*) **before the face of all people** (*peoples*), as lying open to their acceptance also.

32. A light to enlighten (*for revelation to*) **the Gentiles.** This is a still more distinct statement of the design to extend the benefits of salvation to all the peoples, so that none should be left without a knowledge of the will of God and the way of life. His declarations are as explicit as those of Isaiah, and in respect to evangelical largeness, quite throw the utterances of Mary and Zacharias (ch. 1) into the shade. The universal scope of the mercy in Christ is thus indicated at his first appearance among men.—**And the glory of thy people Israel.** What a glory if only they had so accepted the offered blessing, that the rest of the world should have looked up to that nation as the perpetual leaders of salvation!

33. And Joseph and his mother marvelled (*were marvelling*). Joseph, in a later Greek text, in place of *his father,* betrays the care of men to speak more precisely than the inspired writer had done. They *were wondering* at what he was saying,

52 LUKE. [Ch. II.

34 And Simeon blessed them, and said unto Mary his mother, Behold, this *child* is set for the *a* fall and rising again of many in Israel; and for *b* a sign which shall be spoken against;
35 (Yea, *c* a sword shall pierce through thy own soul also,) that the thoughts of many hearts may be revealed.
36 And there was one Anna, a prophetess, the daughter of Phanuel, of the tribe of Aser: she was of a great age, and had lived with an husband seven years from her virginity;

34 the things which were spoken concerning him; and Simeon blessed them, and said unto Mary his mother, Behold, this *child* is set for the falling and the rising of many in Israel; and for a sign which is spoken
35 against; yea and a sword shall pierce through thine own soul; that the thoughts out of many hearts may be
36 revealed. And there was one Anna, a prophetess, the daughter of Phanuel, of the tribe of Asher (she was ¹ of a great age, having lived with a husband seven

a Isa. 8:14; Hosea 14:9; Matt. 21:44; Rom. 9:32, 33; 1 Cor. 1:23, 24; 2 Cor. 2:16; 1 Pet. 2:7 3....*b* Acts 28:22....*c* Ps. 42:10; John 19:25.—¹ Gr. *advanced in many days.*

both as coming from a stranger, and because of the boundless extent of benefits which he predicted from it, reaching to the ends of the world.

31. And Simeon blessed them, (*invoked God's blessing on them*)—**and said unto Mary**—to her in particular, as if with a divine perception of her peculiar relation to the child, and certainly with a prophetic foresight of her future experiences—**Behold this child is set for the fall and rising again** (*falling and rising up*) **of many in Israel. Is set**—is *placed, appointed.* **The fall and rising again,** may be taken as referring to the same, or to different persons. In the former view the phrase would foretell the moral prostration into which many would fall; the repentance and humiliation which they would experience, when made conscious of sin, in the light of the Messianic preaching, and the elation of spirit, a rising up of the heart, through pardon, justification, and adoption, which in that light would be found possible. In the latter, and more probably correct view, **the fall** was to happen to the worldly, proud, self-righteous, and obstinately unbelieving—the scribes and Pharisees and rulers generally, who would be crushed, and carry down the nation with them—while yet many of the lowly, penitent, seeking ones would rise through faith in Jesus to true dignity, happiness, and glory; and in the end a great multitude of the nation, yea, "all Israel should be saved" (Rom. 11:26. Comp. Isa. 8:14; Rom. 9:32, 33; 1 Cor. 1:23, 24; 1 Pet. 2:7, 8).—**And for a sign which shall be spoken against.** Omit **which shall be.** How true this was in the first age, on the part of both Jew and Gentile, is obvious to every one. "Gainsaying," in Rom. 10:21, is the action of those who were doing what is here predicted. It culminated in the taunts and ribaldry of the day of crucifixion, when he who was given as **a sign** (Matt. 12:39, 40) of God's counsel concerning his kingdom, was rejected in favor of an infamous malefactor.

35. Yea, a sword shall pierce through thy own soul also. The Revision properly omits the parenthesis, and substitutes "and" in the beginning for **also** at the end. This clause joins closely with the preceding, and the following one depends on this. **A sword shall pierce,** strictly, *go through,* etc., is a metaphor to express strongly the pangs which would rend the mother's heart, in view of that contradiction of sinners against her Son (Heb. 12:3), under which she would see him expire on the cross. The order of the Greek words makes this only a complementary phase of the suffering to Jesus himself; he is set for a sign spoken against, and through thy own soul also will go a sword.—**That the thoughts** (*reasonings,* or *process of thought*) **of** (*out of*) **many hearts may be revealed.** That, distinctly equivalent to *in order that.* It is of the divine purpose that as a result of Christ's death of agony, the views and conclusions of men concerning him should be brought to light in their words and conduct. So it proved from the Day of Pentecost.

36–38. Testimony of Anna, a Prophetess.

36. And there was one Anna, a prophetess—a successor to Hannah and Hulda and Deborah, of the olden time—proving again, how, at this turning period of the Jewish history, the special sources of communication from heaven to men, were opened anew.—**Daughter of Phanuel, of the tribe of Aser** (*Asher*)—showing that in the obliteration of tribal boundaries, the lineage of women also was, in some cases at least, accurately preserved.—**She was of a great age, and had** (*having*) **lived with a husband seven years from her virginty.**

CH. II.] LUKE. 53

37 And she was a widow of about fourscore and four years, which departed not from the temple, but served God with fastings and prayers *a* night and day.
38 And she coming in that instant gave thanks likewise unto the Lord, and spake of him to all them that *b* looked for redemption in Jerusalem.
39 And when they had performed all things according to the law of the Lord, they returned into Galilee, to their own city Nazareth.
40 *c* And the child grew, and waxed strong in spirit, filled with wisdom: and the grace of God was upon him.

37 years from her virginity, and she had been a widow even unto fourscore and four years), who departed not from the temple, worshipping with fastings and
38 supplications night and day. And coming up at that very hour she gave thanks unto God, and spake of him to all them that were looking for the redemption
39 of Jerusalem. And when they had accomplished all things that were according to the law of the Lord, they returned into Galilee, to their own city Nazareth.
40 And the child grew, and waxed strong, 1 filled with wisdom: and the grace of God was upon him.

a Acts 26: 7; 1 Tim. 5: 5....b Mark 15: 43; ver. 25; ch. 24: 21....c ch. 1: 80; ver. 52.——1 Gr. *becoming full of wisdom.*

37. And she was a widow of about fourscore and four years. Rather, *even unto eighty-four years.* The description emphasizes her single marriage and long widowhood. She had been married but a short time, and ever since had remained a widow, which was regarded as religiously honorable to her. The reckoning of her age at this time is a little uncertain. The English Revision, in rendering "she had been a widow even for," etc., would suppose her full age to have been at least one hundred and five years. The Greek seems hardly to warrant, certainly does not necessitate, the "even for," and the intention of the writer more probably was to say that, after being left a widow in early life, she had lived as a widow even on to eighty-four years of age. So Meyer, Godet, Farrar.—**Which** (*who*) **departed not from the temple**—was there whenever it was open to worshipers.—**But served God** (*worshiping—performing service to God*) **in fastings and prayers** (*supplications*) **night and day.** Fastings were a main part of the practical righteousness of that day, treated by our Lord (Matt. 6: 16. ff.) as standing on a level with almsgiving and prayer. They were not commanded in the divine law; only one in the year, on the Day of Atonement, being required. Some others had been brought in to commemorate great national calamities; and in the ascetic system of the Pharisees two weekly fasts, on Monday and Thursday, had become sacred among them. The special word used for **prayers** here, "*supplications,*" or entreaties, implies special earnestness and fervor. **Night and day** marks the continuance of worship in the temple, and may possibly mean that she had a place of lodging in the temple enclosure, though this can be only conjecture; and the probable view is that, being there late and early, "all the time," as we say, she spent parts of the night, as well as the day time, in her devotions.

38. And she coming in (the verb was translated "came upon" ver. 9, see note) **that instant** (*at that very hour,* when, namely, Simeon was speaking of the Christ-child), **gave thanks likewise unto the Lord.** She thanked God for his wonderful gift, **and spake of him to all them that looked for** (*the*) **redemption in** (*of*) **Jerusalem.** Redemption of Jerusalem was equivalent to the consolation of Israel, for which Simeon waited (ver. 25), only not so directly referring to the person of the Messiah. The language impliesthat there were numbers of pious expectants in the city—**all them**—and Anna, as a prophetess, would now be able to assure them that the redemption was drawing nigh. [The tense of the verb translated **spake** indicates continued action—*was speaking*—doubtless to one after another, or to group after group, as she had opportunity to do, as devout persons came into the temple courts—persons whom she knew to be waiting for the redemption of Jerusalem.—A. H.]

39. RETURN OF THE HOLY FAMILY TO NAZARETH. All things according to the law, particularly the purification, and the presentation of the child (ver. 22-24).—**They returned into Galilee, to their own city Nazareth.** Luke writes as if entirely unaware of the visit of the wise men, the flight into Egypt, the recall, and the intention of Joseph to settle in Judea—incidents of this period mentioned by Matthew (2: 1-23).

40. BODILY AND SPIRITUAL DEVELOPMENT OF JESUS. And the child grew, and waxed strong. Or, *was strengthened,* physically, after the manner of other children; whether with freedom from those accidents and maladies to which most are subject, we are left to conjecture. Perhaps the negative is involved in the statement that "he bare our sicknesses" (Matt. 8: 17).—**Filled with wisdom**—more exactly, *becoming filled.* There was as truly normal a strengthening and ex-

41 Now his parents went to Jerusalem *every year at the feast of the passover.
42 And when he was twelve years old, they went up to Jerusalem after the custom of the feast.
43 And when they had fulfilled the days, as they returned, the child Jesus tarried behind in Jerusalem; and Joseph and his mother knew not *of it*.
44 But they, supposing him to have been in the company, went a day's journey; and they sought him among *their* kinsfolk and acquaintance.
45 And when they found him not, they turned back again to Jerusalem, seeking him.
46 And it came to pass, that after three days they found him in the temple, sitting in the midst of the doctors, both hearing them, and asking them questions.

41 And his parents went every year to Jerusalem at 42 the feast of the passover. And when he was twelve years old, they went up after the custom of the feast; 43 and when they had fulfilled the days, as they were returning, the boy Jesus tarried behind in Jerusa- 44 lem; and his parents knew it not; but supposing him to be in the company, they went a day's journey; and they sought for him among their kinsfolk 45 and acquaintance: and when they found him not, 46 they returned to Jerusalem, seeking for him. And it came to pass, after three days they found him in the temple, sitting in the midst of the ¹doctors, both

a Ex. 23:15, 17; 34:28; Deut. 16:1,16.—1 Or, *teachers.*

pansion of his intellectual powers and endowments as of his bodily frame. He advanced in knowledge of his Father's works and will and ways and word, and in the right application of such knowledge to the conduct of life, for himself and others, for time and eternity. (Isa. 11:2 f). **And the grace of God was upon him** (John 1:14). He enjoyed the fruits of God's favor in all his experience. It was the necessary result of the fact just before stated. This prepares us for the remarkable relation concerning him in the next paragraph.

41-51. ATTENDANCE ON THE PASSOVER AT TWELVE YEARS OF AGE.

41. Now (*and*) **his parents went to Jerusalem every year at the feast of the passover.** This was required of every male Jew above twelve years of age (Ex. 23:15; Deut. 16: 1-8; 1 Sam. 1:3, 21). After the building of the temple, the Passover could be celebrated nowhere but in Jerusalem. It began on the 14th of the month Abib, afterward Nisan, and continued through an entire week. Women were allowed, in the later ages even recommended, to attend; and in regard to younger children, it was probably optional with parents to take them or not.

42. And when he was twelve years old. At this age, the Jewish boy began to assume a position in the community which he did not occupy before. He was now called "a son of the law"; began to practice the fastings, and prescribed prayers; to wear the phylactery, like adult men. Scrupulous, but not Pharisaic regard for the Mosaic law, is marked in the piety of this family.

43. Fulfilled the days, viz., the well-known seven (Ex. 12:16).—**The child** (*boy*) **Jesus tarried behind in Jerusalem; and Joseph and his mother knew not of it.** We are left uncertain whether it was unawares to the boy that they departed without him. Nor does anything indicate whether this was his first visit to Jerusalem at the Passover. It may have been only the first at which anything specially noteworthy occurred.

44. They went a day's journey—*i. e.*, without making special effort to find him. This day's journey would be but a few miles, perhaps not more than six or eight.—**The company** was what we should call a caravan, made up of the inhabitants of Galilee, who, for greater security from marauders, would join sometimes scores, if not hundreds, of families journeying slowly to and from the holy city. In order to rest during the heat of noontide, it was their custom to start before light in the morning. To get all together on the road, and to settle arrangements for the night's encampment, might occupy a considerable part of one day.—**And they sought him.** The Greek is nearly like our "tried to hunt him up."—**As their kinsfolk and acquaintance** may have been widely scattered through the train, the task would go on slowly and imperfectly; and, even after the halt for the night, was continued in vain. The boy was not with them.

45. And when they found him not, there was nothing to do but to go back to Jerusalem, **seeking him.** Some make this clause simply mean "to seek him there"; but it may suppose a search on the way back, as well as after they arrived. The next morning they would begin their scrutiny of the city. From the question of Jesus (ver. 49), we may, perhaps, infer that they did not go directly to the temple; but in the course of the day they reached the place.

46. The phrase, **after three days,** reckoning them to begin with the departure of the company, would bring us near to the close of

47 And *all that heard him were astonished at his understanding and answers.
48 And when they saw him, they were amazed: and his mother said unto him, Son, why hast thou thus dealt with us? behold, thy father and I have sought thee sorrowing.
49 And he said unto them, How is it that ye sought me? wist ye not that I must be about *my Father's business?

47 hearing them, and asking them questions: and all that heard him were amazed at his understanding 48 and his answers. And when they saw him, they were astonished: and his mother said unto him, ¹ Son, why hast thou thus dealt with us? behold, thy 49 father and I sought thee sorrowing. And he said unto them, How is it that ye sought me? knew ye

a Matt. 1:24; Mark 1:22; ch. 4:22, 32; John 7:15, 46....*b* John 2:16.——1 Gr. *Child.*

the third day, according to our way of speaking. But with the Hebrews, one day, with any part of the day before and after it, would freely be called three days. Meanwhile Jesus, enjoying the hospitality of some who would be interested in his character and manners, was availing himself of the religious privileges afforded at the temple, which he would be able to compare with the worship and instruction of the rural synagogue of Nazareth. In some one of the courts of that great and splendid structure, some of the renowned rabbis of the day were frequently found teaching the disciples, who sat below them, reverently drinking in the wisdom that fell from their lips. The names of a crowd of these teachers of the law have come down to us. It is sufficient to mention the illustrious Hillel, Nicodemus, "the teacher of Israel" (Revision), and Joseph of Arimathea. It is possible, also, that Gamaliel, Paul's future teacher, may have been now pursuing his preparatory studies for his life work. [Is it more likely, in view of the language which Luke employs (Acts 5:34 ff.), to describe his position, a few years later, that Gamaliel was already a member of the Sanhedrim, and therefore one of the teachers or rabbis, if present at all on this occasion?—A. H.] If not of these, of such men we are to think when we read that his parents found Jesus sitting in the midst of the doctors (*teachers*). An ordinary boy of twelve years, however religious, would be little at home in such a place, and would at the most wait outside the circle, to catch what instruction he could. Jesus was not only in the midst of them, but apparently one of the ring of disciples—**both hearing them and asking them questions.** Here is opened a wide field for the imagination, in which expositors have freely expatiated, touching the attitude and manner of the child, the topics on which he discoursed and asked questions. The narrative does not indicate that he discoursed. We are simply told that he listened to them and asked them questions. This was the manner of teaching at the time. Purely oral, it was catechetical in its nature, by question and answer, yet involving some liberty of following out trains of thought suggested, and the proposal of personal ideas, in the way of questions at least.

47. That he thus intimated views of the truth of God quite different from the stereotyped dicta of the ordinary teachers, is plainly taught us, when we are told that **all that heard him were astonished at his understanding**—as displayed in the questions which he propounded, **and answers** which he gave; in both which equally he betrayed his acquaintance with the very spirit of the truth. Everything was consistent with the modesty of youth, while expressing more than the common wisdom of age. Even then he "spake as never man spake."

48. **And when they** (his parents) **saw him, they were amazed.** The Greek verb here denotes a still greater excitement of wonder than that for "astonished" in ver. 47—("amazed," Revision). This freedom and boldness of the child, as it would seem to them, was very different from the retiring modesty to which they had been accustomed. His mother spoke first.—**Son** (*child*), **why hast thou thus dealt with us? Thy father and I have sought thee sorrowing.** Her grieved, motherly kindness speaks in the word "child," and mingles with her sudden joy, in the form of a gentle rebuke, when the look and tone must have been of contentment and admiration.

49. **Why is it that ye sought me** (*were seeking one*)? His mother's words, not simply "have sought thee," but *were seeking*, implied that they had searched the city. His answer says, in effect, Why should you spend time in such a quest?—**Wist ye not** (*did ye not know*) **that I must be about my Father's business?** or "*affairs*"; strictly, "*the things*" of my Father. The latter phrase is given in the Revision by "must be in my

50 And ᵃ they understood not the saying which he spake unto them.

51 And he went down with them, and came to Nazareth, and was subject unto them: but his mother ᵇ kept all these sayings in her heart.

52 And Jesus ᶜ increased in wisdom and stature, and in favour with God and man.

50 not that I must be in my ¹ Father's house? And they understood not the saying which he spake unto 51 them. And he went down with them, and came to Nazareth; and he was subject unto them: and his mother kept all ² these sayings in her heart.

52 And Jesus advanced in wisdom and ³ stature, and in ⁴ favour with God and men.

a ch. 9: 45; 18: 34....*b* ver. 19; Dan. 7: 28....*c* 1 Sam. 2: 26; ver. 40.—1 Or, about my Father's business. Gr. in the things of my Father. 2 O: things....3 Or. age. ..4 Or, grace.

Father's house," and certainly direct examples from the Greek can be more clearly and abundantly adduced of that sense of the phrase. At the same time, expressions like this—the things of God, the things of Cæsar, the things of a child, the things of the Spirit, and (1 Tim. 4: 15), "meditate on these things (see preceding verses); give thyself wholly to them," Greek, "be thou in these things"—are so common, that the phrase here may well have meant, "in the things of my Father," in his affairs, his business. It is said with reason that the other meaning agrees well with his implied correction of them for seeking him elsewhere than in his Father's house; but, if we understand his thought to be that his Father's affairs in Jerusalem had their seat in the temple, we reach the same point, with a broader description of his interest there. The question is somewhat evenly balanced, and we do not think there is a necessity for abandoning the familiar phrase. The other should stand, however, as an alternative rendering. The order of words in the original gives an emphatic prominence to the pronoun I: "that it behooves *me* to be in my Father's business?" His mother had said, Thy father and I have sought thee. Was there, in his phrase "my Father's business," an intimation to her that she should remember who his Father really was?

50. And they understood not, etc. Was it the ambiguity of the clause just considered that perplexed them? If it plainly designated his Father's *house*, the perplexity would be at its minimum. The objection to the truth and consistency of Luke's record of the nativity, which has been based on this verse, and which even Meyer urges, assumes that Joseph and Mary must have clearly understood, from the miraculous birth of Jesus, that he was God's Son in the sense which he seemed to intimate now (and that this is hardly accordant with ver. 33); that there was nothing in the *manner* of his saying to perplex them now, and that all which they had at any time divined concerning him would be present to them at all times, so as to exclude surprise or questionings at any of the prodigious manifestations of the divine child. No one of these assumptions can be upheld. (Compare Godet.)

51. And he went down with them. All appearance of independence which his answer might suggest is dissipated by this immediate exhibition of filial attachment; and the true relation is still more distinctly confirmed in the next clause.—And was subject unto them. He subjected himself, was obedient, habitually, continuously, while abiding with them, as the Greek expression indicates.—But (*and*) his mother kept all these sayings in her heart. This is nearly the same phrase as in ver. 19; only there the verb signifies rather she "was keeping them together," as the materials of more perfect knowledge; and here that "she was keeping them persistently," or each in addition to the preceding. The use of but in the Common Version, is entirely without warrant.

52. SUMMARY ACCOUNT OF THE FURTHER DEVELOPMENT OF JESUS IN HIS INDIVIDUAL LIFE. And Jesus increased (*advanced*) in wisdom and stature. Increased = made progress. In wisdom—that is, in intellectual acquirements and moral adaptation of all to the uses of life. And stature—his physical growth was proportioned to his improvement in the inner man. To translate "in age," which the Greek word would in itself allow, would be inappropriate here, where advancement in age is self-evident.—And in favour with God and man (*men*). Favour is the same as "grace" in ver. 40—the friendly and complacent disposition towards Jesus with which God constantly beheld and helped him, and the good will which such a spectacle of innocence, uprightness, and benevolence awakened in the men of his acquaintance.

How little the gospel narrative was designed to gratify the curiosity of men, appears strikingly from the fact that these few words convey almost everything that is known of Christ during a period of about eighteen years—from the passover visit to Jerusalem until his coming forth to the baptism of John. This is the more noticeable from contrast with the Apocryphal Gospels of the first centuries. They consist very largely of strange and mythical stories of prodigies, often extremely puerile and absurd, which are connected with the nativity and early life of Jesus. And we may easily imagine that fuller knowledge concerning just these years, of which we are told nothing, would have been of special value to us. Here his history, as that of a maturing, and then a ripened private life, might have afforded us examples suited to our own copying, whereas afterward we more easily lose sight of the man in the Messiah. But the first preachers of his truth were too much occupied with him as the Saviour of sinners, the Recoverer of the lost, to allow much space for any other views, however interesting.

REMARK.—The preceding account of the birth and early life of our Saviour has laid the ground for various questions which will often arise as we proceed in our task. They connect themselves with the peculiarity of the nature originated by the immediate action of the Spirit of God upon a woman, as the result of which it could be said "that the Word became flesh," and the offspring could be called, in a unique sense, "the Son of God." It might seem that in this early stage of such a being, the *mode* of that dual entity in one person would betray itself by some utterance or act of the unreflecting child, or the ingenuous youth. Or, could we think, in his case, of an unreflecting child, or, with an implied possibility of the opposite, of an ingenuous youth? Doubtless, if we could, at any period of his life, get any explanation of the enigma, it would be here, through the intimation of something seen or heard by his mother (from whom these narratives concerning him must have come), or the other companions of his domestic life. But we get none. The mystery is fully established with the first manifestation of his rational consciousness. Everything related concerning him obliges us to think that if we had seen him with our own eyes, and directly heard him, our perplexity would have been as great as it is now. Certainly his mother did not understand him yet, as far as we have gone with them. That look of wondering and almost awe-struck delight with which she embraces him in Raphael's "Sistine Madonna," is justified by the weird, unearthly, yet eminently human, glance with which he looks out on us from the immortal canvass. The painter would delude us in regard to the material surroundings, but we can scarcely doubt that, if we had seen her and her infant Son in their lowly domestic hut, we should have stopped in silence, as they do before the picture, to gaze into that divine human reality. But we could not comprehend it. We could, at most, join in the sacred curiosity with which the mother pondered every saying and movement of her child. From this indecision of hers at the time, her testimony concerning him becomes the more convincing to us who have the light of subsequent developments concerning Christ's character and works. That she did not know him as God manifest in the flesh, in a dogmatic sense, gives to her account of his development the force of a moral demonstration that he *was* so, without at all solving the mystery *how*. Had she set out to establish that view, she could hardly have given us a narrative so unintentionally suited to establish it in our thoughts. The phenomenon of a faultless child developing by normal stages into the physical frame of boyhood, youth, manhood; growing with equal pace in strength, distinctness, compass, symmetry of all appropriate intellectual powers; able to receive aid from what helped others, yet often able to give back more to his helpers; interested in the matters which engaged the studies and excited the pleasures of others, while always betraying a consciousness of higher interests than generally occupied them; and with a sensibility that answered, in its emotions, to every perception, every attainment, every communication from without—this he must have been to those who noticed him then. Above all, there was a moral purity and elevation, a fervid glow of religious sentiment, animating every thought and action, and crowning the whole expression of his being. It would seem more than human, more than had been apparent in any prophet; but what was it more, and how was it more? There was no act that could be separately predicated of God, none at all bespeaking corrupted humanity, many which were perfectly human,

CHAPTER III.

NOW in the fifteenth year of the reign of Tiberius Cæsar, Pontius Pilate being governor of Judea, and Herod being tetrarch of Galilee, and his brother Philip tetrarch of Ituren and of the region of Trachonitis, and Lysanias the tetrarch of Abilene,

2 *a* Annas and Caiaphas being the high priests, the word of God came unto John the son of Zacharias in the wilderness.

1 Now in the fifteenth year of the reign of Tiberius Cæsar, Pontius Pilate being governor of Judæa, Herod being tetrarch of Galilee, and his brother Philip tetrarch of the region of Ituræa and Trachonitis, and Lysanias tetrarch of Abilene, in the high-priesthood of Annas and Caiaphas, the word of God came unto John the son of Zacharias in the

a John 11 : 49, 51 ; 18 : 13 ; Acts 4 : 6.

while not merely human. The whole was consistent only with the conception that he was at once God and man. At no time did God act alone, or man suffer alone. Every experience was that of the God-man. His own revelations concerning himself afterward interpret the prior utterances of prophets and angels, with a distinctness to which his mother could not yet, if ever, attain. These revelations, to be sure, while giving us all needed, perhaps all possible, light, might still be expressed in "Behold, I shew you a mystery!" We have the fact that he was at once equally and truly God and man—the two perfectly and inseparably identified, two without confusion of natures one. This oneness of God and man in Jesus of Nazareth our minds can receive as a fact, and our hearts rejoice in. What is behind and below that fact is of the secret things which belong to God. We have seen the fact exhibiting itself in the seclusion of an humble, laborious home, and we shall now see it displayed in the activity, patent to a whole nation, of Christ's brief public career.

PART I. SECT. III. Ch. 3: 1—4: 13. FROM THE BEGINNING OF JOHN'S MINISTRY TO THAT OF JESUS.

1. The public ministry of John the Baptist, including the baptism of Jesus. This account embraces: 1. The date of the beginning of his public work (ver. 1, 2). 2. The nature of it (ver. 3-9). 3. Its effects (ver. 10-17). 4. The fate of John (ver. 18-20). 5. The baptism of Jesus (ver. 21-23). 6. The genealogy (ver. 23-38). 7. The temptation (ch. 4: 1-13).

1, 2. THE DATE. This is given with a particularity quite consistent with the purpose of Luke to "write in order," which would lead him to fix times and places, whenever his resources furnished him the means. He defines this point by six circumstances of ever-narrowing circuit.

(*a*) **The reign of Tiberius Cesar.** This began, strictly, Aug. 19, in the year 767 of the Roman era, on the death of his step-father Augustus, the first emperor. Much use is made of this *datum* in researches concerning the year of Christ's birth. It is the year in which John began to preach and baptize; and if we *knew* at what time in the year he began, and that Jesus was baptized soon enough after he began, and if we disregard the "about" in ver. 24, assuming that Jesus was just "thirty years of age when he began to teach" (ver. 23, Revision), we *might* possibly know that Jesus was born between the 19th of August, 751, and the same day in 752 U. C. For **the fifteenth year of Tiberius** would reach to 781-82 U. C., thirty subtracted from which gives the date just named. But that encounters the difficulty that Herod had then been some time dead; for a heavy preponderance of authority favors the opinion that he died in the spring of 750 U. C., and Jesus was born some time, perhaps near two years, before. In this state of the case, it is convenient to find that Tiberius was, "two or three years" before the death of Augustus, raised by the latter to a partnership in the dominion. This might reduce the fifteenth year of his reign to 779-80 U. C., and retaining all the suppositions before enumerated, would render it possible that he should have been born from four to five years before A. D. 1. With this supposed date agree well the results of what other lines of conjecture have most probability; and we are practically safe in resting in it as a hypothesis. As we have before said (p. 46), all pretence of demonstrating definitely the day, month, and even the year of our Lord's birth, is mere pretence. Geikie (*Life and Words of Christ*, Vol. I., p. 559, note 8), gives the elements of the calculations, expresses his own view, and closes with the sensible remark: "Still the whole subject is very uncertain. Ewald appears to fix the date of the birth as five years earlier than our epoch. Petavius and Usher fix it as on the 25th of December, five years before our era; Bengel, on the 25th of December, four years before our era; Auger and Winer, four years before our era, in the spring; Scaliger, three years before our era, in October; St. Jerome, three years before our era, on December 25; Eusebius, two years before our era, on January 6; and Ideler, seven years before our era, in December."

(*b*) **Pontius Pilate being governor of Judea.** He was procurator, *i. e.*, imperial administrator of the revenues of Judea for ten years, A. D. 25-36.

(*c*) **Herod,** (Antipas, son of Herod the Great), **being tetrarch of Galilee.** A tetrarch was, originally, as the name itself indicates, a governor of a fourth part of what had been a kingdom; now it designated a petty monarch of a small country, dependent on the general dominion of Rome; "a tributary prince, not of sufficient importance to be called a king." (Smith, *Dict. of Bib.*, on the word).

(*d*) **His brother Philip tetrarch of Ituren.** This was a small district northeast of the Sea of Galilee, extending half way to Damascus, settled by Jetur, son of Ishmael (Gen. 25: 15. 16), from whom it took its name—the modern *El-Jedûr*.—**And of the region of Trachonitis.** (*El-Lejah*), nearly identical with the ancient kingdom of Og; a rough, rocky land, as its Greek name signifies, and inhabited still from the earliest times by a wild and predatory race of people. It was situated southeast of Ituren, nearly east of the sea. Around it, on the west, lay the wider country of Hauran (Auranitis), land of Bashan, which also was included in the tetrarchy of Herod Philip.

(*e*) **Lysanias the tetrarch of Abilene.** Since Josephus (Ant., 19: 5. 1), mentions Abilene as called "of Lysanias," about sixty years before this (comp, *Antiq.*, 20: 7. 1), and is supposed by some, in this last passage, to refer to another of the same name, in the time of Claudius Cesar, Luke has, of course, been suspected here of mistaking the time of the rule of Lysanias. Scarcely anything is known of the history of that region during the nearly eighty years between these two dates. The answer to the charge is obvious, that if there *was* another Lysanias in the time of Claudius, it shows that the name, and probably the line, had been kept up through the interval. Either the second one supposed, may, therefore, have been tetrarch twenty years, before (about A. D. 30), or his father, or some other member of the family may, which would be just what Luke relates. If, as is more probable, Josephus does *not* intend a second Lysanias in *Antiq.*, 20: 7. 1, then Luke simply informs us of one, whose existence would otherwise be unknown to us. (See Smith, *Dict. of Bib.*, and Winer, *R. Wörterb*, art. Abilene). Little is known of him or of his country, "Abilene." The latter, however, from the site of its capital, the ruins of which have been identified, must have lain west of Damascus.

The sacred writer, having described the civil state of all the region of country pertaining even remotely to Jerusalem, comes now to the religious rule.

(*f*) **Annas and Caiaphas being the high priests,** (rather, *in the high priesthood of Annas and Caiaphas*). The word in the Greek for **high priest**, is now universally agreed to be singular; but as two men are named, the words can be consistently joined only in the way here given. That the high priesthood is ascribed to both, when only one high priest at a time is contemplated by the law, shows the disorder of the age now before us. Annas is called high priest, (Acts 4: 6; John 18: 19; comp. 13); while in John 11: 49, 51, we are told that Caiaphas was high priest the same year. The explanation seems to be given by the history of that time in Josephus, (*Ant.*, 18: 7. 1; 20: 8. 9). From that we learn that Annas, a rich Sadducee, had been high priest (appointed by a Roman governor), but deposed several years before our date; yet, that being a man of great wealth, ability, and influence, he continued to enjoy much esteem from the people, and had five sons, besides Caiaphas, his son-in-law, successively in the office during his life time. (John 18: 13). Josephus shows, also, with what capricious frequency the office was filled and vacated by the hated Romans, so that it became, apparently, not uncommon for two or more simultaneously to be entitled high priest. The respect in which Annas was held, with the consideration naturally given to such a man by his own sons in the office, would especially conduce to his being called high priest, and sharing in the deliberations of the acting high

3 *And he came into all the country about Jordan, preaching the baptism of repentance a for the remission of sins;

3 wilderness. And he came into all the region round about Jordan, preaching the baptism of repentance

a Matt. 3:1; Mark 1:4....b ch. 1:77.

priest for the time. Compare our practice of still calling an ex-governor or judge by his former title.

The result of this enumeration of contemporary rulers, civil and religious, is to show that the ancient realm of David and Solomon has fallen into a state of distraction and decay, pitifully inferior even to Herod's unprincipled and cruel, but vigorous and powerful, reign; while the religious institutions, representing the law and the prophets of better days, are now the foot-ball of a pagan power, and void of everything like a sincere and earnest life.

The word of God came unto John the son of Zacharias in the wilderness. The wilderness was the region famous as "the wilderness of Judea," called "the deserts" (1:80), into which, as we have seen, John withdrew while yet a boy, and where he had lived, so far as appears, until now. We can easily suppose, therefore, that John had seen very little, in the course of his life, if anything at all, of Jesus, notwithstanding their family relationship. **The word of the Lord came unto** (Greek, "*came to be upon*") **John** Of the manner of this revelation we can know nothing, and may only reverently conjecture. It would seem that he became conscious of the possession of religious truth which he was specially called by God to publish to the people. This was the form of speech by which the prophets in the Old Testament sometimes described the occasion of their most weighty utterances (Joel 1:1; Hos. 1:1; Jer. 4:4). We may learn from the connection in such cases, that the mode of impartation was various—by a dream, a vision, possibly by words heard, or a sudden flash of intellectual light, or deep and prolonged study —and that the constant feature of their experience was a recognition that the truth present to the mind of the prophet was not of his own authorship, but a message from God.

3-9. HIS WORK.—ITS NATURE.

3. And he came into all the country (*round*) **about** (*the*) **Jordan.** This expression implies that he left now the "wilderness," although it bordered closely on the lower end of the Jordan valley, and may have included so much of this as lay near the northern end of the Dead Sea. **The country round about *the* Jordan** was the arid plain which stretched along the river, from a few miles below the Sea of Galilee to the Dead Sea; bounded by the steep wall of the highlands of Bashan and Gilead on the east, and on the west by the more gradual and less elevated slopes of the central ridge which ran north and south through Judea and Samaria. Its ancient name was The Arabah, which is still applied to the southern prolongation of this very remarkable ravine, from the Dead Sea to the Elanitic Gulf. The natives now call the portion extending north from the Dead Sea, even to the sources of the Jordan, *El Ghor.* It was, in its southern portion, for the most part exceedingly barren and desolate, with only small strips and patches of verdure where the river itself gave moisture, being scorched with a tropical heat. Jericho lay in an expansion of its width near the Dead Sea; and besides that, scarcely a town flourished in it. When it is said that John came into all this country, we must understand that he moved from place to place, up and down the river, to meet the convenience of people who lived opposite to, but not near, its several stages.—**Preaching the** (*a*) **baptism of repentance for the** (*unto*) **remission of sins.** This might be paraphrased: "Proclaiming the duty of all people to repent, and on the ground of their repentance to be baptized, and all with a view to the foregivness of their sins." **Preaching** meant, properly, publicly proclaiming what was to be communicated, as news, to the hearer. **Repentance** was the main thing in the requirement of John, explained by him in its grounds (ver. 7), its sanctions (ver. 9), and its varied fruits and manifestations (ver. 10-14); but as it expressed itself visibly in the rite of baptism, this is mentioned first in Luke—the reverse in Matthew. The **baptism** which he preached was an immersion of the professed penitent in water, at first that of the river Jordan (Matt. 3:6), the neighborhood of which John seems to have frequented just because it alone in all that region would furnish the supply of pure water needed for the vast crowds who came to the rite. The word **baptism** is simply the Greek noun written, with slight change, in English letters, because it had been so transferred, not in the earliest Latin versions, but in the *Vulgate*, from which it came into the early religious vocabulary of England. Variety of *modern* usage has unhappily made the English word ambiguous; but that the Greek term expressed the notion of dipping, plunging, immersion, whelming (any one of which terms would suggest the true intent, so far as the New Testament rite is concerned), a scholar learns upon simply consulting the chief dictionaries of the Greek language: Liddell and Scott, Cremer (*Biblical-Theological Lex. of the New Testament Greek*), Grimm (*Clavis*), Rost and Palm's edition of Passow's *Wörterbuch*, Sophocles (*Lexicon of the Byzantine Greek*), Stephanus' *Thesaurus*, etc., etc.; the chief commentaries, Meyer, De Wette, Godet, McClellan (see note on Matt. 28: 19), etc., etc. Or, he may refer, as an example of all, to Conant on *Baptizein*, where all the known instances of the use of the word which could bear on the Scriptural usage are collected and printed, with enough of the context to enable any one to make the right definition for himself. But the plain English reader, with no authority but his Bible, may arrive with equal certainty at the same conclusion, by noticing that wherever the word baptism occurs in the New Testament to denote the Christian rite, he may substitute immersion, or one of the synonomous words, in

RIVER JORDAN.

perfect consistency with the context; thus proving to a demonstration that the meaning not only may be, but must be, what these English words directly convey. He need only reflect that the chances against one of these words being appropriate in five or ten cases, when some other sense had been intended by the Greek, would be innumerable; whereas they are appropriate in every case of the use of the noun or the corresponding verb.

A ceremony of immersion was introduced by John, in connection with his demand for repentance; primarily, it is possible, to signify the moral purification implied in renewedness of heart and life. In the subsequent course of Christian revelation, other meanings, other power, shone forth from the simple and expressive rite. John *may* have seen only its fitness to symbolize the putting away of sin, and the preparation for a life of profound and resolute righteousness. "Repentance" is, etymologically, that change of view and feeling which results from reflection on one's past conduct and inward character, as wrong, and which leads to a radically different course. Chalmers gave a good description of it: "renewedness of mind." Deep moral thoughtfulness on the past, resulting in the effective purpose to so live as to please God, is directly suggested by the Greek word. As such an exercise of the mind must needs occasion much dissatisfaction with oneself, it is not strange that the word is often associated with regret and self-reproach. The thorough renovation of the life-purpose, however, is what the Scripture makes to be its essence. It must be largely because our translation takes the tone of the Latin Vulgate, in which the words for repentance and its cognates express directly the notion of regret, rue, sorrow, that this element of dissatisfied *feeling* has apparently become in many minds the very signification of repentance. It is only an incident of it, more or less of which is of little consequence, if only the practical resolution to serve God with the whole heart is thoroughly established. The essential change of moral state has then taken place. It should be added that the Greek verb to repent may have suggested to Hebrews in Christ's day more of the idea of feeling than to the native Greeks, from its having been used in their Greek translation to render a Hebrew verb, which was appropriate to express deep and painful emotion. [Compare the excellent note of Dr. Conant on Matt. 3: 2, in the Revised Version of the American Bible Union, quarto edition.]

Perhaps the notion of repentance was hardly so comprehensive in John's conception as that which we form under the clearer light of the gospel. He was not the one that should come, and could not offer the immersion in the Spirit. What he would have the people do was to consider their ways, that they might see how far they were from the ideal of duty, piety, and privilege, which their institutions and their Scriptures set before them. That ideal was to be realized under the reign of the Messiah. To undergo such a change as would prepare them to welcome his explicit teachings and control, to prepare them for faith in him—*that* might be acceptable repentance to John.

For remission of sins, *i. e.*, *unto*, in order to, with a view to obtaining, **remission,** or "release from," "forgiveness." The baptism of repentance thus grammatically looked forward to the **forgiveness,** and was not based upon it. If the pledge given in baptism was truly kept, forgiveness would follow at the coming of the Messiah, when this change of mind would have prepared the subject of it for faith in Christ.[1]

It has been made a question whether John found a rite of immersion existing, by which proselytes to Judaism professed their conver-

---

[1] May there not be a better explanation of the words, *unto the remission of sins?* For it is certainly difficult to believe that there was no remission of sins before the historical Christ was known and accepted. It is difficult to see how forgiveness could be withheld from one who had truly turned to the Lord, and was ready to welcome the Christ as soon as he should be revealed. The baptism of repentance looked, we think, to the forgiveness of sins, because entrance upon the new life, symbolized by this rite, was the condition of forgiveness, and because no man enters into that new life without spiritual union with Christ and preparation of heart to rely on his grace. Compare the language of Peter to the multitude in Acts 2: 38, where repentance and baptism upon the name of Jesus Christ are still enjoined, "in order to the forgiveness of sins"; and the words of Peter to Cornelius, Acts 10: 34, 35. The inward change was supposed to be genuine when it led to obedience in the prescribed outward expression.—A. H.

4 As it is written in the book of the words of Esaias the prophet, saying, *The voice of one crying in the wilderness, Prepare ye the way of the Lord, make his paths straight.
5 Every valley shall be filled, and every mountain and hill shall be brought low; and the crooked shall be made straight, and the rough ways *shall be* made smooth;
6 And *b* all flesh shall see the salvation of God.

4 unto remission of sins; as it is written in the book of the words of Isaiah the prophet,
The voice of one crying in the wilderness,
Make ye ready the way of the Lord,
Make his paths straight.
5 Every valley shall be filled,
And every mountain and hill shall be brought low;
And the crooked shall become straight,
And the rough ways smooth;
6 And all flesh shall see the salvation of God.

a Isa. 40:3; Matt. 3:3; Mark 1:3; John 1:23....*b* Ps. 98:2; Isa. 52:10; ch. 2:10.

sion, and were installed members of the select nation. There is no mention, certainly, of any such usage in the Old Testament, nor in the Apocrypha, or in Josephus or Philo, or in the other Jewish writings prior to, or contemporary with, the age of John. Nor have the deepest researches of scholars resulted in any clear proof that anything analogous to baptism then existed. That certain ablutions may have been practiced by proselytes on their coming to the passover, and that, in the first or second century, the custom of immersing proselytes came to be thought necessary, is generally admitted. See the authorities, pro and con, briefly condensed and judiciously estimated in Winer, *Real Wörterbuch*, Art. Proselyten-taufe. A very recent writer, Dr. L. Schultze, says (in Zöckler's *Handbuch der Theologische Wissenschaften*, 1883, p. 494), without qualification, "proselyte baptism is of a later time" — than John. (Comp. Edersheim, *Life of Jesus*, App. XI.)

Again, dogmatic interest has discussed the question whether John's baptism was Christian baptism. It was, and it was not. The act of immersion was the same, when practiced by Christ and his apostles, as when practiced by John, being designated everywhere by the same word. But the significance of the rite, as expressive of a sense of sin and a determination to take a new moral position, so as to be prepared for the reception of the coming of the Messiah—this, on the part of John's disciples, was not just the same as the sentiment, the aim, and the effect with which, after the resurrection of Christ, the believer was baptized into the name of the Father and of the Son and of the Holy Ghost. His sentiment is that of grateful devotion to a Saviour already well known; his purpose is to die with that Saviour to all sin, that he may live with him a new life of holiness; and the effect is the reception, in love and hope, of the end of his faith—the salvation of his soul (Mark 16:16; Acts 2:38; R m. 6:3, 4; 2 Cor. 5:19; 1 Pet. 3:21; 1:8, 9).

4. **As it is written in the book of the words,** etc. The position and work of John is compared with the description, in Isa. 40:3, of the imaginary herald who precedes, and orders the road prepared for, Jehovah at the head of his people, returning joyfully to Jerusalem from their long captivity in Babylon. Here is a figure drawn from the custom of Oriental monarchs, before whom, in their stately procession, the most extravagant pains are taken to clear their path of all impediments and difficulties. The herald, supposed thus to be going before Jehovah to see that the march was made easy for him and his ransomed people, is seen in the gospel to have been a type of John the Baptist preceding the Lord's advent as Messiah, and preparing for him access to the confidence and love of men. John's appearance is the only actual realization of that grand and beautiful description of a herald, as the advent of Jesus alone fulfills that promise of deliverance to distressed and despairing men.

5. The expressions of the prophet, **every valley shall be exalted,** etc., were metaphorical hyperboles, literally applicable only partially even to the preparations made for the most powerful civil or military potentate. We cannot, with any confidence, apply them severally to the particular moral tasks of John as forerunner. They are a poetical expansion and variation of the thought, that John, by promoting sincere repentance, has to make ready the way for Jesus to the hearts of the people whom he comes to save.

6. In the old, temporal deliverance, the manifestation of divine power and faithfulness was to be so conspicuous, that **all flesh shall see the salvation of God**—which, in John's case, would mean that eternal life should be provided for, and offered to, the whole world.

6. **Then said he** (rather, *he said, therefore*),

7 Then said he to the multitude that came forth to be baptized of him, *O generation of vipers, who hath warned you to flee from the wrath to come?
8 Bring forth therefore fruits b worthy of repentance, and begin not to say within yourselves, We have Abraham to our father: for I say unto you, That God is able of these stones to raise up children unto Abraham.
9 And now also the axe is laid unto the root of the trees: ¹ every tree therefore which bringeth not forth good fruit is hewn down, and cast into the fire.

7 He said therefore to the multitudes that went out to be baptized of him, Ye offspring of vipers, who 8 warned you to flee from the wrath to come? Bring forth therefore fruits worthy of ¹ repentance, and begin not to say within yourselves, We have Abraham to our father: for I say unto you, that God is able of these stones to raise up children unto Abraham.
9 And even now the axe also lieth at the root of the trees; every tree therefore that bringeth not forth good fruit is hewn down, and cast into the fire.

a Matt. 3 : 7....*b* Or, *meet for*....*c* Matt. 7 : 19.——1 Or, *your repentance.*

namely, in conformity with his errand to produce repentance, by convincing of sin. **To the multitude that came forth**—strictly, *were coming forth.* They had to leave their homes in the wide circuit of towns and cities to which the tidings of John's preaching had reached, and come forth into the wilderness. But a great many of them, not merely "of the Pharisees and Sadducees" (Matt. 3 : 7), as we should conclude from Luke's account, came to him with no proper sense of what they were doing. It was as if a fashion had soon set in to go and be baptized by the hermit preacher. Not individually, thoughtfully, each in the seriousness and humility of conscious guilt and craving for a better spiritual life; they went in holiday crowds, as Musselman hordes now go, at Easter, to dip themselves in the Jordan.

7. O generation of vipers—John says to them—not "children of Abraham" as ye imagine yourselves; but people of malignant and detestable disposition, not in the least prepared for friendship to the Christ, but needing to be transformed before ye can see him in peace.—**Who hath warned** (*suggested to*) **you to flee from the wrath to come** (or *coming wrath*)? In the spirit of the closing prophecy of the Old Testament, concerning himself, John sees first the "great and terrible day of the Lord," connected with the coming of the Messiah, a day "which shall burn as an oven," a day of wrath to the impenitent and ungodly. He was so stirred by the religious declension and moral corruption of his time, that the penal character of "the day of the Lord," was to him, as to the ancient prophets, very prominent. In this view the Jews also shared, though generally they referred that feature of the day of judgment to the heathen. But in the present case, John seems to see them flocking to him, as if under the delusion that they could avoid the penalties and secure the blessings of the Messiah's advent, by merely sharing in the outward ceremony of his immersion. His question, thus, amounts to this: "Who suggested to you that you could escape from the just consequences of your sins by a mere physical act? Was it the great adversary, whose brood ye are?"

8. Bring forth therefore—since the mere sign of repentance cannot help you, without its transforming operation in your lives— **fruits worthy of repentance.** Such fruits would be inward exercises of the soul—such as hungering after true righteousness, compassion, mercy toward the erring and unfortunate, purity of heart, a humble purpose to wait only on Jehovah in all his requirements and ordinances, a desire for his mercy, and outward conduct consistent with such a state of mind.—**And begin not to say within yourselves,** equivalent to, Do not start with saying; otherwise real repentance will be precluded as unnecessary.—**We have Abraham to** (*for* or *as*) **our father,** and are of course objects of God's favor, and sure of a place in the kingdom of heaven.—**God is able of these stones,** etc. Sooner than recognize you, in your hardness of heart and impenitence, as heirs of his promise to Abraham, God will prepare for that blessing other hearts which you would think as little capable of sharing it as the stones which lie along these banks. Nor can your rejection be long delayed.

9. And now also (*even now*), while ye are so lightly pressing toward an outward hypocritical righteousness, **the axe is laid unto the root of the trees. The trees** represent the proud, self-righteous members of the Jewish nation. **The axe is the symbol of divine punishment.** Its being **laid unto the root** signifies that the "feller" (Isa. 14 : 8) is already come up against them, and holds his instrument directed toward the trunk of one and another, ready to level them with the ground.—**Is hewn down and cast into the fire.** The action is future, the tense is pres-

10 And the people asked him, saying, *What shall we do then?
11 He answereth and saith unto them, ᵇ He that hath two coats, let him impart to him that hath none; and he that hath meat, let him do likewise.
12 Then ᶜ came also publicans to be baptized, and said unto him, Master, what shall we do?
13 And he said unto them, ᵈ Exact no more than that which is appointed you.
14 And the soldiers likewise demanded of him, saying, And what shall we do? And he said unto them, Do violence to no man, neither accuse any falsely; and be content with your wages.

10 And the multitudes asked him, saying, What then must we do? And he answered and said unto them, He that hath two coats, let him impart to him that hath none; and he that hath food, let him do likewise. And there came also ¹publicans to be baptized, and they said unto him, ²Master, what must we do?
13 And he said unto them, Extort no more than that which is appointed you. And ³soldiers also asked him, saying, And we, what must we do? And he said unto them, Extort from no man by violence, neither accuse any one wrongfully; and be content with your wages.

ᵃ Acts 2:37.....ᵇ ch. 11:41; 1 Cor. 8; 14; James 2:15, 16; 1 John 3:17; 4:20.....ᶜ Matt. 21:32; ch. 7:29.....ᵈ ch. 19:8.—¹ See marginal note on Matt. v. 46.....² Or, Teacher.....³ Gr. soldiers on service.

---

ent; strictly, "*is in the act of being cut down and cast into the fire.*" Every fruit tree will yield fruit of some kind, and every man will exhibit some character; unless this be good in God's sight, it will meet only rejection and punishment.

10-17. PARTICULAR TEACHINGS OF JOHN. This general teaching, so well suited to awaken compunction and alarm in hearts of any susceptibility, led some to ask for more particular instruction concerning the fruits required of them.

10. And the people (*multitudes*, Revision) **asked him, saying, What shall we do then?** The answer is, in general, that they should practice love and beneficence to fellow-men in need.

11. Into ver. 11 is doubtless condensed the body of his doctrine applicable to all. It suppresses selfishness, calls out self-denying sympathy, practical love of one's neighbor.

12-14. Specimens of the manner in which the prophet applied the general principle to particular cases of inquiry. **Then there came also publicans.** These were among the first inquirers attracted by John, and most generally prepared to welcome the Saviour at his coming. The office of the publicans, who appear so frequently in the Gospel, namely, that of tax collectors of the revenue required by the Roman Government, was in itself consistent with personal uprightness, and intrinsic worth, on the part of the incumbent. But while it is not really agreeable to the most contented community, in the best governed state, it was for special reasons peculiarly odious, abominable, to the Jews at that time. They had to meet the cost of a burdensome religious system, which should, in God's original plan, have afforded them also civil security and order. In addition, here were the grinding taxes levied for the benefit of a foreign, pagan government, a galling offence to their independence—a flagrant scandal to their monotheistic principle of religion. The instruments for exacting these taxes were Hebrews—more shame to them!—who, by undertaking such service, made themselves renegades, more despicable even than the Romans, whose tools they were. As a rule, men of good character would not put themselves in such a position; and if they did, so little likely were men to hold themselves above what they generally have the credit of being, they would be in great danger of falling to the level of the popular estimation. But that their occupation was not essentially immoral, is indicated by John's not requiring of them unconditionally to quit it. Yet in answering their question he did point out the very peril in which they stood.

13. Exact no more than that which is appointed you. The Roman dominion was made hateful and destructive to its subject provinces, not merely by the severity of its own exactions, but more by the additional extortions of the rapacious collectors (publicans), who, through all stages of the process, from the head farmer of the revenues that undertook to raise them from a whole province, down to the petty local underling, sought to enrich themselves. The people were, to a great extent, at the mercy of these arbitrary minions of a detestable tyranny. The case of a Turkish province, say Armenia, at the present day, affords the life-like parallel to the condition of the Jews, in reference to tax gatherers. John faithfully tells them to refrain from any demands beyond what were included in the law under which they served.

14. And the soldiers likewise. More exactly, *and men in the military service also.* These were apparently Jews engaged in some campaign of which we have no certain account, but not in the Greek called, technically,

15 And as the people were in expectation, and all men mused in their hearts of John, whether he were the Christ, or not;
16 John answered, saying unto *them* all, ⁎I indeed baptize you with water; but one mightier than I cometh, the latchet of whose shoes I am not worthy to unloose; he shall baptize you with the Holy Ghost and with fire:

15 And as the people were in expectation, and all men reasoned in their hearts concerning John, whether haply he were the Christ; John answered, saying unto them all, I indeed baptize you with water; but there cometh he that is mightier than I, the latchet of whose shoes I am not ¹ worthy to unloose; he shall baptize you ²in the Holy Spirit and

a Matt. 3: 11.——1 Or. *sufficient*....2 Or, *with*.

"soldiers."—**Do violence to no man.** Perhaps the meaning is nearly equivalent to *terrify* or *harrass* no man, in order to wring from him what is his.—**Neither accuse any falsely** (*wrongfully*), that is, in order to extort from him his property.—**And**—as the antithesis, observe, to both these prohibitions—**be content with your wages.** In these two cases, the fruit of repentance which the Baptist requires is no more than common morality enjoined in the law of Moses; but it is in such a form, as to each, that the honest attempt to practice it would evince something of self-denial, charity, and the general disposition to do right. On the other hand, the difficulty of even partial obedience to those requirements, and the impossibility of more in one's own strength, would promote humility and awaken a longing for that righteousness which could be found only in "the kingdom of heaven."

15, 16. JOHN'S PROCLAMATION CONCERNING THE MESSIAH. As John had said not a word hitherto, in Luke's report, about the Messiah, it was not unnatural that questions should arise in the popular mind concerning his relation to that personage.

15. And as the people were in expectation—not merely of some word of explanation from John about himself, but, more generally, of the coming of the Messiah—**and all men mused** (*reasoned*) **in their hearts . . . whether** (*haply*) **he were the Christ.** It shows how vague was their preconception of the Christ, that there hovered a universal suspicion (*all men*) that John himself might possibly be "he that is to come."

16. John answered—their unspoken question—**I indeed baptize** (*am baptizing*) **you with water**—and in requiring this as the symbol of moral purification, and the pledge of a new life, you might think me to be performing Messianic functions.—**But one mightier than I cometh**—a potentate so much more exalted than I, that I am not sufficient to perform for him the most menial service.—**The latchet of whose shoes** (*shoe-strings*) **I am not worthy to unloose** —not fit to perform the task of a domestic slave with a rich Roman.—**He** (strongly emphatic, *he himself*) **shall baptize you with** (*in*) **the Holy Ghost** (*Spirit*) **and with fire.** Omit the latter **with.** This will be the work of him whom you are expecting. He will be the Christ. The element of an immersion is naturally preceded by *in*, and that the Greek expresses with the *Holy Spirit.* In measure so ample will he be bestowed on the recipients of this blessing, that they are said to be baptized—immersed—in the Holy Spirit. The word for "in" is not used with the word "water" in the first clause of the verse, according to the certainly correct text, and, although the American Revisers judged that it should be expressed in English, wherever baptism "with" water is spoken of, it is somewhat doubtful whether it should so stand, except in Acts 1: 4. In Matt. 3: 5, also, it stands "baptized in the river Jordan," and that is the normal usage. The Greek view could equally well contemplate the enveloping element, locally, as that in which, or, instrumentally, as that with which, the dipping was effected. And while it is awkward for us to speak of immersing a thing with water, it is simply a matter of familiarity, of idiom; and we need only take a synonomous verb, "to whelm," and it is perfectly natural for us to speak of "whelming with water." **And fire** (without " in " or "with") is part of the promise to the same persons, supposed believers. He will immerse you in the Holy Spirit and fire, in both. Fire may be added as figuratively synonomous with Holy Spirit, in one of his functions, the removal of all that is carnal and sinful in the soul, as, in another view, he supplies all renewing and sanctifying grace. The renewed man is refined, as silver tried in the fire. The Spirit may in this make use of trials and afflictions, sometimes called a fire;

17 Whose fan *is* in his hand, and he will thoroughly purge his floor, and *a* and will gather the wheat into his garner; but the chaff he will burn with fire unquenchable.
18 And many other things in his exhortation preached he unto the people.

17 *in* fire: whose fan is in his hand, thoroughly to cleanse his threshing-floor, and to gather the wheat into his garner; but the chaff he will burn up with unquenchable fire.
18 With many other exhortations therefore preached

a Mic. 14: 4, 12; Matt. 13: 30.

but to think of these as directly intended, is less congenial with John's standing-point. He means, rather, the self-denying and disciplinary efficacy of the Spirit in elucidating and enforcing the truth of God on a partially-sanctified soul. Those who refer the fire to Gehenna—future punishment—must understand the pronoun *you* as equivalent to "some of you," which must then be repeated in thought, and that would require the repetition of "with" (in) before "fire." He will immerse some of you in the Holy Spirit, and some of you in fire. Meyer, on Matt. 3: 11, takes this view, and adds: "Both are denoted as a baptizing (βαπτίζων), since they are the two opposite sides of the *Messianic lustration*, by which, like those baptized, one part are overflowed by the Holy Spirit, the others by hell-fire." With him agree a long series of expositors from the earliest times. An equal number, perhaps, including Calvin and Godet, support substantially the view here advocated. This supposes that John has reserved the mention of hell-fire to the next verse, where he carefully distinguishes that fire by the adjective "unquenchable." It is quite unlikely that there is any direct reference to the tongues "*as of* fire," in Acts 2: 3.

17. **Whose fan is in his hand, and he will thoroughly purge** (*thoroughly to cleanse*) **his** (*threshing*) **floor.**—This floor was a smooth surface of rock or leveled, compacted earth, by preference on an elevation, where the grain was trodden out of the sheaves by cattle, and, after raking off the straw, the grain was separated from the chaff, by repeatedly throwing it up into the breezy air. The fan, by which this tossing up was effected, was a broad and light wooden shovel. The process is an expressive metaphor of that judgment for which the Christ was come into the world (John 9: 39), such that he who believed in him would not be condemned; but he who believed not was condemned already, because he did not believe (ch. 3: 18).—**And will gather the wheat into his garner. The wheat** is the humble, penitent, believing portion of the chosen people, the Simeons and Annas, and Marthas and Marys; **his garner** is the kingdom of the Messiah, with its duties and trials, as well as privileges and blessings here, and its unmixed felicities in the perfected state. **The chaff** indicates the worldly-minded, self-complacent, work-righteous Jews who, having rejected their Messiah, will be rejected by him "in that day," and overwhelmed with deserved irremissible punishment—Chorazin, Bethsaida, Capernaum, the Scribes and Pharisees, and all Gentiles like them. The **unquenchable fire** is probably the "hell fire" (Gehenna of fire) spoken of by our Saviour (Matt. 5: 22; 10: 28). Fire had been adopted by the Old Testament prophets as a symbol of divine punishment for sin and transgression (Isa. 33: 12-14.), and its interminableness to the utterly incorrigible and impenitent was signified by the epithet unquenchable, or everlasting (Isa. 66: 21. ref.). We, after the lapse of a long time, postpone the fulfillment of these declarations to a still future day. It is probable that John and his hearers interpreted his words as about to take effect at the appearing of the Messiah.

18-20. FURTHER WORK AND FATE OF JOHN.

18. **And many other things in his exhortation preached he unto the people.** Rather, *with many other exhortations, therefore*; strictly, *with many and other, i. e.*, different, relating to different subjects, or to different aspects of the same, and expressed in different terms. The preceding statements are regarded as a selection and sample of the teachings with which he warned and stimulated the people to true, practical, heart piety. **Preached** (or, *proclaimed the good tidings*) of the Messiah's near approach to those who waited for him.

How long the active ministry of John continued before the baptism of Jesus, is unknown. The common supposition is, that it was only a few months—about the difference between the age of John and Jesus. But

19 a But Herod the tetrarch, being reproved by him for Herodias his brother Philip's wife, and for all the evils which Herod had done,
20 Added yet this above all, that he shut up John in prison.
21 Now when all the people were baptized, b it came to pass, that Jesus also being baptized, and praying, the heaven was opened,

19 he 1 good tidings unto the people; but Herod the tetrarch, being reproved by him for Herodias his brother's wife, and for all the evil things which Herod had done, added this also to them all, that he shut up John in prison.
21 Now it came to pass, when all the people were baptized, that, Jesus also having been baptized, and

a Matt. 14: 3; Mark 6: 17....b Matt. 3: 13; John 1: 32.——1 Or, *the gospel.*

when we consider what he was to do (Luke 1: 16, 17, 76-79; Matt. 3: 4-6), what he had done (Matt. 3: 5, 6, par.), and the impression that he had made upon all Israel, even to their remote settlements (Matt. 11: 7 ff; 21: 25, 26; Luke 7: 24 ff; Acts 13; 24, 25), it seems quite as likely that his ministry lasted years as months.

19. But Herod the tetrarch being reproved by him, etc. Luke writing to Theophilus "in order," having now finished his account of the public work of John with the people, gathers up what he knew concerning his subsequent fortunes, prior to his death, and tells us at once how his public labors terminated in a prison. **Herod the tetrarch,** that is, Herod Antipas (ver. 1).—**Herodias, his brother Philip's wife.** Omit **Philip's** and read *brother's*. See an account of the affair in Josephus (*Antiq.*, 18: 5. 4). Herod Antipas had taken the wife of his brother, Herod Philip (ver. 1), from her husband, while he was Philip's guest, and formed a pretended marriage with her, on condition of putting away his own wife. For this unhallowed conduct he had, as we here learn, been **reproved** by John, the stern preacher of righteousness, as well as **for all the evils** (*evil things*) **which Herod had done.** The notices of him in Josephus will show that, worthily of his origin, half Edomite and half Samaritan, he had done enough, both in contempt of Hebrew law and customs, and in the promotion of pagan practices, to furnish texts for many rebukes.

20. Added yet this above all—namely, of his evil deeds; nearly equivalent to *capped the climax with this.*—**That he shut up John in prison.** Josephus tells us (*Antiq.*, 18: 5. 2) that this treatment of John, a good man, by Herod, was popularly believed to be the ground of great misfortunes which befell the latter; and that **the prison** was the Castle of Machærus,

near the shore of the Dead Sea; where, in a most dismal region, the ruins of such structures have been recently found. The incarceration really took place, not till a considerable time, perhaps some months, after Christ's baptism. (Comp. John 2: 13; 3: 22, 23; 4: 1). But all this period the Synoptic Gospels leave out of their account. From this moment John is lost to view in the Gospels, except one glimpse (7: 18 ff), and then a reference to the violent death at the hands of Herod (9: 7-9), for whom, however, the stern spirit would not down at his bidding. Some general notice of his character and influence will be more appropriate on 7: 1 ff.[1]

21, 22. Baptism of Jesus. Having thus carried the narrative concerning John to a natural resting-place, the writer comes back to the baptism of Jesus, in connection with which, observe, John is not named. Luke gives some interesting details not mentioned by the other evangelists, while he omits some of theirs.

21. Now when all the people were baptized, it came to pass, etc. It will be noticed that Luke does not, in form, relate the baptism; but assuming that, as known to the reader, he particularly mentions as following it, the descent of the Spirit upon him, with the *Bath Col*, or voice from heaven, and, incidentally, gives two circumstances attending the baptism. The first of these vaguely defines the time of it. It was **when all the people were baptized.** The Greek does not allow us to think of this as equivalent to "when all the people had been baptized," making Jesus the last to whom John administered the rite (comp. John 3: 23), nor, as meaning "when all the people were being baptized," (so Meyer). This would require the Greek infinitive to be in the present tense, as the other would require it in the perfect,

---

[1] We would here call attention to a valuable monograph on John, in the Congregational Union Lecture for 1874: *John the Baptist*, by H. R. Reynolds, D. D., London, 1874. In this large volume almost every aspect of John's character and work is learnedly treated. Interesting and instructive on this subject is also the neglected work of C. S. Matthies, *Baptismatis Expositio Biblica, Historica, Dogmatica*, Berlin, 1840, pp. 44-71, ed. 2.

22 And the Holy Ghost descended in a bodily shape like a dove upon him, and a voice came from heaven, which said, Thou art my beloved Son; in thee I am well pleased.

22 praying, the heaven was opened, and the Holy Spirit descended in a bodily form, as a dove, upon him, and a voice came out of heaven, Thou art my beloved Son; in thee I am well pleased.

while the indefinite preterite simply places the transaction back somewhere in that time when John baptized all the people as they came to him. It gives no hint whether any person was present as a spectator. As one of **the people**, Jesus was baptized among all the rest.—**And praying.** The second circumstance clearly brought out by Luke alone, was, that after the baptism, and evidently (comp. Mark 1: 10, 11) while the Saviour was coming up from his symbolic burial, he was engaged in prayer. This appears from a literally adequate rendering of the Greek: *Jesus also having been baptized, and being in the act of prayer.* We may reverently imagine what was the subject of his requests to his Father. From the fact that this is mentioned as immediately preceding, or rather, simultaneous with the opening of the heavens, is it not intimated that he was looking for some recognition of his Messiahship to be given, and that he earnestly besought this now? At all events it came.—**The heaven was opened.** An ineffable fact is intimated to us in an expression shaped to meet human capacity of comprehension. Jesus saw through the blue depths of ether, into the very home of God.

22. And the Holy Ghost descended in a bodily shape (*form*) like a dove upon him. This was symbolically represented to Jesus and to John, the impartation to the former of the Spirit of God to be his permanent and distinguishing possession, in some sense additional to that element of divinity which pertained to him as the Incarnate Word, sealing and qualifying him for all the functions and experiences of the office of Messiah—Redeemer.—**Shape like a dove,** probably clear, resplendent white, beautifully fit to signify the purity and soaring energy of that power which was to be his, without measure, in the new economy of redemption—the Dispensation of the Spirit. That this bestowment was figured as a dove, a living and complete creature, and that it "abode on him" (John 1: 33), may have been designed to show that the Third Person of the Trinity entire was associated with the Son of man as a permanent endowment, for his personal behalf, and for the salvation of all the subjects of his kingdom.—**And a voice came out of heaven.** It came to Jesus himself, evidently, and probably to John also. There is no intimation, in either of the narratives, that it was audible to any other person. The Jewish theologians designated as *Bath Kol* (*daughter of a voice*), the lowest stage of revelation, after the cessation of prophecy in Malachi, coming through a miraculous voice from heaven. Some have (but without any tangible proof) reckoned this occurrence with that recorded in John 12: 18, also Luke 9: 35, as belonging to that category.—**Thou art my beloved Son.** This was probably the testimony which, or something equivalent, Jesus had desired in his prayer. There had already grown up in his consciousness, when he was twelve years of age (2: 49), the recognition of God as his Father in a special sense. That had doubtless become clearer, with his increase in wisdom respecting all subjects during the years that had passed until now. But now there is given to him further the testimony, which assured him of sonship in the high and peculiar sense of the second Psalm: "Thou art my Son, this day have I begotten thee." It came to him now as an announcement, also, that the moment of his entrance on that office which had brought him hither was come, and the full equipment for its functions had been bestowed. It was his ordination to the office of the Christ of Israel, and Saviour of the world.—**In thee I am well pleased,** rather, *I was well pleased.* The verb is in the aorist, or indefinite preterite, and may rarely be used where a perfect tense would do as well, but not (except the so-called gnomic use, or in similes) for a present. Yet the familiar English present gives an effect so suitable that we are ready to think no other could have been intended, and translators have from the beginning dealt with the phrase as though (with reverence be it spoken) the All-wise had blundered; and commentators have had to labor to show why it might be so. Had they rendered it as a perfect, "I have been well pleased," it might be said, in its favor, that the state of mind expressed plainly continues to the time of speaking. That is so; it is not shown, however, by the tense of the verb, but by the nature of the case, and would be shown with the English preterite just as it is in the Greek. (See Buttman, *Gram. of New Testament Greek*, p. 198; and compare Dr. Conant's note on Matt. 23: 1, Version of American Bible Union, (Quarto Edition.) It may be said, that if we allow the verb to refer us to the past, we do not know to what point to go back; and that may well incite us to more study of the question, but is no reason why we should preclude it. Perhaps the divine thought is: "In the adoption of that plan of human redemption, of which thou wast to be the Mediator and Finisher, I was well pleased with thee." Such references of the aorist tense to counsels of eternity are common. But we would only suggest, not attempt to decide. What recognition and consecration, more satisfactory, could the Son of man have desired, or possibly have received?

NOTE ON THE SIGNIFICANCE OF CHRIST'S BAPTISM.—Since Luke calls John's baptism "a baptism of repentance," thus implying a recognition of guilt on the part of its recipients, while Matthew and Mark tell us expressly that they were baptized "confessing their sins" (Matt. 3:6; Mark 1:5), questions naturally arise touching the baptism of the sinless Jesus. Why should it be sought by him? How could it be allowed by John? Yet neither Mark nor Luke speaks of any doubt felt by the parties to the act, or intimates any of his own. Luke might seem to intend an explanation in some sense by connecting this baptism with that of all the people, as though he felt that Jesus, by reason simply of his being of the people, needed to identify himself with them in their movement toward the Messiah's kingdom. He also (like Mark) places the baptism at such a point in the history of Jesus as to show that the act was regarded as denoting the transition from the private life of the latter to his public and official function. But our surprise remains that he should not have noticed the difference, in respect to this rite, between him who "knew no sin" and the sinful crowds.

A variety of dogmatic answers to the perplexing question have been offered through centuries past. After the plan of redemption had been accomplished, and the full light of revelation thrown upon it, such answers would occur to one and another thoughtful man, and be carried back to the beginning of "the gospel of Jesus Christ" (Mark 1:1). A number of these have been equally and so diversely plausible as largely to cancel each other, and none of them satisfies inquiry, as suggested by the historical record of the event. Could they have been in the minds of the evangelists? Yet it would seem as if something had been in their minds, to account for their reporting the baptism of Jesus as a matter of course.

Must we not suppose that, while they spoke of John's baptism in its ordinary application as significant of a sense of sin, and as a pledge to repentance, they saw also that it was initiatory to the new religious dispensation which was dawning on the world? The repentance professed and promised in this symbol was, if sincere, a prelude to forgiveness of sin at the hands of the Messiah, and to eternal life. But this presupposed membership in the kingdom of the Messiah. This kingdom in its earthly realization involved a social system, a governmental polity, an organization. It would have its distinctive forms and peculiar rule. Into this baptism would introduce its members. Baptism, in other words, was, as the rite guaranteeing repentance, a door of entrance into the kingdom, for those whose hearts had been so prepared. It was thus both and equally an expression and pledge of renewedness of mind on the one hand, and on the other of adherence to the cause and company of the Messiah. It was sufficient for John to present the former aspect in urging it on the wicked and self-righteous multitudes; the latter was that in which it would be equally appropriate to Jesus also. He was to be the head of that very kingdom, and it was fit that he should honor its appointed rites, and especially honor this rite by receiving in connection with it that last requisite sign and bestowment, the dove-like form and the measureless fullness of the Holy Spirit. This, while unnecessary for him, perhaps, in his individual capacity, was the indispensable anointing with the Holy Spirit (Acts 10:38), the *chrism*, by which he became THE CHRIST, and so duly qualified for the unique and supremely exigent office of Saviour for mankind.

Is not this answer to the question which

23 And Jesus himself began to be about thirty years of age, being (as was supposed) *the son of Joseph, which was *the son* of Heli,
24 Which was *the son* of Matthat, which was *the son* of Levi, which was *the son* of Melchi, which was *the son* of Janna, which was *the son* of Joseph,
25 Which was *the son* of Mattathias, which was *the son* of Amos, which was *the son* of Naum, which was *the son* of Esli, which was *the son* of Nagge,
26 Which was *the son* of Maath, which was *the son* of Mattathias, which was *the son* of Semei, which was *the son* of Joseph, which was *the son* of Juda,

23 And Jesus himself, when he began *to teach*, was about thirty years of age, being the son (as was supposed) of Joseph, the *son* of Heli, the *son* of Matthat, the *son* of Levi, the *son* of Melchi, the *son* of Jannai,
25 the son of Joseph, the *son* of Mattathias, the *son* of Amos, the *son* of Nahum, the *son* of Esli, the *son* of
26 Naggai, the *son* of Maath, the *son* of Mattathias, the

a Num. 4: 3, 35, 39, 43, 47....b Matt. 13: 55; John 6: 42.

we are following out (an answer latent in Mark and Luke), expressly sanctioned by our Saviour himself, in his reply to John's statement of the very difficulty which raises our question? John had implied that it was improper for him to baptize one whom his moral instinct, as we might say (not to speak of some acquaintance which he probably had with the holy life that Jesus had led), showed him to be exempt from those sins with which all other men, including himself, were chargeable. Jesus says, in effect: "Lay aside such scruples in this matter *now*. It is not unbecoming to either of us—to thee as implying arrogance, to me as acknowledging inferiority —that I should receive baptism at thy hands. It is altogether fit. I am yet a private person. Thou art, in closing the preparatory economy, to inaugurate the new, and it is incumbent on me formally to assume my official headship of the latter through the ordinance by which all my subjects are to enter in. This is directly required of us both by my Father." Righteousness is, in general, conformity with the declared will of God. The "righteousness" of which our Lord here speaks is thus —and what else can it be?—compliance with God's declared will *in the matter of his baptism*, declared to John as he tells us (John 1: 33), and to Jesus in whatever indication had moved him to go to the baptism, and to pray as he did in coming up from the water. It was thus on both sides the performance of an appointed duty, an act of *righteousness*, perfectly consistent with Christ's complete holiness, if not even assuming it, and resulting in the full discharge of "all" obligation preliminary to his public recognition as the Son of God.

The becomingness, amounting to a solemn obligation on his part to submit to this ordinance, would be clear to our Lord, if *he* saw even then that significance of it to every worthy recipient, which the apostles afterwards discerned as lying in it, namely, a death and resurrection. Paul (Rom. 6: 4, and repeatedly) sees baptism to be a symbol of the believer's burial, consequent upon a death to sin and a resurrection to a new and holy life. To Jesus it would be a symbol of that actual death of shame and agony, a sacrificial death, to which in entering on his Messianic course he consciously devoted himself. It is hard to believe that John did not himself gain this conception of what he did, especially in connection with the Father's testimony to the Sonship of Jesus, when we hear him the next day saying of him: "Behold the Lamb of God, which taketh away the sin of the world."

With the fuller record of Matthew and of John before us, there thus seems plainly a sufficient explanation afforded how Jesus could consistently be baptized, while the rite in general signified a sense of sin, and of the need of a new birth to a holy life. Luke and Mark, not bringing in that additional information, simply, as narrators, leave the facts recorded by them to suggest the explanation. John's baptism was, in its general aspect, a baptism of repentance. But even in this, their readers knew, lay the idea of a baptism of self-consecration to the kingdom of God, and in so far it was appropriate to the sinless Jesus as Head of that kingdom. They, as probably did their sources of information, simply leave the facts to disclose the *whole* significance of the rite.

23-38. GENEALOGY OF OUR LORD. Having reached the point where Jesus steps forth from his private sphere, fully prepared to enter on his work of salvation for the world, our author, mentioning his age, goes on to give his lineage. His motive in doing this was not the same as that of Matthew, who, to prove Jesus the promised seed of Abraham and son of David, the Messiah, King of

27 Which was *the son* of Joanna, which was *the son* of Rhesa, which was *the son* of Zorobabel, which was *the son* of Salathiel, which was *the son* of Neri,
28 Which was *the son* of Melchi, which was *the son* of Addi, which was *the son* of Cosam, which was *the son* of Elmodam, which was *the son* of Er,
29 Which was *the son* of Jose, which was *the son* of Eliezer, which was *the son* of Jorim, which was *the son* of Matthat, which was *the son* of Levi,
30 Which was *the son* of Simeon, which was *the son* of Juda, which was *the son* of Joseph, which was *the son* of Jonan, which was *the son* of Eliakim,
31 Which was *the son* of Melea, which was *the son* of Menan, which was *the son* of Mattatha, which was *the son* of ᵃ Nathan, ᵇ which was *the son* of David,
32 ᶜ Which was *the son* of Jesse, which was *the son* of Obed, which was *the son* of Booz, which was *the son* of Salmon, which was *the son* of Naasson,

27 *son* of Semein, the *son* of Josech, the *son* of Joda, the *son* of Joanan, the *son* of Rhesa, the *son* of Zerubbabel, the *son* of ¹ Shealtiel, the *son* of Neri, the *son* of Melchi, the *son* of Addi, the *son* of Cosam, the *son* of
29 Elmadam, the *son* of Er, the *son* of Jesus, the *son* of Eliezer, the *son* of Jorim, the *son* of Matthat, the *son*
30 of Levi, the *son* of Symeon, the *son* of Judas, the *son*
31 of Joseph, the *son* of Jonam, the *son* of Eliakim, the *son* of Melea, the *son* of Menna, the *son* of Mattatha,
32 the *son* of Nathan, the *son* of David, the *son* of Jesse, the *son* of Obed, the *son* of Boaz, the *son* of ² Salmon,

a Zech. 12: 12....*b* 2 Sam. 5: 14; 1 Chron. 3: 5....*c* Ruth 4: 18, etc.; 1 Chron. 2: 10, etc.—1 Gr. *Salathiel*....2 Some ancient authorities write, *Sala*.

Israel, traces his descent, the first thing, from the ancestor of the nation down, through its royal line, to Joseph, the commonly supposed father of Christ; Luke, from the desire rather to make his readers acquainted with the human derivation of Jesus from God, through the whole line of that humanity which he came to redeem, cannot allow him to pass the point at which it would still be natural to introduce this item, without carrying his parentage back to the first man, and to *his* parentage, namely, to God.

23. And Jesus himself began to be about thirty years of age. This verse should read: *And Jesus himself, when he began to teach, was about thirty years of age.* This is now very generally agreed by scholars to be the meaning of the Greek sentence, only some might prefer to supply, instead of "to teach" in the Revision, "his ministry," or his "work." Luke gives us the age as nearly as his sources of information would enable him; but the term "about" is so elastic in its qualifying power, as to frustrate all attempts to fix the precise age of Jesus at his baptism, or the time which had elapsed since the beginning of John's ministry. The age of thirty was reckoned by both Jews and Greeks as the point of full maturity of the powers of men, both physical and mental, for both sacred and civil functions.—**Being (as was supposed) the son of Joseph, which was the son of Heli,** etc. The order of the Revision, *the son (as was supposed)*, is right. Here we see that Luke begins with Jesus and goes back through a series of progenitors, the natural order of an inquirer into his special parentage: while Matthew, as if following the series of the public records, comes down from a known ancestor to Christ. The existence of this latter kind of records is evident from the fixed custom of resorting for enrollment to each man's own city, (2:3). That the means of tracing the pedigree of a particular individual back were extant also, appears from cases such as that of Anna (2:36), and Paul, (Phil. 3:5). Other differences between the two genealogies are obvious. Matthew makes, from Abraham, three sections of fourteen (twice seven) names, down to Christ; while Luke mentions fifty-four between the same limits, no pairs of which are identical in the two lists, after David, except in the case of Shealtiel and Zerubabel. What was the relation, then, between the two series of names? That there was no irreconcilable difference may be assumed, because there was no such allegation made in the early age when inaccuracy and contradiction, if existing, could easily be demonstrated. The absence, as to us, of all sources from which the two evangelists drew, leaves us to conjecture only how they stood toward each other. Two leading hypotheses have been employed to effect harmony, neither of which is free from serious deficiency, but either of which may help to show that there is no *necessary* incompatibility between the two accounts.

I. Both give an account of the lineage of Joseph, Christ's father, as supposed in his day. Of this supposition there are two varieties. (1) Matthew gives the royal line of David, showing the reigning, or ruling personages, as long as there were such, and their legal heirs, through whom the blood royal came to Joseph, without attempting to give

CH. III.] LUKE. 73

33 Which was *the son* of Aminadab, which was *the son* of Aram, which was *the son* of Esrom, which was *the son* of Phares, which was *the son* of Juda,
34 Which was *the son* of Jacob, which was *the son* of Isaac, which was *the son* of Abraham, *a* which was *the son* of Thara, which was *the son* of Nachor,
35 Which was *the son* of Saruch, which was *the son* of Ragau, which was *the son* of Phalec, which was *the son* of Heber, which was *the son* of Sala,
36 *b* Which was *the son* of Cainan, which was *the son* of Arphaxad, *c* which was *the son* of Sem, which was *the son* of Noe, which was *the son* of Lamech,
37 Which was *the son* of Mathusala, which was *the son* of Enoch, which was *the son* of Jared, which was *the son* of Maleleel, which was *the son* of Cainan,
38 Which was *the son* of Enos, which was *the son* of Seth, which was *the son* of Adam, *d* which was *the son* of God.

33 the *son* of Nahshon, the *son* of Amminadab, ² the *son* of ¹ Arni, the *son* of Hezron, the *son* of Perez, the *son* 34 of Judah, the *son* of Jacob, the *son* of Isaac, the *son* 35 of Abraham, the *son* of Terah, the *son* of Nahor, the *son* of Serug, the *son* of Reu, the *son* of Peleg, the *son* 36 of Eber, the *son* of Shelah, the *son* of Cainan, the *son* of Arphaxad, the *son* of Shem, the *son* of Noah, the 37 *son* of Lamech, the *son* of Methuselah, the *son* of Enoch, the *son* of Jared, the *son* of Mahalaleel, the 38 *son* of Cainan, the *son* of Enos the *son* of Seth, the *son* of Adam, the *son* of God.

a Gen. 11 : 24, 26....*b* See Gen. 11 : 12....*c* Gen. 5. 6, etc.; 11 : 10, etc....*d* Gen. 5 ; 1, 2.——1 Many ancient authorities insert, *the son of Admin;* and one writes, *Admin* for *Amminadab*....2 Some ancient authorities write, *Aram*.

the actual series of his immediate forefathers; while Luke gave just this, the true paternal descent, not concerning himself with the official lineage. This is the view advocated laboriously by Lord Hervey, among many, (see Smith's *Dict. of the Bible*, Am. Ed., p. 884.ff.). He thinks the case so plain, according to that view, that it scarcely needs discussion. "One has only to read them [the two genealogies] to be satisfied of this." "St. Luke's is Joseph's private genealogy." "This is capable of being almost demonstrated." Where a conjecture might be ventured, he says, "it is perfectly certain," etc.

(2.) *Vice versa*, it is maintained with much force that Matthew's word "begat," repeated so many times, implies the actual generation of the several descendants, while Luke's phrase "son of," is freely applicable to one legally brought (by adoption, or otherwise) into the family of David. This supposition is maintained with much fullness of discussion, learning, and confidence, by Dr. J. B. McClellan, in a note to his *New Translation of the New Testament*, (Vol. I., p. 408, ff.)

II. Luke presents the family record of Mary the mother of Jesus, with the design rather of exhibiting our Lord's common descent with all men, according to the flesh, from Adam, the father of all. In doing this he shows incidentally that Mary too was truly of the offspring of David. As the ancient genealogies, Jewish or Roman, would not start from the mother, Luke begins with Joseph (*as representing Mary*), who thus becomes, in a loose sense, son of her (assumed) father, Heli. Some would facilitate this hypothesis by extending the parenthesis in the verse before us, so as to make it, "Being the son (as was supposed of Joseph) of Heli." Thus the sonship of Jesus would be directly referred (through Mary, who could not be named in the series) to Heli, supposed to be her father. The absence, in the Greek, of the article before *Joseph*, which precedes every name in the series after that, slightly favors that view, grammatically. The explanation afforded, however, is on the whole not satisfactory; and if the alternative view, in either aspect of it, did not involve a number of violent assumptions, this would meet with little favor. If it be accepted, no other difficulties are suggested by the comparison with Matthew's pedigree, except that the two lines coincide in the two names, Shealtiel and Zorobabel, about which the difficulty is much the same on either supposition. To the objection that the Jews and Romans took no account of women in their family records, it may be answered that the case of Anna (2:36) shows that a woman's derivation could be traced, as is proved by Paul's case also, ("a Hebrew of Hebrews"), and that Luke cared little about the legal or official record; but much about the connection of Jesus with all that was highest in the Hebrew line, and all that was most ancient in the ancestry of mankind. There might seem a special reason why custom should be departed from in this case, because the Messiah was to be born of a virgin. This would show, also, how the prophecies concerning "the seed of Abraham" were fulfilled, and how "Jesus Christ our Lord" "was made of the seed of David according to the flesh" (Rom. 1:3), and not merely by legal succession; a thing which, as the companion of Paul, Luke might have an interest in maintaining. This view, in the main, is advocated by Godet, preceded by Knapp, Bengel, Spanheim, and others. If we must adopt either of the harmonistic

CHAPTER IV.

AND ^a Jesus being full of the Holy Ghost returned from Jordan, and ^b was led by the Spirit into the wilderness,
2 Being forty days tempted of the devil. And ^c in those days he did eat nothing: and when they were ended, he afterward hungered.

1 AND Jesus, full of the Holy Spirit, returned from the Jordan, and was led in the Spirit in the wilderness during forty days, being tempted of the devil.
2 And he did eat nothing in those days: and when

---

a Matt. 4:1; Mark 1:12....*b* ver. 14; ch. 2:27....*c* Ex. 34:28; 1 Kings 19:8.

---

methods above mentioned, we should hesitatingly decide for the latter, notwithstanding the absence of direct mention of Mary, which alone hinders it from being unquestionably valid. But we prefer to leave the final decision in abeyance, while resting confidently in the accuracy of both accounts, as drawn from sources of evidence open to the writers, but lost to us.

Some differences in the forms of names will be noticed in comparing the Revised with the Common Version. These result, either from following more ancient and better copies of the Greek text in the former version, or from the plan of conforming proper names of ancient personages in the New Testament to those with which we are familiar in the Old.

Ch. 4: 1-13. THE TEMPTATION.

1. Full of the Holy Ghost (*Spirit*) as the result of that singular endowment which he had just received at the baptism; for this is to be understood, in Luke's order, as following close upon that event. That gift becomes the element, support, and moving power of his whole life henceforth (see ver. 13.)—**Returned from** (*the*) **Jordan.** The word translated **returned**, was a favorite with Luke, who used it thirty-two times out of the thirty-five in which it occurs in all the New Testament. It would, here, naturally lead us to the conclusion that Jesus returned to Galilee, from which he had come; and when we read instead, that **he was led by the Spirit into** (*in*) **the wilderness**, we are left in doubt whether this is related as an incident and interruption of the journey back, the account of which is then resumed in ver. 14, with a repetition of **and Jesus returned**, etc., or whether the verb is here used in a different sense, of a separate movement "toward the wilderness," equivalent to "turned away." The former is much more probable, considering that in every other instance the verb (ὑποστρέφω) is distinctly used of the movement back to the place or state from which it began. —**He was led by the Spirit**—strictly, in the Spirit. This shows, as in the parallel passages of Matthew and Mark, that his movements were animated, directed, impelled by the Spirit, which he had received without measure.—**Into** (literally, *in*) **the wilderness.** That he is here said to have been "led *in* the wilderness," shows that our record contemplates a later stage of his experience than that where it was said he was led up" (Matthew), and that the Spirit "driveth him" (Mark), *into* the wilderness. Together they show that his entering upon this trial, and his continuance in it, and through it, were not against, but in obedience to, the influence and control of the divine Power which had sealed and consecrated him to his Messianic office.

2. Forty days. This connects itself primarily with the preceding clause (see the Revision), showing that the impulse of the Spirit was upon him all that time. He was, as it would seem, caused to move from place to place in his solitude. Who can tell the thoughts that occupied his mind? It was equally a period of protracted temptation; for the following clause, **being tempted of the devil**, is also connected with the "forty days." Mark again makes the temptation run through the whole time, while Matthew, overlooking this, fixes attention on the three grand assaults of the adversary, which all the Synoptists speak of as closing up the long season of trial.—**And in those days he did eat nothing.** It was a voluntary fast, consistent with the concentration of the thoughts of Jesus upon themes connected with that work which was now formally devolved upon him. His case was comparable to that of Moses in the mount (Ex. 24:18), and of Elijah on his long journey through the wilderness to Horeb (1 Kings 19:8). We can hardly be mistaken in imagining that there passed under his survey a variety of possible methods for the conduct of his work, and the attainment of its divinely appointed end. And all, we

3 And the devil said unto him, If thou be the Son of God, command this stone that it be made bread.
4 And Jesus answered him, saying, ᵃ It is written,

3 they were completed, he hungered. And the devil said unto him, if thou art the Son of God, command 4 this stone that it become ᵇ bread. And Jesus

a Deut. 8:3—1 Or, a loaf.

may be sure, was in prayerful communion with his Father in heaven.—**And when they were completed, he afterward hungered.** During the long mental toil, not without conflict, he might be comparatively unconscious of physical needs. But when the limit of endurance was reached, there would naturally be an awful craving for food.

3. And the devil said unto him. The same personage is called in Mark, Satan, and in Matthew, the Tempter. Satan, in the Hebrew, meant "adversary," "accuser," and is freely applied to human foes as well as to the accuser before God (Job 1:6). The corresponding Greek word, *Diabolos*, also meant, as an adjective, "accusing," "calumniating"; but with the article (ὁ διάβολος), "the devil," always either (1), the great adversary of God and man, prince of the powers of evil, who tempts man to sin, opposes God in his work of salvation, and leads in all the movements of hostility to Christ; the head, in short, of all spirits and agencies of wickedness and harm, as Christ is of all holy and helpful powers and influences; or (2), any man regarded as possessed of the spirit, and doing the work, of the devil (John 6:70), like to which, although the synonomous Satan is used, are (Matt. 16:23; Mark 8:33). For the purpose of being tempted by him had Jesus, on the threshold of his ministry, been urged out into the horrid solitudes of the desert, with wild beasts for company (Mark 1:13); and of his lures and machinations, had he been more or less conscious, during the meditations and prayers of this period. And the idea of "temptation" here includes every element that ever, in any relation, enters into it. It is the putting him to the test in all his powers, not with that trial which a man is blessed when he falls into (James 1:2), but t.at which has for its malignant aim to lead into sin and its wretchedness. It was as though, now that Jesus had been declared the Son of God, he was to encounter all the wiles and opposition of him whose rule over the souls of men it was his errand to destroy, and thus to demonstrate his personal, intrinsic capacity for the Messianic work, to which, by his baptism, he had been officially consecrated. The Son of God encounters the prince of the demons in a decisive conflict.

We are not told *how* the latter came into contact with Jesus—whether there was any visible form such that a man present would have seen him at all; nor need we speculate on this further than to suppose (which we must, to vindicate our Saviour from the suspicion of originating the temptations to himself), that he was distinctly aware of the actual presence of the arch-enemy. It was a real contest between the Saviour and an external being, distinct to the inward eye, at least, not his own thoughts marshaled against each other.

In the confidence of a pride warranted by numberless victories over the piety of men, from their first ancestor down, that person came to our Lord in his faintness, and unspeakable need of food.

3. And the devil said unto him, If thou be (*art*) the Son of God. The indicative mood (which accords with the correct Greek reading) assumes that the Saviour is such. The tempter is aware of the testimony which has been given from on high to his Sonship; and, whether believing it or not, whether understanding fully what it involves or not, speaks as if he did; and on this fact bases the insidious proposition which he makes: "Son of God, act worthily of thy divine dignity."—**Command this stone that it be made bread.** Strictly, *Speak to this stone, that it may become a loaf.* **This stone** is more vivid than "these stones" in Matthew, singling out some one lying near, which, in size and shape, may have resembled one of their flat loaves. Farrar (*Life of Christ*, I., 129), supposes it may have been one of a kind of "siliceous accretions, sometimes known under the name of *lapides judaici*, which assume the exact shape of little loaves of bread." Compare Stanley (*Sinai and Palestine*, p. 153), for the imitative shapes of minerals found in Palestine. What is the harm of this proposal? Wherein is it a temptation? The sense of it was: "The creative power which pertains to thee as God's Son, for the purposes of his kingdom, employ thou to relieve thyself from personal distress, which

That man shall not live by bread alone, but by every word of God.

5 And the devil, taking him up into an high mountain, shewed unto him all the kingdoms of the world in a moment of time.

6 And the devil said unto him, All this power will I give thee, and the glory of them: for *that is delivered unto me; and to whomsoever I will I give it.

answered unto him, It is written, Man shall not live 5 by bread alone. And he led him up, and shewed him all the kingdoms of ¹ the world in a moment of 6 time. And the devil said unto him, To thee will I give all this authority, and the glory of them: for it hath been delivered unto me; and to whomsoever I

a John 12: 13; 14: 30; Rev. 13: 2, 7.——1 Gr. *the inhabited earth.*

is so incompatible with thy comfort and thy honor." But Jesus knew, perhaps Satan also, that this was the very thing which the Spirit had brought him there to bear, and, in bearing the dreadful trial of his own natural appetite, he was not to be lured by the arts of the tempter. His decision in this, as in the following tests, was significant of a principle which ruled him in all his Messianic life on earth. He would bring fish out of the sea, and multiply the loaves indefinitely to meet the wants of his followers; but when he found no figs on the barren tree, he went on with his own hunger unappeased. He would trust himself to his Father's care.

4. It is written. Thus early does he begin to indicate his intimacy with the Old Testament, his constant use of it, and sense of its value as the storehouse and arsenal for the nourishment and defence of saints.—**That man shall not live by** (rather, *on*) **bread alone.** The remainder of this verse in the Common Version is pretty certainly transferred hither from Matt. 4: 4, where it belongs. In making this quotation, the Saviour recognizes his own perfect humanity (what is true of man in general (ὁ ἄνθρωπος) is true of him), and hence his liability to the conditions, and obligations of humanity. Man's true life is not dependent on the gratification of his appetite for food; even if this should be entirely withheld, the life of the soul, nourished by God's truth, may still go forward and upward. To do his Father's will is already the meat and drink of Christ; and to him will he leave the providing for his wants.

5. And the devil, taking (*leading*) **him up.** Luke does not give the designation whither (see the Revision), although that also in the received text has been added from Matthew's narrative.—**Shewed him all the kingdoms of the world in a moment of time.** Here we may almost certainly see that it is not intended we should understand a literal standing place, whether mountain or tower; or an act of physical vision. The readers of the Gospels knew there were no mountains in that part of the world so high as to give human eyes a view through even the clearest air, over the most exceptionally favorable scene, from the highest peaks to the highest, of more than about two hundred miles diameter. It was, however, to the Saviour, as impressive a sight of all kingdoms, as if he could have been placed where they would lie simultaneously under his natural glance. They were presented, in a splendid phantasmagoria, to the inward vision as if present to the outward view. The unreal character of the display, and at the same time its miraculous impressiveness, is indicated by the addition, **in a moment of time** (strictly, *in a point*). The appeal to our Lord's pure and unselfish ambition, to that desire for intellectual and social superiority, influence, rule, which is called in fallen men "the last infirmity of noble minds," aspiring in his case simply after the widest possible field of beneficence, was doubtless as strong as can be conceived.

6. All this power will I give thee, and the glory of them. The Revision presents the right order and rendering: *"To thee will I give."* The position makes it emphatic: many have desired even a small part of such authority—kings and priests, and philosophers, and have wished in vain; the greatest potentates have possessed but a fragment of it—"but to thee will I give it all." It is the offer of dominion, combining in one the authority of Solomon, Sesostris, Alexander, Cesar, and all that had ever been famous on earth. **The glory of them,** is the glory of all those kingdoms; that is, the power of their governments, the luxury of their courts, and the splendor of their armies; the magnificence of their cities, and number of their towns, palaces, castles, monuments, pictures, statues, libraries; their bustling commerce, and patient agriculture, the source of all. To

Ch. IV.] LUKE. 77

7 If thou therefore wilt *ᵃ*worship me, all shall be thine.
8 And Jesus answered and said unto him, Get thee behind me, Satan: for *ᵇ*it is written, Thou shalt worship the Lord thy God, and him only shalt thou serve.

7 will I give it. If thou therefore wilt worship me, it 8 shall all be thine. And Jesus answered and said unto him, It is written, Thou shalt worship the Lord thy

---

a Or, fall down before me....b Deut. 6: 13; 10: 20.

---

justify so arrogant a proposal, the tempter proceeds with a promise.—**For that is delivered unto me, and to whomsoever I will I give it.** This was false, but well suited to beguile one who did not bear in mind that it was "the father of lies" who was speaking. There was, moreover, then, as there ever has been, a sufficient show of the authority and glory of the world being bestowed on the devotees of Satan, to move multitudes of the ambitious to heed his lying proffers. He is called afterward by our Lord, "the prince of this world," or age; but that is said in view of the voluntary self-subjection of the moral world to him. It may be that he can, and does, so instigate and direct wicked men that they prove more successful, temporarily, in the attainment of worldly advantages. But we know of nothing to support what he here declares to our Lord, that the power and glory of all the earth have been given by God to his supreme adversary to dispose of for the pleasure of the latter, and for his ends. Had he better known, or been more able to appreciate the holy ambition of Jesus to gain *inward* influence over the thoughts and affections of men in all the kingdoms, to rule them only for their eternal advantage, he would not have wasted his impotent craft.

The Saviour could hardly have understood this offer of the prince of the world, as personal to him, in such a sense as not to involve the policy of his cause, the administration of his kingdom. That, also, should flourish and come to prevail throughout all the world, so that the authority of the kingdoms and the glory of them should belong to it, through the gift of that "murderer from the beginning."

7. If thou therefore wilt worship (*pay homage to, or salutations of respect before*) **me, all shall be thine.** Now it appears that there is an important condition to the bestowment of that gift which has been offered so freely. **Thou** is strongly emphatic here again, as if the devil had a favor toward Jesus, so that if *he* would accept it, he would take it from those now in possession of it, and *it*—the authority—**all shall be thine.** We can easily fancy that he thought he had gained the consent of the object of his address. We know that our Lord would not have taken the slightest gift at his hands, however free, or valuable in itself; and we have a proof of it in the fact that he did not exchange one word with him in regard to any proffers, except to reject them abruptly, each by a Scripture text. The condition of reverence to Satan did not require ostensible religious worship, or avowed subordination. It might apparently have been satisfied with a kind, and degree of outward respect which would avoid open hostility, and allow mutual independence. And in the furtherance of the gospel cause—in other words, in the organization and development of Christ's Kingdom—we can imagine it being so understood that if the kingdom of Satan were not attacked and warred against, he would engage that the whole should go under the name of Christ's cause. But our Lord had come into the world to destroy the works of the devil, so that he could hear of no homage; and his "kingdom was not of this world," so that he was not concerned to win the authority or glory of the world. No sooner, therefore, had he heard what the tempter had to propose, than he was ready again with another Scripture.

8. It is written, Thou shalt worship the Lord thy God, and him only shalt thou serve. This Scripture was evidently cited, not only as a defence to the Saviour, but a condemnation of Satan. It may be noticed that the passage is quoted freely, according to its sense as bearing on the present case, not according to the letter. Both the Hebrew, and the Greek Version then commonly in use, have, "Thou shalt *fear* the Lord," etc. **Serve**—at the end, is, in the Greek, the verb which expresses the idea of worship offered in outward prayers and vows, and sacrifices. The aptness and promptness of the answer should be remarked by every Christian. The form of adoration must not

9 ᵃ And he brought him to Jerusalem, and set him on a pinnacle of the temple, and said unto him, If thou be the Son of God, cast thyself down from hence:
10 For ᵇ it is written, He shall give his angels charge over thee, to keep thee:

9 God, and him only shalt thou serve. And he led him to Jerusalem, and set him on the ¹ pinnacle of the temple, and said unto him, If thou art the Son 10 of God, cast thyself down from hence: for it is written,
He shall give his angels charge concerning thee, to guard thee:

a Matt. 4:5....b Ps. 91:11.—1 Or, *wing*.

be offered without its spirit, and neither, except to "the blessed and only Potentate, the King of kings and Lord of lords."

9. A third test was to be applied before the devil would yield to his defeat. **And he brought** (*led*) **him to Jerusalem.** Whether actually, in the body or not, is to be answered according to the view which one takes of the whole series of these temptations. If we regard the preceding as of the nature of a vision, this will naturally be so judged. And the last two temptations are either that, or, considering the tasks involved, and the exhausted condition of the Saviour when they began, they are pure miracles, which forbid all speculation even, as to the manner of their performance. **And set him on a** (*the*) **pinnacle of the temple. The pinnacle,** equivalent to *wing*, or *winglet*, is translated by some, "the parapet." **The temple** is here, as in the great majority of instances, the temple courts, with all their appurtenance of costly and magnificent buildings. (See on 2:27.) At what part of it the pinnacle or parapet is to be located, is not certain; but the nature of the case leads us strongly to think it must have been some well known prominence on the cornice of the outer wall of the outer porch, near the southeastern angle. This was called the Royal Porch, which crowned the foundation wall built up from the depths of the Kidron valley. Thus the depth in this part from the summit of the porch to the bottom of the foundation wall is represented by Josephus as appalling. (*Ant.*, 15, 11, 5.) **If thou be** (*art*) **the Son of God, cast thyself down from hence.** The inducement for Christ to throw himself down, if any could be imagined, would be, probably, on the supposition that he should safely accomplish it, that he might gain renown from this evidence of his wonder-working power. The other tests had assailed his natural bodily appetite, and his ambition for extensive rule. This aims at his Messianic pride. It challenges him again, on the ground of his being the Son of God, to do something becoming such a personage; and, as if presuming on that trust in his Father which Jesus had evinced, it also brings in Scripture as an incitement to the proposed attempt. Note how truly the solicitation corresponds with Satan's suggestion to every tempted soul: "Cast thyself down." He would cast his desired victim down if he could, but can only invite and persuade to what may be yielded or refused. Ullmann, in his classical treatise on the *Sinlessness of Jesus*, (pp. 168, ff. 205 f. T. and T. Clark's Ed.), holds that the stress of the seductive effort of the tempter, in this case, was to induce Jesus to "run willfully into manifest danger." He thinks that this may be and is really a peril to active and ambitious minds, that, full of the importance of their enterprise, they rush toward its execution, trusting that the divine power will bring them safely through the difficulties into which they may plunge. But does anything in all Christ's course suggest the propriety of testing him on that point? Ullmann objects to the view that the Saviour was tempted to perform an *epideictic* miracle; that the narrative says nothing of beholders of his deed being present. But if it does not imply this, why bring him to Jerusalem and to the temple? Especially in Luke, where he has already been "led up" to some high position. The Scripture cited is (against Ullmann) as apposite on this view as on the other.

10. For it is written. The devil also knows the sound of Scripture, but cannot be trusted to convey its sense. **He shall give his angels charge over** (*concerning*) **thee,** etc. The passage cited (Ps. 91:11) was originally designed to set forth the perfect security of the ideally perfect saint in all the services and experiences to which God calls him. It may have often perplexed the reader who compared its glowing and unqualified assurances of the safety and success of godly men, considering how different their lot in life often appears; here we see how, on the supposition that *its conditions as to character*

11 And in *their* hands they shall bear thee up, lest at any time thou dash thy foot against a stone.
12 And Jesus answering said unto him, *a* It is said, Thou shalt not tempt the Lord thy God.

11 und,
On their hands they shall bear thee up,
Lest haply thou dash thy foot against a stone.
12 And Jesus answering said unto him, It is said, Thou shalt not try the Lord thy God.

a Deut. 6: 16.

---

are strictly fulfilled, all becomes literally true. Some think that Satan intentionally left out the clause "in all thy ways," after "shall keep thee," as if he supposed that would suggest to Jesus the sophistry of his application. Saint Bernard says, in reference to what the devil proposed, "This is not *a way*, but a destruction: or, if a way, it is not thine, but his (Satan's)." (See Perowne *On the Psalms*, at this place).

12. It is said—(*has been said*), and so stands, equivalent in sense to "it is written," which perhaps the Saviour would not repeat after the adversary had profaned it. The expression was appropriate, considering that the revelation through Moses was first given to the people orally (comp. Matt. 5: 21, 27). — **Thou shalt not tempt the Lord thy God.** The reference is to Deut. 6: 16. To tempt God, in the sense here intended, is to put oneself in a situation such as to test the power or disposition of God to relieve him of difficulties, or rescue him from destruction. This idea is a legitimate modification of the original one, which was to murmur and hesitate in the way appointed by God; through lack of faith in his ability to sustain one in it. In turning the sentence from the plural into the singular of the person addressed, Jesus may have designed to make it apply to the tempter in relation to himself, as well as to himself in relation to God. The answer settles it that our Lord personally will not use his power for securing his own fame, nor in his Messianic office will he countenance the desire for signs "from heaven," by which possibly worldly favor might be won, apart from faith and hearty obedience.

12. And when the devil had ended all the (*every*) temptation — ("Had spent his last dart" — Bengel) — **he departed from him.** He had brought to bear for the ruin of our Lord, every mode and degree of trial to such a person which the resources of hell would afford. These three typical tests, and every one, not specially mentioned, involved in the six weeks' experience, had proved futile. He was baffled and condemned afresh out of the word of God. Still he did not absolutely relinquish his undertaking.—**For a season**—rather, *until a fit opportunity*. Entirely frustrated for the time, he would await another more favorable, in speaking of which Luke probably had in mind the great crisis of Gethsemane, and the cross, of which our Lord could say to his enemies, "This is your hour and the power of darkness" (Luke 22: 53; John 12: 31; 14: 30; 16: 11. Comp. Heb. 4: 15). We need not, however, exclude the thought of other trying emergencies in the life of the Saviour, where he is reported to have waited with special solicitude on God in prayer.

Matthew gives the second and third temptations in an order the reverse of Luke's. Subjective reasons are given by different authors for preferring one or the other. These can hardly settle anything. Matthew's narrative seems to mark designedly the actual succession by his "then," ver. 5, and "again," ver. 8. This evidence is sufficient, at least, to determine our conclusion in favor of his order, in the absence of arguments to the contrary more decisive than we have seen. Luke probably gives the facts in the arrangement presented in his documents.

NOTE ON THE TEMPTATION.—The doubt, not unfrequently expressed, "whether the Son of God was really capable of being tempted to evil," is sufficiently answered by reference to Heb. 4: 15—"but was in all points tempted like as we are." The fact is beyond question. If the inquiry be, "*how could this be true?*" we have to admit there is a mystery about every experience of that Person which no mere man can reasonably pretend to fully explain. But any special difficulty in the thought of his liability to temptation seems to be obviated by the consideration that, whatever he was more, he was truly and completely a man. As such, he was perfect in all the powers, capacities, and susceptibilities essential to our nature. Among these, as appears from the case of our first parents, is the power of choice between good and evil conduct. Jesus had also the power to perceive the tendency of one act or

13 And when the devil had ended all the temptation, he departed from him *a* for a season.

13 And when the devil had completed every temptation, he departed from him ¹ for a season.

a John 14:30; Heb. 4:15.——¹ Or, *until.*

course of action to afford present gratification to desires and propensities innocent in themselves, and of the alternative action to bring much hardship, cheered only by the smile of God and the consciousness of right. He would, we must suppose, be perfectly sensitive to all the present painfulness of the latter course, and the agreeableness of the former. He might say to himself, "I will take the former"; for Adam said it, and then the awful transformation from innocence to guilt, from holiness to criminality, would have taken place. We do not thus, of course, loose the knot presented in the act of a soul, perfectly blessed in the favor of God and in the practice of the right; yet rejecting the difficult good, and choosing the pleasant evil. We have simply enumerated the steps by which one such soul appears to have reached that baneful choice. It may seem infinitely more improbable that Jesus should take that final step than Adam. But having traced him in imagination to the verge of it, with holiness untouched, we can no more see why he too might not, as Adam did, have allowed the prospect of ease and minor gratification to preponderate, and have said, "Yes, I will take that step too." Then first would he have been tempted like us we are, *not* without sin. Shuddering, we recoil from the awful possibility, and bless God that he resisted the seducer, not merely for himself, but so that in union with him we also may be safe.

God's foreknowledge that he would so triumph, in no way interferes with the question of his ability to succumb.

Another difficulty arises from the account of the Temptation, in that Jesus should parley with the tempter at all. In regard to this, we may, perhaps, not adequately appreciate what the apostle says (2 Cor. 11:14), as if in allusion to this very occasion, "for Satan even fashioneth himself into an angel of light" (Revision). But the important consideration is that the precise end for which the Spirit of God urged him into the desert, was that he might be subjected to the full force of Satan's wiles and assaults. Some reasons for this we may ourselves discern, especially in view of the result, and many more may well have existed in the divine mind. But if there were good reasons for any exposure of Jesus to the adversary, it might be needful that he should have to endure all which hell could adventure. Thus it was not for him to preclude, but to endure abominable propositions.

We may notice again that the result of Christ's triumphant steadfastness against the adversary was not merely the assurance of his superiority to all subsequent possible temptations. It was that, indeed, first of all. It secured that, although the tempter had left him only until a fit season; yet never would Jesus be moved from his position. Never would he employ his Messianic power to relieve himself of privation or any physical distress involved in the accomplishment of all his Heavenly Father's will. Nor would he call down legions of angels to further his Messianic ends, when his Father had appointed that they should be reached by suffering and self-sacrifice. No possibility of power over men through earthly dominion and glory should ever swerve him one hair's breadth from the purpose to gain influence over them by equity, truth and kindness, or not at all. We might be perfectly sure that he would never accept any show of advantage to his cause, however specious, from the ruler of this world, or through connivance with him. But there lay also in Christ's personal victory, as Messiah, over Satan, a perpetual law for his kingdom in its exposure to the antagonism of the world. It should never think it hard that, while distributing heavenly treasures, it must often, in fidelity to God, suffer worldly poverty, and bear worldly pity or contempt. It can never, without forfeiting connection with Jesus, attempt to spread itself more rapidly among men, at the cost of compromise with the spirit of the world, or by the assimilation of its forms to those which distinguish "this world." Nor may it, in the prosecution of its ends, venture on measures not truly warranted by the word of God, presuming that he will deviate from his appointed plan to obviate the consequences of its rashness; especially may it not seek, by pandering to

CH. IV.] LUKE. 81

14 ᵃ And Jesus returned ᵇ in the power of the Spirit into ᶜGalilee: and there went out a fame of him through all the region round about. | 14 And Jesus returned in the power of the Spirit into Galilee: and a fame went out concerning him through

a Matt. 4: 12; John 4: 43....b ver. 1....c Acts 10: 37.

the curiosity, or dazzling the imagination, or astounding the intelligence, of men, to accomplish those effects which can follow only from compunction of conscience and the resulting desire of salvation.

At this point, we reach the close of what our evangelist seems to have regarded the more private and preparatory period of the life of Christ. The Messiah is manifested, the favor of the Father is proved and assured, the machinations of his great adversary are brought to nought.

PART II. THE MINISTRY IN GALILEE. Ch. 4: 14—9: 50.

It had for its object to persuade the people of the Messiahship of Jesus, in the spiritual sense of the more evangelical prophecies, and to win them to trust in him as their Teacher, their Redeemer from the ills which sin had caused to soul and body, for time and eternity; their Saviour, in short, and their King. It resulted in the manifestation of great curiosity concerning him on the part of the masses; in an extensive confidence in his power and willingness to bestow temporal blessings; in wide rumors that he was a prophet, possibly even the risen Elijah; in waves of popular conviction that he was the expected Son of David, come to establish a national and earthly kingdom; and with some humble hearts, in a clear and loving recognition of him as having the words of eternal life. It abundantly demonstrated the spiritual nature, the freshness and blessedness of membership in his kingdom, and resulted in the rejection of it by the great mass of those whom he would fain have saved.

This ministry lasted, probably, near two years and six months. It should be carefully noticed, however, that estimates of the length of Christ's ministry vary between one and three, or even more years, with a fraction of another. That which presupposes three passovers during its continuance, previous to the last, is much more generally adopted, and is that upon which the statement of time for the Galilean ministry was just made. This makes its continuance run three years, and as much more as the baptism preceded the first passover. How far from demonstration all conclusions must stop, is well shown by comparison of two, among the quite recent discussions of the subject. C. E. Caspari, in his *Chronological and Geographical Introduction to the Life of Christ*, pp. 107-254, (T. & S. Clark's Edition, 1875), confidently limits the ministry to two years; Dr. J. B. McClellan, in his *New Translation of the New Testament*, (Vol. I., pp. 539-621, London, 1875), maintains the three years' view. Each is perfectly confident that he sees the exact truth in almost every particular, and is ready to determine not only the year, but the day, and often the hour of the day of occurrences—a great part of which they must, of course, determine differently.

14, 15. Return into Galilee, and general SUMMARY ACCOUNT OF THE OPENING WORK THERE.

14. **Jesus returned.** The narrative begun in ver. 1 is resumed. The verb (comp. ver. 1) is here used in its proper sense, with reference to his having gone from Galilee to the Jordan, to be baptized. We have already seen (ch. 3: 19, 20) that, chronologically, the mention of John's imprisonment should have followed the account of the baptism of Jesus, with a considerable interval. A careful consideration of John's Gospel (1: 29—4: 3), will render it probable that, on the supposition of Christ's temptation following close upon the baptism, he must have returned after that to the Jordan, where John was; that he there attracted to him four scholars (Andrew, John, Peter, Nathanael), with whom he went soon into Galilee, where he made the water wine; that he visited Capernaum, and went to a passover at Jerusalem—purifying the temple, instructing Nicodemus, baptizing in Judea; and that then, learning how the Pharisees were comparing him with John, he left Judea, and went away again into Galilee. It is very likely that the mention of John the Baptist in John 4: 3, implies that he had been lately apprehended, with the approval, if not the aid, of the Pharisees; and that Jesus went into Galilee to escape a similar, premature fate. With that return, this in Luke must

F

15 And he taught in their synagogues, being glorified of all.
16 And he came to ªNazareth, where he had been brought up: and, as his custom was, ᵇhe went into the synagogue on the sabbath day, and stood up for to read.

15 all the region round about. And he taught in their synagogues, being glorified of all.
16 And he came to Nazareth, where he had been brought up: and be entered, as his custom was, into the synagogue on the sabbath day, and stood up to

a Matt. 2:23; 13:54; Mark 6:1....b Acts 13:14; 17:2.

coincide; and in the course of it occurred the very interesting scene of Jacob's well. If the baptism took place in mid-winter, this work in Galilee might have begun in early summer.—**In the power of the Spirit**—mighty, that is, in word and deed, through the possession of that Spirit of God, who was, since the baptism, the director and sustainer of all his activity.—**Into Galilee: and there went out a fame** (*rumor*, or *report*) **of** (*concerning*) **him through all the region round about.** Immediately, as it would seem, the popular mind began to be exercised about his teachings and acts, probably also by tidings of the testimony of John the Baptist to him as the "one greater than he", who was to come after him (John 1.34). The miracles, also, which he performed in the neighborhood (John 2:1 ff.; 4:46 ff.), and his extraordinary conduct at Jerusalem (John 2:15, 23), would be talked about.

15. And he (*he himself*) **taught in their synagogues.** The synagogues, which arose among the Jews in answer to religious wants deeply felt, after the return from the exile, corresponded in many points to the churches of Christian times. The word was indeed ambiguous, like "church," denoting primarily the religious assembly, for whose use the house existed. They were, primarily, as afterward the churches, assemblies, meetings, of those of common faith and sentiment, for the promotion of religious ends. The edifice would seem, from *some* accounts, to have been built strictly after a certain pattern, on an elevated site, with a prescribed orientation, and in a uniform style of architecture. From the nature of the case, however, we may be sure that the size would vary according to the estimated number of the congregation, and the materials and style would be such as they could afford. Recent examination of the ruins of ancient synagogues in Palestine, made by the Exploration Fund Expedition, shows that they stood both on high ground and low, outside of the towns and in their most crowded quarters, with the entrance from various points of the compass. Of course, only the more substantial have left any remains to our day. They were generally rectangular parallelograms in plan, with some remembrance of the form of the tabernacle. Toward their farther end, within, was a chest or ark, containing the sacred rolls of the Old Testament books. This might be screened from the main apartment by a curtain. Forward of this were seats, facing the entrance, for the president and elders of the synagogue.

Still further in front was a platform, on which the reader of the Scriptures stood, between which and the entrance were seats, on one side for the men, and on the other, with a lattice between, for the women, who must be closely vailed. The place was used, not only for religious exercises of the congregation, but for meetings of a judicial character, in which persons were tried for religious offences, and, if convicted, punished.

As a pious Jew, our Saviour regularly attended the synagogue meetings, which afforded him, as we shall soon see, an excellent opportunity to deliver his message; and as they were met with wherever Hebrews were scattered, they were the convenient scene of almost all the earliest apostolical preaching.—**Taught**—or *was wont to teach*, as a custom—expresses in one word what Mark expands into "preaching the gospel of the kingdom of God," etc. (Ch. 1:14, 15). Compare Matthew, who adds that he said, "Repent." (Ch. 4:17). Instruction and persuasion regarding the relations into which men are brought toward God, by the coming of Christ, with the consequent privileges and obligations—this was, and is, the preaching of the gospel. Luke says nothing of miracles wrought, as yet; but from John 4:54, we may conclude that the healing of the centurion's son took place before his first visit to Nazareth.

16-30. HIS VISIT TO NAZARETH, AND PREACHING THERE.

16. And he came to Nazareth, where he had been brought up. What memories on his part are implied in that last statement!

Ch. IV.] LUKE. 83

17 And there was delivered unto him the book of the prophet Esaias. And when he had opened the book, he found the place where it was written,

18 "The Spirit of the Lord is upon me, because he hath anointed me to preach the gospel to the poor; he hath sent me to heal the brokenhearted, to preach deliverance to the captives, and recovering of sight to the blind, to set at liberty them that are bruised,

17 read. And there was delivered unto him ¹the book of the prophet Isaiah. And he opened the ²book, and found the place where it was written,

18 The Spirit of the Lord is upon me,
³Because he anointed me to preach ⁴good tidings to the poor:
He hath sent me to proclaim release to the captives,
And recovering of sight to the blind,
To set at liberty them that are bruised,

a Isa. 61 : 1.——1 Or, *a roll*....2 Or, *roll*....3 Or, *wherefore*....4 Or, *the gospel*.

He had avoided going directly to his former home, the residence of his parents still, perhaps from the feelings expressed (John 4: 44). But his heart must have yearned toward the companions of his early life; and after he found that his proclamation was awakening a lively interest elsewhere, he would not be content until they too had received the "glad news."—**And, as his custom was, he went into the synagogue on the sabbath-day.** This custom could not have been based on any special divine command, but on the reasonableness of it and, doubtless, the felt advantage of mingling with his countrymen in their devotions, and in the reading of the Scriptures. This, as well as the occasions thus afforded for the accomplishment of his mission, would account for and justify his constant practice. The worship in those places was formal and liturgical, a great part of it, doubtless, barren of spirituality; but there would be individuals of a different style, and, on the whole, it was such as the time allowed. Many a disciple of his has found spiritual refreshment, and strength for the tasks of life, from communion with fellow-disciples in acts of worship; not merely when increase of religious knowledge was to be gained, but even where little of instruction was to be looked for.—**And stood up for to read** (omit for). The standing posture was common in reading the Scripture, as expressive of respect. As Jesus rose, he probably stepped to the platform, or *bema*, on one side of the room (see ver. 15). The president of the synagogue would ordinarily select the reader from among the younger men; but when Jesus rose, signifying a desire to perform that service, it was readily granted to him.

17. And there was delivered unto him the book of the prophet Esaias (*Isaiah*). This was in the form of a roll, like a wall-map with us, but of a narrow strip of prepared leather, long enough to allow the whole work to be written on it in columns of convenient width, *running across the long strip*, and following each other — with suitable spaces between — from right to left. The left-hand end was attached to a roller, like that of a map; but, unlike the law, which had two, the other rolls had but that one. Such a book would be opened and closed by unrolling and rolling up again. Thus the Saviour now, holding the roll in his left hand, pulled along the writing with the other, until he **found the place where it was written.** Such being the manner of reading, the verb **found** could hardly mean "chanced upon," as some (Meyer among them) have supposed, and as the verb might in itself indicate. We understand rather that he unrolled until he came to the passage he wanted (Isa. 61 : 1, 2). Doubtless, he selected it with reference to the use he intended to make of it as a text; otherwise it is not obvious why he might not leave it for Providence to select, through any appointed reader. Whether the prophets were divided into sections at that time, to be read in a prescribed order on successive Sabbaths, as the law was, cannot be affirmed with certainty, still less that this passage was the prophetic lesson (*haphtara*) for that Sabbath. The Pentateuch was divided into fifty-two, or, as the length of the year might require, fifty-four paragraphs or sections (*paraseïas*), by reading one of which each Sabbath the whole would be gone over every year. Such is the common account, although high Hebrew authority insists that this course covered two years and a half. (Zunz, *Gottesdienstliche Vorträge*, S. 3 ff.) The reading of the Pentateuch lesson had either ended when Jesus entered, or, more probably, his mind being on this prophecy, he remained quiet through what preceded. On the kinds and order of exercise in the synagogue meetings, see Smith's *Dict. of Bible*, and Geikie, *Life of Christ*, Vol. I., p. 180 ff.; or (more brief), Farrar, *Life of Christ*, Vol. I., 220 ff.

18. The Spirit of the Lord is upon me,

19 To preach the acceptable year of the Lord. | 19 To proclaim the acceptable year of the Lord.

etc. This language, in the mouth of the prophet, was intended directly to comfort the people of Israel in their long captivity in Babylon, and afterward, through the promise of deliverance, restoration to prosperity, and the abundant favor of their God. The Spirit of the Lord is upon the prophet to qualify him for this message of blessing. The predictions had never yet been fulfilled in the history of Israel, and Christ takes up the language anew as having really referred to himself, whatever primary and lower application had been intended by Isaiah.—**Because he hath anointed me to preach the gospel** (*good tidings*) **to the poor.** This is assigned as the cause of the possession of the Spirit of the Lord. It refers to the descent of the Spirit upon him at his baptism (Acts 10: 38).— **Anointed me.** The Greek name Christ— "the anointed," Heb., "Messiah"—is from the verb "to anoint," here used; and the passage is thus equivalent to *has made me Messiah*. The verb is properly in the preterit, **anointed**, as the action is regarded as prior to the sending in the next clause.—**The gospel** (*the good tidings*), means the news that the kingdom of heaven is come, into which all may enter who are prepared for it, especially **the poor.** We may correctly interpret this as implying "in spirit" as its complement, yet we shall see that Luke, in several instances, fails to make that addition, as though he thought it would necessarily be understood that poverty tended to prepare the heart for the heavenly riches (see 6: 20). More important is it to notice that the language is originally Isaiah's, and that in the prophets and in the Psalms, it is familiar that the blessings of God's grace are needed, craved, and enjoyed by the poor more than by those who abound in worldly good. Still, *mere* poverty is nowhere represented as sufficient to secure God's grace.—**He hath sent me**—in consequence of that anointing—**to preach deliverance** (*release*) **to the captives.** The actual captivity of the people in Babylon was a type of the spiritual bondage of men under sin and Satan (John 8: 34; Rom. 6: 16, 20 ff.; 2 Pet. 2: 19). To announce release from this, full and free, with all the consequent peace and joy, and eternal hope, Christ came (Comp. Heb. 2: 14, 15).— **And recovering of sight to the blind.** It should be noticed that Luke omits the clause **to heal the broken hearted,** the second clause in Isaiah's series. It was afterward inserted, to complete the quotation, and became current in the later text—whereas the one before us is brought in for substance from Isaiah 42: 7, in place of "the opening of the prison to them that are bound," in 61: 1. The spiritually blind, to whom Christ proclaims sight, are those who realize their ignorance of the most important truths, and so are ready to welcome *the* truth (John 9: 39), "that they which see not might see."—**To set at liberty them that are bruised.** These words are cited from the Septuagint of Isaiah 58: 6. Another beautiful figure for relief from the wounds and bruises caused by sin.

19. To preach the acceptable year of the Lord. The blessings promised to the Israelites of old were all summed up in a figure drawn from the Year of Jubilee. As in that year liberty was proclaimed to slaves, release to debtors from their penalties, and the restoration of their family estates to dispossessed owners, so joyful a season would be that state of blessedness which should follow upon the exile. In Christ's application, the year of jubilee typifies the Messianic era, the period of the bestowment of a finished and free salvation. **The acceptable year of the Lord** is, in the Hebrew, "*the year of the pleasure of Jehovah*"—that is, the time in which he delights to bless his people. There is evidently nothing in this use of the phrase, "year of the Lord," to warrant the supposition very common among the early Fathers, that Christ's public work lasted but one year. Notice how the quotation stops when it comes to the fearful sentence, "and the day of vengeance of our God." John the Baptist would hardly have left it out.

The section ordinarily read would be much longer than that here quoted. Either the narrative is intended to show merely where the passage is found and how it begins, of which Jesus then read as much as he pleased, or (and this is the common view) that he stopped here of his own authority, having read as much as was necessary. It is not at all unlikely that, in the course of his reading, or the following remarks, Jesus referred to

Cʜ. IV.] LUKE. 85

20 And he closed the book, and he gave it again to the minister, and sat down. And the eyes of all them that were in the synagogue were fastened on him.
21 And he began to say unto them, This day is this scripture fulfilled in your ears.
22 And all bear him witness, and *wondered at the gracious words which proceeded out of his mouth. And they said, ᵇ Is not this Joseph's son?
23 And he said unto them, Ye will surely say unto me this proverb, Physician, heal thyself: whatsoever we have heard done in ᶜ Capernaum, do also here in ᵈ thy country.

20 And he closed the ¹ book, and gave it back to the attendant, and sat down; and the eyes of all in the synagogue were fastened on him. And he began to say unto them, To-day hath this scripture been fulfilled in your ears. And all bare him witness, and wondered at the words of grace which proceeded out of his mouth: and they said, Is not this Joseph's son?
23 And he said unto them, Doubtless ye will say unto me this parable, Physician, heal thyself: whatsoever we have heard done at Capernaum, do also here in thine

a Ps. 45: 2; Matt. 13: 54; Mark 6: 2; ch. 2: 47....b John 6: 42....c Matt. 4: 13; 11: 23....d Matt. 13: 51; Mark 6: 1.—1 Or. *roll.*

other passages of Isaiah which, in the report, became blended with the one first read, as we have seen.

20. And he closed (*rolled up*) **the book, and he gave it again to the minister** (*attendant*). **Minister** is in itself a perfectly proper rendering, meaning a "servant," above the bound and menial grade; but the present familiar use of that word makes it ambiguous in this connection. He was a kind of clerk of the meeting, who had charge of the sacred books, brought them forth at the order of the presiding officer (as in ver. 17), and again returned them to their ark-like case. See the Saviour deliberately, thoughtfully, rolling up the long sheet before he handed it back. **And sat down.** This was the usual posture of the speaker—Rabbi, priest, Levite, or, exceptionally, some other person—who commented on the Scripture lesson, when any such person chose to speak. Usually, we may presume, he was called on by the head of the meeting (as Acts 13:15). This was not, however, an essential part of the services.—**And the eyes of all in the synagogue were fastened on him.** A little delay appears to have followed, after Jesus had resumed his seat, probably now sitting down on the elders' bench, fronting the congregation. What the people had already seen and heard, what they had learned from other places, and, most of all, the passage which he had just read, and the manner of his doing it, would all combine to awaken earnest curiosity as to what might now follow.

21. And he began to say (*began by saying*) **unto them.** How he continued, the narrative does not inform us. Luke gives the theme and the key-note of his discourse, and leaves it to our sympathy with the speaker to fill it out.—**This day is this scripture fulfilled in your ears.** The verb is in the perfect tense. That acceptable year has come. To-day the significance of that prophetic language is fully manifested in the offer which I make to every waiting soul, of salvation, including deliverance from all the evils caused by sin, and the perfect repossession of God's lost favor, for time and eternity.

22. And all bare him witness. Their meetings were not bound to silence on the part of the congregation, as are ours. They, with one consent, gave, in their comments to each other, honorable testimony to the excellence of his discourse. This implies and almost proves that he spoke at some length.— **And wondered at the gracious words,** etc. **Gracious words,** or *words of grace.* "Grace" is here beauty, rhetorical and moral pleasantness, perhaps including also the idea of graciousness, in the freedom and fullness of his offer. This, with the expressions, "The common people heard him gladly," and the report of the officers, "never man spake as this man," fully warrant the belief that our Saviour, without any meretricious arts of speech, had an eloquence of truth, sincerity, simplicity, and affection, which commended his matter to men's conscience and taste. Nothing is said, however, of faith, or any truly religious exercises of their hearts. On the contrary, they manifested unbelief.— **And** (not *but*) **they said,** as if it were perfectly consistent with what had preceded. **Is not this Joseph's son?** In their mouths, this meant: "How is it possible for a man of his birth and education to speak in this way, and to urge such claims for himself?" There was not merely wonder in their question, but a shade of unbelief and refusal. What inference may we draw from their admiring surprise, in regard to the change which Jesus had undergone through his baptism, the reception of the Spirit thereupon, and the discipline of the temptation? It is almost certain that he had often taken part in their synagogue services before.

23. And he said unto them, Ye will

24 And he said, Verily I say unto you, No *a* prophet is accepted in his own country.
25 But I tell you of a truth, *b* many widows were in Israel in the days of Elias, when the heaven was shut up three years and six months, when great famine was throughout all the land;
26 But unto none of them was Elias sent, save unto Sarepta, *a city* of Sidon, unto a woman *that was a* widow.
27 *c* And many lepers were in Israel in the time of Eliseus the prophet; and none of them was cleansed, saving Naaman the Syrian.
28 And all they in the synagogue, when they heard these things, were filled with wrath,

24 own country. And he said, Verily I say unto you, 25 No prophet is acceptable in his own country. But of a truth I say unto you, There were many widows in Israel in the days of Elijah, when the heaven was shut up three years and six months, when there came a 26 great famine over all the land; and unto none of them was Elijah sent, but only to ²Zarephath, in the land 27 of Sidon, unto a woman that was a widow. And there were many lepers in Israel in the time of Elisha the prophet; and none of them was cleansed, but 28 only Naaman the Syrian. And they were all filled with wrath in the synagogue, as they heard these

a Matt. 13:57; Mark 6:4; John 4:44....*b* 1 Kings 17:9; 18:1; James 5:17....*c* 2 Kings 5:14.—1 Gr. *Sarepta.*

surely say (*doubtless ye will say*) **unto me this proverb, Physician, heal thyself.** Seeing their moral blindness, which desires not the opening of its eyes, Jesus anticipates the objection they are ready to urge. **This proverb**—or parallel, illustrative saying—(Greek παραβολή, *parable*), seems intended to express the popular view that one who sets himself up to heal others, should keep himself in good health. Loosely applied here, it might mean, "Thou who demandest confidence as the Messiah, show thyself worthy of confidence, by doing such miracles as the Messiah is to perform."—**Whatsoever we have heard done at Capernaum, do,** etc. It is the first demand, so often repeated, for "signs from heaven," for show-miracles, such as the devil had proposed: "Cast thyself down hence." But in answering him, Jesus had answered all. He saw clearly that there was no feeling of the need of a Healer in their unspoken suggestion, and there was no tendency in miracles as such, mere prodigies, to awaken that heart faith which alone could accept him. Where such faith existed, miracles of loving kindness could be wrought, and only there (Matt. 13; 58; Mark 6:5). That principle in man which makes it hard to see superiority in one with whom we have grown up, here confirms the obstinacy of impenitence.

24. And he said, Verily I say unto you, No prophet, etc. He sadly recognizes the fact that, in spite of his desire to do them good, and of the unspeakable solemnity of the crisis, it happens to him, as before to other messengers of God. They reject him as God's representative, because they have known him as a man. Still they cannot frustrate God's plan. As prophets before have, under God, rendered aid to some and passed by others, as God might please; so will he exercise mercy with discrimination, and not pander to capricious and selfish desires.

25-27. But I tell you of a truth, many widows were in Israel, etc. (See 1 Kings 17: 8-24; 2 Kings 5: 1-15.) The purport of his reference to these historic facts is: My doing some things in Capernaum which I do not here, is quite of a piece with the action of other prophets whom you profess to respect. In my case, as in theirs, it is God's pleasure that decides. In naming as favored cases previously two Gentiles, he does not so much wish to put the inhabitants of Nazareth on a level with heathen (although they may have taken it so), as to intimate in his very first discourse the equal destination of his gospel to all needy souls. That they must be *needy* souls lies in the fact that one of those favored ones was a widow, helpless and famishing; and the other, one who had proved that earthly eminence and power could not relieve him of an afflictive and loathsome malady, and who submitted to profound humiliation, that Jehovah might remove it.—**Three years and six months.** A comparison of 1 Kings 17: 1 ff., and 18: 1 ff., seems to show that the lack of rain was confined to a period of less than three full years; but from James 5: 1, we learn that the view here taken was the one settled upon in the time of Christ. The Old Testament passages are not distinctly incompatible with it.

28. And all they in the synagogue, when they heard these things, were filled with wrath, etc. The order of words in the Revision is better. Little of the Sidonian widow's trustful poverty, or of the Syrian leper's desire for cure, in these breasts. They were enraged because their townsman judged for himself when and where his miracles should be performed, claiming thus an equality with the ancient prophets.—**All they.**

Cн. IV.] LUKE. 87

29 And rose up, and thrust him out of the city, and led him unto the *a* brow of the hill whereon their city was built, that they might cast him down headlong.
30 But he, *b* passing through the midst of them, went his way,
31 And *c* came down to Capernaum, a city of Galilee, and taught them on the sabbath days.

29 things; and they rose up, and cast him forth out of the city, and led him unto the brow of the hill whereon their city was built, that they might throw 30 him down headlong. But he passing through the midst of them went his way.
31 And he came down to Capernaum, a city of Galilee.

a Or, *edge*....*b* John 8:59; 10:39....*c* Matt. 4:13; Mark 1:21.

We might certainly have supposed that some would have exhibited a better mind. We are not, perhaps, *obliged* to understand it as without any qualification. Could possibly any of the family of Jesus—parents, brothers, sisters—have been in that congregation? It is remarkable how little we see of any of them afterward, in plainly friendly relations, till Calvary (John 19:25; his mother), and the prayer-meeting after his resurrection (Acts 1:14; his mother and br thers).

29. And rose up, and thrust him out of their city, and led (more exactly, *were for leading*) **him to the brow of the hill,** etc. The second verb is in a tense which expresses an incomplete action, and does not say that they reached the brow of the hill, but set out for it. A steep cliff of some forty feet in height, on a slope of the hill, above the town, is spoken of by travelers, and visible in the views of the place which are given us. This cliff may have been much higher then, and would easily suffice to cause the death of their intended victim. Their attempt at the destruction of Jesus was not after any form of penalty prescribed in their law, even if any crime had been formally charged; but it was the result of a reckless outbreak of popular wrath.

30. But he, passing through the midst of them, went his way. When the first blaze of their fury subsided, his moral dignity abashed their rage for injustice and murder.

31-41. A SABBATH DAY IN CAPERNAUM.

31. And (*he*) **came down to Capernaum, a city of Galilee.** The last statement would evidently be superfluous for those familiar with Palestine, and is an explanation, like the same concerning Nazareth (1:26), for the benefit of readers strange to the holy land.
—**Capernaum** (in some of the best ancient copies written Capharnaum, meaning Village of Nahum), was then an active town on the western shore of Lake Gennesaret. Like Nazareth, it is unmentioned in the Old Testament, but it had already been the scene of a great miracle of the Saviour (John 4:46 ff.); and from this time onward it is familiar to us as "his own city" (Matt. 9:1; Mark 2:1). Here, if any where, he may be said to have had a residence the next two years or more; at least, to have made it his head-quarters, lodging when there not improbably in the house of Simon (Luke 4:38), which seems, therefore, to be sometimes referred to simply as *the* house. Hence, perhaps, he was thought subject to taxation at this place (Matt. 17:24, 25). This city was thus exceptionally favored with the presence, the teaching, and the beneficent works of Jesus; but instead of profiting accordingly from this privilege, it gained therefrom only a deserved celebrity of woe (10:15). So truly indeed was the place "brought down to hades," early in the Christian era, that, even after the extremely careful explorations of recent years, we are still left dubious which of the fields of ruin scattered along the lake shore once supported the proud and guilty city. Two spots especially dispute the melancholy distinction. *Tell Hum*, a considerable expanse of the fragments of ancient edifices, including the remains of a spacious synagogue, which *may* have been that built by the Roman centurion, lies overgrown with weeds, about two miles west of the mouth of the Upper Jordan. *Khan Minyeh* is two miles, or two and a-half, further south, and shows some traces of the existence there of a former city. Almost all investigators agree that one or the other is the remnant of Capernaum. But which? The grounds of judgment are scanty and indecisive. They are the supposed, but disputable, significance of the two names; a couple of ambiguous allusions in Josephus, (*Life*, 72. *Wars*, 3, 10, 8); the references in the Gospels, which are about equally compatible with either claim; and the two currents of later Jewish and Christian tradition. Of these, it is said that the Jewish makes for Khan Minyeh; the Christian, for Tell Hum. Dr. Edward Robinson, and Lieut. Conder, of the Palestine Exploration Fund, with others,

hold that, in regard to localities there, the Jewish opinion is, where different, much the more trustworthy. On these premises, recent authorities, of course, are divided in judgment. In favor of *Tell Hum* are Winer (*Realwörterbuch*); Ritter (*Geog. of Palestine*); Van de Velde (*Narrative*); Thomson (*Land and Book*); Capt. Wilson (*Recovery of Jerusalem*); Farrar (*Com. on Luke*, p. 200). In favor of *Khan Minyeh* are Porter (*Hand-book of Syria and Palestine*); Dr. Robinson (*Biblical Researches*); Tristram (*Land of Israel*); Macgregor (*Rob Roy on the Jordan*); Lieut. Conder (*Tent Work in Palestine*). Schultz (Herzog und Plitt, *Theol. Real-Encyclopädie*, 2d Ed., Art. Capernaum), leaves the question undecided. So also in Zöcker's *Handbuch d. Theol. Wissen.*, 1883, I., 214. Edersheim, *Life of Jesus, the Messiah*, I., 365, n. 1, doubtfully decides in favor of Tell Hum; but is he warranted in saying that most modern writers agree in fixing the site at this place? On either hypothesis, the place was not far from twenty miles, in a direct line, northeast from Nazareth; and as the latter was on elevated ground, the statement that he **came down,** is strikingly exact. He must descend, not only to the level of the Mediterranean Sea, 1,200 feet or more, but to that of the Lake of Gennesaret, which is 682.5 feet lower. Capernaum lay not far beyond the northern limit of the comparatively smooth tract of country stretching along, and away from, the coast known as the Plain of Gennessaret, from which the lake took one of its names. Josephus celebrates the fertility, and describes the productions of this section, in his account of the destruction of the city Tarichea, and the dreadful slaughter of its occupants, in the War of Titus and Vespasian. (*Jewish Wars*, 3; 10, 7, 8).

And taught (*he was teaching*) **them on the sabbath days** (*on the Sabbath*). The word translated **Sabbath** is very irregular, being used freely in the plural as well as the singular, for a single day, although it might in other places have a plural signification also. Here it is defined as one day (see the Revision) by the fact that all which follows to ver. 43, belongs to one day, and that ver. 43 declares the necessity for him to leave Capernaum and go through the country, preaching. The imperfect tense of the verbs in this verse and the next shows that it was in connection with his teaching that the incident of the demoniac occurred. After this he went out of the synagogue into Peter's house, where he remained until evening (ver. 33, 38, 40).

TELL HUM.

32 And they were astonished at his doctrine: *for his word was with power.
33 *And in the synagogue there was a man, which had a spirit of an unclean devil, and cried out with a loud voice,

32 And he was teaching them on the sabbath day: and they were astonished at his teaching; for his word was
33 with authority. And in the synagogue there was a man, that had a spirit of an unclean demon; and he

a Matt. 7: 28, 29; Titus 2: 15....b Mark 1: 23.

32. And they were astonished at his doctrine (rather, *teaching*). It was not **doctrine** in our modern sense, but his teaching as to its manner and spirit, as well as its matter. What surprised them was that **his word was with power** (rather, *in authority*). (Comp. Matt. 7: 28, 29). They were used to hearing professedly religious truth given out with a careful and ever-repeated reference to the previous Rabbis as the authority. It is hard for us to form an idea of the tyrannical rigor with which the Scribes and Pharisees issued their edicts of instruction, received, of course, with a corresponding servility of mental submission by their hearers. But now they listened to a man who uttered the truth as of his own judgment, and with such reasonableness, and consistency with the simple words of Scripture and with the testimony of their own consciences, that they were amazed.

33. A man which had a spirit of an unclean devil (rather, *demon*). The word **devil** is so strictly singular in the original of the New Testament—invariably representing the one arch-enemy of God and man, Satan, the tempter, prince of the demons—or some man who, as acting like and for him, is called by his name, that the use of it, in this connection, is altogether misleading. It is to be wished, certainly, that we had a more satisfactory word to designate the beings so named; but it seems strange that the English section of the recent revisers should have left in the translation an apparent consent to so great an error. Their marginal reading might well have taken the first place, as it does in various American editions, in accordance with the preference of the American section of the revisers. (See Revision above.) "*Demon*" is nearly one of the two Greek names, written in English letters, and does not necessarily, in classic Greek, imply depravity, as the epithet **unclean** here shows. But no epithet is elsewhere used in the New Testament—the name itself standing for a supernatural spirit, subservient to the devil, and acting in his cause to corrupt and harm, and eternally destroy men. Their origin, and more particular relation to Satan, are not explained. Their number is indefinitely great. These beings, often called "unclean," or evil "spirits," are said to enter into men, who then "have" evil spirits, and are spoken of in the Common Version as "possessed" by them—(the Greek is, *are demonized*). The person so afflicted (for it everywhere appears as a dreadful affliction) has his own faculties of thought, emotion, and will, so usurped by the intruding power, that he speaks as the demon. Again, the consciousness is confused, distracted; and sometimes the human, sometimes the demoniac person, prevails. Violent contortions and spasms of the body, accompanied with excruciating pains, were occasional features of the horrid state. As the phenomena of epilepsy and insanity present many resemblances to the cases of possession reported in the New Testament, some have hazarded the supposition that these were all instances of such merely natural maladies, and that Jesus only accommodated his way of speaking about, and dealing with them, to the popular idea that such maladies were the work of demons. It may not be possible to clear the subject of perplexing mystery, but it is to be borne in mind that the Jewish conception of this matter (originating from their associations with Oriental pagans during the exile, and matured afterwards) regarded the disturbing spirits as the ghosts of wicked men deceased, while the New Testament views them distinctly as supernatural beings, not of human nature, sent hither by the devil, whose extra-mundane place is "the abyss." Whatever might be said on another theory of several occurrences concerning them in the New Testament, some, like that of the Gadarene demoniac, cannot be fully explained on any hypothesis but that Jesus saw in them, and intended his disciples to see, the agents of the devil—his angels of evil and harm to men. He accordingly taught that his work was to contend against and expel them, that his disciples should do the same, and that both he and they might recognize the success of his mission in the subjection of the demons to them.

To the difficulty that we do not see evidence

34 Saying, *a* Let *us* alone; what have we to do with thee, *thou* Jesus of Nazareth? art thou come to destroy us? *b* I know thee who thou art; *c* the Holy One of God.
35 And Jesus rebuked him, saying, Hold thy peace, and come out of him. And when the devil had thrown him in the midst, he came out of him, and hurt him not.
36 And they were all amazed, and spake among themselves, saying, What a word *is* this! for with authority and power he commandeth the unclean spirits, and they come out.

34 cried out with a loud voice,[1] Ah! what have we to do with thee, thou Jesus of Nazareth? art thou come to destroy us? I know thee who thou art, the Holy 35 One of God. And Jesus rebuked him, saying, Hold thy peace, and come out of him. And when the demon had thrown him down in the midst, he came 36 out of him, having done him no hurt. And amazement came upon all, and they spake together, one with another, saying, What [2] is this word? for with authority and power he commandeth the unclean

a Or, *Away*....*b* ver. 41....*c* Ps. 16: 10; Dan. 9: 24; ch. 1: 35.—1 Or, *Let alone*....2 Or, *this word, that with authority . . . come out?*.

of such possession in other times, especially in our own, it has been common to reply that the Satanic agency was then allowed more freely, in order that the Saviour's triumph over it might be signally displayed. That is not an unreasonable answer; but may it not be true, also, that to the all-discerning eye a certain proportion of the cases which we ascribe to merely physical disorders of the nervous system, appear as instances of Satanic perversion through evil spirits? The possessive case in "spirit of an unclean demon," is the possessive of apposition, or definition, equivalent to "a spirit which was an unclean demon."

And (*he*, the demonized man), **cried out with a loud voice**, significant of the awe and fury with which the sight of Jesus filled him.

34. Saying, Let us alone. This should be changed to an interjection of fear and displeasure—*Ah!*—**What have we to do with thee**, etc.? The plural number of the pronoun may indicate that the man speaks for himself and the demon; or that the demon associates himself with his class, as being all threatened by the advent of Christ. He means: Why shouldest thou interfere with us?—**Art thou come to destroy us?** Christ's presence forebodes harm to the infernal spirits. **I**—the demon speaks through the man—**know thee**, etc. Whence this prompt and constant recognition by the demons of the divine character of our Lord? Was it that they had learned it from their ruler; or that pure and perfect goodness revealed itself instantly and infallibly to unmixed evil, as a hostile and punitive power?—**The Holy One of God.** In what sense, precisely, the wicked spirit employed this title, is questionable; probably as equivalent to Messiah.

35. And Jesus rebuked him, saying, Hold thy peace, etc. The unhallowed salutation would aggravate the Saviour's abhorrence. He did not desire lip-homage to his office; least of all would it be welcome from such a source. Hence the injunction, **Hold thy peace.** Strictly, *Be thou muzzled!* "Speak not of knowledge of me!" As to the afflicted man, that the Lord deals not at all with him shows that he is not thought of as criminal in entertaining the unclean spirit; but, as in most such cases, the victim of diabolical malignity. The man who was dispossessed would be left as before the evil power overcame him.—**And when the devil**—(*demon*)—**had thrown him down in the midst,** etc. The departure of the invading spirit was apt to be accompanied with terrible pains. On this occasion he appears to have caused an agonizing wrench of the man's whole frame (comp. Mark 1: 26), by which he was thrown down in the open space in the middle of the synagogue. They probably expected to find him dead; but found him so free from permanent harm when the deliverance had been effected, that they could say he had **hurt him not.**

36. And they were all amazed—that is, *amazement came upon all.* The cure of demoniacs was sometimes attempted by Jewish exorcists, and, as would appear, with a kind of success (Matt. 12: 27, and comp. Jos. Ant., 8. 2. 5). Probably, however, few people had seen even pretended successes of this kind; and, if they had, there were features of this case—the entire absence of every shade of jugglery, the intense earnestness, the religious solemnity, and the single efficacy of the Saviour's simple word of command—for which they were not prepared.—**What a word is this!** The Common Version gives the main sense, but not the form, of the thought. (See Revision). The **word** is that command so imperative and efficacious, which had just been uttered.—**For with authority**—as a personal endowment (as in ver. 32)—**and power**—in the practical exercise of that authority—**he commandeth the unclean spirits**—the people see that what he has done in this case he can and will do in other cases—**and they come out.**

37 And the fame of him went out into every place of the country round about.

38 ᵃ And he arose out of the synagogue, and entered into Simon's house. And Simon's wife's mother was taken with a great fever; and they besought him for her.

39 And he stood over her, and rebuked the fever; and it left her: and immediately she arose and ministered unto them.

40 ᵇ Now when the sun was setting, all they that had any sick with divers diseases brought them unto him and he laid his hands on every one of them, and healed them.

37 spirits, and they came out. And there went forth a rumour concerning him into every place of the region round about.

38 And he rose up from the synagogue, and entered into the house of Simon. And Simon's wife's mother was holden with a great fever: and they besought 39 him for her. And he stood over her, and rebuked the fever; and it left her: and immediately she rose up and ministered unto them.

40 And when the sun was setting, all they that had any sick with divers diseases brought them unto him; and he laid his hands on every one of them,

a Matt. 8 : 14 ; Mark 1 : 29.....Matt. 8 : 16 ; Mark 1 : 32.

37. And the fame of him went out—(*i.e.*, "a noise," or *rumor, concerning him*) **into every place of the country round about.** It was not clear and intelligent information, but a varying and mixed popular talk, such as is apt to follow so strange occurrences, and well suited to draw general attention to Christ. It is worthy of notice that the first miracle reported by Luke is the expulsion of a demon. The victory over Satan, which he had achieved in the wilderness, is repeated in the case of Satan's emissaries and his works.

38, 39. HEALING OF PETER'S WIFE'S MOTHER.

38. And he arose out of the synagogue, and entered into Simon's house. From Mark 1: 29, we see that Andrew lived with his brother Simon, in Capernaum. That the house is called Simon's, does not prove, indeed, that he owned it, but renders this extremely probable. It was doubtless a lowly abode, as that of a plain fisherman. Luke has not named him before; but he either intentionally leaves to his readers to supply that this was the well-known apostle, Simon Peter, or, unconsciously, as in other cases, alludes to facts which he does not relate. Peter was, as we see, a married man; nor is there the slightest reason to suppose that his wife was dead at this time, as some Romanists have urged. We have reason, rather, to conclude from 1 Cor. 9: 5, that she subsequently accompanied him on his missionary tours.—**Simon's wife's mother was taken** (*holden*) **with a great fever**—confined to her bed, as appears from Matt. 8: 14, and Mark 1: 30. It is thought that Luke's medical discrimination is seen in referring this disease, as specially violent, to one of the two classes into which fevers were divided, "the great" and "the small." Galen, on "The Different Fevers," in Wetstein on this passage.—**And they besought him for her**—rather, questioned him about her. The Greek verb shows that they did not have to repeat the question, or wait an answer. They might well hope that, after what they had just seen of his superhuman power, and what he had previously done in their city (ver. 23), he would, if his attention were called to her case, heal her also. And he did. What he would not do at Nazareth, or elsewhere, merely to display power, and gratify curiosity, he could not help doing in answer to the even faintly trustful faith of needy hearts.

39. He stood over her—as a physician kindly examining her case—**and rebuked the fever**—recognizing a personal principle of evil in the diseases afflicting men.—**And it left her.** She was instantly restored to health. **And immediately she arose.** Thus proving the reality and miraculous suddenness of the cure. —**And ministered unto them**—probably by preparing the Sabbath evening meal for Jesus, Peter, and their companions; thus proving that she consecrated her restored strength to the faithful discharge of the duties incident to her position.

40, 41. AN EVENING AND NIGHT (?) FILLED WITH HEALING ACTS OF MERCY.

40. Now (*and*) **when the sun was setting**—the earliest moment when it would be thought allowable on the Sabbath; they did not wait until the sun was entirely down.— **All they that had any sick with divers diseases brought them unto him.** What a scene presented itself to the Saviour's compassionate glance! What a number and variety of the physical "ills which flesh is heir to," when a whole community gathered their sick, and maimed, and crippled, and blind, and dumb, before the Great Physician, each one most anxious to attract his merciful look! It was one of those opportunities, fortunate even in the time of Christ's earthly mission, when the streams of healing mercy flowed

41 ᵃ And devils also came out of many, crying out, and saying, Thou art Christ the Son of God. And ᵇ he rebuking *them* suffered them not ᶜ to speak: for they knew that he was Christ.
42 ᵈ And when it was day, he departed and went into a desert place: and the people sought him, and came unto him, and stayed him, that he should not depart from them.
43 And he said unto them, I must preach the kingdom of God to other cities also: for therefore am I sent.

41 and healed them. And demons also came out from many, crying out, and saying, Thou art the Son of God. And rebuking them, he suffered them not to speak, because they knew ᶠ that he was the Christ.
42 And when it was day, he came out and went into a desert place: and the multitudes sought after him, and came unto him, and would have stayed him, 43 that he should not go from them. But he said unto them, I must preach the ᵍ good tidings of the kingdom of God to the other cities also: for therefore was I sent.

a Mark 1: 34; 3: 11....b Mark 1: 25, 34; ver 34, 35....c Or, *to say that they knew him to be Christ*....d Mark 1: 35.——f Or, *gospel*.

freely from the fountain, and when those who needed it appreciated their privilege. Faith in his ability to heal disease, at least, was solidly established, and many might be ready to gain this blessing, who refused his more precious offers to their souls.—**And he laid his hands on every one of them**—as he had done also on the mother-in-law (ver. 39), from what we read in Matthew and Mark. This was not a necessity in order that he might effect the cure, but it was well suited to bring the beneficiaries into a personal relation with him, when they were brought forward, every one separately, and to certify to rude minds that the benefit really came from him.—**And healed them.** So that we are permitted to imagine a considerable town (allowing due latitude to the phrase "*all* they that had") cleared, for one happy hour, of all sickness and bodily plagues.

41. **And devils**—(*demons*)—**also came out of many.** A repetition of the scene in the synagogue. This is mentioned separately, as a crowning exercise of power and mercy, but as closely connected with the general work of bodily cure. The possessed, like the sick, appeal to compassion.—**And he, rebuking them, suffered them not to speak.** The extorted confessions of his Messiahship are again sternly silenced, and now distinctly for the reason that **they knew that he was the Christ,** and were forward to declare it.—**For** is distinctly equivalent to *because.* Had he desired that fact concerning himself to be bruited abroad, he would not desire to have it rest on the testimony of "unclean demons"; but we see many evidences that he did not wish it to be talked about, in the existing temper of the populace; but rather that it should be revealed quietly to the reflection and faith of prepared souls.

42, 43. PREPARATION FOR A PREACHING TOUR THROUGH GALILEE.

42. And when it was day—that is, the morning of that day which had begun at sunset on the Sabbath evening (ver. 40). It was very early in the morning (Mark 1: 35).—**He departed and went into a desert place.** Mark also teaches what we might infer from the account here, that he *went out and departed into a solitary place,* to pray (Mark 1: 35), and also that he was engaged in prayer there when **the people** (*multitudes*) **sought him,** etc. The multitudes were prompted and guided, as would appear (Mark 1: 36) by Simon and those with him, who might have learned the intention of Jesus to leave that neighborhood—**And came unto him**—implies in the Greek that there was some pains required to reach him, and they did not stop until they found him; or, possibly, that they found him in prayer, and should have remained aloof, but in their urgency came quite up to him. **And stayed** (*would have stayed*) **him**—the tentative imperfect,—**that he should not depart from them.** He had proved himself so useful to them, that they would fain have kept him with them permanently. What amount of interest in his higher mission there may have been among them for the moment, no one can tell; but we may suppose that if a year later there had been in the town as many righteous men as would have saved Sodom for Abraham, they would have averted that awful denunciation (10: 15) which singled out this city, as pre-eminent in unbelief, for signal ruin.

43. And (*but*) **he said**—seeing clearly the greatness of his work and the shor.ness of his opportunity—**I must preach the kingdom of God to other cities also.** It was the necessity laid upon him by the very nature of his mission, which constituted the **I must.**—**Preach.** The word (κηρύσσω), properly rendered "preach," in the next verse, is not used here, but a more specific term (εὐαγγελίζομαι), *to announce as good news.* For the definition of **the kingdom of God**—the theme of this

44 *d* And he preached in the synagogues of Galilee. | 44 And he was preaching in the synagogues of ¹Galilee.

CHAPTER V.

AND *b* it came to pass, that, as the people pressed upon him to hear the word of God, he stood by the lake of Gennesaret, | 1 Now it came to pass, while the multitude pressed upon him and heard the word of God, that he was

a Mark 1 : 39....*b* Matt. 4 : 18 ; Mark 1 : 16.——1 Very many ancient authorities read, *Judæa.*

joyful announcement, see on 6: 20. The designation of it in Luke is uniformly as here; so in Mark, while Matthew much more commonly calls it "the kingdom of heaven." **Other cities**—should be "*the other cities,*" marking the gracious design of Jesus to leave none without instruction and invitation.—**For therefore am I sent; or, *because: for this was I sent*.** This announcement of the good news of salvation to all whom he could reach, was a part of the object for which his Father had sent him from his own bosom, and on which he cheerfully came forth out of heaven (Mark 1 : 38).

4: 44—7: 50. THE MISSIONARY EXCURSION THROUGH THE PROVINCE OF GALILEE. From the point which we have now reached, we may recognize a topographical distribution of the ministry of our Lord in Galilee, running on to 9: 51, when he finally takes up his slow movement toward Jerusalem. It is divided into two preaching circuits—the first narrower, not extending apparently to places more than about a day's walk from the western shore of the Sea of Galilee, while the second aimed to reach all the more distant localities, even those east of the lake, and far north toward Cesarea Philippi. Thus here an announcement is made of a season of preaching in the synagogues, in the course of which no localities are mentioned until 7: 1, when he enters again into Capernaum, from which he may have been not far at any point. He does not tarry there at that time, but is presently at Nain; and in 8: 1, he sets out on a new excursion, to visit every city and village with his joyful proclamation. By the aid of the other evangelists, we are able to fix the place and the chronological order of some of the events recorded, more definitely than the documentary or oral authority necessible to Luke enabled him to do. The exhibition of Christ's teaching and work was his leading aim, subordinately to which we see him grouping the facts, in topographical circles of labor, according to a distinct conception, and not inconsistently with the other accounts.

One prominent result of the first circuit is the selection of the twelve apostles.

4: 44. And he preached (*was preaching*) **in the synagogues of Galilee.** This is a general description of the nature of his work, and of the usual seats of it, during the period, of indefinite duration, occupied by chapters 5–7. Some might not unreasonably prefer to connect it with the two preceding verses, as denoting, in a summary and provisional way, the issue of that preparation, which these chapters go on to describe in detail. Preaching was, in this stage of the gospel, the public announcement of the truth concerning the advent of the kingdom of God, with men's privilege and duty in regard to it; and the synagogues offered everywhere the most convenient and appropriate place, as at Nazareth and Capernaum, for the proclamation.

Ch. 5. 1-11. CALL TO DISCIPLESHIP OF PETER (Andrew also.—Matt. 4: 18), **JAMES AND JOHN.**

1. And it came to pass, that, as the people (*multitude*) **pressed upon him.** This narrative is best to be thought of as the first of the incidents of that period of evangelizing labors summarily described in 4: 44. From a comparison of Mark 1: 20, 21, it is extremely probable that what here follows actually took place more immediately after our Lord's coming down from Nazareth, before the Sabbath whose history we have just considered. Luke must, we think, have placed it at Capernaum, since the boat into which he entered (ver. 3) was Simon's. So we see that, after having spoken of his continuous missionary work as about to begin, he pauses to describe the special call of certain disciples, as explaining their subsequent companionship. For it is to be noted that hitherto, so far as appears from Luke, and from other Synoptics, our Saviour has moved about and taught, alone. We hear of no associate with him at Nazareth, and Peter is named in 4: 38, as a stranger. **To hear** (*and heard = were hearing*) **the word of God.**

What Jesus spoke concerning himself and the kingdom, was God's word, because God gave it to him to speak, and because it was a constant revelation of God's holy and merciful name. **He stood by the lake of Gennesaret.** This lake, on the surface and borders of which so many incidents of our Saviour's public ministry took place, is mentioned in the Old Testament as the Sea of Chinnereth, and Chinneroth; and in the New Testament as the Sea of Galilee—in Matthew, Mark and John; and Sea of Tiberias, in John 21:1; but in Luke, only, as the Lake of Gennesaret. It is an expansion of the smooth sand, or, in part, of coarse pebbles and shingles of rock, surrounds the entire lake, reaching to the foot of the mountain. On this space grows luxuriantly a tropical vegetation, including fine palm trees, near the ancient Tiberias, while the mountain slopes are bare of verdure, furrowed with deep ravines, canyons, or *Wadys*, and desolate, except as brightened by patches of grass for a season in spring. The climate, as might be expected in such a hollow, is oppressively hot and unhealthy in summer; at other seasons, pleasant and even delightful.

In our Saviour's time, the neighborhood of

LAKE OF GENNESARET.

Jordan, filling a portion of its bed lying in that wonderful chasm through which, as described on 3:3, the river runs its entire length. The sheet of water is thirteen miles long and six broad; its depth reaches, in places, 165 feet. The water is clear, comparatively cool, and excellent for drinking. It is still, as in ancient times, teeming with fish. The mountains which border the Jordan below, to the Dead Sea, enclose this lake also, rising steeply to the height of perhaps a thousand feet on the eastern side. On the west, the ascent is more gradual and not so high, even at the southern end; while toward the north it sinks, as we have seen, into the Plain of Gennesaret. A narrow beach of this lake was the most thickly peopled, and most prosperous part of Palestine. Large towns almost crowded each other along the western shore, and the water itself was alive with hundreds of boats for fishing, for freight, for pleasure, and sometimes for war. The productiveness of the fisheries; the fertility of the plain before mentioned, and of other parts in the neighborhood; and the traffic of caravans and cargoes passing between the Mediterranean and Damascus, or the farther east—gave employment to multitudes of people, among whom chiefly our Saviour taught and labored through his public life. The lake is now lonely—its shores almost void of inhabitant. A single boat has for many

2 And saw two ships standing by the lake: but the fishermen were gone out of them, and were washing *their* nets.
3 And he entered into one of the ships, which was Simon's, and prayed him that he would thrust out a little from the land. And he sat down, and taught the people out of the ship.
4 Now when he had left speaking, he said unto Simon, ᵃ Launch out into the deep, and let down your nets for a draught.
5 And Simon answering said unto him, Master, we have toiled all the night, and have taken nothing: nevertheless at thy word I will let down the net.
6 And when they had this done, they inclosed a great multitude of fishes: and their net brake.
7 And they beckoned unto *their* partners, which were in the other ship, that they should come and help

2 standing by the lake of Gennesaret; and he saw two boats standing by the lake; but the fishermen had gone out of them, and were washing their nets.
3 And he entered into one of the boats, which was Simon's, and asked him to put out a little from the land. And he sat down and taught the multitudes
4 out of the boat. And when he had left speaking, he said unto Simon, Put out into the deep, and let down
5 your nets for a draught. And Simon answered and said, Master, we toiled all night, and took nothing:
6 but at thy word I will let down the nets. And when they had this done, they inclosed a great multitude
7 of fishes; and their nets were breaking; and they beckoned unto their partners in the other boat, that they should come and help them. And they came, and filled both the boats, so that they began to sink.

a John 21 : 6.

---

years represented the lively throng that crossed and circled under the Saviour's eye, while scanty ruins cumber the sites of the busy cities of old, and weigh down the dust of their inhabitants. Travelers dispute whether the scene can now be called beautiful or pleasant; but curiosity will always be piqued by such a body of water, lying so deep, in such a basin of rock whose lofty summits rise but little above the level of the "great sea"; and even undevout hearts are tenderly stirred by memories of the walks and works and prayers of the Lord Jesus, which the scene naturally evokes.

2. Two ships (*boats*) **standing by the lake**—drawn out on the shore. The size of this lake would scarcely allow what we call ships, for any use; and these were fishers' boats, with a sail, but without deck, unless at the ends, and mainly propelled by oars. Josephus says there were, at that time, four thousand vessels on the lake.—**But the fishermen were gone out of them, and were washing** (perhaps, rather, *had washed*) **their nets.** The true text is uncertain. The preterit tense of the second verb would imply that the washing was ended; the imperfect that it was going on.

3. And he entered into one . . . and prayed him (Simon) **that he would thrust out,** etc. The reason for this lay in the statement that **the people pressed upon him** (ver. 1), and that he himself was standing on the shore. That was a very inconvenient position for addressing the great throng whom the reports concerning him had drawn together. **And he sat down and taught the people** (*multitudes*) **out of the ship.** The sitting posture was usual for the religious teacher, as we have seen (4: 20); but probably here the unstable position of the boat may have been a chief reason. Having wrought miracles the night before, he now gave the people the message which those were suited to prepare for and to confirm.

4. Now (*and*) **when he had left speaking, he said unto Simon, Launch out into the deep**—verb in the singular, addressed to Peter as captain—**and let down your nets**—plural, of the crew—**for a draught.** The **nets,** from their Greek name, were cast-nets—one of which might be thrown out by each hand on the boat, with the aim to surround as many fish as possible.

5. Master, we have toiled all the night, and have taken nothing. The word Master (ἐπιστάτης), is properly, superintendent, commander, not *rabbi* or teacher (διδάσκαλος), which would be familiar to Jews, but not to Greeks. This designates Jesus with reference to his authority, which would better suit Peter's present view. Luke uses it several times, and he alone in the New Testament. Peter's answer delicately hints that there cannot be much use in trying again by daylight, when the more favorable night-time has brought no luck. — **Nevertheless** (*but*) **at thy word I will.** Jesus had said, Let down *your* nets. Peter, who was in command, says, **I will let down the net** (*nets*). Theophylact says, "Before believing, Peter exercises faith in Christ."—Meyer.

6. Their net (*nets*) **brake** (*were breaking,* ready to break). This result can hardly be called, in the strictest sense, a miracle, except as being "a miracle of knowledge."—Godet. It was a wonder of that class where a remarkable, but not supernatural, event was divinely effected at such a time and place, in the history of revelation, as unmistakably to indicate the interposition of God.

7. Their partners which were in the

96 LUKE. [CH. V.

them. And they came, and filled both the ships, so that they began to sink.

8 When Simon Peter saw *it*, he fell down at Jesus' knees, saying, ^aDepart from me; for I am a sinful man, O Lord.

9 For he was astonished, and all that were with him, at the draught of the fishes which they had taken:

10 And so *was* also James, and John, the sons of Zebedee, which were partners with Simon. And Jesus said unto Simon, Fear not; ^bfrom henceforth thou shalt catch men.

8 But Simon Peter, when he saw it, fell down at Jesus' knees, saying, Depart from me; for I am a sinful

9 man, O Lord. For he was amazed, and all that were with him, at the draught of the fishes which they

10 had taken; and so were also James and John, sons of Zebedee, who were partners with Simon. And Jesus said unto Simon, Fear not; from henceforth

a 2 Sam. 6: 9; 1 Kings 17: 18....*b* Matt. 4: 49; Mark 1: 17.

---

other ship—the other of the two, namely, mentioned in ver. 2. The **partners** were James and John, the sons of Zebedee (ver. 10; comp. Matt. 4: 21; Mark 1: 19). **Filled both the ships**—(*boats*)—etc. That the catch of their several nets should have been sufficient for this, without supposing any miracle of the multiplication of the fish, will not seem at all incredible to one who reads the account of Josephus.—*Jew. Wars*, vol. iii. 10, 7; Robinson, *Phys. Geog.*, p. 204, 5; Tristram, *Land of Israel*, p. 426; Thomson, *Land and Book*, p. 79-81; Ritter, *Geog. of Pal.*, vol. ii. 250; McGregor, *Rob Roy on the Jordan*, ch. xx.; Porter, *Handbook*, vol. ii. 409; and the authorities cited in Winer, *Real-wörterbuch*, under word Fische.

8. When Simon Peter, etc.—rather, *And Simon Peter, when he saw it,* **fell down,** etc. It was a natural expression of that solemn awe, and sense of unworthiness, which at all times attended the extraordinary manifestation of God's presence to mortals (Judges 13: 22, 23; 2 Sam. 6: 9; 1 Kings 17: 18), and which we still feel at those moments when we are suddenly made sensible of the near exercise of his holy, though gracious power. Meyer finds Luke inconsistent with himself in showing Peter thus affected after the exhibitions he had had, the day before, of Christ's divine authority. But, while a more full acquaintance with all the circumstances is to be desired, we may note that it is not said Peter was present on that afternoon, even at his own house. And if he certainly were, who can prescribe when, to the varying moods of a man's mind, and in the diverse circumstances surrounding him, he must most properly experience those agitations of his profoundest being which mark the turning points of life, and determine eternal destiny? This revelation of divinity, in his own sphere of duty, and after we know not what cogitations, came home to him. His first feeling was that of his personal sinfulness, which made a manifest inconsistency with the holiness of the Lord, so that he prostrated himself with the confession—**I am a sinful man.** It is eminently congruous with that sense which Peter afterward felt of Christ's redeeming grace, that he should have been a particularly wicked man in his unregenerate days, and not above the proverbially low level of morality where the followers of his craft used to be found. His prayer was, in form, that of the Gadarenes after the healing of their demoniac (8: 37); but who does not feel that Peter would have been inconsolably afflicted if Jesus had taken him at his word? [Is it not possible that Peter's mind reverted to his distrust of Christ's knowledge or power when told to launch out and cast in the net? Though he obeyed the Master, he did it with very little faith; and now his sinful lack of trust overwhelmed him with shame. He felt himself to be exceedingly unworthy before his holy and heart-reading Lord.—A. H.]

9, 10. For he was astonished, etc. More exactly, *Amazement held him, and all that were with him*—**and so was also James and John.** The feeling of each would be deeper, being common with that of the rest. **And Jesus said unto Simon.** The others do not appear in this call as given by Luke, yet it is evident from the partially parallel and briefer narratives of Matthew and Mark, that Jesus, at some point in the scene, gave the call to the whole four. Had we all the facts implied in the three accounts, in their order, we *might* be able to see that they cover proceedings of parts of two days; that the call to the four was given the day before the Sabbath in Capernaum, while the washing of the nets took place on the morning of the day after the Sabbath, with the Saviour's discourse to the people, the miraculous draught, and the address to Peter, separately reminding him that he was henceforth to follow a new life. **Fear not**—that very sense of sinfulness which prostrated him, being accompanied with penitence and a desire of a better life, was a reason why

11 And when they had brought their ships to land, *b* they forsook all, and followed him.
12 *a* And it came to pass, when he was in a certain city, behold a man full of leprosy: who seeing Jesus

11 thou shalt ¹ catch men. And when they had brought their boats to land, they left all, and followed him.
12 And it came to pass, while he was in one of the cities, behold, a man full of leprosy: and when he

a Matt. 4: 20; 19: 27; Mark 1: 18; ch. 18: 28.....*b* Matt. 8: 2; Mark 1: 40.——1 Gr. *take alive*.

he need not dread the presence of God. From **henceforth thou shalt catch**—(Gr. *take alive*)—**men**. The Greek represents it as Peter's permanent work: "shalt be taking men." The change of Peter's sentiment and purpose, wrought through the view of his past life, was suited to fit him all the better for that different work, and constituted in God's gracious providence the turning point of his career. "So far thus, but **henceforth**."

This great draught of fishes, in connection with the call of the first four disciples, presupposes some previous acquaintance with the men, although they have not before appeared in the Synoptical Gospels. The Gospel of John supplies the lacking information. From that, we learn that of the number who had become attached to John the Baptist, at the Jordan, in such relation as to be called his disciples, or scholars, before our Lord's return to the Jordan after the temptation, were three of these four men. First, two (John 1: 36-43), Andrew and John, moved by the Baptist's testimony, make themselves acquainted with Jesus where he was then lodging, and become convinced that they have found the promised Messiah; and so persuade Simon of this that he, too, attaches himself to the Lord.

Afterward, Philip and Nathanael enter into the like relation of provisional discipleship; and, returning with the Teacher to Galilee, they, some or all—some "disciples" at least—were present with him at the wedding in Cana (John 2: 2), in a short sojourn at Capernaum (ver. 12), on his journey to Jerusalem at the Passover (ver. 17), and on the way back through Samaria (4: 27). After this, it would appear that they separated to their several places and occupations. It may bring us nearer to the reality if we assume that these disciples, at least that Peter did *not* accompany Jesus to that first passover. We then have a natural explanation why Mark, who was Peter's interpreter, did not mention occurrences of that journey, with which the apostle was personally unacquainted. Matthew could say nothing of them of his own knowledge, and Luke would,

for such reasons, find nothing about that time in his Galilean sources. John, from his acquaintance with the high-priest (John 13: 15), appears to have been more at home, on some account, in Jerusalem; and this may be why he dwells on facts pertaining to Judea, where the others were strangers, while they give the Galilean narrative. Nothing is reported intimating that their scholarship to Jesus involved the necessity of constant attendance. It was not till the morning of the Sermon on the Mount, that he appointed them, "that they might be with him." But now his cause has reached that stage where, as we may suppose, he saw the need of companionship and help; the necessity for putting in training, also, men who, with further instruction and apprenticeship, might become qualified to assume larger responsibilities, and take charge of his interests when he should be taken away. Such was the significance of the call of the fishermen on the lake. They are not yet apostles; only scholars, selected out of a number, now constantly increasing, who, in some sense and to some extent, recognized in Jesus a "Teacher sent from God," perhaps even a Messiah; but with great diversity of intellectual and spiritual appreciation. The promise to these men, that they should be "fishers of men"—catchers of souls unto eternal life—might afterward find in their thoughts typical illustration, and perpetual confirmation from the success of that haul to which their Master sent them, under circumstances so unpromising. They accept his call—and what a difference resulted in the subsequent course of their lives, in their experiences on earth, in their memory among men, and in their eternal destiny!

11. **They forsook (or, *left*) all, and followed him.** Boats, nets, all worldly goods, and business cares, ceased from the moment to engage their thoughts. Not necessarily that they left things in disorder, or without properly arranging the affairs of their families; but that everything now was turned to the one purpose of discipleship to Christ.

12-16. CURE OF A LEPER.

12. When he was in a certain city (*one*

fell on *his* face, and besought him, saying, Lord, if thou wilt, thou canst make me clean. 13 And he put forth *his* hand, and touched him, saying, I will; be thou clean. And immediately the leprosy departed from him.

saw Jesus, he fell on his face, and besought him, saying, Lord, if thou wilt, thou canst make me clean. 13 And he stretched forth his hand, and touched him, saying I will; be thou clean. And straightway the

of the cities)—namely, of those contemplated in 4: 44. Luke, who, from his purpose to write "in order," would fain have given definite places and dates, was often obliged, nevertheless, from the lack of particular information, to content himself with a general indication of the scene and the time.—**A man full of leprosy.** Leprosy, of which, as of other diseases, there were various species, was particularly prevalent in Egypt, Syria, and different parts of the Levant. The symptoms of it, as afflicting the Israelites, after their long and degraded servitude in Egypt, and the manner in which it was to be treated, are minutely laid down in Leviticus 13 and 14. It appeared on the surface, as a disorder of the skin, in whitish spots, or patches, which naturally spread by slow degrees, and became confluent, covering, at last, the entire body. Meantime, it wrought inwardly also, until the whole physical system was corrupted, even to the marrow of the bones. The disease was hereditary, and was regarded as incurable by medicines; yet the provisions of the law seem to suppose the possibility of spontaneous cure in cases where leprosy had been declared present. During its continuance, it had the effect: (1) Personally, of rendering its subject extremely miserable. When it was fully developed, he was a living mass of corruption, an offence to himself as well as others, troubled with incessant pains by day, and sleep-scaring dreams by night, and with no hope of recovery to health. (2) Socially, it cut him off from intercourse with others, except such as were similarly afflicted. This was, apparently, more from fear of ceremonial pollution than of contagion. The disease is often spoken of as highly contagious (so in Godet), but it is not expressly so called in the Bible. Naaman was in an official position, incompatible with natural abhorrence of infection. Physicians dealing, on the east coast of Africa, with what is now regarded as the "leprosy of the Jews," declare its contagiousness very problematical; and, in the case before us, the man was "in a city," not, apparently, precluded from proximity to others. It may be noted also, as a curious fact, that in the law (Lev

13:13), the leper in whom the disease had proceeded to such an extent that it had "covered all his flesh," should be declared clean by the priest. But, according to the law, he must wear a distinctive and squalid dress—specially a covering over the upper lip, and must constantly indicate his state, by crying: "Unclean! Unclean!" (3) Ceremonially, it thus rendered him "unclean," and cut him off from all participation in the religious rites of the congregation, and even ejected him from the camp. It was thus treated in the Levitical system as a symbol of sin. The rigorous exclusion from society, originally practiced, seems now to have been considerably modified. **Full of leprosy**—so long and badly affected with the disease, that his whole body was tainted, and he, naturally, hopeless of relief.—**Who** (properly, *but*) **seeing Jesus** (*he*) **fell on his face**—thus indicating his reverence, his sense of personal unworthiness, and his appeal for mercy. This latter appears distinctly in his uttered prayer—**Lord, if thou wilt, thou canst make me clean.** Of the Lord's ability to do even this, he was fully convinced, from what he had seen and heard of his wonderful works. But what he mentions first is the doubt which disquiets him—Will he cure me? He had heard of no instance of the healing of a leper, and perhaps this good physician shared so fully in the popular aversion and disgust, that he would not sully himself by contact with so odious a wretch as himself. He evidently hopes, but can base his petition, which he hints, rather than expresses, only on an **if.** —**Make me clean.** The cure of leprosy is often spoken of as a purification, in reference to its defiling character; sometimes as a healing, regarding it as a disease; and again, as a departure, the evil being personified, when the plague has ceased.

13. And he put (*stretched*) **forth his hand, and touched him.** Instantly the response came, by an act first, as had the sufferer's prayer, as if to show that the Lord was as willing and ready as he was able, to bless; and as giving to the suppliant a most encouraging proof of sympathy and kindness. No fear of contagion or defilement should

14 ᵃAnd he charged him to tell no man: but go, and shew thyself to the priest, and offer for thy cleansing, ᵇaccording as Moses commanded, ᶜfor a testimony unto them.
15 But so much the more went there a fame abroad of him: ᵈand great multitudes came together to hear, and to be healed by him of their infirmities.
16 ᵉAnd he withdrew himself into the wilderness, and prayed.

14 leprosy departed from him. And he charged him to tell no man: but go thy way, and shew thyself to the priest, and offer for thy cleansing, according as 15 Moses commanded, for a testimony unto them. But so much the more went abroad the report concerning him; and great multitudes came together to 16 hear, and to be healed of their infirmities. But he withdrew himself in the desert, and prayed.

a Matt. 8: 4... b Lev. 14: 4, 10, 21, 22... c Matt. 4: 25; Mark 3: 7; John 6: 2....d Matt. 14: 23; Mark 6: 46.

hinder him from answering to the felt and trustful sense of dependence on his help.— **I will: be thou** (*made*) **clean**. This word, and not the friendly touch, was what issued in the beneficent change.—**And immediately the leprosy departed from him**—a proof of Christ's power and kindness, more impressive, perhaps, more significant of his condescension and superiority to the prejudices of his day, than any which he had before given. Could any one doubt, after this, his willingness to relieve every bodily woe, or to cleanse from that moral guilt and pollution so fitly represented by the leper's case?

14. And he charged him to tell no man. We are not told the reason for these repeated charges to the objects of his mercy, that they should not publish what he had done for them. It may, probably, have been that he saw a tendency, in that region, to fix attention on his works, to the neglect of his word, and to build on them a temporal and carnal expectation concerning his kingdom. He would have the former bear testimony, indeed, to his Messiahship, but only as they might be interpreted by the latter, through the study of meditative and believing souls.— **But go, and shew thyself to the priest,** etc. Our Lord was careful not to violate, but to honor, the law given by Moses, while he lived under it. This advice was conformable to the prescription in Lev. 14: 2, 10, 21, the reasons for which are obvious in that connection. **And offer for** (concerning, or in relation to) **thy cleansing**—make the offering required in connection with thy ceremonial purification. The **testimony** would result from the priest's declaration of his restored health—**unto them,** namely, his relatives and acquaintances; not a testimony to the priests in Christ's behalf, as the man was forbidden to tell that Christ had done it.

15. But so much the more went there a fame abroad of (or, *concerning*) **him, etc.—** The more, that is, in proportion to the strictness with which Jesus had enjoined silence. Luke does not expressly lay the blame on the healed leper, as does Mark, whose whole account is particularly graphic. The course of the man was doubtless very natural—too natural to evince much spiritual grace. It is one of the many proofs that the faith of those who flocked to Christ might have reference only to his power of physical beneficence. In this case, if the great multitudes had come together mainly to hear Christ's proclamation of the good tidings, many would think the man's mistake venial. Some have, indeed, strange to say, immorally supposed that the object of the prohibition was that a louder rumor concerning him might go forth. There does not seem to have been need of effort, at this time, to attract numbers to be healed of their infirmities.

16. And (*but*) **he**—*he* himself, amid all this thronging of excited thousands—**withdrew himself into the wilderness, and prayed.** This was what came of the cleansed man's imprudent and disobedient zeal (Mark 1: 45). Our Lord could not, for a time, "enter openly into *a* city," but was in retirement in desert, solitary places in the gullied mountains of Galilee, partially similar to those in which John the Baptist abode in Judea (1: 80).—**And prayed** (*was praying*)—spent the time of his retirement in seeking spiritual rest, and light from heaven in regard to these dubious manifestations of popular sentiments concerning him. It is the second of nine instances in which Luke, alone of the evangelists, presents the Saviour as engaged in prayer (3: 21; 6: 12; 9: 18, 28, 29; 22: 32, 41; 23: 46). [*I. e.,* No one of these nine instances is mentioned by any other Evangelist.—A. H.] With these may be mentioned the retirement spoken of in 4: 42, which we learn from Mark 1: 33, was for prayer. One who looks at these instances, in their connection, will see that they all pertain to serious and important occasions of Christ's life, and work.

17 And it came to pass on a certain day, as he was teaching, that there were Pharisees and doctors of the law sitting by, which were come out of every town of Galilee, and Judæa, and Jerusalem: and the power of the Lord was *present* to heal them.

17 And it came to pass on one of those days, that he was teaching; and there were Pharisees and doctors of the law sitting by, who were come out of every village of Galilee and Judæa and Jerusalem: and

17-26. Cure of a Paralytic.

17. On a certain day (literally, *one of those days*)—in which he was preaching in the synagogue of Galilee (4:44). Luke probably could not name the time more definitely. From Mark (2:1-12), we learn that the place was Capernaum, although this seems as little known to Luke as was that of the preceding miracle. [Is it at all certain that Luke would have specified the day and place, if he had known them? Or that he made any attempt to give all the minute points of the history with with which he had become familiar? A. H.]—**He was teaching**—after the manner shown us at Nazareth. This was a branch of the work of preaching.—**Pharisees.** This sect, which here first appears in Luke, sustained a very important relation to the work of our Lord. They were a small class, scattered through the land, but clustered especially in Jerusalem and the other cities, and large towns, pre-eminently distinguished by their zeal for the strict ritual observances of their hereditary religion. Originating (we know not precisely how or where) in that dark and barren period which followed the close of the Old Testament revelation, they *separated* themselves, in profession and practice, from the mass of the nation, as these did from the rest of mankind. Their name, **Pharisees,** or Separates, signified this claim to peculiar sanctity, or Hebraistic righteousness. Their aim was, doubtless, as much political as religious, in this consistent with the ancestral policy of their nation; only they had fallen on a very bad stage of the national condition, which they made it their supreme business to conserve. With no change from the triumphant period of the Maccabæan monarchy, except toward the multiplication of requirements and increased rigor in their observance, they made religion and patriotism to consist in the practice of an all-comprehensive and unyielding ritual. They insisted on the perpetuation of every particle of rite and ceremony which had been handed down to them, and found authority in reputed traditions for whatever seemed further necessary to support what they already had. These traditions were an oral law (so-called), derived [as was claimed] from Moses, through the succession of Rabbis, of equal authority with the law written, and so related to it that when the reqirements of the former conflicted with the precepts of the latter, those must prevail. Failure, in any point, to keep the whole sacred form, was a sin; practical compliance with all the traditions was a clear title to salvation. They had, in part by development of the teachings and intimations of the Old Testament and, in part by the aid of philosophical speculations, domestic and foreign, constructed loose doctrinal systems. These included, beside the clear theology of their Scriptures, fixed opinions concerning the existence and agency of superhuman spirits, good and evil, the immortality of the soul, a future retribution involving eternal rewards and punishments, and especially, the future Messiah and his reign. The patriotic quality of their religious zeal made them impatient of foreign restraint on their nation, particularly impatient of the Roman government, and ready to encourage turbulence and insurrection, on the least prospect of success.

The stress which they laid on the punctilious observance of outward rites, mostly of mere human origin, encouraged spiritual pride, and an assurance of work-righteousness which looked down on less scrupulous and common people as contemptible and profane. Their idea of the nature of religion appears to have been accepted by a multitude in the respectable classes, who did not belong to the party; and it was doubtless generally held by those who looked for the Messiah, that, under his reign, they would of course be distinguished with pre-eminent honor and rewards.—**Doctors of the law.** Whether these (νομοδιδάσκαλοι) were distinct from the class called lawyers (νομικοί), is not altogether clear. The names are probably only two designations of the one office—that of guarding, expounding, applying the law. The class would naturally be in close sympathy with the Pharisees, even when they did not belong to their body.—**Which were come out of every town** (*village*)—showing how widely they were distributed. They had evidently

CH. V.]   LUKE.   101

18 *And, behold, men brought in a bed a man which was taken with a palsy: and they sought *means* to bring him in, and to lay him before him.
19 And when they could not find by what *way* they might bring him in because of the multitude, they went upon the housetop, and let him down through the tiling with *his* couch into the midst before Jesus.
20 And when he saw their faith, he said unto him, Man, thy sins are forgiven thee.

18 the power of the Lord was with him ¹to heal. And behold, men bring on a bed a man that was palsied: and they sought to bring him in, and to lay him
19 before him. And, not finding by what *way* they might bring him in because of the multitude, they went up to the housetop, and let him down through the tiles with his couch into the midst before Jesus.
20 And seeing their faith, he said, Man, thy sins are

a Matt. 9 : 2; Mark 2 : 3.——1 Gr. *that he should heal.* Many ancient authorities read, *that he should heal them.*

assembled by concert, and were **sitting by**—in the room where he was teaching, to observe what Jesus would say and do. His fame as a prophet and mighty worker had spread so widely, and risen so high, that the ruling authority in the religious sphere would deem it necessary to have definite information about him. This may account for the sudden and impressive apparition of these dignitaries on the field of his operations. Some suppose that the time was near the second passover in his ministry (John 5:1), and that the populous caravans moving to or from the feast, might furnish the number of Pharisees and doctors who now manifest themselves. In any case, those who were from Judea and Jerusalem must have come expressly to carry out an arrangement planned beforehand.—**And the power of the Lord was present to heal them.** The translation here is difficult, not only on account of the different forms of the text noted in the margin of the Revision, but also because of the conciseness of the expression. It might be roughly given somewhat more literally (following the preferable text), "And there was a power of the Lord for him to heal:" **The Lord** (κυρίου, without the article equivalent to God); "for," or "in order to," his working cures. As the presence of many seeking cures showed great faith in him as a bodily healer, so power was given him to meet the emergency. It was a time like that first Sabbath evening in Capernaum (4:40), and like the subsequent hour when the messengers of John the Baptist were present (7:21). The case of the paralytic is particularly detailed, not as exhausting the record of his activity then, but because of a special lesson which it taught.

18. And, behold, men brought in (on) **a bed a man which was taken with a palsy** (*that was palsied*). The interjection **behold** indicates the surprise occasioned by the event, that a man as helpless toward moving himself, through the severity of his disease, as if

he were dead, should be brought by four men (Mark 2:3), and with so much pain placed before the Saviour. The **bed** was a couch or pallet, scarcely more than a stretcher in our hospital practice.

19. And when they could not find by what way, etc. Mark vividly describes the crowd that thronged the house and all the space about the door (2:1 f.).—**They went upon the housetop.** The roofs were generally nearly level, and were reached by a flight of stairs, either outside, from the street, or within, from the open court, or area, about which the more considerable houses were usually built.—**And, let him down through the tiling,** etc. This may mean only that they passed him through a trap-door in the roof, although Mark's account would seem to imply that some removal of the roof was necessary—a "digging through" that, or some partition, before they could reach the Saviour. The narratives are too brief to allow us to bring the scene clearly before us. Thomson, in the *Land and Book* (Vol. II., pp. 6-8, 1st Ed.), tells us that breaking through the roof is of frequent occurrence in that country now. Jesus may have been in the upper chamber or attic, where meetings were held (Mark 14:15; Acts 1:13; 9:39); but various other views are entertained.

20. And when he saw their faith, he said unto them (omit *unto them*), **Man, thy sins are** (equivalent to *have been*) **forgiven thee.** Faith is visible in its works; and, if ever apparent, it was manifest in that scene. **Their faith** must here include that of the sufferer himself. And his faith, at least, must have beheld in Jesus the Physician of diseased souls also. It is most probable that he was conscious of having brought the malady on himself by wicked transgressions, and for this cause was distressed in conscience and heart. To such a state of mind, at any rate, Christ first addressed himself.—**Man**—mortal, child of Adam, and subject to affliction.

21 ^a And the scribes and the Pharisees began to reason, saying, Who is this which speaketh blasphemies? ^b Who can forgive sins, but God alone?

21 forgiven thee. And the scribes and Pharisees began to reason, saying, Who is this that speaketh blasphemies? Who can forgive sins, but God alone?

_{a Matt. 9:3; Matt. 2:6, 7....b Ps. 32:5; Isa. 43:25.}

Mark expresses it more affectionately, "Child," and Matthew adds to that, "Cheer up." It may well have been a young man. **Thy sins are** (*have been*) **forgiven thee.** The verb is a perfect. On the manifestation of thy repentance and faith, the condemnation all for which he came? Certainly he had received a benefit in comparison with which a mere physical cure was paltry, and perhaps his heart was fully content; but there was more reserved for him.—**The scribes.** The word "scribe," originally "writer," perhaps copyist

LETTING DOWN IN A BED.

against thee has been canceled. It had been foretold (1:77) that Jesus would bring "salvation to his people through the remission of their sins." But this is the first distinct declaration by him of this form of blessing. It is made now, doubtless, because of a special preparation for it in this sufferer's heart; and also, perhaps, that an important effect might be produced on the Pharisees who were present. We are not told the result of this in the soul of the pardoned man. Had he received of the law," in the New Testament designates one who, by professional learning, was conversant with the law, and skilled in questions concerning it. The office dated from the time of "Ezra the scribe." They were in sympathy with the Pharisees, and might belong to their body; and were highly esteemed. It is very probable that the word here is strictly synonomous with "doctor of the law" (ver. 17).

21. Began to reason, saying—possibly to each other, in suppressed tones—**Who is**

22 But when Jesus perceived their thoughts, he answering said unto them, What reason ye in your hearts?
23 Whether is easier, to say, Thy sins be forgiven thee; or to say, Rise up and walk?
24 But that ye may know that the Son of man hath power upon earth to forgive sins, (he said unto the sick of the palsy,) I say unto thee, Arise, and take up thy couch, and go into thine house.
25 And immediately he rose up before them, and took up that whereon he lay, and departed to his own house, glorifying God.
26 And they were all amazed, and they glorified God, and were filled with fear, saying, We have seen strange things to-day.

22 But Jesus perceiving their reasonings, answered and said unto them, ¹What reason ye in your hearts?
23 Whether is easier, to say, Thy sins are forgiven thee; 24 or to say, Arise and walk? But that ye may know that the Son of man hath authority on earth to forgive sins (he said unto him that was palsied), I 25 say unto thee, Arise, and take up thy couch, and go unto thy house. And immediately he rose up before them, and took up that whereon he lay, and de-26 parted to his house, glorifying God. And amazement took hold on all, and they glorified God; and they were filled with fear, saying, We have seen strange things to-day.

Or, Why.

this which speaketh blasphemies? To speak blasphemies would, of course, vitiate all claims to Messiahship, or to a prophetic character, and would besides bring him under the jurisdiction of the Sanhedrin at Jerusalem as a heinous criminal. The blasphemy which they professed to see lay in his assuming a function (to forgive sins), which belonged only to God, as is plain from the following question. Their complaint is, therefore, more directly, that he pretends to wield the authority of God.—**Who can forgive sins, but God alone?** Since the fact of sins being forgiven is not apparent to the senses, there was room for them to deny it; and their implication is that his words to that effect are merely a false, and therefore a blasphemous, sound.

22. But when Jesus perceived their thoughts,—(*reasonings*)—which he might do from their actions and looks, without hearing their words, even if words were used—he **answering said, What reason ye in your hearts?** He answered their thoughts, unspoken to him at least. What objections do ye make? Do ye need proof that I can forgive sins?

23. Whether is easier, to say, etc. Not certainly, to pronounce those sentences; but which of the two is more within the compass of a power below God's, to remit sins by a word, or by a word to work a manifest miracle of healing?

24. But that ye may know that the Son of man hath power, etc. The Saviour's admirable argument is: You deny that I perform a divine function, the effects of which you cannot see; I will perform one equally divine, as yourselves admit, and the effect of which you cannot fail to see, by instantly restoring to complete health this helpless and hopeless invalid.—**The Son of man,** is the name by which Jesus most commonly desig-

nates himself, and which his disciples never in the Gospels apply to him. In what view he felt this appropriate to him, has been much discussed. Probably no one statement would cover all his reasons. It expressed the deep consciousness of full participation in the nature of those whom he came to redeem, and may have been chosen to win their confidence more readily and completely. At the same time, the constant distinction, *the* Son *of* man, which no mere mortal would think of assuming, could hardly fail to suggest that he who assumed it was something more than man, and might lead some to think that he regarded himself as the long-expected "seed of the woman," who should bruise the serpent's head. This is more likely to be a Scriptural source of the idea than the phrase in Daniel 7: 13: "One like a Son of man," although this passage may have entered into the formation of the title. (See Cremer, *Bibl. Theol. Wörterbuch,* 2 Ed. p. 563 f., or English Translation). —**I say unto thee, Arise.** To smooth the abrupt transition to this address to the paralytic, the narrator has inserted the preceding parenthesis.

25. And immediately he rose up before them, etc.—Thus carrying out to the letter the injunction which the Saviour had designedly made particular, that the fact of his healing might be impressively clear. Three distinct stages of the free activity of the immovable paralytic are marked.—**Glorifying God**—as indeed he, if ever any man, had reason to do. Others who had corrupted and broken down their bodies by evil courses, have had to bear the physical penalties, even when their sins were forgiven. Some in his day were healed of physical maladies, but failed of the spiritual renewal which Jesus had to bestow. This man, rejoicing in both forms of blessing, might well glorify God. And not he alone.

26. And they were all amazed (strictly,

27 ᵃAnd after these things he went forth, and saw a publican, named Levi, sitting at the receipt of custom; and he said unto him, Follow me.
28 And he left all, rose up, and followed him.
29 ᵇAnd Levi made him a great feast in his own house: and ᶜthere was a great company of publicans and of others that sat down with them.
30 But their scribes and Pharisees murmured against ᵈhis disciples, saying, Why do ye eat and drink with publicans and sinners?

27 And after these things he went forth, and beheld a publican, named Levi, sitting at the place of toll, and
28 said unto him, Follow me. And he forsook all, and
29 rose up and followed him. And Levi made him a great feast in his house: and there was a great multitude of publicans and of others that were sitting at
30 meat with them. And ¹the Pharisees and their scribes murmured against his disciples, saying, Why do ye eat

ᵃ Matt. 9: 9; Mark 2: 13, 14....ᵇ Matt. 9: 10; Mark 2: 15....ᶜ ch. 15: 1.—1 Or, *the Pharisees and scribes among them.*

---

amazement held them all). It is a very strong expression of the wonder produced by what had occurred.—**And they glorified God,** as explained in 2: 20.—**And were filled with fear**—another instance of the awful solemnity occasioned by the divine presence (2: 9).

27-32. CALL OF LEVI (Matthew) TO DISCIPLESHIP. And after these things—not necessarily on the same day—**he went forth** —apparently to the shore of the lake, where he would always find plenty of people—**and saw a publican**—on the publicans, see on 3: 12—**named Levi, sitting at the receipt of custom** (*place of toll*)—toll-house, or custom-house. It is almost the universal opinion that **Levi** is only another name of the disciple who, as one of the twelve apostles, is called Matthew in all the Synoptical Gospels. Reasons for this conclusion are: (1) That the call of Levi is so formal and similar to that of Simon and Andrew, James and John, as to indicate that he was to be one of the twelve, whereas no Levi is mentioned among that number. (2) That Matthew records his own call (9:9) as following close upon the healing of the paralytic, and under circumstances identical with those attending the call to Levi; and that the Saviour was at a feast "in the house," immediately afterward, as he is here at a "reception" given him by Levi, at which, in both accounts, very many publicans were present, and the same complaints were made against Christ, and silenced by the same answer. (3) These circumstances so indubitably point to identity of the person bearing the two names, that we only mention, without ascribing much independent weight to it, the steadfast tradition from the earliest times in favor of this supposition. Any shade of remaining improbability is removed by the frequency of double names to the same person in Scripture. Levi might very naturally pass from Levi to Matthew, when abandoning his dis-

reputable vocation, and entering on a new and consecrated life.

28. And he left all, rose up, and followed him. To follow Christ, in that day, was not simply to believe on him; but, literally, to leave one's ordinary place and to go with him. Why Jesus should single out Levi from all the publicans about the lake, we can only conjecture. Doubtless, there was some reason, in his natural endowment, his education, and business training, the quality of his faith, manifested possibly in former interviews, which showed him fit to be one of the more intimate circle of Christ's scholars. His obedience to the call was as prompt as that of the four previously called (ver. 11, where see the note).

29. And Levi made him a great feast (Greek, *reception*) **in his own** (omit, *own*) **house.** This itself shows that he did not abandon his place recklessly, and without time to faithfully close up his affairs. It appears that he was a man of means, so far as to own a house, and to be able to entertain a large company in it. The feast was made by him in honor of the man who had, he felt, honored and blest him; while it gave opportunity, also, to many of his own class to become acquainted with Jesus, and feel the power of his influence. **A great company** (*multitude*) **of publicans and of others.** Recall the number of towns, the denseness of population, and abundance of traffic about the lake (**ver. 1 f.**), and it will not seem strange that a **multitude** (Greek, *a crowd*) of revenue officers could be summoned at short notice.— **And of others**—these could not have been respectable people in the eyes of strict Jews; but we do not know how far the more mixed population of "Galilee of the Gentiles" might generally so view them. Matthew and Mark express directly the Jewish sentiment—calling them "sinners."

30. But their scribes and Pharisees— *i. e.,* those who lived among that people.

31 And Jesus answering said unto them, They that are whole need not a physician; but they that are sick. 32 ᵃI came not to call the righteous, but sinners to repentance. 33 And they said unto him, ᵇWhy do the disciples of John fast often, and make prayers, and likewise *the disciples* of the Pharisees; but thine eat and drink?

31 and drink with the publicans and sinners? And Jesus answering said unto them, They that are whole have 32 no need of a physician; but they that are sick. I am not come to call the righteous but sinners to repentance. 33 And they said unto him, The disciples of John fast often, and make supplications; likewise also the *disciples* of the Pharisees; but thine eat and drink.

a Matt. 9: 13; 1 Tim. 1: 15....b Matt. 9: 14; Matt. 2: 18.

This is as likely to be the intended meaning as that given in the Revision—*the Pharisees and their scribes*—there is room for doubt.—**Murmured against his disciples** —with whom they felt more free than with the Master; but it was he of whom they complained (Mark 2: 16). It was enough that our Lord would hold any intercourse with such people; but that he **sat down with them** at the table, namely, to eat with them, greatly aggravated the offence. (Compare the charges against Peter, Acts 11: 3.)

31. Jesus answering said—speaking in place of the disciples whom they had addressed. **They that are whole**—in sound health—**need not a physician; but they that are sick.** This self-evident proposition contains the substance of his reply in a form so impersonal as neither to excite nor allow any debate. If Jesus is a Soul Physician, they cannot deny that his place is with the morally diseased. He claims that that was his office.

32. I came not (*am not come*) **to call the righteous, but sinners to repentance. Righteous** is without the article, as well as **sinners**, in the original equivalent to "righteous persons." This interprets the preceding maxim so as to complete the Saviour's defence. In the sphere of his curative operation, **sinners**—represented by the publicans and their associates—are **the sick; repentance**, the restoration to health which he effects. His mission to the world contemplates no other objects. We need suppose no sarcasm upon the Pharisees in the mention of **righteous** persons, any more than an intention to ascribe to them true righteousness. **Righteous** are mentioned by contrast simply to set forth more clearly the character to which he, as a Saviour, brings blessing. There is place for him only where there is sin—moral ruin, the germs of eternal death. If his opposers had complained of his companying with the publicans, *rather than with them*, they might have felt a sting in his reply. As it was, he set forth a precious truth, which might reach their hearts, too— if not utterly incorrigible—and which, as it gave encouragement to the vile and outcast of that day, has been the balm of healing to thousands in every age who realized that they were sick through sin.

33-39. EXPLANATION ABOUT FASTING Matt. 9: 14-17; Mark 2: 18-22. There is nothing in Luke's account here to hinder our supposing that what follows belongs, chronologically, with the preceding event. Christ's indifference to their ceremonial distinctions of caste, may have attracted attention to his neglect of their ritual fasting. Yet we cannot be sure, from the mere juxtaposition in the narrative, that this was so.

33. And they (indefinite for "people," doubtless, of the Pharisaic sort), **said unto them, The disciples** [omitting **why,** because it is not found in the best supported text.—A. H.] **of John fast often, and make prayers** (*or supplications*), **and likewise the disciples of the Pharisees.** Fasting was enjoined in the law of Moses only as a national duty, and that only for one day in the year—the day of atonement. Individuals fasted voluntarily throughout their history, in emergencies which made it natural. Prophets sometimes called the whole people to fast, with prayers and acts of humiliation, to avert calamities and propitiate God. After the cessation of prophecy, the hierarchical authorities established, in commemoration of national afflictions, successively, several annual fasts; and in the later growth of hard ceremonialism and work-righteousness, two weekly fasts—on Mondays and Thursdays— had been made a necessity for all who would cultivate conspicuous godliness. John the Baptist seems, in this respect, to have gone with the prevailing tendency to the uttermost. From the connexion in which he had placed himself with Jesus, the people may have been more struck with the laxness of the latter. They mention first, at all events, the discrepancy between his practice and that encouraged by John, then that of the Phari-

34 And he said unto them, Can ye make the children of the bridechamber fast, while the bridegroom is with them?
35 But the days will come, when the bridegroom shall be taken away from them, and then shall they fast in those days.
36 *And he spake also a parable unto them; No man putteth a piece of a new garment upon an old; if otherwise, then both the new maketh a rent, and the piece that was *taken* out of the new agreeth not with the old.

34 And Jesus said unto them, Can ye make the sons of the bridechamber fast, while the bridegroom is with them? 35 But the days will come; and when the bridegroom shall be taken away from them, then will they 36 fast in those days. And he spake also a parable unto them; No man rendeth a piece from a new garment and putteth it upon an old garment; else he will rend the new, and also the piece from the new will not

a Matt. 9: 16, 17; Mark 2: 21, 22.

sees. We see here that adherents of John, his scholars, or disciples, maintained a separate standing after the "one mightier than he" had come, and he himself had been laid aside from work. We shall meet with them once or twice more; and the fact of their continuance as John's disciples, is of interest in connexion with the incidents in Acts 19: 6.—**The disciples of the Pharisees,** were those who were in study and training for membership in their sect, and, perhaps, included those who went with them, mainly, in principle and practice, without bearing their name. John's disciples, we see, made the days of fasting occasions of special prayer—*supplications*—which would differ in aim and spirit from those of the Pharisees, if, as would appear, these also joined prayers with fasting. Such being the type of piety then most highly approved, it was natural that Christ's total neglect of their traditional observances should appear to many strange and shocking. **And he** (Jesus) **said unto them,** speaking in the manner of patient, even tender, instruction. **Can ye make the children** (*sons*) **of the bridechamber fast while the bridegroom is with them? The** *sons* **of the bridechamber** are intimate friends of the bridegroom—his "groomsmen" who, after escorting the bride to her new home, remained in attendance throughout the feast, which might, in more eminent families, last seven days. The whole time was a season of joy and hilarity. To practice fasting under such circumstances, the Saviour says, is impossible. It would be a monstrous impropriety. Fasting is not consistent with a joyous state of mind.

35. But the days will come (omit the article before *days*), *but days will come*. Here the Saviour pauses, as if musing on the bereavement and sadness of the time, which he foresees, and begins anew (inserting *and* before *when* of the Common Version): (*and*, **when**

the bridegroom shall be taken away from them, then shall (*will*) **they fast.** In this Jesus makes himself the bridegroom who has come to take as a bride the kingdom given him by his Father, and whom the disciples wait upon in this relation. But this wedding will be interrupted in the progress of the feast; he, the chief personage, will be taken from the company by violence; and, in the sorrow of his bereaved friends, fasting will find its place.

The teaching condensed in this illustration is, that in his kingdom fasting is for Christ's disciples a voluntary thing, which may be useful in its season, and will be practiced by them spontaneously, as an aid to devotion, when they mourn the absence of their Lord.

36. And he spake also a parable unto them—to illustrate, as would appear, the radical incompatibility between the prevailing system of proscriptive, compulsory, external service to God, and the free heart-worship which he had come to introduce. **No man putteth a piece from an old garment,** etc. Through this verse the textual evidence constrains us to adopt the rendering of the Revision. *No one rendeth a piece from a new garment*—(cloak)—*and putteth it on an old garment*—(cloak, etc). The language represents a man as *tearing* a piece out of a new cloak to patch an old one. In doing this he has torn and mutilated the new, and fails to match the old. The *piece* in the first clause becomes equivalent to "a patch" in the last. "Patch," indeed, is the natural signification of the word.—The **new garment,** or cloak, stands for the gospel system of religion, consisting essentially in the worship of the Father in spirit and in truth, as contrasted with the old system, then in practice, of salvation by outward works. The **piece** of the former may be any particular privilege of the New Testament, as, for example, freedom in the matter of fasting. Putting this on the old system, would be the re-

37 And no man putteth new wine into old bottles; else the new wine will burst the bottles, and be spilled, and the bottles shall perish.
38 But new wine must be put into new bottles; and both are preserved.
39 No man also having drunk old *wine* straightway desireth new; for he saith, The old is better.

37 agree with the old. And no man putteth new wine into old ¹wine-skins; else the new wine will burst the skins, and itself will be spilled, and the skins will perish. But new wine must be put into fresh wine-
38
39 skins. And no man having drunk old *wine* desireth new: for he saith, The old is ¹good.

CHAPTER VI.

AND ª it came to pass on the second sabbath after the first, that he went through the corn fields; and his disciples plucked the ears of corn, and did eat, rubbing them in their hands.

1 Now it came to pass on a ²sabbath, that he was going through the cornfields; and his disciples plucked the ears of corn, and did eat, rubbing them

a Matt. 12: 1; Mark 2: 23.——Many ancient authorities read, *better*....2 Many ancient authorities insert, *second-first*.

quiring of those who still held to that system in other respects, to adopt this view and practice. It would be taking a part of the gospel out of its proper relations, and showing it in glaring incongruity with all the stiffness and legality round about it. Thorough repentance, and sincere faith in the gospel, were, in short, pre-requisite to the possession of any one of the peculiar prerogatives of the Christian character.

37. And no man putteth new wine into old bottles. The **bottles** referred to were skins of the smaller animals, drawn off skillfully, so as to cause no ruptures except at the neck and above the feet. These skins, properly tanned and tied up tight, except one aperture, are still used in the East, as they then were, for holding and transporting water, milk, wine, and other liquids. The only objection to the name "wine skins," of the Revision, is that they were not designed specifically for wine. The Saviour now alludes to what must have been another familiar fact of every-day life. These skins, with use, would become brittle; and the expansion of gases in the fermentation of new wine, would be very likely to burst them sooner than if they were fresh.

38. So new wine would require **new bottles** (fresh skins). Even these, evidently, could not be tightly closed on new wine till fermentation was well advanced. In this the **new wine** means the free, filial spirit and expansive energy of the new kingdom; the **old bottles**, the men of legal, ceremonial piety, represented by John's disciples, and the more devout Pharisees. They cannot, while standing on the ground of a national ritualistic devotion, receive the proper conception, still less can they cherish the true spirit of the gospel. This demands men who have been "born again," by a fundamental transformation of views, sentiments, and principles of life.

39. The Saviour does not here pass a sweeping condemnation on the old piety which had been brought to his notice in contrast with his own. He does not deny that it also had an excellence for its time: but was different from the gospel, and incompatible with it. It must be entirely given up, in principle, to make way for the gospel. Yet he can understand the reluctance of the doubting and perplexed to make an instant and radical change of view and practice. Hence the next illustration. **No man also (and no man) having drunk old wine,** etc. **The old is better** (*good*); that is, palatable, pleasant to the taste (χρηστός). Our Saviour could appreciate the force of hereditary belief, the prejudices in favor of sacred custom, the memories of religious attainments won, and of devout experiences enjoyed, through the legitimate use of the Mosaic system. Take the case of John's disciples—more excusable, certainly, for doubt as to his Messianic claims than their Master, whom yet he was more than ready to excuse (7: 24 ff.). We may see that it deeply, tenderly engaged his thought. He would regret that the better tendency in them did not prevail, would hope that it might grow stronger; but he saw how natural it was that they should hesitate to break away from all the outward pomp and ceremonial of religion—a burdensome and crushing, but time-hallowed ritual, which had descended to them from Ezra and from Moses, and in the midst of which they supposed that heroes and prophets and saints had lived and died.

Ch. 6. 1-5. THE SON OF MAN LORD OF THE SABBATH.

1. It came to pass on the second sabbath after the first—more exactly, *a second-first Sabbath*. The word so translated is not met with elsewhere in Greek, except in allusion to this passage; nor has any place in Jewish literature been cited where the idea is expressed. Hence a grand field for speculation; and abundant ingenuity has been exercised to conceive of a series of Sabbaths, such that some one in it might naturally be called the "second-first." Nothing worthy of confidence has resulted. More than a dozen schemes, probably, have been proposed, according to each of which, if we *suppose* that a certain Sabbath was called "first," a certain other might be known as "second-first." It is not worth while to repeat them. The case is precisely as if an English writer should now, without the slightest explanation, mention a second-first Sunday; and people should set themselves, centuries afterwards, to make out what Sunday he meant. Of course, the case might be such that readers at the time and place of writing would readily perceive the sense, and the clue be entirely lost afterward. This is not very probable in the case before us, seeing that the difficulty was noticed so early that the solution would then have been discoverable.

If we might unhesitatingly follow the Revision, we should be at once relieved of embarrassment. That agrees with excellent authority of manuscripts and versions; but they are liable to suspicion as being possibly attempts to obviate a great perplexity by leaving out the troublesome word. Still, we do not wonder that the Revisers, with the support of Tregelles, and Westcott and Hort's text, inclined rather to the view that the strange adjective had crept in by mistake. A common conjecture has been that some one early put in the margin of his copy, at this place, "first," with reference to the "other sabbath" in ver. 6; and that, then, he or some other one, noticing the mention of a Sabbath in 4: 31, corrected by writing "second." So it stands in some manuscripts, "second" "first." As this would be nonsense, a copyist may easily have combined them so as to make a possible sense, as ignorant, probably, as we are, how it was to be understood. We know that marginal notes, such as here supposed, were transferred to the text by copyists who believed them to have been omissions in the previous copy. And it is worthy of notice what evidence of the care of transcribers, in setting down just what they found, is afforded by the retention in so many manuscripts of this perplexing word. Tischendorf had dropped it; but in his last edition restored it, in spite of the authority of his favorite Sinaitic Manuscript. The question of its genuineness remains doubtful, but with as strong reason as we can often have that a mistake had crept into the text, as early as our first copies.

The fact that they were plucking heads of ripe, or nearly ripe, grain on this day, may guide us to the season of the year in which it fell. If we knew whether the grain was barley (ripe in Judea at the Passover), or wheat (offered in the temple at the Feast of Pentecost), and if we knew just how the times of ripening in the sultry Plain of Gennesaret compared with that on the hills of Judea, we could come very near it. We may thus set aside several of the conjectures which have been hazarded; and, if obliged to guess, we might say, with many, that, as the Feast of Pentecost came seven weeks after the paschal Sabbath, the seven *ordinary* Sabbaths of those weeks would probably be known as the first, second, third, etc., and that, when the Passover Sabbath came on a Friday, that also might be called the first, making the ordinary weekly Sabbath a second-first. Here every one may take what seems to him best. Westcott and Hort (Appendix, p. 58) cite Jerome on this passage, as saying (we translate): "A brazen face often interprets what it does not know, and, when it has persuaded others, assumes that it itself also does know. When I once asked my teacher, Gregory Nazianzen, to explain what the 'second first Sabbath in Luke' meant, he playfully replied, 'I will teach you about that in the church, where, while all the people applaud me, you will be obliged, against your will, to know what you know not, or, at least, if you alone keep silence, you alone will be set down as a fool.'" (Ep. 52, p. 263).

He went (equivalent to *was going*) **through the corn fields**—(the article may be omitted, and **corn fields** must, of course, be understood in America in the sense of grain-fields of barley or wheat). **His disciples plucked the ears of corn** (*heads of grain*) **and did eat, rubbing.** The disciples only appear to have been hungry (Matt. 12:1), and took of the grain. It shows us to what fare our blessed Saviour and his chosen friends were sometimes reduced. Their

2 And certain of the Pharisees said unto them, Why do ye that *which is not lawful to do on the sabbath days?
3 And Jesus answering them said, Have ye not read so much as this, *what David did, when himself was a hungered, and they which were with him;
4 How he went into the house of God, and did take and eat the shewbread, and gave also to them that were with him; *which it is not lawful to eat but for the priests alone?
5 And he said unto them, That the Son of man is Lord also of the sabbath.

2 in their hands. But certain of the Pharisees said, Why do ye that which is not lawful to do on the 3 sabbath day? And Jesus answering them said, Have ye not read even this, what David did, when he was 4 an hungred, he, and they that were with him; how he entered into the house of God, and did take and eat the shewbread, and gave also to them that were with him; which it is not lawful to eat, save for the 5 priests alone? And he said unto them, The Son of man is lord of the sabbath.

a Ex. 20: 10....b 1 Sam. 21: 6....c Lev. 24: 9.

taking the grain thus, "with the hand, and not with the sickle," was perfectly warranted by the law (Deut. 23:25). The grain, when ready to harvest, would require no "labor" in shelling it out with their hands.

2. Certain of the Pharisees—whom we shall find henceforth on the alert to detect something criminal in Jesus—were, in some manner, watching now. **That which is not lawful to do on the sabbath days**—*day* (comp. on 4: 31). They probably included both the plucking and the shelling out in the alleged violation of the Sabbath. This they could do consistently with the oppressive tendency of the Rabbis to multiply and sharpen the specific application of the Mosaic laws, and especially of the important law of the Sabbath. Thus they had, of course, proscribed reaping and threshing grain, and then had found picking off ears to be a kind of reaping, and rubbing out the grains a kind of threshing, both equally prohibited. If the *walking* of the Saviour had been objected to, we should probably have had a special mention of that; so their journey must have been a short one.

3. Have ye not read so much as this—among the many Scriptural proofs of the innocence of my conduct. The verb is a preterit—*Did ye not even read?* Mark, with a more decided shade of irony, "Did ye never?" Surely, this should have attracted the attention of such zealous devotees of the law. **What** (equivalent to, *that*) **David did when himself was a hungered** (*was hungry*), **and they that were with him?** (See 1 Sam. 21: 3-6, for the history). He puts himself parallel to David, and his disciples to the companions of David.

4. How he went into the house of God —this was the successor to the original tabernacle, the temporary scene of divine worship, which was then at Nob. **Shewbread**—Hebrew, "bread of the face," "presentation bread," which stood constantly before the face of Jehovah, in the Holy Place in his house. It is called also in the Hebrew, "bread of setting forth," or "of array" (1 Chron. 9: 32; Neh. 10: 33); and here in Luke (literally) "the loaves of the setting forth," in allusion to the formal ranging of the twelve loaves, on the Table of Shewbread, in two rows (or piles) of six each.—**Which** (*loaves*) **it is not lawful to eat, but for the priests alone?** When the new loaves were placed there each Sabbath, they were to remain sacred to the Lord until replaced the next Sabbath. Then they fell to the lot of the priest, as representing him, but could be eaten by no other person (Lev. 24: 5, 6, 9; Comp. 21: 22). The Saviour finds a parallel to his own case in the fact that David violated the letter of the law in eating, and letting his friends eat, what was forbidden to any but the priests. The language of 1 Sam. (21:6) implies, moreover, that he did this on a Sabbath; "for the shewbread was taken away from before the Lord, to put that bread, in the day when it was taken away," and that was a Sabbath. (So Farrar on the passage).

5. Having shown by the example of David, that the ceremonial law must give place to the claims of necessity and mercy, the positive to the moral in God's requirements (Matt. 12:7), he goes further. The Son of man (see on 5: 24), is Lord also (or *even*) of the sabbath. The purport of this in this connexion must be that his judgment as to what is right on the Sabbath warrants his disciples, and justifies his disciples in what they were doing. As he is the source of authority for the Sabbath, his authority forestalls all questions of the Pharisees and others. This need not mean that he could, by his *fiat*, make right what the Sabbath command had specifically forbidden, to one under his circumstances, but that what he saw fit to do, or allow others to do, could not have been specifically forbidden

6 ᵃ And it came to pass also on another sabbath, that he entered into the synagogue and taught; and there was a man whose right hand was withered.
7 And the scribes and Pharisees watched him, whether he would heal on the sabbath day; that they might find an accusation against him.
8 But he knew their thoughts, and said to the man which had the withered hand, Rise up, and stand forth in the midst. And he arose and stood forth.
9 Then said Jesus unto them, I will ask you one thing: Is it lawful on the sabbath days to do good or to do evil? to save life or to destroy it?

6 And it came to pass on another sabbath, that he entered into the synagogue and taught: and there was
7 a man there, and his right hand was withered. And the scribes and the Pharisees watched him, whether he would heal on the sabbath; that they might find
8 how to accuse him. But he knew their thoughts; and he said to the man that had his hand withered, Rise up, and stand forth in the midst. And he arose
9 and stood forth. And Jesus said unto them, I ask you, Is it lawful on the sabbath to do good, or to do

ᵃ Matt. 12:9; Mark 3:1; see ch. 13:14; 14:3; John 9:16.

to those in their circumstances. From his practice and permission, the true idea of the Sabbath in his time was to be derived.

It will be noticed that for this occasion, at least, Christ puts the law of the Sabbath on the same footing as that of the shew-bread. Could he have done this of the necessarily and absolutely moral commandments? The question that has been raised, whether the Lord here gave any intimation of the abrogation of the Sabbath, must be answered in the negative, except as it may have suggested the abrogation *in fulfillment* of the whole Mosaic law. Considering how prominently the people then ranked the law of the Sabbath, they could not fail to apply what he said of this to their whole system. It was all, he maintained, subject to his lordship, and had no authority but what he allowed. And this was, beyond all question, to claim the rank of the Messiah.

6-11. A MIRACLE OF HEALING ON THE SABBATH. Parallels — Matthew 12: 9-14; Mark 3: 1-6.—**On another Sabbath.** From Matthew and Mark, we learn that the event took place on a Sabbath. Luke states that it was a different Sabbath from that just before mentioned. How long after the other, is not stated. It may have been very soon, or the succession here may have been designed to multiply evidences of Christ's superiority to the merely ritual requirements (fasting; minute scruples about the Sabbath) of the Pharisaic religion.—**He entered into the synagogue**—that, namely, of the place where he then was.—**Whose** (literally, *and his*) **right hand was withered** — emaciated (from palsy?) and useless. Being his right hand, it was a great affliction to him, and rendered his such a case as all knew would appeal strongly to the sympathy of our Lord. What a testimony was in their expectation!

7. **And the scribes and** (*the*) **Pharisees** —(were watching)—**him**—while he was teaching, to see **whether he would heal on the sabbath.** The Received Greek text says, "will heal"; the critically corrected text, *heals;* equivalent to makes a practice of healing. Even this would be a violation of their hair-splitting prohibitions of liberty on that day.—**That they might find an accusation against him.** How serious an accusation it would be, appears from the fact that the Jews in Jerusalem for this reason "persecuted Jesus, and sought to slay him, because he had done these things (healed the impotent man) on the Sabbath day" (John 5:16).

8. **But he** (*he himself*) **knew their thoughts**—(*reasonings*)—all those machinations which aimed to catch him in the trap of their absurd and cruel traditions, and to put him to death. He knew them and determined to meet them boldly, and contrast with their anxious and hypocritical rules for fettering the Sabbath, the freedom of a vivifying love. —**And he arose and stood.** The word **forth** is an addition to the Greek, proper before, but not in this clause. Forth from the seats of the meeting-house, at the command of our Saviour, came the poor man out into the open space, and stood, observed by all, not knowing what to expect, while Jesus exposed the hearts of their religious leaders, his adversaries.

9. **I will ask you**—(omit **will** and **one thing**)—thus calmly engaging their attention and that of the audience, while he makes them, tacitly or openly, confess that he is beneficently right, and they murderously wrong (that is, to benefit or to harm). **To do good or to do evil?** What is the real use and divine intent of the Sabbath? But why does the Saviour propose and repeat an alternative question? Why speak of doing evil, *i. e.*, harm? And of killing? Did any one maintain that it was lawful to do this; or that one

10 And looking round about upon them all, he said unto the man, Stretch forth thy hand. And he did so: and his hand was restored whole as the other.
11 And they were filled with madness; and communed one with another what they might do to Jesus.
12 *And it came to pass in those days, that he went out into a mountain to pray, and continued all night in prayer to God.

10 harm? to save a life, or to destroy it? And he looked round about on them all, and said unto him, Stretch forth thy hand. And he did so: and his hand was restored.
11 But they were filled with ¹madness; and communed one with another what they might do to Jesus.
12 And it came to pass in these days, that he went out into the mountain to pray; and he continued all night

a Matt. 14 : 23.——1 Or. *foolishness.*

must do it if he did not do what was good and helpful? Some have supposed that he meant "I must do one or the other. To heal this poor man's hand, by which he earns his livelihood, is in effect to save his life; and in effect I not only harm him, but destroy his life by failing to heal him. This, however, though the view is sustained by Godet, seems forced and quibbling. It would afford no answer to their probable argument that the work of mercy could wait till the next day; nor does it account for the "madness" which his question excited in their breasts. Better refer one branch of the alternative in both questions to him, the other to his enemies. I propose to do a good thing, and to save a life by restoring to this man the ability to work, and by arresting the spread of his malady; you are scheming even to kill me (comp. John 5: 16); a most wicked deed. Which of us is to be condemned? There was no reply.

10. And looking round about upon them all—very deliberately, so as to note the expression of every one; and with a look, no doubt, of triumphant confidence, but in which there was mingled anger against his malignant adversaries, and sorrow for the hardness of their hearts (Mark 3: 5).—**He said unto the man** (Revision, *unto him*), **Stretch forth thy hand.** He would have everything open and above board. There should be no room for allegations of jugglery or deception of any kind. The healing change was to take place in the eyes of the congregation. This preliminary act might involve an exercise of faith, even the attempt to raise his disabled hand; yet it is not said that the malady impaired the power of his arm.—**And he did so.** His hand was raised in the presence of them all, a withered hand.—**And his hand was restored**—not "had been" restored, but at that moment underwent the change. They saw it withered until a certain moment; the next moment it was sound and well—"whole as the other," in Matthew's account, which in some copies of the text is added

here. The Revision omits it, with the support of excellent authority. Matthew's phrase suggests that the man may have held up the other hand, also, to view, to show that they were both alike.

11. And they—the scribes and Pharisees—**were filled with madness**—primarily, *dementia,* which may be either "lack of reason," "folly," "insanity," or, as we often call it now, **madness**, expressing itself in raving efforts to harm Jesus.—**And communed** (*talked*) **one with another what** (*as to what*) **they might do to Jesus.** Here, first, we find the criticism of the Pharisees ripened into a hatred which would never rest until it had found a pretext and means to destroy him. The position of freedom which he had now taken toward the traditions concerning Sabbath observance, implying as it did supreme contempt for all their paltry "hedges" about the genuine law, was tantamount to a claim to the Messiahship, and this to a declaration that *they* must retire from their leadership of the people, with all its honors and emoluments.

12-19. Appointment of Twelve Apostles.—Parallels—Matt. 12: 15; 10: 2-4; 4: 24, 25; Mark 3: 7-19.

From the statements of Matthew and Mark, following the preceding narrative, it appears that, when he perceived the malice of his adversaries, our Saviour retired from their neighborhood to the border of the lake. There his fame soon drew great multitudes around, and scenes were frequent such as are described in verses 17-19 of the present chapter.

12. It came to pass in those days. Luke points to the period when the persecution of the Master had become manifest in its murderous malignity, proving the need of preparation for the continuance of his cause when this hostility should have wrought its deadly work. They were days, too, when the growing multitudes who flocked to him, to see and hear, and be healed, made it neces-

13 And when it was day, he called *unto him* his disciples: "and of them he chose twelve, whom also he named apostles;

13 In prayer to God. And when it was day, he called his disciples: and he chose from them twelve, whom also

a Matt. 10:1.

sary that he should have assistance in the present necessary labors. It was under such circumstances **that he went into a** (*the*) **mountain to pray.** His resorting to the **mountain**—equivalent to *wilderness* (5:16);—was for the sake of more complete retirement than he could command in the populous flat lands near the sea. What particular mountain is intended has been much debated, and without any certain conclusion. It seems not unlikely that, in contrast with the lake shore, the elevated tract which, as we have seen (5:1), almost everywhere rises back of it, might be called the mountain, although Meyer denies that *the mountain* (τὸ ὄρος) can be taken in that sense as equivalent to the German *Gebirge*, "mountain region." We do not see how it could help meaning just that, often, in the mouths of the people below. Even if we must understand it of a particular elevation, it would be only a peak, or knob, rising out of the general mountain surface. Such a knoll, or a pair of them, was fixed upon, as early as the time of the Crusades—Stanley, *Sinai and Palestine;* but Jerome had indicated the same opinion (Eph. 4:1) ad Marcel—as being so suitable to the indications of locality in the Gospels, as to deserve to have been the scene of the Sermon on the Mount; and so it has been generally recognized in modern times as the Mount of the Beatitudes. The Arabs call it *Karun Hattin*, horns of Hattin, as rising from the edge of the Plain of Hattin. It is two or three miles in a direct line, southwest of Tell Hum (Capernaum?). On the plateau, he retired at night, from his disciples to some higher point, such as one of the horns of Hattin, **to pray, and continued all night in prayer to God.** Luke is, we have already seen, more particular than the other Evangelists to mention instances of this felt human need and privilege on the part of Jesus, connecting each with some obvious emergency in his life. The choice of his apostles was such an emergency now. He had gathered about him a large company of disciples, or scholars, pupils; but what twelve of them would be most competent for the high and peculiar service for which he must now provide?

Eternal consequences depended on the decision. The prosperity and possible defeat of his cause hung in the balance. The fate of men to the latest ages would be determined by his choice. It is easy, and perhaps not irreverent, to imagine our Saviour bowed before his Father then, under the blue sky, and mentioning, one by one, the men of whom he thought as possibly suitable for the first missionary work.

The whole night was spent in this solemn communion with the Father; and only with the morning dawn was he ready for the work of the day.

13. And when it was day—with the early streaks of morning, according to the habits of that country, to begin work with the opening light—**he called his disciples**—(omitting **unto him**, Revision)—that is, the company that in a general sense bore that name. Did they probably suspect his object, or what consequences were involved in this convocation? If they did suspect, what emotions must have filled their minds while waiting in the Master's presence! We have only to suppose that the statement of Matthew (5:1), "He went up into the mountain," refers to his ascent of the plateau the night before; and that he omits all mention of the further retirement to a higher hill, bringing in the designation of the twelve in a different connection (10:3, 4), and all appearance of discrepancy between Matthew and Luke is cleared away.—**And of them he chose twelve.** The number was in all probability fixed with reference to the twelve tribes of Israel. The Teacher chose them, as we see, with great care and discrimination, guided by his previous observation of their capacities, and with the light given in answer to his prayers. Those who were not taken for the peculiar service now desired, were not rejected for other duties of discipleship, but were, by the very omission distinctly confirmed in these.—**Whom also he named apostles.** Before they had borne the name of "disciples" only, in common with all the rest; now they took the additional title appropriate to their specific function—APOSTLES. This name (equivalent to missionaries), while perfectly consistent with their vocation, "that

14 Simon, (*a* whom he also named Peter,) and Andrew his brother, James and John, Philip and Bartholomew, 15 Matthew and Thomas, James the *son* of Alpheus, and Simon called Zelotes,

14 he named apostles; Simon, whom he also named Peter, and Andrew his brother, and James and John, 15 and Philip and Bartholomew, and Matthew and Thomas, and James *the* son of Alpheus, and Simon

a John 1: 42.

they might be with him" (Mark 3: 14), expresses the object of that intimacy, namely, that he might send them forth on occasions, to act in his stead, and ultimately to replace his visible agency on the earth. The full intent of their calling is given (Mark 3: 14, 15).

14. Simon, who is named first in all the four catalogues of the twelve—**whom he also named Peter**—thus, apparently, first applying to him the designation which had been predicted on his first visit to Christ at the Jordan (John 1: 42). Some think, however, that the surname was added at a subsequent period, on occasion of Peter's confession (Matt. 16: 18), and is here spoken of as then given. The solemn roll-call went on, not necessarily in the precise order of either of the recorded lists. It could not have been in the order of all, as they differ among themselves, in minute particulars, while preserving in the main a remarkable agreement. We seem to see that, as the twelve were selected out of the mass of the disciples, so there was a discrimination among them into three groups of four names, according to the Saviour's estimate of them in some respect.—**And Andrew his brother.** He had been first in recognizing Jesus as the Lamb of God, according to the instruction of his previous master, John the Baptist, and was the means of bringing his brother Simon to the Lord (John 1: 35, 42). Perhaps his conversion of his brother was the most important service to the cause of Christ which he ever rendered, and may have been the chief reason why, in Matthew and Luke, he stands next to Peter on the roll (comp. Mark 3: 25; Acts 1: 13). [Is it certain that Simon was "converted," in the present sense of that word, by Andrew? Is it not more probable that both these had been baptized by John, "confessing their sins," and prepared in heart to follow the Christ as soon as he should be made known to them? That they were "waiting for the consolation of Israel"? If so, Andrew had an easy task to lead Simon to Jesus. (Comp. John 1: 40, 41, and notes on that passage).—A. H.]—**James and John,** sons of Zebedee. *James* is mentioned first, as is plausibly supposed, on account of age.

John was, beyond reasonable doubt, the unnamed one of the two that stood with John the Baptist, when the latter pointed out Jesus as the Messiah (John 1: 40), and who then sought the company of Christ. We have no clear evidence that James also had seen him before the memorable draught of fishes (Luke 6: 1, 11). These four are grouped (Andrew sometimes last) as the first quaternion, whenever the names of the twelve are recited. Three of them were repeatedly distinguished by the special intimacy of Jesus at interesting crises of his history.—**Philip and Bartholomew.** We read (John 1, 43) that after Andrew, John, and Peter had found Jesus, he (Jesus) next findeth Philip, whose name also here appears among the twelve. Then we are told (ver. 45) that Peter found Nathanael, in a way so similar to the case of Andrew and Peter, as to suggest that these two also may have been brothers. At least it is hard for us to think, from the description of Nathanael, then, that he was not marked for an apostle. And in John 21: 2, we do find him named among several apostles as though he certainly was one of them. But in his natural place on the lists of names we find everywhere Bartholomew, without the slightest clew to his origin, the circumstances of his call, or to any incident of his discipleship. Something of this we naturally expect concerning one standing so high in the series of names. For such reasons, and further because the designation here given is merely a Hebrew patronymic, equivalent to son of Tolmai, the greatly prevalent opinion has been that his real personal name was Nathanael.

15. Matthew (Levi, the publican), **and Thomas,** the despondent doubter (John 20: 25), who gained for us a special proof of our Lord's resurrection (ver. 28). These make up the second quaternion, of which Philip always comes first, with some changing of the position of all the other three. **James the son of Alpheus,** heads the third group. He is, with good reason, supposed to be the one called "James the less"—rather, "the little" (Mark 15: 40), and was probably overseer of the Church in Jerusalem, after the murder of

H

16 And Judas *the brother* of James, and Judas Iscariot, which also was the traitor.
17 And he came down with them, and stood in the plain, and the company of his disciples, *b* and a great multitude of people out of all Judea and Jerusalem, and from the sea coast of Tyre and Sidon, which came to hear him, and to be healed of their diseases;

16 who was called the Zealot, and Judas the [1] *son* of James, and Judas Iscariot, who became a traitor; and he came down with them, and stood on a level place, and a great multitude of his disciples, and a great number of the people from all Judæa and Jerusalem, and the sea coast of Tyre and Sidon, who came to

a Jude 1....*b* Matt. 4:25; Mark 3:7.——[1] Or, *brother*. See Jude 1.

James, son of Zebedee. His father was probably not the Alpheus, father of Levi (Matthew), mentioned (Mark 2:14). (See Hackett, in Smith's B. D., p. 73). **Simon called Zelotes.** The commonness of his name made necessary a distinguishing epithet. Zelotes, meant a zealot, and was given to him, doubtless, because he had belonged to that party of fanatical patriots, who, since the days of the Maccabees, had burned with a flagrant hatred of foreign domination. They were on the alert for every possible opportunity of resistance and insurrection, and by their mad excesses contributed much, at a later period, to the miseries of the capture of Jerusalem by Titus. The designation "Canaæan" (not "Cananite") in Matthew and Mark, is the Aramæan equivalent to Zelotes.

16. And Judas the brother (rather, *the son*) **of James.** Judas (Greek for Judah) was one of the most common of Jewish names. *The son* is not expressed in the Greek; but the ellipsis in such cases is so uniformly thus, that we should need stronger proof that the relationship was different than can be drawn from Jude 1:1, to warrant our substituting **brother** here. His place in the catalogue of Matthew is occupied by Lebbaeus, and in that of Mark by Thaddaeus, warranting the belief that in that age of various names, he was so differently called, perhaps at different times and in different relations. His father is likely to have been the James last mentioned above [? A. H.].—**And Judas Iscariot, which also was the traitor**—rather, *who became* (turned out) *a traitor*. This name naturally stands last in all enumerations, as Peter's first. His surname is probably the Greek pronunciation of *ish Kerioth*, "man of Kerioth," a town mentioned in Joshua 15:25. Of the other apostles, we are not told here what they did; and, with the exception of Peter, James, and John, no record is left to us of more than some little incident—a question asked, a word or two spoken. Even of the excepted three, **their whole** certain history is given in the

New Testament. Without fame, they taught and toiled; lost individually in the body of "the apostles." Known unto God only were the details and the abundance of their labors, and the poignancy of their sufferings, cheerfully borne FOR THAT NAME. Their record is on high. But Judas, the last on the list, is here commemorated as the author of a deed which no other companion of Christ could fail to recall with a shudder, whenever his name was repeated; he "became a traitor." Why Jesus should have chosen him as one of his messengers, it may be appropriate to consider at a later period. Had we seen him at this point, he would probably have seemed specially likely to be useful in certain respects; and, generally, of as fair a promise as any of the twelve.

17-19. WORKS OF MERCY, PRELIMINARY TO THE SERMON ON THE MOUNT.

17. And he came down with them, and stood in the plain (rather, *a level place*). As this last clause is expressed in the Common Version, we must, in order to avoid distinct contradiction with Matthew 5:1, understand the discourse which follows, against all the preponderating reasons to the contrary, to be different from the one in Matthew. But the Revision gives the exact and proper rendering of our verse—not **in the plain**, as opposed to "on a mountain," but *on a level place* (ἐπὶ τόπου πεδινοῦ), which might be on a mountain; and, indeed, necessarily implies comparison with hilly land. The "horns of Hattin," previously described, perfectly meet the conditions here, and so might a variety of other places on that high, but very uneven table-land west of the Sea of Galilee. Jesus, having gone up, the previous day, on the elevated and solitary plateau, as Matthew describes, had passed the night on a higher summit, whither he had called his disciples, we know not how many; and, after choosing out the twelve apostles, now came down and stood, that is, occupied a position, on the level surface of the plateau, which, travelers say, would accommodate

18 And they that were vexed with unclean spirits: and they were healed.
19 And the whole multitude a sought to touch him: for b there went virtue out of him, and healed them all.

18 hear him, and to be healed of their diseases; and they that were troubled with unclean spirits were healed.
19 And all the multitude sought to touch him: for power came forth from him, and healed them all.

a Matt. 14: 36....b Mark 5: 30; ch. 8: 46.

some two thousand men. The plateau was 1,000 feet higher than the lake. The *Kurun* ridge was elevated above the plateau about forty or fifty feet, to one approaching from the lake; but on the side toward the Plain of Hattin, sloped down steeply about four hundred feet. Such was the scene of the Sermon on the Mount. **The company** (Greek, *a great crowd*) **of his disciples.** Matthew also, while placing the Sermon on the Mount early in his Gospel, presupposes a wide extent of previous preaching, and a large gain of disciples, such as Luke has brought us to in a more nearly chronological order of the events (Matt. 4: 23-25). But discipleship here means necessarily no more than acceptance of the truth of Christ's Messiahship, in many cases no more than a belief that he was a "Teacher sent from God" (John 3: 2). Their understanding of his real character, and the depth of their conviction, varied indefinitely with the various scholars, and with the same one at different times. (See, for the state of things a little later, John 6: 60, 66, 67.)—**And a great multitude of the people.** The range of country from which the throng assembles, is greater than any previously named, showing the constant extension of the reports concerning him.—**Came to hear him**—that they might make up their minds as to his character and requirements; some, doubtless, with hearts prepared to put themselves under those spiritual teachings of which they had caught hints.—**And to be healed of their diseases.** Many would have no higher aim or faith than this; but we would hope that, in a large proportion of those who received physical benefits, there would arise, also, the sense of spiritual needs, and the experience of spiritual satisfaction. Trust in the great Healer, rewarded by unspeakable gains of bodily health and comfort, would naturally open their hearts to the offer, from the same source, of soundness and rest to sin-sick, troubled, and laboring souls.

19. And the whole multitude sought to touch him. It was another of the occasions when "the power of the Lord was with him to heal" (5: 17), and when great faith on the part of the needy gave scope for its exercise. There may have been much superstition with the faith, leading them to think that physical contact was necessary to secure the desired boon, especially as the dense throng around him would hinder those more distant from perceiving the manner of his work. When they came near, they would find that **there went virtue** (*power*) **out of him, and healed them all**—not mechanically, but of his own will, in answer to their genuine, but often unenlightened faith. (Comp. 8: 43 ff.)

20-49. THE DISCOURSE ITSELF. In regard to this, we agree with those who hold it to be an abridged report of the same discourse which Matthew gives more nearly in full (ch. 5-7). The obvious superficial difficulty from the apparent diversity of locality, is set aside by a consideration of the facts above presented (ver. 17). Other objections growing out of the substance and form of parallel teachings in the two reports, are analogous to those which arise wherever independent accounts, of varying fullness, are given as of the same transaction or discourse. On the other hand, we infer that they were different reports of the same discourse from these circumstances, namely, that the two begin with beatitudes and end with the parable of the wise and foolish builders; that between these two extremes, Luke also gives the law of the new commonwealth, without needing, as did Matthew, to compare or contrast this with the old law; and brief applications of this law to the conduct of his followers, without contrasting the hypocritical practices of workers under the fossilized law of the Scribes and Pharisees. Add, that both are directly followed by the account of the healing of a centurion's servant in Capernaum. In Luke, we have the Manifesto of the Messiah, not distinctly in his character of Royal Lawgiver, but more generally, in that of a compassionate Saviour, Expounder of the principles of his kingdom, and Teacher of the way of life.

20-26. THE CHARACTER AND BLESSEDNESS OF HIS FOLLOWERS CONTRASTED WITH THE CHARACTER AND WOES OF THE OPPOSITE CLASS.

20 And he lifted up his eyes on his disciples, and said, *Blessed *be ye* poor: for yours is the kingdom of God.

20 And he lifted up his eyes on his disciples, and said, Blessed *are* ye poor: for yours is the kingdom

a Matt. 5:3; 17:5; James 2:5.

20. And he lifted up his eyes on his disciples—a formal introduction to the following account.—**Blessed be** (*are*) **ye poor.** The address here is direct, to the disciples before him, and not apophthegmatic, about such, as in Matthew. This seems to suit better with the actual relation of the parties in question. The disciples were generally poor in worldly wealth, and the crowd, probably almost all, of humble rank in the gradations of society. To them he speaks, on the supposition that they put themselves under his teaching, and yield him allegiance as head of the expected kingdom. **Blessed**=happy : happy are ye. Not that their poverty is in itself happiness; but that *they* are not hindered by the abundance of worldly goods from realizing their spiritual needs; are aided, rather, by their lack of them to turn from the world, and seek the treasures in heaven. This qualification of the idea of poverty, as calculated to make more sensible the deficiencies of spiritual excellence, or lack of true righteousness, which is here implied, is directly expressed by Matthew: "Blessed are the poor in spirit," as, indeed, it must be expressed, when the general, proverbial, form of the beatitudes was adopted. That which was not true of "poor" as such, holds directly of those whom the Saviour addresses as "*ye* poor." Ye, who, coming to learn of me, and put yourselves under my guidance, are poor in worldly goods. Perhaps the style in Matthew only faintly implies that which in Luke is most conspicuous, simple poverty.—**For yours is the kingdom of God.** Luke and Mark constantly designate the **kingdom** as **of God**, while Matthew commonly calls it "the kingdom of heaven." The latter conforms more to the later Jewish usage, in avoiding the direct name of God, where possible, and indicating him by the word "Heaven," his abode personified. The phrase had naturally arisen from the reflection of pious men on the idea of a theocratic state, in which Jehovah was to rule over an obedient and faithful people, according to laws and instructions emanating from himself, and resulting in a holy character and corresponding blessedness. As the theocratic nation, instead of actually approximating to the idea, receded constantly further from it, it rose ever more brightly to prophetic vision as a reality of the future, in connection with the presence and influence of that mysterious Rod or Shoot from the stem of Jesse, about whom clustered all the intimations of a Messiah. Daniel (2:44; 7:14, 18, 27), had fixed this conception in the form of a kingdom, established by God, glorious, powerful over all others, and everlasting. In the Wisdom of Solomon (10:10), we find mention plainly of a Kingdom of God.

The term had been much worked over by Jewish theologians, and was familiar in the language of piety at the time of Christ. He had only to clear it of misconceptions and errors, and absurdities, of earthliness and narrowness, in order to make it a fit vehicle of the true idea of spiritual and eternal salvation. In his lips, it stood for the complex and sum of blessedness designed by his Father in eternal counsels, and about to be realized through his mediation. It brings to our thoughts the whole sphere of Christian welfare under the figure of a state, in which God reigns (Kingdom of God), through the agency of Jesus (Kingdom of Christ, Eph. 5:5), over souls renewed, through repentance and faith in Jesus, by God's own Spirit, and consecrated to his service without reservation or drawing back for time and for eternity. The law of this Kingdom is love—love binding each soul to God in supreme devotion, and to every fellow-soul, as God's child and image, in all affectionate, sympathizing offices of help.

John had spoken of this Kingdom as near, "at hand." Jesus, at the beginning of his public work, announced it in the same way (Matt. 4:17; Mark 1:15); but after his preaching has resulted in conversions and the attachment of hearts to him, he freely refers to it as present, while yet much that is said of its fruition is expressed in the future tense, as if all present experience of it was only inchoate and prelusive. It was constituted when a troubled soul first truly heeded the injunction, "Repent and believe the gospel; for the kingdom of God is at hand," thus accepting the rule, and offering himself as the subject,

Ch. VI.] LUKE. 117

21 ᵃ Blessed are ye that hunger now: for ye shall be filled. ᵇ Blessed are ye that weep now: for ye shall laugh. | 21 of God. Blessed are ye that hunger now: for ye shall be filled. Blessed are ye that weep now: for ye

a Isa. 55: 1; 65: 13   Matt. 5: 6....*b* Isa. 61: 3; Matt. 5: 6.

of God in Christ. Then began that blessed society of souls with the Saviour, which crowns all other worthy unions and relationships, or makes up for them when they do not exist. It has grown by the accession of every following soul that has broken away from the hard reign of the world, and its prince, to find peace and rest under the easy yoke of the Son of man. We are taught to pray that it may continue thus to spread, until it shall have embraced all the nations within its general sway, and the will of Our Father shall be done on earth as it is in heaven. May he hasten that consummation!

To give the character of a society, a rule, a state, a kingdom to the individual relation of a believing soul to Christ, some outward organization, some badge of membership, seems essential. To answer important purposes, this relation must, in its temporal continuance, be represented visibly. As emerging from the Hebrew polity of the Old Testament, "the kingdom of God" could not naturally mean a purely spiritual relation, a mere "psychological kingdom"; but must have a form, institutions, polity, adapted to its spiritual nature, as the old form was to its social and religious intention. And the whole teaching of the New Testament is consistent only with the hypothesis of such an outward, visible body of the saved. What its pattern should be, we could not tell beforehand. But "the reason of positive institutions in general is very obvious, though we should not see the reason why such particular ones are pitched upon, rather than others." (Bishop Butler, *Anal.* Pt. 2, ch. 1). The "church" is not, according to the definition of the word, identical with "the kingdom," but when the removal of the Lord from the earth left the latter without hope of adequate organization during "the life that now is," the church ideally came into the place of the kingdom, and inherited the institutions and polity by which its reality was to be manifested to itself and to the world. The ideal church or congregation is represented by each particular church, and has for its practical aim to call out of the world, and train to perfection, those whom the Father has given to the Son, that they may be fit members of the glorified state.

Thus, even on earth the essentially inward, personal, spiritual relation of the subject to his king may be more or less perfectly expressed in an outward, organic communion. In such a communion, provision is ideally made for assuring happiness to the Lord's "poor," in the supply of many of their earthly wants, the fulfillment of reasonable, but unsatisfied desires. This we see in the practice of the earliest disciples, after the Day of Pentecost, and in a degree through all the ages since. Doubtless, the Master's intention for such help even here has yet to be more perfectly answered. Enough, to show that it is in no mockery that he says: "Happy are ye, poor, for yours *is* the kingdom of God." But everything that *is*, at the best is only preliminary to a more glorious hereafter—a state in which lies so much of the blessedness, as to warrant its being called also "the kingdom of heaven." There is its capital city, the throne of its King, the scene of its full, eternal development and felicity. There, at all events, those poor, whom Jesus here blesses, will thankfully own themselves rich, in the friendship of a glorified Redeemer, and the perfected society of all God's chosen.

21. Blessed are ye that hunger now—addressed not to another class of persons, but to the same, regarded as suffering that want which is involved in the poverty just characterized.—**For ye shall be filled**—points to that future, abundant satisfaction of all right and holy desires, which is assured to all subjects of the kingdom.—**Blessed are ye that weep now; for ye shall laugh.** This weeping is a sign and fruit of the poverty, and the laughing is a translation into outward symbol of the spiritual joy of the kingdom.—**Now**—in all these declarations, names the period preliminary to the complete revelation of the reign in Christ, to the glories of which all these traits of character are also prerequisite, and the future tense of the promises looks forward to that perfected character and happiness.—These three traits correspond to three of the first found in

22 ᵃ Blessed are ye, when men shall hate you, and when they ᵇ shall separate you *from their company*, and shall reproach *you*, and cast out your name as evil, for the Son of man's sake.
23 ᶜ Rejoice ye in that day, and leap for joy: for, behold, your reward *is* great in heaven: for ᵈ in the like manner did their fathers unto the prophets.
24 ᵉ But woe unto you ᶠ that are rich! for ᵍ ye have received your consolation.
25 ʰ Woe unto you that are full! for ye shall hunger. ⁱ Woe unto you that laugh now! for ye shall mourn and weep.

22 shall laugh. Blessed are ye, when men shall hate you, and when they shall separate you *from their company*, and reproach you, and cast out your name as
23 evil, for the Son of man's sake. Rejoice in that day, and leap *for joy:* for behold, your reward is great in heaven: for in the same manner did their fathers
24 unto the prophets. But woe unto you that are rich!
25 for ye have received your consolation. Woe unto you, ye that are full now! for ye shall hunger. Woe *unto you*, ye that laugh now! for ye shall mourn and

a Matt. 5; 11; 1 Pet. 2: 19; 3: 14; 4: 14....b John 16: 2....c Matt. 5: 12; Acts 5: 41; Col. 1: 24; James 1: 2....d Acts 7: 51....
e Amos 6: 1; James 5; 1....f ch. 12: 21....g Matt. 6: 2, 5, 16; ch. 16: 25....h Isa. 65: 13....i Prov. 14; 13.

Matthew, but not in the same order. Lest any should fall away from discipleship, or shrink from embracing his cause, through fear of trials which experience had now proved they were likely to meet, he shows that the suffering of persecution for his sake is also a ground of rejoicing.

22. Blessed are ye, when men shall hate you, etc. Friendship to him was sure to draw the hatred of the world, and, eminently, that of the religious leaders of that time.—**Separate you from their company,** by excommunication from their synagogues, and the refusal of social intercourse.—**Cast out your name as evil**—probably, by some formula of execration, as if the very mention of their names was of evil (baneful) tendency. —**For the Son of man's sake.** On the title, see on 5: 24. The blessing is assured only to afflictions borne, on account of true allegiance to him. And the same condition is implied with the fore-mentioned poverty and hunger.

23. Rejoice ye in that day, and leap for joy. The day of contempt and cruelty toward his followers, Jesus seems to see as if present; so sure is it to come. "Blessed *are* ye when men *shall* hate you," etc. Then, instead of regarding it as an occasion of grief and mourning, rejoice, rejoice exceedingly.— **Leap for joy,** is, etymologically, the same as to "exult," rejoice triumphantly. What can make such a course reasonable or possible? Simply a due consideration of what is involved in connection with the Kingdom of God. That does not allow any one to fail of a spiritual reward for all sacrifices in its behalf.—**Your reward is great in heaven.** That is, in the perfected state of the kingdom, when its temptations, trials, discipline, have given way to rest, fruition, perfect peace. These will be more abundant and more richly appreciated in the case of men who have most bravely borne most of those.—**For in like manner did their fathers unto the prophets.**—A practical proof from history that this is so. The prophets are applauded now; who would not bear what they endured to be honored as they are honored? They, surely, inherit eternal blessedness; but in their day they were treated, at the hands of the fathers of your persecutors, with the same abuse which threatens you. Your reward shall be like that of the prophets.

24. The four traits of character thus positively presented as belonging to those who enter the kingdom, are further illustrated by contrast with four opposite characteristics of those who can have no part or lot therein; and to the four blessings are opposed four corresponding woes. Of these, Matthew makes no mention.

Woe unto you that are rich. A certain proportion of the company assembled, might consist of those social and religious magnates, whom we have seen lurking around the Saviour as conspirators and spies—men who commonly belonged to the wealthy, or the comfortable portion of society. That he thus directly addressed them is more probable than that he simply imagined such as listening to him. It was a case like that of John the Baptist denouncing the Pharisees and Sadducees (Matt. 3: 7). Not as rich, merely, but as the wordly, proud, self-satisfied, and unrepenting rich, are they miserable.—**For ye have received your consolation**—all that was possible for you of joy and comfort, ye have had here on earth; and the bliss of the kingdom henceforth ye cannot know.

25, 26. The two classes of verses 25 and 26, are precisely antithetical to the two in ver. 21, 22, and their destinies are diametrically opposite. Abundance and mirth for a season, and a good report from the world, will be followed with a famine of spiritual peace, and with

26 *Woe unto you, when all men shall speak well of you! for so did their fathers to the false prophets. 27 *But I say unto you which hear, Love your enemies, do good to them which hate you, 28 Bless them that curse you, and *pray for them that despitefully use you. 29 *And unto him that smiteth thee on the *one* cheek offer also the other; *and him that taketh away thy cloak forbid not *to take thy* coat also. 30 *Give to every man that asketh of thee; and of him that taketh away thy goods ask *them* not again. 31 *And as ye would that men should do to you, do ye also to them likewise.

26 weep. Woe *unto you*, when all men shall speak well of you! for in the same manner did their fathers to the false prophets. 27 But I say unto you who hear, Love your enemies, 28 do good to them that hate you, bless them that curse you, 29 pray for them that despitefully use you. To him that smiteth thee on the *one* cheek offer also the other; and from him that taketh away thy cloak 30 withhold not thy coat also. Give to every one that asketh thee; and of him that taketh away thy goods 31 ask them not again. And as ye would that men

a John 15; 19; 1 John 4: 5....b Ex. 23: 4; Prov. 25: 21; Matt. 5: 44; ver. 35; Rom. 12: 20....c ch. 23: 34; Acts 7: 60....d Matt. 5: 39....e 1 Cor. 6: 7.../Deut. 15: 7, 8, 10; Prov. 21: 26; Matt. 5: 42....g Matt. 7: 12.

dishonor and mourning forever.—**For so (***in the same way***) did their fathers to the false prophets.** Numerous men, in the Old Testament, pretending to be sent by God, spoke "smooth things" to the people, leading them into sin and final ruin. But the unbelieving and ungodly honored them, and now they are held in infamy.

27-36. THE LAW OF THE NEW SOCIETY IS UNIVERSAL LOVE.

27, 28. But I say unto you which hear, Love your enemies. The statement of the fundamental principle of their lives and conduct, as his subjects, had been prepared for in the more detailed discourse in Matthew, by elaborate contrast with the law of Moses. Here it comes in abruptly, but with evident allusion to those things previously said. In Matthew (5: 21-27, 31), the Master had repeatedly told them, "Ye heard that it was said to them of old time"; here his language is, "*I* say to you that are hearing." I lay down the law for you as members of the new religious state. The essence of it is, that whereas ye have understood the old requirements to be a partial good-will toward certain persons, on certain conditions, and not to others, or otherwise, ye are now to love all men and treat them lovingly.—**Do good to them which hate you.** The love here enjoined is, essentially, good-will—desire for the true happiness of others. It expresses itself in prayer to God for their welfare, in kindness of word—blessing—and in benevolence of act. That it is to be cherished toward **enemies, those which hate you**, and **despitefully** (abusively) **use you**, is as much as to say that it is to be cherished toward everybody, without exception. Its scope should be as universal as the bounty of God, and its limitations, if any, should be analogous to those which would restrain him.

29, 30. And unto him that smiteth thee, etc. These paradoxical instances seem designed to impress vividly on the follower of Jesus that he must, as such, bear suffering and injustice, without retaliation or failure of good will. Casuistry may revel in questions started by these precepts, concerning predicaments in which those to whom the Saviour spoke could never be placed. But we may interpret, in practical life, the rules of Christ by his own example, and that of his apostles. This will confirm what might be understood beforehand, that the love to one must harmonize with the love to all others; that love is not identical with gratification of the wishes of its object, but may sometimes necessitate refusal, and resistance to importunities and injuries; that love toward a person, or persons, is consistent with appealing to right laws against such, for restraint and correction. Love itself suggests these qualifications, and authoritative example sustains them. With ideally perfect men, such as the Saviour contemplated, and in an ideal society, there would, of course, be no difficulty; but in every case, toward even the most harmful of men, love must not fail. We must sooner bear harm and injustice than sacrifice good will, like that of Christ himself.

31. And as ye would that men should do to you, etc. The Golden Rule here comes into a setting more obviously appropriate, where it looks back to the whole presentation of the law and duty of the kingdom. In respect to what the law of *love* requires of us in particular cases, the Master gives us a short and easy formula, by which we may solve many problems. It is needed only when we find no specific rule, in reason or revelation, to govern our action. In such an emergency, to determine what we should do toward a fellow-man, we may judge what we should

32 *For if ye love them which love you, what thank have ye? for sinners also love those that love them.
33 And if ye do good to them which do good to you, what thank have ye? for sinners also do even the same.
34 *And if ye lend *to them* of whom ye hope to receive, what thank have ye? for sinners also lend to sinners, to receive as much again.
35 But *love ye your enemies, and do good, and *lend, hoping for nothing again; and your reward shall be great, and *ye shall be the children of the Highest: for he is kind unto the unthankful and *to* the evil.
36 *Be ye therefore merciful, as your Father also is merciful.
37 *Judge not, and ye shall not be judged: condemn

32 should do to you, do ye also to them likewise. And if ye love them that love you, what thank have ye?
33 for even sinners love those that love them. And if ye do good to them that do good to you, what thank have ye? for even sinners do the same. And if ye lend to them of whom ye hope to receive, what thank have ye? even sinners lend to sinners, to receive
35 again as much. But love your enemies, and do *them* good, and lend, ¹ never despairing; and your reward shall be great, and ye shall be sons of the Most High: for he is kind toward the unthankful and evil.
36 Be ye merciful, even as your Father is merciful.
37 And judge not, and ye shall not be judged; and condemn not, and ye shall not be condemned: re-

a Matt. 5: 46.....*b* Matt. 5: 42.....*c* ver. 27.....*d* Ps. 37: 26; ver. 30.....*e* Matt. 5: 45.....*f* Matt. 5: 48.....*g* Matt. 7: 1.——1 Some ancient authorities read, *despairing of no man.*

like, and what we should think right (both these elements must enter into our judgment) to have done to us by him, if our relations were reversed. *That* we should do to him as the relations stand. The Golden Rule takes the place of no other commandment, least of all the command to love; it determines simply how a more general commandment applies to a special case.

32-34. Love that is partial or mercenary is not the love which engages the favor of the Lord.—**For** (rather, *and*) **if ye love them which love you, what thank have ye?** etc. Even mercenary self-interest prompts ungodly, unregenerate men to shows of love which promise profitable returns. What Christ enjoins is an unselfish, self-sacrificing good will. To do a favor in hope merely of a *quid pro quo,* is not the kindness of the kingdom. To lend for the sake of receiving a legal equivalent, is good business policy, but no indication of the spirit proper to Christ's followers.

35. But love ye your enemies—the direct and positive inculcation of ver. 27 ff., is resumed.—**And do** (*them*) **good, and lend**—do all that has been enjoined.—**Hoping for nothing again** (rather, *never despairing,* or, "despairing in nothing"). This is the undoubted meaning in usage of the participle translated in the Common Version—**hoping for nothing again.** The correct rendering encourages pure charity with a hope of return, but not earthly—*never despairing* of a profitable return—in *spiritual* gains.—**And your reward shall be great**—namely, in the kingdom of heaven (ver. 20 ff.). This gives a better text than the Common Version, for charity sermons; but let anniversary preachers and the representatives of benevolent institutions note how and where the reward for *Christian* beneficence is to be paid. The Saviour's compensation for service to him, and sacrifices in his cause, is better than worldly good; it is an increase of the spirit of beneficence and sacrifice to all eternity.—**And ye shall be the children** (lit., *sons,* without the art.) **of the Most High.** By a familiar Hebrew figure, the word "sons" was employed to signify "partakers of the character of," e. g., Belial, wisdom, etc. Thus here, "sons" of God, because evincing a spirit, a character, like God's, of free, benevolent love. —**For he is kind unto** (lit., *toward*) **the unthankful and to the evil** (rather, *unthankful and evil*). How few of all the race of men could have lived and had opportunity of happiness, had their Creator and Preserver looked for worthiness and gratitude, not to say recompense, in them.

36. Be ye (*become ye,* or prove yourselves —**therefore** omitted, as in 'Revision) **merciful** - compassionate or pitiful — **as your Father also is merciful.** The Greek does not so abruptly bid us to *be* possessed of so divine a trait, but exhorts us to advance to ever greater perfection in it—to *become* such. So shall we act worthily of our sonship, and not otherwise.

37. Judge not (the true text has *and* before *judge*), **and ye shall not be judged,** etc. Passing over, in this connection, all the rich instruction of Matthew 6, much of it suggested by Jewish customs, Luke brings this precept in directly as a part of the law of love. It forbids the disposition and habit of sitting in judgment on the motives and conduct of others, as inconsistent with that love which is the essence of the Christian character, and which "hopeth all things"

not, and ye shall not be condemned: forgive, and ye shall be forgiven;

38 a Give, and it shall be given unto you; good measure, pressed down, and shaken together, and running over, shall men give into your b bosom. For c with the same measure that ye mete withal it shall be measured to you again.

38 lease, and ye shall be released: give, and it shall be given unto you; good measure, pressed down, shaken together, running over, shall they give into your bosom. For with what measure ye mete it shall be measured to you again.

a Prov. 19: 17....b Ps. 79: 12,....c Matt. 7: 2; Mark 4: 24; James 2: 13.

(1 Cor. 13: 7). It is not merely unfavorable judgment, condemnation, but the habit of judging at all, that is to be avoided. The verb here, as in all these precepts, but one, denotes not a single act, but a practice or custom of action. The censorial spirit should be suppressed. It cannot be Christ's intention to prevent our forming those opinions about others by which we must guide our own conduct, nor our pronouncing in particular cases on the character of manifest action, and the character of the disposition from which it springs; especially not our exercising judgment when officially required (1 Cor. 5: 12). Such judgment Jesus himself requires (Matt. 7: 6), where Bengel says, "a dog is to be regarded as a dog, a swine as a swine." (See ver. 42.) Not only his own conduct, but that of his apostles, will furnish numerous instances of right and necessary judgment. Only, no judgment but in love and good will, and where needful to help; while judging as a habit, and for no practical good, is a contradiction to love. The practical criterion may be found in 1 Cor. 13: 4-6. Some think the Saviour was warning against the faults of Pharisees and scribes; but unless he had before him people less addicted to the fault in question than the generality of his disciples since, there was no need of his aiming outside of them.—**And ye shall not be judged.** This declaration holds good, to a great extent, even in the present life—the censorious man is the object of censure. But it is a light thing to be judged of man's judgment; and this, like all the other indications of future treatment in the discourse, had reference to the sentence of the Son of man on his throne, in the last day. Then, as the merciful shall obtain mercy, the hard, critical, unloving character will meet an opposite judgment. *And* (see the Revision) **condemn not,** etc. This, which is really implied in the preceding, needed to be distinctly stated, that it might be clearly seen that unnecessary judgment of all kinds was forbidden, and then, *a fortiori*, such judgment as involved condemnation. To this the habit of passing sentence on others in one's mind is apt to come. **Forgive** (better, *release*), **and ye shall be forgiven** (*released*)—it is not a case of personal injury which needs to be forgiven, but of pronouncing sentence. Rather, *release* or "absolve" the person concerned from inculpation, where love and duty do not demand the unfavorable judgment. With this qualification, most of the judgments of Christians against their brethren would be avoided.

38. **Give**—what? All possible help, by word, deed, sympathy, and material contributions. It is a comprehensive re-statement of the law of love, in practice. It follows upon the immediately preceding, as if the Saviour would say, Ye shall not only not do those harmful things, but instead shall render assistance to every brother whom you can aid. —**And it shall be given unto you; good measure,** etc. This is not a mercenary offer, but, as "it is more blessed to give than to receive," this is a promise of that blessing in abundance. The **measure** is thought of as a dry measure, and it is **good** in the sense of being ample, which the following clauses are familiarly adapted to prove.—**Shall men give into your bosom**—in the time of complete retribution, although something of this recompense goes with the kind deed here and now. The word **men** is not only not in the original text, but leads away from the true sense. The subject of the verb is our indefinite "they" (French, *on;* German. *man*), and points vaguely to those (perhaps angels) who shall carry the final judgment into effect.—**Bosom**, is that bag-like fold into which the loose outer robe then worn (mantle or shawl) fell, as it was thrown around in front over one shoulder. In this they often carried a moderate quantity of goods. Ruth, by taking off her mantle ("veil"), made it serve to bear a heavy load (Ruth 3: 15).— **For with the same measure that ye mete (*measure*) withal, it shall be measured to you again.**—According to the quantity of love which ye exhibit toward

122   LUKE.   [Ch. VI.

39 And he spake a parable unto them; ^aCan the blind lead the blind? shall they not both fall into the ditch?
40 ^bThe disciple is not above his master: but every one that is perfect shall be as his master.
41 ^cAnd why beholdest thou the mote that is in thy brother's eye, but perceivest not the beam that is in thine own eye?
42 Either how canst thou say to thy brother, Brother, let me pull out the mote that is in thine eye, when thou thyself beholdest not the beam that is in thine own eye? Thou hypocrite, ^dcast out first the beam out of thine own eye, and then shalt thou see clearly to pull out the mote that is in thy brother's eye.

39 And he spake also a parable unto them, Can the blind guide the blind? shall they not both fall into a
40 pit? The disciple is not above his ¹ master; but every one when he is perfected shall be as his ¹ master.
41 And why beholdest thou the mote that is in thy brother's eye, but considerest not the beam that is in
42 thine own eye? Or how canst thou say to thy brother, Brother, let me cast out the mote that is in thine eye, when thou thyself beholdest not the beam that is in thine own eye? Thou hypocrite, cast out first the beam out of thine own eye, and then shalt thou see clearly to cast out the mote that is in thy brother's

a Matt. 15 : 14....b Matt. 10 : 24; John 13 : 16; 15 : 20....c Matt. 7 : 3....d See Prov. 18 : 17——1 Or, *teacher*.

others, will love be returned to you by God and good men.

39–43. The train of thought running through these verses, and constituting them properly one paragraph, is not narrowly definite, but seems to be in general the necessity of a hearty, sincere, vitalizing appropriation, by each member of the kingdom, of its characteristic principle of love. This must be held in the spirit of the kingdom, not in the formal, self-righteous, hypocritical way of the Pharisees, but in humility, sympathetic kindness, and purity of heart.

39. And he spake also a parable unto them. This formula "and he spake also," is used by Luke often to mark the beginning of a new topic. We accordingly see no clear logical connection between the *parable* and what has just been said. Godet ingeniously points out that ver. 41, 42 follow naturally in the train of ver. 37, 38. True, and if *they* had been found here, we should have said that connection was natural. As it is, we must admit that if the verses before us were a part of this discourse (comp. Matt 15 : 14), the logical link on which they hung has not been given us. He begins a new train, naturally leading through to ver. 42. **Parable** is, in this place, an illustrative simile.—**Can the blind,** etc.— The Saviour, in the Greek, individualizes his case. *Can possibly a blind man guide a blind man?* The connection in which the same illustration is used in Matthew 15 : 14, shows that there the Pharisees and their like are aimed at—their dry, jejune, hide-bound, traditional repetitions of the truth, even when it was truth, having no power to enlighten or move toward holiness. They were doomed to destruction themselves, and would lead any who trusted to them down to the **ditch**—(*pit*) i. e., of Gehenna—with them.

40. The disciple—scholar—**is not above his master**—teacher. If you put yourselves to school under Pharisees, you will be no better, in understanding divine things, no more honest in religious practice, than they.—**But every one that is perfect** (*when he is perfected*), etc., has been completely schooled, drilled, trained, so that he is such as they would like to have him, shall be **as his master**—has become as perfect a Pharisee as the other. Nothing more.

41, 42. Warning against the *assumption* of piety and righteousness. Having reference still, perhaps, to the practice of the Pharisees, as self-righteous, fault-finding, insincere teachers, Christ would not only not have his friends become pupils of the Pharisees, but he would prevent them from adopting their ways or spirit.

41. The beam that is in thine own eye, is an extravagant, almost ludicrous emblem of the gross faults and blemishes of the inculpated class (considering their pretensions and greater means of knowledge), as compared with the ignorance and consequent error of common men, which are but a **mote**—a bit of chip, a minute sliver, or particle of dust—**in thy brother's eye.** A man of that sort should rid himself, by repentance, confession, and humble amendment of life, of his own unrighteousness, before assuming to correct the trivial errors of his brethren.

42. The word **brother** shows that Jesus has in view the relation of members of his kingdom, and is concerned lest the spirit of Pharisaism should establish itself there.— **Thou hypocrite!** points to a possible dissembler among his followers also, and the need of sincerity, humility, and love, in order that one may **see clearly** whether a brother is really in fault, and how rightly to correct him (comp. Gal. 6 : 1), "in the spirit of meekness, lest thou also be tempted."

43. For a good tree bringeth not forth corrupt fruit, etc. The Revision gives the

43 For a good tree bringeth not forth corrupt fruit; neither doth a corrupt tree bring forth good fruit. 44 For *every tree is known by his own fruit. For of thorns men do not gather figs, nor of a bramble bush gather they grapes. 45 *A good man out of the good treasure of his heart bringeth forth that which is good; and an evil man out of the evil treasure of his heart bringeth forth that which is evil: for *of the abundance of the heart his mouth speaketh. 46 *And why call ye me, Lord, Lord, and do not the things which I say? 47 *Whosoever cometh to me, and heareth my sayings, and doeth them, I will shew you to whom he is like: 48 He is like a man which built an house, and digged deep, and laid the foundation on a rock: and when the

43 eye. For there is no good tree that bringeth forth corrupt fruit; nor again a corrupt tree that bringeth 44 forth good fruit. For each tree is known by its own fruit. For of thorns men do not gather figs, nor of a 45 bramble bush gather they grapes. The good man out of the good treasure of his heart bringeth forth that which is good; and the evil man out of the evil treasure bringeth forth that which is evil: for out of the abundance of the heart his mouth speaketh. 46 And why call ye me, Lord, Lord, and do not the 47 things which I say? Every one that cometh unto me, and heareth my words, and doeth them, I will 48 shew you to whom he is like: he is like a man building a house, who digged and went deep, and laid a foundation upon the rock: and when a flood arose, the stream brake against that house, and could

a Matt. 7: 16: 17....b Matt. 12: 33....c Matt. 12: 35....d Matt. 12: 34....e Mal. 1: 6; Matt. 7: 21; 25: 11; ch. 13: 25....f Matt. 7: 24.

verse more exactly. **Corrupt** = unsound, rotten; figuratively, what is unfit and spoiled for its proper use. In Luke's presentation of the simile, if, as the **for** indicates, a logical connection is preserved, the tree stands for the disciple as a teacher, who is **good** when he truly reflects the humility, sympathy, equity, and loving-kindness of the Master. The **fruit** is his power through word and deed to help others toward greater perfection, the legitimate influence, in short, of character and life, **good**, necessarily, if those are good. In Matthew, also, the corresponding passage (7: 17, 18) is connected with cautions against false prophets, but with peculiarities in the application.

44. **For every** (or *each*) **tree is known by his** (*its*) **own fruit**, etc. An axiom of unquestionable truth, looking both backward and forward, on which the whole argument of these verses rests. It is simply exemplified in the reference to the thorn and bramble bush; as these, so every one bears fruit after its kind.

45. **A** (*the*) **good man**, etc. He now takes the place of the good tree, the analogy necessarily failing in some respects. He is, through God's grace, good by virtue of a store of right principles and motives of action, from which, as from an inward treasure, he brings forth good words, good deeds, good influence of every kind. The **heart** is the beneficent store-house of all lovely and helpful supplies, and so proves itself **good**. Conversely of the opposite character—**the evil**—the selfish, hard, unloving, malignant **man**—the products of his heart correspond with the inward contents.—This must be so, **for of** (*out of*) **the abundance of the heart his** (each man's) **mouth speaketh**. Doubtless if the Saviour had gone into details, he might have said that the actions and desires of the man, as well as his words, are only specimens of **the abun**-

dance = overflow—**of the heart**. It does not mean that the definite subjects which most engage a man's interest will be necessarily most talked about by him, but that the moral quality of his heart will determine the quality of his discourse and conduct.

46-49. CONCLUSION: THE NECESSITY OF PRACTICAL OBEDIENCE TO THESE TEACHINGS.

46. And why call ye me, Lord, Lord—thus professing yourselves my disciples, members of the kingdom of God—**and do not the things which I say?** It is as great a delusion as to think of a thorn bush as bearing figs, or of a man as **good**, when the manifest outcome of his heart is evil. Professions and pretense are not sufficient; there must be the proved, practical reality of a heart submissive to my will. **Whosoever cometh to me, and heareth my sayings**—puts himself in the attitude of a disciple—**and doeth them**—that is, shows himself a disciple indeed. Here the clause, **and doeth them**, requires the whole emphasis. The Saviour describes a man who puts himself as a pupil under him, not to acquire merely an understanding of his principles, not to know the gospel as he might know some abstract science, but that he may acquire an art—as one might acquire the art of playing the organ—the art, namely, of holy living, and practical conformity to the declared will of Christ. He learns, in order that he may **do**, and by doing proves that he has learned indeed.—**My sayings** are the precepts and instructions of the foregoing discourse, capable of being condensed into one word—love; but that again easily expanding into the law of all piety, purity, goodness, true righteousness.

48. He is like a man which built (lit.,

flood arose, the stream beat vehemently upon that house, and could not shake it; for it was founded upon a rock.
49 But he that heareth, and doeth not, is like a man that without a foundation built a house upon the earth; against which the stream did beat vehemently, and immediately it fell; and the ruin of that house was great.

not shake it: ¹because it had been well builded.
49 But he that heareth, and doeth not, is like a man that built a house upon the earth without a foundation; against which the stream brake, and straightway it fell in; and the ruin of that house was great.

1 Many ancient authorities read, *for it had been founded upon the rock;* as in Matt. vii. 25.

building) **a house.** It is the perfect security of such a disciple's position that Jesus would illustrate. He may be thought of as establishing a character that is to be tested by fearful exigencies, or a hope of everlasting life, firm enough to stand against seductions, and assaults of men and Satan, through life and in death. It is his house which he is rearing, the home and refuge and defence of his peace, which can allow no doubt to hang over the question of its solidity and safety. It is worse than nothing, if not safe. **And digged deep** (or lit., *went deep*), **and laid the foundation on a rock.** The Greek is, *a* foundation on *the* rock. It is as if Christ were thinking of a site where the surface earth was known to be light and sandy, but resting, at no very great depth, on a wide, extending rock. The prudent builder took all needed pains to reach that, before beginning to lay his wall. He acted as though he understood the perils of the region, and would leave no chance of being undermined. The lower levels about the Sea of Galilee, or the plains at the foot of hills and mountains anywhere there, would meet the suppositions.—**And when the flood arose**—as was liable to be the case any year. The description at this point is much less fully developed than in Matthew's report. But **the flood**=freshet—implies the "rains," which fell copiously on the higher lands, and descending in rivulets, formed a **stream**=river, which, overflowing its banks, **beat vehemently upon that house.** These natural occurrences represent the trials and temptations which vehemently threaten the Christian's character, at times, and tend to undermine his hope. But if he has gone down to Christ's own "sayings," and grounded his life in obedience to them, he shall stand. **And could not shake it**—to say nothing of overthrowing it—**for** (in the Revision, *because*) **it was founded upon a rock** (or better, *it had been well builded*). It is surprising that so careful and learned a writer as Scrivener should (*Plain Introduction*, Ed. 2, p. 473), have objected to this change of the text, on the ground of an incongruity between the present participle (οἰκοδομοῦντι), at the beginning, and the perfect infinitive (οἰκοδομῆσθαι) at the end of the verse. He who had begun well with the foundation had gone on well through every stage of the erection.

49. But he that heareth and doeth not —the Greek plainly means *he that heard and did not*—the past tense supposes the end to have come, and turns our view back on a lost opportunity. "In that day" it will appear that he who merely heard the teaching of Jesus, without yielding up his heart and life to its power, was not saved from an eternal loss.—**Without a foundation built a house on the earth**=sand (Matt. 7: 26)—merely on hearing, knowledge, profession. A neighbor, perhaps, to the prudent man, he built carelessly, in spite of a good example. Against his house, also, the swollen river dashed, and it endured not at all.—**Immediately it fell; and the ruin of that house was great.** In his case, the outward events signify different trials, in part, from those which beset the Christian—pre-eminently the final judgment. How different the effect, eternity alone can tell. "A single lost soul is a *great ruin* in the eyes of God. Jesus, in closing his discourse, leaves his hearers under the impression of this solemn thought. Each of them, while listening, might think that he heard the crash of the falling edifice, and say within himself: This disaster will be mine, if I prove hypocritical or inconsistent."—Godet.

When we ask what, precisely, was symbolized by *the* **rock,** in this closing parable, it is common to say, "Christ himself; Christ, by virtue of his atoning sacrifice, the ground of our eternal hope." And this undoubtedly expresses a most important and blessed truth of theology. But is it *directly* taught here? What is it that the wise builder reaches by his process of digging and going deep, as compared with the other man? Is it not obedience, the actual *doing of the things commanded* by Jesus? Surely, he who accomplished that founded on the rock.

It may be said that Christ is elsewhere named the rock. True; but not regarded as a foundation. The apostle tells us (1 Cor. 10: 4), that the Spiritual Rock, yielding the gushing spring which followed the Israelites through the wilderness, was Christ, the source of all grace and blessing to his disciples. Elsewhere, he is called "the chief corner-stone" (not Rock) of the spiritual building, his church; but the apostles and prophets are "the foundation," as the conveyers of his truth and spirit. Pre-eminent among the apostles, at a certain moment, Peter, as foremost in faith, is called the "Rock," who is to become a foundation for the church. Christ neither calls himself so, nor is so called by any other in the New Testament.

But, it will still be asked, Can there be such obedience as we can safely build on, without faith in Christ? Emphatically, No. That we might infer from consideration of the true nature of gospel obedience, and we are saved the trouble of thinking it out for ourselves by the divine philosophy of the plan and process of salvation, crystallized for all ages, in Romans 3: 21-26. But here it becomes us to notice that Jesus chooses rather (the reasons why, we need not now inquire after) to have us think of *love*, and that not as a mere subjective state of feeling, but a practical carrying out of his precepts, as the solid rock. As there could not be this obedient love without faith, so there could not be that truthful acceptance of Christ and his grace, without love. Theoretically, there may be a natural precedence of faith, to other exercises of the soul, as love and hope; actually and chronologically, love is as early in its origin, and at least as truly comprehends the rest. All shall abide, thank God! but the greatest is love.

Whatever may have led the Saviour to so exalt obedience springing from love, in this paragraph, the same consideration guided him throughout the whole discourse. Not a word in it directly of faith, from beginning to end; not a word directly of atonement; not a word directly of pardon. It has often been commented on as a remarkable deficiency in so elaborate a programme of the kingdom of heaven, which we have come to think of as scarcely anything but faith and pardon. It only shows how gradually the *theory* of gospel salvation developed itself even in the teachings of our Lord. It is the spirit of the gospel in exercise among the members of his kingdom, on which he now entirely, and always principally, insists—the humility, the sense of spiritual need, the sorrow for sin, the disposition of universal love, the sacrifice of self, and beneficence like that of God. As there is always a practice before an art, and generally an art before the science, Christ now teaches the practice of holy living, which was the great end of his coming; and requires it to be cultivated as an art, suggesting the materials of a science, which, if needed, will come in due time. So, largely, throughout the gospel. Here are the practical elements of faith, afterwards taken up into the more systematic statements of the Apostle Paul; but let us not forget that they are, indeed, taken up there. Christ teaches us what we must do and be, and at the close of his teaching, after much added about faith and the Spirit that should be given, seems to forget all but the living aspects of our duty to love, when he declares on what principle he will pronounce the eternal judgment (Matt. 25: 40, 45; John 15: 10). Nor does Paul fail to see this, also, showing that to those who seek it by patient continuance in well doing, and to no others, will God render eternal life. (See Rom. 2: 7.)

We are told that this is no more than was taught and required of men by the ancient prophets. What need of teaching more; if only men could be led to be and do what the prophets required, "to do justly, and to love mercy, and to walk humbly with thy God"? But how differently is this taught by Christ! His life, free from every taint of sin, and shade of infirmity, such as marred the best of prophets, interprets and enforces the precepts which appeal to men's consciences and reason. In the light of his out-beaming holiness, they feel their sin, and are urged to repentance. His merciful sympathy encourages and guides the effort necessary to maintain the upward and arduous grade of life. His calmness and serenity amid opposition, danger, and privation, inspire them with strength to bear; and love, answering in their hearts, draws them to leave all and follow him.

Thus, even when Jesus taught them substantially what old prophets had, more or less distinctly taught, the truth at his lips had a

CHAPTER VII.

NOW when he had ended all his sayings in the audience of the people, *he entered into Capernaum.
2 And a certain centurion's servant, who was dear unto him, was sick, and ready to die.
3 And when he heard of Jesus, he sent unto him the elders of the Jews, beseeching him that he would come and heal his servant.

1 After he had ended all his sayings in the ears of the people, he entered into Capernaum.
2 And a certain centurion's ¹servant, who was ²dear ³unto him, was sick and at the point of death. And when he heard concerning Jesus, he sent unto him elders of the Jews, asking him that he would come

a Matt. 8: 5.—1 Or. *bondservant*....2 Or. *precious to him*. Or, *honourable with him*.

power and efficacy which they could not attain. The final explanation is that the Teacher himself was more than they. He was a prophet—God's *spokesman*—*and* he was the Messiah, in whom God himself spoke. He does not explicitly so name himself in this discourse, it is true; but to every thoughtful soul he raises or warrants the conviction that he is such. What he enjoins, he enjoins as a Divine Lawgiver, who does not need to support himself on former precepts, but whose "I say unto you," is authority of itself. What they have to suffer in his service is to be borne "for *the Son of man's sake.*" That they shall not themselves lack strength, is proved by the power which has just been given to the apostles (Mark 3: 15), even "to cast out demons." The authority of the Messiah guaranteed the promises of blessedness in the kingdom of heaven. All this fell short of the fullness of mature gospel teaching mainly in its failure to answer *how* such infinite blessings could be conferred on sinful souls, and to apply the peculiarly affecting motive which lies in a clear perception of Christ's dying love for them.

Ch. 7: 1-10. Return to Capernaum; Healing of the Centurion's Servant.

1. Now when (omit **now**) **he had ended . . . he entered into Capernaum**—This is the first mention of Capernaum since the commencement of his tour of labors (4: 44). As far as he could be said to have a residence, or even head-quarters, Capernaum seems to have been the place (4: 31; Matt. 4: 13)—in Peter's house more probably than in that of his own parents. His stay here now was brief (ver. 11), and can scarcely be regarded as an end of his expedition through the province. Matthew also makes a visit to Capernaum follow directly upon the Sermon on the Mount—an additional proof of the identity of the discourse reported by both writers, and rendering it very likely that the mountain where it was delivered was near Capernaum.

2. And a certain centurion's servant, who was dear unto him, was sick. A centurion, according to the meaning of the term, was a military officer, commanding one hundred men—of a rank, therefore, in the Roman army, analogous to that of captain with us. This man was probably in the service of Herod Antipas, and may have been a Roman, or, with equal probability, some Greek or Oriental, trained in the Roman manner. He was, perhaps, "a proselyte of the gate," one who accepted the principles of the Jews in the main, and followed some of their customs. Had he been circumcised, thus becoming a "proselyte of righteousness," they could not have distinguished between him and "our nation."—He had a **servant**—strictly, a bond-servant, or slave. Slaves were very numerous at that time throughout the Roman Empire. The Hebrews had long ceased from making slaves of their own people, but still held those of other nations. Among the Greeks and Romans they were, for the most part, of races as white as their owners, often whiter; sometimes of equal, or even superior, culture, and capable of serving the masters in close intimacy, involving important trusts, and consistent with high mutual esteem and friendship. So here, the centurion's servant **was dear unto him.** The adjective means, primarily, "valuable," "precious," then "held in honor," "esteemed." It might therefore possibly be understood as denoting pecuniary worth, or capacity for usefulness; but the whole tenor of the narrative consists better with the idea of personal esteem and affection, naturally suggested by the word **dear.** He was sick—bed-ridden, as we learn from Matthew; and his description of the complaint leads us to think of something like a very bad rheumatism. And he was at the point of death—**ready to die**—a death, too, of very great suffering, from which any friend would specially desire to have him spared.

3. And when he heard of (*concerning*) Jesus—what wonderful works of healing he

4 And when they came to Jesus, they besought him instantly, saying, That he was worthy for whom he should do this:
5 For he loveth our nation, and he hath built us a synagogue.
6 Then Jesus went with them. And when he was now not far from the house, the centurion sent friends to him, saying unto him, Lord, trouble not thyself: for I am not worthy that thou shouldest enter under my roof:
7 Wherefore neither thought I myself worthy to come unto thee: but say in a word, and my servant shall be healed.

4 and save his ¹servant. And they, when they came to Jesus, besought him earnestly, saying, He is
5 worthy that thou shouldest do this for him: for he loveth our nation, and himself built us our syna-
6 gogue. And Jesus went with them. And when he was now not far from the house, the centurion sent friends to him, saying unto him, Lord, trouble not thyself: for I am not ²worthy that thou shouldest
7 come under my roof: wherefore neither thought I myself worthy to come unto thee: but ᵃsay the

1 Gr. *bond-servant*....2 Gr. *sufficient*....3 Gr. *say with a word*.

had wrought, even in desperate cases —**he sent unto him the** (omit the) **elders of the Jews**—heads, probably, of a synagogue of the place, and a sort of religious magistrates. These might be more persuasive messengers than ordinary servants; and they, in consideration of his personal friendliness, were ready to do for him what they would ordinarily spurn to do for a centurion.—**Beseeching** (*asking*) **him**—that is, the centurion asking through the elders. (Comp. Matthew).

4. **Heal his servant**—*save* is more exact than *heal*. Salvation in Scripture designates deliverance, rescue, restoration, of all kinds, individual or national, bodily or spiritual, and in all degrees, from the termination of any transient trouble to the removal of guilt, condemnation, and wrath, and the full fruition of God's favor to all eternity. Here the verb is a compound, to express special earnestness; equivalent to, that he would bring him through safe.—**He was** (*is*) **worthy for whom he should do this** (preferably, *that thou shouldest do this for him*). It was not natural for a Jew of that day to plead for favors in behalf of a Gentile, but the generosity of this convert made him an exceptional case. They were even willing to apply for him to Christ, whom many of their rank had now come to regard as an object of hatred and abhorrence. But we ought not to charge upon all, even of the Scribes and Pharisees, that hostility which prevailed among them as a class. We see, indeed, almost to the last, that prominent Jews under the pressure of affliction humbly beseech his temporal aid.

5. **For he loveth our nation, and he** (*himself*) **hath built us a synagogue**, (or, *our synagogue*). This last fact would be a sufficient proof to them of love to their nation, and indeed it was a rare, though by no means unparalleled, thing, that a man in his station should show such favor to Jews. His interest in their religion would incline him to friendliness and fraternity in other respects, and his defraying the whole expense of building their church was the fruit of it. Our (Greek, "the") **synagogue**—not necessarily the only one in the town, but that with which these elders were connected.

6. **Then Jesus went with them.** Had he measured the objects of his healing love by their standard of worthiness, few of the thousand works of his beneficence would ever have been performed. But the elders had gained the case of their client with Jesus, when they showed him a sufferer whom he might reach, and friends longing for his help. They illustrate how, many times, men who had no personal interest in Christ have conveyed his blessing to others. He had almost reached the centurion's home, when the latter **sent friends to him**—relatives, or the inmates of his own house.—**Saying unto him,** he saying again through his deputies. **Lord, trouble not thyself**—namely, by coming so far out of thy way. We can only harmonize this with the desire in ver. 3, that Christ should "come and heal," by supposing that the elders had expressed *their* sense of what he wished, or, that he afterwards reflected that actually visiting his house was unnecessary. It will be noticed that in Matthew, where the delegation is entirely unnoticed, nothing is said about requesting Jesus to go to the centurion's house.—**For I am not worthy** = fit, of that moral worth which would make it suitable.

7. **Wherefore neither thought I myself worthy to come unto thee.** Plainly a different, but not incompatible, report of the transaction from the one followed by Matthew. The thought back of this is, that it is not necessary for Jesus to visit the house, and that the sender has no social or moral claim to war-

8 For I also am a man set under authority, having under me soldiers, and I say unto one, Go, and he goeth; and to another, Come, and he cometh; and to my servant, Do this, and he doeth it.
9 When Jesus heard these things, he marvelled at him, and turned him about, and said unto the people that followed him, I say unto you, I have not found so great faith, no, not in Israel.
10 And they that were sent, returning to the house, found the servant whole that had been sick.
11 And it came to pass the day after, that he went into a city called Nain; and many of his disciples went with him, and much people.

8 word, and my ¹servant shall be healed. For I also am a man set under authority, having under myself soldiers: and I say to this one, Go, and he goeth; and to another, Come, and he cometh; and to my ¹servant, Do this, and he doeth it.
9 And when Jesus heard these things, he marvelled at him, and turned and said unto the multitude that followed him, I say unto you, I have not found so great faith, no, not in Israel.
10 And they that were sent, returning to the house, found the ¹servant whole.
11 And it came to pass ²soon afterwards, that he went to a city called Nain; and his disciples went with

---

1 Or, boy....2 Gr. bond-servant....3 Many ancient authorities read, on the next day.

---

runt him in asking for anything in the least superfluous. It is not merely humility which thus speaks, but an apprehension that Jesus might think it less suitable that the man of another nation, a Gentile, and of a secular calling, should approach him, than the religious representatives of Christ's own people.— **But say in a word**—a word spoken by Christ at a distance will be all sufficient. Did even he believe that the word need not be spoken aloud? that the inaudible will of the Saviour would infallibly accomplish the desired result? So it proved. **And my servant shall be healed** (rather, *Let my servant be healed.*) The Greek is still rather petition than prediction. [The reading is doubtful. B. and L. have ιαθήτω = *Let—be healed;* but א A C D R, αθήσεται = *Shall be healed.*—A. H.]

8. For I also am a man set under authority, etc. The reason involved in this lies in the fact that Christ commands the agencies of healing, as he himself directs his soldiers to do his errands, and is obeyed. He states his own position humbly; the point is that he exercises authority, but he is careful to say, that his is no supreme authority, as is Christ's I am myself, though under the control of higher officers, yet, in my low sphere, in command, so that with a word, "Come," or, "Go," or, "Do this," I secure that my will is done. How much more will a word from thee suffice for all that I desire! No human example could more expressively set forth the power that lay in a command than the order of a Roman officer and master. What he was in these rude, earthly relations, he sees Jesus to be in the supernatural and spiritual sphere.

9. When Jesus heard these things, he marvelled at him. Wonder and admiration at such clear, unqualified faith, held him for a moment, and he rejoiced in the omen of future triumphs of his truth among the Gentiles of the remotest regions. (See Matt. 8: 11).

A great crowd had followed the Saviour, eager to see what would happen at the house of the officer. Jesus would have them all apprehend the full significance of the Gentile's faith. He turned, therefore, to face them, and secure their attention, and said: **I have not found so great faith, no, not** (not even) **in Israel.** The excellency of the centurion's faith seems to have lain in his clear persuasion of the ability of Jesus to do miracles of cure by a mere word of command. In previous cases, as in that of rebuking the fever of Peter's mother-in-law, it had been necessary for him to lay his hands on them, or touch the blind eyes, or the bound tongue, and allow them to touch his garment. These were accommodations to weakness prevalent among the Jews, to which this Gentile was entirely superior. He saw that the power lay in the Spirit of Jesus, so that whatever that willed to be done, was done. And his confidence was justified.

10. And they that were sent . . . found the servant whole—in sound health. This was a case of faith in the healing power of Jesus promptly answered and highly honored by the Great Physician. That the officer recognized in him the Saviour of souls, we are not told; but if he did, it does not seem natural that he should have failed to encourage the coming of Jesus to his house, that he might share his spiritual instruction and grace.

11-17. Resurrection of the Son of the Widow at Nain. This event is not reported by either of the other evangelists. The question naturally rises, why Luke should have preserved what Matthew and Mark passed by. The most obvious answer is, that, supposing them all to have had the report of it, the special object of Luke alone made this record important to him. That special object, in this part of his writing, we suspect to have been to mark the climax of

Ch. VII.] LUKE. 129

Christ's manifestation of himself. He had just given proof of his power to heal mortal diseases by a word, even by an act of his will. That had followed upon the announcement of his high claims as Messiah, and of the corresponding duties and privileges of his adherents as constituting the kingdom of God. It had been preceded by a number of miracles specially selected to show his power over Satan's kingdom (4:31-37); over all manner of diseases (4:38-41); over the kingdom of nature (5:1-11); over leprosy, emblem of man's sin (5:12-16); over paralysis, emblem of man's helplessness (5:17-26); over prevailing prejudice and groundless moral distinctions, in the special calling of a publican (5:27-32); over the morally crippling fetters of tradition, in the elucidation of the principles of fasting (5:33-39), and the Sabbath (6:1-11). But in all this, up even to the great exercise of his restorative and delivering power preceding his Sermon on the Mount (6:17-49), where the people felt it necessary "to touch him," that they might share the outstreaming virtue (as it seemed to them), there was a certain poverty of apprehension concerning his character and ability, above which we are lifted at once, in the faith of the centurion: "Give command only, and whatever thou biddest shall be done." Here is a beginning of receptivity, and that in the case of one of the Gentiles—happy omen!—to which the Saviour may now reveal still more of himself. Hence the presentation, next, of our Lord's dominion over death.

11. And it came to pass the day after (or, Revision, *soon afterwards*), **that he went to a city called Nain.** This city, which still

NAIN.

exists under the same name, *Nein*, was situated twenty-four miles nearly south of Capernaum. This was a long distance for Jesus to have walked by the "next day," and the preponderance of authorities, in our judgment, supports the Revision. In either view, knowing how much the Saviour would find to do in passing that distance through a populous country, we see the urgency with which he pressed to "preach the good tidings of the Kingdom of God to the other cities also" (4:43).—**And many of his disciples went with him, and much people** (*a great mul-*

I

12 Now when he came nigh to the gate of the city behold, there was a dead man carried out, the only son of his mother, and she was a widow: and much people of the city was with her.
13 And when the Lord saw her, he had compassion on her, and said unto her, Weep not.
14 And he came and touched the bier: and they that bare *him* stood still. And he said, Young man, I say unto thee, ^aArise.
15 And he that was dead sat up, and began to speak. And he delivered him to his mother.
16 ^bAnd there came a fear on all: and they glorified God, saying, ^cThat a great prophet is risen up among us; and, ^dThat God hath visited his people.

12 him, and a great multitude. Now when he drew near to the gate of the city, behold, there was carried out one that was dead, the only son of his mother, and she was a widow; and much people of the city
13 was with her. And when the Lord saw her, he had compassion on her, and said unto her, Weep not.
14 And he came nigh and touched the bier: and the bearers stood still. And he said, Young man, I say
15 unto thee, Arise. And he that was dead sat up, and began to speak. And he gave him to his mother.
16 And fear took hold on all: and they glorified God, saying, A great prophet is arisen among us: and,

a ch. 8: 54; John 11: 43; Ac's 9: 40; Rom. 4: 17....*b* ch. 1: 65....*c* ch. 24: 19; J hn 4: 19; 6: 14; 9: 17....*d* ch. 1: 68.

titude). Now and henceforth, we find him frequently accompanied by a crowd of disciples and others on his journeyings.

12. Behold—a sad and striking encounter at the gates of the city. The town stood on the side of the Little Hermon mountain, and was reached by a steep, rocky ascent, through this one gate.—**There was a dead man carried out**—more literally, *there was carried out one who was dead.*—**Was carried out** = was in the act of being carried out.—**The only son of his mother, and she was a widow.** The case was thus a peculiarly sorrowful one, and had evidently excited deep interest among the people of the town; for **much people** (*a considerable crowd*) **of the city was with her.** It was doubtless no uncommon thing for Jesus to meet a funeral, and we do not know that on any other occasion he interfered with the course of nature under such circumstances. But now, apart from the solemn shock of disputing the way with a corpse through the gate of the city wall, the circumstances of this death becoming known to him, would be peculiarly suited to touch the sympathetic heart of the Son of man. "Mourning for an only son" was a type of the sorest grief. Jesus himself signalized the love of his Father in giving his only begotten Son for the salvation of the world. And now an only son, followed by his mother, and she a widow, probably indigent and dependent on him for support—what element of the pathetic was wanting?

13. And when the Lord saw her, he had compassion on her. As we might expect, he did not wait for faith; her distress evoked his pity, and pity moved him to comfort.—**He said unto her, Weep not.** He was probably a stranger to her, and his words would naturally first occasion wonder, or even fear. It would be rude and cruel if he stopped with that. However it may have been with the mother, none of those who had been with him in Capernaum could have lacked faith that he could, or hope that he might, do even this wonder of mercy, and restore the dead to life.

14. And he came nigh and touched the bier (*coffin*) in which, with the lid removed, the body seems to have been carried on a bier. The Greek word is not that appropriate to a bier, but to a coffin. The object of the act was to arrest their movement. As before, in touching the leper, Jesus now ignored the ceremonial scruples against even indirect contact with the dead. The bearers stopped, in suspense, we must presume, about what was to happen.—**And he said**—addressing the dead youth, over whom as yet only a cloth would rest, in his coffin—**I say unto thee, Arise.** It was the voice which shall one day summon the nations under ground forth to the judgment bar. Will they hear? This "one that was dead" heard.

15. And he that was dead sat up, and began to speak. Performing plainly the deeds of a living man, he proved that life had gone forth in that command. **And he delivered [***gave***] him to his mother.** What a present! How simple the relation! It leaves us free to imagine the look, the manner, the tone, the language, with which Jesus would convey the unparalleled gift. And her emotions! She had lost her only son, and now he was hers again by a direct gift of God. As for the multitude, surely there could never again be a doubt that here was the Messiah, and that the Messiah was divine! Alas for the obstinacy of prejudice, and the slowness of men to realize how great a boon God has sent them in Jesus Christ!

16. And there came a fear on all—or, *And fear took hold on all*—the natural effect of such a manifestation of supernatural power.

17 And this rumour of him went forth throughout all Judea, and throughout all the region round about.
18 ªAnd the disciples of John shewed him all these things.
19 And John calling *unto him* two of his disciples

17 God hath visited his people. And this report went forth concerning him in the whole of Judæa, and all the region round about.
18 And the disciples of John told him of all these
19 things. And John calling unto him ¹two of his

ª Matt. 11 : 2.....1 Gr. *certain two.*

(Comp. 1: 12; 2: 9; 5: 8, 9). **And they glorified God**—clearly recognizing a marvelous instance of his power and mercy, yet by no means apprehending how near he was to them in it.—**A great prophet is risen up among us**—was true, and expressed the highest conception to which the mass, even of those who knew most about Jesus, had yet attained. (Comp. 9: 18, 19, and par. John 6: 66). They saw in him what Nicodemus saw—"a teacher sent from God"; some, even a spokesman for God (prophet); but with diverse ideas as to his rank and relation to the Messiah. Even in this they saw proof that "God hath visited his people." From the days of Samuel to those of Malachi, pious Jews had looked on the presence among them of Jehovah's prophets, as a token of his own presence and favor, and their absence as a cause for regret and mourning. Now, after a famine of the direct prophetic word for four hundred and fifty years, with no "open vision" (1 Sam. 3:1), the appearance of a great prophet, one who, with a word merely, accomplished what Elijah did only with great pains and protracted exertion (1 Kings 17: 21), was a joyful proof of God's visitation.

17. And this rumor of him [or, *report concerning him*] **went forth throughout all Judea, and throughout all the region round about.** Some have scented a mistake in this mention of Judea, when the Saviour was yet in Galilee. But he was in the extreme southern part of that province, if not actually within the border of Samaria; and what was to be particularly stated was, that whereas already the rumor concerning him had spread widely through Galilee, this wonderful work of his carried the word southward into Judea and Samaria, and the country beyond Jordan. Besides the simple delight which Jesus had in acts of mercy, assuaging pain, preserving life and useful strength, and even restoring life where this might be, he certainly attached an evidential value to these deeds of his, as proving his character and disposition, and would rejoice in having them widely known and truthfully interpreted.

18-35. John the Baptist in Prison Sends Messengers to Jesus. Christ's Testimony of Him. Matt. 11: 2-19.

It suits admirably with what we have supposed to be the plan of this portion of Luke's narrative, that this incident should be presented just here, to carry forward, another step, the revelation of our Lord's Messiahship. John's state of mind may well have been not very different, at that time, from that of other thoughtful observers of the course of Jesus. At all events, we can see that if the design of Luke were to select such facts in his career as would bring his readers by degrees, analogous to the actual stages, to a full recognition of Christ as the Son of man, his procedure is happily adapted to that end. Christ's dealing with John aims to satisfy an honest doubter of this truth, without, at the same time, deviating from his settled policy of letting the facts work their own way to the understanding and hearts of men.

18. And the disciples of John shewed him of all these things. Thus "the report concerning him (ver 17) went forth" beyond Judea, even to the dismal rock-fastness of Machærus (*Makor*), east of the Dead Sea, where we left the Baptist in confinement (3:19,20), perhaps (as we cannot reach certainty concerning the dates) about eighteen months before. The word brought to him of the remarkable works of Jesus, such as, if correctly reported, were worthy of the Messiah, yet not all that the pious had expected of him, greatly disturbed his mind. What was he to conclude about the true character and office of this extraordinary personage? It is evident that his imprisonment was not so rigorous as altogether to prevent the access of his disciples and friends, and he must have had other intelligence of Jesus since they were last near each other at "Ænon, near Salim."

19. And John, calling unto him two of his disciples—thus showing his state to have been not unlike that of Paul, at Cesarea, according to Acts 24 : 23.—**Sent them to Jesus,**

sent *them* to Jesus, saying, Art thou he that should come? or look we for another?
20 When the men were come unto him, they said, John Baptist hath sent us unto thee, saying, Art thou he that should come? or look we for another?

disciples sent them to the Lord, saying, Art thou he 20 that cometh, or look we for another? And when the men were come unto him, they said, John the Baptist hath sent us unto thee, saying, Art thou he that

---

(or, *the Lord*). We have here, and in the preceding statement, another evidence that some who had embraced the teachings of John still adhered to him, and were distinguished from the disciples of Jesus. Whether they also recognized Jesus as the Messiah, and only waited on John from friendly regard, and to aid him in his afflictions, or from some other cause, we do not know. Saying—the Greek participle is singular=to say, John speaking through them.—**Art thou he that should come** (or, *cometh*), **or look we for** (are we to expect) **another?**

20. Arriving where he was, these men faithfully proposed their master's question. The phrase, "The coming one," or *He that cometh*, was a familiar designation of the Messiah. After the incidents of the Baptism, and the previous intercourse of the families of the two at the period of John's nativity, it seems so strange, on a superficial reading, for John now to doubt whether Jesus was the Messiah whom he had predicted and pointed out, that commentators have put various violent twists upon his language, to make it consistent with some other purport. But we have only to remember that John, though a prophet, and Christ's herald, was "a man of like passions with us," to clear the subject of peculiar difficulty. At once we notice that John has such confidence in Jesus, that he is sure he can have from him the clearing up of his perplexities. If the latter is not himself the Messiah, he can explain what is yet to be looked for. John seeks his instruction. Recall now that in our reflections on John's work in ch. 3, we have seen that, as near as he came to Christ, he was far from that view of him which Jesus distinctly presented of himself in his first reported discourse, at Nazareth. The leading features of the work of him that was to come, are seen by the herald in quite other proportions from what the course of Jesus for now many months had realized. The unfruitful trees had not been cut down; the grain had not been winnowed from the chaff, nor was the unquenchable fire kindled to his view. He probably saw no tendency toward any of these results. Not

one prominent element of the prevailing conception of the reign of the Messiah, could he recognize in the proceedings of Jesus.

Had he been allowed to share the Saviour's company, to receive the silent influence of his example, and his truth, to ask for explanations, and to hear reasons, we may be sure that his mental state would have been very different. But he had not only lacked the privileges of the humblest of the Lord's disciples, he had, on the contrary, been left to pine, and fret out his spirit in cruel incarceration, brought on him by righteous zeal in the very cause which he was sent to promote.

That John should, in these circumstances, have wavered, and been seriously shaken in his conviction that Jesus of Nazareth was the end of the law and the prophets, the restorer of the kingdom to Israel, is not profoundly surprising. He was indeed a special, and for certain uses, an inspired messenger of God. So was Elijah; and Elijah also lost confidence in the methods and the cause of God; he sulked, as we might say, and thought it hard that the Lord did not carry on his work according to the prophet's views. Moses, again, and Jeremiah had their times of great despondency, and no doubt would have then gladly sought light in their perplexities if there had been one like Jesus at hand.

Let us notice now what John asks, and what it implies.—**Art thou he that cometh?** The position of **thou** in the Greek is strongly emphatic, in anticipation of the next clause. What is implied, suppose the answer to be in the affirmative? Something like, "Let me be assured of the fact. I lack satisfactory evidence." Not, "Let these messengers of mine have the evidence." That, if John were clear in his own mind, would have been a clumsy, if not an insincere way of indicating his desire. And, without discussing the other expedients for avoiding the scandal of a great prophet falling short of a perfect, unintermittent, imperturbable faith in former divine indications which are becoming fulfilled in a sense which the prophet did not put upon them, it is enough to say that the Saviour's kind and faithful hint in verse 23

21 And in that same hour he cured many of *their* infirmities and plagues, and of evil spirits; and unto many *that were* blind he gave sight.
22 ᵃThen Jesus answering them said unto them, Go your way, and tell John what things ye have seen and heard; ᵇhow that the blind see, the lame walk, the lepers are cleansed, the deaf hear, the dead are raised, ᶜ to the poor the gospel is preached.
23 And blessed is *he*, whosoever shall not be offended in me.
24 ᵈAnd when the messengers of John were departed, he began to speak unto the people concerning John, What went ye out into the wilderness for to see? A reed shaken with the wind?

21 cometh, or look we for another? In that hour he cured many of diseases and ¹ plagues and evil spirits; and on many that were blind he bestowed sight.
22 And he answered and said unto them, Go your way, and tell John what things ye have seen and heard; the blind receive their sight, the lame walk, the lepers are cleansed, and the deaf hear, the dead are raised up, the poor have ² good tidings preached to
23 them. And blessed is he, whosoever shall find none occasion of stumbling in me.
24 And when the messengers of John were departed, he began to say unto the multitudes concerning John, What went ye out into the wilderness to be-

a Matt. 11: 4....b Isa. 35: 5....c ch. 4: 18....d Matt. 11: 7.—1 Gr. *scourges*....2 Or, *the gospel.*

shows that it was John who was in danger of stumbling against the Christ.—**Or look we for another?** This may have meant only, "or not." The whole meaning would thus be, "If thou art not Messiah, thou art nothing; and we must simply wait until he comes." But the words used suggest rather that John questioned, not whether Jesus was an eminent messenger from God, but only whether, as there were some who held that the forerunner would come in one character, some in another, there might not be two, and so Jesus only a second forerunner like himself.

21. Our Lord might have answered him categorically, "Yes, I am"; but this would have been contrary to his chosen course at that time and in that region (comp. his way with the woman at Jacob's well), and would have been less honorable to John, and less helpful than the method he took.—**And** (should be omitted, also **same**) **that hour he cured many of their infirmities** (or, *diseases*, **and plagues, and of evil spirits**—put here compendiously among the bodily cures—**and unto** (or, *on*) **many that were blind he gave** (or, *bestowed*) **sight.** Thus he gave to John, through his disciples, to see the powers ascribed in prophecy to the Christ fully operative in him. Taking advantage of the presence of a "great multitude" (ver. 11), among whom would be, according to all experience, a number desirous to be healed of their maladies, the Lord varied and multiplied his benefits to such, in a way which could not fail to suggest to John the prophetic descriptions of Messianic blessings. (Comp. Isa. 29: 18; 35: 5, 6; 60: 1-3.)

22. These things they were to **tell** (or, *report to*) **John.** The variety of benefits flowing from his work is enumerated with a force and vivacity scarcely to be imitated in English. Omitting the article to show that these are merely specimen cases, and the noun to fix attention on the diverse maladies, he says, **blind see; deaf hear; lame walk; lepers are cleansed; dead are raised.** This might all have passed before the eyes of John's deputies. And so, from the phrase, **What ye have seen and heard**, we may suppose that these acts of Christly grace were accompanied with instruction concerning his main object on earth, and announcements of the more precious gifts which he had to bestow. This caps the climax of the list of benefits. That **to the poor** (*to poor people*) **the gospel is preached.** Such was generally, no doubt, the relation in which, to our Saviour's view, his temporal and spiritual favors stood to each other. The announcement of the good news crowned all.

23. **And blessed** (happy) **is he, whosoever shall not be offended** (*shall find no occasion of stumbling*) **in me.** Here is the tender and faithful admonition by which Jesus intimates to John that he recognizes the motive of this deputation, and encourages him to renewed trust, notwithstanding the difference of the Master's procedure from what the forerunner had expected. So much the latter would naturally feel that he had deserved and would be thankful for.

24. But our Lord seemed, in a manner, to regret he had said a word which could even look to others like reflecting upon the course of his faithful and much-tried herald. **And when the messengers of John were departed.** Matthew's word more directly breathes the feeling: "While they were going." Immediately, as if he could not wait, **he began to speak unto the people** (or, *multitudes*) **concerning John**—the object being to bear witness to his exalted character and function, and to indicate his relation to

25 But what went ye out for to see? A man clothed in soft raiment? Behold, they which are gorgeously apparelled, and live delicately, are in kings' courts.
26 But what went ye out for to see? A prophet? Yea, I say unto you, and much more than a prophet.
27 This is he, of whom it is written, *a* Behold, I send my messenger before thy face, which shall prepare thy way before thee.
28 For I say unto you, Among those that are born of women there is not a greater prophet than John the Baptist: but he that is least in the kingdom of God is greater than he.

25 hold? a reed shaken with the wind? But what went ye out to see? a man clothed in soft raiment? Behold, they that are gorgeously apparelled, and live 26 delicately, are in kings' courts. But what went ye out to see? a prophet? Yea, I say unto you, and 27 much more than a prophet. This is he of whom it is written,
Behold, I send my messenger before thy face, Who shall prepare thy way before thee.
28 I say unto you, Among them that are born of women there is none greater than John: yet he that is ¹ but

---

a Mal. 3:1.——¹ Gr. *lesser*.

---

himself.—**Began to speak**—implies a formal and important saying, one really, as we see, containing the highest commendation that had ever been passed on a man. How gladly would we know that it had been reported to the Baptist in all its fullness and strength!—**What went ye out into the wilderness for to see** (better, omitting **for,** *to behold*)? and, as the result, "what did ye actually behold?" He would recall to his hearers the impression which they had received concerning John, from attending on his preaching. The Received Text (corrected according to the best manuscripts by Westcott and Hort, and the Revision, to the preterit form of the verb, as in the Common Version), gives the verb in the perfect, with a large number of authorities, and as approved by Tischendorf. It is very probable that the Received Text is right, and was early changed to conform to Matthew. The translation of that would be: "What have ye been out," etc. The difference is interesting, as if there were two translations of the same Aramaic original of Christ's words. The Aramaic would not, by the form of the verb, distinguish between *preterit* and *perfect*. The interrogative form is adapted to excite attention, and the repetition of the question, again and again, before resting on the true answer, increases curiosity, and guides constantly nearer to the truth.—**A reed shaken by the wind?** The reed rises to the thought as one of the features of the vicinity of the Jordan; but the metaphorical use of it is to denote an unstable, vacillating man, such as John might seem from this recent message to him. Did you find John such a man?

25. **But** (since not that) **what went ye** (or, *have you been*) **out for to see?** To "behold" was used to express the first aim of their curiosity; **to see,** is sufficient in repeating the reference.—**A man clothed in soft raiment? Soft**—made of fine and delicate stuff. This is figurative for a man of nice tastes, and luxurious habits, and dainty requirements, such as might become impatient and desponding from the hard fare of the prison. Was John such? Would you thus have had to go into the wilderness to find him?—**Behold, they which are gorgeously apparelled, and live delicately** (in luxury), **are in kings' courts**—in the palaces. Such were the false prophets in the courts of the kings of old. You did not find the hermit preacher in such places.

26. **But what,** etc. The way is now prepared for the true answer.—**A prophet? Yea, I say unto you, and much more than**—something over and above—**a prophet. A prophet.** He was spokesman for God, to intimate his plan of redemption at its culminating point, and to prepare men's minds for the reception of the crowning gift of the God of grace to men. In every respect in which Elijah or Isaiah was a prophet, the title was applicable to John. He was **much more than a prophet,** because to him had fallen the office of installing the Messiah in his position, and pointing him out to men as the bearer of the Spirit, the Bridegroom of his congregation, the atoning Lamb.

27. **This is he of whom it is written,** etc. Jesus here refers to John the same prophecy in which his work had been foretold by the angel to Zacharias (1:17), and by Zacharias himself in his prophetic psalm (1:76). (See on those places.)

28. **I say unto you, Among them that are born of women**—as if he had said, Among all human beings that live, or that ever lived since the first pair—**there is not a greater prophet than John the Baptist.** The Revision is perhaps right in omitting **prophet** here, the best very early sources of information sustaining them, while yet the considerations leading the other way are strong enough to have induced Tischendorf,

29 And all the people that heard *him*, and the publicans, justified God, ᵃ being baptized with the baptism of John.

30 But the Pharisees and lawyers rejected ᵇ the counsel of God against themselves, being not baptized of him.

29 little in the kingdom of God is greater than he. And all the people when they heard, and the publicans, justified God, ¹ being baptized with the baptism of 30 John. But the Pharisees and the lawyers rejected for themselves the counsel of God, ² being not bap-

a Matt. 3: 5; ch. 3: 12....*b* Acts 20: 27.——1 Or, *having been*....2 Or, *not having been*.

against his favorite Sinaitic manuscript, to retain the word. It is, at all events, in the character of a prophet that the Saviour ascribes to John this high praise. Let it be duly weighed, that we may appreciate the eminence of Christian discipleship—**But he that is least in the kingdom of God is greater than he. Least**—properly, "less," or "smaller." The adjective is a comparative in the Greek, yet the main sense may not be very different from that of our Common Version. It is not clear with whom the lesser Christian is compared in Christ's thought. Some think with John, the disciple occupying a lower, less important place in the kingdom than John did in the Old Dispensation. He is still greater than John, having a better understanding of the principles and constitution of that kingdom, and having shared differently and more largely that renewing, sanctifying, comforting Spirit which John saw to belong to the future. More probably, however, the comparison intended is with other members of the kingdom. That one, no matter who, that is inferior to his brethren in knowledge and spiritual gifts, yet has some true experience of the knowledge of Christ, as the giver of instantaneous, complete, free, eternal, salvation, *he* is nearer to the ideal of a saint than John. Who takes to heart this truth? Who really believes and understands that, as a Christian, however humble, he stands more close to God, as it respects knowledge of his ways, and interest in his grace, than did John the Baptist? Yet he stood as near as David, or Abraham, or any Old Testament saint. The member of the kingdom may, indeed, look back to them as encouraging witnesses to the power of faith (Heb. 12: 1), while yet he looks forward and upward to Jesus himself, as the first specimen and perfect exemplar of our faith, our responsibility, and our blessedness (ver. 2 ff).

29. And all the people that (or, *when they*) **heard him** (that is, John,) **justified,** etc. This is a continuation of Christ's discourse (not, as some have understood it, an interpolation of a bit of the history of Luke,) in which he shows how John's call was slighted by the leaders of the nation. The common **people,** free from the ambitions and prejudices of the wealthy, proud, and respectable, felt their need of repentance, and **justified God** by acknowledging the rightfulness of his claim upon them, and were baptized as a declaration of their renewedness of mind, and pledge of life consistent with such a delaration. Even **the publicans,** and they particularly, hindered by no figment of self-righteousness, freely heard the summons of John. They thus **justified God** (Ps. 51: 4) by owning themselves sinners, and honoring his way for their obtaining pardon. There is, in this language, a further intimation of the extent and power of John's influence upon the people at large. They were **all** affected by it, and we seem to see that, if the religious leaders had joined, and aided the movement, Jesus would have found a nation prepared for his coming.

30. But the Pharisees and lawyers rejected (annulled, frustrated) **the counsel of God against themselves, being not baptized of him. The counsel of God** was that the nation, heartily repenting, and manifesting a purpose of spiritual amendment, should accept the teaching and authority of the Messiah, who would then make of them the nucleus of the new kingdom. For this, the people showed themselves ready; but their religious guides and governors, when once they saw the true nature of this plan, unwilling to humble themselves and abdicate the influential positions they held, rejected the teaching of Jesus, and so frustrated the plan. This he could declare, because he by this time perceived that the mass would go with them. They did this **against themselves**—*i. e.,* to their injury and undoing. "For themselves" (Revision), as equivalent to "so far as they were concerned," is grammatically justifiable, and logically, it is involved in the common rendering. But the point seems to be that Christ sadly admits that their course has set aside God's plan of mercy toward the nation, but would distinctly point out that while all suffer, the

31 And the Lord said, "Whereunto then shall I liken the men of this generation? and to what are they like? 32 They are like unto children sitting in the marketplace, and calling one to another, and saying, We have piped unto you, and ye have not danced; we have mourned to you, and ye have not wept. 33 For ᵇJohn the Baptist came neither eating bread nor drinking wine; and ye say, He hath a devil.

31 tized of him. Whereunto then shall I liken the men 32 of this generation, and to what are they like? They are like unto children that sit in the marketplace, and call one to another; who say, We piped unto you, and ye did not dance; we wailed, and ye did 33 not weep. For John the Baptist is come eating no bread nor drinking wine; and ye say, He hath a

a Matt. 11:16....*b* Matt. 3:4; Mark 1:6; ch. 1:15.

rulers, whose influence has secured this result, will specially feel the ruin that must follow. They have decided **against themselves.**

31. Whereunto then shall I liken the men of this generation? **Then** (equivalent to therefore), seeing that they thus treated my predecessor just as they are now treating me.—**And to what are they like?** He studies as he speaks, inquiring of himself what comparison might truly set forth their strange conduct. In a moment it becomes clear to him.

32. They are like unto children, etc. He recalls a childish sport which he must have watched often with interest, and had probably shared in himself, when he gathered with his mates in the square, equivalent to **market place,** of the towns. The details would be familiar to his hearers. It seems that they had reduced to something like a definite game, plays which in a less regular way have amused young children in every country and time—"playing wedding," and "funeral." The Saviour refers to a case where they had divided into two sections, one to give the music and direct the movements, the other to carry out the play; but when the first proposed the "wedding," the others would not have that, and yet peevishly refused to join in playing "funeral" also. The first set then say, **We have piped unto you** (made joyful music), **and ye have not danced; we have mourned to you** (*wailed*, sung a dirge), **and ye have not wept**—broken forth in lamentation. The Revision rightly gives the verbs in the preterit. These speakers seem intended to represent John and Christ, as endeavoring, in different tempers and ways, to induce their countrymen to embrace God's word; the immovable and impenitent nation are the other section who hang back, and consent, as a whole, to the invitation of neither herald. It is objected to this, the common explanation, that it makes Jesus and John a part of the men of that generation, inappropriately. Hence Meyer (*not* De Wette; Godet, on the passage) supposes the speakers here to stand for the Jewish people; and those addressed, for John and Jesus Christ. But surely it is those addressed who are to blame. And when did the people ever manifest any desire to win over their teachers? Godet curiously makes the two sets of children represent John and his adherents on the one side, and Jesus with his disciples on the other, who mutually complain that their leading is not followed, while yet he would have the fault lie with "the moral insensibility and carping spirit in Israel," whereby the opposite teachings are paralyzed. This, at least, is what we make out of the translation, not having the original at hand. We might understand it as if John and Jesus, with their disciples, in one group, were reckoned as belonging to that generation. But there is no need of stickling for the letter of the simile, more than in many other parables, e. g., that of the Sower. Understand the Saviour as saying, "The case with this generation in their relation to me is like that of children playing—one part faithfully trying to promote the pleasure of all, the other (strictly, that which represents the men of this generation) captious, sullen, responding to no kind of proposal that is made for their recreation." That the generation should be likened to a set of children, and then identified with only a portion of them, is not unlike the comparison of the kingdom of heaven to a sower sowing seed on various soils, and afterward confining the similitude to the seed, the soil, and the crop. The one point to be illustrated is the refusal of the Jews to enter the kingdom, as urged either by the ascetic and rigorous demands of John, or by the gentle and more urbane invitations of Christ.

33. For—he speaks now in application of the figure to them. Ye heeded neither the dirge nor the dance—**for John the Baptist came**

34 The Son of man is come eating and drinking; and ye say, Behold a gluttonous man, and a winebibber, a friend of publicans and sinners!
35 a But wisdom is justified of all her children.

34 demon. The Son of man is come eating and drinking; and ye say, Behold, a gluttonous man, and a winebibber, a friend of publicans and sinners! And wisdom 1 is justified of all her children.

a Matt. 11 : 19.—1 Or, was.

(or, *is come*) **neither eating bread** (or, *eating no bread*), etc. "His meat was locusts and wild honey"; a proof of extreme temperance and self-denial.—**And**—not "but"; "and of course."—**Ye say, He hath a devil** (*demon*); "it is the devil's message, not God's." This is not the language of those who are piping cheerfully to John, and wishing that he would more fitly present the cause of the Lord, as Meyer's view of the Saviour's simile supposes, in which view Lange and Van Oosterzee unite. It is the language of hatred, scorn, rejection.

34. The Son of man is come eating (that is, bread), **and drinking** (that is, wine) —living in a natural, human way, as becomes the Son of man, the ideal of humanity.—**And ye say, Behold a gluttonous man** (*a glutton*), **and a winebibber** (a toper). Does he mean, Ye are "lamenting" to me that I do not take a more serious view of the true religion? He means, Ye are determined not to accept God's call to his kingdom, no matter through whom he invites you.

35. But (*and*) **wisdom is** (*was*) **justified of all her children.** "But," in the Common Version, is one of the few instances in which earlier translators would fain have mended, and not simply rendered, the inspired word. Doubtless the Evangelist might have used "but," and we could not have challenged its propriety; but it would have been with quite a different effect from that produced by "and." Ye did so, and so, and so, over against God's repeated proposals, *and* [all the same] wisdom was justified. The **wisdom** intended is that counsel of God by which he provided that John the Baptist should go before the Messiah, in the spirit and power of Elijah, to prepare the way, and that Jesus, the Christ, should follow him. The **children of wisdom** are, by the common Hebrew figure (see on 6: 35), those who in practice conform to God's infinitely wise plan, and find salvation. While the great mass act the foolish and wicked part, some have accepted the proffered grace, more by far than would have done so otherwise. Their course showed that they recognized the **wisdom** of God's method,

and has thus **justified** it—practically declared it a right method; and in their example every reasonable beholder has the evidence that it was wisdom that so planned. Thus wisdom was justified by—more exactly, "from," in consequence of, "by reason of," all her children, from the beginning, whether gained by the ministry of John, or by that of Jesus. Matthew has in the parallel passage, "her works," according to the text of Tischendorf, and Westcott and Hort, her accomplished results, as equivalent to "the believing and obedient disciples she has won."

The wisdom here celebrated lies, it will be noticed, in the association of the forerunner with Christ in the plan of God. This may warrant us, before parting finally with the account of that hero of the faith, in recalling, summarily, the leading aspects of his service to the cause of Christ.

REMARKS ON THE MISSION OF JOHN THE BAPTIST. Given such a moral and religious tate as that of the Jews, "in the day of John's shewing unto Israel," to reveal effectually to the people God's doctrine of salvation for them—this was the problem then to be solved. A salvation from sin, of the stain or burden of which they were not conscious; consisting in spiritual conformity to God's Spirit, of which they had no conception; of sincere and spontaneous obedience of the heart to him, instead of mere outward works, in compliance with rules laid down by men who had usurped the place of the divine Law-giver. It was a problem to drive the wisest of men to his wit's end. Of this problem, John in his work enacted the solution.

1. Its first word was repentance. Repent ye. It had often been said by prophets of the early days, from Joel down, in reference to particular acts of transgression, and passing states of alienation from Jehovah, and sometimes with a transient success. But even in Malachi we witness a prevalent condition of mind to which the idea would be strange; and ever since the favored people have gone further and further away from it. John found them puffed up with pride, resting on birthright, as though, because they were physi-

cally descended from faithful Abraham, they were sure of heaven, without regard to their own faithlessness and departure from the teachings of their prophets. They were sunk in a soulless formality, content with an anxious routine of outward performances, some of which had once made a part of the skeleton of a preliminary system of religion, but were now mere scattered dry bones. On points of dispute as to these minutiæ, they divided into sects, each thinking itself holier than others, all careless of the weightier matters, judgment, mercy, and righteousness toward the helpless poor and ignorant among them. Now the solitudes of the wilderness and the deep ravine of the Jordan reverberate with the voice of one calling aloud, Repent, ye! What he meant was, as people soon found, that they must humbly recognize their sinfulness, and change for the better their views of God and of themselves—change their purposes, their conduct, their lives. They must attain to a devotion of the heart to God, and this must prove itself in dispositions of equity and kindness toward fellow-men. This announcement was sounded out by such a voice, and with such accompaniments of character, ceremonial, and scenery, as roused the minds of the nation, like an electric shock, to a consideration of the nature of acceptable service to God; that is, of religion worthy of the name.

2. He gave concentration and point to the vague expectation of a Messiah, by declaring his kingdom "at hand." The previsions of him described in the Biblical prophets appear to have been forgotten or overlooked in the popular religious literature of the people for some centuries. We search the Greek apocryphal books (properly so called), without finding an indubitable trace of Messianic hope. Josephus gives no intimation of such a thing in all his writings. But in 2 Esdras (not found in Greek, but brought down into our English apocrypha from Latin and other translations), the Book of Enoch, the Psalms of Solomon, etc., we see that speculation was rife, before John's time, concerning a wonderful Avenger and Deliverer, who was to come for the rescue and glorification of Israel. The views concerning him were, at times, expressed in apocalyptic images, suggested, perhaps, by the Book of Daniel, and of a mystical wildness and indistinctness of purport, to which the visions of our New Testament Revelation are transparency itself. These were well calculated to excite deeply the popular imagination, and give occasion for infinite diversity of particular expectations. In the Targums, or Chaldee translations (more properly, paraphrases) of parts of the Old Testament, a more rational presentation of views like those of the true prophets must have been at this time somewhat widely known. The result of it all was that, while a very extensive perturbation of thoughts existed about a great Anointed One, ere long to make his appearance, there was little definiteness of anticipation, with no helpful influence on the conduct of those who entertained it, and in the case of great multitudes no interest at all.

On an age so situated fell the proclamation of John the Baptist: "Repent ye; for the kingdom of heaven is *at hand.*" At first no mention is separately made of the King. But he would be suggested as a matter of course. And that he was *at hand!* Thousands who had scarcely believed in him even while they dreamed and talked of him, would find the conception taking the distinctness of a reality, when awakened by the summons: Repent, for the *kingdom is at hand.* Its nearness would inspire an unwonted interest as to its character, and the qualifications for citizenship therein. But we may be certain that all the Jews who were really least fit for it would be most sure of their right to it, simply as Jews. This delusion it was, as we have seen, John's first object to scatter; and he soon caused it to be understood that there was but one way into that kingdom, namely, repentance and the confession of sin. A Jew, not less than if he were a Gentile, Pharisee and publican alike, must submit to this condition, publicly professing, in the sacred immersion, his need of moral purification, and pledging himself to a different life. And this, without distinct mention of the king, but only of the kingdom. But, "as John fulfilled his course," he said, "there cometh one mightier than I, and of a dignity which I am not worthy to serve." This was his initial definition of the Christ. And he added such description of the Messianic office as was, indeed, little adequate to a full appreciation, but all that was necessary to prepare for his reception, with those who were waiting for his salvation. Or

35 ᵃAnd one of the Pharisees desired him that he would eat with him. And he went into the Pharisee's house, and sat down to meat.

36 And one of the Pharisees desired him that he would eat with him. And he entered into the Pharisee's

a Matt. 26 : 6 ; Mark 14 : 3 ; John 11 : 2.

finally, if such persons queried *how* they could obtain through the future King and Judge, that pardon, purity, peace, and holiness which they felt distressingly needful, he pointed to Jesus passing by, one day, and said: "Behold the Lamb of God, who taketh away the sin of the world."

3. He gained to his ministry a number of disciples, who were so prepared in heart and understanding, as to be comparatively ready for the call of Christ to come with him, and to constitute the nucleus of that unique society which, once begun, was to spread over all lands, continue throughout all time, and in eternity still to subsist as the Kingdom of Heaven. True, Jesus received them little advanced toward completeness of discipleship with him. They would still need much care and teaching, much patient training and apprenticeship to his service; but nothing that they had learned from John would have to be unlearned; they would only require that additional tuition and supply of the Spirit, which their Master himself had been conscious of lacking, in the presence of Jesus. Five, at least, of the twelve were thus, as we know, made ready for the Lord by his herald; and it is highly probable that a large proportion of the remainder had been first with John, and that the same was true in regard to the whole of his converts.

4. John continued to the last to lend the weight of his testimony to the support of Jesus as his successor and superior, "at ‚Enon, near Salim"; even in his last despondent embassy he sent to him as the one to whom he might apply for decisive explanation; and that his trust in Christ remained throughout his life, we have touching evidence in the report, that when he was dead, "his disciples went and told Jesus." That death so moved the mass of the people that Josephus, laying aside his studied reticence concerning the whole gospel history, tells us they thought it the occasion of God's displeasure against Herod, his murderer, as manifested long afterward in a bloody defeat of the latter in a battle with king Aretas, his former father-in-law.

So deep was the impression of a divine mission on John's part that, at the very close of Christ's life, the proudest magnates of Jerusalem dared not question it; and long afterward, in the remote regions of Pisidia, Paul could hope to gain interest in his message concerning Jesus, by reminding his hearers of John's precursory testimony in his behalf.

In all these respects, his public life was a work of leveling the way of the Christ, and making his paths straight. Very different, we repeat, would have been the task of the Master, if his servant had not helped powerfully to make ready a people prepared for the Lord.

36–50. JESUS, IN THE HOUSE OF A PHARISEE, FORGIVES A PENITENT WOMAN'S SINS. This is one of the precious revelations concerning Jesus as the Saviour of the outcast, for which we are indebted entirely to the narrative of Luke. And, while we would refrain from asserting what was the connection in the evangelist's mind of the several topics of which he treats, we think it not unlikely that this incident is placed here as a finishing evidence of the Messiahship of Jesus. He who had healed the centurion's servant with a word, raised the widow's son, given John proof that he was the Coming One, now demonstrates his exercise of the highest functions of the Son of man in forgiving sins also. True, he had before forgiven the sins of the paralytic, as he had before healed many; but just as we saw the cure of the centurion's servant to be a grade above the previous healings, so this forgiveness was an act of mercy purely to the soul's need of a peculiarly guilty woman, the very type of "a sinner," apart from all connection with bodily ailments, which might before have disguised the character of the act.

Although the name of his host here was the same as that of the proprietor of the house mentioned (John 12 : 1 ff), where also a woman anoints him in the course of a meal; still the circumstances of the two men (one a Pharisee, the other a leper), and the character and relations of the two women (a sister of Lazarus, "a sinner"), forbid our

37 And, behold, a woman in the city, which was a sinner, when she knew that *Jesus* sat at meat in the Pharisee's house, brought an alabaster box of ointment,

38 And stood at his feet behind *him* weeping, and began to wash his feet with tears, and did wipe *them* with the hairs of her head, and kissed his feet, and anointed *them* with the ointment.

37 isee's house, and sat down to meat. And behold, a woman who was in the city, a sinner; and when she knew that he was sitting at meat in the Pharisee's house, she brought ¹ an alabaster cruse of ointment,

38 and standing behind at his feet, weeping, she began to wet his feet with her tears, and wiped them with the hair of her head, and ² kissed his feet, and

1 Or, *a flask*....2 Gr. *kissed much.*

thinking the two accounts to refer to the same occasion.

36. And one of the Pharisees desired (*asked*) **him that he would eat with him.** This incident belongs, chronologically, to a period when the attitude of the Pharisees had not yet become so flagrantly hostile to the Lord as to prevent some friendly intercourse between them. Nor, indeed, need we suppose that, even later, every one bearing the name of Pharisee was so inflamed with their characteristic hatred of Jesus as personally to wish him harm, or to destroy hope in the latter of some benefit to the Pharisee. The meal here treated of was not apparently a formal and elaborate entertainment; but there were other guests present (ver. 49). **Sat down to meat** (*reclined at table*). It is necessary, in order that what follows may be clearly intelligible, to bear in mind that the custom among Greeks, Romans, and Orientals, in Christ's day, was to recline at table, leaning on the left elbow, extended at full length on a broad couch or settee, with the face toward the table, and the feet sloping backward, across the couch, so as to be easily reached by one approaching from the rear.

37. And, behold—a notable fact is to be reported.—**A woman in the city, which was a sinner** (the Revision, rightly, *a woman which was in the city, a sinner*). There is thus brought suddenly before us a woman who was known in the city as being, in the worst sense, "a sinner." That she could approach the table in a respectable house, especially the house of a scrupulous Pharisee, is to be explained only from the freedom, elsewhere brought to view in the Gospels, with which people went in and out of the abodes of their neighbors, and observed what was taking place in them. The same custom frequently surprises and annoys travelers in the East at the present day.—**When she knew that Jesus sat at meat** (reclined, as in ver. 36), **brought an alabaster box,** etc. She knew something about Jesus before, and must have been instructed by his teachings, melted by his gracious sympathy with sinners, and moved to profound repentance and desire for the assurance of pardon. This we see from what follows. The **alabaster box** is called in the Revision "a cruse," which is better; but the original simply says, "an alabaster." This was the name of a vessel, made of that material—a vase, jar, or broad-mouthed bottle, suitable for holding the fragrant cosmetic here called **ointment.** It was much in vogue at that time among all more civilized peoples, as promotive of health, and pleasant to the senses of sight and smell, and so an indispensable accompaniment of banquets and all festive occasions. It was used on the hair and face in great profusion, compared with anything familiar now, and, probably, with a much greater outlay of expense.

38. And stood at his feet behind him, weeping.—His feet were bare, according to custom; for, even if men wore sandals on the street, these were laid aside on entering a house; and, regularly, the feet were washed by a servant, as the first act of hospitality to a visitor. This was also a sort of necessity, in order that they might not soil the carpets, or the cushions on which they reclined at the table. What was said above of the manner of this reclining shows how she could best reach Christ's feet standing behind him. —**Weeping**—from sorrow on account of her sinful life; partly, also, with thankfulness and complacency toward him who had led her to amendment, and opened to her a prospect of peace and hope.—**And began to wash** (*wet*) **his feet with** (*her*) **tears.** **Wash** is not warranted by the Greek, but *wet* or "moisten." This may have been unintentional, although it was, more probably, an act symbolic of the most humble devotion to his service. Washing another's feet was performing a menial office, and would be voluntarily undertaken only as a sign of affectionate regard. The same sen-

Ch. VII.]   LUKE.   141

39 Now when the Pharisee which had bidden him saw it, he spake within himself, saying, *This man, if he were a prophet, would have known who and what manner of woman this is that toucheth him: for she is a sinner.
40 And Jesus answering said unto him, Simon, I have somewhat to say unto thee. And he saith, Master, say on.
41 There was a certain creditor which had two debtors: the one owed five hundred *pence, and the other fifty.
42 And when they had nothing to pay, he frankly forgave them both. Tell me therefore, which of them will love him most?

39 anointed them with the ointment. Now when the Pharisee that had bidden him saw it, he spake within himself, saying, This man, if he were ¹ a prophet, would have perceived who and what manner of woman this is that toucheth him, that she is a
40 sinner. And Jesus answering said unto him, Simon, I have somewhat to say unto thee. And he saith,
41 ² Master, say on. A certain lender had two debtors: the one owed five hundred ³ shillings, and the other
42 fifty. When they had not *wherewith* to pay, he forgave them both. Which of them therefore will

a ch. 15: 2.... b See Matt. 16: 28.——1 Some ancient authorities read, *the prophet*. See John 1: 21, 25....2 Or, *Teacher*....3 See marginal note on Matt. 18: 28.

timent was further expressed by her next act.—**And did wipe them with the hairs of her head, and kissed his feet**, etc. In putting her hair to such a use, she literally laid that which is the glory of a woman (1 Cor. 11:15) at the Saviour's feet. The verb **kissed** is a compound in the Greek, denoting special tenderness of regard, and the tense of this and the following verb shows that the actions were continued and repeated, as though she could not desist. The ointment, which she would not venture near to pour on the head, as was usual, she lavished, as a treasure of respect, on her Saviour's feet. It was a very unusual, and, to the Pharisee, we may suppose, an astounding, a horrifying scene.

39. He, differing from many members of his sect, was too courteous to remark upon it to Jesus; but **he spake within himself, saying, This man, if he were a prophet, would have known** (*would know*) **who,** etc. The Pharisee finds no fault with the morality of the Saviour, but thinks he must be mistaken, and so incurs contamination, which he would not do if he were a prophet. The prophet shares divine knowledge; Jesus, therefore, does not deserve the reputation which he widely enjoys.

40. His conclusion must have been shaken when the latter, **answering the unspoken thought of his heart**, proceeded to explain the meaning of his conduct.—**Simon**—a name very common among the Jews, originating in the Hebrew for Simeon, slightly changed to assimilate it to a familiar Greek proper name.—**I have somewhat to say unto thee.** With this "polite introduction," as Bengel well styles it, the Saviour begins one of those easy and familiar specimens of discourse, which, particularly in the Gospel of Luke, betray a character of geniality—one

might almost say, of humor, colloquial freedom, and gentle, good-natured seriousness, as distinct as that of Socrates in the Apology and Crito.

41. **A certain creditor** (*lender*) **which had two debtors.** Two—the one representing the guilty woman, the other, the Pharisee, in their relation to God.—**The one owed five hundred pence, and the other fifty.** The "penny" of our Gospels (Greek, δηνάριον, nearly an exact transliteration of the Lat. *denarius*), is estimated in the margin of our Bibles (Matt. 18: 28), at seven and a half pence English (the Revision more exactly, eight and a half), or about seventeen cents of our money. This is correct, measuring by the weight of silver contained in the Roman coin, at the price of silver in our coins. But if we measure it by its equivalent in labor, and in the products of labor at that day, its value was very much greater—as much as a dollar, or nearly an English crown. Thus, it was the pay for a day's work in a vineyard (Matt. 20: 2), for a day's entertainment of an invalid at an inn (Luke 10: 35), and two hundred pennyworth of bread was thought of as sufficient for a lunch of "five thousand men, besides women and children" (Mark 6: 37). The proper translation of such words occasions special difficulty; but we shall not err from the intention of our Saviour's apologue here, if we substitute "dollars" in place of "pence."

42. **And** (omit *and*) **when they had nothing to pay** (the Revision is more correct), **he frankly forgave** (freely gave it to) **them both**—on consideration simply of their poverty and helplessness.—**Tell me, therefore,** (omit this and read) **which of them therefore**—in consequence of such favor received (See Greek Text) **will love him most?** With great skill Jesus obliges the Pharisee to pass judgment on himself, which the latter seems

142 LUKE. [Ch. VII.

43 Simon answered and said, I suppose that *he*, to whom he forgave most. And he said unto him, Thou hast rightly judged.
44 And he turned to the woman, and said unto Simon, Seest thou this woman? I entered into thine house, thou gavest me no water for my feet: but she hath washed my feet with tears, and wiped *them* with the hairs of her head.
45 Thou gavest me no kiss: but this woman, since the time I came in, hath not ceased to kiss my feet.
46 ᵃ My head with oil thou didst not anoint: but this woman hath anointed my feet with ointment.
47 ᵇ Wherefore I say unto thee, Her sins, which are many, are forgiven; for she loved much: but to whom little is forgiven, *the same* loveth little.
48 And he said unto her, ᶜ Thy sins are forgiven.

43 love him most? Simon answered and said, He, I suppose, to whom he forgave the most. And he said
44 unto him, Thou hast rightly judged. And turning to the woman, he said unto Simon, Seest thou this woman? I entered into thine house, thou gavest me no water for my feet: but she hath wetted my feet
45 with her tears, and wiped them with her hair. Thou gavest me no kiss: but she, since the time I came
46 in, hath not ceased to ¹kiss my feet. My head with oil thou didst not anoint, but she hath anointed my
47 feet with ointment. Wherefore I say unto thee, Her sins, which are many, are forgiven; for she loved much: but to whom little is forgiven, *the same* loveth
48 little. And he said unto her, Thy sins are forgiven.

a Ps. 23:5.....b 1 Tim. 1:14....c Matt. 9:2; Mark 2:5.——1 Gr. *kiss much*.

already to suspect, by his hesitation, in admitting an obvious truth.

43. I suppose that he, to whom he forgave (the) most. This answer prepares the way for the application of the supposed case to the conduct of the two actual debtors toward God. This follows in ver. 44-47, in such manner as to show that the woman it is, compared with him, who has loved most her gracious benefactor.

44-46. Seest thou this woman? The question intimates at once that she was as the greater debtor, and that he loves less. **Thou, she,** often repeated, keep up the comparison. The **water for the feet, the kiss** of salutation, the beautifying and refreshing cosmetic **oil for the head,** are referred to as ordinary tokens of hospitality, the omission of which, especially of the feet-washing, appears more like a cold indifference to Christ than the narrative otherwise would lead us to imagine. Simon's deficiency the grateful woman had done her best to supply. For the lacking water, she had given her tears; for the towel, her hair; for the kiss of salutation on the cheek, multiplied kisses of tender gratitude on his feet; for the mere oil for his head, she had lavished a costly *unguent* on his feet.

47. Wherefore I say unto thee, Her sins, which are many—many as they are—etc. **Wherefore** (on account of which) must be connected with **I say,** and not with "her sins are forgiven." Grammatically it anticipates the appositional clause, "because she loved much." He does not declare that her sins are forgiven on account of this practical love which she has exhibited; but that, on account of this he is warranted in declaring that her sins **are forgiven.** Rather *have been forgiven;* for the verb in Greek is in the perfect tense. She has been forgiven. It may be known from the fact that she loves. Were one to press the force of the preterit sense, "she *loved*," he might find in it a shred of argument for her love as the antecedent ground of her pardon. But it need be thought of as antecedent only to the conduct she has just exhibited. She loved before she came in; and love it is which shows forth in all these actions. We need not hesitate to think that the Saviour *might have* said that her forgiveness came in consequence of her love, love itself being only a phase of faith; but the order of the words, the perfect tense of the verb, the drift of the parable where the debtors' love is consequent on their forgiveness, and the explicit declaration in ver. 50, all warrant the conclusion that here also, as everywhere else, in all the Scripture, he recognizes her faith as the condition of that forgiveness which her love bespeaks. **Because she loved much.** The much (love) is correlative to "the many" (sins). Her *many* sins have been forgiven, hence she loved *much,* which explains the remarkable demonstration of gratitude and reverence she has now made. **But to whom little is forgiven**—he who is not conscious of having been forgiven much—**the same loveth little**—the debtor who owed fifty pence. Even he would love somewhat; and loving somewhat would make some demonstration of it. "Much forgiveness much love, little forgiveness a little love," warrants the inference: No love, no forgiveness. And to the Pharisee, Christ had said: I entered into thy house, thou gavest me *no* water, *no kiss, no* ointment for my head. He was left to make the application.

48. And he said unto her—not having before addressed her directly—**Thy sins are**

Cн. VII.]   LUKE.   143

49 And they that sat at meat with him began to say within themselves, ᵃ Who is this that forgiveth sins also?
50 And he said to the woman, ᵇ Thy faith hath saved thee; go in peace.

49 And they that sat at meat with him began to say within themselves, Who is this that even forgiveth sins? And he said unto the woman, Thy faith hath saved thee; go in peace.

ᵃ Matt. 9:22; Mark 5:34; 10:52; ch. 8:48; 18:42.——1 Or, among.

---

forgiven. That state of grace in which her love had proved her to be, Jesus attests for her assurance and comfort. Blessed assurance! "Then was our mouth filled with laughter, and our tongue with singing."

49. And they that sat at meat with him (the Pharisee's guests) **began to say within themselves**—in a similar spirit to that at 5: 21, but apparently with less rancor, after the demonstrations of divine authority which have now been multiplied—**Who is this,** etc?

50. Jesus, paying no attention to their carping thoughts, continues his word to the woman.—**Thy faith hath saved thee.** This sentence, while showing that the forgiveness of her sins was her salvation, explains also that the instrumental ground of the forgiveness was her faith. This faith is a peculiar exercise of the mind involving the action of the intellect and the heart alike, and not complete without a revolutionary determination of the will. We may, perhaps, come nearer to apprehending its nature by trying to imagine its origin in her, than by attempting an abstract definition. She had probably seen and heard Jesus before. Some word of his had opened to her view the folly of her course and the sinfulness of her character, so as to fill her with shame and anxious forebodings. While thus led to reproach herself, she saw further that this teacher was not without sympathy for the fallen and lost, which might reach even to a case like hers. Some things which we know that he uttered, would even seem as if it was indeed such as she, the outcasts of respectable and sanctimonious society, that he specially yearned to bless. She may have received some great sanative or other temporal benefit at his hands. She could not fail to be aware that he required repentance, a radical, practical, perpetual cessation from sin, and that his whole invitation looked to a course of arduous self-sacrificing pursuit of a spirit and character and life like his. This was hard; but it was right, and the opposite course was abominable. In his example she saw how even the hardness of it was glorified, its sacrifices rich enjoyments, its losses true gains, its labors rest. In him she saw not only a perfect and encouraging pattern of all this; but one able and ready to aid and lead even her into the blessedness of a like experience. She was unworthy to think so; but she would even trust. She would mould her life into conformity with his requirements, and at a distance she would follow his footsteps, and hope that at last God would accept her as one of his faithful pupils. All this, and more and deeper thoughts than this, we see to have been struggling within her, and moving her to show her gratitude and devotion in this venturesome approach to his feet, merely, at the Pharisee's table. It was love which burst into tears at the sight of him. It had been faith when she first trusted that she might, and decided that she would, give her poor life to his direction; and let him draw the boundary line between the two affections who can. Or, we may say that it was all *one act of repentance, in hope of the Kingdom of God at hand.*—**Go in peace.** The Greek is strictly, "*Go into peace.*" Peace is conceived of as a state which one entering is to go forward in, so as to realize, ever more and more, that rest and serenity of soul which follow pardon, and deepen finally into eternal rest.

CHAPTER VIII.

AND it came to pass afterward, that he went throughout every city and village, preaching and shewing the glad tidings*of* the kingdom of God: and the twelve *were* with him,

2 And *a* certain women, which had been healed of evil spirits and infirmities, Mary called Magdalene, *b* out of whom went seven devils,

1 AND it came to pass soon afterwards, that he went about through cities and villages, preaching and bringing the ¹ good tidings of the kingdom of God, 2 and with him the twelve, and certain women who had been healed of evil spirits and infirmities, Mary that was called Magdalene, from whom seven demons

a Matt. 27 : 55, 56.....*b* Mark 16 : 9.——1 Or, *gospel.*

8: 1-3. ANOTHER PREACHING CIRCUIT THROUGH GALILEE.

1-3. It is probable that the passage gives a summary sketch of the activity of our Saviour during what remained of the Galilean ministry, closing at ch. 9: 50. The previous tour, since 4: 44, may have extended only through the nearer parts of the country, as far as to Nain, while this reached the stranger territory on the other side of the Lake, and the neighborhood of Cesarea Philippi (in Matthew and Mark, the borders of Tyre and Sidon also). Matthew and Mark make a new excursion begin with the sending forth of the twelve; Luke, to say the least, gives no decisive indication that he so conceived that mission; and if we make a division in this Gospel at the end of our present chapter, we must do it from extrinsic considerations. It is not easy to say with what special view Luke selected or arranged his matter. If we think the object hitherto to have been a practical demonstration, furnished to the people, of Christ's Messiahship and of the Messianic character as that of a divine Saviour of lost souls, we may perhaps say that the further design here is, while clinging to the same thread, to show the diverse effects of this demonstration on the mass, and on the chosen few; the separation from the world caused by the reception of his truth; and the necessity of making provision for the continuance of his work, when the Messiah—astounding announcement!—should be violently cut off. The crowds drawn toward the Saviour increase, but his failure to assume earthly dominion chills mistaken zeal; and upon the first clear recognition of his Christhood follows the first shocking prediction of his painful, dishonored death. The latter part of the period is spent in ranging the territory not Jewish, adjacent to Galilee, as if intent on avoiding arrest by the hostile rulers, until the time for his being received up had fully come.

1. And it came to pass afterward—that is, after the events just related, regarded as closing up the preceding circle of evangelistic labors (4: 44; 7: 50). The starting point is not named, but naturally to be thought of as Capernaum. The "soon" of the Revision is almost too specific an addition, yet the Greek marks what follows us so following that nothing comes between, and no time is lost.—**That he** (*he himself*) **went throughout every city and village** (*journeyed throughout by city and village*). The sentence describes the Saviour as traversing the country with the aim of most completely reaching the people, and especially making sure that no city or village should be neglected. It was as though he would not have one soul left unvisited by the light of salvation.—**Preaching and shewing the glad tidings of the kingdom of God.** Two phases of the one perpetual work of declaring the truth concerning salvation. **Preaching,** as explained in ch. 3: 3, gives the work according to its manner; **shewing,** etc., according to its subject matter and its quality to the recipient soul. Jesus announced his message, in an important sense, as a new thing, a message which treated of the Kingdom of God, its presence, its principles, its blessedness, tidings concerning which were good news.—**And the twelve were with him,** viz., journeyed about with him. They did not always all accompany the Saviour, or it would hardly be mentioned in a particular case. They were serving their apprenticeship to the work on which he would soon send them forth alone.

2, 3. And (with him) **certain women, which had been healed of evil spirits and infirmities**—that is, journeyed about with him. This presents a new phase in the ministry of Jesus, not mentioned by the other evangelists, and helping us to see more clearly two things. 1. The poverty of Christ and his apostles, and how they were enabled to give themselves unremittingly to the work, involving as it did considerable expense for their maintenance. Some of the apostles

(James and John, Peter and Matthew), may be supposed to have had some means; but whether, if so, domestic requirements left them any surplus free for the common support, we have no evidence. Jesus could say, not long after this, "The Son of man hath not where to lay his head." But these women, as we see, accompanied him on this excursion for the purpose of giving support and aid to the company, as might be required. May we not take it as a specimen of the assistance rendered at all times by those who believed on him, when the ordinary resources of hospitality proved deficient? 2. The superiority of Jesus to the prejudice of his day against women. We see evidence of this prejudice in the correct statement, in John 4: 27, that his disciples "wondered that he talked with *a* woman." While the Jewish Scriptures and secular literature celebrated the excellence of the virtuous woman, the rabbis of Christ's day thought it scandalous to speak to a woman in public. But our Saviour manifested in this, as in other respects, a supreme indifference to distinctions—of sex, as of nationality, rank, occupation, character—between human beings in the presence of his gospel. The spectacle of his company in their travels would seem a strange one, anywhere, at any time. How much more strange then, when, in the synagogue, the women were latticed off in a part of the house separate from men, and might not appear in the streets, unless when they vailed all but the eyes. But with the treatment of women by Christ began a revolution which has resulted in a social and domestic condition as different from the best then known as it is possible to conceive. And so unassailable was the purity of his character, that his kindness and courtesy toward women appears not to have raised a breath of calumny against him on the part of those who were forward to urge every charge that could impair his influence, or sully his name.

These women seem all to have received special benefits at the hands of our Lord, in cures of maladies and relief from evil spirits; and this had naturally prepared them for the effectual reception of his soul-renewing message. The feeling of personal attachment to a physician who has cured one of some sore disease, was exalted and spiritualized here toward one whom they regarded as the author of to them of eternal salvation, also, from the ills which ruin a soul. The names of a few of them are rescued from earthly oblivion for us; the many others are well known to God. One, indeed—**Mary, that was called Magdalene**—does not appear here only. She is often mentioned subsequently in connection with the life, the death, the resurrection, of our Lord. Yet of her previous history we know nothing at all, except what is implied in this sentence. The epithet, **Magdalene**, signifies that she had lived, probably been born, at Magdala, *Migdal-el*, watch-tower of God, a place on the west side of the Sea of Galilee, the present *El-Mejdel*, an hour's walk south of Capernaum. An untrustworthy tradition, unfortunately embodied in a chapter heading of our Bible, on ch. 7, has identified her with the "woman who was a sinner" in that chapter, so that, although that heading was without any real authority, many people now are surprised to be told that there is not a particle of proof in favor of such a view. There had, indeed, seven demons gone out of her through Christ's merciful command. That they were spoken of as seven, shows that the demoniac influence over her had been seven-fold powerful and distressing. We must combine in imagination all that we know of the helplessness of epilepsy and the ravings of insanity, distinctly recognized as the result of an abhorrent intrusion into the inmost centre of the soul, to form any proper idea of that from which she had been delivered. But this did not imply peculiar guilt. Her case had been pitiable, not criminal.— **Joanna wife of Chuza, Herod's steward.** This man's office, manager of the business affairs of Herod Antipas, was one of high respectability, and it has been conjectured that he was the nobleman whose son Jesus had miraculously healed at Capernaum (John 4: 27), in his early ministry. It may have been so. That his wife should be free to accompany her benefactor, suits better with the supposition that she was now a widow; and that she was able thus to render him aid proves that not merely the worldly "poor" were even then happy in their participation of the kingdom of God.—**Susanna** (the word in Hebrew means "a lily), although her name is preserved, is really no more known to us than the **many others** who are not even designated separately, but "whose names are

146 LUKE. [CH. VIII.

3 And Joanna the wife of Chuza, Herod's steward, and Susanna, and many others, which ministered unto him of their substance.
4 ᵃ And when much people were gathered together, and were come to him out of every city, he spake by a parable:
5 A sower went out to sow his seed: and as he sowed, some fell by the way side; and it was trodden down, and the fowls of the air devoured it.

3 had gone out, and Joanna the wife of Chuza, Herod's steward, and Susanna, and many others, that ministered unto ¹ them of their substance.
4 And when a great multitude came together, and they of every city resorted unto him, he spake by a 5 parable: The sower went forth to sow his seed: and as he sowed, some fell by the way side; and it was trodden under foot, and the birds of the heaven de-

a Matt. 13: 2; Mark 4: 1.—1 Many ancient authorities read, *him.*

written in the book of life."—**Which ministered unto him of their substance.** We may understand from this, more specifically, that they purchased, with their means, the food and other necessaries, when needful, prepared the food, paid the expense of lodgings, and the fare of boats across the lake. Imagination aids us to see the sacred company traveling and halting by turns, and listening or aiding, as Christ diligently accomplished his mission, in city by city, and village by village, showing the glad tidings.

4-15. PARABLE OF THE SOWER.

4. And when much people (or, *a great multitude*) **were gathered together** (or, *came together*). It was at a point of time when the ministry of Jesus was still attracting great attendance, perhaps greater than before, in consequence of this systematic and more formal dissemination of the word, of which we have just spoken. The extraordinary character of his retinue would make a deeper impression. The multitude now spoken of was apparently the people of the neighborhood where he was.—**And were come to him out of every city**—better, *and they were coming to him,* etc. These were the additional crowds furnished by the several cities he had visited. They may well be supposed to have represented a great variety of ideas and states of heart concerning Jesus and his work. The genuine believer, whether more clearly enlightened in his truth, or drawn to him as yet only by a heart-experience of the benefit of his instruction and sympathy, would jostle the proud and malignant Pharisee, while around them clustered every modification of indifference, curiosity, or active inquiry touching the great wonder of their time. Popular enthusiasm prevailed through it all, naturally occasioning anxiety, and involving peril, as well as encouragement, to the cause of Jesus. Hence, he **spake by a parable.** The Greek word for **parable,** re-appearing with little change in the English vocable, is derived from a verb which signifies to place a thing beside another for the purpose, among others, of comparison. We have had the noun already more than once in the sense of a simile or comparison (4:23; 5:36; 6:39), *i. e.*, a mental placing of two things side by side, that the one less clear may be understood from a consideration of the other. But here we have the first instance in our Gospel of a **parable,** in that special sense, in which Jesus frequently used it, at once to veil and to unveil, fundamental truths concerning his kingdom. It is hard to draw a definition of it, so as to comprehend all its features, and to exclude all other forms of illustrative simile. It differs from many similes in not confining itself to a single instance of character or conduct, and in not looking outside of the Kingdom of God. It is an allegory, except that it generally intimates, more or less distinctly, what it is designed to set forth. It always takes the form of a story, relating some occurrence consistent with the customs of human conduct, or an operation of natural laws, suited to explain the principles of the Kingdom of God, its claims, requirements, promises, and its growth See a good definition in Grimm's Clavis Nov. Testamenti, ed. 2, (under the word παραβολή).

5. A (rather *the*) **sower went out to sow his seed.** A comparison with Matthew and Mark shows that the Teacher, to get out from the press of the crowd, had entered a boat, and spoke, sitting in the boat at a convenient distance from the shore. Neander supposed that the use of the article, *the* sower, was explained by imagining Jesus, as he sat, to have pointed to some farmer actually engaged at the moment in sowing his field, on a neighboring slope. It is quite sufficient, however, to understand the article as indicating the representative of a class. (P. Buttmann, *Gr. Gram.* § 124, 1).—**And as he sowed, some fell**- Gr. *one fell.* Mark and Luke individualize the experience—"one," "another," "the other," (Mark 4. 8), "the others," while Matthew throughout, uses the plural number correctly given in the version of the Ameri-

Ch. VIII.] LUKE. 147

6 And some fell upon a rock; and as soon as it was sprung up, it withered away, because it lacked moisture.
7 And some fell among thorns; and the thorns sprang up with it, and choked it.
8 And other fell on good ground, and sprang up, and bare fruit an hundredfold. And when he had said these things, he cried, He that hath ears to hear, let him hear.
9 ^aAnd his disciples asked him, saying, What might this parable be?
10 And he said, Unto you it is given to know the mysteries of the kingdom of God: but to others in parables; ^bthat seeing they might not see, and hearing they might not understand.

6 voured it. And other fell on the rock; and as soon as it grew, it withered away, because it had no moisture.
7 And other fell amidst the thorns; and the 8 thorns grew with it, and choked it. And other fell into the good ground, and grew, and brought forth fruit a hundredfold. As he said these things, he cried, He that hath ears to hear, let him hear.
9 And his disciples asked him what this parable 10 might be. And he said, Unto you it is given to know the mysteries of the kingdom of God; but to the rest in parables; that seeing they may not see,

a Matt. 13: 10; Mark 4: 10....*b* Isa. 6: 9; Mark 4: 12.

---

can Bible Union—**By the way side**—along the way, or road. The Saviour seems to have had in mind a narrow path, leading through the arable field, such as the one in which the disciples were walking when they plucked the ears of grain on the Sabbath, without fences to define it, and on which some seeds would inevitably fall, as the sower scattered them in the vicinity. Here, lying in plain sight on the hard, worn surface, they would be liable to be trodden by passing men and beasts, and to be picked up by the ever-present birds.

6. And some (*another*) **fell on a rock** (lit. *the rock*), etc.—**Moisture** here, and depth of earth in the other Synoptics, complement each other, and show that we are to think not of a soil filled with loose stones; but lying in a thin layer over a flat surface of rock. The warmth of this bed would cause the seed to start more promptly than elsewhere; but would also, after the rains ceased, speedily end its growth.

7. And some (*another*) **fell among thorns** (*the thorns*), i. e., into places already occupied by the seeds and roots of thorny weeds. These springing up rankly with it, as their nature is, would outstrip the more useful plant, overshadow, and stifle it.

8. And other (*another*) fell on good (or, *into the good*) **ground**—ground free from weeds, deep and mellow, of which there was a portion in the field. And this seed **sprang up** (*grew*), **and bare fruit a hundred-fold**—a hundred grains for the one. The well-known fertility of the better soils in Palestine, would have easily furnished cases of production as great as this, which is put here, however, merely as a vivid account of a great yield.—**He that hath ears to hear, let him hear.** Let every one use all his faculties for understanding what I have said.

9. And his disciples asked him (omit *saying*) **What might this parable be?** To us, now, it seems so plain that a child would scarcely need to ask its meaning. But if we consider that Jesus had previously indicated clearly the design of all similar illustrations, while, as yet, he had here left them with the bare story of a man sowing a field, with its various incidents, we shall not wonder that they were perplexed. From the answer which follows, we may see that the question was more comprehensive than as stated by Luke. It included also, in Matthew and Mark, an inquiry why the Lord used the parabolic mode of teaching. We may well suppose that the question had a somewhat more specific aim, to ascertain why the Lord used this way of teaching *now*, when he had for a year and a half, or more, spoken undisguisedly all his thoughts. The Saviour replies first to the latter, and then explains this particular parable.

10. And he said, Unto you it is (has been) **given** (*i. e.*, by God, in awakening in you a spiritual desire for the truth, and faith in me as your teacher), **to know the mysteries of the kingdom of God. Mysteries** in the New Testament mean generally deep truths concerning salvation, which, having been hitherto concealed from human understanding, at most only shadowed forth in dark sayings and enigmatic rites of the Old Testament, are now plainly displayed in the proclamation of the gospel. The sum of this parable was one of the **mysteries**, and the fact that those disciples had been prepared through grace to know them, made it appropriate and pleasant for Jesus to impart to them the desired explanation.—**But to**

11 ᵃNow the parable is this: The seed is the word of God.
12 Those by the way side are they that hear; then cometh the devil, and taketh away the word out of their hearts, lest they should believe and be saved.

11 and hearing they may not understand. Now the 12 parable is this: The seed is the word of God. And those by the way side are they that have heard; then cometh the devil, and taketh the word from their heart, that they may not believe and be saved.

ᵃ Matt. 13:18; Mark 4:14.

others (better, *the rest*) in parables (is the truth exhibited); that seeing they might not see, etc. *The rest* are the indifferent and morally insusceptible mass. The truth should be put before them in forms of expression which, if they really desired to feel its power, would contain light and life to them also. They should look on its embodiment in the character and life of the Lord. But through their worldly self-satisfaction they should catch no glimpse of the life in him, and the most vital teachings should convey no intended sense at all. Such a course was specially appropriate, not to say indispensably necessary now. The suspicion and ill-will of the Pharisaic magnates, of which we saw nothing during the first period of his Galilean ministry, had passed into the stage of murderous hostility. They were watching every utterance of his, not with the slightest intention or desire of profiting thereby; but that they might catch from him some word which they could wrest into a ground of accusation against him. On the other hand, the readiness of the turbulent multitude to become excited about his Messiahship, as equivalent to an earthly royalty promising gratification to their carnal aspirations, made it important for him to weigh his words, and to dispense the truth in such form as was best suited to convey it to the conscience and heart of earnest inquirers. Others might see it, and seeing, not perceive (Mark 4:12). It is their own fault. They choose not to interest themselves in the ends which they are aware Christ's words propose. The continuance of such refusal increases their inability, by the regular operation of a natural law under which God has placed men, and the result, therefore, may truthfully be said to be designed by him. This is the force of **that** in the sentence: "in order that" **seeing they might not see.** The parables have, for one object, to hide the most important truth so that those who wish not to see it shall become, while they so wish, more blind, and those who long for the truth shall, at the same time, see it more brightly.

11. Now—answering the question expressed in ver. 9—**the parable is this.** Every one will notice in the explanation following, with what rhetorical boldness Jesus disregards the exactness of respondence between his exegesis and the terms of the parable, contenting himself with such statements as should certainly guide the popular apprehension to his meaning.—**The seed is the word of God.** He leaves us to infer that the sower with whom he began is himself primarily, and secondarily his disciples, continuing and extending his work.

12. (*And*) **those by the wayside are they that hear** (better, *those who have heard*). The sense is more forcibly expressed than if he had stopped to say, "The hard-trodden soil of the path in the parable represents some hearts on which the word of the gospel falls without making the least impression." It will be noticed also that, by the same felicitous carelessness of rhetoric, our Lord makes the men whose hearts are soil into which the truth is planted, themselves the plants that spring up from it. Again, one seed was specified in the parable in each soil, while a plurality of men now take its place. They *have heard;* the sounds entered their ears, and have excited the sense which is naturally attached to them in their earthly applications. But meeting no desire for religious understanding and impulse; encountering, rather, a state of mind entirely absorbed, and satisfied with what occupies it, the true intent of the communication made is utterly lost. It is as if birds picked up the seed, or a heavy foot crushed it. This again results from criminal carelessness. Of this Satan takes advantage, and employs all his influence to encourage such fatal indifference to the truth. Such, doubtless, were a large part of our Lord's hearers, as they are the largest part, at ordinary seasons, of every congregation where the word of Christ is now proclaimed. And it is still, no doubt, true:—**Then cometh the devil**—little suspected, and apparently little needed in the pre-determined stolidity of the mass.—**And taketh away the word out of**

Ch. VIII.] LUKE. 149

13 They on the rock *are they*, which, when they hear, receive the word with joy; and these have no root, which for a while believe, and in time of temptation fall away.
14 And that which fell among thorns are they, which, when they have heard, go forth, and are choked with cares and riches and pleasures of *this* life, and bring no fruit to perfection.

13 And those on the rock *are they* who, when they have heard, receive the word with joy; and these have no root, who for a while believe, and in time
14 of temptation fall away. And that which fell among the thorns, these are they that have heard, and as they go on their way they are choked with cares and riches and pleasures of *this* life, and bring no fruit to

(rather, *from*—it had not effectually entered) their heart. He has only to amuse them with scenes of imaginary pleasure, or occupy them with any worldly memories or expectations, to hinder all legitimate religious advantage.—**Lest they should** (or *that they may not*) **believe and be saved.** Should they give even thoughtful attention to Christ's truth, their interest in it might be excited, their consciences might be roused, their desires for pardon, peace, and a more worthy life be kindled; they might take Jesus as their guide, and be led to real welfare for time and eternity.

13. They on the rock, etc.—(rather, *And those on the rock*). The second class of hearers, whose heart is symbolized by the rock with a light coating of mellow soil, differs from the preceding in certain respects. They have some curiosity, at least, concerning the word. They give some attention. They form an idea of advantages to be gained by adherence to Christ; desire them, as they conceive of them; think they accept them on Christ's terms; rejoice in this thought. But when removed from the influences which encouraged them, they find that the new course involves trials; that the repentance required is a constant mortification of all evil desires; they find stumbling-blocks in all difficulties; forget their transient joys, and fall away as quickly as they embraced the truth. The plant of faith *sprang up* in them, but could not strike a tap-root.—The **time of temptation**—is any state of outward circumstances which puts the staying power of faith to the test, and offers allurements to give it up. Every experienced observer knows that instances of such superficial and transient discipleship are sadly common still; but will be surprised, perhaps, that the Master ascribes to such "belief," even **for a while.** But they do believe some part of the truth, but not all; and not the main things, and hence not anything long.

14. And that which fell among (*the*) **thorns, these are they, which, when they have heard,** etc. Notice the different form of expression, and more correct, rhetorically

in the first clause. Still our Lord goes forward in the second as if he had said, "those who fell." The vital point of comparison in all these instances is of the hearers to the soils. And here we have to think it out. "The ground which received the seed, is an emblem of those souls which received the word into the midst of distracting cares," etc. This class differ from the second—first, in that the growth of faith proceeds somewhat further. It is supposed that the seed of truth has sprung up in them, and gone on almost to a mature plant. Secondly, the causes of barrenness now are internal; not as before, outward onsets of persecution or temptation; but the truth has, in some apparently fortunate moment, found lodgment in a heart ordinarily occupied with **cares and riches and pleasures of this life** (*this* should be omitted). **Of life,** qualifies all the preceding nouns. The **cares** of life are the anxieties and solicitudes, from whatever cause, harassing the mind in the experiences of daily life. The **riches** of life are worldly wealth, regarded as engrossing much thought; and the **pleasures** of life are mentioned, both because they satisfy the ordinary desires of men, and dull the capacity for higher ambitions and enjoyments. The heart already occupied with either of these kinds of experience, and especially if occupied by them all, mingled or in succession, has no room for the hospitable entertainment of purposes and activities involving improvement in holiness, and reaching out toward eternity. These may find partial place, for a season, but they lack air and light, and the natural disposition not being suppressed, are finally stifled, before the fruits of earnest struggle with sin, and a Christ-like love to others are developed. *Go forth*, in the Common Version, is rightly transposed and rendered—*As they go on their way*, i. e., in the progress of their life, as opportunity is given for the operation of the discordant principles within them—**they are choked**—in respect to their more promising tendencies—**and bring no fruit to perfection.** It is the case of an experience where there has been such an

15 But that on the good ground are they, which in an honest and good heart, having heard the word, keep *it*, and bring forth fruit with patience.
16 *a* No man, when he hath lighted a candle, covereth it with a vessel, or putteth *it* under a bed; but setteth *it* on a candlestick, that they which enter in may see the light.

15 perfection. And that in the good ground, these are such as in an honest and good heart, having heard the word, hold it fast, and bring forth fruit with patience.
16 And no man, when he hath lighted a lamp, covereth it with a vessel, or putteth it under a bed; but putteth it on a stand, that they that enter in may see

a Matt. 5: 15; Mark 4: 21; ch. 11: 33.

effect of gospel truth as to give indications like those of a true conversion, and not afterward so plainly falsified as entirely to forbid hope that there may be a better principle lingering within, while yet carking cares, the love of money, and rampant self-indulgence, in whatever forms, are so indubitably present, that clear and decided evidences of a gracious state are never seen.

15. Those compared to the excellent ground into which a seed fell, these are **they, which** (*such as*) **in an honest and good heart,** etc. **Honest** stands for a Greek adjective, meaning, properly, "beautiful," suited to represent outwardly that which is inwardly **good.** So we speak of a "handsome" character = noble, excellent, fine; a beautiful soil, as the ground is here called. The heart here described following in the series of those already characterized by comparison to the soils, is **honest,** or honorable, or beautiful, **and good,** in that it is mellow for the ready reception of the truth, deep to give the springing plant permanent standing room, vacant of unfriendly growth to allow ample expansion and undivided nutriment. Apart from metaphor, the goodness and moral beauty of the heart here described lies in its desire to know the truth, its candor in recognizing God's word concerning sin and redemption as the truth, and its readiness and earnestness to give that truth due influence over the conduct and dispositions which make up the life. Such hearts **having heard the word,** and embraced the truth with faith and love, **keep it,** i. e., *hold it fast,* not allowing it to be snatched away by the devil, nor dried up with the first heat of temptation, nor choked by more cherished purposes and habits of life. **—And bring forth fruit.** The plant comes to complete development of itself, and bears grain in corresponding abundance.—**With patience**—endurance through all hindrances and trials; constancy which yields to no temptation to desist; perseverance which stops not until the end is reached. This is what none of the other plants had. The first made no start; the second barely started; the third attained a somewhat protracted, but sickly and inefficient life; the fourth continued through all the normal stages, and held out till the full ripening of the crop. The Saviour saw all these classes of hearers before him when he spoke the parable; and we would fain hope that he sees some of the last class also even yet.

The parable of the Sower, the most comprehensive in its range of instruction of all the parables, suggests many questions which it leaves to be answered, on a comparison of other Scripture, by an enlightened theology. What is the explanation of the difference in the quality of hearts here signified? What the relation between the operation of the human powers and of God in his grace, in determining the results of the presentation of truth in each case? As Christ contents himself with setting forth the actual facts everywhere attending the publication of his truth, "the glad tidings of the kingdom," we need notice only that the fundamental character of the announcement, as requiring repentance, and offering forgiveness, and expecting gratitude, forbids our ascribing any particle of *merit* to any heart that receives it. We may add, that, so far as appears, the less beautiful hearts needed only to employ and direct aright their capacities for receiving and appropriating the word, in order to bring forth fruit also. Finally, the seed of divine truth germinates, when it does germinate, and springs up, and grows, and brings fruit to perfection, only through the vivifying influence of God's genial Spirit, operating and empowering, at the start, through every stage of increase, and in the final harvest. This is as the warmth, the sun, the air, the shower, to the growth of the grain.

16-18. JESUS APPENDS TO THE PARABLE AN ADMONITION TO SPREAD THE KNOWLEDGE AFFORDED BY HIS PARABLE.

16. And (or, *but*) **no man when he hath lighted a candle** (*lamp*), etc. The connec-

17 *For nothing is secret, that shall not be made manifest; neither *any thing* hid, that shall not be known and come abroad.

18 Take heed therefore how ye hear: *b* for whosoever hath, to him shall be given; and whosoever hath not, from him shall be taken even that which he seemeth to have.

19 *c* Then came to him *his* mother and his brethren, and could not come to him for the press.

20 And it was told him *by certain* which said, Thy mother and thy brethren stand without, desiring to see thee.

17 the light. For nothing is hid, that shall not be made manifest; nor *anything* secret, that shall not be known
18 and come to light. Take heed therefore how ye hear: for whosoever hath, to him shall be given; and whosoever hath not, from him shall be taken away even that which he ¹ thinketh he hath.
19 And there came to him his mother and brethren,
20 and they could not come at him for the crowd. And it was told him, Thy mother and thy brethren stand

---

a Matt. 10: 26; ch. 12: 2....*b* Matt. 13: 12; 25: 29; ch. 19: 26....*c* Matt. 12: 46; Mark 3: 31.——1 Or, *seemeth to have*.

---

tion with the preceding is, I have opened to you in private the mystery of the kingdom, through the explanation of the parable. But this knowledge in you is as a light, kindled in order that it may shine abroad; and you are with all earnestness to diffuse it as widely as possible.—The **candle** is not mentioned in antiquity; lamps of a rude idea, although often graceful in form, were used instead. The **candlestick** (rather, *stand*) was a holder for the lamp, analogous to our candlestick.— **Bed** means a couch or divan at the side of the room, a seat by day, and sleeping-place at night.

17. **For nothing is secret** (or, *hid*), etc. All that is now a mystery to the worldly crowd is opened to those prepared, for the very purpose that they may publish it to all who will receive it, that it may in the end be universally understood.

18. **Take heed therefore**—seeing it is your high office, as light-bearers for the benighted, to dispense the truth from me—**how ye hear**—that ye hear attentively, understandingly, appreciatively, that all who resort to you may see the light as I give it forth.—**For whosoever hath, to him shall be given.** A stimulus to such careful appropriation of divine truth. No one has this who does not accept it with reverence, love, and obedience. Even a little thus appropriated assures increase, as in the principles of all science and art.—**And whosoever hath not, from him,** etc. The teacher who assumes to know— **seemeth to have** (*thinketh he hath*)—what he has not learned at the right source, nor in the way of due reflection and practical use, will, so continuing, become manifest even to himself as an impostor.

19-21. HE GIVES PREFERENCE TO HIS TRUE DISCIPLES OVER NATURAL KINDRED. (Comp. Matt. 12: 46-50; Mark 31-35.)

19, 20. **Then** (*and there*) **came to him his mother and his** (omit *his*) **brethren.**

The same occurrence, we may assume, as that recorded in Matthew and Mark. The brothers of Jesus (their names are given in Matt. 13: 55), who frequently appear in company with his mother, were, doubtless, sons of Joseph and Mary, born, as well as some sisters (Matt. 13: 56), after him. This view agrees perfectly with previous intimations (Matt. 1: 25; Luke 2: 7), and with every mention of them, as well known to his fellow townsmen (Matt. 13: 55; Mark 6: 3), as not for a time believing in him (John 7: 5), but afterward among his disciples (Acts 1: 14), where Mary is again associated with them. The existence of any supposition counter to this is due to the superstitious, not to say blasphemous, honor which very early began to be ascribed to Mary, and to the utterly unhebraic, antichristian, and irrational notion of the superior sanctity of celibacy. In view of the matured fruit of both these germs of error, we are not favorably impressed with any opinion to which they have given origin. But after the first hint of the perpetual virginity of Mary had been imagined, there began to be a necessity to put some non-natural sense on the texts concerning Christ's brothers and sisters, above cited. Hence the baseless conjectures that they were children of Joseph by a former wife, or by a supposed levirate marriage of Joseph with a supposed widow of his supposed brother Clopas; or that they were cousins, as being children of this Clopas and a sister of Mary. Any one who desires to puzzle himself with the intricate tangle of guesses in support of these theories, may consult Smith's *Dict. of Bible, Art.* Brothers, where their vanity is exposed, as it is also by Meyer, Godet, Farrar, Alford, McClellan, and others. But any one content with the plain intimations of Scripture, that Mary had other children (Matt. 1: 25; Luke 2: 7); and that those among whom Jesus and his brothers had grown up thought it strange that he should be so unlike them (nothing

21 And he answered and said unto them, My mother and my brethren are these which hear the word of God, and do it.
22 ᵃNow it came to pass on a certain day, that he went into a ship with his disciples: and he said unto them, Let us go over unto the other side of the lake. And they launched forth.

21 without, desiring to see thee. But he answered and said unto them, My mother and my brethren are these who hear the word of God, and do it.
22 Now it came to pass on one of those days, that he entered into a boat, himself and his disciples; and he said unto them, Let us go over unto the other side of

---

a Matt. 8: 23; Mark 4: 35.

---

strange, if they were more distant relatives); and that no instance is adduced to show that, in Greek, cousins, as such, were ever called brothers; and that all four evangelists speak of them, repeatedly, precisely as if they thought them his own brothers, Luke also in the Acts, and Paul in 1 Cor. 9: 5; and that no important reason is apparent why they should not have been such—no one considering these things will have occasion to seek further.

The object of their present attempt to reach Jesus appears, from Mark 3: 21, to have been to take him in charge, perhaps put him under restraint, as not in his right mind. When they saw the great commotion made among the people by his preaching and works, they went out to lay hold on him; for "they said, He is beside himself." (Compare ver. 31 ff.) This does not necessarily breathe hostility, but only an honest fear that he was going crazy, and needed to be taken care of. But it does, of course, show that they lacked proper insight into the plan of their brother, and sympathy with the spirit of his work. Their mistake was less excusable than that of Festus concerning Paul (Acts 26: 24 f). Whether Mary shared the error of her sons, cannot be positively affirmed. Some think she had, like John the Baptist, become seriously perplexed by his failure to realize her conception of his destined course; (comp. John 2: 31). But it is equally probable that she may have accompanied her sons only in sympathy with Jesus, and to moderate their attempts upon him.— **And could not come at him for the press** (or, *crowd*). The crowd itself, such as it was, might confirm their supposition that fanaticism or frenzy was at work in him. Luke (and Matthew) gives no account of the place. Mark (3: 20), shows that it was in a house. They had to content themselves with sending word through the multitude that they were outside, and desired to speak with him. Had he not understood their disposition towards him, and probable design in coming, we should expect him to have given more attention to their request. In no view can we make his course seem consistent with that worshipful reverence which Romanists and their copyists profess for Christ's mother. Over him, as if absorbed in delight that some before him were receiving his word into honest and good hearts, all natural attachments lost their power. Common interest in the Kingdom of God was a closer and more tender tie.

21. And he answered . . . My mother and my brethren (brothers) **are these which hear the word of God, and do it.** Spiritual relationship is more to me than flesh and blood. A noble privilege, that the believer may feel himself nearer to the blessed Lord, than if he were merely a son of the same mother, or even that happy mother herself, in the mere natural relationship.

22-25. He Stills a Tempest on the Lake. (Compare Matthew 8: 23-27; Mark 4: 35-41.)

22. On a certain day—literally, *On one of those days*—namely, those occupied by that preaching tour which Jesus was now accomplishing. Mark enables us to see that it was the day on which he had spoken the parable of the Sower.—**He went into a ship** (or, *a boat*), etc. At what point he embarked is not certain, but it was on the west side of the lake. Did the former fishermen among his disciples retain some interest in a boat, which they could command? Did Zebedee favor his sons and their Master with the use of one? Had they to pay the fare in one, out of the slender remnant of some private resources, or by the liberality of helping men and women? We cannot tell. It seems to have been the only way in which our Master's tiresome pedestrianism was ever relieved, until he crossed Olivet, and entered Jerusalem riding on an ass.—**Let us go over unto the other side,** etc. East of the Lake of Gennesaret lay a region rough and wild, which, although within the bounds of the Promised Land, had been scarcely, more than in name, possessed by Israel, and was now occupied by a heterogeneous and comparatively barbarous popu-

LUKE. [Ch. VIII.

23 But as they sailed, he fell asleep: and there came down a storm of wind on the lake; and they were filled *with water*, and were in jeopardy.
24 And they came to him, and awoke him, saying, Master, Master, we perish. Then he arose, and rebuked the wind and the raging of the water: and they ceased, and there was a calm.
25 And he said unto them, Where is your faith? And they being afraid wondered, saying one to another, What manner of man is this! for he commandeth even the winds and water, and they obey him.
26 *a And they arrived at the country of the Gadarenes, which is over against Galilee.

23 the lake: and they launched forth. But as they sailed he fell asleep: and there came down a storm of wind on the lake; and they were filling *with water*,
24 and were in jeopardy. And they came to him, and awoke him, saying, Master, Master, we perish. And he awoke, and rebuked the wind and the raging of
25 the water: and they ceased, and there was a calm. And he said unto them, Where is your faith? And being afraid they marvelled, saying one to another, Who then is this, that he commandeth even the winds and the water, and they obey him?
26 And they arrived at the country of the ¹Gerasenes,

---

a Matt. 8:28; Mark 5:1.—1 Many ancient authorities read, *Gergesenes*; others, *Gadarenes*; and so in ver. 37.

---

lation. Only a few villages and strongholds were scattered near the eastern shore. The Saviour desired to give them also the benefit of his teaching and of his salutary works. He wished that no dark spot within the field of his permitted labors should be left unblest with the heavenly light.

23. As they sailed, he fell asleep. The day had been a busy one, and was now far advanced. Mark, indeed, strongly intimates that the disciples hurried him away, just "as he was in the ship," where he had been through the day's preaching, and without waiting for further preparation, in order that he might rest. Once away from the waiting crowds, the natural desire for sleep would come upon him; and he lay down on a bench at the stern, with a cushion for a pillow, and was presently sound asleep. How sound, appears from what follows; and herein we see a striking evidence of the Saviour's full participation with us in the experiences of humanity.—**And there came down a storm of wind on the lake**—an occurrence still very common, and easily accounted for, by the difference in elevation and temperature between the deeply depressed and sultry sea-level, and the cool summits of the steep, surrounding hills. Gullying ravines guided the currents of cold air from the snow-clad mountains at the north, down to supply the place of the rarefied air above the water. The effect on the little lake is often exceedingly formidable. The waves rise to heights which would hardly seem possible on so limited a surface. (See *Sea of Galilee*, by Capt. Wilson, R. E., p. 265, in *Recovery of Jerusalem*, ed. by Walter Morrison. The same in *Our Work in Palestine*, p. 185 f. See also MacGregor, *Rob Roy, on the Jordan*, p. 330, and p. 408 f.) Immediately there was danger to the little bark. —**They were filled** (*becoming filled*) **with water, and were in jeopardy.** The water was probably breaking over already into the boat in places.—**Master, Master**—the same peculiar term spoken of on 5:5. Both their haste and their confidence in the Saviour's judgment and will, appear in the brevity of their statement.—**We perish.** What a contrast is recognizable in the deep composure of the sleep of Jesus and the angry turbulence of the storm; between the frightened excitement of his followers and the quiet self-possession with which he, being waked, **rebuked the wind and the raging—surge—of the water**, addressing them as though they were intelligent creatures, or under the control of such. (Compare 4:39; Ps. 106:9.) —**And there was a calm.** More suddenly, even, than it rose, the tempest ceased.

25. Where is your faith? He implies that they had faith, at least had had it; but what is become of it? This is surely an occasion when it ought to be at hand, and in use. They probably took little heed of the rebuke to them at the moment; but they took a new lesson of the power of their Master, which might profit them another time.—**And they being afraid, wondered** (*marvelled*). The gigantic tumult of the elements, and their own consternation, prepared them for an impression of Christ's majesty at this moment, greater than was occasioned by his raising the widow's son to life.—**What manner of man** (or, *Who then*—seeing that he does such things) **is this! for** (or, *that*) **he commandeth even the winds**, etc. That = seeing that—more appropriately than "for," justifies their hushed inquiry. The form of direct command to the powers of nature, rather than this silent exercise of his will, had been peculiarly suited to impress their thoughts.

The boat, with Christ and his disciples in the midst of an angry sea, has been recognized as a fit emblem of his church in trouble, through all her history.

26-39. The Demoniac at Gergesa. (Matt. 8:28-34; Mark 5:2-20.)

27 And when he went forth to land, there met him out of the city a certain man, which had devils long time, and ware no clothes, neither abode in *any* house, but in the tombs.

26. And they arrived at (Greek, *sailed into*) **the country of the Gadarenes** (or, *Gergesenes*), &c. There is peculiar difficulty in determining what the name of these people was in the Gospel as first written. We have respectable authority in each of the three Gospels, for all the three names—Gergesenes, Gadarenes, Gerasenes. Gadara is supposed to

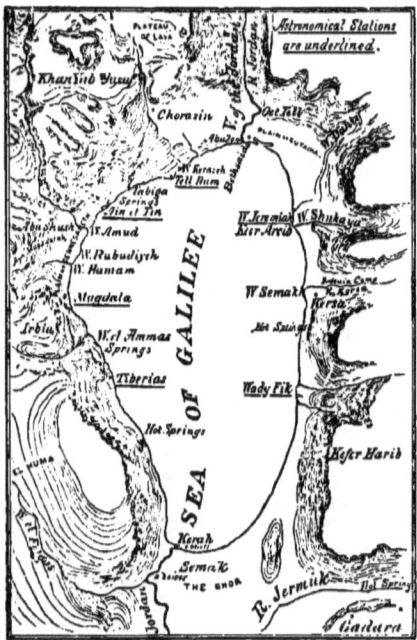

be represented by the ruins found at *Um-keis*, or *Mkes*, ten or twelve miles southeast of the Lake of Gennesaret; and Gerasa, by the place now called Gerash, some fifty miles from the lake in the same direction. It is evident that the "country" must, in either case, have borne the name of the prominent city for a long distance around, even to the shores of the lake. It is reported farther by travelers that there is no place on the eastern shore where a herd could run down the slope directly into the sea, except near the remains of a small town about southeast of Capernaum, now called *Kersa* (see chap. above). This led

27 which is over against Galilee. And when he was come forth upon the land, there met him a certain man out of the city, who had demons; and for a long time he had worn no clothes, and abode not in *any*

Dr. Thomson (*The Land and the Book;* and Porter, *Handbook of Syria and Palestine*, p. 401 f., Wilson in *Recovery of Jerusalem*, p. 286 f., and MacGregor, p. 324 and p. 409 f.), to the very probable conclusion that here was anciently the town called Gergesa; at all events that near it must have occurred the events relating to the demoniac, and that this was "the city" (ver. 34). On this supposition we may conjecture that the comparative obscurity of this town, perhaps its destruction in the devastating wars soon after, led early copyists, in their perplexity about the place, to vary between names drawn from the two better known cities, Gadara and Gerasa, and that from Gergesa. This last is adopted in our passage by Tischendorf, "Gergesenes," and we think rightly, although Westcott and Hort sustain the Revision in "Gerasenes."—**Over against Galilee.** The course of their voyage had been (towards *Kersa*) nearly east. Here Jesus landed among rude, half-heathen people, among whom, however, the Jews might have such a preponderant influence that his errand would still be to "the lost sheep of the house of Israel."

27. And when he went forth to (*upon the*) **land.** As it was late in the day when they sailed, we may suppose that Jesus and his company spent the night on the boat, and, whether so or not, that the incident about to be mentioned took place not until the next morning.—**There met him out of the city a certain man**—viz., of Gergesa. A *man out of the city*, in the sense that he had belonged there when he was fit to live among people.—**Which had devils** (*demons*), and the most miserable specimen of that unhappy class presented to us in the Gospels. (See in regard to them on 4:33.) The words **long time** belong to the next clause. *And for a long time he* **ware no clothes**—Greek, "he did not put on an outer garment." It was a horrible apparition, not unlike, in appearance, the most dreadful cases to be met with in our asylums, who frequently tear off their clothing.—**Neither abode in any house, but in the tombs.** Being driven from the habitations of men, and with no such place of refuge as Christian charity has made common in its time, the vacant and unused tombs, so

28 When he saw Jesus, he cried out, and fell down before him, and with a loud voice said, What have I to do with thee, Jesus, *thou Son of God most high?* I beseech thee, torment me not.

29 (For he had commanded the unclean spirit to come out of the man. For oftentimes it had caught him; and he was kept bound with chains and in fetters; and he brake the bands, and was driven of the devil into the wilderness.)

30 And Jesus asked him, saying, What is thy name? And he said, Legion: because many devils were entered into him.

28 house, but in the tombs. And when he saw Jesus, he cried out, and fell down before him, and with a loud voice said, What have I to do with thee, Jesus, thou Son of the Most High God? I beseech thee,

29 torment me not. For he was commanding the unclean spirit to come out from the man. For 1 oftentimes it had seized him; and he was kept under guard, and bound with chains and fetters; and breaking the bands asunder, he was driven of the

30 demon into the deserts. And Jesus asked him, What is thy name? And he said, Legion; for many de-

1 Or, *of a long time.*

---

frequently met with, especially on hill-sides, in Palestine, and of which many are said to remain in the vicinity of the spot Kersa (see MacGregor, *Rob Roy on the Jordan,* p. 410), would furnish him a fit and acceptable lair

28. When he saw Jesus, he cried out—a verb is used which signifies, specifically, "to croak," "to give a hoarse scream," "to shout vociferously." It was at first the inarticulate expression of his rage and hatred and fear, at the sight of one whose presence, he instinctively felt, foreboded no good to him.—**And fell down before him**—not as a man, but as one demonized; to denote, in his conscious inferiority, abject deprecation.—**What have I to do with thee,** etc.=Why shouldest thou meddle with me? Why not leave me alone? This is the prayer of his unholy dread, in the presence of self-revealing holiness and divine authority.—**Jesus, thou Son of the most High God.** That he should recognize the person before him as Jesus, does not oblige us to ascribe to him supernatural discernment. Although our Lord had never, so far as appears, been in that neighborhood before, yet the place was easily in sight of the shore, not six miles off, where most of his mighty works had been done, including the expulsion of many demons. Doubtless, there had been much talk of this within the hearing of the possessed sufferer, and much discussion held as to the Messiahship of the mighty adversary of Satan. And in calling him **Son of the most high God,** we cannot be certain that the demon, speaking through the man, meant otherwise than to use a title understood to characterize the Messiah. No one at that time gives evidence of having more than an incipient apprehension of the unfathomable depth of truth which spiritual reflection would gradually discover in it.—**I beseech thee, torment me not.** Send me not to the place of torment. The demon felt that Christ's presence threatened punishment to him. Indeed, already the notice had been served upon him.

29. For he has commanded (rather, *was commanding*) **the unclean spirit,** etc. We may note here that Christ speaks as though he conceived the spirit to be one. Compare the form of the address in Mark.—**For**—indicating the reason for Christ's command—**oftentimes it had caught** (or *seized*) **him; and he was kept bound with chains and in fetters**—like a case of chronic insanity, of the most violent and even dangerous type. Not only like such a case, but one where the Satanic power had actually produced such bodily disorder as necessitated extreme derangement of the mind. This description applies to him while yet retained in the town —in chains and *under guard.*—**And he brake the bands**—perhaps, more than once—**and was driven of the devil into the wilderness** (better, *by the demon into the deserts*— deserted, solitary places, where he met Jesus (comp. "dry places," 11: 24). Such was the case which had engaged Christ's compassionate concern.

30. And Jesus asked him, saying, What is thy name? The most effectual way imaginable to call into exercise what fragment of reason might be in the man, and to soothe the excitement under which he labored.— **And he said, Legion,** etc. **Legion** in the Roman military organization was analogous to regiment or brigade, with us. This name may have been assumed by the man, to signify his persuasion, not only that he was possessed by a multitude of evil spirits (a Legion consisted normally of six thousand men), but that their fiendish power over him was as rigorous and irresistible as that of the Roman arms over her conquered provinces. We have noted above in the case of Mary Magdalene (8: 2), that the severity of the disorder resulting from possession was explained

31 And they besought him that he would not command them to go out ᵃ into the deep.
32 And there was there a herd of many swine feeding on the mountain: and they besought him that he would suffer them to enter into them. And he suffered them.
33 Then went the devils out of the man, and entered into the swine: and the herd ran violently down a steep place into the lake, and were choked.
34 When they that fed them saw what was done, they fled, and went and told it in the city and in the country.
35 Then they went out to see what was done; and came to Jesus, and found the man, out of whom the devils were departed, sitting at the feet of Jesus, clothed, and in his right mind: and they were afraid.

31 mons were entered into him. And they intreated him that he would not command them to depart
32 into the abyss. Now there was there a herd of many swine feeding on the mountain: and they intreated him that he would give them leave to enter
33 into them. And he gave them leave. And the demons came out from the man, and entered into the swine: and the herd rushed down the steep into the lake,
34 and were drowned. And when they that fed them saw what had come to pass, they fled, and told it in
35 the city and in the country. And they went out to see what had come to pass; and they came to Jesus, and found the man, from whom the demons were gone out, sitting, clothed and in his right mind, at

---

a Rev. 20: 3.

---

by the number of alien spirits, and on that principle this man feels himself the abode of a legion of them. Jesus had treated the Satanic power as one (ver. 29), and so the Evangelists had spoken of it; but from this point it will be observed that the account proceeds on the man's own supposition that they were many. The man's view would chime with that generally entertained at the time; and the Saviour might well forego the attempt to correct an error on this incidental point, in those circumstances.

31. And they besought him that he would not command them to go out into the deep (or *abyss* = "the bottomless pit" of Rev. 9: 1, 11; 11: 7). Anything was preferable to the infernal state.

32. And there was there a herd of many swine feeding.—This proves the heathen character of portions of the population in that neighborhood. **The mountain** was that which appears in the pictures of the Sea of Galilee, as we look across from the western shore.—**And they besought him,** etc. The unclean animal would suit the unclean nature, and here seemed an escape from being sent back to perdition.—**And he suffered them**—granted their prayer, and disappointed their aim.

33. Then went the devils out of the man—(better, *And the demons came out from the man*). In a subject so entirely outside the limits of ordinary human experience, no authoritative explanation can be added to the simple statement of the word. Whether the view on which the Saviour has spoken to the demon in the man as a single being, was the correct one, or the man's crazed imagination that he was possessed by an army of them, we cannot properly *understand* the effect on the swine—"they were about two thousand" (Mark 5: 13). The possession of dumb brutes by one or many rational, but infernal spirits, must remain a mystery to us. Godet, on the passage, declares that "the influence exerted by the demons on the herd was, in no sense, a possession. None but a moral being can be morally possessed." But might there not be a possession in the case of the swine that was not moral? He seems to think of some panic of terror started in some way at that time, which was believed by those who shaped the popular narrative to be the result of the transfer of the demoniac power to them. This is far from satisfactory, as are the other conjectures which have been hazarded to clear up the mystery. Enough, that the man was completely rescued, and the unclean spirit, in being allowed his desire, was most effectually remanded to the abyss.

34. And when they that fed them saw, etc. As they were "a great way off" from the position of Jesus (Matt. 8: 30), the panic among the swine, and their total destruction, must have come as a prodigious surprise.—**They fled**—ran away from the scene in terror, reporting everywhere in town and country, the loss of the property, and the almost miraculous circumstances attending it.

35. The people, thus aroused, went in numbers, of course, to the scene, and **came to Jesus**—perhaps having heard nothing about him in connection with the matter—**and found the man, out of whom the devils were departed, sitting**—(the word, *sitting,* belongs here); this itself was wonderful in the case of one who had been so unceasingly restless and violent, ready for mischief, "so that none could pass through that way" (Matt. 8: 28).—**Clothed**—this was another proof of change (comp. ver. 27); now some one had furnished him necessary garments

Cн. VIII.] LUKE. 157

36 They also which saw *it* told them by what means he that was possessed of the devils was healed.
37 *a* Then the whole multitude of the country of the Gadarenes round about, *b* besought him to depart from them; for they were taken with great fear: and he went up into the ship, and returned back again.
38 Now *c* the man out of whom the devils were departed besought him that he might be with him: but Jesus sent him away, saying,
39 Return to thine own house, and shew how great things God hath done unto thee. And he went his way, and published throughout the whole city how great things Jesus had done unto him.

36 the feet of Jesus: and they were afraid. And they that saw it told them how he that was possessed with 37 demons was 1 made whole. And all the people of the country of the Gerasenes round about asked him to depart from them; for they were holden with great fear: and he entered into a boat, and returned. 38 But the man from whom the demons were gone out prayed him that he might be with him: but he sent 39 him away, saying, Return to thy house, and declare how great things God hath done for thee. And he went his way, publishing throughout the whole city how great things Jesus had done for him.

a Matt. 8:34....*b* Acts 16:39....*c* Mark 5:18.——1 Or, *saved.*

---

and he wore them like other men.—**In his right mind, at the feet of Jesus.** This is the Greek order of the last clause, and closes the series of facts according to their ascending importance in the history of the affair—quiet, clothed, mentally sane, and employing his restored faculties in reverently, thankfully waiting upon the teachings of his benefactor. **—And they were afraid.** Another instance of the awe and dread produced in minds conscious of sin, by the manifestation of Christ's divine character and power.

36. They also which saw it—a different set from the swine-herds who had carried away the report; the disciples, and, perhaps, others with them.—**Told them by what means** (or *how*) **he that was possessed of the devils** (or *with demons*) **was healed** (Greek, saved). Here **how** is emphatic. The swine-herds had borne some word about the demoniacs (Matt. 8:33), but apparently nothing about Christ's relation to them. This, we should naturally suppose, would have awakened in them a thankful interest in him, and opened the way for fruitful labors there on his part. A great deliverance had been mercifully and miraculously granted to an afflicted countryman and neighbor, and the vicinity cleared of a great burden and danger. But with this, they now learned of Christ's connection with the drowning of the swine, which alone awakened any interest in their minds, and that in the way of repulsion to Jesus.

37. Then (or *And*) the whole multitude —of the community, without distinction of Jew and Gentile—**besought (*asked*) him to depart from them; for they were taken (*holden*) with great fear.** Not now a holy, or even religious awe, but a selfish, worldly, mercenary, fear. This was their prayer to him who, as they knew, only waited for a desire from them to heal their sick, and save their lost souls. Their prayer was heard, and the only opportunity ever to be afforded them for blessings, directly at the hands of Jesus, was lost. **And he went up into the ship** (*entered into a boat*) **and returned.** It is not improbable, as we have seen on ver. 27, that Christ had passed the night after the storm, on board the boat, so that the cure of the demoniac would have taken place early the next morning, and this return have begun before noon.

38. One touching and instructive incident occurred as he was leaving. The saved man **besought** (or, *prayed*) **him that he might be with him.** Every disciple of Christ can enter into the feeling with which he would plead not to be deprived of that company in which he had found a boon more precious than life. How could his faith stand, if he were soon left to himself? What a comfort, if he could bask at all times in the light of that life-beaming face! His prayer, too, was doubtless answered—heaven will show—yet not as he had conceived it.—**Jesus sent him away** from his bodily presence, although he had called others to leave all and go with him. He wished his disciples in many spheres and places. Those whom he did not take with him, however, were still to serve him as truly as those whom he took. And all alike might be "with him" in the closest sympathy while they were engaged in promoting his work in the world.

39. Return to thine own (or, *thy*) **house, and shew,** *declare,* (or, *relate,*) etc. We see thus that a privilege was granted him which had been withheld from many who seemed more favored. They were forbidden to speak of Christ's mercies. The reason probably was that there was no danger in the Gergesene country of an unhealthy excitement, and there was no other way of spreading the gospel news there. The redeemed man was

40 And it came to pass, that, when Jesus was returned, the people *gladly* received him: for they were all waiting for him.
41 *a*And, behold, there came a man named Jairus, and he was a ruler of the synagogue: and he fell down at Jesus' feet, and besought him that he would come into his house:
42 For he had one only daughter, about twelve years of age, and she lay a dying. But as he went the people thronged him.
43 *b*And a woman having an issue of blood twelve years, which had spent all her living upon physicians, neither could be healed of any,

40 And as Jesus returned, the multitude welcomed him; for they were all waiting for him. And behold, there came a man named Jairus, and he was a ruler of the synagogue: and he fell down at Jesus'
42 feet, and besought him to come into his house; for he had an only daughter, about twelve years of age, and she lay a dying. But as he went the multitudes thronged him.
43 And a woman having an issue of blood twelve years, who [1] had spent all her living upon physicians,

a Matt. 9:18; Mark 5:22....*b* Matt. 9:20.——[1] Some ancient authorities omit, *had spent all her living upon physicians and.*

allowed to do for Jesus what the latter could not do for himself, being driven out of the country.—**And he went his way, and published** (or, *publishing*)—not only in his house, but—**throughout the whole city**—and (according to Mark, ver. 20), in Decapolis, a district of country named as possessing ten cities—**how great things Jesus had done unto him.** The man might not have been competent, in the Master's judgment, for a missionary work abroad, or for doing anywhere the work of a teacher and defender of the faith, while yet admirably fitted to do the common work of Christians, in a private and familiar sphere, the work, namely, of testifying to his own happy experience of God's saving power and mercy. Notice that he understands what God had done for him to have been done by Jesus.

40-56. RETURN TO THE WEST SIDE OF THE LAKE, AND SOME REMARKABLE WORKS THERE. Matt. 9: 18-22; Mark 5: 21-34.

40. When Jesus returned (omit was), the multitude gladly received him. It is doubtful whether **welcomed** is preferable to "gladly received" of the Common Version.—**For they were all waiting for him**—this intimates that the place was Capernaum, where he had left many people gathered. He meets a great change in the attitude of the people from that of those he had left scarcely an hour's sail away, and no doubt welcome to himself, even though he found so much of mere earthly interest in their expectation of healing and outward benefit to themselves and their friends. Some would also be concerned about tidings of the kingdom. Scarcely had he reached the throng of people on the shore, when his aid was in demand.

41. And behold, there came a man named Jairus, etc. The interjection notifies us that there was something surprising in it. To contemporaries the name itself might suggest the explanation, but the fact of his being a ruler of the synagogue there, and that he approached Jesus with the most humble reverence, and with unmistakable signs of confidence that he, and he alone, could do him a favor of the greatest importance, was well suited to attract general attention. As one of the rulers of the synagogue, Jairus belonged to the highest class of the community. That class were generally now so excited against our Lord, that we must suppose this man to have been unusually exempt from their prejudices, or to have been driven by mere stress of parental solicitude for a dying child, to suppress them. In either case his conduct proves a real conviction in his mind of a truly divine power in Jesus to relieve suffering and heal disease. His need was, indeed, a sore one.

42. He had one only daughter—when Nathan would express the extremity of the poor man's tenderness for his one ewe lamb, he said, it "was unto him as a daughter"—**about twelve years of age**—old enough to have found a deep place in a father's heart—**and she lay a dying.** Truly his agony might well get the better of much pride and reluctance, to secure the only possible help for him on earth. How many thousands of distressed parents have since wished that their Saviour were accessible to them, as he was to men when he was on the earth, well assured that he could not then refuse them aid! But he can give comfort even now. We do not need to be told that the prayer of the ruler, that Jesus should **come into his house,** was granted. They are on the way. The multitudes previously collected, now following him and growing, might have impeded their passage through the most ample streets; but in the contracted ways of an Oriental town, they **thronged**—literally, "choked"—**him** in their close packed mass. This gave opportunity for another miracle within a miracle—a miracle by stealth.

43, 44. A woman having an issue of

Ch. VIII.] LUKE. 159

44 Came behind him, and touched the border of his garment: and immediately her issue of blood stanched.
45 And Jesus said, Who touched me? When all denied, Peter and they that were with him said, Master, the multitude throng thee and press thee, and sayest thou, Who touched me?
46 And Jesus said, Somebody hath touched me: for I perceive that a virtue is gone out of me.
47 And when the woman saw that she was not hid, she came trembling, and falling down before him, she declared unto him before all the people for what cause she had touched him, and how she was healed immediately.
48 And he said unto her, Daughter, be of good comfort: thy faith hath made thee whole; go in peace.

44 and could not be healed of any, came behind him, and touched the border of his garment: and immediately the issue of her blood stanched. And Jesus
45 said, Who is it that touched me? And when all denied, Peter said, ¹ and they that were with him, Master, the multitudes press thee and crush thee. But
46 Jesus said, Some one did touch me: for I perceived that power had gone forth from me. And when the
47 woman saw that she was not hid, she came trembling, and falling down before him declared in the presence of all the people for what cause she touched
48 him, and how she was healed immediately. And he said unto her, Daughter, thy faith hath ² made thee whole; go in peace.

a Mark 5: 30; ch. 6: 19.—1 Some ancient authorities omit *and they that were with him*....2 Or. *saved thee.*

---

blood twelve years, and in such a case that, after spending all her living on physicians, she was worse than ever, **came behind him.** She must have worked her way, following the human current, so as to reach him without being seen—at least, as she supposed. She might have thought he would deem her touch pollution, yet believed that she must touch him, to receive any help. Thus she was able to **touch the border** ("hem," or "fringe") **of his garment,** that is, of his outer, shawl-like mantle. This robe was required by the law (Num. 15: 38 f.) to be made with a fringe of the depending threads of the warp (the cloth being further secured from raveling by a narrow blue ribbon), which the Jew was required to wear as a distinctive badge. The robe being folded with care, so that it would fall in two corners in front, and two behind, the woman touched it, probably at one of these corners, behind him. We may suppose it to have been true humility, in part, that led her to seek the boon secretly, which she believed Jesus able to impart, and partly, the influence of superstition, and regard for the customs of her time. Even such faith should not fail of success.—**Immediately her issue of blood stanched.** She was conscious that after so many years of mortifying pain, fruitless expenditures, and disappointed hopes, she was again well.

45. But she had not, as she supposed, stolen a cure. **Jesus said, Who** (or, *Who is it that*) **touched me?** He was aware of the seizure of his garment, and in the manner of it recognized the touch of faith, which he had answered with the healing influence. But he would know more distinctly who was the person that had received the blessing, in order to the moral advantage of that person, and to show to all that there was no magical efflux of power from his person. All about him denied that they had touched him, in the sense of intentionally taking hold of him; and the disciples thought it quite impracticable, in such a jam, to find out who in particular had come in contact with him.

46. But Jesus insisted, **Somebody hath touched me** (*did touch*)—designedly took hold of me; and the touch was efficacious—**for I perceive that virtue is**—read, as in Revision: *I perceived that virtue,* here =healing power, *had gone out from me.* This is adduced as a reason of his knowledge of the touch. The full explanation would involve an understanding of the mystery of Christ's person, beyond what we possess. Enough that we see it was not by any magical virtue in his garments, or his body itself; but from the centre of his spiritual being, and in answer to faith in him as the Physician, that the power had gone forth. Mark tells us that he was meanwhile looking around to see "who she was that had done it." This, strictly taken, shows that he knew the person was a woman. Jesus had to learn many things like other men, by inquiry, experiment, and search.

47. And when the woman saw that she was not hid, (that what she had done and experienced was known), **she came trembling**—in her new-found happiness, recalling the precept of the law (Lev. 15: 19, 25), and the cruel horror of women on the part of the Rabbis; (see Geikie, 1: 530), and, perhaps, fearing that she had actually committed a *theft* of what was to her more precious than rubies—**and falling down before him, declared,** etc. Thus she furnished to the whole multitude a new mode of proof of the unfailing abundance of grace in Christ, to meet the need of every sufferer.

48. And he said unto her—instead of the

49 ᵃ While he yet spake, there cometh one from the ruler of the synagogue's *house,* saying to him, Thy daughter is dead; trouble not the Master.
50 But when Jesus heard *it,* he answered him, saying, Fear not: believe only, and she shall be made whole.
51 And when he came into the house, he suffered no man to go in, save Peter, and James, and John, and the father and the mother of the maiden.
52 And all wept, and bewailed her: but he said, Weep not; she is not dead, ᵇ but sleepeth.
53 And they laughed him to scorn, knowing that she was dead.
54 And he put them all out, and took her by the hand, and called, saying, Maid, ᶜ arise.

49 While he yet spake, there cometh one from the ruler of the synagogue's *house,* saying, Thy daughter
50 is dead; trouble not the ¹ Master. But Jesus hearing it, answered him, Fear not: only believe, and she
51 shall be ² made whole. And when he came to the house, he suffered not any man to enter in with him, save Peter, and John, and James, and the father of
52 the maiden and her mother. And all were weeping, and bewailing her: but he said, Weep not; for she
53 is not dead, but sleepeth. And they laughed him to
54 scorn, knowing that she was dead. But he, taking

a Mark 5: 35....*b* John 11: 11, 13....*c* ch. 7: 14; John 11: 43.——1 Or, *Teacher*....2 Or, *saved*.

reproof which she had feared, or severer penalty—**Daughter**—the unwonted kindness of this address must itself have scattered her fears—**thy faith hath saved thee**—it, not any outward contact, is what has secured for you this great deliverance at my hands.—**Go in** (unto) **peace** (comp. 7: 50).

49-56. THE CASE OF JAIRUS' DAUGHTER RESUMED.

49. While he yet spake, there cometh one from the ruler of the synagogue's house, etc. Some delay had taken place, and meantime the child had died. Matthew (ver. 18), overlooking this second message included by anticipation, the substance of both in the father's original statement. The thought of the messengers now was that, as the child was dead, there was no longer scope for the power of Jesus.

50. But when Jesus heard—hearing, but "not heeding" (Mark 5: 36 Revision)—**he answered him**—met his despairing thought. —**Fear not, believe only.** It would require of him a higher exercise of faith indeed; but he may understand that all things are possible to him that believeth.—**And she shall be made whole** (Greek, *be saved,* to wit, from death).

51. And when he came into the house, etc. **Into the house** means probably into the court, or yard, of the house; but possibly we might substitute "unto the house;" while **to go in,** has reference to the apartment of the house, in a strict sense, where the child lay.—**Except Peter,** etc.—enough to serve as witnesses of the state of the child, and of her restoration, but not a throng to disturb the solemnity befitting the scene. The parents represented the general community, the three apostles the body of the disciples. On four different occasions the Saviour made such a distinction among the apostles, and in every case it was this same three, here, at the Transfiguration (9: 28 par.), in Gethsemane (Matt. 26: 37 par.), and (with the addition of Andrew) on the Mount of Olives (Mark 13: 3)—that were favored with his more intimate association. It is probable that not merely priority in the line of their discipleship, but also greater congeniality of character, and ability to profit by his more intimate intercourse, determined this uniformity of selection. Are there like reasons of difference still?

52. And all—those about the couch of death —**wept,** etc., (better, *were weeping and bewailing*) **her.** So soon had the usual practices of mourning etiquette begun; strange indeed to us, yet whether more unreasonable than much with which we are familiar, would require an impartial observer to decide. The *weeping* was a dolorous, rather than tearful, series of ejaculations, and the *wailing* was beating of the breast, rending the outer garment, tearing out the hair, with outcries, in which neighbors joined. Professional mourners were also hired to go through the requisite performances. All this our Saviour now rebuked, saying—**Weep not; she is not dead, but sleepeth.** That he meant this figuratively (comp. John 11: 11; 1 Cor. 15: 6, 51; 1 Thess. 4: 13), is scarcely to be doubted from ver. 49, 52, esp. 55, and from the whole spirit of the narrative. It was natural that he should so speak here, both because he purposed to restore her immediately to life, and to signify the impropriety of the din and uproar they were making. They, understanding him literally, ridiculed his saying, little knowing that they were contributing to a more unquestionable proof of his divine power.

54. We learn from both Matthew and Mark that he had them removed from the room.— And took her by the hand, and called, saying, Maid, arise. The clause—**And he put them all out**—is to be omitted. Mark

55 And her spirit came again, and she arose straightway: and he commanded to give her meat.
56 And her parents were astonished: *but he charged them that they should tell no man what was done.

55 her by the hand, called, saying, Maiden, arise. And her spirit returned, and she rose up immediately: and he commanded that *something* be given her to
56 eat. And her parents were amazed: but he charged them to tell no man what had been done.

CHAPTER IX.

THEN *b* he called his twelve disciples together, and gave them power and authority over all devils, and to cure diseases.
2 And *c* he sent them to preach the kingdom of God, and to heal the sick.
3 *d* And he said unto them, Take nothing for *your* journey, neither staves, nor scrip, neither bread, neither money; neither have two coats apiece.
4 *e* And whatsoever house ye enter into, there abide, and thence depart.

1 AND he called the twelve together, and gave them power and authority over all demons, and to cure
2 diseases. And he sent them forth to preach the
3 kingdom of God, and to heal ‖ the sick. And he said unto them, Take nothing for your journey, neither staff, nor wallet, nor bread, nor money; neither have
4 two coats. And into whatsoever house ye enter,

a Matt. 8: 4; 9: 30; Mark 5: 43....*b* Matt. 10: 1; Mark 3: 13; 6: 7....*c* Matt. 10: 7, 8; Mark 6: 12; ch. 10: 1, 9....*d* Matt. 10: 9; Mark 6: 9; ch. 10: 4; 22: 35....*e* Matt. 10: 11; Mark 6: 10.—‖ Some ancient authorities omit, *the sick.*

gives the very Aramæan phrase which he used, *Talitha cumi.* Luke gives the translation. The taking her by the hand, we suppose to have been just a token of the affectionate interest which Jesus felt in a child cut down as a flower, and whom he would restore to life. His simple, vernacular words pierced the dull, cold ear of death, and the first object of her returning consciousness would be the image of her Restorer, holding her by the hand.

55. And her spirit came again (*returned*), etc. The historical reality of the whole transaction, and the calm reasonableness of Jesus in it all, appear from his natural concern about her sustenance, in directing that there should be given her to eat.

56. And her parents were astonished. Mark gives a very strong expression of their surprise. They probably had seen nothing previously of such mighty works of Jesus; and although the father had gone to entreat from him a miracle, the actual occurrence of it could never cease to be wonderful.—**But he charged them to tell no man what was** (*had been*) **done.** Contrast this with ver. 39, and see note on 5: 14. An additional reason for reticence now, as in some other cases, might be, the injury to the character of the person saved, if she became the subject of great notoriety and corresponding attention.

1–6. THE TWELVE APOSTLES COMMISSIONED AND SENT FORTH. (Matt. 10: 1, 5–16; Mark 6: 7–13.)

1, 2. The place from which the apostles were sent forth is not indicated. In Mark, Nazareth appears to be the last preceding note of locality. They had now been long enough with the Master, sharing his special instruction, to warrant their being sent abroad by themselves, on a kind of trial tour, partly to prove them for the work which must before long devolve wholly on them, and partly to reach the inhabitants of Galilee more thoroughly in their pitiable need (Matt. 9: 36), than Jesus could himself do before he must leave that favored region forever.—**Then** (rather, *And*) **he called his** (*the*) **twelve disciples** (omit **disciples**) **together**—separating them from other disciples and strangers. —**And gave them power and authority.** The **power** was intrinsic authority to meet all Satanic agencies and the maladies of men, while **authority** was the liberty and full permission to use this ability as the occasions which Christ specified should arise.—**Over all** (*the*) **devils** (literally, *demons*); mentioned first to make conspicuous their antagonism to the devil, his emissaries, and all his work.— **And to cure diseases.** They were, like their Master, to care for the health of both body and soul. The former, as really as the latter, was a matter of deep concern to our Lord; and although we truly say that his chief and ultimate aim was benefit to souls, no one can set limits to what he would have done simply to relieve men from bodily woe. For the sake of mutual support and comfort, the disciples were sent in pairs (Mark 6: 7), and the means put into their hands to use were the preaching of **the kingdom,** the antidote to all spiritual disorders, and actual healing of the sick, according to the power which had been imparted (ver. 2).

3, 4. The special precepts enjoined in these verses have all one intention, to fix the care of the apostles exclusively on the accomplishment of their task, while they left themselves entirely to God's providence, which would

L

5 *And whosoever will not receive you, when ye go out of that city, ᵇshake off the very dust from your feet for a testimony against them.
6 ᶜAnd they departed, and went through the towns, preaching the gospel, and healing every where.
7 ᵈNow Herod the tetrarch heard of all that was done by him: and he was perplexed, because that it was said of some, that John was risen from the dead;
8 And of some, that Elias had appeared; and of others, that one of the old prophets was risen again.

5 there abide, and thence depart. And as many as receive you not, when ye depart from that city, shake off the dust from your feet for a testimony
6 against them. And they departed, and went throughout the villages, preaching the gospel, and healing everywhere.
7 Now Herod the tetrarch heard of all that was done: and he was much perplexed, because that it
8 was said by some, that John was risen from the dead; and by some, that Elijah had appeared; and by others, that one of the old prophets was risen

a Matt. 10: 14.....b Acts 13: 51.....c Mark 6: 12... d Matt. 14: 1; Mark 6: 14.

provide for their necessary support.—The **staves** (*staff*, singular), **scrip** (or *wallet*), **bread, money,** would all be naturally thought needful for a journey; but they were to drop all the solicitude which providing and preserving such things would occasion, and learn how entirely they could depend on their Father in heaven.—The **coat** was the under-garment, at once shirt and tunic, or long vest, covering the man to the knees, or lower. In particular, they were not to be squeamish about the kind of house in which they might have transiently to lodge. Any house of hospitable people was good enough to shelter them for the time, and there they were to remain while they staid in the neighborhood, and **thence depart** when their work there was done.

5. But the Master foresaw that not every city or house would receive his disciples in a hospitable manner. Their visit, like his own, would effect a moral discrimination, a "judgment" among the people, by which the "worthy" would be separated from those "not worthy" of the gospel (Matt 10: 11. 13).—When leaving those of the latter class, Jesus commands them—**Shake off the very** (omit **very**) **dust from your feet for a testimony against them.** The action would be a most expressive token of their utter alienation from the Kingdom of God, whose heralds thus refused to carry with them on their sandals so much as a particle of the dust from their ground.

6. These directions they faithfully fulfilled, **and went through the towns** (better, *throughout the villages*). As no mention is made of cities, we may infer that, in the circuits which Jesus had already made through Galilee, the cities and towns had been chiefly visited, and that these messengers occupied themselves with the smaller places, in order that the glad tidings might reach every needy soul.—**Everywhere,** is to be understood with

the necessary and obvious limitation to Galilee. It is an instance of young ministers being exercised and tested, first, on more retired fields.

7–9. PERPLEXITY OF HEROD.

7, 8. **Now** (or, *And*) **Herod the tetrarch heard of all that was done** (*the things that were done*). While the six pairs of apostles were prosecuting their mission of beneficence to body and soul (comp. Mark 6: 12, 13), our Lord was busy by himself, or with other associates, accomplishing the work for which he was sent (4: 43). All this taking place within the narrow limits of a section of the dominion of Herod Antipas, lying about his chief residence at Tiberias, could not fail to reach his ears, and engage his attention. Very naturally he was much perplexed. The most superficial view of the facts would account for that, and when we add the popular rumors, the manifest excitement of the mobile Galileans, who held him culpable (as Josephus tells us) for killing John the Baptist, we may read, in Luke's expression, a still deeper significance. Fear was mingled with his perplexity, although this is brought out much more distinctly in the other accounts, while Luke, merely hinting the fear, makes the perplexity prominent.—**Because that it was said of** (*by*) **some, that John was risen from the dead, and of** (*by*) **some,** etc. Those who spoke of John, must have been persons unaware that he had so directly described Jesus as the one mightier than he, who was to come after him, or they would not have needed to suppose John risen from the dead, that he should be able to do things which he never did in his mortal state (Mark 6: 14). Some, not quite so deeply impressed, thought **that Elijah had appeared. Appeared,** not risen—as he had been translated, that he should not see death. This view directly connected Jesus in their minds with the Messiah, as about to appear

9 And Herod said, John have I beheaded: but who is this, of whom I hear such things? *And he desired to see him.

10 ᵇ And the apostles, when they were returned, told him all that they had done. ᶜ And he took them, and went aside privately into a desert place belonging to the city called Bethsaida.

9 again. And Herod said, John I beheaded: but who is this, about whom I hear such things? And he sought to see him.

10 And the apostles, when they were returned, declared unto him what things they had done. And he took them, and withdrew apart to a city called

a ch 23: 8....b Mark 6: 30....c Matt. 14: 13.

(comp. Mal. 4: 5), and involved an explanation of his miraculous efficiency. So, with that of those who did not go higher in their conjecture than **one of the old** (ancient) **prophets**, supposed to be risen to life again.

9. To these diverse opinions or surmises, Herod replies as not satisfied. **John have I beheaded.** The sense is, "It cannot be John; as for him, he is certainly dead, for I put him to death." The *I* is strongly emphatic. The idea of resurrection on his part, or that of the prophets, does not affect him much. And yet, if not John, who could it be?—**Who is this, of** (i. e., *about*) **whom I hear such things?** It is a mystery, and to his godless, but superstitious disposition, a trouble as well as a doubt.—**And he desired** (*sought*) **to see him.** So had he been perplexed about John, when alive (Mark 6: 20), when he used to hear him gladly. But Jesus evidently avoided him, never apparently having entered Tiberias, near which he spent so much time. Matthew and Mark, it will be noticed, report a subsequent stage of his reflections, when he had become persuaded that John was really risen from the dead.

The passing allusion in ver. 9, is all that Luke gives us concerning the tragical end of the great forerunner. Matthew and Mark, the latter most fully, relate the sad and shameful particulars. Melancholy, indeed, was the closing stage of that bold, energetic, and zealous career. If it were the only case of the kind, we should find in it an impeachment of the equity of God's providence. But we know rather, that it was an instance of a general rule of providence, that the greatest characters, and those that play the most important parts in the history of human redemption, must purchase their eminence by suffering, and end their days, often, with slight evidence of the greatness of the work they have wrought. Disappointment, persecution, and worldly dishonor, attended the experience of prophets, apostles, and their Master himself, as well as of exalted

specimens of pious fidelity in the subsequent time, quite to our day. But none of them would have desired our pity. They were happy even in their sufferings, and would have spurned the highest worldly felicity as an alternative. They had regard to the recompense of the reward; but more moving was the word: "Happy are ye, for so persecuted they the prophets who were before you, and into whose company you thus come!"

10-17. RETURN OF THE TWELVE, AND FEEDING OF THE FIVE THOUSAND. (Comp. Matt. 14: 13-23; Mark 6: 30-44; John 6: 1-14.)

10. And the apostles, when they were returned. How long they were absent cannot be told—probably some weeks, but not months. **Told him what things they had done.** The Greek verb intimates that they gave him a narrative. To have the particulars of their report would have been very interesting, and surely instructive. From Mark 6: 12, 13, we may confidently infer what, for substance, it must have been. We are later told (10: 17), what it was which had specially impressed the seventy in their analogous experience. **And he took them and went aside** (*withdrew*), etc. This, as we shall see, expresses rather what he desired and aimed at, than what he accomplished. His motive seems to have been, partly, the desire of rest for them, probably also for himself (Mark 6: 31), and partly that he might, with them, consider deliberately their report for instruction and encouragement to them. For this there was no opportunity, amid the multitude of "comers and goers" (Mark), where they were.—**Privately**—the Revision says "apart," which, in the sense of "by themselves," is correct; but the Common Version gives the intention and spirit. They went by boat, starting from some one of the numerous points on the western side of the lake.—**The city called Bethsaida.** Putting together this and the "desert place" of Matthew and Mark, we see that the design was to reach the unoccupied plain east of the

11 And the people, when they knew it, followed him: and he received them, and spake unto them of the kingdom of God, and healed them that had need of healing.
12 ᵃAnd when the day began to wear away, then came the twelve, and said unto him, Send the multitude away, that they may go into the towns and country round about, and lodge, and get victuals: for we are here in a desert place.
13 But he said unto them, Give ye them to eat. And they said, We have no more but five loaves and two fishes; except we should go and buy meat for all this people.
14 For they were about five thousand men. And he said to his disciples, Make them sit down by fifties in a company.

11 Bethsaida. But the multitudes perceiving it followed him: and he welcomed them, and spake to them of the kingdom of God, and them that had
12 need of healing he healed. And the day began to wear away; and the twelve came, and said unto him, Send the multitude away, that they may go into the villages and country round about, and lodge, and get provisions: for we are here in a desert
13 place. But he said unto them, Give ye them to eat. And they said, We have no more than five loaves and two fishes; except we should go and buy food for
14 all this people. For they were about five thousand men. And he said unto his disciples, Make them

a Matt. 14: 15; Mark 6: 35; John 6: 1, 6.

mouth of the Jordan, at the northern end of the lake. There, two miles up the river, lay the new city of Bethsaida, called specially "Bethsaida Julias"—Julia's Bethsaida, because Philip the tetrarch had built it in honor of the emperor's daughter, Julia. Some ruins of it are supposed to be recognized now, bearing the name *Et Tell.* This city, being east of the Jordan, was in Gaulonitis, and distinct from Bethsaida of Galilee (John 12: 21). Reland (*Palaestina*, p. 653 ff.), completely established the double reference of the name. (See Josephus, *Ant.*, 18: 2, 1; 18: 4, 6; *Wars of Jews*, 2: 9, 1; 3: 10, 7.) The expectation of finding rest there, on the Saviour's part, was disappointed.

11. And the people, (lit., *the multitudes*), **when they knew it**—namely, that they had sailed for Bethsaida—**followed him "on foot"** (Matt. and Mark), and reached the place before him. A glance at a good map will show that the distance around the curve of the lake, was so little in excess of the straight course of a vessel from one of the northwestern harbors, that the pedestrians might outwalk the boat if it encountered a calm, or an adverse wind. Weary as he was, and longing for quiet with his disciples, instructed also as to the vain curiosity which moved many of them (John 6: 26), still **he received** (i. e., *welcomed*) **them,** in hope of good to some, and **spake unto them of the kingdom of God.** Here was a text suggestive of hours of discourse, that the truth m'ght be made intelligible, and sent home to individual hearts; and the discourse was diversified by practical mercies; for **them that had need of healing he healed.** Thus a good part of the day may have been spent.

12. Then came the twelve, and said unto him, Send the multitude away, etc.

The solitude which would have been an excellent place for the conference and rest of a few, became now an occasion of anxiety to the apostles. What was this throng to do for food, and lodging for the night? Nothing appeared but that they should be got to scatter among the neighboring villages and farmhouses—what to do there, perhaps the apostles did not see clearly; but the charge would, at least, be removed from them. They intimate their opinion to Jesus in a tone as if, rather, he had been disciple and they the master.

13. Give ye them to eat. Ye is emphatic. Do not send them off, in an uncertainty, to others; provide a meal for them yourselves. It was one of those paradoxical precepts by which Jesus often arrested attention, and made truth and duty more impressive. The disciples were almost shocked, and thought they proved the impossibility of compliance, by showing that they had scarcely half food enough for a meal for themselves.—**We have no more but five loaves** (biscuits) **and two fishes**—and there was probably a touch of irony in the addition—**except we should go and buy meat** (food) **for all this people.** This would have required, as they estimated, an outlay equivalent to two hundred dollars now (Mark 3: 7; comp. on 7: 41). They had a treasurer (Judas), and a common fund in a wallet, to meet inevitable expenses; but we may well doubt whether it ever contained two hundred pence (denaries) at once. Nothing less would answer now.

14. For they were about five thousand men—not human beings, but **men** (ἄνδρες), not counting women or children. Our Lord had in mind not merely to satisfy the natural want of this great throng for food, which excited his compassion, but to give also a fresh demonstration of his power over nature, while

15 And they did so, and made them all sit down.
16 Then he took the five loaves and the two fishes, and looking up to heaven, he blessed them, and brake, and gave to the disciples to set before the multitude.
17 And they did eat, and were all filled: and there was taken up of fragments that remained to them twelve baskets.

15 ¹sit down in companies, about fifty each. And they
16 did so, and made them all ¹sit down. And he took the five loaves and the two fishes, and looking up to heaven, he blessed them, and brake; and gave to the
17 disciples to set before the multitude. And they did eat, and were all filled; and there was taken up that which remained over to them of broken pieces, twelve baskets.

1 Gr. recline.

he illustrated symbolically the destination of his disciples to dispense spiritual nourishment to famishing souls. Hence he makes them the medium and agents through whom this great benefit shall be wrought.—**Make them sit down** = recline—**by fifties in a company** (rather, *in companies*—lines or rows), like those at the tables of a banquet, only much more numerous.—**By fifties** = fifty in each. The preparation was deliberate, orderly, and becoming to a meal, even the simplest, in the presence of the Lord. They were required to recline on the grass, and not take, as might happen, whatever any one could reach. Mark, as in so many instances, *pictures* the scene, showing the people arranged in "companies" (Greek, banquets), indicating that there was a decorous breaking up of the throng into regular groups, suitable for sociability, and convenient to be supplied. This may imply the placing of each group in the form of a three-sided hollow square, after the manner of a festive table; and such a supposition is favored by the other descriptive word in Mark, "ranks" (Greek, garden beds (πρασιαί), See Homer, *Odys*, 7: 127, in the garden of Alcinous).

15. The plan was carried out by the disciples, and we may almost see them seated in companies, of fifty each, on the green grass of early spring. MacGregor (*Rob Roy on the Jordan*), studying the subject on the spot, supposes the arrangement to have been in one parallelogram of fifty files, each of one hundred men, making one hundred ranks. This is less conformable to the description given in the text.

16. When all were regularly seated, and quiet, **Jesus took the five loaves . . . and blessed. Blessed,** when spoken of things, as here, means thankfully prayed that God's favor might accompany the use of them. Our Lord's habit of so doing before meals, signified at once his own gratitude for daily supplies, his desire that all might conduce to the best accomplishment of his work in life, and his sense of the propriety of such feeling and practice on the part of all who receive God's gifts.—**And brake, and gave to the disciples to set before the multitude.** The loaves, as we have seen, were rather biscuits, crackers, or pilot-bread, and the fishes, probably salted, dried, and somewhat brittle, so that breaking was a natural way of dividing them into parts.

17. And they did eat, and were all filled. Never had so vast a satiety resulted from so meagre a visible supply. As to the manner of it, no one can do more than conjecture, how the quantity in the hands of Jesus, or from his hands, grew to meet the often returning baskets, in the hands of the ministering disciples—perhaps many more than the twelve—until the last rank of the remotest company had been visited once and again, and all had enough. Then the supply on hand was many times greater than it had been in the first place.—**And there was taken up of fragments that remained to them** (rather, *that which remained over to them of broken pieces*—Revision), **twelve baskets.** The **broken pieces** are not so well thought to be "fragments" left by the eaters, as pieces broken by Christ, and ready for them if they had wanted more. Perhaps no one considered it then, but the apostles must often have seen afterwards, how they had, on that grassy waste, been conveying, in an emblem, their Saviour himself, as they were then doing in reality, through his word and Spirit, to the hungry, famishing souls of men. And they were not long in learning that in his one person was provision appropriate to the needs of each particular soul, and more than ample for the needs of all. Of that, also, a store always remains over, and the last heart that pants for pardon and holiness will have no reason to doubt that he also may eat and be satisfied.

The baskets used on this occasion were probably such as the Jews commonly carried about with them, in heathen neighborhoods at least,

18 a "And it came to pass, as he was alone praying, his disciples were with him: and he asked them, saying, Whom say the people that I am?

18 And it came to pass, as he was praying apart, the disciples were with him: and he asked them, saying,

a Matt. 16: 13; Mark 8: 27.

perhaps more to make sure of having unpolluted food and clothing, than for any other convenience. Juvenal, *Sat.* 3: 14, speaks of the basket (using the same word as here), and bundle of hay, as the characteristic token of a Jew, amid the mixed population of Rome. The size, therefore, if indeed there was a uniform size, was not such as to be inconvenient for constant use, further than which we have nothing to guide our judgment. The four Evangelists employ the same term, among the several for naming different kinds of baskets, and some early Greek lexicographers, though long subsequent to Christ's day, speak of the *cophinus* as "a capacious vessel."

18-27. PETER DECLARES JESUS TO BE THE MESSIAH. THE LAW OF DISCIPLESHIP. Compare Matt. 16: 13-20.

This narrative supposes a considerable time to have elapsed, and space to have been traveled, since the one with which we have just been occupied. There we had the parallel reports of the *four* Evangelists. Careful study of the other three shows that the feeding of the five thousand marked a very important crisis in the Saviour's life. The mistaken enthusiasm of the multitude in favor of one who seemed to them repeating the wonder of Moses in the bestowment of the manna, would brook no longer delay in having him declare himself the Messiah and deliverer of the Jewish nation. We read, therefore (John 6: 15), that he, knowing that they are about to come and seize him, to make him a king, *flees* again into the mountain himself alone. The other Gospels say that before doing this he *compelled* his disciples to go on board the vessel, and precede him to the other side. This, Luke passes over, as do all the Synoptics the discourse at Capernaum the next day (John 6: 22), so important in dispelling the delusions of the crowd, and thinning their number. Nor does Luke allude to any of the long series of important movements of the Lord, recorded in Mark 6: 45—8: 26, and the parallel portions of Matthew. Some weeks, not improbably months, must have passed. The Saviour, still seeking retirement, had gone from Capernaum to the country of Tyre and Sidon, to the west of Galilee, thence eastward across the Upper Jordan, and around through Decapolis, to the eastern border of the lake, where he again fed a hungry company of four thousand, beside women and children; thence to the southern or western shore, from which he next sails to Bethsaida Julias once more, and apparently on his journey to the far north, which brought him where the present section of Luke again brings him before us.

There is not only an omission of all this by this Evangelist, but he does not even name the scene of what he here relates. Both Matthew and Mark, however, inform us that it was "in the parts," "among the villages" "of Cesarea Philippi," which lay near the sources of the Jordan, at the foot of Mount Hermon, the southern point of the gigantic Lebanon range.

18. And it came to pass, as he was alone praying. *Alone:* (Greek, κατὰ μόνας, on lonely [ways]) means "apart from the public view." **The disciples were with him**—of his company, but not, necessarily, at the moment close by him, as at Gethsemane. While he courted solitude, he might well desire to have them near. Great concerns were on his mind. He was about to leave Galilee, the chief scene of his labors for two years past and upward, to return to it no more. He was leaving it for Jerusalem, that favored and guilty city, outside of which it was not permitted that a prophet should die. The hostility of the ruling Jews had reached that point of decision and unscrupulousness, which showed that they would not stop short of his death, while the worldly motives and the fickleness of the crowds, gave no promise of a present turning of the people to him. He himself was going to Jerusalem to die. And on his disciples, now partially tested, must devolve the task of carrying forward the enterprise which he had begun. This affecting and *testing* truth must now be revealed to them. How would they endure it? How did their idea concerning him compare with the popular view? And what precisely was this? These subjects must have lain weightily on his heart in that prayer which Luke, alone again of the Evangelists, has mentioned. Close after the prayer it probably was (Mark

19 They answering said, *a* John the Baptist; but some say, Elias; and others *say*, that one of the old prophets is risen again.
20 He said unto them, But whom say ye that I am? *b* Peter answering said, The Christ of God.
21 *c* And he straitly charged them, and commanded *them* to tell no man that thing;
22 Saying, *d* The Son of man must suffer many things, and be rejected of the elders and chief priests and scribes, and be slain, and be raised the third day.

19 Who do the multitudes say that I am? And they answering said, John the Baptist; but others say, Elijah; and others, that one of the old prophets is 20 risen again. And he said unto them, But who say ye that I am? And Peter answering said, The Christ 21 of God. But he charged them, and commanded them 22 to tell this to no man; saying, The Son of man must suffer many things, and be rejected of the elders and chief priests and scribes, and be killed, and the third

a Matt. 14: 2; ver. 7, 8....*b* Matt. 16: 16; John 6: 69....*c* Matt. 16: 20....*d* Matt. 16: 21; 17: 22.

says simply on the way) that **he asked them, saying, Whom say the people** (*who do the multitude say*) **that I am ?** Momentous question! Should we not expect, after the excitement consequent on the feeding of the five thousand, that the people generally must speak of him as the Messiah? But the spiritual and enlightening discourse in Capernaum (comp. John 6: 66) had prepared us for the answer which now comes.

19. John the Baptist—some still rate him so high as to suppose that the Messiah is soon to follow—**But some**—giving him a less exalted rank — say, **Elias** (*Elijah*)—next in pre-eminence to John—**and others**—merely —**that one of the old prophets is risen again**—any one that may chance. No climax, but a regular descent from John the Baptist. Not one voice reported from among the multitude—and the disciples had enjoyed a wide opportunity to learn the popular views—declared for the Messiahship of Jesus. Notice that this report from the "multitude" does not preclude the assurance that in private circles, like the home of Lazarus and Mary, a clear, though partial, recognition of Christ's true character, wrought its blessed effects. Notice, also, that the least appreciative did not deny to Jesus the character of a prophet; like the honored ones of former days.

20. But it is hard for us, following carefully this narrative, to avoid the feeling that it was with a degree of anxiety that Jesus now came home to the twelve themselves.—**But whom say ye that I am ? Ye is**, in the Greek, strongly emphatic, as if it read: "Ye, however, say me to be whom?" Perhaps he cared, after all, very little about the multitude, whose ideas of a Messiah he knew could not correspond to him, but everything about the judgment of his apostles, on whom so much depended in the further presentation of his work. If they were right, all would yet come right. Happily, their answer was in a different tone.—**Peter, answering** —as usual, spokesman for the body, who had all been questioned—**said, The Christ of God.** This is the laconic sum of the fuller reply, as reported in Matthew, "The Christ, the Son of the living God."—**The Christ**= "the Anointed One"="the Messiah."—**Of God**—foreordained, promised, predicted, given, manifested, by God. This was enough. In it lay the tiny seed which should grow to become a tree of life, and spread until its branches filled the whole space under the heavens.

21. How little matter it made, comparatively, that the multitudes did not call him Messiah, appears from the injunction which follows. They themselves had not come to their conclusion concerning him by any process of natural reasoning; it was a revelation, not from flesh and blood, not through the operations merely of any logical understanding, but direct from the Father of Jesus in heaven (Matt. 16: 17).

21. And (rather, *but*) **he straitly**—strictly —**charged them, and commanded them to tell no man that thing** (better, *tell this to no man*). They might hear the whole truth concerning the Messiah, but to the multitude it would now be only a stumbling-block. Gradually, at the best, and as God's providence should unfold the whole truth, could any of these receive it. And could even they, the apostles, to whom God had revealed the fact, could they bear the explanation of the fact?

22. This was now to be tested, by his **saying, The Son of man must suffer many things,** etc. His lot is not to be, in the earthly sense, a happy one; but a lot of suffering. This, itself, would be a hard saying to those who held the ordinary views of the Messiah, as a royal and glorious personage. But there was more to be told in the same strain, and Jesus brings out the particulars in appalling words.—**And be rejected of the elders,** etc. Instead of himself becom-

23 ^a And he said to *them* all, If any *man* will come after me, let him deny himself, and take up his cross daily, and follow me.
24 For whosoever will save his life shall lose it: but whosoever will lose his life for my sake, the same shall save it.

23 day be raised up. And he said unto all, If any man would come after me, let him deny himself, and take 24 up his cross daily, and follow me. For whosoever would save his life shall lose it; but whosoever shall

a Matt. 10: 38; 16: 24; Mark 8: 34; ch. 14: 27.

ing popularly the source of religious authority, and controller of the customs of worship, he is to be cast out, excommunicated by the most highly esteemed of the nation, paragons of sanctity and righteousness, as men supposed.—**And be slain**—with their approval, of course. This he told them as a reason for keeping silent in regard to his Messiahship, to other people. And although he added— **And be raised the third day.** It was long before they even understood the meaning of that, not to speak of finding comfort in it. How little the multitude were as yet ready for any right acknowledgment of Jesus as the Christ, according to his true plan, appears convincingly when we read in Matthew and Mark, that even Peter was shocked at hearing him speak of his future rejection and death, and that he felt at liberty to contradict and rebuke his Lord.

23-27. THE LAW OF DISCIPLESHIP TO CHRIST. Matt. 16: 24-28; Mark 8: 34—9: 1.

23. The germ, at least, of a great truth was now distinctly lodged in their hearts, without actually shaking their attachment to him; and when they joined again the outside throng, from whom they had temporarily withdrawn, **he said to all**—to the crowd as well as to his chosen—**If any man will come after me, let him deny himself.**—To come after Christ was to become his disciple, which, in typical cases, involved the actual leaving of other interests to go with him wherever he went. In this relation of teacher and pupil, he, as the custom was, went first in their travels, and thus the expression "to go after him" was a literal statement of the fact (comp. 14: 25-27). Afterward it became a metaphorical description of attachment to Christ, when there was no outward change of place, but only an inward change of relation toward him. So we, by a natural transfer of ideas, speak of following Christ as equivalent to leading a Christian life. This really involves all that there is of it. But to make explicit what might fail to appear, he adds—**Let him deny himself.** This means more, far more, than we frequently intend when we speak of denying oneself; the giving up something we value, refraining from something we could desire, that some more worthy or important end may be gained The merest worldling and epicurean may do that, often must do it, as a prudent worldling. It means more than that we should subdue our baser propensities, and be governed by reason and conscience in all that we do. That is the aim of philosophy; and he who should have succeeded in it would not, in Christ's sense, have denied himself, but only indulged his better self. The Master means that one in becoming his disciple must renounce altogether the claim and disposition to be his own man; acknowledge him as Proprietor, Teacher, Leader, Lord; giving himself away entire, judgment, reason, as well as passion, propensity, desire, and will, to one who is seen to be alone worthy to direct and employ all.—**And take up his cross daily.** Here again we have, by speaking of the toils, burdens, disappointments. and sorrows of life as "our crosses which we have to bear," grievously belittled the Saviour's meaning. He had these also, but they were not his cross. His cross was the heavy stake which he set out to carry from Pilate's judgment-seat to Calvary, that he might hang on it to die. Such scenes all men were familiar with where the cruel punishments of Rome were known. The expression now used was probably proverbial, and there was signified by it that the true disciple must follow his Lord, ready to yield life itself for his cause. He should walk —**daily**—constantly, with the cross, metaphorically, on his shoulder, devoting the body of sin in him to merited death, and the natural life to extinction when fidelity to Christ should require it. **And**—so let him—**follow me.** This, and nothing less, is to follow him.

24. This severe requirement Jesus justifies and explains. **For whosoever will**—wills, is resolved to—**save his life shall lose it.** The man that prizes the natural life so as to withhold it from Christ, who requires the giving of it up, may retain it longer than otherwise here, but will lose it as the ground for the

25 a For what is a man advantaged, if he gain the whole world, and lose himself, or be cast away?
26 b For whosoever shall be ashamed of me and of my words, of him shall the Son of man be ashamed, when he shall come in his own glory, and in his Father's, and of the holy angels.
27 c But I tell you of a truth, there be some standing here, which shall not taste of death, till they see the kingdom of God.

25 lose his life for my sake, the same shall save it. For what is a man profited, if he gain the whole world,
26 and lose or forfeit his own self? For whosoever shall be ashamed of me and of my words, of him shall the Son of man be ashamed, when he cometh in his own glory, and *the glory* of the Father, and of the
27 holy angels. But I tell you of a truth, There are some of them that stand here, who shall in no wise taste of death, till they see the kingdom of God.

a Matt. 16: 26; Mark 8: 36....b Matt. 10: 33; Mark 8: 38; 2 Tim. 2: 12....c Matt. 16: 28; Mark 9: 1.

eternal welfare, the life alone worth living for.—**But whosoever will lose his life for my sake**—yield it up in the fulfillment of my will concerning him—**the same shall save it**—shall rejoice eternally and the more richly in the blessedness of heaven.

25. Such self-sacrifice is consistent with the true advantage of every man.—**For what is a man advantaged** (or *profited*) **if he gain the whole world, and lose** (or *forfeit*) **himself.** A more exact translation would be "in having gained," "in having lost," etc. The Greek shows that the Saviour now looks back on an opportunity lost, on a ruin accomplished. What are we to say of the advantage, when it appears that a man in gaining as he did, supposably, the whole world, for the space of his subsequent stay on earth, has **lost**—thrown away, himself, or *forfeited*—suffered the loss of, **himself**—been mulcted of eternal life? The case of Dives in the parable (ch. 16), is a slight approach to a parallel. Excluded from heaven, what is eternal existence to him but endless bankruptcy of joy, of proper life!

26. The principle stated on which such disastrous failure takes place—**For whosoever shall be ashamed of me,** etc. He is thinking of those within the circle of gospel privilege, and sees that the root of their refusal to embrace his service lies in pride, or the feeling of shame at being reckoned followers of one who has, and offers so little, of what the natural mind esteems. The shame of such on the part of the Son of man will appear in his refusal to recognize them when even they would regard his favor as an honor and a blessing.—**When he shall come in his own glory. Own** is not warranted by the Greek.—**His glory**—is that impression of divine excellence, the "form of God," of which he emptied himself at the Incarnation, but which he resumed with added honor at his Ascension, which he will wear at his Second Advent, and which we think of as an ineffable radiance or splendor.—**And in his Father's**—the tokens of dignity and rule lent to him by his Father, that he may represent him in the throne of eternal judgment.—**And**—the glory—**of the holy angels**—who will constitute the celestial retinue with which he will come to receive his faithful ones to himself. For the palpable implication is, that by as much as that illustrious epiphany will bring shame to the unbelievers who have been ashamed of him, will it announce glory and recompense to all who have clung to him in his humble earthly manifestation

27. But I tell you of a truth, The remark plainly implies that an important statement is to follow. The conjunction **but** stands for a Greek particle, adapted to connect the sentence to the preceding without sharply deciding whether the relation is one of agreement="and," or of opposition="but." It depends entirely on the translator's view of this relation whether he renders it "and" or "but." "And" might be used in this case, unless it would mar the train of thought. It probably would show more directly the train of thought, which seems to be, in brief, "and some now here will be alive to see that glorious coming." **But**—suits better with the supposition that what is to be said relates to something more or less different from the preceding. "But I say to you truly, another kind of a coming of the kingdom will take place sooner." This would be convenient for the expositor, of our time, who does not see that the predicted coming actually took place before the eyes of any then living. But it would greatly belittle the dignity and weight of this closing declaration to assume, even here in Luke, that it contemplates something else than what has just been spoken of. In the parallel reports of Matthew and Mark, there is no shadow of doubt that the previous topic is continued.

We thus, indeed, meet a very serious difficulty of interpretation, but not more so than we often encounter in studying the apparent dates and chronological relations of events announced in unfulfilled prophecy. Christ speaks as a prophet, and reveals future facts of great spiritual importance, to occur in an increasing, but never completed development. With them may mingle other facts, also foretold, which may be described physically, and which have their distinct occasions in the calendar of earth. Hence, the perplexity to our understanding, and hence, the light to our faith.—**There be** (*are*) **some** (*of those*) **standing here which shall not** (or, *by no means*) **taste of death**, etc. The aim of this statement seems to be, pretty clearly, to cheer and sustain the disciples under the present and immediately threatening contrast of circumstances, to that glory which shall yet be revealed to them. Be not discouraged; the time is not long. Not all of you will see it during the term of your natural lives, but some will.—**To taste of death**—is "to die," according to the usage, familiar in Hebrew and in Greek, of employing "taste" to signify "experience," "be cognizant of," "have a share of."—**Shall not**—most certainly shall not.

Because *all* that Jesus had spoken of as pertaining to his glorious advent, and *as* he spoke of it, did not take place during that generation, infidel critics have found our Lord not a truthful foreteller. For the same reason, the most reverent expounders have been greatly perplexed, and felt it necessary (many of them), to force the language of our verse to refer to something apart from the glorious coming. Thus, some have contended that the reference in the prophecy is to the Transfiguration, occurring a week after these words were spoken, and related here, in the next paragraph. This, if regarded as a complete explanation, would not, indeed, be incongruous with the limitation of the vision to **some** of those standing there, as only three of them saw the glorified Saviour; but it was not such a coming, if any at all, as involved the putting to shame of those who had refused Christ. Others think of the resurrection of Christ from the dead, as here foretold; or, the bestowment of the Holy Spirit on the Day of Pentecost; or, the establishment of the Church among Jews and Gentiles; or, the destruction of Jerusalem, regarded both as an infliction of Christ's displeasure against the apostate and wicked nation, and a deliverance of the gospel from their effective hostility, "contrary to all men" as they were. Generally, the advocate of one of these hypotheses rejects the rest; and in attempting to make a complete explanation, becomes confused, strained, and inadequate. Why may we not suppose them all, and whatever else was experienced toward the realization of the kingdom within the next forty or fifty years, during which some of Christ's believing hearers would be alive and remain? Would not all this amount, according to our Lord's frequent way of speaking, to such a coming as would answer to his prophecy here? That he could not have been reasonably understood as promising that the winding up of the administration of his cause on earth would take place within a life-time, we may believe from the fact that he had already spoken parables which presupposed a longer continuance, and afterwards spoke still more decidedly. But he knows that the full consummation is to be; and in prophetic vision he sees stages of its progress stretching out before him, with the destruction of Jerusalem more definitely marked as associated with the deliverance of his friends and punishment of his enemies. The accomplishment of so much may well appear as not only a great progress, but as a specimen and earnest of the full work, though this stretches on in a further unfolding into eternity. Looking at the whole, Jesus speaks in the language which we refer entirely to the coming which is to attend the extinction of nature and the consummation of this age. When he looks at a lesser portion of it, he speaks of what will be accomplished before all his hearers see death.

To our feelings there naturally seems such a distance between this last-named modicum of blessedness, largely clouded with imperfections and troubles, that we doubt whether it could be called a coming at all, in comparison with the remaining glory. But it might not have appeared so to the Saviour, and might not appear so to us, if we could think of the matter apart from those physical images of effulgent splendor, crowns, angelic forms, and archangelic trumpets, in which it is now necessary for us to frame ideas of heaven. Peter (2 Pet. 1: 16-18) certainly found, even in the Transfiguration, a pledge and sample of the heavenly glory (the power and *coming*—Parousia) of the Lord; yet who can doubt that he saw a still more impressive glory in the mediatorial majesty displayed through

28 ªAnd it came to pass about an eight days after these sayings, he took Peter and John and James, and went up into a mountain to pray. | 28 And it came to pass about eight days after these sayings, he took with him Peter and John and

a Matt. 17:1; Mark 9:2.

the Holy Spirit at Pentecost, and in all his triumphs of that age. It is not a subject for measurements and statistics; but we can easily believe that to celestial vision the difference between the gospel glory of the last years of John, the beloved disciple, and the fifteenth year of Tiberius, was more remarkable than that between those years and the end of the world. The apostles died in hope of something still better; but they knew, and had given the proof to many, that the Kingdom of God was come.

Some would reconcile the language of our verse with the subsequent facts, by assuming the promise to be conditioned on the repentance of the Jews as a nation (and comp. Acts 3:19 ff.); and others (to mention no more) think the words may have been spoken on a different occasion, but then assigned, at an early period, in the common memoir of Christ's sayings, to this connection as apposite, and so transmitted to us. We prefer the view above sketched, that he spoke in ver. 27 of the same manifestation of his kingdom as in ver. 26, but in an earlier stage of it, and without noting the chronological gradation.

Every one may see how this difficulty itself proves the composition of the Synoptic Gospels during the generation contemporary with the Lord.

28-36. THE TRANSFIGURATION. Matt. 17:1-13; Mark 9:2-13.

28. **And it came to pass about an eight days after these sayings.**—All the Synoptists are particular to mark the date of this very important event in the life of our Lord, and all, doubtless, mean one week, two excluding the days of the two events, and naming six days, Luke including the two and naming eight. (The article an should be omitted). As the locality of the preceding discourse appears to have been the same as that of Peter's confession, which was the neighborhood of Cesarea Philippi, we may conclude that the scene of the Transfiguration was some mountain in that vicinity. It is thus natural to think of some spur or slope of Hermon, which Jesus and his disciples had often gazed on, towering gloriously in the far north, as they traversed the neighborhood of the Sea of Galilee. A tradition of little trustworthiness designates Mount Tabor, on the southern border of Galilee. Were there any proper authority for this representation, six days' time would have allowed the journey from the Upper Jordan; but the Saviour seems to be rather seeking retirement, and avoiding premature arrest now, and when Mark next gives an indication of place (9:30), he says, "coming out from thence, they journeyed through Galilee."—**He took with him Peter and John and James**—the three select and often favored apostles (8:51). He probably desired the support of their presence, as at Gethsemane (though now with far different feelings), because of the object before him.—**Went up into a mountain to pray.** This statement prepares us to expect again some important development in the progress of his mission. What he had lately said to his disciples, and they to him, had brought the revelation possible for him to make to them by word during his earthly stay, nearly to completion. "To all," also, he had laid down the essential conditions, practically considered, on which they must share the Messianic salvation. The result would be to excite a great fermentation of thought in all minds that were not like the hard-trodden road-bed to the seeds of his truth. To cherish, enlighten, and guide the infant faith would now be necessary; and to this end, some manifestation of the true glory of his reign, as opposed to the carnal splendor and majesty of which men dreamed, and of the real blessedness of his subjects, might powerfully contribute. The souls of the chief apostles being confirmed, would serve even now as a nucleus of imperturbable faith to the rest; and their testimony, to be given after the resurrection, would supply to all what would then be necessary to sustain confidence, and rouse enthusiasm, in the midst of self-denial, and sacrifice of worldly aims. The Saviour's prayer, accordingly, may have had this for its object, that he might himself have fresh evidence of his Father's approbation and support, in the sacrifice of himself which he had soon to com-

172   LUKE.   [Ch. IX.

29 And as he prayed, the fashion of his countenance was altered, and his raiment *was* white *and* glistering.
30 And, behold, there talked with him two men, which were Moses and Elias:
31 Who appeared in glory, and spake of his decease which he should accomplish at Jerusalem.
32 But Peter and they that were with him *were heavy with sleep: and when they were awake, they saw his glory, and the two men that stood with him.

29 James, and went up into the mountain to pray. And as he was praying, the fashion of his countenance was altered, and his raiment *became* white *and* dazzling. And behold, there talked with him two men,
31 who were Moses and Elijah; who appeared in glory, and spake of his ¹decease which he was about to accomplish at Jerusalem. Now Peter and they that were with him were heavy with sleep; but ²when they were fully awake, they saw his glory, and the

a Dan. 8:18; 10:9.—1 Or, *departure.*....2 Or, *having remained awake.*

plete; and, moreover, that his brethren might be suitably strengthened for their share in the trials of which he had apprised them.

29. And as he prayed (better, *was praying*, in the very course of his prayer), **the fashion of his countenance was altered** (Greek, *became an other*). An intolerable glory shone on the face of Moses, when he came down from communication with Jehovah in the mount. On the face of Jesus now shone, we may suppose, that brightness of glory, or its counterpart to mortal eyes, which was the very image of his substance, and in which angels had recognized "the form of God" (Phil. 2:6; Heb. 1:3; 2 Pet. 1:16). The change seems to have affected his whole person; for, we are told that **his raiment was** (or *became*) **white and glistering** (*i. e., dazzling*). **And** is absent from the Greek; *dazzling* or **glistering** interpret the word **white**.

30. And behold—a marvelous fact—**there talked with him two men, which** (οἵτινες) **were Moses and Elijah.** From the usual force of the compound relative rendered **which**, we might judge that the two attendant beings were known as men, because they were found out to be Moses and Elijah=seeing that they were. But this may be one of the rare cases in which some authorities take the compound as identical in sense with the simple relative=who. Special significance might have attached to the presence of Moses and Elijah. The special lesson in the appearance of just these two, at this time, lay in the fact that they represented the law and the prophets, or the whole preparatory Dispensation of the national religion. Elijah, in a crisis of their history, had triumphantly opposed himself to the idolatrous perversion of the true worship, and, by providing for the training and support of prophets, had secured the continuance of a qualified line of these ministers of Jehovah, down to Malachi.

31. Who appeared in glory—suitable to those who should commune with the glorified Saviour, and indicative of the eternal felicity, in the heavenly state, of those who have faithfully served God on earth. Their state was thus a great encouragement to those who still struggle here below.—**And spake of his decease which he should** (*was about to*) **accomplish at Jerusalem.** Christ in conference with the great law-giver and the typical prophet, about his approaching death! Their theme was not, then, the majesty of his destined reign; but the preliminary sufferings of the Christ. Yet they did not treat his end *as* death; but a departure, a **decease** (ἔξοδος), a cessation and going out from that state of humiliation to which he had condescended, into the blessedness from which they had just come. Compared with this, the pains and earthly shame would be as nothing (comp. Heb. 12:2). This was the consummation of all that the law and the prophets had portended; and the disciples might well be reconciled to the strange and shocking announcement which Jesus had made to them concerning his fate, when they saw it recognized as the result aimed at in all the anterior revelation of God. **Which he** *was* about to **accomplish**—strictly, *to fulfill.* It was not merely that he would experience this departure, that it would happen to him; but that his death, with all that should precede and follow on earth, should fulfill God's appointment of humiliation, pain, and shame for him, as well as the consequent honor and reward in his resurrection and ascension to glory. All this was involved in the thought of fulfilling his **decease,** or departure. (See Kypke, *Observ.* on the passage).—**At Jerusalem**—a pathetic touch; the place where he ought to be hailed and enthroned as Zion's promised king (13:33).

32. But (or *Now*) Peter and they that were with him were heavy (*had been weighed down*) **with sleep.** The verb is in the pluperfect, and the statement has reference to a time prior to the scene which they had just witnessed. It is intended to explain that the disciples were not asleep at this time, as might naturally be suspected, seeing that

Сн. IX.] LUKE. 173

33 And it came to pass, as they departed from him, Peter said unto Jesus, Master, it is good for us to be here: and let us make three tabernacles; one for thee, and one for Moses, and one for Elias: not knowing what he said.
34 While he thus spake, there came a cloud, and overshadowed them: and they feared as they entered into the cloud.
35 And there came a voice out of the cloud, saying, ᵃThis is my beloved Son; ᵇ hear him.
36 And when the voice was past, Jesus was found alone. ᶜAnd they kept *it* close, and told no man in those days any of those things which they had seen.

33 two men that stood with him. And it came to pass, as they were parting from him, Peter said unto Jesus, Master, it is good for us to be here: and let us make three ¹tabernacles; one for thee, and one for Moses, and one for Elijah; not knowing what he 34 said. And while he said these things, there came a cloud, and overshadowed them: and they feared as 35 they entered into the cloud. And a voice came out of the cloud, saying, This is ²my Son, my chosen: 36 hear ye him. And when the voice ³came, Jesus was found alone. And they held their peace, and told no man in those days any of the things which they had seen.

ᵃ Matt. 3:17....ᵇ Acts 3:22....ᶜ Matt. 17:9——1 Or. *booths.* 2 Many ancient authorities read, *my beloved son.* See Matt. 17:5; Mark 9:7. 3 Or, *was past.*

---

it was in the night (ver. 37). It was no dream, no mere vision; they had been drowsy.—**And when they were awake**—rather, *but having kept awake.* (See Grimm's *Clavis* on the sense of this very rare verb).—**They saw his glory, and the two men**, etc., in the manner related in the preceding verse. The manifestation had been intended for them as much as for Jesus, and they had not to depend on his report of what occurred; but saw it for themselves, and received the proper impression which such an occurrence was suited to make (2 Pet. 1:18 ff.).

33. And it came to pass, as they departed (or *were parting*) **from him**—before Moses and Elijah had actually left—**Peter said to Jesus, Master, it is good for us to be here** (rather, *it is a good thing that we are here*).—It would seem that he spoke with some hazy idea of securing a longer stay of the celestial visitants. This is indicated by the close connection with what follows.—**And**—since we apostles are here, and have the strength for it—**let us make three tabernacles** (*tents,* Greek σκηνάς)—here, probably of branches of trees and shrubs, booths. It is precarious interpreting the language of Peter, when we are directly told that he knew not what he said; but it is much as if he had thought, at a flash, that, with suitable shelter, the company might be continued, to the honor of Jesus and the benefit of his disciples.—**One for thee**, etc. They are quite content themselves to remain in the open air.

34. While he thus spake (literally, *while he said these things*), **there came a cloud, and overshadowed them.** The description suggests that sublime veil of Jehovah's majesty which rested over the tabernacle in the ancient days, when it went and where it rested, like which, this shadow of God now enveloped the Father. On a moonlight night, it would still be seen as a cloud, and in the day-time or night we may well believe that the divine indwelling would give a radiance that made it "bright" (Matt. 17:5). No wonder that **they feared**—were thrilled with trembling, worshipful awe—**as they entered into the cloud**—that is, felt themselves embraced within its mysterious folds.

35. What it all portended was evident when **there came a voice out of the cloud, saying, This is my beloved Son** (*the chosen*, is probably the true reading); **hear** (*ye*) **him.** Thus is assured to the Lord Jesus once more, and with reference to that stage of his course which now opens, the approbation, and sympathy of God, his Father, and to the disciples, a divine authority for all which he declares, requires, or predicts.

36. And when the voice was past (rather, *came*), **Jesus was found alone.** With the dying away of that sound the whole phenomenon reached its consummation. God had ratified the proposed fulfillment of the law and the prophets, in the death and glorification of Jesus as his Son, at Jerusalem. The same cloud which had borne the voice, took back the two messengers from the world of those who live eternally.—**And they kept it close** (Greek, *were silent*), **and told no man in those days**, etc. **In those days** they did not tell it, because Jesus (Matt. 17:9) commanded them to say nothing about this wonderful revelation, until he should have risen from the dead. The possible reasons for such an injunction have been spoken of in remarks above, on ver. 28. The disciples could only wait for a distinct idea of what was meant by his rising from the dead, but they faithfully observed his direction. Meantime, we may be assured that their own confidence in their Master, as an all-sufficient Saviour, would be greatly fortified.

37 ªAnd it came to pass, that on the next day, when they were come down from the hill, much people met him.
38 And, behold, a man of the company cried out, saying, Master, I beseech thee, look upon my son: for he is mine only child.
39 And, lo, a spirit taketh him, and he suddenly crieth out; and it teareth him that he foameth again, and bruising him hardly departeth from him.
40 And I besought thy disciples to cast him out; and they could not.
41 And Jesus answering said, O faithless and perverse generation, how long shall I be with you, and suffer you? Bring thy son hither.
42 And as he was yet a coming, the devil threw him

37 And it came to pass, on the next day, when they were come down from the mountain, a great multitude met him. And behold, a man from the multitude cried, saying, ¹Master, I beseech thee to look
38 upon my son; for he is mine only child; and behold,
39 a spirit taketh him, and he suddenly crieth out; and it ²teareth him that he foameth, and it hardly departeth from him, bruising him sorely. And I besought thy disciples to cast it out; and they could
40 not. And Jesus answered and said, O faithless and perverse generation, how long shall I be with you,
41 and bear with you? bring hither thy son. And as he was yet a coming, the demon ³dashed him down,
42 and ⁴tare *him* grievously. But Jesus rebuked the unclean spirit, and healed the boy, and gave him

a Matt. 17: 14; Mark 9: 14, 17.—1 Or, *Teacher*....2 Or, *convulseth*....3 Or, *rent him*....4 Or, *convulsed*.

37-42. A Demoniac Child whom the Apostles were not Able to Cure. Compare Matt. 17: 14-21; Mark 9: 14 ff.

In all the Synoptics, this event follows immediately upon the Transfiguration.

37. The next day, when they were come down from the hill (*mountain*). They finished the night there. Now they passed suddenly from the glory and felicity of heaven to the sins and misery of earth.— **Much people** (*a great multitude*) **met him.** From Mark, who gives this occurrence with much greater detail, we learn that the case of the demoniac boy, whom the disciples could not heal, had given the Scribes occasion to dispute with them, probably in relation to the power, which they and their Master claimed, to cast out demons.

38, 39. And, behold, a man of the company (literally, *from the multitude*) **cried out**—in a tone of great earnestness of desire, and deep distress — **saying, Master** = teacher — **I beseech thee, look** (or, *to look*) **upon my son**, etc. It was, indeed, a very pitiful case—an only son, a circumstance which, as we have before seen, appealed powerfully to the only begotten Son of the heavenly Father (7: 12). This child was worse than dead, unless the help of the Great Physician could avail for him also. He was subject to paroxysms of epileptic insanity, so violent in their manifestations, as we read in ver 39, that his life must have been a distress to himself and a heavy affliction to all his friends. **Teareth** = wrenches with convulsions; **bruising** = cramping, crushing.

40. And I besought thy disciples to cast him (*it*) **out; and they could not.** This, according to all the records, was what moved the Lord to the utterance of disappointment and rebuke in the next sentence.

41. O faithless = unbelieving—**and perverse** (Greek, *twisted*) **generation.** It does not seem necessary to confine the broad term, **generation**, with Meyer, to the groups of disciples, only nine at the most, including neither of the most eminent. Doubtless, it was their failure which grieved him—a failure resulting, too, in great measure, from their weakness of confidence in that power and authority which they had received from him to meet such demands. But where were the signs of faith among those around, without which Christ himself seldom or never attempted these mighty works? The feeling, therefore, with which he uttered his complaint, and the very object addressed, was wider than the handful of derelict disciples, although with them he was specially grieved. Their perverseness was the result of obscure and feeble faith, and appeared in a lack of harmony of life and conduct with their privileges and obligations. They must surely have done better in the excursion on which they had been sent out (see ver. 6). Or, had they been so dependent on Peter, James, and John?— **How long shall I be with you, and suffer you?** Until when must I be? The tone is as if he had meant to say, I cannot remain here always; how long will it be before I can lay the burden down, secure that others will bear it successfully? But it was not in the nature of Jesus to let a suffering and prayerful soul go unrelieved, whoever might be to blame; and he said to the anxious father—**Bring thy son hither.** This address to him, as if in continuance of the preceding language, shows that, in Luke, almost certainly, Christ did not speak that to the disciples alone.

42. And as he was yet a coming, the devil (*demon*) **threw him down** (caused him to fall as if his bones were broken), **and tare** (wrenched, convulsed) **him**, as if it would

down, and tare *him*. And Jesus rebuked the unclean spirit, and healed the child, and delivered him again to his father.
43 And they were all amazed at the mighty power of God. But while they wondered every one at all things which Jesus did, he said unto his disciples,
44 *a* Let these sayings sink down into your ears: for the Son of man shall be delivered into the hands of men.
45 *b* But they understood not this saying, and it was hid from them, that they perceived it not: and they feared to ask him of that saying.
46 *c* Then there arose a reasoning among them, which of them should be greatest.

43 back to his father. And they were all astonished at the majesty of God.
But while all were marvelling at all the things
44 which he did, he said unto his disciples, Let these words sink into your ears: for the Son of man shall
45 be delivered up into the hands of men. But they understood not this saying, and it was concealed from them, that they should not perceive it: and they were afraid to ask him about this saying.
46 And there arose a reasoning among them, which

---

a Matt. 17: 22....*b* Mark 9: 32; ch. 2: 50; 18: 34....*c* Matt. 18: 1; Mark 9: 34.

---

rend him limb from limb. Mark gives an interesting conversation of the Saviour with the poor father, suited to develop at once his sense of necessity and his faith; but Luke and Matthew go straight to the cure. As on other occasions, the near presence of Christ caused violent access of the malady, betraying special malignity on the part of the evil spirit. As if it had been a challenge from the prince of the demons, the Son of man met it calmly with a reproof, not of the child. —**And Jesus rebuked the unclean spirit** —as being the personal, conscious, intentional cause of all this ill—**and healed the child**— even by the rebuke banished the infernal troubler.—**Delivered him** (or, *gave him back*) **again to his father.** Compare the manner of it with that of the restoration of the widow's only son at Nain (7: 15. 16).

42. And they were all amazed at the mighty power of God—his majesty (2 Pet. 1: 16, Greek), the glorious manifestation of his power. The mouth of the scribes was shut again, and the truth concerning the divine efficiency of Jesus shone forth bright from the cloud which the ill success of certain disciples had thrown over it.

43-45. CHRIST AGAIN PREDICTS HIS SUFFERINGS IN VAIN. Indeed, it would seem that he recognized again, in this outburst of adoration signs of an unhealthy and misdirected enthusiasm, which he instantly set himself to correct.—**But while they wondered**—at the moment they began to express their astonishment—**he said unto his disciples**—they being peculiarly liable, after what had recently occurred, to conceive wrong expectations.

44. Let these sayings sink down into your ears—give them your profoundest consideration, let them reach your heart—**for the Son of man shall be delivered into the hands of men.** Luke does not repeat the saying fully, as do the other Synoptists, leaving readers to supply from the previous prediction (ver. 22), that the result of his being given up would be his death, to be followed by a resurrection. All this, as regarded the Messiah, was a mystery to them.

45. They understood not this saying —could attach no consistent sense to the declaration. Not only did they not understand it; **it was** (=had been) **hid** (*concealed*) **from them that they perceived it not** (or, *should not perceive it*). It was afterward seen that there had been a divine purpose in this ignorance and incapacity of theirs, really a concealment of the amazing truth until they should be able to receive it without too great a shock, and with great benefit and joy.— **And they feared to ask him of that** (or, *about this*) **saying.** Although they did not understand it, there was a disastrous intimation in his words, which awed them into silence.

46-48. THEIR AMBITION REPROVED BY THE EXAMPLE OF A CHILD. Matt. 18: 1-5; Mark 9: 33-37.

Mark expressly names Capernaum as the scene of this occurrence, where Matthew also (17: 24) places the affair of the tribute-money, which immediately preceded this. **Then there arose a reasoning**—an argument— **among them.** Meyer would render this sentence, "and there came in a reasoning in them"; *i. e.*, in their hearts. This view is undoubtedly favored by the fact that Jesus is said in the next verse to know "the reasoning of their heart," which seems as if nothing had been said. If Luke were our only narrator of the facts, that rendering and interpretation would hardly be objectionable. From the other narratives, however, we know that something was said, and the translation in the

47 And Jesus, perceiving the thought of their heart, took a child, and set him by him,
48 And said unto them, *a* Whosoever shall receive this child in my name receiveth me; and whosoever shall receive me receiveth him that sent me: *b* for he that is least among you all, the same shall be great.
49 *c* And John answered and said, Master, we saw one casting out devils in thy name; and we forbade him, because he followeth not with us.

47 of them was the ¹greatest. But when Jesus saw the reasoning of their heart, he took a little child, and
48 set him by his side, and said unto them, Whosoever shall receive this little child in my name receiveth me: and whosoever shall receive me receiveth him that sent me: for he that is ²least among you all, the same is great.
49 And John answered and said, Master, we saw one casting out demons in thy name; and we forbade

---

a Matt. 10: 40; 18: 5; Mark 9: 37; John 12: 44; 13: 20.....*b* Matt. 23: 11   12.....*c* Mark 9: 38.   See Num. 11: 28.——1 Gr. *greater.*
.....2 Gr. *lesser.*

---

text is quite as likely to be correct. The matter of the reasoning was as to **which of them should be greatest**—or, more exactly, *might possibly be greater.* Matthew suggests a natural occasion for such rivalry, in the distinction which had just been given to Peter in miraculously catching the fish which furnished the required tribute-money. Luke makes no reference to such an incident, and simply shows the disciples as engaged in a comparison of their respective capacities for high office in the kingdom of the Messiah. The Greek comparative "greater," not "greatest," implies that the discussion was not as to a gradation of the apostles from highest to lowest, but as to fitness among them for the chief place. Which of them, over against the rest as a body was greater, viz., than they all. The final effect is superficially the same, as he that was greater *than* all others would be greatest of all; but the Greek point of view was different. The Greek, no more than English, would use a comparative when the *thought* was of a superlative. (See Winer, *Grammatik*, 5 Aufl. S. 280). Obviously, any reasoning among them on this subject betrays a sad failure to realize the nature of true eminence in the service of the Master. This, however, does not appear to have disheartened him, as did the failure of faith to heal the lunatic boy.

47. Perceiving the thought of their hearts—which fairly implies here in Luke, that it was expressed; because how could a *reasoning*, of the nature of a debate, enter in simultaneously in many hearts without a word spoken? He **took a child** (*little child*) **and set him by him.** This means that he caused the child to sit, or stand, close beside himself, as he sat, in the position of nearest attachment, with the disciples in a semicircle around him (Matthew and Mark), but further off.

48. Whosoever shall receive this (*little*) **child in my name**, etc. **In my name**—that is, on the ground that he bears my name, professes himself a disciple of mine. Hence, this little child is named simply as representing the character, in certain respects, of a true disciple (comp. Matt. 5: 5). The receiving such a child is to humble oneself like it, and in that proportion to become truly great. (See on 14: 11). The little child is a type, not indeed of moral purity and freedom from sin, but of the absence of such ambition and desire of superiority over others, in rank, as was now clouding the character of his chosen servants. —**Receiveth me**—who am present in every disciple, as much in the humblest and most insignificant, as in the noblest and most exalted. Not only so, but **receiveth him that sent me**—who is present in me, as I am in the believer. In view of such a truth, how paltry seem all contentions about grades of religious merit.—**For he that is least** (properly, less, smaller, namely, than others) **among you all, the same is great.** He that humbleth himself will be exalted in the assignment of places in Christ's kingdom. Whatever other virtues shall be taken into account, nothing will be honored in the absence of the child-like remoteness from selfish ambition. How could it be otherwise, when the Vicegerent himself receives the name that is above every name, and the worship of the universe, on the ground of such humility and condescension as it would be utterly impossible for any other being to exhibit? Observe that Jesus does not deny, rather confirms, that there are gradations of rank in his perfected reign, but bestowed on principles directly opposite to those which commonly prevail in the allotments of this world.

49, 50. INTOLERANCE REPROVED. Mark 9: 38-41.

49. And John answered and said, Master, we saw, etc. **Answered**—inasmuch as his remark had reference to the phrase which Jesus had used, "in my name." The beloved disciple is reminded of an occurrence in which he perhaps had done wrong. It surprises us at first that John

50 And Jesus said unto him, Forbid *him* not: for *a* he that is not against us is for us.

50 him, because he followeth not with us. But Jesus said unto him, Forbid *him* not: for he that is not against you is for you.

a See Matt. 12 : 30 ; ch. 11 : 23.

should have to confess this particular fault, from the impression of gentleness and charity which his Gospel is apt to give concerning him. But some expressions in his Epistles warrant the appellation, Son of Thunder (Mark 3 : 17), and render probable the account of his vehement indignation against the heretic Cerinthus, even in his extreme old age.— **Casting out devils** (*demons*) **in thy name.** The latter clause stands first in the Greek, showing that it recalls the words from the preceding verse.—**And we forbade him, because he followeth not with us.** It is implied in the Greek that their prohibition was effectual, and stopped the work. The stranger appears to have been doing, but in an unobjectionable way, what certain "vagabond Jews" attempted at Ephesus, during the ministry of Paul there. Whether the man mentioned here effected the cures which he attempted, is not quite certain, but that he did, more probable. The mere fact that he had not formally joined the company of those who went about with Christ, as of his company, would not seem to preclude the idea, when we learn that "many" will say to Jesus in the last day, "in thy name, we cast out demons, when we lived on the earth." Indeed the Lord seems (Mark 9 : 39) to admit that he did a miracle in his name. In that time, this delegation of power to work wonders of healing in the name of Christ might, in various ways, subserve his cause, even though the faith were only partial, but sincere as far as it went. Doubtless, he also would see that an unrestrained practice of this kind might lead to much evil; but he could make due allowance for peculiar circumstances, and he saw, at all events, that the spirit in which the disciples had grudged any participation in the authority of their Master was not right.

50. And Jesus said unto him, Forbid him not.—Whatever their motive was, he did not encourage the bluff suppression of efforts that were even ostensibly put forth in furtherance of his cause. But he gives a reason for his injunction which is of general interest.—**For he that is not against us** (*you*), **is for us** (*you*). *You* is the better supported reading. Jesus might naturally speak thus, as the counsel was for their future guidance, and on them would soon devolve the whole charge of the gospel. The principle laid down is not contradictory, but a complement to that in Matt. 12: 30—"he that is not for me is against me." Both are true, but with different aspects. When Christ thinks of his cause as demanding the heart homage, and practical submission, of every soul, then neutrality is hostility to him. When he thinks of it as a system of means by which knowledge concerning him is to be diffused and faith promoted, then any form of external co-operation, even the absence of opposition, counts as an aid. Paul in Rome, when it was a question of Christ being made known so, or not at all, to the dying multitude, rejoiced that he was preached, if it must be, from the most detestable motives (Phil. 1 : 15 18).

PART THIRD.—THE FINAL DEPARTURE FROM GALILEE, AND JOURNEY TO JERICHO, ON THE WAY TO JERUSALEM. 9 : 51—18 : 35.

According to the plan of the composition of Luke's Gospel, which we have hitherto traced, we have reached the period where the revelation of the Messiah is become as complete as it is likely to be during his earthly life. The unworldly character of his mission, the necessity that it should end in a violent death at the hands of the chief religious authorities of the nation, and the requirement of self-sacrifice on the part of those who would share the blessings of his rule, have all at least been plainly stated. Provision has been made for the carrying forward by others of the work which he has begun. Luke now begins his account of the journey which he makes from Galilee to Jerusalem, that he may reach the appointed end. There is a great number of events, and a large amount of instruction included within the terms of this journey, much of which is peculiar to this Gospel. A number of the items contained in it might have belonged, in the actual order of their occurrence, to an earlier time; and it is a question for harmonizers, in parallel reports, what

M

51 And it came to pass, when the time was come that ᵃ he should be received up, he steadfastly set his face to go to Jerusalem.
52 And sent messengers before his face: and they went, and entered into a village of the Samaritans, to make ready for him.
53 And ᵇ they did not receive him, because his face was as though he would go to Jerusalem.
54 And when his disciples James and John saw *this*,

51 And it came to pass, when the days¹ were well-nigh come that he should be received up, he stedfastly set his face to go to Jerusalem, and sent messengers before his face: and they went, and entered into a village of the Samaritans, to make ready for him.
53 And they did not receive him, because his face
54 was *as though he were* going to Jerusalem. And when his disciples James and John saw *this*, they said, Lord, wilt thou that we bid fire to come down

ᵃ Mark 16:19; Acts 1:2....ᵇ John 4:4, 9.—1 Gr. *were being fulfilled*.

order of time is the more probable. But in our narrative all comes in as part of the incidents of a slow, thronged journey, which the writer aims to keep before our minds by occasional restatements of the fact, as at 13:22; 17:11.

Whether the beginning of this journey was the same as that of his departure from Galilee to attend the Feast of Tabernacles (John 7:1, 10), the autumn before his death, or, whether that had taken place before, with the stay about Jerusalem, till the Feast of Dedication, in the beginning of winter (John 10:22), and the raising of Lazarus, are much and very variously discussed by the harmonists. (See a collection of the discrepant views in McClellan, *New Testament*, I., 452-65, where we have also, of course, a triumphant *demonstration* of the "absurdity" and "skepticism" of the best of them, and the infallible certainty of his new view.)

51-56. HE SETS FORTH, IS REFUSED ENTERTAINMENT IN A SAMARITAN VILLAGE.

51. When the time was come that he should be received up. A more exact rendering of this part of the verse would be—And it came to pass, *when the days of his being taken up were becoming filled* ("were receiving completion."—McClellan). His being **received up** implies his death and resurrection, but expresses his ascension to heaven. The text presupposes that there was a definite time for this, of which the Saviour was aware, distant a certain number of days, which number was running out, drawing to a close, more exactly, becoming fulfilled, or filled up, so that when the last one was past, his ascension would take place. The clause fixes the time of what follows as indefinitely near to the close of Christ's stay on earth, and, while implying all the pains that should precede, represents his destined departure as finally glorious.—**He steadfastly set his face to go to Jerusalem.** He = *himself*—in antithesis to the "messengers" next spoken of. His "**decease**" (ver. 31), which included his ascension

or assumption, must be accomplished there, and knowing the time to be near, and foreseeing the sufferings which were involved, perhaps dissuaded also by opposition of his disciples (Matt. 16:22), he needed to "set his face as a flint" that he might not be deterred. While there is nothing in the language here to absolutely prevent this setting out from being the same as that in John 7:10, still it agrees better with the supposition of a later time, not earlier than that of the festival of the dedication, at which Jesus was present in Jerusalem, apparently as an interlude in the main journey.

52. And sent messengers before his face, etc.—as a necessary incident of his journey. It supposes that he had planned the route which he would pursue, for some distance in advance, and sent them forward, not essentially as religious heralds, but to provide for the reception and entertainment of himself and his company. It is probable that the women mentioned in 23:49, 55, were now with him.—**And they went and entered into a village of the Samaritans**—not that it was his plan to go directly, and by the nearest road, requiring only three or four days; but along the border of Galilee it might be sometimes convenient for him to lodge in a Samaritan village. Nor was there anything in the general habits of Samaritans, at that time, to prevent his doing so. He might fairly have anticipated treatment as favorable as he had received on his way northward, at Sychar (John ch. 4), more than two years before. These people, however, would not **receive him**—allow his messengers to procure entertainment for him—**because his face was as though he would go to Jerusalem.** Why it should have made a difference in their treatment that he was going *to* rather than *from* Jerusalem, is not apparent, unless they grudged the honor that the presence of the great wonder-worker and supposed Messiah would carry to the rival centre of worship.

54. And when his disciples James and John saw this, they said, etc. Another

they said, Lord, wilt thou that we command fire to come down from heaven, and consume them, even as *Elias did?
55 But he turned, and rebuked them, and said, Ye know not what manner of spirit ye are of.
56 For *the Son of man is not come to destroy men's lives, but to save *them*. And they went to another village.
57 *And it came to pass, that, as they went in the way, a certain *man* said unto him, Lord, I will follow thee whithersoever thou goest.
58 And Jesus said unto him, Foxes have holes, and

55 from heaven, and consume them¹? But he turned
56 and rebuked them². And they went to another village.
57 And as they went in the way, a certain man said unto him, I will follow thee whithersoever thou
58 goest. And Jesus said unto him, The foxes have

---

a 2 Kings 1 : 10, 12....h John 3 : 17; 12 : 47....c Matt. 8 : 19.——1 Many ancient authorities add, *even as Elijah did*....2 Some ancient authorities add, *and said, Ye know not what manner of spirit ye are of. Some, but fewer, add also, For the Son of man came not to destroy men's lives, but to save them.*

---

phase of the Boanerges. They blaze forth even beyond Peter. They were incensed at the indignity put upon their Lord, and that by Samaritans. The addition to their question—**as Elijah also did**—fails of the approbation of the Revision, and is omitted by Tischendorf, Tregelles, and Westcott and Hort. We probably must submit to the loss, yet it seems very strange that the disciples should suggest the punishment of burning, if they were not thinking of Elijah's vengeance on his pursuers (2 Kings 1 : 9, 14); and if they were thinking of that, it would be natural that they should indicate it.

55. But he turned and rebuked them. The original text appears to have stopped with this, judging by the external evidence; but the remainder of the verse, if not true, is so well feigned, that it looks more like genuine than is often the case with a spurious clause. It would be very much like the Master to turn to account such an opportunity for emphasizing the different spirit of the gospel from that of the piety of Elijah's time.

56. And they went to another village. It may have seemed to those irate disciples a tame way of meeting such an insult; but it was the Saviour's way, and in it he illustrated the spirit of his precepts to them in Matthew 10 : 23. There can scarcely be a doubt that the former part of this verse was added long after Luke's time. The **other village** was, no doubt, on the Galilean side of the border, with which view the Greek word for *another* particularly agrees. (See Grimm, *Clavis*, p. 177 a.) Our Lord did not force his blessings on any one.

57-62. THE FAITH OF THE PROFESSED DISCIPLES PUT TO THE TEST. Two of the cases here brought before us are mentioned by Matthew also, but in a different connection (8 : 19 ff). Although reported together, they may have occurred at intervals, and been grouped on account of the similarity of the teaching; and any time would seem a suitable one for such an incident to occur. The first case was that of a scribe—of a class, therefore, who did not often show favor toward the claims of Jesus. He comes as a volunteer. The accession of such a man to the ranks of the disciples, would be a gain as desirable, to human view, as the conversion, in our time, of a noted unbeliever and leader of society.

57. A certain man said unto him, Lord, I will follow thee whithersoever thou goest. His profession and promise were unexceptionable. There was no reservation. He would go with the Saviour where he should choose. We hardly see why he was not welcomed joyfully. But the Lord seems to have thought that he protested too much. There was danger, at least, that he spoke on the supposition, after all, that he would be led to ease, and honor, and power. His disposition would be better known to himself if such a delusion were distinctly dispelled. The answer, at all events, was consistent with this view of his need.

58. Jesus said unto him, Foxes have holes, and birds of the air (literally, *heaven*) **have nests** (Greek, *dwelling-places*); **but the Son of man hath not where to lay his head.** This is the most touching utterance of the Saviour left on record, concerning the hardness of his earthly lot, in respect to the outward means of comfort, on which life itself depends. At Capernaum, he seems to have had a lodging in a particular house, almost as if it were his own. Even that was not his own, and elsewhere he was entirely dependent on the hospitality which Providence might throw in his way. The statement was chill enough to nip the sprouting zeal of the scribe; and we hear nothing of his actually following a step.

58. And he said unto another, Follow

birds of the air *have* nests; but the Son of man hath not where to lay *his* head.

59 *a*And he said unto another, Follow me. But he said, Lord, suffer me first to go and bury my father.

60 Jesus said unto him, Let the dead bury their dead: but go thou and preach the kingdom of God.

61 And another also said, Lord, *b* I will follow thee; but let me first go bid them farewell, which are at home at my house.

62 And Jesus said unto him, No man, having put his hand to the plough, and looking back, is fit for the kingdom of God.

holes, and the birds of the heaven *have* *1*nests; but the Son of man hath not where to lay his head.

59 And he said unto another, Follow me. But he said, Lord, suffer me first to go and bury my father.

60 Lord, suffer me first to go and bury my father. But he said unto him, Leave the dead to bury their own dead; but go thou and publish abroad the kingdom

61 of God. And another also said, I will follow thee, Lord; but first suffer me to bid farewell to them that

62 are at my house. But Jesus said unto him, No man, having put his hand to the plough, and looking back, is fit for the kingdom of God.

---

a Matt. 8: 21....*b* See 1 Kings 19: 20.——1 Gr. *lodging-places.*

---

me. This man did not offer, but was solemnly called, much in the same manner as the chief apostles had been. But he did not respond in the spirit of those who took the summons of Jesus as paramount to all other duties.—**He said, Lord suffer** (=permit) **me first to go and bury my father.** This was certainly in itself a very reasonable request. Our Lord would himself have been the first to reprove the lack of a disposition to care for the remains of a father. But there was now another call on the man even more pressing. Either Christ could not tarry for the funeral, which is extremely likely, or it was necessary for the hesitating convert to receive a startling intimation of the extent and depth of the devotion involved in discipleship. The lesson to him would at the same time impress all hearers with the strictness of Christ's demands. **Let the dead bury their** (*own*) **dead.** It thus appears that there were others by whom, as Jesus saw, the funeral rites might be duly performed. By a play on the word he calls them dead, as being alive only to the world and its perishing interests, and reminded his hearer of the dreadful nature of that state from which he was called to flee at all hazards.—**Their** *own* **dead**—as if the naturally dead belonged to the spiritually dead.—**But go thou and preach** (*publish abroad*) **the kingdom of God.**—Christ must have seen in this man a real faith, however halting, and a talent to make him a useful herald of the gospel, if once he could be brought wholly into that work. Indeed, he belonged (Matt. 8: 21) to the class of disciples, in some sense of the word; and from the spirit of this narrative we could easily believe, if there were any proper authority for it, the old tradition mentioned by one of the fathers, that this man was the future Philip the Evangelist.

61. And another also said, Lord, I will follow thee; but let me first (the verb is the same as *suffer*=permit, in ver. 59) (omit **go**) **bid farewell to them which are at home at my house. At home,** or, **at my house,** in the last clause is superfluous in the English, and not warranted by the Greek. Either one is enough. Another case of procrastination—of promise to follow Christ after a while. But what Jesus asked, and asks, is immediate consecration. His plea for delay, though asking nothing reprehensible, was of less weight than the preceding. Like that, it intimated indecision. His feeling was an inclination, not a determination.

62. No man having put his hand to the plough (Greek, *on a plow*) **and looking back, is fit for the kingdom of God.**—The teaching is, that service to the Lord in labors to promote the kingdom of God, to spread his gospel and win new subjects for the heavenly king, must be whole-hearted, undistracted by lower cares. This is illustrated by an agricultural metaphor. As the plowman needs to look straightforward, to cut a good furrow, so the fit, well-adapted servant of the Lord must direct all attention to the work which he gives him to do.

The whole section is an application, in typical cases, of the instruction in ver. 23 above.

These three men were all candidates, not for discipleship merely, which might have allowed them to remain at home, but for that public ministry for Christ, which required men to leave home and all counter engagements, and be ready, when taught and qualified, to do his errands anywhere. The principle of undivided devotion is applicable, with modifications, to the case of every Christian; the forms in which it is here set forth address themselves particularly to ministers of the gospel, actual or intended.

CHAPTER X.

AFTER these things the Lord appointed other seventy also, and *sent them two and two before his face into every city and place, whither he himself would come.
2 Therefore said he unto them, *The harvest truly is great, but the labourers are few; *pray ye therefore the Lord of the harvest, that he would send forth labourers into his harvest.
3 Go your ways: *behold, I send you forth as lambs among wolves.

1 Now after these things the Lord appointed seventy¹ others, and sent them two and two before his face into every city and place, whither he himself was about to come. And he said unto them, The harvest is plenteous, but the labourers are few: pray ye therefore the Lord of the harvest, that he send forth
3 labourers into his harvest. Go your ways: behold, I

a Matt. 10: 1; Mark 6: 7....b Matt. 9: 37, 38; John 4: 35 ...c 2 Thess. 3: 1....d Matt. 10: 16.——1 Many ancient authorities add, *and two; and so in ver. 17.*

Ch. 10. 1-12. MISSION OF THE SEVENTY.
1. After these things the Lord appointed other seventy (*seventy others*) **also.**—These things are the circumstances attending the departure from Galilee, and particularly what has just been related concerning the proposed preachers of the kingdom of God.—**Seventy**—in allusion to the seventy elders of Moses (Num. 11: 16).—**Others also**—in reference to the twelve whom he had previously appointed as apostles. The number was large, that they might rapidly accomplish, in a short time, throughout Southern Galilee, but more especially beyond the Jordan, the work which had been done in Northern Palestine. Some ancient authorities make the number seventy-two, as some texts number the elders under Moses also; other supposed antecedents of the number (the traditional seventy languages, seventy palm trees, Jewish Sanhedrin), are merely fanciful.—**And sent them two and two before his face**, etc.—They were to go in pairs, as did the twelve (see on 9: 2 ff.).—**Into every city and place.**—They were to visit every place, whether city, village, or farm house—**whither he himself would** (*was about to*) **come.** The purpose was, as afterward appears, to prepare people for his coming, so that they might receive, without delay, such benefit as was possible for them, from his necessarily hasty passage. It was, in some sense, a repetition, on a small scale, of the function of John the Baptist in a wider relation.
2. The harvest truly is great (*plenteous*), **but the laborers are few.**—Even in reference to the fields then lying open before them on the road to Jerusalem, the declaration had a pathetic significance. So it had been wherever he went since the "ripe" harvest fields at Sychar (John 4: 35). The harvest was ample, and the laborers, even now

that he had called seventy others, were few to meet the demand. We may infer that he had no more that he could hopefully send out for such work. And, if we suppose his mind to have gone forth over the world, then lying in wickedness, and along the generations out of whom should come the other sheep of his, not of that flock, how must his soul have been burdened with the thought of the mere handful of reapers to whom he must leave the task!—**Pray ye therefore the Lord of the harvest**, etc. A prime object of the laborers is to concern themselves about an increase of their number. That the harvest is God's, gives them good ground for praying him to do what they cannot of themselves accomplish. The injunction may mean, " Pray that God will prosper you in winning men to faith in me, some of whom will become light-bearers to others, or also, that he may incline some who already believe to such ardor of love and zeal, that they will, without reserve, give themselves up to the ministry of the gospel. God is the source from which such gifts must come; and as Christ was much in prayer with reference to the twelve (comp 6: 12 ff.), so he would have them wait on God, even while they themselves worked by instruction and exhortation toward the same end. **Send forth**—strictly, "thrust forth"; the Greek implies urgency, almost compulsion, as though much reluctance would have to be overcome. Send *forth*, not, specifically, from Judea, still less from heaven (Godet), but from the seclusion or earthly engagements of private life.—**Into his harvest.** There is indeed a work of sowing and culture, as well as of reaping, but it is encouraging that there is harvesting in it, and that this is really its characteristic feature.
3-4. Go your ways: behold, I send you forth as lambs in the midst of

4 *Carry neither purse, nor scrip, nor shoes; and
*salute no man by the way.
5 *And into whatsoever house ye enter, first say,
Peace *be* to this house.
6 And if the son of peace be there, your peace shall
rest upon it: if not, it shall turn to you again.
7 *And in the same house remain,* eating and drinking such things as they give; for *the labourer is
worthy of his hire. Go not from house to house.
8 And into whatsoever city ye enter, and they receive
you, eat such things as are set before you:
9 *And heal the sick that are therein, and say unto
them, *The kingdom of God is come nigh unto you.
10 But into whatsoever city ye enter, and they receive you not, go your ways out into the streets of the
same, and say,
11 *Even the very dust of your city, which cleaveth
on us, we do wipe off against you; notwithstanding be
ye sure of this, that the kingdom of God is come nigh
unto you.

4 send you forth as lambs in the midst of wolves.
Carry no purse, no wallet, no shoes; and salute no
5 man on the way. And into whatsoever house ye
6 shall ¹enter, first say, Peace *be* to this house. And
if a son of peace be there, your peace shall rest upon
7 ²him; but if not, it shall turn to you again. And in
that same house remain, eating and drinking such
things as they give: for the labourer is worthy of
8 his hire. Go not from house to house. And into
whatsoever city ye enter, and they receive you, eat
9 such things as are set before you: and heal the sick
that are therein, and say unto them, The kingdom
10 of God is come nigh unto you. But into whatsoever
city ye shall enter, and they receive you not, go out
11 into the streets thereof and say, Even the dust from
your city, that cleaveth to our feet, we do wipe off
against you; howbeit know this, that the kingdom

a Matt. 10: 9, 10; Mark 6: 8; ch. 9: 3....*b* 2 Kings 4: 29....*c* Matt. 10: 12....*d* Matt. 10: 11 ...*e* 1 Cor. 10: 27....*f* Matt. 10: 10;
1 Cor. 9: 4, etc.; 1 Tim. 5: 18....*g* ch. 9: 2....*h* Matt. 3: 2: 4: 17; 10: 7; ver. 11....*i* Matt. 10: 14; ch. 9: 5; Acts 13: 51; 18: 6.
—— 1 Or, *enter first, say*....2 Or, *it.*

---

wolves. Here, eminently, they were taking up their cross daily. Not a flattering introduction to their work, if there were faint-hearted men among them; but honest, and as stimulating as it was sincere, to such as had any share of the Master's own spirit. They were at once guarded against romantic illusions, roused to energy, and prepared to profit by his preliminary counsels. These are contained in ver. 3–11, and in their spirit have been expounded in Notes on 9: 1–5.

4. This verse corresponds to verse 3, there. But notice here an enhanced intensity of direction as given in the Revision: "Carry *no* purse, *no* wallet, *no* shoes (sandals)." The prohibition of salutations by the way, is to prevent delay, in mere gossip, and specially, perhaps, in the formal and tedious character of their *salaams* of courtesy, wherever they greeted each other at all. (But see Smith, *Dict. of the Bible*, p. 2795).

5. Peace be to this house—the common formula of salutation among the Jews, with whom "peace" comprehended all blessing, and welfare, as it is among the Mahometans now, in their *Salaam*=Hebrew *Shalom*.

6. And if the (*a* in Revision) **son of peace be there.** A *son of peace* is a peaceable man, one filled with the spirit of peace (6: 35; Matt. 9: 15; 13: 38). He would be known as such if he met this greeting with a like spirit. —**Your peace shall** (*will*) **rest upon it**—your salutation, implying a prayer for his welfare, will take effect in blessings from above. **But if not, it shall turn to you again**—Greek, "will turn back upon you." What you had wished for him you shall receive yourselves.

7. The sense of the first member of verse 7, is substantially the same as that of 9: 4; which see.—**For the laborer is worthy of his hire.** This obvious truth might free their minds from scruple in receiving the hospitality of the house; "eating and drinking" such things as they gave.—**Go not from house to house.** This is plainly implied in the preceding clause; but Jesus thought it of practical importance enough to state it plainly.

8. And into whatsoever city ye enter, and they receive you—when the welcome of the particular house speaks the sentiment of the community, the course of conduct recommended is doubtless the same as was to be pursued in reference to a single house; but here detailed once for all.

9. Heal the sick that are therein—both as a satisfaction to Christ-like sympathy with suffering, and to prepare hearts for a more ready acceptance of the greater boon of spiritual healing and eternal life.—**And say unto them, The kingdom of God is come nigh unto you**—so near, that is, in its announcement and invitation, as actually to reach you (ἤγγικεν ἐφ' ὑμᾶς).

10, 11. In case of a refusal to receive them, the direction is equivalent to that which was given to the apostles (9: 5), only more intense. An almost word for word rendering of the Greek sentence may help to apprehend the vehemence: Going out into the streets of it, say, Even the dust which cleaveth to us out of your city on our feet we wipe off for you.—**Notwithstanding, be ye sure of this, that the kingdom of God is come nigh.** That which should have been an opportunity of salvation, is to be noted as a ground of pecu-

12 But I say unto you, that *it shall be more tolerable in that day for Sodom, than for that city.
13 ᵇ Woe unto thee, Chorazin! woe unto thee, Bethsaida! ᶜ for if the mighty works had been done in Tyre and Sidon, which have been done in you, they had a great while ago repented, sitting in sackcloth and ashes.
14 But it shall be more tolerable for Tyre and Sidon at the judgment, than for you.
15 ᵈ And thou, Capernaum, which art ᵉ exalted to heaven, ᶠ shalt be thrust down to hell.

12 of God is come nigh. I say unto you, It shall be more tolerable in that day for Sodom, than for that 13 city. Woe unto thee, Chorazin! woe unto thee, Bethsaida! for if the mighty works had been done in Tyre and Sidon, which were done in you, they would have repented long ago, sitting in sackcloth 14 and ashes. Howbeit it shall be more tolerable for 15 Tyre and Sidon in the judgment, than for you. And thou, Capernaum, shalt thou be exalted unto heaven?

a Matt. 10: 15; Mark 6:11....b Matt. 11: 21....c Ezek. 3: 6....d Matt. 11: 23....e See Gen. 11: 4; Deut. 1: 28; Isa. 14: 13; Jer. 51: 53..../ See Ezek. 26: 20; 32: 18.—1 Gr. powers.

liar condemnation, and an occasion of eternal regret. The rejection of gospel privileges is itself the proof that they have been mercifully offered.

12. I say unto you (omit that), **It shall be more tolerable in that day for Sodom, than for that city.** The guilt of refusing the salvation of Christ will seem more heinous, in the light of eternity, than the blackest moral corruption on the part of those who knew nothing of pardoning grace. —**That day** was—since the earliest prophets, Obadiah (s) and Joel (3:18), the stereotyped designation of a period of judgment connected with the Messiah's reign, when the people of God should be suitably blessed, and his enemies visited with condign vengeance. The idea of it grew more clear and definite in the history of revelation, until in the mouth of Jesus (Matt. 7: 22), and his apostles (2 Tim. 1: 12, 18; 4: 8), it is distinctly the day of eternal judgment at his second coming.

13-16. Doom of the Unrepenting Cities.

The thought of the guilt of such a city as he has been imagining recalls to his heart the case of the cities among whom most of his mighty works had been done, and many of his most moving discourses uttered, and which he had now been obliged to leave finally in their impenitence and ruin.

13. Woe unto thee, Chorazin! Woe unto thee, Bethsaida! Chorazin.—Ill-omened name, mentioned only in the denunciation of our Lord, yet so mentioned as to show that there had been a history of blessings offered, and so received as to make them only a curse. The ruins of the place, now called *Kerazeh*, have quite recently been identified almost beyond question, lying about two miles off the Lake of Gennesaret, nearly north of *Tell Hum*, and almost due west from the mouth of the Upper Jordan. Of the **Bethsaida** here spoken of, called Bethsaida of Galilee (John 12: 21), as distinguished from Bethsaida Julias, mentioned 9: 10, we know scarcely anything except the name. Its site is variously conjectured by travelers, while all agree that it was situated in the neighborhood of Capernaum and Chorazin.—**For if the mighty works had been done in Tyre and Sidon which have been** (*were*) **done in you** —showing that they are selected because they had been the scene of so much of the Saviour's manifestation of his power and grace—**they had** (*would have*) **repented,** etc. From such allusions to abundant deeds and words of Jesus, in two of the cities visited by him, of which the Gospels give us no particular account, we get an inkling of the volumes of unwritten gospel which are registered in heaven.—**Tyre and Sidon** had been regarded by the ancient prophets as types of wicked communities, in respect to their idolatry, and luxury, and moral corruption. Even they would have been moved, the Saviour says, to sorrow for their iniquity, and to reformation of life, had they shared such revelations of the love and mercy of God as had the cities of Galilee. Their mourning would have been like that of Job in intensity (Job 2:8), and of Nineveh (Jonah 3: 5-8), **sitting in sackcloth and ashes** (Comp. Esther 4: 1-3; Jer. 6: 26).

14. Even these cities will be crushed under a less heavy load of self-condemnation and divine inflictions than Chorazin and Bethsaida —**at the judgment.**

15. There was a city more criminal still than these.—**And thou, Capernaum, which art** (rather, *shalt thou be*) **exalted unto heaven?**—The interrogative form of the sentence is required by present evidence concerning the Greek text—How shall it be with *thee?* As thou hast abounded above all other cities in instruction and motives to repentance and holiness, through the more frequent presence of thy citizen, the Messiah, art thou to be correspondingly eminent amidst the honors

16 ᵃHe that heareth you, heareth me; and ᵇhe that despiseth you despiseth me; ᶜand he that despiseth me despiseth him that sent me.
17 And ᵈthe seventy returned again with joy, saying, Lord, even the devils are subject unto us through thy name.
18 And he said unto them, ᵉI beheld Satan as lightning fall from heaven.

16 thou shalt be brought down unto Hades. He that heareth you heareth me; and he that rejecteth you rejecteth me; and he that rejecteth me rejecteth him that sent me.
17 And the seventy returned with joy, saying, Lord, even the demons are subject unto us in thy name.
18 And he said unto them, I beheld Satan fallen as lightning from heaven.

---

a Matt. 10: 40; Mark 9: 37; John 13. 20....*b* 1 Thess. 4: 8....*c* John 5: 23....*d* ver. 1....*e* John 12: 31; 16: 11; Rev. 9: 1; 12: 8, 9.

---

and felicity of his reign? Nay, rather—**thou shalt be thrust** (*brought*) **down to hell**=*Hades*. *Hades* may be here a metaphor to express the lowest imaginable depth, according to that representation of the ancient mythologies, which made the abode of Hades open as far below the surface of the earth as heaven—the sky, or the ethereal firmament—is above it. This would be to the Greek mind the greatest possible perpendicular measure, from heaven to Hades. As the Greek name for the world of the dead had become naturalized in Palestine, since the rule of Alexander the Great, we may well suppose that the Greek conception of it might be so familiar as to warrant allusions to it, although the Hebrew conception of Sheol, the abode of the dead, as modified during the four or more centuries after the close of the Old Testament, was commonly expressed by the word, in Christ's time. But the whole sentence may be taken as it usually has been, not metaphorically, but literally: Capernaum instead of rising into heaven shall be brought into Hades, in one section of which is the region of punishment. What hinders this from being entirely satisfactory, is that *unto* Hades is strictly "as far as to Hades," implying a special depth of descent, while the other cities equally were brought down to the lower world, literally, and "to undergo punishment in Gehenna" (Meyer on Matt. 11: 23). Then they, pre-eminently, "will begin to say, We did eat and drink in thy presence, and thou didst teach in our streets," but instead of finding any comfort in the remembrance, it will inflict the sharpest sting of all upon their souls.

16. He that heareth you heareth me, etc. On the identity of his followers with Christ, and of himself with his Father (see on 9–48). The statement resumes the address to the seventy which had been interrupted at ver. 12. What could now more powerfully impress his ministers with the terrible responsibility laid upon them, than the truth that, as his message had involved eternal life and death to its objects, so would theirs to the people that should hear them.

17–20. Report of the Seventy.

17. And the seventy returned.—How long a time had elapsed since their mission began, and where they found the Master on their return, are matters of doubt. Some weeks probably had been required to visit every city and place whither it was in his plan to come himself, and it has been supposed, with much probability, by a great many harmonizers, that all which is recorded in John 7: 11–10: 39, or a part of it, took place on an incidental and private journey to Jerusalem during the interval. Such a supposition gives a convenient place and time for the visit to Martha and Mary (verses 38-42 of this chapter). Luke, however, writes without any apparent knowledge of that journey. If we adopt the view proposed, the seventy, having gone southward through Perea, the country beyond the Jordan, might have met Jesus in or near Jerusalem, or at or near Jericho, as he went across thither again (John 10: 40). Then we are entirely free to imagine the course of his travel and labors during the considerable period before he re-appears at Jericho on the final ascent to Jerusalem (18: 35). **With joy, saying, Lord, even the devils** (*demons*) **are subject**=subjected, as often as we meet them—**unto us through** (*in*) **thy name.** The verb is in the present tense, and expresses what goes on in their experience. "Nineteenth century English" would be, "are being subjected."—**Through thy name**—when we bid them, on the ground of thy authority, to depart. They had been sent to heal the sick and to preach (ver. 9), and they either understand all sickness to be the work of evil spirits, or the cure of demoniacs is so prominent in their thoughts, as to cast all the rest into the shade. Certainly this function would express most vividly their power against the adversary, and there might naturally be a special satisfaction in this branch of their success, after the failure (9: 36–43).

CH. X.]   LUKE.   185

19 Behold, *I give unto you power to tread on serpents and scorpions, and over all the power of the enemy; and nothing shall by any means hurt you.
20 Notwithstanding, in this rejoice not, that the spirits are subject unto you; but rather rejoice, *because your names are written in heaven.
21 *In that hour Jesus rejoiced in spirit, and said,

19 lightning from heaven. Behold, I have given you authority to tread upon serpents and scorpions, and over all the power of the enemy; and nothing shall
20 in any wise hurt you. Howbeit in this rejoice not, that the spirits are subject unto you; but rejoice that your names are written in heaven.
21 In that same hour he rejoiced ¹in the Holy Spirit,

<small>a Mark 16: 18; Acts 28: 5....b Ex. 32: 32; Ps. 69: 28; Isa. 4: 3; Dan. 12: 1; Phil. 4: 3; Heb. 12: 23; Rev. 13: 8; 20: 12; 21: 27.
....c Matt.11: 25.—1 Or, by.</small>

---

18. Their joy met an answering emotion in the heart of Jesus. **And he said unto them, I beheld Satan as lightning fall** (or *fallen*) **from heaven.** The order of the Greek is, more nearly, "I was beholding Satan as lightning out of heaven fallen." The connection of the words, rather, and the consistency of ideas, very decidedly, requires "out of heaven" to be referred to "lightning." The participle "fallen" agrees with "Satan." The time to which this beholding is to be referred back has been variously determined. The verb is in the imperfect tense—strictly, "I was beholding." There is no reason for putting it back of the hour when he sent them forth, but it may point either to that or to the subsequent period of their absence. Christ has observed them in spirit, has known their labors and their success. The language might be paraphrased, "During the course of your mission I had such a vision of its success against the prince

SCORPION.

of the demons, that it was as if I viewed him already fallen with the swiftness of a lightning flash, from heaven, and prostrate in utter defeat."—It may be that, if we had a fuller description of this scene, we should see that this peculiar form of expression referred to a meditation into which the Saviour had been thrown by the report of the seventy, rousing himself from which, he said, "I was beholding," etc.—In any case, he has gained, in the result of this trial mission of such as he might expect to be the ordinary ministers of his gospel, a triumphant assurance of victory over all the power of evil, decisive and everlasting.

19. Behold, I give unto you power (*have given you authority*) **to tread on serpents and scorpions,** etc. This opens the secret of that efficiency which had surprised and delighted them. I have given you the power, although I did not expressly mention it.—**Serpents and scorpions** may be merely types of physical perils which they will escape in his service (comp. Acts 28: 3-6), but more probably are metaphorical for all forms of evil agency which they may encounter.—**The enemy**—is, ultimately, the devil. He is, indeed, fallen in the divine purpose and promise; but will yet cause many a fearful, though unavailing, struggle.

20. Notwithstanding, in this rejoice not, that the spirits are subject unto you, etc. The ability to overcome them is compatible with exclusion from the glorified kingdom (Matt. 7: 22, and see on Luke 9: 49). It brings rather an obligation, not to pride and elation of spirits, but to corresponding holiness, and meetness for eternal life.—**But** (omit rather) **rejoice, that your names are written in heaven.** To be enrolled among the citizens of the eternal city, as he assumes to be the case with them, *that* is a proper subject of joy. The figure is based on the fact that in ancient states a register was kept of the names of all who were entitled to the privileges, and bound by the obligations of citizenship. The same conception lies in Ex. 32: 32, 33; Dan. 12: 1; Phil. 4: 2. It is the outward counterpart to God's hidden counsel of election. But as from the earthly register a name unworthy of the city could be erased, so it is by faith and patience only that any particular saint can make his election sure (2 Pet. 1: 10). But such assurance raises the humblest saint to a position of honor and joy above that of the most talented, successful, and honored servant, merely as such.

21-24. TRIUMPH OF JESUS ON OCCASION OF THIS REPORT.

21. In that (*same*) **hour Jesus** (rather, *he*) **rejoiced** (exulted) **in spirit** (or, *the Holy Spirit*). The Greek verb denotes a lively,

I thank thee, O Father, Lord of heaven and earth, that thou hast hid these things from the wise and prudent, and hast revealed them unto babes: even so, Father; for so it seemed good in thy sight.

22 *a* All things are delivered to me of my Father: and *b* no man knoweth who the Son is, but the Father; and who the Father is, but the Son, and *he* to whom the Son will reveal *him*.

and said, I ¹thank thee, O Father, Lord of heaven and earth, that thou didst hide these things from the wise and understanding, and didst reveal them unto babes; yea, Father; ²for so it was well-pleasing in 22 thy sight. All things have been delivered unto me of my Father: and no one knoweth who the Son is, save the Father; and who the Father is, save the Son, and he to whomsoever the Son willeth to reveal

a Matt. 28 : 18 ; John 3 : 35 ; 5 : 27 ; 17 : 2....*b* John 1 : 18 ; 6 : 44, 46.—1 Or, *praise*....2 Or, *that*.

exalted, triumphant joy. Everything in the paragraph shows how peculiarly he was stirred with delight at the evidence he had received of the future progress of his kingdom through his ministers. The reasons are quite conclusive in favor of the addition of "Holy" before "Spirit." Without it we think of that human spirit which distinguished the person of Jesus, "spirit of holiness" (Rom. 1:4), which was, indeed, in perpetual identity with the divine Word, but to which the epithet "Holy" associates the Third Person of the Trinity, though not given as yet so distinctly to the saints.—**And said, I thank thee, O Father, Lord of heaven and earth.** The word for **thank,** expresses here, comprehensively, not merely thanksgiving, but praise, adoration, and all worshipful acknowledgment. The whole soul of Jesus was drawn out in celebrating the grace of him who was now seen to be Lord of the Universe, and Father of our Lord, at the proof of his coöperation with these plain, unlettered men, who had prospered in their work against the adversary, through his name, despite the unbelief and opposition of the wise and religious of the nation. His Sonship to that God was now a peculiar source of delight and comfort to him.—**That thou hast hidden** (*didst hide*) **these things from the wise and prudent** (*understanding*), **and hast revealed** (*didst reveal*) **them unto babes**—the simple-minded, and void of worldly wisdom. Some would soften this by interjecting in the first number an "although"; "although thou didst hide," etc. But that is none of Christ's. He praises God for it all.—**Thou hast hid**—better, *didst hide*—not just now. We are referred back to the divine purpose of salvation "before the foundation of the world," when it was so planned that the way should be made so plain that even babes might follow it, while the worldly wise and self-sufficient would despise it for its very plainness and facility. Thus only did God hide it from the one class, who would not have

real salvation, in any case, and reveal it to the simple-minded and docile, "babes," such as all must be to whom salvation is possible.—**These things**—as we have implied, are the doctrine and saving power of the gospel, as illustrated in the prosperous work of the seventy, and particularly in their own enrollment in the register of heaven.—**Even so** (or, *Yea*), **Father, for** (or, *that*) **so it seemed good** (or, *was well pleasing*) **in thy sight.** We must understand the sentence to be continued, and bring in "I thank thee" again after **Father.** So—resumes the whole preceding statement, and *that* is a preferable connective. It is the Amen of the Saviour's reverent meditation on his Father's plan.—**It seemed good.**—*Was well pleasing*—is truer and stronger. It is of the same radical sense, as "I am well pleased" (Matt. 3: 17; 17: 5; Luke 3: 22). That God was pleased to have it *so*, is the matter of all Christ's rejoicing.

22. Having been addressing his Father, he proceeds in the tone of absorbed meditation: **All things are** (rather, *were*, when I was sent forth) **delivered to me of my Father.**—Of that glorious scheme of salvation God, when it was adopted, made me the administrator, and gave over into my hands all things pertaining to its execution.—**And no man** (no one, **knoweth who the Son is, but the Father, and who the Father is, but the Son,** etc. This illustrates the completeness of Christ's possession of the **all things** pertaining to salvation. Salvation involves the return of a lost sinner to God the Father, from whom he has strayed, which takes place only as he is guided by the Son to a clear and definite knowledge of him. Through the Son alone can he so know to whom he must come in repentance for reconciliation. But how is the lost one to come to the Son for guidance? Only by the Father, yet unknown, inwardly moving and directing him to the Son as the only Revealer of God. Men may doubtless in some sense know God apart from Christ, even his eternal power and Godhead (Rom. 1: 20), but

LUKE.

23 And he turned him unto *his* disciples, and said privately, ᵃBlessed *are* the eyes which see the things that ye see:
24 For I tell you, ᵇthat many prophets and kings have desired to see those things which ye see, and have not seen *them*; and to hear those things which ye hear, and have not heard *them*.
25 And, behold, a certain lawyer stood up, and tempted him, saying, ᶜMaster, what shall I do to inherit eternal life?
26 He said unto him, What is written in the law? how readest thou?

23 *him.* And turning to the disciples, he said privately, Blessed *are* the eyes which see the things that ye
24 see: for I say unto you, that many prophets and kings desired to see the things which ye see, and saw them not; and to hear the things which ye hear, and heard them not.
25 And behold, a certain lawyer stood up and tried him, saying, ¹Master, what shall I do to inherit eter-
26 nal life? And he said unto him, What is written in

---

a Matt 13:16....*b* 1 Pet. 1:10....*c* Matt. 19:16; 22.35.——1 Or, *Teacher.*

---

to reach that intimate recognition of him as a person, just and merciful, holy and compassionate toward sinners, interested in our welfare, and ready as well as able to supply all our spiritual needs, which is involved in this idea of him as the Father—*that Jesus declares impossible except as a man arrives at it through the experimental knowledge of himself.* We first see God as a Father through the divine love and sympathy of the Son. "He that hath seen me hath seen the Father" (John 14:9; comp. ver. 7). The Father's influence, unrecognized as such, troubles, humbles, softens, inclines, the soul into a readiness for the instruction and invitations of the Son, having embraced whom it exclaims in happy amazement, "Now I know God indeed; the Father has been in it all." This is as true a revelation as ever was made to mortals—the uncovering to the heart of what was before entirely concealed; a double revelation, in which God discloses his Son in Jesus of Nazareth, and in the same flash, shows in the author of the soul's penitence, and anxiety, and prayer, God himself, real, apprehensible, adorable, and adored, the Father of our Lord Jesus Christ, chiefest among ten thousand, and altogether lovely.

23. And he turned him unto his disciples, and said privately. Privately—to them alone, because what he had to utter applied in its full sense only to them, and the Master would have them take it in its full sense. Hence, he takes pains that they alone should hear. **Blessed** (*happy*) **are the eyes which see the things that ye see.**—The meaning is, in other words: Happy are ye in sharing the revelation of the mystery of salvation through the gospel, and beholding something of its blessed fruits in the conversion of some.

24. For I tell you (or *say unto you*) **that many prophets and kings** (omit have) **de-sired.**—This was suited to deepen their sense of the value of their privilege. The most pious and mightiest of former days had looked forward to brighter knowledge of God's ways and a holier life for his saints. They were sure it would come, but of its precise character, as of its time, and its medium, they could form no adequate conception. Another intimation of the superior advantage of the Christian position.

25-37. PARABLE OF THE GOOD SAMARITAN. THE OCCASION OF IT. 25-29.

25. And behold, a certain lawyer stood up and tempted him. The place is unknown. What a **lawyer** was, is explained on 7:30. This one **stood up**, perhaps out of a sitting crowd, to address the Saviour. **Tempted** means, here, not necessarily more than "put him to the test" as to his soundness in doctrine and reasoning power; but probably in the hope of showing his own superiority, and possibly with the expectation of trapping him in his reply. It is enough to suppose that the lawyer was curious to know what answer the new Teacher would give to the old moot question which he proposed to him. He has the air neither of a trifler, nor a man concerned about a matter of serious search, to him—**Saying, Master, what shall I do,** etc. The word **do**, is emphatic, the Greek being more literally: "By having done what shall I inherit?" Here we see that eternal life was a topic familiar to Jewish theologians, which, as votaries of the law, they would hope to gain by works.

26. Whether the man felt much or little earnestness in his question, the subject was one of momentous importance, and gave Jesus an opportunity to impart an important lesson to all who were present.—**He said unto him, What is written in the law?** As he was a lawyer, and as the gospel presupposed a right view of the claims of God's

27 And he answering said, *a* Thou shalt love the Lord thy God with all thy heart, and with all thy soul, and with all thy strength, and with all thy mind; and *b* thy neighbour as thyself.
28 And he said unto him, Thou hast answered right, this do, and *c* thou shalt live.
29 But he, willing to *d* justify himself, said unto Jesus, And who is my neighbour?
30 And Jesus answering said, A certain *man* went down from Jerusalem to Jericho, and fell among thieves, which stripped him of his raiment, and wounded *him*, and departed, leaving *him* half dead.

27 the law? how readest thou? And he answering said, Thou shalt love the Lord thy God *1* with all thy heart, and with all thy soul, and with all thy strength, and with all thy mind; and thy neighbour as thyself.
28 And he said unto him, Thou hast answered right: 29 this do, and thou shalt live. But he, desiring to justify himself, said unto Jesus, And who is my 30 neighbour? Jesus made answer and said, A certain man was going down from Jerusalem to Jericho; and he fell among robbers, who both stripped him and

a Deut. 6:5. *b* Lev. 19. 18. *c* Lev. 18:5; Neh. 9. 29; Ezek. 20: 11, 13, 21; Rom. 10: 5....*d* ch. 16: 15.—1 Gr. *from*

law, Jesus meets him on his own ground. He had, in effect, asked, "Which precepts in particular must I keep, to be sure of standing well with God in the judgment?" Christ's question to him is in effect: "What dost thou, as a student of the law, understand to be the essence of it?"—**How readest thou?** *How dost thou make out its meaning?*

27. And he answering said, Thou shalt love the Lord thy God with all thy heart, etc. He does not grope among the secondary and special precepts; but, like Christ himself (Matt. 22:40), goes straight to the heart of the matter, and gives it in its two phases as expressed in Deut 6: 5; 10: 12; Lev. 19: 18.

28. And he said unto him, Thou hast answered right. We can hardly imagine him to have answered better, as to the demand of the law. He had himself answered his own question. "What good thing must I do?" He must love God perfectly, and his neighbor as much as himself. We can suppose him to see, by this time, if he sincerely sought the way of life, that his question should have been: *How* shall I do that which I know must be done to have a good title to eternal life? But the Lord deals with him yet as though he was in perplexity concerning the *what?* Thy understanding is correct, thou hast no need of further light.—**This do** (continually *practice*) **and thou shalt live** (eternally). **This,** namely, love God and fellow man; **do,** really *practice;* cherish and exercise such love at all times, and in prescribed measure, and thou art sure of heaven. This declaration was at once sincerely truthful—appropriate to the man's religious position, and a sentence of condemnation to him in that position. For to **do this** required that he should have already kept that law, without failure or deficiency, for one single instant, from his earliest consciousness. This he could not pretend to have done, in the face of the confessions of sin on the part of the most eminent saints in his Bible. But supposing him to have come so far right, it would be necessary for him to go forward to the end in immaculate obedience to the divine rule, in all its depth and breadth of significance. How impossible this was, appeared in the fact that he was now groping after the thing needful to do, and mean time not certain of being in the safe way. Still he must see that the Saviour's principle held good. Do this completely, perpetually, without intermission or error, and thou shalt live.

29. The question which the lawyer had put is now fully answered. But he could not allow himself to be so easily silenced. He was in danger of seeming foolish, to have expressed doubt in so clear a matter; and to retrieve his position before the people, in other words—**willing** (*resolved*) **to justify himself**—for having so ostentatiously asked a question which he has himself answered easily, he **said unto Jesus, And who is my neighbor?**—He would thus make it seem as though this was the point of his perplexity, which Jesus had not yet cleared up. He might well feel, too, that in the various antagonistic decisions of the doctors touching the application and limits of the term "neighbor," he had proposed a puzzle which would test the Galilean teacher indeed. But our Lord was not to be caught, nor turned aside into any mere speculative and hair-splitting disputes. The true intent of the law is shown by an example of neighborliness, which at the same time illustrates the spirit of the gospel, as it lived and wrought in the breast of its divine Founder.

30-37. The Parable.

Jesus answering (taking him up—not the usual word for answering), **said.**—The correct text omits **and.**—**A certain man went** (*was going*) **down from Jerusalem to Jericho,** etc. The Saviour frames a narrative to exemplify his thought, in perfect consistency with all that we know of the circumstances supposed. The road from Jerusalem went *down* literally, to Jericho, the descent in less than twenty miles being about 3,500 feet. It was also a very dangerous road, lying much of the way in a deep ravine, through soft rocks in which caves and chambers abounded, affording shelter to miscreants, who from them sallied forth to prey upon travelers. It is still the capital city of the nation, and **Jericho** was "the city of palm trees," near the mouth of the Jordan; this and nothing more seems to have been intended.—**And fell among thieves** (*robbers*), as many had done before him, and have since, down even to our own day. (See Stanley, *Sinai and Palestine;* Porter, *Handbook;* Ritter, *Geog. of Pal.*, iii. 11; *Dict. of Bible*, p. 1266). The famous Order of Knights Templar originated in the middle

WAY TO JERICHO.

necessary to have an escort in passing over that road, on which atrocious outrages, amounting sometimes to murder, have been perpetrated within a life-time past. Of travelers there were many, passing between the cities of Jerusalem and Jericho, and to and from the lands beyond the Jordan. We need seek for no deeper meaning in the terms used in this verse than the most obvious ones.— The **certain man**—was just a man, and, since he started from Jerusalem, with nothing said to the contrary, a Jew.—**Jerusalem** meant ages, in a combination of Christian champions to guard this perilous pass, and assist travelers needing aid. **Which** (*both*) **stripped him of his raiment**—after taking what other property he had—**and beat him**—either because he resisted, or out of mere wantonness—**and departed, leaving him half dead**.—Had they murdered him there would have been no need of help, and his injuries must be of sufficient seriousness to present a strong claim for mercy; hence **half dead.** Surely he needed a neighbor.

31 And by chance there came down a certain priest that way: and when he saw him, *he passed by on the other side.
32 And likewise a Levite, when he was at the place, came and looked on *him*, and passed by on the other side.
33 But a certain *b*Samaritan, as he journeyed, came where he was; and when he saw him, he had compassion *on him*,
34 And went to *him*, and bound up his wounds, pouring in oil and wine, and set him on his own beast, and brought him to an inn, and took care of him.

31 beat him, and departed, leaving him half dead. And by chance a certain priest was going down that way: and when he saw him, he passed by on the other side.
32 And in like manner a Levite also, when he came to the place, and saw him, passed by on the other side.
33 But a certain Samaritan, as he journeyed, came where he was: and when he saw him, he was moved with
34 compassion, and came to him, and bound up his wounds, pouring on *them* oil and wine; and he set him on his own beast, and brought him to an inn, and

a Ps. 38: 11....*b* John 4: 9.

31. And by chance (Greek, *by a concurrence*, or, *coincidence*) **there came down a certain priest** (or, *a certain priest was going down*). This was a most natural thing, as Jericho was a priest-city, and at the termination of their weekly "course" at Jerusalem, some priests would be frequently traveling homeward by that route. The priest was, by virtue of his office, nearest in position to the seat where Jehovah sat, and should have shared most largely in the spirit of true religion. If any man on earth might reasonably be expected to lend a helping hand to the wounded traveler, a countryman, and also of the seed of Abraham, this priest was he. But he was the most remote from any such disposition.—**He came and looked on him and passed by on the other side.**—He could not help seeing him; but as the sufferer lay on the other side of the road from that on which he happened to be walking, perhaps a little off from the narrow way, proper, he did not even cross it to ascertain more particularly what the case was.

32. The Levite who followed him, after an interval, belonged also to the priestly tribe—stood next in order of the divine service, and was under a like obligation to exhibit the holiness and moral loveliness of their religion. But his course only helps to demonstrate that official holiness has little to do, necessarily, with that of the heart. It would be impossible for him to do less than the priest; he did, in fact, somewhat more, and worse. Or, does the Saviour mean to paint his conduct a shade lighter, when he makes him, after reaching the place, cross the way and look on him, and then pass by? Hardly. The man only added a cold and heartless curiosity. Both probably had to invent excuses, such as commentators have often imagined, to parry the thrusts which even their consciences must have launched against them. The Greek text followed by the Revision makes the conduct of the Levite almost a simple repetition of that of the priest. The authority for this, although strong, does not seem decisive. It is evident that the wounded wretch will find no neighbor among his own countrymen. And now, having prepared his hearers by the exhibition of two cases of the most shocking absence of the spirit inculcated by the law, he shows its exercise in the case of one at the opposite pole of their ceremonial righteousness.

33, 34. But a certain Samaritan, as he journeyed, came where he was.—We have not now to learn what a repugnance there was, amounting often to the most intense abomination, between the Samaritans and the Jews. The origin of the former race, their intrusion into the very heart of the Holy Land, the rivalry which had existed between them and the orthodox Jews, may be read in any Dictionary of the Bible. The southern border of their territory was not far north of this road, and with all their mutual hatred, there was nothing, under the Roman rule, to hinder their traveling through each other's country. The business of this Samaritan took him down toward the Jordan, and he was riding on an ass, whereas the others had apparently been on foot. When he came opposite the wounded man, instead of acting as the priest, and the Levite had done, especially as the Jews would expect a Samaritan to act, he acted simply as a man. He not only **went to him**—but, with cost, and inconvenience, and delay to his journey, rendered to him all forms and degrees of attention and help that would have been appropriate on the part of a near personal friend who was unstinted in means, and at complete leisure. First, and most helpful of all, **he had compassion.** That genuine sympathy for the suffering, which is more than all outward acts and appliances, bespoke itself in everything he said and did. **He bound up his wounds, pouring in** (*on them*) **oil and wine.** This was according to

35 And on the morrow when he departed, he took out two ᵃpence, and gave *them* to the host, and said unto him, Take care of him; and whatsoever thou spendest more, when I come again, I will repay thee.
36 Which now of these three, thinkest thou, was neighbour unto him that fell among the thieves?
37 And he said, He that shewed mercy on him. Then said Jesus unto him, Go, and do thou likewise.

35 took care of him. And on the morrow he took out two ¹shillings, and gave them to the host, and said, Take care of him; and whatsoever thou spendest more, I, when I come back again, will repay thee.
36 Which of these three, thinkest thou, proved neighbour unto him that fell among the robbers? And
37 he said, He that shewed mercy on him. And Jesus said unto him, Go, and do thou likewise.

a See Matt. 20: 2.—1 See marginal note on Matt. 18: 28.

the approved practice of Jewish pharmacy (Isa. 1:6). The injured parts, restored to their proper place, were mollified, and stimulated to recuperation. Happily, the knapsack of the traveler could furnish, from his provision for the road, all that was wanted for this simple surgery. The next thing was to get the patient forward to a place of safety and rest. So he **set him** (lifting him up, *ἐπιβιβάσας*) **on his own beast, and brought him to an inn** (trudging along on foot himself), **and took care of him.** This was more like an inn in modern times—a caravanserai or khan (Greek, *πανδοχεῖον*)—than that described in connection with our Saviour's birth (2: 7). Its proprietor was a private individual, not the government, and supplies could be procured which the lodger did not already possess. The ruins of one extensive inn of this kind are mentioned by travelers (see Porter's *Hand-book*, I., 181), as existing on this road, and, probably, near the scene which Jesus had in mind. It is called *Khan el Ahmah*.

35. Having giving his own time and attention to his patient the rest of that day, **On the morrow**—as he went forward to accomplish his delayed journey—**he took out** (Greek, "threw down") **two pence** (=two dollars; see on 7: 41), **and said, Take care of him; and whatsoever thou spendest more, when** (*I when*) **I come again, I will repay thee.** He appears to intend to pay in full for the care of an invalid at an inn for two days, by which time he hoped to be back. But if he should be delayed, or if additional needs should appear, he provides for every contingency — **I** (emphatic; you need not hold the sick man to account, I) **will repay thee.** Could generosity go farther?

36, 37. APPLICATION.

36. **Which** (omit **now**) **of these three, thinkest thou, was** (*proved himself*) **neighbour,** etc. The Revision well substitutes *proved himself* for **was** here. The Greek verb is that which primarily signifies "to become," but which in many places is almost ="to appear as," "to turn out" so and so. By the question, the Saviour again puts it upon the lawyer to answer himself. With more than Socratic skill, he thus often, instead of stating his own judgment or a practical point, led or compelled his collocutors to develop their own thoughts into distinctness.

37. **And he said, He that shewed mercy** (*the* mercy) **on him.** The Greek article is hardly idle here. He would not speak the hated name, Samaritan, but substitutes a description which itself evinces his own narrowness and lack of true neighborly love. The Saviour, in drawing from the lawyer the definition of "neighbor," has it not in a direct and formal shape. Had he himself been obliged to give it, he would, perhaps, have said, Thy neighbor is, in the sense of God's law, every human being. But he was intent, as always, on a practical lesson. He would not unnecessarily shock prejudice. He allows the lawyer to take the one remaining step of inference, that, as the good Samaritan was neighbor to the wounded Jew, the latter was, in that very fact, neighbor to him; that a Jew would fulfill the law in showing mercy to a distressed Samaritan, and, of course, to any other man needing sympathy and aid. He could not, in short, keep that law which he had professed a desire to understand without acting toward any needy man on earth as the Samaritan did. So Jesus brings the lesson home to him.—**Go, and do thou likewise.** This reverts again to the first question, "What must *I* do to inherit eternal life?" Christ had replied as to the first table; he has now as to the second.

REMARK.—It is curious, at first sight, that the lawyer seemed to have no perplexity touching the great commandment of perfect love to God, while he was not altogether clear as to the requirement toward fellow-men. Yet he may have been sincere in this. Our Saviour and his apostles, whenever they would

38 Now it came to pass, as they went, that he entered into a certain village: and a certain woman named *Martha received him into her house.
39 And she had a sister called Mary, [b] which also [c] sat at Jesus' feet, and heard his word.
40 But Martha was cumbered about much serving, and came to him, and said, Lord, dost thou not care that my sister hath left me to serve alone? bid her therefore that she help me.

38 Now as they went on their way, he entered into a certain village; and a certain woman named Martha
39 received him into her house. And she had a sister called Mary, who also had sat at the Lord's feet, and
40 heard his word. But Martha [1] cumbered about much serving; and she came up to him, and said, Lord, dost thou not care that my sister did leave me to serve alone? bid her therefore that she help me.

a John 11: 1 ; 12: 2, 3....*b* 1 Cor. 7: 32, etc....*c* Luke 8: 35; Acts 22: 3.—1 Gr. *distracted.*

inculcate the observance of the law, without stating its whole requirement, specify by naming the commandments of the second table, never those of the first alone (Matt. 19:17; parallels, Rom. 13: 9; Gal. 5: 14; Jas. 2: 8). The reason may be that, while either branch of the one dual commandment involves the other, it is easier for us to imagine that we have kept the first when we have not, than it is that we have kept the second. Hence John, in his First Epistle, applies to Christian profession the test furnished by the law of love, in both directions (2: 10 and 5: 2), but much more fully dwells on the need of love towards our brother, and the proof from this that we love God, and are born of God.

38-42. A VISIT AT THE HOUSE OF MARTHA AND MARY.

38. Now it came to pass as they went, that he entered into a certain village. As this family were, about this time, living at Bethany (John 11: 1; 12: 9. comp. ver. 1), near Jerusalem, we cannot doubt that that was the village mentioned, although Luke does not name it. Some have thought it necessary to place this incident back, on a former journey; but, as we have stated on 9: 51, and on ver. 17, above, there is nothing in Luke inconsistent with the supposition of a brief visit of Jesus to Jerusalem, unnoticed in this Gospel, while the seventy were preparing the way for him in Perea. At such a time, he reached this village, going to or from Jerusalem over the eastern slope of the Mount of Olives.—**And a certain woman named Martha received him into her house.** It was a house which our Lord must have often visited before. A brother of the two women, named Lazarus, was at this time, or had been recently, so intimate with him as to be known as he whom Jesus loved. Not long after this time it must have been, when the Master was summoned from beyond the Jordan (John 10: 40; 11: 1 ff.), with the word that this friend was very sick; on which occasion was wrought one of the most marvelous and beneficent works which Christ performed on earth—the raising of that friend from death to life. Faint as is the picture of his intercourse with the family at Bethany, we easily see more evidence of its being a real home to him, when he was in that neighborhood, than any other place, even "his house" in Capernaum. To it we shall see him, a little later, retiring every night for repose and sympathy, from the labors, debates, oppositions, and hostile plots that were culminating in the arrest, the sham trial, and the cross.

We know little of the internal relations of the family. Lazarus appears as without a wife—perhaps a widower. Martha appears as the older sister. Some think her to have been the wife of one Simon, who had been a leper, whose house was known as his after his decease (Matt. 26: 6; Mark 14: 3. Comp. John 12: 1). The house is here called "her house," and she is seen to be housekeeper.

39. And she had a sister called Mary, which also sat at Jesus' (probably, *the Lord's*) **feet,** etc. The *also* intimates that she had first participated in the care for suitably entertaining Jesus, as implied further in Martha's phrase, "she hath left me." But while Martha prosecutes further domestic preparations, Mary now feels the opportunity of hearing the instruction of the Master too precious to be lost for such a cause. She "seated herself" at Jesus' feet, after the manner of scholars before the Rabbi.—**And heard** (was listening to) **his word.** She evidently was not willing to let one syllable of it drop.

40. But Martha was cumbered about much serving = the domestic ministry (see 4: 39). The Greek says: "She was distracted," her mind drawn in opposite directions; yet no one can deny that "cumbered" is a very congruous substitute. She had planned a task of hospitality which was becoming a burden to her; and partly, we may suppose, apprehending failure, and partly piqued that her sister should be *idly* enjoying more of the privilege of Christ's company,

41 And Jesus answered and said unto her, Martha, Martha, thou art careful and troubled about many things;
42 But *one thing is needful: and Mary hath chosen that good part, which shall not be taken away from her.

41 But the Lord answered and said unto her, ¹Martha, Martha, thou art anxious and troubled about many things; ²but one thing is needful: for Mary hath chosen the good part, which shall not be taken away from her.

a Ps. 27:4.——1 A few ancient authorities read, *Martha, Martha, thou art troubled* : *Mary hath chosen*, etc....2 Many ancient authorities read, *but few things are needful, or one*.

she came (*up*)—suddenly presented herself—**to him and said, Lord, dost thou not care**, etc. She inaptly assumes that he is to charge himself with the right behaviour of the family. She implies that he is in fault in encouraging her sister's fault. On this ground, therefore, she instructs him what he is to do in the matter. **Bid her therefore that she help me.** Literally, "speak to her therefore, in order that she may take hold with me." It must have been mortifying to Mary, and an unpleasant scene to the others who were present. Never did the divine-human sympathy, forbearance, and tact of Jesus, more decidedly shine out. He saw instantly how natural was Martha's feeling, though petulant; gave her full credit for the hospitable and pious motive which drove her to superfluous toil on his account; yet sadly felt how much better was Mary's way of profiting by his presence with the family. All this and much more, which no language but his own can convey, speaks in his affectionate, half-playful, yet faithful, and even solemn reply.

41. And Jesus (*But the Lord*) **answered and said unto her, Martha, Martha**—surely she was already grieved with herself, although he must have sadly smiled as he looked her in the eye—**thou art careful** (full of cares, *anxious*) **and troubled** (perturbed in mind, or fretted) **about many things**—the respectability of the entertainment, the gratification of our appetite, etc.—**But one thing is needful**—namely, a supreme interest in the kingdom of heaven. The next sentence, following close upon and expounding this, should have guarded every one from the truly jejune idea, that Jesus speaks here directly of provision for the table, as if "one dish," "one article of food," were meant, and the Saviour said that was all that was necessary. Some have thought he played upon this lower meaning in presenting the spiritual and all important truth. We see no evidence of such reference at all; only this, all the expenditure of our time and strength and care should have one aim, "the kingdom of God and his righteousness." **For** (not *and*) **Mary hath chosen that good part which** (=such that it, ἥτις) **shall not be taken away from her.** The **good part** is evidently the same as the **one thing** which is needful. The "for," if a correct reading of the Greek, implies that a thought lies unexpressed after, **one thing is needful**, namely, "there your sister is right, and I cannot reprove her"—for Mary chose out the good part, portion, or share, out of the many things that attract our desire and exertions. A **good**, because a supremely useful, portion, including the full, eternal salvation of her soul. It, and it alone, **shall not be taken away from her.**

This little narrative takes us into the midst of a domestic incident of the life of Jesus, more purely domestic than any other in the Gospels. Yet where shall we find a more attractive picture of him? Where does his presence seem more truly a blessing than at this evening family entertainment? From what formal discourse of his could we more clearly derive three of the most important religious lessons than from this fireside intercourse? 1. The supreme importance of the attainment of his salvation—**one thing is needful**. 2. The hindrance to this from undue subjection to the cares of life—**thou art anxious and troubled about many things**. 3. The decisive influence upon it of personal choice—**Mary hath chosen that good part.**

Still we must not suppose that Jesus means to preclude anxious Martha from all share in that part. Her words and conduct in John 11:20 ff. forbid the thought. She also recognized in him the Messiah, the all-powerful Judge of the last day. But hers was, after all, more of an Old Testament faith, which was estimated by its outward works, and anticipated a salvation to come; while Mary found her salvation present in the presence, the truth, the example of the Master, his very spirit, which she desired more and more fully to imbibe. They were to each other as the

CHAPTER XI.

AND it came to pass, that, as he was praying in a certain place, when he ceased, one of his disciples said unto him, Lord, teach us to pray, as John also taught his disciples.
2 And he said unto them, When ye pray, say, ^a Our

1 AND it came to pass, as he was praying in a certain place, that when he ceased, one of his disciples said unto him, Lord, teach us to pray, even as John 2 also taught his disciples. And he said unto them, When ye pray, say, ¹ Father, Hallowed be thy name.

a Matt. 6: 6.——1 Many ancient authorities read, *Our Father, who art in heaven.* See Matt. 6: 9.

two Epistles: one of James, the teacher of fidelity, labor, obedience; and one of John, breathing light, gladness, and love.

Ch. 11: 1-13. FURTHER INSTRUCTION CONCERNING PRAYER.

1. And it came to pass, that as he was praying in a certain place. As in many designations of time and place by our author, especially in this section of his work, "a certain" seems to mean "some place, not necessary to be more definitely pointed out." Our Saviour, who was always in a spirit congenial to prayer, was often engaged in the definite act. This fact was patent to his disciples, and is especially noticed by Luke. His supplications were sometimes audible, as at Gethsemane, probably here also, and from the attention which they excited, at a time when prayer, in some style, was a very common phenomenon, we must conclude that the matter, or the manner, or both, of his prayers, was such as to impress others with a sense of their own deficiency. Evidently it did so here. His prayer made them feel that they could not pray aright. We may profitably speculate as to the qualities by which it produced that effect.—**When he ceased, one of his disciples said unto him, Lord, teach us to pray, as John also taught his disciples**—or, *even as John,* etc. We cannot easily suppose that those who had heard his particular instructions on the mount concerning prayer, but a few months before, would need to be informed how they ought to pray. This raises the question whether we have here the source and true occasion of the Lord's Prayer in Matthew, as some suppose. We think it more probable that it was original in both connections. To assume a frequent repetition of his sayings, on the part of Jesus, within the short compass of one of the Gospels, is unreasonable; but if we imagine the question to have been asked by one who had more recently joined him, it was very natural that he should give the substance of the former prayer. That it is the same *only in substance,*

shows that it was neither intended by Christ, nor understood by the first disciples as an obligatory form.—**As John also taught,** etc. The Jews were punctilious in the forms of prayer. Three times a day those in Jerusalem resorted to the temple courts to join in repeating the prayers there, or, where that was impracticable, they engaged in prayer wherever they might be, sometimes taking pains to be overtaken by the appointed hour, in the public squares, or at the corners of the streets. In this, as in the matter of fasting, John the Baptist may have shared the prevailing custom. But he would necessarily feel the inadequacy of the common formulas to express that higher, more spiritual view of God's service which he inculcated. He may have given his scholars patterns, or even liturgical forms of prayer; but they would breathe the spirit of the publican in the parable, rather than of the Pharisee, expressing the desire of forgiveness, and of aid and direction in the purpose to live a new and more spiritual life. But to one who had come, from John's leadership, under the immediate influence of Jesus, and had drunk in something of his free spirit, so as, in the kingdom of heaven, to have risen above the spirit of his former master, the whole system of John would seem as hide-bound and insufficient, as to John's disciple the modes of the Jews had seemed. Hence his present position. He little realized that in the directness, the simplicity and trustfulness of that, he was practicing the Master's own art of prayer, to a degree. But so he really was, and his prayer was instantly answered.

2. And he said unto them—teaching all, while he fulfilled the request of the one—**When ye pray, say, Father** (omit **Our,** and **which art in heaven**), **hallowed be thy name.** This shorter form of the address is abundantly supported by the best authorities. The prayer was simplicity itself, yet divinely comprehensive of all which a suppliant soul can need.—**Father!** The single word sets before us the object of our prayer in that very

Father which art in heaven, Hallowed be thy name. Thy kingdom come. Thy will be done, as in heaven, so in earth.
3 Give us day by day our daily bread.

3 Thy kingdom come.[1] Give us day by day [2] our daily

1 Many ancient authorities add, *Thy will be done, as in heaven, so on earth.* See Matt. 6: 10....2 Gr. *our bread for the coming day;* or, *our needful bread.*

relation which is best suited to draw our hearts toward him in reverence, trust, love, devotion. The fuller statement in the Sermon on the Mount, "Our Father, which art in heaven," adds ideas of exaltation and dignity, and signifies directly our fraternity with all disciples in our petition. This latter thought is suggested here by the plural "us" of the petitioners; and the single word—**Father**—has a depth of tenderness in it, which no addition can bring nearer to the heart. The term had been seldom used in addressing God in the Old Testament, and only to denote him distinctly as the Father of the nation—Israel; more frequently in the Apocrypha, but associated with other epithets and descriptions, significant of coldness and formality.—**Hallowed be thy name**—let us and every one who speaks thy name (which may all the nations do!) think of it with that holy regard which is due to the Being and character which it represents. The name of God stands familiarly in Scripture for his divinity, character, in short, for himself. To hallow the name, is to treat God as holy, in thought concerning him, in the sentiments of the heart, the words of the lips, the conduct of the life.—**Thy kingdom come.** On the significance of the phrase, "Kingdom of God," see note on 6: 21. That it should come, involves the accession of an ever greater number of willing, obedient subjects, till the number of God's chosen shall be made complete; and, secondly, that those who belong to it should abound more and more in its appropriate spirit, and do works meet for such a relation, until it shall appear in holiness and perfection, answerable to that of its exalted Head. Not merely extensive, but intensive development, is thus involved in the prayer. This is further indicated by the additional petition—**Thy will be done as in heaven, so in earth**—which belongs strictly in Matthew, though by some transcribers brought into early copies of Luke, also. The Revision omits it here.

3. Give us day by day our daily bread. Thus we have, following two petitions looking to God's glory, and the glory of his kingdom, one based upon our temporal needs, to be followed by two more, relating to our spiritual interests. This petition relating to personal want comes first, because the support of life is the condition of all activity, use, and felicity, even spiritual. It is but one, that we may not dwell upon temporal interests, and is limited to what is strictly essential, bread—without concern for luxury, or even comfort. Some have thought that to bring in the mention of mere physical food, in this connection, was not worthy of the Saviour, and have labored to allegorize it into a spiritual supply; but surely many of Christ's hearers then, and in every age, would not think it unfit to ask the heavenly Father for their necessary food; and Farrar, on the passage, well says, "That this prayer is primarily a prayer for needful earthly sustenance, has been rightly understood by the heart of mankind." An occasion for much speculation as to possible abstruse meanings has been found in the singularity of the term translated **daily**. Being met with nowhere else in the Greek language, except in the parallel passage, Matt. 6: 11, and in late references to these, the first recourse would be to the earliest translations. But of these, the Latin renders "daily" (*quotidianum*), with which one form of the Syriac (Curetonian) substantially agrees; but the common Syriac gives "needful." The etymology, also, is ambiguous. Some suppose the adjective (ἐπιούσιος) to come from the verb (ἐπιέναι), and so to mean "pertaining to the coming"; that is, the coming day, or time; others give the meaning, "adapted to nature, or, being" (as if from ἐπὶ ὤν, or, ἐπὶ οὐσία). This last would easily come to the sense of necessary, essential; and notwithstanding the serious objection, that we ought then to find the *iota* elided before a vowel, we still think (and especially in view of the number of similar cases adduced by Cremer (*Bib. Theol. Lexicon*), that this is the most probable of the derivations proposed. Nothing, however, is so certain as to require us to change the familiar rendering, **daily**. The full discussion of the

4 And forgive us our sins; for we also forgive every one that is indebted to us. And lead us not into temptation; but deliver us from evil.

4 bread. And forgive us our sins; for we ourselves also forgive every one that is indebted to us. And bring us not into temptation.[1]

[1] Many ancient authorities add, *but deliver us from the evil one* (or, *from evil*). See Matt. 6:13.

Greek word (ἐπιούσιος), is admirably condensed in Dr. Conant's Note on Matt. 6:11 (Am. Bible Union's Version of Matthew, 4to edition), and more at large in Lightfoot on *Revision;* Tholuck, *Sermon on the Mount;* McClellan, *New Testament,* I., 632-647; Cremer, *Bibl. theolog. Wörterbuch der neuetest. Gräcität,* 239-242.

4. And forgive us our sins. The forgiveness of our sins is the first, greatest, ever present spiritual necessity of our souls. That those should no longer stand charged to our account, in the book of God's remembrance, but be canceled, blotted out, and put as far away from him as the east is from the west, is the perpetual condition of our peace. The Saviour does not here explain the ground on which pardon can consistently be granted to the sinner, but he mentions a disposition or state of the heart, which necessarily goes with faith in Christ, as precedent to it—the disposition, namely, to forgive those who have injured us. (Comp. the fuller statement Matt. 6:14, 15.)—**For we** (add, *ourselves*) **also forgive,** etc. The prayer is put into the mouth of those who are already disciples, and who, therefore, although conscious of remaining sinfulness, share with the Master something of that charity which they wish to have exercised toward them.—**Who is indebted to us.** Here the counterpart, between men, of **our sins** toward God, is regarded as a debt, *i. e.,* an obligation on the part of our neighbor to do or to refrain from something, failing of which he is liable to penalty at our hands. Matthew shows our sins against God as "debts" for which we are holden to make satisfaction. It will be noticed that "trespasses," familiar from the Episcopal Prayer-book form of prayer, is not in either form of the Lord's Prayer in the Bible. Rev. J. H. Blunt, *Annotated Book of Common Prayer,* London, 1868, gives, on page 31, various forms of the Lord's Prayer prior to the sixteenth century, in none of which do we find "trespasses"; but he quotes one from the King's Prymer, of the year 1538, which has that word, then made familiar to the English ear by Tyndale's Version of 1534. Tyndale alone of the English translators has used it.—**And lead us not into temptation.** Being once forgiven, the disciple dreads to incur other sins. He knows also his own liability to error, and his need of God's gracious care to hold him secure. It can hardly be a prayer to be kept from that testing by which one's genuine character is brought to light (Ps. 139:23 f.) and his virtues exercised, the endurance of which is declared to be an eminent blessing (James 1:2, 12). It is rather against that solicitation to sin which arises from the seductive influence of forbidden things on our weaker, unspiritual propensities and affections. This influence we need not ask God to refrain from directly exerting upon us, for he tempteth not any man, in this sense (James 1:13). That comes from God's arch-enemy, and ours, against which our Lord especially directed his disciples to pray and to watch (Matt. 26:41; Luke 22:40, 46), at that hour which was "the power of darkness." The prince of darkness alone can be thought of as shaping the circumstances of our life, so as by them to incite in us evil dispositions and conduct. What we pray to God for is, that he will, in his all powerful providence, so guide our way that we may escape the tempter's snares. It is but putting into a prayer what Paul assured his Corinthian brethren God would do for them (1 Cor. 10:13).

This view of Satan as the author of the temptation deprecated would be supported by the translation, in Matthew, by the Revision of the following clause, "*but deliver us from the evil one.*" This clause is, however, rejected, on good grounds, from Luke's report, by the most eminent and conservative editors of the Greek text.

Whether, supposing the clause to be genuine, we should translate "evil" or "the evil one," is a question on which the reasons for and against either alternative are so delicately balanced that we can hardly be sure which way they preponderate. If those in favor of the Revised rendering are a shade more weighty, the difference is scarcely enough to warrant any change, not absolutely necessary, in this peculiarly hallowed passage.

5 And he said unto them, Which of you shall have a friend, and shall go unto him at midnight, and say unto him, Friend, lend me three loaves;
6 For a friend of mine in his journey is come to me, and I have nothing to set before him?
7 And he from within shall answer and say, Trouble me not: the door is now shut, and my children are with me in bed: I cannot rise and give thee.
8 I say unto you, *a* Though he will not rise and give him, because he is his friend, yet because of his importunity he will rise and give him as many as he needeth.
9 *b* And I say unto you, Ask, and it shall be given you; seek, and ye shall find; knock, and it shall be opened unto you.

5 And he said unto them, Which of you shall have a friend, and shall go unto him at midnight, and say
6 to him, Friend, lend me three loaves; for a friend of mine is come to me from a journey, and I have nothing to set before him; and he from within shall
7 answer and say, Trouble me not: the door is now shut, and my children are with me in bed; I cannot
8 rise and give thee? I say unto you, Though he will not rise and give him, because he is his friend, yet because of his importunity he will arise and give
9 him ¹ as many as he needeth. And I say unto you, Ask, and it shall be given you; seek, and ye shall

a ch. 13: 1, etc.... *b* Matt. 7: 7; 21: 22; Mark 11: 24; John 15: 7; James 1: 6; 1 John 3: 22.——1 *Or, whatsoever things.*

5–13. ENCOURAGEMENT TO PRAYER.

The request to be taught to pray, *i. e.*, how to pray, is now granted; but, with the best of models, the Saviour knew that the right disposition was still more essential, including a real sense of need, and the free, child-like trust in God, which goes spontaneously, promptly, to him, and waits boldly, perseveringly, for the desired blessing. Hence it is that, after giving a specimen of what they should ask for, and in what style of language, he now adds a lesson of encouragement to freedom and urgency in prayer.

5–8. And he said unto them, Which of you shall have a friend, etc. The story of successful application to a fellow-man for needed favor, is told in a form of homely and vivid reality, and in words of the utmost familiarity, and even of conversational carelessness. The sentence is not grammatically consistent, but with ver. 8 changes from the interrogative to the declarative form. It becomes regular only by some such expedient as, at the seventh verse, to substitute for "and he" "but who," or, "who nevertheless." Yet the intent of the whole is beyond all danger of mistake.

The object is to show that in our human relations, constancy in entreaty may, even under the greatest discouragements, secure needed benefits. So the man in trouble is supposed to go to his friend **at midnight**—the least favorable hour in the whole twenty-four, to expect any exertion at the hand of a plain, unsophisticated man who sleeps in the night, and to whom rest is sweet. The first application does, indeed, meet with little success.—**The door is now shut**—otherwise the applicant might enter and help himself without troubling his friend.—**And my children are with me in bed.** *The* bed, in an ordinary house, would commonly be the divan built along one or more sides of the living room, which served as a seat, or lounge, during the day. He could not rise from this without disturbing the children, and so more seriously frustrating the night's repose. But we are to suppose the petitioner, who will not take No, for an answer, to persevere, until he finally prevails. His conduct did not seem, to the Saviour who pictures it, praiseworthy in any other light than as the simple expression of a deeply felt necessity; for when he speaks of the man as obtaining by his **importunity** what mere friendship would not grant, the Greek word signifies properly "discourtesy," "impudence," "shamelessness." He asked for the loan of **three loaves**, either because from their small size it was thought so many might be required by a hungry man, or, as some think, for the appearance of bounty—one for the traveler, one for the host, and one as a reserve. As the result of his rough urgency he will receive all that he needs, and apparently on more favorable terms than he had proposed. **He will give him as many as he needeth.**

The argument of this illustration is, that if the reluctance of a drowsy man may be thus overcome by the persistent and strenuous entreaty of a neighbor, much more will God's willingness to bless be moved by the sincere, urgent, and unremitting supplication of those who need his aid. He may cause them to wait until their faith is exercised, and they are better prepared, in every way, to appreciate the boon; but in due time it will come, either in form as they have desired, or as they would desire, knowing what God knows.

9. This verse applies the parable to the hearers.—**And I say unto you, Ask, and it shall be given you.** The statement is without qualification, as of a universal and infallible proposition. Yet the asking must not be a mere hasty request, expressive of a light and fleeting desire, but a reverently

10 For every one that asketh receiveth; and he that seeketh findeth; and to him that knocketh it shall be opened.
11 *If a son shall ask bread of any of you that is a father, will he give him a stone? or if *he ask* a fish, will he for a fish give him a serpent?
12 Or if he shall ask an egg, will he offer him a scorpion?
13 If ye then, being evil, know how to give good gifts unto your children; how much more shall *your* heavenly Father give the Holy Spirit to them that ask him?

10 find; knock, and it shall be opened unto you. For every one that asketh receiveth; and he that seeketh findeth; and to him that knocketh it shall be 11 opened. And of which of you that is a father shall his son ask a loaf, and he give him a stone? or a 12 fish, and he for a fish give him a serpent? Or *if* he 13 shall ask an egg, will he give him a scorpion? If ye then, being evil, know how to give good gifts unto your children, how much more shall *your* heavenly Father give the Holy Spirit to them that ask him?

a Matt. 7:9.——1 Some ancient authorities omit, *a loaf, and he give him a stone?* *or*.

bold (Heb. 4:16) insistence on the petition, growing out of a want which can take no refusal. This is denoted by the term, **seek,** which, in this connection, may mean, "try to find the most promising way of access, or the most effectual plea to move the divine compassion," but probably signifies only a more intense, vigilant, vehement solicitude for the needed favor.—**Knock**—viz., at the door of God's store-house of blessings, is a term undoubtedly suggested by the preceding parable, and denotes a continuance, and increase of urgency; corresponding to which—**it shall be opened unto you,** signifies the finding access to the supplies of grace for which we pray.

10. Verse 10 simply relates, in a general form, for the encouragement and guidance of all, the truth which had been so vividly addressed to the disciples.

11-13. As if the Saviour could not leave a topic of such vital importance to the Christian life, he adds to the preceding inducements to prayer, the argument drawn from the readiness of an earthly father to grant the natural desires of his children. The Revision, in verses 11, 12, keeps nearer to the form of the expression in the Greek.—**Bread, fish,** and **eggs** were common staples of diet among the people, and the antithetical mention of **bread**=a loaf, and **a stone; fish, serpent; egg, scorpion,** rests on the deceptive resemblance of those objects in the respective pairs. The question is shrewdly shaped to show that no father could so mock the desire of his child for necessary food.

13. If ye then, being evil—as ye naturally are ("a shining proof of original sin," says Bengel, on Matt. 11:13)—**know how to give good gifts unto your children**—as exemplified in the articles of food—**how much more shall your heavenly Father give the Holy Spirit to them that ask him?** The argument is again from the less to the greater. God is a spiritual Father to them that trust in him. According to this analogy, rather than that of a sovereign, governor, or judge, we are encouraged to think of him, and to believe that he is just as full of affection and sympathy for us, just as ready to comfort and help, as the tenderest parent on earth can be, while his ability is greater by all the difference between earth and heaven, where he rules from the throne of the universe.—**Give the Holy Spirit**—not to the exclusion of needed temporal good, but as the sum of all spiritual blessing, which being bestowed, all other things really indispensable will be added—**to them that ask him,** in the spirit and manner, of course, of the preceding instruction and encouragements. As it is not all ostensible prayer which fulfills these conditions, so only a part comes within the scope of the promise. We need not wonder, therefore, that in spite of the fullness of God's offered stores, so much formal prayer remains unanswered.

Although several of the petitions of the Lord's Prayer may be more or less nearly matched by similar, detached sentences from thoughtful men, Hebrews, or of the classic nations, or of those of further Asia, its originality and uniqueness will never be impaired until they can *all* be found, severally complete and combined in so divine proportions as, like this prayer, to express appropriately the daily wants of the humblest child, while they include everything which the most diversified and exigent experience has occasion to seek from God. Further, they must be found so composed, in such an atmosphere of trust, love, and obedience, on the one hand, and of almighty, paternal care and affection on the other, as this context exhibits, before they can pretend to the place in human hearts of "Our Father, which art in heaven."

What view of God so exalted as not to find expression in the tender title, Father? What

14 ªAnd he was casting out a devil, and it was dumb. And it came to pass, when the devil was gone out, the dumb spake; and the people wondered.
15 But some of them said, ᵇ He casteth out devils through Beelzebub the chief of the devils.

14 And he was casting out a demon *which was* dumb. And it came to pass, when the demon was gone out, the dumb man spake; and the multitudes marvelled.
15 But some of them said, ¹ By Beelzebub the prince of

a Matt. 9 : 32 ; 12 : 22....*b* Matt. 9 : 34 ; 12 : 24.——1 Or, *In.*

bond of brotherhood so close and solemn as that of which every one is conscious when he deliberately says, in his prayer to God, "give *us*;" "forgive *us*;" "lead *us*"? Surely the whole lies involved in even the briefest form of the Lord's Prayer.

This teaching binds us to pray first of all, and with supreme concern, for the glory of God, and the universal establishment of his kingdom in Christ. To this it subordinates *all* desires for personal blessings. But it not only allows, it encourages us, to pray for what is essential to life, and strength for God's service—the bread, the fish, the egg of daily sustenance. With even more confidence may we ask for the forgiveness of our sins, and for preservation from all evil. And what more can be thought of, fit to be desired of God, which is not by implication contained in these few words?

And how can *such* prayer fail of fulfillment? Even the hard, skeptical, and cynical Juvenal, after satirizing all human prayers and wishes, allows to human weakness such requests as we can grant ourselves. The Lord's Prayer shows us a scheme of petitions comprehending everything, which we may offer to our Heavenly Father, with the fullest assurance that he cannot help granting us these or what we might prefer, if we so pray.

14-26. From His Casting Out an Evil Spirit, the Scribes and Pharisees Take Occasion to Blaspheme.

14. And he was casting out a devil (*demon*), **and it was dumb.** The event seems to be the same as that recorded in Matthew 12: 22 ff.; and implied in Mark 3: 19 ff., where the connection in Mark would lead us to think that it occurred much earlier than the period of the present journey. Matthew speaks of the demoniac as both blind and dumb. We may note here again the confounding of the alien spirit with the person afflicted. The latter was dumb, but the defect of speech is ascribed to the demon which had caused it. The strongly continuative form of the verb, **was casting out**—may have been used with the feeling that the hostile observers were meanwhile watching him. **The people** (*multitudes*) **wondered.**—All three narratives of this affair suppose a great throng to have been present, most of whom were probably at the time strangers to such works of Jesus. Hence their wonder at the miracle. The interest manifested by such numbers would be likely to specially exasperate his adversaries.

15. But some of them—the Pharisees, Matthew; scribes from Jerusalem, Mark—**said, He casteth out devils**—*demons*—etc. The Revision gives the right order of words.—**Beelzebul** (which is the correct spelling of the word), was a designation of Baal, the chief deity of the Phenicians and Canaanites generally. The worship of this abominable idol-god had been formerly introduced among the Israelites by Ahab, in the northern, and Ahaz in the southern kingdom. One of the many special names appropriated to him (Baal-peor, Baal-berith, etc.), in different localities and relations, was Baal-zebub (2 Kings 1:1) = god of flies; *i. e.*, having power over, and able to drive away, flies. At a later period, pious Jews, now thoroughly cured of idolatry, but remembering the seductive power of this temptation from Baal-peor down, appropriated the name to the chief of the evil spirits, Satan; and, to make it more offensive to their people, changed it slightly, by a play upon the sound, from Beel-zebub to Beel-zebul, meaning, as many think, "dung-baal." (See Winer, *Real wörterbuch*, s. v. Beelzebub.) The charge is, accordingly, that Jesus was in collusion with the prince of evil, and only pretended to work against the latter, while using against the minions of Satan power lent by Satan himself. Such a charge would be unspeakably wicked, if uttered hypocritically, when they did not believe it; but still more profoundly depraved when they actually believed the most manifest divine beneficence to be Satanic craft. Here, at least, sincerity in their accusation intensified its guilt. It proved such an utter obliteration of the sense of holiness as that they could regard that and the work of the devil as one thing.

16 And others, tempting *him*, ᵃ sought of him a sign from heaven.
17 ᵇ But ᶜ he, knowing their thoughts, said unto them, Every kingdom divided against itself is brought to desolation; and a house *divided* against a house falleth.
18 If Satan also be divided against himself, how shall his kingdom stand? because ye say that I cast out devils through Beelzebub.
19 And if I by Beelzebub cast out devils, by whom do your sons cast *them* out? therefore shall they be your judges.

16 the demons casteth he out demons. And others, try-
17 ing *him*, sought of him a sign from heaven. But he, knowing their thoughts, said unto them, Every kingdom divided against itself is brought to desolation;
18 ¹ and a house *divided* against a house falleth. And if Satan also is divided against himself, how shall his kingdom stand? because ye say that I cast out de-
19 mons ² by Beelzebub. And if I ² by Beelzebub cast out demons, by whom do your sons cast them out?

a Matt. 12: 38; 16: 1....b Matt. 12: 25; Mark 3: 24....c John 2: 25.——1 Or, *and house falleth upon house*.....2 Or, *in*.

16. And others, tempting him, sought of him a sign from heaven. This, as appears, came from a different quarter. The writer brings before us two assaults upon the Saviour, on different grounds, before the latter gives his answer to either. This needs to be borne in mind, to appreciate the subsequent narrative. These men starting, perhaps, from the allegation of the others, that he had done this miracle through power from below, ask ironically, that he should give them some proof of his mission from God by a miracle out of heaven (compare the opinion of Theoph. quoted by Meyer, on Matt. 16: 1). But the expression was often used by them to signify some particularly striking display to the senses of supernatural action, such as the voice from heaven (see examples out of Rabbinical literature in Wetstein on Matt. 16: 1), or, the manna descending out of heaven (John 6: 30, 31), as distinguished from changes and phenomena pertaining to the earth. Notice of this challenge Jesus defers to ver. 29, after he has dealt with the accusation of conspiracy with the devil. This latter he refutes by two arguments: 1, it is contrary to obvious fact in all analogous cases of earthly practice (ver. 17, 18); and 2, to their judgment on the exorcisms effected by the Jews themselves (ver. 19). This leaves as the only true explanation (ver. 20), "by the finger of God."

17. But he, knowing their thoughts—apparently not having heard their words—**said unto them, Every kingdom divided,** etc. The maxim is at the same time an axiom, and needs no discussion, only to be applied.

18. If Satan also be divided against himself. The verb is preterit=was divided, to wit, in the action which I just performed, and this regarded as a specimen of a series. So in Matt. 12: 26, the exact rendering is, "If Satan is casting out Satan, habitually, through me, he was divided against himself," namely, when he entered upon such a plan. The argument, then, is: "If Satan, habitually by my agency, fights against his own emissaries, there is plain belligerency within his dominion—the most destructive imaginable.—**How shall his kingdom stand?** It "hath an end" (Mark 3: 26). **Because ye say that I cast out devils** (*the demons*) **through Beelzebub.** This refers his argument and its conclusion to the charge they had made, and witnesses to his indignation at the monstrous injustice which they had done him. That was aggravated by the partiality and inconsistency of their course.

19. And if I by Beelzebub cast out devils (*the demons*), **by whom do your sons cast them out?** There were, in that day, exorcists among the Jews who had the credit of casting out demons from the possessed, and whom, from our Lord's way of referring to them, we must suppose to have actually given relief to some of this afflicted class, perhaps only occasional, partial, temporary relief (Acts 19: 13 ff., Jos. *Ant.*, 8: 7, 5). Many suppose, but unnecessarily, that Jesus intends merely an *ad hominem* argument, sufficient to silence his adversaries, since they supposed their own exorcists to possess this power.—**Therefore shall they be your judges.** Unless their own sons were in league with Beelzebub, there was no ground for charge against him. Whatever might be the fact as to the Jewish exorcisers, the uniform surprise manifested at Christ's power over demons showed that his work was a veritable "sign," nevertheless, from the promptness, the facility, and efficacy of its performance, and especially from the moral atmosphere which he threw around him, and the spiritual change which often appeared in those delivered by him. It was evident to all but the obstinately blind, that the power of God wrought through him.

20. But if I with the finger of God

20 But if I ᵃ with the finger of God cast out devils, no doubt the kingdom of God is come upon you.
21 ᵇ When a strong man armed keepeth his palace, his goods are in peace:
22 But ᶜ when a stronger than he shall come upon him, and overcome him, he taketh from him all his armour wherein he trusted, and divideth his spoils.
23 ᵈ He that is not with me is against me; and he that gathereth not with me scattereth.
24 ᵉ When the unclean spirit is gone out of a man, he walketh through dry places, seeking rest; and finding none, he saith, I will return unto my house whence I came out.

20 therefore shall they be your judges. But if I by the finger of God cast out demons, then is the kingdom
21 of God come upon you. When the strong man fully armed guardeth his own court, his goods are in
22 peace: but when a stronger than he shall come upon him, and overcome him, he taketh from him his whole armour wherein he trusted, and divideth his
23 spoils. He that is not with me is against me; and
24 he that gathereth not with me scattereth. The unclean spirit when ᶠ he is gone out of the man, passeth through waterless places, seeking rest; and finding none, ᵍ he saith, I will turn back unto my

ᵃ Ex. 8: 19....ᵇ Matt. 12; 29; Mark 3. 27....ᶜ Isa. 53: 12; Col. 2: 15....ᵈ Matt. 12: 30....ᵉ Matt. 12: 43.—1 Or. it.

cast out devils (*the demons*). **With the finger of God** is, in Matt. 12: 28, "by the Spirit of God"—both phrases being figurative, for "by the power of God." The hypothetical opening of the sentence, with **if,** most strongly assumes that the case is so. —**No doubt** (or, *Then*) **the kingdom of God is come upon you.—Come upon,** nearly =has overtaken, has surprised **you.** The Saviour ascribes such importance to this class of his mighty works, as to maintain that they of themselves prove him to be the Messiah and head of the new kingdom. Where he was, it was. It was not something to be expected merely; but was essentially present. That it had come **upon,** not merely "among" or "unto" them, implied that they were not ready for it, and that it came with a shadow of hostility to the system which they upheld.

21, 22. Having refuted the blasphemous accusation of ver. 15, he now describes his procedure against Satan.

21. When *the* (not **a**) **strong man** (*fully*) **armed keepeth** (or, *guardeth*) **his palace,** etc.—*The* **strong man** stands for Satan, who, before the coming of Christ, holds the souls of men in **peace**=securely, in his power (as illustrated by the demoniacal possessions) as being **his goods**—or possessions, in **his palace**—which is the abode of fallen men.

22. But when a stronger than he (namely, Christ, the Lord) **shall come upon him,** etc.—**Come upon** is not the same verb in the Greek as in ver. 20, but means simply "to attack." Christ came upon the adversary decisively in the experience of the temptation, and overcame him.—**He taketh from him all his armor**—strictly, his panoply—**wherein**=*in which*—**he trusted.** He strips him of his power of offence and defence—**and divideth his spoils.** It would simplify the figure if we could suppose the "panoply" to

be the retinue of demoniac spirits, Christ's treatment of one of which (ver. 14) had given occasion to the discourse; but the idea of a complete armor seems too broad for that. "Dividing the spoils" is appropriating them to himself, possibly assigning them to the disciples as trophies of their work; and **the spoils** are the souls, called "his goods" in the preceding verse, now noted as having been taken captive by him.

23. In this contest between Christ and the devil, all men are enlisted, and should be enlisted on the side of Jesus.

23. He that is not with me is against me. The remark holds good pre-eminently as to that portion of his hearers who had charged him with being in league with Beelzebub. The first member of the verse presents a figure drawn from military relations, the second from the practice of harvesting.—**He that gathereth not with me**—the grain that should enrich my garner—**scattereth** abroad — wastes the harvest, and does what he can to frustrate my design of salvation. The harmony between this and the converse, superficially discrepant proposition in 9: 50, was pointed out on that verse.

24-26. The Saviour was led by his reflections on the terrible malignity which had now been evinced against him, to find in the subject of demoniacal possession an apt illustration of the degeneracy of the Jewish nation, as compared with what it had been at a former time. The people, as cured, in the time of Ezra and Nehemiah, of their easily besetting sin of idolatry, and turned to the service of Jehovah with undivided purpose of heart, is **the man** out of whom **the unclean spirit** is gone. The same people, as they now present themselves to his view, hardened in unbelief, formality, pride of legalism, hatred of the Messiah, amounting even to blasphemy against the Holy Spirit, is the man repos-

25 And when he cometh, he findeth it swept and garnished.
26 Then goeth he, and taketh to him seven other spirits more wicked than himself; and they enter in, and dwell there; and *the last state of that man is worse than the first.
27 And it came to pass, as he spake these things, a certain woman of the company lifted up her voice, and said unto him, ᵇBlessed is the womb that bare thee, and the paps which thou hast sucked.
28 But he said, Yea, ᶜrather, blessed are they that hear the word of God, and keep it.
29 ᵈAnd when the people were gathered thick to-

25 house whence I came out. And when ¹ he is come,
26 ¹ he findeth it swept and garnished. Then goeth ¹ he, and taketh to him seven other spirits more evil than ² himself; and they enter in and dwell there: and the last state of that man becometh worse than the first.
27 And it came to pass, as he said these things, a certain woman out of the multitude lifted up her voice, and said unto him, Blessed is the womb that bare thee, and the breasts which thou didst suck. But he said, Yea, rather, blessed are they that hear the word of God, and keep it.
29 And when the multitudes were gathering together

a John 5 : 14; Heb. 6 : 4; 10 : 26; Pet. 2 : 20,....*b* ch. 1 : 28, 48,....*c* Matt. 7 : 21; ch. 8 : 21; James 1 : 25....*d* Matt. 12 : 38, 39.——
1 Or, it....2 Or, itself.

sessed by **the unclean spirit,** and in a condition so much more desperate than before, that it is as if the returned demon had brought with him seven others beside himself to dwell there.

24. When the unclean spirit is gone out of *the* (not a) **man**—in a definite case, imagined as effected through the exorcism of the Jews.—**He walketh** (or *passeth*) **through dry** (*waterless*) **places, seeking rest.** This was the vulgar idea (compare Baruch, 4 : 35; Tob. 8 : 3), that unclean spirits haunted desert spots, where no water was, especially the sites of ruined and abandoned cities (compare Isaiah 13 : 21; 34 : 14; Rev. 18 : 2).—**And finding none, he saith, I will return,** etc. Something like this was the desire of the demons in Legion (8 : 31, 32), to be allowed to enter into the swine, rather than to be sent adrift absolutely unhoused. When he says **to my house,** he is not aware of having been authoritatively and effectually expelled. He came out, and may, if he pleases, return. There is typified the superficial and transient amendment which the people experienced in ancient times, as seems to us more probably intended, or, under the preaching of John the Baptist.

25. And when he cometh he findeth it swept and garnished. Such is the description of the supposed patient, restored to his right mind. That the house is **swept** = clean, and all its furniture and utensils in proper and beauteous order, **garnished,** implies what Matthew expressly adds, that it is "empty," strictly, "at leisure," ready for an occupant. This signifies that when the old idolatrous practices of the nation ceased, no divine spirit of true repentance, faith, heart obedience, had taken its place.—**Then goeth he and taketh to him seven other spirits,** etc. This sets forth the confirmed incorrigibleness of the Jewish people, now further than ever from any general disposition to seek their God, and wasting the remnant of their day of grace in machinations against their only Saviour. Truly, **the last state of that man is worse than the first.**

27, 28. THE TRUE GROUND OF HAPPINESS.

27. As he spake these things, a certain woman of the company (*out of the multitude*) **lifted up her voice.** This would seem to have been before he had fully completed his discourse, which he resumes in ver. 29. The woman's admiration might well be excited both by the matter and manner of our Lord's discourse. She may have wished to show him that however cruelly he was rejected by the leaders, and neglected by the mass, there were some at least who sympathized with him, and would fain do him honor. In this she was only the mouth-piece of a great many of the common throng.—She **lifted up her voice,** either that she might make herself heard by Jesus, **out of the multitude,** or, in order to testify the more impressively to all around her honor to the Lord.—**Blessed is the womb that bare thee, and the paps** (*breasts*) **which thou hast sucked** (or, *didst suck*). "Her sentiment is good, but she speaks after the manner of a woman."—*Bengel.* What a happiness to have been the mother of such a son! So, first of all, feels her mother's heart.

28. But he said—not able or disposed to question the blessedness of such a relationship, but much concerned that she and all should more highly appreciate the privilege of hearing him.—**Yea rather, blessed are they that hear,** etc. There is a blessing indeed in the outward kinship, but chiefly in the believing submission of the heart to that truth which I bring from God (compare 8 : 19-21).

29-36. CONTINUATION OF THE DISCOURSE

gether, he began to say, This is an evil generation: they seek a sign; and there shall no sign be given it, but the sign of Jonas the prophet.

30 For as *Jonas was a sign unto the Ninevites, so shall also the Son of man be to this generation.

31 ᵇThe queen of the south shall rise up in the judgment with the men of this generation, and condemn them: for she came from the utmost parts of the earth to hear the wisdom of Solomon; and, behold, a greater than Solomon *is* here.

32 The men of Nineveh shall rise up in the judgment with this generation, and shall condemn it: for they repented at the preaching of Jonas; and, behold, a greater than Jonas *is* here.

unto him, he began to say, This generation is an evil generation: it seeketh after a sign; and there shall no sign be given to it but the sign of Jonah.

30 For even as Jonah became a sign unto the Ninevites, so shall also the Son of man be to this generation.

31 The queen of the south shall rise up in the judgment with the men of this generation, and shall condemn them: for she came from the ends of the earth to hear the wisdom of Solomon; and behold, ¹a greater than Solomon is here.

32 The men of Nineveh shall stand up in the judgment with this generation, and shall condemn it: for they repented at the preaching of Jonah; and behold, ¹a greater than Jonah is here.

a Jonah 1: 17; 2: 10.... *b* 1 Kings 10: 1....*c* Jonah 3: 5.——¹ Gr. *more than*.

INTERRUPTED AT VERSE 26. He is now ready to notice the demand made (ver. 16) for a sign from heaven. (See on that verse.)

29. And when the people were gathered thick together—better, *the multitudes were gathering together unto him.* He may not improbably have found additional reason for expressing himself on the topic proposed, in this streaming toward him of throngs more eager to see his wonderful deeds, and even to hear what he might have to say, than to give him the well-earned confidence of their hearts.—**He began to say**—a formula which intimates the opening of an important discourse. Indeed, there is no intimation in our Gospel of any cessation of the train of discourse here begun, until 13: 10. **This** (add *generation*) **is an evil generation.** Evil, in that it refuses the clear manifestation of God's presence in him, in his teachings, his life, and his familiar miracles, and grossly demands displays of physical power. **They seek** (Greek, *it seeketh*) **a sign, and there shall no sign be given it.** The word **sign** is used here in that special and ostentatious sense in which some of them had presumptuously demanded it. No such sign would Christ condescend to give them. There was, indeed, one event yet to take place concerning him, which, although far enough from their present thought, even they would have to admit was a sign from heaven—namely, his resurrection. Hence he adds, **Except the sign of Jonas**—the sign, that is, which lay in the history of Jonah.

30. For as Jonas was (literally, *became* = proved to be, turned out) **a sign unto the Ninevites, so**, etc. As Jonah's coming forth from a three days' stay in the belly of the whale, as if alive from the grave, was a sign to the men of Nineveh that Jehovah had indeed sent him, so Christ's return from the dead, after three days, would be—the verb points to the future—a sign irrefragable that God had sent him as the Messiah. (Compare Acts 2: 32, 33.)

31. The mention of the Ninevites, who repented at the preaching of Jonah, might have recalled to the thought of Jesus the sad contrast of the effect of his mission upon his own generation, in general. Hence the following comparisons.—**The queen of the south**= Sheba, 1 Kings 10: 1—**shall rise up in the judgment with the men**—men, distinctively, not human beings—**of this generation.** She will rise in company with them, woman though she was, on the same footing with them before the judgment bar.—**And shall condemn them**—by recalling how earnest she was to gain knowledge of Solomon's wisdom "concerning the name of Jehovah" (comp. 1 Kings 10: 9).—**From the ends of the earth.** Sheba = Sabæa, in Arabia Felix, was at that time practically a great way off from Jerusalem. She put herself to great trouble and expense to seek wisdom at a long distance.—**And, behold, a greater than Solomon is here.** At your very door, within the hearing of your ears, is one offering treasures of wisdom and grace, of which Solomon had nothing; and ye listen to him only to cavil, to disobey, to hate.

32. The men of Nineveh shall rise up (—*stand up*), etc. These were probably mentioned before the queen of the south, as the order is in Matt. 12: 41, but Luke's arrangement consults chronology and rhetorical climax.—**They shall** *stand up*—side by side—**with this generation**—so much more favored, in respect to the knowledge of the true God, and the teachings of his Son—**and shall condemn it**—by the contrast of their example.—**For they repented at the preaching of Jonas** (Jonah 3: 5); **and, behold, a greater than Jonas is here.** Yet this generation has not repented, and is not

33 ᵃ No man, when he hath lighted a candle, putteth it in a secret place, neither under a ᵇ bushel, but on a candlestick, that they which come in may see the light.
34 ᶜ The light of the body is the eye: therefore when thine eye is single, thy whole body also is full of light; but when thine eye is evil, thy body also is full of darkness.
35 Take heed therefore, that the light which is in thee be not darkness.
36 If thy whole body therefore be full of light, having no part dark, the whole shall be full of light, as when the bright shining of a candle doth give thee light.
37 And as he spake, a certain Pharisee besought him

33 No man, when he hath lighted a lamp, putteth it in a cellar, neither under the bushel, but on the stand, that they that enter in may see the light.
34 The lamp of thy body is thine eye: when thine eye is single, thy whole body also is full of light; but when it is evil, thy body also is full of darkness. Look therefore whether the light that is in
35 thee is not darkness. If therefore thy whole body be full of light, having no part dark, it shall be wholly full of light, as when the lamp with its bright shining doth give thee light.
37 Now as he spake, a Pharisee asketh him to ᵈ dine with him: and he went in, and sat down to meat.

a Matt. 5: 15; Mark 4: 21; ch. 8: 16....b See Matt. 5: 15....c Matt. 6: 22.——1 Gr. *breakfast*.

going to repent, even after the more than Jonas has risen triumphantly from actual death.

33-36. THE LIGHT OF THE KNOWLEDGE OF CHRIST.

The mention of Christ as the source of true wisdom, superior to Solomon, the preacher of God's truth greater than Jonas, carries with it the thought of the privilege of those who most directly share his instruction, and are filled with light from him. They are as lamps that have been lighted.

33. No man when he hath lighted a candle (*lamp*), **putteth it in a secret place** (or *cellar*), **neither under** (not **a** but *the*) **bushel,** etc. So it is not the design of God, in distinguishing the disciples with the knowledge of the gospel, that they should personally, selfishly, unprofitably to others, appropriate this light to themselves, but that they should conspicuously exhibit, and beneficently impart it to others about them who need it (comp. Matt. 5: 14-16). *Light* is a well-known symbol of saving knowledge.

34. To fully acquire this salutary light they need an inward faculty of heart, understanding, conscience, adapted to its reception. This is here signified by the figure of the bodily eye.—**The light of the body is the eye.** The metaphor is only half expressed, requiring, to complete it, the addition, "so is there also an inward organ, a power of the soul, which discerns between truth and error, right and wrong, and which recognizes duty, and in its normal condition should safely guide the moral life." But as the bodily eye, in order to perform its function well, must be sound and healthy—**single** —simple, unperverted, true—so the mental faculty must work clearly, sincerely, and according to the reality of moral things.

This is implied, with the force of great brevity, in the caution of verse 35, which speaks of a light within, requiring careful attention, lest what is the appointed medium of moral light, guiding to proper conduct, should convey error, rather, and involve the life in darkness.

35. Take heed (literally, *look*), **therefore, that the light which is in thee** the moral judgment, which is designed to indicate the way of right living) **be not darkness**—so dull and inefficient through misuse, as to furnish no illumination, and not even to welcome the light afforded from without it. The Greek says, *is* **not darkness**—carrying a strong intimation that attention will show this to be the fact.

36. The discourse comes back to the outward image, leaving the application to the spirit to be made by us.—**Therefore**—seeing that such is the relation of the eye to conduct—**if thy whole body therefore be full of light,** etc. The body may be regarded here as standing for the whole man, body and soul, irradiated by "the light that is in thee." The case is that of a man whose discernment of right and duty is so clear and unerring, and his preference for it so unhesitating, that he may be said to have **no part dark;** there is no failure to perceive, no inclination to practice evil. What is asserted of this subject, that—**the whole shall be full of light**—can avoid the appearance of tautology only by emphasizing "whole" in the first sentence, and "full of light" in the second. The Greek for "full of light" is "light" (adjective), "bright," "luminous."—If thy *whole* body therefore be light, having no part dark, the whole will be—*light*=there will be light and nothing else—**as when the bright shining of a candle** (better, *the* **lamp,** with its bright shining), **doth give thee light.** *The lamp,* here, is the house lamp, under the radiance of which a person in the room is completely illuminated.

to dine with him: and he went in, and sat down to meat.
38 And *when the Pharisee saw *it*, he marvelled that he had not first washed before dinner.
39 *And the Lord said unto him, Now do ye Pharisees make clean the outside of the cup and the platter; but *your inward part is full of ravening and wickedness.
40 *Ye fools, did not he that made that which is without make that which is within also?
41 *But rather give alms of such things as ye have; and, behold, all things are clean unto you.

38 And when the Pharisee saw it, he marvelled that he had not first bathed himself before ¹dinner.
39 And the Lord said unto him, Now do ye Pharisees cleanse the outside of the cup and of the platter; but your inward part is full of extortion and wickedness.
40 Ye foolish ones, did not he that made the 41 outside make the inside also? Howbeit give for alms those things which ²are within; and behold, all things are clean unto you.

a Mark 7:3.....*b* Matt. 23:25.....*c* Tit. 1:15.....*d* Isa. 58:7; Dan. 4:27; ch. 12:33.——1 Gr. *breakfast*....² Or *ye can*.

37–41. The Hypocritical Scruples of a Pharisee.

37. And as he spake, a (certain should be omitted) **Pharisee besought** (or, better, *asketh*) **him to dine** (Greek, *breakfast*) **with him.** The succeeding narrative follows directly upon the account of the preceding discourse (ver. 15-36). The Pharisee, who invites him, may have been hitherto ignorant of the special teaching and character of Jesus, and now curious to learn more about him; or, he may have been on the look-out for opportunity to entrap him; or, possibly, from a more liberal mind, simply desirous to cultivate the society of the great Teacher. If his subsequent course will allow it, we should prefer this last supposition. In either case Jesus was ready to embrace any opportunity of intercourse by which he might spread more widely the good tidings of the kingdom.— **And he went in, and sat down to meat.** The meal to which he was now invited was not properly the formal dinner, but the first meal of the day—a breakfast or lunch.

38. Even thus—when the Pharisee saw it—that he reclined without any formality— **he marvelled that he had not first washed before dinner.** The Greek for **washed** means (ἐβαπτίσθη) "been immersed," "dipped." Rev. J. B. McClellan, an eminent scholar of the Church of England, translates "dipped himself," rightly as to the main sense; yet the verb is in the passive, and implies rather that the bath was thought of as effected through the agency of a servant. The same author translates the analogous passage (Mark 7:4), "And after market, except they dip themselves"—a proper middle voice—"they eat not;" on which his note is, "Greek, *baptizein* Matt. 28:19 ref., (which references see in this Com. on 3:3). 2 Kings 5:14, he DIPPED himself seven times in the Jordan; parallel—wash thyself 5:10; Luke 11:38; Heb. 9:10; Judith 12:7, 8; she DIPPED herself in the fountain, and came in clean.—Sirac, 34:25). He that DIPPETH himself after touching a dead body; A. V. washeth. Justin, *Trypho*, 46. Trypho, the Jew, said it was even now possible to keep such Jewish ordinances as the Sabbath, circumcision, new moons, and DIPPING (or, BAPTIZING), of one-self after touching things forbidden."

39. The wonder of the Pharisee was probably expressed in the Saviour's hearing.— **Now do ye Pharisees cleanse,** etc. **Now** indicates a conclusion="now I see," "now it is evident." Ye make yourselves clean, by external ceremonies, as one would do who should, with these dishes from which we eat, wash the outside only.—**But your inward part is full of ravening** (or *extortion*) **and wickedness;** your mind and heart are wholly set on selfish gain, however unjust, and the gratification of evil desires.

40. Ye fools, did not he that made that which is without (*the outside*), **make that which is within** (or *the inside*) **also?** Does not common sense teach that God the Creator has at least as much care about the internal state of things (including men), as the external?

41. But rather (*How be it,* Revision), unfavorable as your course looks, there is a better way possible for you.—**Give alms of such things as ye have.** The Greek admits of three possible renderings, all, however, serving to impress the same lesson, namely, cherish the spirit of charity, love, mercy (Matt. 9:13; 12:7), and you will have no need of external purifications. 1. The Common Version understands the participle (τὰ ἐνόντα, from ἔνι), as meaning "the things that are present," "that are on hand" (comp. Col. 3:11; James 1:17). 2. "Those things which are within," as the Revision (from ἔνειμι). This refers to the contents of their dishes, the "cups and platters," and the precept is: "Give as alms what you thus squander in luxury; cultivate the

42 *But woe unto you, Pharisees! for ye tithe mint and rue and all manner of herbs, and pass over judgment and the love of God: these ought ye to have done, and not to leave the other undone.

42 But woe unto you Pharisees! for ye tithe mint and rue and every herb, and pass over justice and the love of God: but these ought ye to have done,

a Matt. 23 : 23.

spirit of self-denying charity, and all will be right with you." This is preferable to the previous translation, and connects itself with the mention of the "within" and "without." 3. Take the participle as an accusative case of specification: "as to what is within," now meaning the mind and disposition ("your inward part,") "give alms,"=practice true religion, **and behold**—a wonderful effect—**all things**—outside and inside—**are clean unto you.** Number 2 is grammatically simple, and by so much to be preferred. The Saviour is not, of course, stating fully the way of sanctification; but only setting over against their outward legality the spiritual, inward,

backed up by other Pharisees present. At all events, he had received an impression of

RUE.

their formality, hypocrisy, and utter lack of love to God or man, which bound him to expose its hollowness.

42. But woe unto you, Pharisees! This **woe** combines grief, warning, and threatening. It is three times repeated against the Pharisees.—**For ye tithe mint and rue and all manner of herbs** (*every herb*); the sin was essentially in what they left undone; but this extravagant legality which led them to go beyond the requirements of their written law, so as to tithe the very weeds of their gardens, was itself a sad indication of their conception of righteousness.—**And pass over** (neglect, or fail to exercise) **judgment and the love of God. Judgment** (Hebrew, *mishpat*) is, here, that course of conduct which right judgment prescribes=right conduct, justice, and which God has commanded. —**These** (viz. judgment and the love of God)

MINT.

self-denying, beneficent nature of acceptable service to God. "Love is the fulfilling of the law" (Rom. 13: 8).

42-52. DENUNCIATION OF THE PHARISEES AND LAWYERS.

The disparagement of Christ's freedom of conduct by his host (ver. 38), may have been

43 *a* Woe unto you, Pharisees! for ye love the uppermost seats in the synagogues, and greetings in the markets.
44 *b* Woe unto you, scribes and Pharisees, hypocrites! *c* for ye are as graves which appear not, and the men that walk over *them* are not aware *of them*.
45 Then answered one of the lawyers, and said unto him, Master, thus saying thou reproachest us also.
46 And he said, Woe unto you also, *ye* lawyers! *d* for ye lade men with burdens grievous to be borne, and ye yourselves touch not the burdens with one of your fingers.
47 *e* Woe unto you! for ye build the sepulchres of the prophets, and your fathers killed them.
48 Truly ye bear witness that ye allow the deeds of your fathers: for they indeed killed them, and ye build their sepulchres.

43 and not to leave the other undone. Woe unto you Pharisees! for ye love the chief seats in the synagogues, and the salutations in the marketplaces.
44 Woe unto you! for ye are as the tombs which appear not, and the men that walk over *them* know it not.
45 And one of the lawyers answering said unto him, *f* Master, in saying this thou reproachest us also.
46 And he said, Woe unto you lawyers also! for ye lade men with burdens grievous to be borne, and ye yourselves touch not the burdens with one of your fingers.
47 Woe unto you! for ye build the tombs of
48 the prophets, and your fathers killed them. So ye are witnesses and consent unto the works of your fathers: for they killed them, and ye build *their*

a Matt. 23: 6; Mark 12: 38, 39....*b* Matt. 23: 27....*c* Ps. 5: 9....*d* Matt. 23: 4....*e* Matt. 23: 29.—*f* Or, *Teacher.*

ought ye to have done, and not to leave the other (Greek *those*) undone, or neglected, *i. e.*, so far as they might be required, or were to be, done at all. The right disposition was necessary to allow any value to external performances.

43. The uppermost seats (or, chief sittings) **in the synagogues**, were the official bench on which the elders sat, facing the congregation. (See on 4: 14.) The fault condemned in this verse was ambition for showy preëminence, and the applause of men.

44. Hypocrisy, covering gross immorality and corruption of heart. **Ye are as** (*the*) **graves which appear not,** etc. To come in contact with a grave, or tomb, was eminently defiling. To have come too near one, unaware, would greatly offend the scrupulousness of a strict Jew. This, since graves were irregularly scattered about, and the distinguishing marks of their presence would in time become obliterated, was a peril to which every one was liable. Hence nothing could be a more expressive symbol of moral corruption and hatefulness than a hidden grave. Such, the Saviour says, were the conspicuous religionists of that time—an unsuspected body of corruption and source of moral defilement.

45. Then answered one of the lawyers, and said unto him, Master, thus (or, *in saying this*) **thou reproachest** (dost insult) **us also.** On the relation of the lawyers to the Pharisees and scribes, see on 7: 30. As educated to their function, they may have thought themselves, and actually been regarded, more respectable than the Pharisees. This man seems to have supposed that Jesus had not meant to include lawyers in the same condemnation as the Pharisees, which his language might imply, and that, if his attention was called to it, he would correct the mistake. But the Lord had made no mistake. He had spoken according to character and to facts; and to whomsoever these pertained, for them his words were intended.

46. Woe unto you also, ye lawyers (or, *lawyers also*)*!* Whether as morally corrupt or not, the lawyers were in some respects peculiarly culpable, because they multiplied commandments and requirements, as if a part of the divine law. They were fabricators of tradition, which Christ hated, and so loaded **men with burdens grievous to be borne** —precepts hard, or even impossible, for the people to comply with.—**And ye yourselves touch not,** etc. Their utter failure to keep their own commandments made their course all the more cruel to the people.

47. While professing great reverence for the former prophets, their spirit is one of intense and murderous hostility to those who come in the character of those prophets, and so they prove themselves children, indeed, of those who killed the prophets. To build **the sepulchres**=*tombs*—**of the prophets**, might be to their credit, if they acted from a sincere desire to honor them. But when it was done from a hollow disposition to connect their own names with revered monuments, it simply evinced their likeness to those who murdered the prophets. Unbelievers killed them, and unbelievers built their tombs. It is a case of fathers and children dealing with God's prophets.

48. Truly ye bear witness, etc.; (according to the best text: *So*=*therefore*—*ye are witnesses*) viz., that your fathers killed the prophets—*and consent to* **the deeds of your fathers.**—*Consent to* means "are well pleased with," "take pleasure in" (Rom. 1: 32). The Saviour intimates that it would be more pru-

49 Therefore also said the wisdom of God, a I will send them prophets and apostles, and *some* of them they shall slay and persecute:
50 That the blood of all the prophets, which was shed from the foundation of the world, may be required of this generation:
51 b From the blood of Abel unto c the blood of Zacharias, which perished between the altar and the temple: verily I say unto you, It shall be required of this generation.

49 *tombs*. Therefore also said the wisdom of God, I will send unto them prophets and apostles; and *some* of 50 them they shall kill and persecute; that the blood of all the prophets, which was shed from the foundation of the world, may be required of this generation; from the blood of Abel unto the blood of Zachariah, who perished between the altar and the ¹sanctuary: yea, I say unto you, it shall be required

a Matt. 23: 34....b Gen. 4: 8....c 2 Chron. 24: 20, 21.—1 Gr. *house*.

dent for them to leave the tombs of the prophets neglected and forgotten, than by hypocritical appearances of honor to them, to call up the remembrance of their slaughter at the hands of men like-minded with these men.— **They indeed killed them, and ye build,** etc.—**Their sepulchres**, "though supposed, is not expressed in the Greek. Your building is the natural sequence of their killing."

49-51. Therefore also said the wisdom of God, I will send, etc. What is intended by **the wisdom of God,** is very obscure. We should naturally understand it to designate some Book or portion of the Old Testament. Not only, however, is there no Book so named, but when we look for a saying like what is here given, we find nothing very nearly similar. A variety of hypotheses have been suggested to meet the difficulty. In Matthew 23: 34 ff., the same declaration for substance is ascribed to Christ himself: "Behold I send," etc., and some have supposed that Jesus here means the wisdom of God speaking through him. He cannot, of course, be here quoting himself on a former occasion, then, because the two reports are of the same discourse. And if we could allow the entirely unparalleled circumlocution of "the wisdom of God" for "I," the preterit tense "said" hinders; for it should be "says." Some would have it that an Apocryphal Book, now lost, called "Wisdom of God," is cited here, but the utter singularity of such a proceeding by Christ properly excludes this conjecture, even if we had some intimation that any such Book had been lost. Godet and others imagine that in the early church, the "Proverbs of Solomon" were called simply Wisdom, or Wisdom of God (comp. apochryphal Wisdom of Jesus son of Sirach, Wisdom of Solomon), and that then the quotation is from the closing verses of the first chapter. This is "clutching out of the air" a fancy, more pleasant, perhaps, than the acknowledgment of ignorance, but not so profitable. Somewhat more probable, in our judgment, is the supposition that Christ has in mind here several passages of the Old Testament, partly historical (as 2 Chron. 24: 18 ff.; 36: 14 ff.), partly predictive (as Prov. 1: 15 ff.), taking the main sense of which, as appropriate to his own present use—"I send unto you" (Matt. 23: 34), he throws it back into the purpose of God, which the history simply fulfilled. As he was thus adapting to himself what God in his wisdom had planned and executed, he might express himself in such way that the thought would be both "the wisdom of God said I will send," and "I will send." One other view may be suggested, that Jesus, seeing all this abuse and murder of the ancient prophets to be but a type of what the early ministers of the New Testament were to meet, simply declares that this also was a part of God's plan. The wisdom of God=God, in his wisdom, said, viz., within himself, I will send, etc. As God would do this through Christ, the mode of his expression might have allowed the equivalent report, I send, etc. This would be an unparalleled form of statement with our Lord, but in no other sense unnatural. These conjectures are ventured merely as such, where nothing but conjecture is possible, and where room for conjecture seems exhausted. It must be left as a very dark expression. The **prophets** spoken of are those of the New Testament Church (Eph. 4: 11), and they are mentioned before **apostles** (comp. "messengers," 2 Chr. 36: 15), not because of superior rank, for in the New Testament they everywhere stand second, but to bring Christ's ministry into obvious association with that of the Old Testament as the objects of a continuous persecution.—**And some of them they shall kill and persecute.** This was literally fulfilled within the period of the inspired history.— Acts 13: 1-3; 2 Cor. 11: 23 ff.; 1 Thess. 2: 14 f.

50. That the blood of all the prophets, etc. All the prophets that had been slain in

52 *Woe unto you, lawyers! for ye have taken away the key of knowledge: ye entered not in yourselves, and them that were entering in ye hindered.
53 And as he said these things unto them, the scribes and the Pharisees began to urge *him* vehemently, and to provoke him to speak of many things;

52 of this generation. Woe unto you lawyers! for ye took away the key of knowledge: ye entered not in yourselves, and them that were entering in ye hindered.
53 And when he was come out from thence, the scribes and the Pharisees began to ¹press upon *him* vehemently, and to provoke him to speak of ²many

a Matt. 23 : 13.——1 Or, *set themselves vehemently against him....*2 Or, *more.*

---

the world were slain by the Jewish people, and these men might be held responsible for the guilt, as every generation must inherit the consequences of the conduct of every preceding generation of their line.

51. But Jesus, looking at the spirit of his contemporaries as that of all hostility to true piety, the genuine spirit of Cain, includes **Abel** among the prophets, and charges them with the murder of the first righteous man, recorded in the first book of their Bible, and of **Zacharias**—the last recorded, in the last book, as it stood in the order of the Jewish Scriptures, namely, in 2 Chron. 24: 20 ff.— **Verily, I say unto you, It shall be required,** etc.—The certainty of prophetic foresight, and the tenderness of national sympathy, both speak in this repetition of the solemn and dreadful truth. Each generation had, indeed, experienced something of the consequences of its own, and of the former sins; but in a peculiar sense would the penalty of all fall on this generation, because it was to be the last on its ancestral ground, and was to perish most miserably. There were those then living who could witness and suffer the unspeakable horrors of the war of Titus, including the siege and destruction of their idolized capital.

52. **Woe unto you, lawyers!**—Christ returns to the enumeration of their sins, and emphasizes their darkening and perversion of the teachings of their Scripture. In that, rightly understood and applied, lay the knowledge which should serve as a key to open the door of the kingdom of heaven.— **Ye have taken away the key of knowledge**—namely, the key to unlock the kingdom of heaven, which key consists in knowledge. The possessive case is one of apposition, like "the city of New York." Right knowledge of the teaching of the Old Testament, as John the Baptist would have led them to see it, was suited to prepare for the reception of Jesus. But such knowledge, the lawyers, through their hard, formal, lifeless interpretations, and through the multiplication of burdensome traditions, had precluded, had **taken away** from the sight of those who depended on them for light.—**Ye entered not in yourselves**—a truth of fearful significance to them personally, but which is mentioned to signalize a truth that weighed still more heavily on the heart of our Lord, that they had, by their errors and willfully false instructions, led away a multitude of simple souls, ready to enter upon the way of life.—**And them that were entering in ye hindered.** The Saviour recalls "the crowds," "multitudes," that have hung on his teaching, and been melted by his beneficence, and who seemed at times to have ranked themselves under his banner, as his disciples, and sharers of his kingdom. But around them the Scribes and Pharisees and lawyers have lurked, watching, reproving them for their attachment to Jesus, making light of his claims, contradicting what he taught, and even charging him in his holiest self-manifestations with being the agent of the devil. What wonder, then, that he should once and again have been grieved to see many of his disciples go back, and walk no more with him? And when we think how powerfully these religious leaders had hindered the saving influence of Jesus over the mass of his nation, is it strange that his denunciation now, on the very verge of the national opportunity, should thunder and blaze against them?

53, 54. FURTHER SNARES LAID FOR JESUS BY THE SCRIBES AND PHARISEES.

53. **And as he said these things unto them** (better, *and when he was come out from thence*); the Revision conforms to the text as restored according to the best authorities. The Pharisees followed him out, full of animosity, and eager still to harm him.—**The Scribes** (=*lawyers*) **and the Pharisees began to urge** (=*press upon*) **him vehemently**—by words and acts of enraged hostility—**and to provoke him to speak of many things.**—The rare Greek verb here used would seem to mean "to urge to speak

54 Laying wait for him, and ᵃ seeking to catch something out of his mouth, that they might accuse him.

CHAPTER XII.

IN ᵇ the mean time, when there were gathered together an innumerable multitude of people, insomuch that they trode one upon another, he began to say unto his disciples first of all, ᶜ Beware ye of the leaven of the Pharisees, which is hypocrisy.

2 ᵈ For there is nothing covered, that shall not be revealed; neither hid, that shall not be known.

3 Therefore, whatsoever ye have spoken in darkness shall be heard in the light; and that which ye have spoken in the ear in closets shall be proclaimed upon the housetops.

54 things; laying wait for him, to catch something out of his mouth.

1 In the mean time, when ¹ the many thousands of the multitude were gathered together, insomuch that they trode one upon another, he began to ² say unto his disciples first of all, Beware ye of the leaven 2 of the Pharisees, which is hypocrisy. But there is nothing covered up, that shall not be revealed; and 3 hid, that shall not be known. Wherefore whatsoever ye have said in the darkness shall be heard in the light; and what ye have spoken in the ear in the inner chambers shall be proclaimed upon the house-

a Mark 12:13....*b* Matt. 16:6; Mark 8:15....*c* Matt. 16:12....*d* Matt. 10:26; Mark 4:22; ch. 8:17.——1 Gr. *the myriads of*.....2 Or, *say unto his disciples, First of all beware ye.*

off-hand," and so McClellan translates; why, is explained by the next clause.

54. Laying wait for him, and seeking (all the best editors omit *and;* most omit *seeking*) **to catch something out of his mouth.** They hoped to induce him to say something without premeditation, which they could make a ground of accusation against him. This purpose is expressed in the last clause of the Common Version, with slender support of the authorities. What conduct of theirs could better justify his denunciations of them?

Ch. 12: 1-3. WARNING AGAINST THE PRINCIPLES OF THE PHARISEES.

1. In the mean time, when there were gathered together an innumerable multitude of people (better Revised Version, *when the many thousands*—Greek, *myriads*—*of the multitude were gathered together*). During the period of the preceding discourse the people, hearing that Jesus was in that place, had been assembling from various quarters, (11:29), and now constituted a vast throng about him.—**Insomuch that they trode one upon another,** in the eagerness of each one to get nearest to him.—**He began to say,** a phrase which, as we have repeatedly seen, intimates the opening of an important discourse.—**Unto his disciples first of all.** Many prefer to connect **first of all** with what follows: first of all beware, etc.; but as this speech is interrupted by address to others (ver. 13, ff.), and turns entirely from the disciples (13; 1, ff., we may as well refer the phrase to them in this place: to the disciples first, to others afterward.—**Beware ye of the leaven of the Pharisees, which is hypocrisy. Leaven** was an apt symbol of any active principle calculated to spread its influence, and bring surrounding objects into correspondence with itself, (13:21; 1 Cor. 5:6).

Jesus had used it before (Matt. 16:12), to denote the "teaching" of the Pharisees, that which they taught, their characteristic principles, which determined their spirit and conduct. Here also it means the same. Jesus had just had a very impressive specimen of that spirit and conduct, which had led him to portray them in the unflattering colors of his rebuke. Had he been moved also by the discovery that the seeming courtesy of his invitation, 11:37, had been all part of a stratagem to involve him in hostilities with the religious authorities? This may possibly have entered into his reasons. The reason why they should beware of what distinguished these sanctimonious notables was that it was **hypocrisy.** Not their hypocrisy, separately, but their principles and teachings, as being all hypocritical, insincere, canting, a pre-eminent specimen of hypocrisy. The Greek (ἥτις) for **which is,** means strictly, "*seeing that it is,*" thus marking the fact as a reason for being on one's guard against the thing. Every view that he took of their character and proceedings, in the fuller report of Matthew (23:13, 15, 23, etc.), called forth the appellation, "hypocrites"! No one could be infected with their leaven without being a hypocrite, and nothing of this would he have in his kingdom.

2. *But* (not **For**) **there is nothing covered** (*up.*—Revision), **that shall not be revealed,** uncovered, etc. Every pretext is sure to be stripped off; every imitation of truth to be exposed in its real falseness; every counterfeit of honesty and goodness to be branded as spurious; all sham righteousness to be held up as base and pernicious fraud. This result will be reached, if not before, at the day of judgment, and it will be reached in the case of those who claim to be my disciples, as well as in that of the Pharisees and their like.

3. Therefore, whatsoever ye have

Ch. XII.] LUKE. 211

4 "And I say unto you ᵇmy friends, Be not afraid of them that kill the body, and after that have no more that they can do.
5 But I will forewarn you whom ye shall fear: Fear him, which after he hath killed hath power to cast into hell; yea, I say unto you, Fear him.

4 tops. And I say unto you my friends, Be not afraid of them that kill the body, and after that have no
5 more that they can do. But I will warn you whom ye shall fear: Fear him, who after he hath killed hath ¹power to cast into ²hell; yea, I say unto you,

a Isa. 51:7, 8, 12, 13; Jer. 1:8; Matt. 10:28....b John 15:14, 15.——1 Or, authority....2 Gr. Gehenna.

spoken (*ye said*) **in** (*the*) **darkness,** etc. In applying the general remark to his disciples, by way of conclusion, **therefore,** he views them in reference to all their words, private conversation, as well as public discourse, as a revelation of their character; and demands that all shall be sincere and truthful. **The darkness,** in which some of their words will have been spoken, is the state of imperfect discernment of character and tendencies in the present life; and **the light is the full** publicity of the day of judgment. Simply parallel to these expressions are, **in the ear in closets,** and **on the house tops,** respectively. They are two pairs of metaphors for a state of ignorance, and one of knowledge, of its concealment, and of complete manifestation. The preterit tense, *ye said,* puts the hearer at the point of final disclosure—what at that time it will be seen that ye said, etc. It is hard, with Meyer and others, to confine this to the preaching of the apostles, and make **the darkness** mean the privacy necessitated by persecution, and **the light** the liberty of proclamation which they would afterwards enjoy.

4-12. GOD WILL PROTECT AGAINST THE HATRED AND DANGER WHICH FRANK SINCERITY IN THE UTTERANCE OF THE TRUTH WILL INCUR.

4. And I say unto you my friends. The disciples are still addressed; but a new and important branch of the discourse opens. **My friends,** must have had a touching significance to him and to them, after the treatment which he had just received from the Pharisees.—**Be not afraid of them that kill the body, and after that have no more that they can do.** Men may, in their displeasure at your fidelity to the truth, put you to death. (So they did afterward to James, Peter, Paul, and many such). But their rage cannot go beyond the bounds of natural life, readiness to lose which, for Christ's sake, is one of the known conditions of discipleship (9: 23-25). The actual loss of it was, moreover, according to Christ's teaching and the belief of the early Christians, the more speedy attainment of the higher heavenly life (Phil. 1:21-23). There would be even to them a dread of that physical wrench which parts soul and body, a sorrow for the loss to those who loved them; but deeper fear of death they did not feel.

5. But I will forewarn (better, *warn*) **you,** etc. The Saviour seems to say, Ye are indeed in peril; fear is an inevitable incident of thoughtful human experience; whichever course ye take, ye will excite displeasure. But much depends on whose fear ye cherish, and whose hatred ye brave.—**Fear him which, after he hath killed hath power to cast into hell.** This undoubtedly describes God, who inflicts the final penalty for sin, toward whom that "fear which is the beginning of wisdom" is, even under the gospel, a reasonable state of mind, and most reasonable in the face of temptation to disobey him. Several modern expositors, among them even Stier and Van Oosterzee, have strangely understood that Jesus here inculcates on his disciples the fear of Satan. If any one needs argument that, after God has "delivered us from the power of darkness, and translated us into the kingdom of his dear Son" (Col. 1:13), we need more in order to avoid all harm, than to fear God, he may read the words of Alford on Matthew 10:28, which is quoted also by the American editor of Lange on our passage.—**Yea, I say unto you, Fear him.** An emphatic repetition to intimate the solemnity of the subject. **Hell** (γέεννα) is the place and state of the impenitent sinner in the eternity to come. The Greek word was intended to be a mere transliteration of the Hebrew, *Ge-Hinnom;* valley of Hinnom; shortened from the valley of the son, or sons, of Hinnom (Josh 15:8; 2 Kings 23:10). This was the name of the deep valley, or ravine, which runs along the west and south side of Jerusalem. According to some authorities, the name was applied also to some portion of the valley of Kidron, east of the city. (Smith's *Dict. of Bib.,* Art. Tophoth. *Recovery of Jerusalem,* p. 259.) It was naturally a pleasant and fruitful scene; and, as such, doubtless, was appropriated by corrupt and apostate

6 Are not five sparrows sold for two *a* farthings, and not one of them is forgotten before God?
7 But even the very hairs of your head are all numbered. Fear not therefore: ye are of more value than many sparrows.
8 *b* Also I say unto you, Whosoever shall confess me before men, him shall the Son of man also confess before the angels of God:

6 Fear him. Are not five sparrows sold for two pence? and not one of them is forgotten in the sight of God.
7 But the very hairs of your head are all numbered. Fear not: ye are of more value than many sparrows.
8 And I say unto you, Every one who shall confess ¹ me before men, ² him shall the Son of man also confess

a See Matt. 10: 29....*b* Matt. 10: 32; Mark 8: 38; 2 Tim. 2; 12; 1 John 2: 23.——¹ Gr. *in me*....² Gr. *in him*.

kings to the idolatrous worship of Baal and Moloch, with all the cruelties involved in it. (2 Chron. 28: 3; 33: 6; Jer. 7: 31; 19: 2-6.) A particular portion of the valley, called Topheth, or Tophet, was specially polluted by this pagan worship. King Josiah, and others, took great pains to defile the spot, so as to prevent a repetition of the wickedness, by depositing there the carcasses of beasts, and bodies of executed criminals, and making it the dumping-ground of all refuse and filth of the city. It thus became an abomination to all pious Jews, and is reported, in Talmudic traditions, to have been made still further horrible by the presence of perpetual fires, which were necessary to consume the pestiferous offal. Although this last statement is denied by Dr. Edward Robinson and others (impliedly by Winer, *Realwörterbuch*, Art. Hinnom), the traditions seem to fall in with the necessities of the case, as some such consumption of the refuse must have been necessary to the health of the city, and to its ceremonial purity. If only from the remembrance of the fires of Moloch, the valley was called later, "Gehenna of fire." To it, specially to Tophet, Isaiah probably refers (66: 24), when he speaks of the carcasses of transgressors there, and says, "their worm shall not die; neither shall their fire be quenched." He expressly names the place (30: 33), when he says, symbolically, that the Lord hath widened and deepened it, to make it capable of holding all that should be buried there (comp. Jer. 7: 31-33), and adds, "the breath of the Lord, like a stream of brimstone, doth kindle it." Thus early was the natural conception of this horrid place becoming fit to represent the scene of future punishment to God's enemies. The idea of such punishment was not yet distinctly revealed; but it became clearer with the progress of revelation in the Old Testament. In the Apocalyptic Book of Enoch, dating from not earlier than 100 B. C., the Messianic judgment on the wicked is made to take place in an accursed valley, which is for those who shall be accursed to eternity. (See the passage cited in Smith,

Dict. of the Bib., p. 880.) When, therefore, our Saviour needed a term to denote his view of the future condition of those who died disobedient to God, the name of that opprobrious valley was ready to his hand. *Gehenna*, suggestive of the fires of shameful and cruel idolatry, of reeking corruption, and, probably, also, of perpetual flames and smoke, and offensive odors, would be as expressive a symbol of the place of eternal punishment, as would be the banquet with Abraham, the thrones of honor, the Father's house with its many mansions, of the scene and circumstances of the eternal felicity of the saints.

6. Are not five sparrows sold for two farthings? only about four mills apiece; a sum too small for us to represent by any coin, though it is probable that its purchasing power may then have been greater than that of one cent now.—**And not one of them is forgotten before** (or, *in the sight of*) **God**. What a proof of the sleepless vigilance and care of the Creator for all, even the least, of his creatures!

7. But—so far from his forgetting a sparrow—**even the very hairs of your head are all numbered;** have all been counted. Such is his attention to his created things, merely as such.—**Ye are of more value than many sparrows.** Ye are more than mere creatures—servants, children, redeemed ones, who will far less be left uncared for than they. The argument is of the same force as that in Matthew 6: 26-30.

8, 9. These verses add another, not less powerful, incentive to fidelity to Christ, drawn from the experiences of the last day. **Whosoever shall confess me before men.** To confess Christ is to avow one's faith in him as being that which he claims to be, Messiah and Saviour, and to render to him in practice that religious recognition which is due. This involves self-denial always, generally something of sacrifice, and sometimes the hazard of life; but not for naught. The recompense is to be ample.—**Him shall the Son of man also confess;** *i. e.*, recognize as a faithful

9 But he that denieth me before men shall be denied before the angels of God.
10 And *whosoever shall speak a word against the Son of man, it shall be forgiven him: but unto him that blasphemeth against the Holy Ghost it shall not be forgiven.
11 *And when they bring you unto the synagogues, and *unto* magistrates, and powers, take ye no thought how or what thing ye shall answer, or what ye shall say;
12 For the Holy Ghost shall teach you in the same hour what ye ought to say.

9 fess before the angels of God: but he that denieth me in the presence of men shall be denied in the
10 presence of the angels of God. And every one who shall speak a word against the Son of man, it shall be forgiven him; but unto him that blasphemeth
11 against the Holy Spirit it shall not be forgiven. And when they bring you before the synagogues, and the rulers, and the authorities, be not anxious how or
12 what ye shall answer, or what ye shall say: for the Holy Spirit shall teach you in that very hour what ye ought to say.

a Matt. 12: 31, 32; Mark 3: 28; 1 John 5: 16....*b* Matt. 10: 19; Mark 13: 11; ch. 21: 14.

and worthy disciple, entitled to the eternal honor and reward which will lie in the manifestation of the divine favor before the universe. Such recognition, in that day and scene, will outweigh all the temporal pleasures and honors of all the generations that will have lived on earth.

Then will he own my worthless name
Before his Father's face.

9. But he that denieth me, etc. The opposite to this confession, on the part of the wicked, is expressed by denying Christ before men; *i. e.*, either formally or practically refusing to give him the reverence, trust, obedience, and love which he claims; and by his denying the unbeliever to be entitled to his favor when the angels are assembled for the eternal judgment. The statement needs little explanation, but much serious thought.

10. Blasphemy of the Holy Spirit. This verse meets us abruptly, without clear evidence of connection with the context. It may quite possibly have been transferred, in the document followed by Luke, from the connection after 11: 23,=Matthew 12: 32; Mark 3: 29. There the subject of blasphemy against the Holy Spirit was obviously in place (comp. Luke 11: 15). The former half of our verse, about speaking against the Son of man, is sufficiently apposite to the preceding thought of denying him, to account for the whole having been placed here; although the second half requires the other connection. A man might speak against the Son of man, in his humiliation, so different from what was generally expected of the Messiah, through personal misinterpretation of the prophecies, through the effect of erroneous teaching on the part of respected but perverse religious guides, or through the power of unthinking prejudice. This would not presuppose incorrigible stubbornness of unbelief. It was what in some measure pertained to almost every one who came to him. Light might pierce through it, love might melt it, further evidence turn it to faith. Then it could be forgiven. **But unto him that blasphemeth,** etc. Not but that this also would be forgiven, if in its case there could be that repentance and faith on which all forgiveness depends. But blasphemy against the Holy Spirit appeared, in the only case of which we have a description, in a state of mind which by speech confounded God and the devil, ascribing the work of the former to the latter, his opposite, and his arch-enemy (11: 15 and par.). What repentance could there be for a mind to which the clearest manifestations of God's holiness and kindness appeared to be diabolical conduct? To such a person the acts and character of Beelzebub would be just as well suited to awaken penitence and faith as those of Christ himself.

11. Continuation from ver. 9. It is assumed that, as afterward happened a thousand times, they will be delivered **unto the synagogues.** This had a certain jurisdiction, with power to inflict minor penalties, in religious causes.—**And unto magistrates** (strictly, *magistracies*) **and powers** (*authorities*), terms which cover all sorts of government, civil and religious, Jewish or heathen. —**Take ye no thought** (*be not anxious*—have no care) **how or what thing ye shall answer.** This does not prohibit the exercise of their faculties in the way of preparation to meet charges, so far as this was practicable without perturbation and loss of peace; but does forbid whatever would unfit them for calm and clear subserviency to the Holy Spirit.

12. For the Holy Ghost (*Spirit*) **shall teach you in the same hour** (namely, when ye are called to plead) **what ye ought to say.** This is no warrant, to those who undertake to teach men the way of life, to depend lazily on divine ability. Such are likely to

13 And one of the company said unto him, Master, speak to my brother, that he divide the inheritance with me.
14 And he said unto him, *Man, who made me a judge or a divider over you?
15 And he said unto them, *Take heed, and beware of covetousness: for a man's life consisteth not in the abundance of the things which he possesseth.

13 And one of the multitude said unto him, ¹Master, 14 bid my brother divide the inheritance with me. But he said unto him, Man, who made me a judge or 15 a divider over you? And he said unto them, Take heed, and keep yourselves from all covetousness: ² for a man's life consisteth not in the abundance of the

a John 18:36....*b* 1 Tim. 6:7, etc.—1 Or, *Teacher*....2 Gr. *for not in a man's abundance consisteth his life, from the things which he possesseth.*

be left without any ability at all. But it encourages Christ's servants who are exposed to persecutions for their sincere and frank fidelity to him to wait on him for needed aid in defending themselves. They are not assured of deliverance from their peril, but **what they shall say** for the honor of the cause will not fail them. We have the justification of such counsel in subsequent history. In the accounts of persecution in the Acts and Epistles, and in reading the testimony of Christian confessors and martyrs in all the subsequent ages, we can see how wonderfully common men and women were enabled to answer their accusers, so as nobly to honor "the name," whether they were saved from harm or not. Often have their simple, hearty, patient confessions of the Saviour, proved more powerful arguments for his truth than the most logical and eloquent treatises of its undistressed professors.

13-21. A Warning Against Covetousness.

13-14. The occasion. **And one of** (out from among) **the company** (*multitude*) **said unto him, Master, speak to my brother, that he divide the inheritance with me.** The man appears to have been so impressed with the authority and reasonableness of the Saviour's words, that he conceived the idea of turning these to account in a matter of worldly interest to him, quite aloof from the line of the Teacher's proper work. What the particulars of his grievance were we can only conjecture. There was a dispute about the partition of an estate, in which he was interested, with his brother. His complaint was not, in form, that he could not get an equitable, but that he could not get any, division. It would not have been consistent with the usual course of Jesus to assume, in any such case, the function of a temporal magistrate. Here he appears to have seen evidence of a greediness for gain, which simply suggested to him a lesson of general prudence and piety.

14. And he said unto him, Man, who made me a judge or a divider over you? This was all the answer vouchsafed to the man, and, by its severity of tone, showed that the thing desired was impossible. But for him was, doubtless, intended a large share of what was added for the mass of the audience. **And he said unto them, Take heed, and beware of** (*keep yourselves from every kind of*) **covetousness.** Greed for more of worldly good, of wealth, and apparently with the added quality of intense selfishness, and disregard for others' rights, is the Scriptural conception of **covetousness**. It is throughout spoken of as a very bad thing, classed with the meanest vices and ungodliness, equivalent even to idolatry in heinousness (Rom. 1:29; 1 Cor. 5:10; Eph. 4:19—lit., work all uncleanness with *covetousness*—5:3; Col. 3:5; 2 Pet. 2:3, 14 al). It was the very antithesis of Christ's own disposition, who "emptied himself" of the glories of heaven; and he wisely took this opportunity to notify all, that his disciples must guard themselves against it; and he supports his prohibition by a reason which might have force with merely temporal prudence. **For a man's life consisteth not in the abundance of the things which he possesseth.** Life is to be understood, primarily, in its natural sense, earthly existence (comp. ver. 20). But this existence is of value as an opportunity for welfare; real happiness. And this depends on soundness of body and mind, the proper regulation of the desires, and the harmony of all our tendencies and experiences with our relations to God and the world. It certainly does not consist in "the abundance of worldly possessions." That may occasion great and peculiar care and anxiety, and prompt to even more insatiable greed, without the slightest power to gratify one of the nobler aspirations of a human soul. Its characteristic craving is simply for *more* of what has already proved itself vanity. All this the Saviour intimates in the parable which he proceeds to speak to them.

16 And he spake a parable unto them, saying, The ground of a certain rich man brought forth plentifully:
17 And he thought within himself, saying, What shall I do, because I have no room where to bestow my fruits?
18 And he said, This will I do: I will pull down my barns, and build greater; and there will I bestow all my fruits and my goods.
19 And I will say to my soul, *Soul, thou hast much goods laid up for many years; take thine ease, eat, drink, and be merry.
20 But God said unto him, Thou fool, this night ᵇ thy soul shall be required of thee: ᶜ then whose shall those things be, which thou hast provided?
21 So is he that layeth up treasure for himself, ᵈ and is not rich toward God.

16 things which he possesseth. And he spake a parable unto them, saying, The ground of a certain rich man 17 brought forth plentifully: and he reasoned within self, saying, What shall I do, because I have not 18 where to bestow my fruits? And he said, This will I do: I will pull down my barns, and build greater; and there will I bestow all my corn and my goods.
19 And I will say to my ¹ soul, ¹ Soul, thou hast much goods laid up for many years; take thine ease, eat, 20 drink, be merry. But God said unto him, Thou foolish one, this night ² is thy ¹ soul required of thee; and the things which thou hast prepared, whose 21 shall they be? So is he that layeth up treasure for himself, and is not rich toward God.

a Eccles. 11: 9; 1 Cor. 15: 32; James 5: 5....b Job 20: 22; 27: 8; Ps. 52: 7; James 4: 14....c Ps. 39: 6; Jer. 17: 11....d Matt. 6: 20; ver. 33; 1 Tim. 6: 18, 19; James 2: 5.——1 Or, life....2 Or. they require thy soul.

16-21. PARABLE OF THE RICH FOOL.
16-17. The ground of a certain rich man, etc. It is not a bad man, according to the standard of the world—whether of the church also?—that the Saviour sets before us. He does no direct, positive harm to anybody, ("and men will praise thee when thou doest well for thyself," Ps. 49: 18); he simply prospers pecuniarily for himself, without a thought of obligation to God, or care for fellow-men. We see him at the forks of his road, when in deep reflection.

17. What shall I do? Had his question meant, "What shall I render to the Lord for all his benefits toward me?" and had he said: "I will employ my teeming wealth in such manner as safely, prudently, to better the temporal and spiritual condition of as many as I can of my fellow-creatures, especially of those by whose aid I have prospered," he would have been a wise and a rare man. But when he consumes his time and thought in projects for the larger accumulation and safe bestowal of the treasures that stream in upon him, meantime only anticipating sordid, swinish happiness, which is never to come to him, we recognize a common sort of man, and are prepared for the judgment that God will pass upon him.

19. When he shall have reached the point where his overflowing abundance is all housed, and made secure against moths and rust and thieves, then he promises himself that he will lie thus to himself: **Soul**—meaning his appetite, his capacity of animal activity and gratification— **thou hast much (many) goods laid up for many years.** What a sarcasm upon himself, in this application of the term "good," in his circumstances! Even to his low grade of anticipated pleasure there is one condition of which he has not thought, i. e., breath. But that is in another's hand. (See Dan. 5: 23, last sentence.)

20. But God said unto him—perhaps through some significant twinge, or shock, to his physical frame, interpreted by a reproving conscience.—**Thou fool, this night** (which has already begun) **thy soul shall be required of thee** (Greek, they are demanding back from thee thy soul). His time for repentance is past, and God's messengers are already charged to summon him to his account. So far from having a vast store of gratifications for his soul, his soul itself is not his own; and, regarded as his organ of pleasure, is now reclaimed by God.—**Then whose shall those things be which thou hast provided?** And the things which thou didst prepare, whose shall they be? This indicates the spirit of the original better than the Common Version. That thy soul is taken from thee forbids that thou shouldst have any good of them, and whose are they to be? "He heapeth up riches and knoweth not who shall gather them." (Ps. 39: 6.)

21. So is he that layeth up treasure for himself, and is not rich toward God. Laying up, or amassing, **treasure** for one's self is to gather merely for personal use and gratification, as did the Rich Fool. To be **rich toward God** is to do the things that please him, so as to stand high in his gracious favor; which is "the treasure in heaven," "the fruit that increaseth to your account." (Phil. 4: 17; Revision, comp. ver. 19, and Rom. 10: 12.) This is impartially open to the man who has no worldly possessions, and its full fruition, beginning at the day of Jesus Christ, will continue through eternity. But the death of every prosperous worldling is only another instance of the man to whom God said, **Thou fool!**

22 And he said unto his disciples, Therefore I say unto you, ᵃTake no thought for your life, what ye shall eat; neither for the body, what ye shall put on.
23 The life is more than meat, and the body *is more* than raiment.
24 Consider the ravens: for they neither sow nor reap; which neither have storehouse nor barn; and ᵇGod feedeth them: how much more are ye better than the fowls?
25 And which of you with taking thought can add to his stature one cubit?

22 And he said unto his disciples, Therefore I say unto you, Be not anxious for *your* ¹ life what ye shall eat; 23 nor yet for your body, what ye shall put on. For the ¹ life is more than the food, and the body than 24 the raiment. Consider the ravens, that they sow not, neither reap; which have no store-chamber nor barn; and God feedeth them; of how much more 25 value are ye than the birds! And which of you by being anxious can add a cubit unto ² the measure of

a Matt. 6: 25....*b* Job 38: 41; Ps. 147: 9.——1 Or, *soul.*——2 Or, *his stature.*

22–34. INSTRUCTION TO THE DISCIPLES CONCERNING EARTHLY GOODS. This is closely parallel to what Matthew includes in the Sermon on the Mount. Authorities differ as to its connection. On the whole, it seems most likely that Luke has the right order, and that Matthew, for special reasons, gave it in his sixth chapter.

22. The preceding discourse had been addressed to the multitude; now **he said unto his disciples, Therefore**—considering the truth that life consists not in abundant possessions—**I say unto you, Take no thought for your life.** In older English, **thought** meant care, anxiety, trouble of mind. "Here's pansies; that's for *thought.*"—*Hamlet.* "Lest he *take thought* and kill himself."—*Julius Cæsar.* This is designed simply to guard against all and every distraction of mind that would hinder undivided attention to present duties. These, for the Christian, centre in the kingdom of God; and that he is to seek first. But he is forbidden to give care, or even thought, to what may be in the future, which God holds in his own hand, and by study about which the present might be lost. Such is clearly the key to the whole instruction in Matthew, as seen in 6: 34: "Take no thought for the morrow." (Comp. Meyer on Matt. 6: 25, 34, and Dr. Conant's note on ver. 25.) This reference to the future is implied also in Luke, where care for the life, etc., is care for its continuance and future well-being. The rendering "be not anxious" of the Revision is preferable to **take no thought,** as now likely to be understood; but, on the other hand, it should not imply that *care* not amounting to *anxiety* was allowed the disciples for to-day.—**For your life.** The word translated life is ambiguous. Meaning originally breath, then the principle of life, or the condition of being alive, it passed naturally into that of the "soul," as the basis of sense and all animal functions. It might with equal propriety be translated here "soul," as it is in ver. 19, 20 regarded as the principle of the natural life.—**What ye shall eat.** This goes closely with the preceding: Be not concerned in the interest of your soul, or life, as to whence food and drink are to come, to sustain and prolong it.—**Neither for the body**—the material tenement in which the soul is housed, or organ through which the life acts and manifests itself.

23. The reason by which that injunction is sustained is intimated, rather than drawn out. **For the life is more than meat** (better, *the food*), etc. Add that God has given the more important gift, the end, to which the others are only means; and we see that, in reason, he cannot withhold the latter while the former should last.

24. This is illustrated, first, by the care which God has for the inferior creatures of his hand. Having made them, and, presumably, for the accomplishment of his purpose, he does not let them fail of sustenance until that purpose is fulfilled. How much less, then, shall rational creatures, whom he has not only made in his own image, but entrusted with a great service to be performed for himself, fail of support while earnestly engaged in that? The ravens have none of those resources which the man in the parable was so absorbed in acquiring—**store-house** (or *store-chamber*), **nor barn,** with fruits and goods bestowed therein.—**And God feedeth them;** present supplies are never wanting.

25, 26. The argument in regard to support is confirmed by an appeal to common sense: **Which of you by taking thought,** etc.,—by any study or care, can prolong his life one day beyond the limit it would reach in the quiet, resigned, and cheerful endeavor to do God's will? We much prefer the marginal reading, "age" (term of life), to **stature,** in the text. It is much more commonly the meaning of the Greek, and better suited here to the train of thought, which all has reference to the prolonging of life by food and clothing.

Cн. XII.] LUKE. 217

26 If ye then be not able to do that thing which is least, why take ye thought for the rest?
27 Consider the lilies how they grow: they toil not, they spin not; and yet I say unto you, that Solomon in all his glory was not arrayed like one of these.
28 If then God so clothe the grass, which is to day in the field, and to-morrow is cast into the oven; how much more *will he clothe* you, O ye of little faith?
29 And seek not ye what ye shall eat, or what ye shall drink, neither be ye of doubtful mind.
30 For all these things do the nations of the world seek after: and your Father knoweth that ye have need of these things.
31 ª But rather seek ye the kingdom of God; and all these things shall be added unto you.

26 his life? If then ye are not able to do even that which is least, why are ye anxious concerning the
27 rest? Consider the lilies, how they grow: they toil not, neither do they spin; yet I say unto you, Even Solomon in all his glory was not arrayed like one of
28 these. But if God doth so clothe the grass in the field, which to-day is, and to-morrow is cast into the oven; how much more *shall he clothe* you, O ye of
29 little faith? And seek not ye what ye shall eat, and what ye shall drink, neither be ye of doubtful mind.
30 For all these things do the nations of the world seek after: but your Father knoweth that ye have need
31 of these things. Howbeit seek ye ¹his kingdom,

a Matt. 6. 33.——1 Many ancient authorities read, *the kingdom of God*.

Increased stature would contribute nothing to this. Who could expect, or at all desire, to add a foot and a half to his bodily height? But to lengthen by "a span," or **a cubit**, by the same kind of figure, one's age, or lifetime, many have desired, and worried themselves, to bring about. One near to death is reported to have said: "Millions of money for an *inch* of time!" It would seem no great thing to add to an age of thirty or of sixty years, another year, a half year, or a month; but to extend an ordinary stature by one half-yard could not well be called "that thing which is least."

27, 28. As the case of the ravens might reprove anxiety about food, so might the lilies about clothing. **They toil not, neither do they spin**—to provide for future needs; they take no thought for the morrow, but simply live as they were made to live. There is no good reason to doubt that the word translated **lilies** was used to denote some species of the flower which we so name. We cannot tell which species of the liliaceous blossoms found in Palestine is intended, some of them exceedingly gorgeous in colors, and some of exquisite fragrance. These flowers, without care on their part, but by the Creator, just because he desires them so, are clothed in beauty and splendor, such that even **Solomon, in all his glory, was not arrayed like one of these.**

28. If then—better, *but if*—**God** (*doth*) **so clothe the grass which is to-day in the field,** etc., the argument is still more impressive than that drawn from the birds. The lilies are treated as only a part **of the grass,** or coarse herbage, which, in the scarcity of other fuel, was often cut, and, being soon dried in the torrid sun, was used for culinary fuel, and especially for heating their ovens, or kilns. So the **lilies** had not even a sentient existence, like the **ravens**, but they were often of no use to any one, blooming **in the** field, away from view, and that only for a short time. And yet they were clothed with marvelous beauty, so long as God appointed them to flourish.—**O ye of little faith.** Did our Lord speak in pity or in anger? Perhaps in something of both. He probably saw them slow to accept the instruction which he was the more patiently trying to impress upon them; but he knew too well how hard it is to rise above our natural concern for the future welfare of our natural life, not to mingle sympathy with his displeasure.

29. And seek not ye what ye shall eat, etc. The Greek lays strong emphasis on *ye;* and do not ye, more than the ravens and the lilies seek. This closes up and condenses (comp. the "therefore" in Matthew) the whole series of directions.—**Neither be ye of doubtful mind,** is another way, in conclusion, of forbidding the taking thought, or being anxious about the means of continued life and comfort.—**Of doubtful mind;** "uncertain," "in troubled suspense," are familiar meanings of the Greek word, more suited to this connection than "elated," "high-minded," which Meyer and some others approve.

30. So important is the topic of the discourse, that our Lord cannot leave the statement just made, as the outcome of a train of reasoning, without an argument of its own.—**For all these things do the nations of the world seek after;** and the aspirations of his disciples should be directed toward other objects than those desired by common Gentiles.—**And** (or, *but*) **your Father knoweth that ye have need of these things;** and therefore you may unhesitatingly trust that he will supply them as you need. **Your** is emphatic; they (the Gentiles) have none such, and try to make themselves their Providence.

31. But rather, (*howbeit*), although it is unnecessary and wrong for you to make those things an object of concern;—**seek ye the**

32 Fear not, little flock; for *it is your Father's good pleasure to give you the kingdom.
33 *Sell that ye have, and give alms; *provide yourself bags which wax not old, a treasure in the heavens that faileth not, where no thief approacheth, neither moth corrupteth.
34 For where your treasure is, there will your heart be also.
35 *Let your loins be girded about, and *your lights burning;

32 and these things shall be added unto you. Fear not, little flock; for it is your Father's good pleasure
33 to give you the kingdom. Sell that ye have, and give alms; make for yourselves purses which wax not old, a treasure in the heavens that faileth not, where no thief draweth near, neither moth destroyeth.
34 For where your treasure is, there will your heart be also,
35 Let your loins be girded about, and your lamps

a Matt. 11 : 25, 26....b Matt. 19 : 21; Acts 2. 45; 4 : 34.....c Matt 6 : 20; ch. 16 : 9; 1 Tim. 6 : 19.....d Eph. 6 : 14; 1 Pet. 1 : 13....e Matt. 25 : 1, etc.

kingdom of God; (rather, *his kingdom*); let your supreme and constant labor be to share in and promote that.—**And all these things**—which pertain to the support of the natural life—**shall be added unto you;**—that is, ye shall have them besides the essential, spiritual, and eternal blessing of membership in the kingdom of God. In seeking that we seek all.

32. Fear not, little flock. The Saviour evidently saw that it was very hard for his disciples to receive, with hearty trust, the consoling but unworldly doctrine which he preached. He states it accordingly in a still more assuring form, grounding their hope wholly on the eternal love of God.—**It is your Father's good pleasure** (*your Father was well pleased*) **to give you the kingdom.** That God was their Father, and that in the electing purpose, according to which they became disciples, he eternally designed to **give** them part in the finished kingdom—what could more effectually relieve them of anxiety, and enable them to concentrate attention on their work?

33. Sell that ye have, and give alms. Instead of thought about what you are to get, rid yourselves of what you have of those things that distract your minds. By giving them as alms, they become not only no incumbrance, but a positive source of divine favor and eternal fruition.—**Provide**—(*make for*) **yourselves bags**—*purses*), etc. For heavenly riches one needs imperishable receptacles, that is, figuratively, that they should be laid up with God; and **a treasure in the heavens that faileth not,** etc. This treasure can be nothing other than the gospel righteousness, following upon faith in Christ; but which, while it is a present possession of the believer, is increased by all labors and sacrifices, for the Lord's sake, especially by kindness and charity to those in need. It is here spoken of as the assured material of future blessedness, and so laid up in heaven. (See on ver. 31, last clause.) This is the only unfailing treasure. "What I gave away I keep," said a pious bankrupt; "and what I kept I have lost." The principle applies to all sacrifices of self-gratification for Christ and his cause.

34. For where your treasure is, there will your heart be also. The maxim emits light for every soul, and gives a powerful motive for turning all possessions into a heavenly lodestone to our hearts. Its truth is self-evident, that where our treasure, the chief matter of interest to us, is, there our thoughts and affections, our hearts, will centre.

REMARK.—Three things are to be considered on the foregoing teaching, in its general tenor, and, particularly, in the directions of ver. 22, 29, 33:

1. That our Lord addresses his disciples with special reference to their then existing circumstances and duties. They were professedly consecrated, without any reserve, to the furtherance of his kingdom. The advancement of it was their whole aim. If any disciples are differently situated toward him and his work, a corresponding modification of his precepts and promises might be required in their case.

2. What he assures them of, temporally, is a present sustenance so long as God would have them continue in his service. Has this ever failed any? Further expectations were not warranted by his words.

3. Such instruction would make a different impression on men living in a dark and troublous time, and with a bright confidence that the glories of the future recompense were very soon to be realized, from that which we generally receive in a time of settled prosperity, where the blessed appearing of our Lord and Saviour recedes further from our thought in proportion as it draws actually nearer.

35–40. WATCHFULNESS FOR THE LORD'S RETURN.

35. Let your loins be girded about, etc.

36 And ye yourselves like unto men that wait for their lord, when he will return from the wedding; that when he cometh and knocketh, they may open unto him immediately.
37 ᵃ Blessed *are* those servants, whom the lord when he cometh shall find watching: verily I say unto you, that he shall gird himself, and make them to sit down to meat, and will come forth and serve them.
38 And if he shall come in the second watch, or come in the third watch, and find *them* so, blessed are those servants.
39 ᵇ And this know, that if the goodman of the house had known what hour the thief would come, he would have watched, and not have suffered his house to be broken through.
40 ᶜ Be ye therefore ready also: for the Son of man cometh at an hour when ye think not.

35 burning; and be ye yourselves like unto men looking for their lord, when he shall return from the marriage feast; that, when he cometh and knocketh,
37 they may straightway open unto him. Blessed are those ¹servants, whom the lord when he cometh shall find watching: verily I say unto you, that he shall gird himself, and make them sit down to meat,
38 and shall come and serve them. And if he shall come in the second watch, and if in the third, and
39 find *them* so, blessed are those *servants*. ²But know this, that if the master of the house had known in what hour the thief was coming, he would have watched, and not have left his house to be ³broken
40 through. Be ye also ready: for in an hour that ye think not the Son of man cometh.

a Matt. 24: 46....*b* Matt. 24: 43; 1 Thess. 5: 2; 2 Pet. 3: 10; Rev. 3: 3; 16:15....*c* Matt. 24: 44; 25: 13; Mark 13: 33; ch. 21: 34, 36; 1 Thess. 5: 6; 2 Pet. 3: 12.——1 Gr. *bondservants*....2 Gr. *But this ye know*....3 Gr. *digged through*.

The heavenly treasure will become fully ours at the return of the Son of man, in the fully manifested glory of his reign. The figure which he here uses was finely suited to express a state of readiness for activity and efficient service, when the outer garment was a loose, shawl-like robe, which must be confined about the waist whenever exertion and free movement were required.—**And your lights** (*lamps*) **burning**. As Jesus is about to represent, in a figure, his future advent as occurring in the night, readiness to meet and serve him is denoted by having the lamps burning.

36. And ye yourselves like unto men that wait for their lord. The disciples are conceived of as, after Christ's departure from the world, in the case of servants sitting up for their master's return from a late banquet, in order that, at his coming, they may let him in without delay, with due ceremony, and may render him all needed and appropriate service. (Comp. the parable of the Ten Virgins.) As a failure to be in readiness would bring reproach and disgrace on such servants, so vigilance and promptness would receive honor and praise. This latter idea is expressed in the next verse with a warmth which shows that the antitypical truth blends itself with the earthly figure.

37. Verily I say unto you, that he shall gird himself, etc. Surely it is not the thankfulness of any human master which speaks in this declaration; but it is the friendship which Christ will display to the faithful disciples whom he shall find awake and waiting through all the delay of his return.

38. And if he shall come in the second watch, or come (rather, *and if*) **in the third**, etc. The **watch** was a military division of the night, covering the hours occupied by each of the four relays of guards stationed from 6 P. M. to 6 A. M. Before the Roman rule, the Hebrews seem to have made but three periods, giving four hours to each. The first watch, ending at 9 P. M., is not named here, because, in a case like that supposed, the Lord could not be expected so early; but **the third** might come within the time of absence. Such intimations should, it would seem, have guarded the early Christians from the overconfident expectation of an immediate reappearance of the Master. Their teaching was, rather, that peculiarly blessed would those servants be who might have to wait, even into the morning hours of the night of his absence.

39. The Saviour employs another illustration, to show the necessity of perpetual readiness for his coming, which will steal on men "as a thief in the night." **And** (rather, *but*) lest ye should suppose it safe to lay aside vigilance for any one hour,—**this know**—give it due consideration; unless we prefer the alternative reading of the Revision: "but this ye know." **That if the good man** (*master*) **of the house had known what hour the thief would come**. For **would come** the Greek is *cometh*—"is wont to come," which, as the thief has no particular hour, cannot be known. Hence heedlessness at any moment is likely to be at the wrong moment; and proved so, in the case of the supposed householder who went to sleep and was robbed. **The good man** is not any definite, known one, but the one who stands for the whole class of careless, plundered people. The lesson of the implied parable is that, as the precise time of Christ's advent cannot be known, unremitting vigilance and perpetual preparation are required.

40. That lesson is explicitly and solemnly stated.

41 Then Peter said unto him, Lord, speakest thou this parable unto us, or even to all?
42 And the Lord said,*a* Who then is that faithful and wise steward, whom *his* lord shall make ruler over his household, to give *them their* portion of meat in due season?
43 Blessed *is* that servant, whom his lord when he cometh shall find so doing.
44 *b* Of a truth I say unto you, that he will make him ruler over all that he hath.
45 *c* But and if that servant say in his heart, My lord delayeth his coming; and shall begin to beat the menservants and maidens, and to eat and drink, and to be drunken;

41 And Peter said, Lord, speakest thou this parable unto us, or even unto all? And the Lord said, Who then is ¹ the faithful and wise steward, whom his lord shall set over his household, to give them 43 their portion of food in due season? Blessed is that servant, whom his lord when he cometh shall find 44 so doing. Of a truth I say unto you, that he will set 45 him over all that he hath. But if that ²servant shall say in his heart, My lord delayeth his coming; and shall begin to beat the menservants and the maidservants, and to eat and drink, and to be

a Matt. 24 : 45 ; 25 : 21 ; 1 Cor. 4 : 2....*b* Matt. 24 : 47....*c* Matt. 24 : 48.——1 Or, *the faithful steward, the wise* man *whom, etc*....2 Gr. *bondservant.*

41–48. SPECIAL APPLICATION OF THESE TRUTHS TO THE APOSTLES.

41. Speakest thou this parable unto us, or even to all? The parable was probably that which was spoken (ver. 35-38), rather than the half-expressed comparison in ver. 39. Considering that Jesus had been long speaking, sometimes to Pharisees, to lawyers, to the multitude, to his disciples, Peter might naturally be at a loss whether this portion of it was addressed specially to all actual or possible disciples, or to the doubly chosen twelve. The question may have expressed some curiosity—not without a shade of assumption—whether the apostles would really be distinguished, "in the regeneration" (Matt. 19:28), above the mass of believers, according to ver. 37.

42. Who, then, is that faithful and wise steward, etc. The Greek is nearly as in the margin of Revision: the faithful steward, the prudent [one]. The Saviour answers not directly, but by a return question sets Peter and all to consider what was becoming to his servants of apostolic rank; and especially to one to whom, as to Peter, a certain pre-eminence, even in this office, had been already assigned.—The **steward** is not exactly one of the servants of the former parable, brought forward again, but stands for a servant of Jesus, in a different, a more specific, relation. His master is here supposed to be absent for a prolonged stay, and to be testing certain servants, by placing them in charge over fellow-servants during this period; that, on his return, he may be able to give all his affairs into the hands of the one who has proved himself worthy. The question, therefore, says, in effect, to Peter: Instead of asking whether that parable is spoken to you, as you must know that in some sense it is, ask yourselves, rather, what qualities each of you apostles should exhibit, in his position as a steward over my household; and especially thou, Peter, in order to meet with honor at my return. **Household,** here, is the body of domestic servants (Latin, *familia*), sometimes very numerous, constituting the service of a great proprietor at that time.—**Portion of meat** (*food,* rations).—**In due season,** that is, for the day, on the day ; for the week, in the week, etc. To do this punctually and well required the steward to be **faithful,** and the faithfulness supposes prudence. He must be **wise** to see what is needed, and to have ready in supply the requirement for constantly recurring needs, and dispense everything so equitably that all concerned shall be satisfied, and the work of the place go forward efficiently.

43. If the servants before described were happy and honored because of merely watching and readiness, a higher reward would seem appropriate to this one who shall be found **so doing;** that is, prudently and faithfully administering the important business entrusted to him. The Saviour thus answers the question of the preceding verse, by showing what character that steward will evince.

44. His reward will be great according to his fidelity and proved efficiency. He will be promoted to a higher charge: **He will make him ruler** (Greek, *set,* or establish, *him*) **over all that he hath.** The talent which he has manifested and cultivated shall have scope for its eternal exercise in a nobler, happier sphere. The principle of recompense is like that, "Be thou ruler over ten cities," only still more free.

45. But if (omit **and**) **that servant shall say in his heart,** etc. The disgrace and punishment of the servant who, in his place as a steward, is neither faithful nor wise, will be as conspicuous and miserable as the reward of the other is blessed and glorious. **My lord delayeth his coming,** so that I can take time

45 The lord of that servant will come in a day when he looketh not for *him*, and at an hour when he is not aware, and will *ᵃcut him in sunder, and will appoint him his portion with the unbelievers.
46 And ᵇ that servant, which knew his lord's will, and prepared not *himself*, neither did according to his will, shall be beaten with many *stripes*.
48 ᶜ But he that knew not, and did commit things worthy of stripes, shall be beaten with few *stripes*. For unto whomsoever much is given, of him shall be much required; and to whom men have committed much, of him they will ask the more.

46 drunken; the lord of that ¹ servant shall come in a day when he expecteth not, and in an hour when he knoweth not, and shall cut him ²asunder, and 47 appoint his portion with the unfaithful. And that ¹ servant, who knew his lord s will, and made not ready, nor did according to his will, shall be beaten 48 with many *stripes*; but he that knew not, and did things worthy of stripes, shall be beaten with few *stripes*. And to whomsoever much is given, of him shall much be required: and to whom they commit much, of him will they ask more.

a Matt. 24: 51.....b Num. 15: 30; Deut. 25: 2; John 9: 41; 15: 22; Acts 17: 30; James 4: 17.....c Lev. 5: 17; 1 Tim. 1: 13.——1 Gr. bond-servant....2 Or, *severely scourge him*.

for mischief and pleasure. It contains another intimation that Jesus *may* tarry long—so long that his apostle, or other minister, may forget that he is himself only a steward, and act as if he were master of the place.—**And shall begin to beat the men-servants,** etc. In the decline of faith through long waiting, the natural passions may re-assert themselves; self-indulgence, intemperance, and tyranny may take the place of self-denial and Christ-like love. In the sphere of the ministry, from the Pope down to the lowest grade of a men-made hierarchy of every communion, such degeneracy has been so often witnessed as to prove a divine prevision in the warning which Christ left on record. Church history shows that what is here spoken of as a hypothetical possibility, became, and has continued, a familiar reality, and imparts a sad significance to the threat of penalty in the next verse.

46. For, however he may have concluded otherwise, **the lord of that servant will come;** he will come, in effect, by death, in a thousand cases; to some, at last, in his glorified person.—**In a day when he looketh not for**—(*expecteth not*) etc.—the terrible surprise!—**And will cut him asunder.** Such treatment of the guilty steward would be according to the severe and barbarous modes of inflicting the death penalty in ancient times (1 Sam. 15: 33; 2 Sam. 12: 31; Dan. 2: 5; and ample proofs relating to other nations in Wetstein on Matt. 24: 51). Nor is it inconsistent with this view, that the threatening adds: **And will appoint him his place with the unbelievers**—("the hypocrites" Matt. 24: 53). We have only to suppose that the thought passes from the figure to the reality, leaving the parable, or hovering between it and its religious signification, joining to the sentence of bloody death that of the banishment of the deathless soul from God and heaven. The rendering of "severely scourge," in the margin of Revision, has been adopted by many authorities, including Grimm (*Clavis*, under the word διχοτομέω), and is sufficiently warranted by Greek usage to be accepted, if we were constrained to take what follows as relating to temporal punishment; but we are not.

47. And that servant which knew his lord's will and prepared not—(omit *himself*), — *made not ready,* that is, for his lord's due reception at his return—**neither did according to his will**—in the general administration of his office—**shall be beaten with many stripes,** etc. A statement of the general principles of divine punishment. Its severity will vary according to the measure of light against which sin has been committed.

48. But he that knew not. The preterit tense in both sentences looks back from the day of judgment. Of whatsoever servant of Christ it shall then appear that he knew not, during his term of service, his Master's will; that is to say, in his specific requirements and prohibitions, and who cannot, therefore, have sinned against full light; but who, nevertheless, **did things worthy of stripes,** as being in violation of the essential principles of service, suggested by reason and conscience, he **shall be beaten with few stripes.** His punishment will be correspondingly light.—**For**—*and*—to state the principle in the most general way—**unto whomsoever much is** (*was*) **given, of him shall be much required.**—*Was given,* during his period of earthly discipleship.—Much of opportunity, ability, knowledge, to further the cause of the Master, by increasing the welfare of men.—**And to whom men** (more vaguely, *they*) **have committed** (they *committed*) **much, of him they will ask the more;** more, namely, than of him who had not the same powers and means. It may signify, also, "more than he would otherwise have been expected to return."—**They indi-**

49 ᵃ I am come to send fire on the earth; and what will I, if it be already kindled?
50 But ᵇ I have a baptism to be baptized with; and how am I straitened till it be accomplished!
51 ᶜSuppose ye that I am come to give peace on earth? I tell you, Nay; ᵈbut rather division:
52 ᵉFor from henceforth there shall be five in one house divided, three against two, and two against three.
53 The father shall be divided against the son, and the son against the father; the mother against the daughter, and the daughter against the mother; the mother in law against her daughter in law, and the daughter in law against her mother in law.

49 I came to cast fire upon the earth; and ¹ what do I
50 desire, if it is already kindled? But I have a baptism to be baptized with; and how am I straitened
51 till it be accomplished! Think ye that I am come to give peace in the earth? I tell you, Nay; but
52 rather division: for there shall be from henceforth five in one house divided, three against two, and
53 two against three. They shall be divided, father against son, and son against father; mother against daughter, and daughter against her mother; mother in law against her daughter in law, and daughter in law against her mother in law.

a ver. 51....b Matt. 20: 22; Mark 10: 38....c Matt. 10: 34; ver. 49....d Mic. 7: 6; John 7: 43; 9: 16; 10: 19....e Matt. 10: 35.——1 Or, *how I would that it were already kindled!*

cates the persons concerned indefinitely, consistently with the idea of a general maxim, while in reality it is Christ's own agency which has commissioned and reclaims.

49-53. Trials to be Endured by Christ and his Followers.

49. I am come (exactly, *came*) **to send fire on the earth.** The painful thought is forced on the mind of Christ, by a foresight of the trials and troubles which were to be encountered by his disciples in exercising that fidelity which he had just enjoined.—**Fire** is an emblem of that excitement of minds, for and against, which the operation of his truth will of necessity cause. As this was foreseen in the counsels of redemption to be a necessary incident to the realizing of its glorious results, it might be said that to bring it to pass had been a design of his coming from heaven to earth.—**And what will I, if it be already kindled?** The translation should rather be: *And how I wish it were already kindled!* The warrant for this may be found in Meyer's note on the passage, and in Grimm's *Clavis* (under τίς, 1. e. γ; δ, I. 4). The reason for this wish lay in the foreseen necessity of the sufferings on his part which must intervene, and which he would fain have already endured. The fire could not fully blaze until the "offence of the cross" to a hostile world was added to its agony to himself. Not till then would the pains of Gethsemane and Calvary be over.

50. But—it is now quite otherwise—**I have a baptism to be baptized with**—an experience of sufferings to be endured, comparable to nothing so well as to immersion in a flood of distress. "A baptism to be baptized with" is a solecism of English speech, which nothing but unreflecting familiarity could have made tolerable to our ears. The Greek idiom would easily allow a construction nearly equivalent; but the sense is, in English, "an immersion to undergo." To be immersed, overwhelmed, in business, pleasure, cares, trouble, sufferings, is a figure of rhetoric very familiar to us; how familiar it was to the Greek may be seen from the numerous examples in Conant's *Baptizein, its Meaning and Use* (pp. 43–67).— **And how am I straitened until it be accomplished!** Paul could afterward speak of being in a strait between his desire to be more immediately with Christ, and his conviction of the importance of his remaining longer in the work on earth. So here, Christ feels himself greatly **straitened** (the verb is the same as Paul used). The pains of death already, in anticipation, "got hold upon" him, and the prospect was dreadful to the Son of man. But, on the other hand, it was his Father's will, and equally his own, that he should thus suffer, and for that hour had he come into the world. How inevitable that he should be sore pressed by these conflicting considerations, until the end had come.

51. Suppose (*think*) **ye that I am come to give peace on the earth?** Are ye so mistaken as to think that all will be quietness and harmony among men, as the result of my mission? Yet the end was to be peace (1: 79; 2: 14). —**Nay; but rather division.** The **rather** is better left out. (Comp. Matt. 10: 34, "but a sword.") The Greek (ἀλλ ἤ) emphasizes **division** as the result of Christ's coming; so much more conspicuously prominent now, in view of the intense opposition which is ready to put him to death, and will mark the path of the early gospel with the blood of his saints. **Division** alone is what he proceeds to speak of.

52. Henceforth—from the date of his resurrection, which is just at hand—**there shall be five in one house divided.** This was the saddest aspect of the separating power of his truth, the breaking up of the concord of fami-

[Cн. XII.] LUKE. 223

51 And he said also to the people, "When ye see a cloud rise out of the west, straightway ye say, There cometh a shower; and so it is.
52 And when ye see the south wind blow, ye say, There will be heat; and it cometh to pass.
56 Ye hypocrites, ye can discern the face of the sky and of the earth; but how is it that ye do not discern this time?
57 Yea, and why even of yourselves judge ye not what is right?
58 ᵇWhen thou goest with thine adversary to the magistrate, ᶜas thou art in the way, give diligence that thou mayest be delivered from him; lest he hale thee to the judge, and the judge deliver thee to the officer, and the officer cast thee into prison.

54 And he said to the multitudes also, When ye see a cloud rising in the west, straightway ye say, There cometh a shower; and so it cometh to pass. And when ye see a south wind blowing, ye say, There will be a ¹scorching heat; and it cometh to pass.
56 Ye hypocrites, ye know how to ²interpret the face of the earth and the heaven; but how is it that ye know not how to ²interpret this time? And why
58 even of yourselves judge ye not what is right? For as thou art going with thine adversary before the magistrate, on the way give diligence to be quit of him; lest haply he drag thee unto the judge, and the judge shall deliver thee to the ³officer, and the

a Matt. 16:2....b Prov. 25:8; Matt. 5:35....c See Ps. 32:6; Isa. 55:6.——1 Or. hot wind....2 Gr. prove....3 Gr. exactor.

lies. Herein is foreseen the *whole* long, sad, even bloody, story of social and civil persecution, dissension, and strife, arising from the propagation of the gospel. In some families, they would stand fewer, two on his side, opposed by three hating them; in others, the proportions would be reversed; but discord, wherever there was partial or diverse reception of his truth.

53. The statement is made more pathetic by specification: the believing **son** will be persecuted by his worldly **father**; the **daughter**, likewise, by her **mother**; in other cases, these positions of the parties will be inverted; and so through all the tender relations of life. For ages after Christ, this prediction was a literal description of facts; and not a year has elapsed, until now, in which it did not apply to certain instances of hatred on the part of relatives toward followers of Christ. Yet, while he is the occasion of all this, it is not his spirit which hates and contends, but which rather suffers hatred and opposition, for his name's sake, at the hands of those otherwise nearest and dearest. This very dissension involves necessarily a condemnation of all who rage against the Lord, and against his Christ.

54–59. BLINDNESS OF THE PEOPLE GENERALLY TO THE APPROACH OF SUCH A CONDEMNATION.

The long address to his disciples is ended.

54, 55. **And he said also to the people** (*multitudes*), **When ye see a cloud rise out of**—properly, *rising in*—**the west,** etc. They were quick to note the indications of coming weather, and to interpret them, so as to regulate the conduct prudently. The great Mediterranean Sea lay to the west of them; hence, a cloud rising in that quarter would be charged with moisture, and might well bring rain.—**The south wind** reaches Palestine from over the torrid wilderness of Arabia; and when it continues for a time, it becomes a **heat** (a *scorching heat*), the baleful "simoom" of those parts, dreaded by man and beast.

56. **Ye hypocrites.** The charge of hypocrisy rested on their willing blindness, in the religious sphere, to tokens more plain from revelation than these signs which their own reason had collected from the phases of nature. Doubtless, the teachers and leaders were principally intended; but "the doctrine of the Pharisees, which is hypocrisy," had more or less influenced the mass.—**Ye can discern**—scrutinize, so as to form a correct judgment about—**the face of the sky and of the earth** (*or, the earth and the heavens*), a skill which they were bound in consistency to exercise in more important matters.—**How is it that ye do not discern this time** (*season*), namely, that in which Christ's presence with them—having been preceded by John, and fulfilling the ancient prophecies by his teaching and his works—proved that now was the crisis of the nation's destiny. This they might have seen if they would.

57–59. THE SELF-EVIDENT NEED OF REPENTANCE AND PREPARATION FOR THE JUDGMENT.

57. **And why even of yourselves judge ye not what is right?** Had they duly considered what a sign Jesus was, they would have found in him a mighty motive and aid to repentance and peace with God. And even though they shut their eyes to this, why do they not, from the teaching of Scripture, as it is open to all; from reflection on past sins and God's forbearance to them personally, as well as from the indications of an approaching visitation on the people, repent and turn to God in obedience and love?

58. **When thou goest** (rather, *For as thou art going*—since such is already the fact) **with**

59 I tell thee, thou shalt not depart thence, till thou hast paid the very last ᵃ mite.

59 ¹ officer shall cast thee into prison. I say unto thee, Thou shalt by no means come out thence, till thou have paid the very last mite.

CHAPTER XIII.

THERE were present at that season some that told him of the Galilæans, whose blood Pilate had mingled with their sacrifices.

1 Now there were some present at that very season who told him of the Galilæans, whose blood Pilate

a See Mark 12: 42.——1 Gr. *exactor*.

---

thine adversary to the magistrate. The **magistrate** can be none other than God, who must also, perhaps as represented by Christ, be the **adversary**. The illustration is introduced to enforce the obligation on their part to become reconciled with God in "this time." Ver. 56, to judge and do what is right. Ver. 57. According to the supposition of the parable, the creditor had the right to seize his delinquent debtor where he might find him, take him before a magistrate, and, on proving his case, have him condemned to imprisonment, until the claim was satisfied. The details of the application may be variously filled out; but the lesson is perfectly obvious. —**Art in the way**—before thou hast reached the bar of God, the supreme **magistrate**— before whom thou must appear—**give diligence that thou mayest be delivered from him;** *be quit of him* (Revision). This may be effected with our adversary, God, by humble, penitent acknowledgment of "our debts," and the plea for forgiveness, according to the gospel (Matt. 6: 12; Luke 18: 13. 14).—**Lest he** —wearied with "thy hardness and impenitent heart," close the door of conciliation—**and hale thee unto the judge.** He who might have been a magistrate to pacify, is now only a *judge* to condemn.—**And the judge deliver thee to the officer,** etc. The **officer**—exactor—is in effect the bailiff, or constable, who will see that the sentence is duly carried into effect. The prison is Gehenna, hell, to which the verdict of the last day will consign those careless sinners who have trifled away their day of visitation.

59. I tell thee, thou shalt not (*shalt by no means*) **depart thence till thou hast** (*have*) **paid the very last mite.** The mite was the smallest coin then in use, probably one-half the value of the "farthing" (ver. 6). The Saviour's discourse, starting with the case of the Jews threatened with national destruction, through their rejection of him, has turned into a most solemn declaration of the remediless ruin which hangs over every one living unreconciled to God. If the language in this verse does not absolutely preclude the idea of a payment of the debt in prison by one who was unable and unwilling while the chance was afforded him, yet, when we think that the debt to God consists of sins, to be cancelled and undone, we feel that under the figure employed, the impossibility of payment could not be more impressively set forth.

1-5. THE NECESSITY OF REPENTANCE ENFORCED BY OCCURRENCES OF THE DAY.

1. (*Now*) **there were present at that** (*very*) **season some that told him,** etc. They were probably visitors from Jerusalem, who reported, as a matter of news, without any particular feeling on the subject, an incident of recent occurrence there. The time was just as he had completed the long series of discourses running through chapters XI and XII, and while he was yet in the place where he had given the instruction concerning prayer, 11: 1 ff, in the same place, as well as **at that** *very* **season.** McClellan (*New Testament*, p. 552), who teems with novelties of harmonization, and can hardly allow any event of the Gospels to fail of assignment to its precise day and hour, here, on the ground that Luke does not say "at that same *hour*," but "*season*," will see no reference at all to the preceding chapter, but whirls our passage back to a *passover season*, at the time of Luke 5: 16, 17, and of the interval between John 4: 54 and 5: 1. The event narrated is not mentioned elsewhere; but we see that Pilate, the Roman Procurator, had visited upon certain Galileans, guilty of we know not what crime, a bloody slaughter. There is no indication that they were supposed to have been heinously criminal; but a circumstance of their punishment which peculiarly impressed the Jewish imagination was, that in the temple courts they were actually engaged in offering sacrifices at the moment when they were cut down, so that their blood, sprinkling the parts of the victim, could be said to have been **mingled with their sacrifices.** The

2 And Jesus answering said unto them, Suppose ye that these Galileans were sinners above all the Galileans, because they suffered such things?
3 I tell you, Nay: but, except ye repent, ye shall all likewise perish.
4 Or those eighteen, upon whom the tower in Siloam fell, and slew them, think ye that they were *a* sinners above all men that dwelt in Jerusalem?
5 I tell you, Nay: but, except ye repent, ye shall all likewise perish.
6 He spake also this parable; *b* A certain man had a fig tree planted in his vineyard; and he came and sought fruit thereon, and found none.
7 Then said he unto the dresser of his vineyard, Behold, these three years I come seeking fruit on this fig tree, and find none: cut it down; why cumbereth it the ground?

2 had mingled with their sacrifices. And he answered and said unto them, Think ye that these Galileans were sinners above all the Galileans, because they 3 have suffered these things? I tell you, Nay: but, except ye repent, ye shall all in like manner perish.
4 Or those eighteen, upon whom the tower in Siloam fell, and killed them, think ye that they were 1 offenders above all the men that dwell in Jerusalem?
5 I tell you, Nay: but, except ye repent, ye shall all likewise perish.
6 And he spake this parable: A certain man had a fig tree planted in his vineyard; and he came seek-7 ing fruit thereon, and found none. And he said unto the vinedresser, Behold, these three years I come seeking fruit on this fig tree, and find none: cut it down; why doth it also cumber the ground?

a Matt. 18: 24; ch. 11: 4....*b* Isa. 5: 2; Matt. 21: 19.—1 Gr. *debtors.*

Galileans were particularly fierce, turbulent, and intractable, and gave the Roman authorities a large proportion of their trouble in governing the nation.

2. Our Lord's answer shows how ready he was to turn an item of current news into a lesson of duty toward his kingdom. **Suppose ye that these Galileans were sinners above all the Galileans, because they** (*have*) **suffered such** (*these*) **things?** The verb **were** represents the Greek verb "to become," "prove oneself," "turn out to be"; so that the question seems to refer to the opinion betrayed in John 9: 2: Did they prove themselves great sinners by the fact that they have suffered these things?

3. Except ye repent, ye shall all likewise (*i. e., in like manner*) **perish. Likewise** might mean no more than "also." This might be intended specially for the Galilean portion of the crowd which accompanied him. They were noted for their turbulence and fractiousness in the State. *In like manner* does not probably point to the identical method of punishment, although it has often been noted how literally multitudes of the nation, including some, it may be, to whom Christ was speaking, perished in the same way, at the destruction of Jerusalem. It is enough that being also sinners, they were to perish as those sinners had; as surely, as dreadfully, as irremediably. The expression, **ye shall all . . perish,** as truly indicates Christ's judgment that all men are sinners as would any explicit and dogmatic statement to that effect.

4. Or—to take another similar case—**those eighteen,** etc. Another fact, outside of all other historical record. **Siloam** was a pool, south of Jerusalem, fed by the fountain Siloah. Whether **the tower** was an independent structure, or one connected with the wall of the city, and as to anything definite about it, we are without information. Its fall, from whatever cause, had, at some previous time, caused the death of eighteen persons, and may have also led to the opinion that those persons were specially guilty before God—**sinners** (Greek, *debtors*) **above all** (*the*) **men that dwell in Jerusalem.**

5. The denial is the same in regard to them as in regard to the Galileans; and the truth which is thus declared in relation to the two extremities of the country, all in Galilee and all in Jerusalem, may surely apply to all men everywhere. Repentance is essential to salvation.

6-9. THE JEWISH NATION A BARREN FIG TREE.

6. And he spake this parable—following up, and bringing to a close, this long line of various discourse. The lack of any appearance in the nation of that repentance which he had just declared necessary, may have guided to this admonition. **A certain man had a fig tree planted in his vineyard,** etc. Spare ground in the vineyard would, from the preparation which it had received, furnish the most desirable site for other fruit trees also. The fruit of the fig tree was very highly esteemed in the pomology of the Hebrews, and was thus a suitable symbol of the chosen people of God (Jer. 24: 3; Hos. 9: 10; Matt. 21: 19). Placed in a situation most favorable for the growth of moral excellence, they should have yielded fruit in lives of piety and obedience.

7. But such fruit God had **come seeking** again and again, **and found none.** This condenses the history of that people from the days of the Judges. **The three years** are not to be understood literally, but represent gen-

8 And he answering said unto him, Lord, let it alone this year also, till I shall dig about it, and dung it:
9 And if it bear fruit, *well:* and if not, *then* after that thou shalt cut it down.
10 And he was teaching in one of the synagogues on the sabbath.
11 And, behold, there was a woman which had a spirit of infirmity eighteen years, and was bowed together, and could in no wise lift up *herself.*

8 And he answering saith unto him, Lord, let it alone this year also, till I shall dig about it, and dung it:
9 and if it bear fruit thenceforth, *well;* but if not, thou shalt cut it down.
10 And he was teaching in one of the synagogues on 11 the sabbath day. And behold, a woman who had a spirit of infirmity eighteen years; and she was bowed together, and could in no wise lift herself up.

erally the period (being itself a long period to wait for figs on a mature tree) through which God had looked in vain for repentance and holiness.—**Cut it down.** The Greek form of the verb implies instant urgency. It would have the excision done at one stroke.—**Why cumbereth it the ground?** Better as the Revision. **Cumbereth,** as now used, hardly conveys the sense so well as "render useless," "sterilize." (Farrar). While it yields no fruit, it occupies ground which might be profitably taken for something else. **The dresser of the vineyard** stands for Jesus Christ.

8. He, with the natural tenderness of a man for a tree on which he has lavished long care, pleads for a short delay—**this year also**—covering the forty years before the destruction of Jerusalem, that he may try still further expedients, the last resources of his art, to bring it to fruitfulness.

9. And if it bear fruit (*henceforth=for the future*), though it has been barren in the past. The difference between the two versions here depends on a transposition of "after that," in the Common Version, to the previous member as "henceforth," according to both the proper meaning of the Greek, and to the order of the most approved MSS. The possibility, not to say likelihood, that it still will not bear, chokes the gardener's utterance. The sentence remains unfinished by the rhetorical figure called *aposiopesis;* **well** is put in by the translators to weaken and complete it. What could more touchingly indicate the yearning tenderness with which our great High Priest, in heaven, intercedes with his Father for the salvation of those in whose behalf he died? **And if not, then after that** (omit **then after that**) **thou shalt cut it down;** let thy command (ver. 7) be executed. The vine-dresser does not say, "I will cut it down," but consents that it shall be done. "He will cease to remonstrate."—Bengel.

In this parable, the vineyard is the goodly land, with its civil and religious institutions, originally assigned to Israel. The fig tree is the chosen and favored people. The vine-dresser is Jesus Christ. The failure to produce fruit, as sought, is the obstinate rejection of God's ways by that people, their worldliness, hypocrisy, and unbelief. The cumbering the ground is their standing in the way of its occupancy by men more willing and able to render acceptable service to God. The cutting down is the approaching destruction of the existing state and nation, delayed for **this year also,** that they might have full opportunity to repent and accept the Messiah; but which, it is intimated by the agitation of the gardener, will then have to come. But, like all the parables which were primarily adapted to the case of temporal Israel, this one also has its obvious applications to the case of any men who have failed to render to God just love and service.

10-17. A MIRACULOUS CURE ON THE SABBATH GIVES FRESH OCCASION FOR THE DISPLAY OF HYPOCRISY.

10-13. The miracle. The mention of some synagogue, not more definitely specified, is the first decisive hint of a change of scene, further than from the outside to the inside of a house, or *vice versa,* since the mention of "a certain place." (11: 1.)

10. On his journeys the Saviour still sought **the synagogues,** and turned to account the opportunities of **the Sabbath.** He was teaching here, in conformity with the practice seen in 4: 16.

11. A woman which had a spirit of infirmity eighteen years. We have before seen that demoniacs and persons otherwise diseased frequented the synagogues. They might sometimes seek there, not the contributions of the charitable, but the light and comfort of religious worship, in their habitual weakness and pain. This **spirit of infirmity** was probably conceived of as a demon, whose influence resulted in that peculiar feebleness under which she suffered. She was **bowed together**—"bent double," as it is often said. Whether her symptoms were those of palsy, or of chronic

[Ch. XIII.] LUKE. 227

12 And when Jesus saw her, he called *her to him*, and said unto her, Woman, thou art loosed from thine infirmity.
13 ᵃAnd he laid *his* hands on her: and immediately she was made straight, and glorified God.
14 And the ruler of the synagogue answered with indignation, because that Jesus had healed on the sabbath day, and said unto the people, ᵇThere are six days in which men ought to work: in them therefore come and be healed, and ᶜnot on the sabbath day.
15 The Lord then answered him, and said, Thou hypocrite, ᵈdoth not each one of you on the sabbath loose his ox or *his* ass from the stall, and lead *him* away to watering?
16 And ought not this woman, ᵉbeing a daughter of Abraham, whom Satan hath bound, lo these eighteen years, be loosed from this bond on the sabbath day?
17 And when he had said these things, all his adversaries were ashamed: and all the people rejoiced for all the glorious things that were done by him.

12 And when Jesus saw her, he called her, and said to her, Woman, thou art loosed from thine infirmity.
13 And he laid his hands upon her: and immediately she was made straight, and glorified God. And the ruler of the synagogue, being moved with indignation because Jesus had healed on the sabbath, answered and said to the multitude, There are six days in which men ought to work: in them therefore come and be healed, and not on the day of the
15 sabbath. But the Lord answered him, and said, Ye hypocrites, doth not each one of you on the sabbath loose his ox or his ass from the ˡstall, and lead him
16 away to watering? And ought not this woman, being a daughter of Abraham, whom Satan hath bound, lo, *these* eighteen years, to have been loosed
17 from this bond on the day of the sabbath? And as he said these things, all his adversaries were put to shame: and all the multitude rejoiced for all the glorious things that were done by him.

ᵃ Mark 16: 18; Acts 9. 17....ᵇ Ex. 20: 9....ᶜ Matt. 12: 10; Mark 3: 2; ch. 6: 7; 14: 3....ᵈ ch. 14: 5....ᵉ ch. 19: 9—l Gr. *manger*.

rheumatism, is uncertain. The severity of her malady is indicated by the words, **and could in nowise lift up herself**, or, "and could not lift herself up entirely," as Meyer and some prefer.

12. The sight of such misery appeals again irresistibly to the compassion of our Lord. It was itself a prayer.—**He called her to him**—as an expression of his friendliness—**and said unto her, Woman, thou art loosed from thine infirmity.** This form of expression was specially appropriate, when the trouble was as if she had been bound down with cords.

13. And he laid his hands on her. This gave to the unspiritual thought of the woman and of the rest an apprehensible medium through which the healing grace might appear to flow.—**And immediately she was made straight** (literally, *was straightened up*), a palpable proof that the Satanic bondage was broken; and, considering how long she had been held fast in it, a mighty token of the present power of God. **And glorified God**—rendered to him that praise and thanksgiving which so wonderful and beneficent a deed deserved.

14-17. The hypocrisy.

14. And the ruler of the synagogue (ch. 8: 41) **answered with indignation,** etc. We have seen before (ch. 6: 1-11) how Pharisaic legality had made a crime of healing sickness on the Sabbath. This ruler did not venture a direct reproof to Jesus, but, in a cowardly way, tried to scourge him over the backs of the people. The people were upbraided, because, forsooth, one of their number had listened to a word of mercy which relieved her of the distress of half a life-time. He professes

to honor Scripture.—**There are six days in which men ought to work.** True; but there had been no stroke of work; no one had even come to the place for the purpose of being bodily saved. A word spoken, the stretching out of a hand, a straightening of herself upon the part of the woman—that was all.

15. Well might the Lord say, **Thou hypocrite** (rather, *Ye hypocrites*), addressing the class of which this ruler was a specimen.—**Doth not each one of you on the sabbath loose his ox,** etc. These things they did, and it would have been wrong for them not to do them. But it made their hypocrisy appear all the more glaring. Did they say that mercy required them to prevent the suffering of dumb brutes?

15, 16. Hear the Saviour's answer: **Ought not this woman**—not merely a human being, but also **being a daughter of Abraham**—and thus appealing strongly to the pity of a ruler of a synagogue for the seed of Abraham—**whom Satan hath bound**—viz.: by his unclean spirit (v. 11), the abominable tyrant—**lo, these eighteen years**—not for one single day, as with the ox—**be loosed from this bond on the sabbath day?**

17. And when he had (better, *as he*) **said**—before he had finished—**these things, all his adversaries were ashamed** (or, *put to shame*). Well might they be; for their assumption of special piety had been shown hollow and insincere, due entirely to causeless malignity toward him.—**And all the people** (literally, *multitude*) **rejoiced,** etc. We can see that a large and increasing measure of popular favor attended the Lord as he drew nearer the end of this journey, and the end of

18 a Then said he, Unto what is the kingdom of God like? and whereunto shall I resemble it?
19 It is like a grain of mustard seed, which a man took, and cast into his garden; and it grew, and waxed a great tree; and the fowls of the air lodged in the branches of it.
20 And again he said, Whereunto shall I liken the kingdom of God?
21 It is like leaven, which a woman took and hid in three b measures of meal, till the whole was leavened.

18 He said therefore, Unto what is the kingdom of 19 God like? and whereunto shall I liken it? It is like unto a grain of mustard seed, which a man took, and cast into his own garden; and it grew, and became a tree; and the birds of the heaven lodged 20 in the branches thereof. And again he said, Where- 21 unto shall I liken the kingdom of God? It is like unto leaven, which a woman took and hid in three 1 measures of meal, till it was all leavened.

a Matt. 13 : 31 ; Mark 4 : 30....b See Matt. 13 : 33.——1 The word in the Greek denotes the Hebrew seah, a measure containing nearly a peck and a half.

his life. They saw, at least, that he was the friend of the common people; they were hopefully awaiting further developments concerning him, and *rejoiced* at this and **all the glorious things that were done by him**, not less heartily because of the discomfiture of their blind guides.

18-21. TWO PARABLES ILLUSTRATING THE GROWTH AND EXTENSION OF THE KINGDOM OF GOD.

They are given by Matthew and Mark, in a different connection. They were probably preserved as separate sayings in the treasure of apostolic memories of Christ, and were brought into our several Gospels in such relations as their respective sources suggested. We can hardly trace any link of thought between these parables and what precedes.

18. Unto what is the kingdom of God like? We behold the deliberation and rhetorical search of the mind of Jesus for that feature of the kingdom which would serve as a ground of classification, and afford a comparison suitable to the present aim of his discourse.—**And whereunto shall I resemble** (better, *liken*) **it?** This question would, of course, be answered with the other. We know beforehand that he is in pursuit of an image to represent the advancement of his truth, from its then merely germinal condition, to the possession and control of all men's minds in all the earth.

19. We seem to hear him say: I have it; **it is like a grain of mustard seed.** The smallness of this seed, "smaller than all the seeds" (Matt. 13 : 32), was well suited to symbolize the diminutive compass of his cause at the time. It comprised, so far as we are distinctly aware, himself and some hundred, more or less, who had so caught the true idea and spirit of his mission, that they might charitably be regarded as the germ of what it was to become.—**Which a man**—standing for God—**took and cast into his** (*own*) **garden** —meaning the Jewish Theocracy.—**And it grew, and waxed a great tree**, etc. The contrast between the mustard seed and the full grown herb is very striking, even with us; but in Palestine the expansion is much greater. Under favorable conditions it takes almost a shrubby character, becoming, in appearance, a small tree. Thomson (*Land and Book*), Tristram (*Nat. Hist. of the Bible*), and Hackett (Smith's *Dict. of Bib.*, p. 2043, and *Illustrations of Script.* 131 f.), speak of seeing the mustard plants growing to the height of the rider on his horse, and with branches strong enough to support birds, which actually **lodged** in them. There seems no need of the doubt and its solution, offered by Stanley (*Sinai and Pal.*, p. 419 n.) This lodging in the branches is not, necessarily, nesting there, but perching there at night, and at other times, when resting in the shade. This parable is a prophecy of the vast expansion, in point of numbers, which the little handful of his disciples then apparent would experience in the course of ages.

20. And again he said, Whereunto, etc. Thinking now of another aspect of the increase of the kingdom.

21. It is like leaven, which a woman took and hid in three measures of meal —where it operated—**till the whole was leavened.** Nothing could be better adapted than this homely figure to signify that holy contagion, by which the spiritual principle of a new life, once planted by God in the heart, spreads and grows, until all the faculties and affections are entirely pervaded by its influence, and brought into a meetness for heaven, according to the pattern of Christ. And not only so, but its power goes out into all kindred souls with which it comes in contact, contributing to their transformation, while it also receives helpful impulse from them. The process is described in Ephesians 4 : 11-16, the result being, that from Christ, the Head, "the whole body, fitly framed and knit together, through that which every joint supplieth,

22 ᵃ And he went through the cities and villages, teaching, and journeying toward Jerusalem.
23 Then said one unto him, Lord, are there few that be saved? And he said unto them,
24 ᵇ Strive to enter in at the strait gate: for ᶜ many, I say unto you, will seek to enter in, and shall not be able.
25 ᵈ When once the master of the house is risen up, and ᵉ hath shut to the door, and ye begin to stand without, and to knock at the door, saying, ᶠ Lord, Lord, open unto us; and he shall answer and say unto you, ᵍ I know you not whence ye are:

22 And he went on his way through cities and villages, teaching, and journeying on unto Jerusalem.
23 And one said unto him, Lord, are they few that are saved? And he said unto them, Strive to enter in by the narrow door: for many, I say unto you, shall seek to enter in, and shall not be ʰ able.
25 When once the master of the house is risen up, and hath shut to the door, and ye begin to stand without, and to knock at the door, saying, Lord, open to us; and he shall answer and say to you, I know you

a Matt. 9: 35; Mark 6: 6....*b* Matt. 7: 13....*c* See John 7. 34; 8: 21; 13: 33; Rom. 9: 31....*d* Ps. 32: 6; Isa. 55. 6 ...*e* Matt. 25: 10....*f* ch. 6: 46....*g* Matt. 7: 23; 25: 12.——1 Or, *able, when once.*

according to the working in due measure of each several part, maketh the increase of the body unto the building up of itself in love" (Revision). The self-propagating quality of leaven, or yeast, made it a fit symbol of the vital principle of Christianity, whose spontaneous diffusion through the whole being of the individual believer, and so, eventually, of all believers, was to be set forth. It is intrinsically as appropriate to denote the spread of a bad influence as of a good. Hence, Paul could use it as an image of sin, when viewed in reference to its contagiousness (1 Cor. 5: 6, 7). It was directed to be put away from the houses of the Jews during the seven days of the Passover every year, to commemorate the haste with which the fathers (Ex. 12: 34-39) forsook the land of bondage, with their dough unleavened in their baking-troughs. Leaven was not regarded by them as essentially bad. It was an element of their ordinary food, and was as much commanded, therefore, to be used and eaten on the Feast of Pentecost (Lev. 23: 17), as to be avoided during the Passover.

22-30. FURTHER INCIDENTS OF THIS SOLEMN JOURNEY.

22. And he went through the cities and villages (omit the before cities) **teaching, and journeying towards Jerusalem.** This statement brings afresh to the reader's mind that Jesus was still on his last journey to the holy city, and shows how careful he was to reach each town, and so to evangelize the whole region.

23. Then said one (*and one said*) **unto him, Lord, are there** (better, *they*) **few that be** (*are*) **saved?** It is as likely as not that this was the inquiry of a nominal disciple, whose zeal ran rather to unpractical and insoluble speculations about religion, than to the earnest exercise of faith and love. To such questions Jesus never returned categorical answer, but made them texts for useful lessons.—**And he said unto them.** Unto them, because he knew that the inquirer had been a spokesman for others, or simply because all might be profited by his reply. This is, in substance, that it was of no consequence about the number that were attaining to salvation, but of supreme importance that each man should make sure that he himself was saved.

24. Strive to enter in at the strait gate: (better, *through the narrow door*). Salvation, —the kingdom,—is conceived of as a house, now the scene of a banquet (ver. 29), which can be entered only through a *narrow* door.— Strive implies the necessity of strong exertion, such as was required to win a valuable prize from a powerful and practiced antagonist—carry through a successful contest. The narrowness of the portal signifies the necessity for humility, repentance, and self-denial; and implies that only the soul stripped bare of pride, and luxury, and worldly ambition, can pass through.—**For many, I say unto you, will seek to enter in.** Seek is the designation of a feeble effort, which, perhaps, looks rather for a broad door. Some desire and endeavor after heaven will be roused in the minds of a multitude who shall hear the gospel, but who will put forth no adequate endeavor.—**And shall not be able:** with so little of the spirit of faith and self-sacrifice. But the full significance of the future tense in these verbs must include the idea of a seeking which will prove ineffectual, because it comes in place of the striving, when even that would be too late. When, and how, is explained in the following verses.

25-27. When once the master of the house is risen up—from the sitting posture, in which he had waited until the return at night of the proper inmates—**and hath shut to the door**—for the security and rest of the night. The master of the house here is evidently the Lord Jesus in his ascended glory in

26 Then shall ye begin to say, We have eaten and drunk in thy presence, and thou hast taught in our streets.
27 ᵃBut he shall say, I tell you, I know you not whence ye are; ᵇdepart from me, all ye workers of iniquity.
28 ᶜThere shall be weeping and gnashing of teeth, ᵈwhen ye shall see Abraham, and Isaac, and Jacob, and all the prophets, in the kingdom of God, and you yourselves thrust out.
29 And they shall come from the east, and *from* the west, and from the north, and *from* the south, and shall sit down in the kingdom of God.
30 ᵉAnd, behold, there are last which shall be first, and there are first which shall be last.

26 not whence ye are; then shall ye begin to say, We did eat and drink in thy presence, and thou didst teach in our streets; and he shall say, I tell you, I know not whence ye are; depart from me, all ye workers of iniquity. There shall be the weeping and gnashing of teeth, when ye shall see Abraham, and Isaac, and Jacob, and all the prophets, in the kingdom of God, and yourselves cast forth without.
29 And they shall come from the east and west, and from the north and south, and shall ¹sit down in
30 the kingdom of God. And behold, there are last who shall be first, and there are first who shall be last.

a Matt. 7: 24; 25: 41; ver. 25....b Ps. 6: 8; Matt. 25: 41....c Matt. 8: 12; 13: 42; 24: 51....d Matt. 8: 11....e Matt. 19: 30; 20: 16; Mark 10: 31.—1 Gr. recline.

the heavenly mansion, to which he has admitted those (after the judgment) who had any claim to be recognized as his.—**And** (*when*) **ye begin to stand without**—after the door of heaven is closed upon all who did not strive in time to enter in—**and to knock** —as if they had a right to enter without having striven—**and** (*when*) **he**—from within, without seeing them, but finding their voices strange, and knowing that his household is complete—**shall answer and say unto you, I know you not whence ye are:** Combining the sense of Matthew 7: 23; and 25: 12. —**Whence ye are**—where ye belong; certainly not to me, or to my house.

26. Then shall ye begin to say. Begin, as if they were going on with an argument, which, however, is soon cut short.—**We have eaten and drunk in thy presence, and thou hast taught in our streets.** They cannot say what some will, who, nevertheless, will be equally rejected: "Did we not prophesy by thy name, and by thy name cast out devils, and by thy name do many wonderful works? (Matt. 7: 27. Revision.) If only they might be able to add to their plea, "And we repented at thy word and believed thy gospel!" Then would they now have been in the palace. Without striving, or even seeking at the proper time, they had trusted to mere national and other external connections with the Messiah, as sufficient to secure for them his eternal favor. They have made their request; and when refused, have supported it by the only semblance of argument possible—as good as multitudes will offer, who go to the judgment impenitent, and trusting only to an external connection with the church, its ordinances, or its preaching—and now they hear the final denial and denunciation.

27. But he shall (*will*) say, I tell you I know you not whence ye are. Ye never manifested yourselves to me, and I do not recognize you as mine.—**Depart from me, all ye workers of iniquity.** Not having been workers of righteousness, they were, of necessity, workers of iniquity; more so, rather than less, because of their former enjoyment of religious advantages, which they had utterly neglected.

28. There—in that outer void to which they must depart—**shall be (*the*) weeping and gnashing of teeth.** "The article points to the well-known (super-eminent) misery reigning in hell (Matt. 8: 12, 13, 42, 50, al.)."—Meyer. The Greek has the article, also, before "gnashing" and "teeth"; but the English idiom does not require them. The weeping betrays pain; the gnashing of teeth, rage. And this, not on account of the separation from God and Christ only: **when ye shall see Abraham**, etc. The sight of the felicity of all the ancient worthies, including **the prophets** whom their fathers killed, and whose tombs they themselves hypocritically beautified, while they find themselves, who were of that earthly company, "getting thrust out," will give a special pungency to their **weeping and gnashing of teeth.**

29. And they shall come from the east, and from the west, and from the north, and from the south—converts to the Lord from among all the Gentiles—**and shall sit down** (*recline at table*) **in the kingdom of God.** This will be a great aggravation of the penalty on those who regard the heathen as dogs, and have no doubt that they themselves, as natural descendants of Abraham, are entitled to share in the heavenly banquet. The Greek tersely omits **from the** in the four cases, except **from** in the first—*from east and west, and north and south.*

30. And behold there are last—namely,

CH. XIII.] LUKE. 231

31 The same day there came certain of the Pharisees, saying unto him, Get thee out, and depart hence; for Herod will kill thee.

32 And he said unto them, Go ye, and tell that fox, Behold, I cast out devils, and I do cures to day and to morrow, and the third day *a* I shall be perfected.

33 Nevertheless I must walk to day, and to morrow, and the *day* following: for it cannot be that a prophet perish out of Jerusalem.

34 *b* O Jerusalem, Jerusalem, which killest the prophets, and stonest them that are sent unto thee;

31 In that very hour there came certain Pharisees, saying to him, Get thee out, and go hence: for 32 Herod would fain kill thee. And he said unto them, Go and say to that fox, Behold, I cast out demons and perform cures to-day and to-morrow, 33 and the third *day* [1] I am perfected. Howbeit I must go on my way to-day and to-morrow and the *day* following: for it cannot be that a prophet perish 34 out of Jerusalem. O Jerusalem, Jerusalem, that killeth the prophets, and stoneth them that are sent unto her! how often would I have gathered thy

a Heb. 2:10....*b* Matt. 23:37.——1 Or, *I end my course.*

Gentiles who will embrace the gospel—which shall be first—who, in the day of final account, will stand on the same footing as those from Abraham's posterity who *first* believed. They will be reckoned perfectly equal in the gospel, the last first, and the first last; and individual superiority, in any instances, will depend on degrees of faith, which are possible for Jew and Gentile alike.

31-33. IN EXPOSING THE CRAFT OF HEROD ANTIPAS, JESUS AGAIN PROPHESIES HIS NEARLY APPROACHING END.

31. **The same day** (more correctly, *in that very hour*) **there came certain of the Pharisees, saying unto him,** etc. The Pharisees, as a class, had long been so inflamed with anger against him, that they would fain have put him to death. His transparent innocence, and the good will of the people toward him, hindered that purpose; and to prevent the still further strengthening of that good will, the Pharisees of some neighborhood in Perea set themselves to scare him away from them. **Get thee out and depart hence**—proceed on your journey—**for Herod will** (lit., *wishes to* or *would fain*) **kill thee.** They may not have been warranted in thus speaking for Herod; but as Jesus had been for some time now within his dominion, and exciting an ever-widening ferment of thought among the people, the tetrarch may have been much in earnest to be rid of him. Nor is it in the least inconsistent with this, that he had, as we afterwards learn, been desirous to see Jesus (23:8). Thus Herod and the Pharisees would have a like interest in driving the Saviour off.

32. That he saw a stratagem in the message, is intimated by the metaphor of the fox. **Go ye, and tell that fox.** His cruelty, sensuality, and lack of conscience, would have warranted his being called a wolf; but the slyness of the present effort suggested, naturally, the character of the fox.—**Behold, I cast out devils** (*demons*), **and I do cures to-day and to-**

morrow. I go forward in the way which I have pursued, of spiritual and physical beneficence, for a short time longer. **And the third day I shall be** (lit., *I am*) **perfected.** I am coming to my end, and that end is perfection as a Saviour. The point which he contemplates is that at which he afterward said, "It is finished." The days are understood literally by Wieseler and Meyer; but so minute a specification does not seem consistent with the solemn elevation of the sentiment, and would be irreconcilable with the subsequent facts. What he aims at is, to indicate to Herod that, while he should not be turned aside from his plans, the latter had nothing to fear concerning any prolonged stay in his kingdom. This is more particularly stated; and, at the same time, the Pharisees are notified that their desires are not to fail of accomplishment, when he adds that during these three days also he must be journeying on to his death in Jerusalem.

33. **Nevertheless**—that is all true, but—**I must walk** (*go on my way*), the same verb as "go hence" (ver. 31)—travel on, pursue my journey—**to-day and to-morrow, and the day following.** This short time (the same as in ver. 32) must suffice to take me to Jerusalem—keeping up my wonted work as I travel.—**I must** expresses his solemn sense of the divine appointment to death, which he had voluntarily assumed.—**For it cannot be that a prophet perish out of Jerusalem.** The profound irony of a heart wounded by insults, yet concerned more for the wrong-doers (see next verse) than for the injuries to itself. Jerusalem has this high prerogative, and an indefeasible claim to inflict death on God's prophets of all the ages. This cry, wrung from an anguished soul, does not, of course, take note of such rare exceptions as that of John the Baptist.

34. LAMENTATION OVER JERUSALEM.

34. **O Jerusalem, Jerusalem.** The mention of the city, as necessarily the scene of

how often would I have gathered thy children together, as a hen *doth gather* her brood under *her* wings, and ye would not!

35 Behold, [a] your house is left unto you desolate: and verily I say unto you, Ye shall not see me, until *the time* come when ye shall say, [b] Blessed *is* he that cometh in the name of the Lord.

children together, even as a hen *gathereth* her own 35 brood under her wings, and ye would not! Behold, your house is left unto you *desolate*; and I say unto you, Ye shall not see me, until ye shall say, Blessed *is* he that cometh in the name of the Lord.

CHAPTER XIV.

AND it came to pass, as he went into the house of one of the chief Pharisees to eat bread on the sabbath day, that they watched him.

1 And it came to pass, when he went into the house of one of the rulers of the Pharisees on a sabbath to

a Lev. 26: 31, 32; Ps. 69: 25; Isa. 1: 7; Dan. 9: 27; Mic. 3: 12....*b* Ps. 118: 26; Matt. 21: 9; Mark 11: 10; ch. 19: 38; John 12: 13.

his death, draws from him, very naturally, this pathetic apostrophe; which may have been repeated, nearly in the same words, on that equally appropriate occasion where Matthew brings it in (23: 37 ff.), in the Temple, two days before our Lord's death. **Which killest** (rather, *killeth*) **the prophets, and stonest** (*stoneth*) **them that are sent unto thee** (rather, *her*). The exalted tenor of the feeling runs into the parallelism of Hebrew poetry. What a description of that city, which had once been, in the estimation of inspired psalmists, "beautiful for situation, the joy of the whole earth"; "the city of the great king"; in whose palaces "God is known for a refuge." Isaiah had already seen something of the degeneracy, when he was constrained to declare: "Righteousness dwelt in her, but now murderers." For such guilt, terrible retribution must follow. This prospect was the more heart-rending to Jesus, regarded as the sequence of all his pains and solicitude for her welfare. **How often would I have gathered thy children**—inhabitants—**together, as a hen doth gather her (***own***) brood under her wings, and ye would not. I would, and ye would not.** God's pleasure in men's salvation leaves them free, nevertheless, as they are, alas! too often disposed, to persist in the course of ruin. The sentence beautifully intimates our natural helplessness in ourselves, Christ's yearning desire to make us safe and holy and happy, and our foolish preference for misery and peril and sin.

35. Behold, your house. The object of address changes now to be the people of Jerusalem; and **your house** must mean the city, Jerusalem itself.—**Is left unto you.** The verb is in the present tense—is in the act of being left. The word **desolate** does not belong to the text of Luke, and need not be added. The city is being left to you, will be completely given up by God, at the death of your Messiah, and then it will be seen how you will keep it. **Ye shall not** (by no means shall ye) **see me, until the time come when ye shall say** (better, *until ye say*, or, "*until it come that ye say;*" so Tischendorf still).—**Blessed is he**, etc. This cannot be limited to the welcome of the multitudes when he entered into Jerusalem soon afterwards (Matt. 21: 9; Mark 11: 9; John 12: 13; comp. Luke 19: 38), because the other evangelists ascribe the same utterance to Christ after that entrance had taken place. It here points to the Parousia, or second advent of our Lord. Before that should occur, the Jewish nation would believe and turn to their Messiah (Rom. 11: 25-27). Then, when they were prepared to receive him with penitent and joyful adoration, would they again see the Son of man return in glory to assume manifest and eternal dominion. See how Peter (Acts 3: 19-21) urges his countrymen to expedite this glorious consummation, by speedy repentance and faith.

Ch. 14. 1-6. IN THE HOUSE OF A PHARISEE HE HEALS ON THE SABBATH, AND CONFOUNDS HIS OPPOSERS.

1. And it came to pass, as (or, *when*) **he went into the house of one of the chief** (lit., *of the rulers of the*) **Pharisees;** *i. e.*, of a Pharisee who enjoyed recognized leadership in that sect. We might suppose that after the rude experience of chapter 11: 37-54, Jesus would be backward to place himself again in such company. But even that occasion had served for the deliverance of important truth; and on another (7: 36-47), he had met with a great opportunity in a Pharisee's house. As he was invited now (ver. 12) by one in a different place, who might have worthy motives, and a kinder personal feeling, he would not neglect a possible opening for the furtherance of his mission.—**To eat bread on the (***a***) Sabbath day. To eat bread**—to take a meal, meant

Сн. XIV.]   LUKE.   233

2 And, behold, there was a certain man before him which had the dropsy.
3 And Jesus answering spake unto the lawyers and Pharisees, saying, ᵃ Is it lawful to heal on the sabbath day?
4 And they held their peace. And he took *him*, and healed him, and let him go;
5 And answered them, saying, ᵇ Which of you shall have an ass or an ox fallen into a pit, and will not straightway pull him out on the sabbath day?
6 And they could not answer him again to these things.

2 eat bread, that they were watching him. And behold, there was before him a certain man who had
3 the dropsy. And Jesus answering spake unto the lawyers and Pharisees, saying, Is it lawful to heal
4 on the sabbath, or not? But they held their peace. And he took him, and healed him, and let him go.
5 And he said unto them, Which of you shall have ¹an ass or an ox fallen into a well, and will not
6 straightway draw him up on a sabbath day? And they could not answer again unto these things.

a Matt. 12:10....*b* Ex. 23:5; Deut. 22:4; ch. 13:15.—¹ Many ancient authorities read, *a son*. See ch. xiii. 15.

here to participate in an extensive entertainment (ver. 7). This was consistent with even Pharisaic rigor of Sabbath observance. Nehemiah 8: 10 f., shows this in respect to a day of the highest sanctity; and Tobit (2:1) shows it in the case of a man typical for his piety, on the Sabbath. The feast in John 12: 2 must have been on the Sabbath; and Wetstein, on our passage, gives copious proofs of the use of the Sabbath for social entertainments. (Comp. also Lightfoot, *Exercit.*, on this passage.) The food was, in such cases, prepared on the day before.—**They watched** (or, *were watching*) **him.** They—they themselves, emphatically marks the Pharisaic company as a party over against him.

2. And, behold, there was a certain man before him which had the dropsy. We cannot know whether he was one of the family, or one of the guests; or one who had stolen in, as it was easy with their customs to do (see on 7: 37), either from a general curiosity, or, most probably of all, from the hope of receiving help of the wonderful healer. However he came there, there he was, a sufferer who greatly needed, even if he did not expect, aid. "And they were watching him," as on a former occasion (6: 7), probably to see whether this case of suffering would move him to attempt a cure.

3. And Jesus answering—to their inquiring thoughts—**spake unto the lawyers and Pharisees**—whom we saw closely associated in 7: 30 also—**saying, Is it lawful to heal on the Sabbath day** (omit **day**, and add, *or not*, A B D L). Seeing that they were lurking to catch him in a violation of the law of the Sabbath, he would have preliminarily a distinct consideration of this point.

4. And they held their peace. Either they saw that they could make no rational objection to his beneficent purpose, or they contemptuously refused any notice of his question.—**And he took him**—in hand—**and healed him, and let him go**; *i. e.*, sent him away cured. This last statement strongly supports the supposition that the man had come in uninvited, to get this blessing. He should not be disappointed, at all events.

5. And answered them—the evidence favors the reading, *And he said unto them*, **Which of you shall have an ass** rather, according to A B E G M S U V, etc., *a son*) **or an ox fall into a pit** or, *well*), **and will not straightway pull him out** (literally, *draw him up*) **on the sabbath-day?** The authority is stronger for the word *son* in the Greek text. The sense thus is, "shall have a son or even an ox." Wetstein: "If either a son, who is dearer, and more easily drawn out, or even an ox, which is of less worth, and more difficult to extricate." The word translated **pit** (or, *well*), is appropriate to a tank, or cistern, or collection of water from a spring, and does not necessarily imply that the pit or hole now contains water. Obviously a child was more liable to such an accident than an ass, and Wetstein's quotations on the passage prove that the idea was familiar in the discussions of the Jewish rabbis. Thus, in the tract *Bava Kama*, of the Mishna (v. 6), "if an ox or an ass fall into a well—a son or daughter, a servant or maid." *Yoma*, viii., 6, 7: "Danger to life always banishes the sabbath." F., 84, 2: If "one fishing (on the sabbath) sees a child fallen into a pit, he removes the sand and brings him out." It is very likely that this passage was early adapted in some copies to ch. 13: 15. The argument of the Saviour in his question is the same which we have studied in the connection just cited. (Comp. Matt. 12: 11.)

6. And they could not answer him again to these things. The net-work of bondage for the unthinking mass, which they had woven by their traditions, proved but a cobweb before the glance of a truly seeing and searching soul.

7 And he put forth a parable to those which were bidden, when he marked how they chose out the chief rooms; saying unto them,
8 When thou art bidden of any *man* to a wedding, sit not down in the highest room; lest a more honourable man than thou be bidden of him;
9 And he that bade thee and him come and say to thee, Give this man place; and thou begin with shame to take the lowest room.
10 *a* But when thou art bidden, go and sit down in the lowest room; that when he that bade thee cometh, he may say unto thee, Friend, go up higher: then shalt thou have worship in the presence of them that sit at meat with thee.
11 *b* For whosoever exalteth himself shall be abased; and he that humbleth himself shall be exalted.
12 Then said he also to him that bade him, When thou makest a dinner or a supper, call not thy friends, nor thy brethren, neither thy kinsmen, nor *thy* rich neighbours; lest they also bid thee again, and a recompence be made thee.

7 And he spake a parable unto those that were bidden, when he marked how they chose out the 8 chief seats; saying unto them, When thou art bidden of any man to a marriage feast, 1 sit not down in the chief seat; lest haply a more honourable man 9 than thou be bidden of him, and he that bade thee and him shall come and say to thee, Give this man place; and then thou shalt begin with shame to take 10 the lowest place. But when thou art bidden, go and sit down in the lowest place; that when he that hath bidden thee cometh, he may say to thee, Friend, go up higher: then shalt thou have glory in the pres- 11 ence of all that sit at meat with thee. For every one that exalteth himself shall be humbled; and he that humbleth himself shall be exalted.
12 And he said to him also that had bidden him, When thou makest a dinner or a supper, call not thy friends, nor thy brethren, nor thy kinsmen, nor rich neighbours; lest haply they also bid thee again,

a Prov. 25: 6, 7.....b Job 22: 29; Ps. 18: 27; Prov. 29: 23; Matt. 23: 12; ch. 18: 14; James 4: 6; 1 Pet. 5: 5.——1 Gr. recline not.

7-11. A Lesson of Humility to the Guests.

The Saviour's mind appears not at all ruffled by this scene; for he proceeds, with that seriousness, tempered by good-nature, which we have noticed in the parable of the Unjust Judge, to impart counsels of great moment—first to the guests:

8-10. When he marked how they chose out the chief rooms. Certain places at the table, in their formal meals, were then, as now, regarded as more honorable, and so were assigned by the host, according to the dignity of his guests. These Christ noticed, as many an observer has since, that some of his companions at the table **chose out** for themselves. His parable is simply a piece of advice, enforced by a reference to the natural consequences of two supposed courses of conduct. It is in the form and tone of an instruction in etiquette, in which we may see the Saviour affable, thoroughly social, and while assuming, as of course, the position of a teacher, yet masking it simply and kindly, by a homely urbanity of phrase and illustration, which divests it of all arrogance and stiffness. **Room,** in ver. 7, 8, of the Common Version, seat; *i. e.*, couch, on which they reclined, not sat; in ver. 9, 10, place. **Worship,** ver. 10, is honor, respect.

11. What the Saviour spoke with express reference to a marriage feast, all would of course understand as applying to all similar occasions. But in this verse we may see how easily in his conversation counsels of worldly prudence, even in minor affairs, might glide into a sermon of the highest spiritual significance, and of universal cogency.—**For whosoever exalteth himself shall be abased,** (literally *humbled*)—"brought low," (ch. 3: 5), **and he that humbleth himself shall be exalted.** To exalt oneself is to make much in thought and conduct of one's claims to the esteem of others; to humble oneself is to rate high the claim of others. The Saviour's saying is probably true, in the best sense and in the long run, even "in the corrupted currents of this world," and might have been expressed in the present tense. But by putting it in the future, he carries our thoughts to that great day for which all other days were made. The frequency with which he repeated this declaration shows his sense of its importance, perhaps also of the special need of its reiteration, that his disciples might begin to realize how much of *his* religion lay in humility and self-abnegation. James and Peter echo the sentiment of the Master in their Epistles (James 4: 10; 1 Peter 5: 6); but both, as was natural for them, more in the manner and spirit of the Old Testament.

12-14. Advice to His Entertainer.

12. Then said he (*and he said*) **also to him that bade** (*had bidden*—invited) **him**—when he marked that he, after the ordinary manner, had invited to his table relatives and friends, the rich and comfortable. **When thou makest a dinner or a supper, call not thy friends,** etc. **Dinner**—in the same sense as in ch. 11: 38. **Brethren**—brothers, in the proper sense. That he does not mean absolutely to prohibit such courtesies and gratifications is beyond question, both from the nature of the case, and from the fact that Jesus was now, and not unfrequently, present at such meals. He gives as the reason, that

13 But when thou makest a feast, call *the poor, the maimed, the lame, the blind:
14 And thou shalt be blessed; for they cannot recompense thee: for thou shalt be recompensed at the resurrection of the just.
15 And when one of them that sat at meat with him heard these things, he said unto him, *Blessed is he that shall eat bread in the kingdom of God.
16 *Then said he unto him, A certain man made a great supper, and bade many:
17 And *sent his servant at supper time to say to them that were bidden, Come; for all things are now ready.
18 And they all with one consent began to make excuse. The first said unto him, I have bought a piece of ground, and I must needs go and see it: I pray thee have me excused.

13 and a recompense be made thee. But when thou makest a feast, bid the poor, the maimed, the lame, 14 the blind: and thou shalt be blessed; because they have not wherewith to recompense thee: for thou shalt be recompensed in the resurrection of the just.
15 And when one of them that sat at meat with him heard these things, he said unto him, Blessed is he 16 that shall eat bread in the kingdom of God. But he said unto him, A certain man made a great supper; 17 and he bade many: and he sent forth his ¹ servant at supper time to say to them that were bidden, 18 Come; for all things are now ready. And they all with one consent began to make excuse. The first said unto him, I have bought a field, and I must needs go out and see it: I pray thee have me ex-

a Neh. 8:10, 12....b Rev. 19:9....c Matt. 22:2....d Prov. 9:2. 5.——1 Gr. bondservant.

entertaining others in this way affords no scope for a truly religious disposition. It is all consistent with the mercenary views of worldly ambition.—Lest (haply) they also bid thee again, and a recompense be made thee. He would have men moved by something higher than an earthly quid pro quo.

13. But when thou makest a feast—(strictly, a reception)—call the poor, etc. Thus he would fain stimulate his host to religious thought and enterprise, as he had his fellow guests, by an apt comment on the circumstances of the moment. "So may you hold a reception which which will conduce to your spiritual and eternal interests."

14. And thou shalt be blessed. The course which I recommend will not fail of its reward, although not such as the world admires or covets; a reward consisting in the enrichment of the soul, to be experienced in its fullness only in the completed kingdom of God, and coming necessarily from his hand.—For (or, because) they cannot recompense thee: for thou shalt be recompensed at the resurrection of the just. God himself will own the debt at the day of judgment, on the principle of Proverbs 19: 17; Matthew 25: 40. The time is when the just, or righteous—of whom the host shall then be one—shall be raised in "the resurrection of life." It is assumed that in adopting the unselfish, beneficent course, now advised, the Pharisee will do it in the general spirit of faith, and obedience to the precepts of Christ.

15-24. PARABLE OF THE GREAT SUPPER.
15. And when one of them that sat at meat with him heard these things, he said unto him. The Saviour's discourse had evidently suggested in this man's mind thoughts concerning the Messianic kingdom, as had been his intention. How far his

thoughts corresponded with the reality, we cannot clearly know; but they became the occasion of further interesting and important explanations.—Blessed is he that (whosoever) shall eat bread in the kingdom of God. Christ went into the Pharisee's house (ver. 1) "to eat bread" (compare Gen. 43: 25; 1 Sam. 20: 24), and the satisfaction attending this meal with Jesus appears to have led the man to say in effect, "What a fine thing it would be to do this in the presence of God!" The joy of a feast on earth suggests, as we have before seen, various figures of the heavenly blessedness. His tone probably implied that he took for granted that the blessedness would be his. Hence the bearing of the Saviour's reply, which, without following up the nature or extent of that felicity, teaches very impressively that multitudes who were expecting it would be disappointed, and that all who attained to it must do so without delay.

16 A certain man made a great supper, and bade—invited—many. This invitation was preliminary, according to a custom of that part of the world, and signified specifically that those who received it were to be in readiness when definitely summoned. He who makes the supper represents God, preparing for the Jew first, and also for the Gentiles, the salvation of the Messianic kingdom.

17. The final call to come goes forth through John the Baptist, who is the servant sent forth at supper time to say, Come, for all things are now ready. This invitation Jesus himself continued and sharpened, saying, "The time is fulfilled, and the kingdom of God is at hand; repent ye and believe the gospel. (Mark 1: 15.)

18-20. And they all with one consent began to make excuse—to beg off. These are the leading Jews, to whom, as in the case of Nicodemus, the message specially appealed,

19 And another said, I have bought five yoke of oxen, and I go to prove them: I pray thee have me excused.
20 And another said, I have married a wife, and therefore I cannot come.
21 So that servant came, and shewed his lord these things. Then the master of the house being angry said to his servant, Go out quickly into the streets and lanes of the city, and bring in hither the poor, and the maimed, and the halt, and the blind.
22 And the servant said, Lord, it is done as thou hast commanded, and yet there is room.
23 And the lord said unto the servant, Go out into the highways and hedges, and compel *them* to come in, that my house may be filled.

19 cused. And another said, I have bought five yoke of oxen, and I go to prove them: I pray thee have me excused. And another said, I have married a
21 wife, and therefore I cannot come. And the [1] servant came, and told his lord these things. Then the master of the house being angry said to his servant, Go out quickly into the streets and lanes of the city, and bring in hither the poor and maimed
22 and blind and lame. And the [1] servant said, Lord, what thou didst command is done, and yet there is
23 room. And the Lord said unto the [1] servant, Go out into the highways and hedges, and constrain *them*

1 Gr. *bondservant.*

---

because on their decision the course of the nation would so largely depend. And they, with a form of apology, but a heart of contempt, refused the call. Their reasons all make their failure to come depend on some temporal interest of their own, and in no case on anything which could reasonably stand in the way. The third, **I have married a wife,** is perhaps the most plausible, and has a color of support in the law (Deut. 24: 5); but this was neither a summons to war, nor to any business. To plead a recent marriage as a reason for not attending a festive entertainment, was as frivolous as the other pretexts.—**Have me excused**—not meaning "get me excused," "cause my excuse to be accepted," but hold, or, regard, me as one who has made a satisfactory excuse, whose regrets are accepted. This is addressed in the parable to the servant; but, in the application, the servant is Christ. His interpretation of the **I cannot come** in all these cases would be, as in 13: 34, "and ye would not."

21. *And the* (not, so that) **servant came, and shewed** (*reported to*) **his lord these things.** The lamentation of Jesus over the doomed people, as in ch. 13: 34, may have been the burden of many of the reports made by him to God in the hours which he spent in prayer.—**Then the master of the house being angry.** What could be more suited to raise in the breast of a holy God feelings of sore displeasure, than the scornful rejection by lost men of grace provided for them with such pains, and commended to them by the affectionate, self-sacrificing sympathy of his dear Son?—**Said to his servant, Go out quickly into the streets,** etc. Give the invitation now to the lower grades of the people in particular—morally speaking, to the publicans, the sinners, the harlots, "this multitude, that know not the law," and in the estimation of the Pharisees, "are accursed."—Bible Union Version. John 7: 49.

22. Lord, it is done as thou hast commanded (lit., *what thou didst command is done*). Does this mean that the servant had done a second errand, in fulfillment of the direction in ver. 21, or, that he instantly replied on receiving that command, "It is already done"? There are some considerations in favor of the latter view. The emphatic position in the Greek of the verb "it is, *i. e.*, has been done," favors it, as does the consistency of the view with Christ's spontaneous readiness to adopt the measure which his Father will approve. If only the verb "command" were in a present tense, ["what thou commandest," or, "hast commanded," there could be no objection. But as it is, correctly, in the Revision, *what thou didst command* (viz., in ver. 21), at a time prior to this second announcement of the servant, seems to oblige us to understand that the servant has been out again. It shows us Jesus as having made converts chiefly from among the more humble and needy class of the people, and as having done all he could, **and yet there is room.** What pathos in this sentence, considered as Christ's report of his life's work!

23. And the lord said unto the servant, Go out into the highways and hedges, and compel them to come in. This invitation reaches beyond "the city" (ver. 21), and is intended for the Gentiles, who are destined, in the first instance, to compose the chief citizenship of the kingdom. This command is to be executed by Jesus through his apostles and other ministers.—**The highways and hedges** represent the region outside of "the city," which stands for the theocracy; and that it is among the hedges, in the shelter of which the unemployed rustics would lounge, that the invitation is to find acceptance, shows

24 For I say unto you, a That none of those men which were bidden shall taste of my supper.
25 And there went great multitudes with him: and he turned, and said unto them,
26 b If any man come to me, c and hate not his father, and mother, and wife, and children, and brethren, and sisters, d yea, and his own life also, he cannot be my disciple.
27 And e whosoever doth not bear his cross, and come after me, cannot be my disciple.
28 For f which of you, intending to build a tower, sitteth not down first, and counteth the cost, whether he have *sufficient* to finish it?
29 Lest haply, after he hath laid the foundation, and is not able to finish it, all that behold it begin to mock him,
30 Saying, This man began to build, and was not able to finish.

24 to come in, that my house may be filled. For I say unto you, that none of those men that were bidden shall taste of my supper.
25 Now there went with him great multitudes: 26 and he turned, and said unto them, If any man cometh unto me, and hateth not his own father, and mother, and wife, and children, and brethren and sisters, yea, and his own life also, he cannot be my 27 disciple. Whosoever doth not bear his own cross, 28 and come after me, cannot be my disciple. For who of you, desiring to build a tower, doth not first sit down and count the cost, whether he have *wherewith* to complete it? Lest haply, when he hath laid a foundation, and is not able to finish, all that be-30 hold begin to mock him, saying, This man began to

a Matt. 21:43; 22:8; Acts 13:46....*b* Deut. 13:6; 33:9; Matt. 10:37....*c* Rom. 9:13....*d* Rev. 12:11....*e* Matt. 16:24; Mark 8:34; ch. 9:23; 2 Tim. 3:12....*f* Prov. 24:27.

---

that "not many wise" men after the flesh, "not many mighty, not many noble," of the heathen, could be expected soon to fill up the vacuum of the church. The direction to **compel them to come in**, like the "quickly" of ver. 21, has reference to the shortness of the time, now that the supper is waiting. It indicates the need of that urgency of proclamation and persuasion which we see exemplified in the work of Peter and Paul, and the other most faithful ministers of the word; but not at all of that earth-born zeal, in church and state, which has often abused the Lord's word, as a warrant for violence against those who refused to profess a belief that they did not hold.—**That my house may be filled.** God's merciful purpose to save an innumerable multitude should not be frustrated, although the Jews of that time, or any man of that or any generation, might slight the offered opportunity, and count himself unworthy of eternal life. While there is room and a welcome for all, some will be found to take the place of any that refuse.

24. For I say unto you, That none of those men which were bidden shall taste of my supper. How fearfully the purport of this decree was realized in the experience of that and the following generation, history shows, written in lines of blood. Did Christ's questioner (ver. 15) receive the intended explanation as to whether many are being saved?

25-35. The Terms of Discipleship Again Stated and Illustrated.

25, 26. And there went great multitudes with him. He had resumed his course toward Jerusalem, and the accompanying crowds continue, or even increase. He was doubtless aware that few, comparatively, understood really for what they were following him. Hence the necessity of making known to them all what he had before told the apostles, of the conditions of his service. —**And he turned**—so as to face the throng, being himself in advance—**and**—after they had gathered within hearing—**said unto them, If any man come to me,** i. e., to rank himself among my disciples—**and hateth not his father,** etc. There is no reason for softening the definition of "hate," here and in ch. 16: 13; Matt. 6: 24; John 12: 25, so as to make it mean "to love less." Understand only that Christ speaks with reference to a case very common in the experience of the first disciples, when near relations stood in hostility to the claims of the gospel; and to follow one was to come in conflict with the other. Here it was not a lesser attachment to the party opposed to him, that he would have; but utter separation, disfavor, hatred. There must be no divided devotion. This would require great sacrifice often; but he may not shrink, but must even hate his own life, as explained in next verse.

27. Whosoever doth not bear his (*own*) cross—as I must bear mine—**and come after** —obey and imitate—**me, cannot be my disciple** (comp. on 9: 23). Thus must he "**hate his own life,**" when to keep it he would fail in duty to the Saviour. This principle is thus distinctly stated, in order to make sure that no one shall think of entering on his service under any mistake as to what it involves.

28-30. For—this is confirmatory of that implied need of deliberation—**which of you, wishing to build a tower,** etc. The two illustrations here given show what common prudence requires of a man in commencing a work of importance and difficulty in the

31 Or what king, going to make war against another king, sitteth not down first, and consulteth whether he be able with ten thousand to meet him that cometh against him with twenty thousand? 32 Or else, while the other is yet a great way off, he sendeth an ambassage, and desireth conditions of peace. 33 So likewise, whosoever he be of you that forsaketh not all that he hath, he cannot be my disciple. 34 ᵃSalt *is* good: but if the salt have lost his savour, wherewith shall it be seasoned?

31 build, and was not able to finish. Or what king, as he goeth to encounter another king in war, will not sit down first and take counsel whether he is able with ten thousand to meet him that cometh against him with twenty thousand? 32 Or else, while the other is yet a great way off, he sendeth an ambassage, and asketh conditions of peace. 33 So therefore whosoever he be of you that renounceth not all that he hath, he cannot be my disciple. Salt therefore is good: but if even the salt have lost its savour,

ᵃ Matt. 5: 13; Mark 9: 50.

affairs of this world. How much more in the courses which directly determine eternal consequences! The building of **a tower** may be named as symbolical of providing a refuge for oneself, a place of safety, to which the assured favor of God may be likened, or the proved character of gospel righteousness, on which that favor depends. The details of the figure are drawn true to life; but in the application, the mockery of beholders must be referred to the amazement and pity which God and holy beings feel at the view of a profession of discipleship dishonored, and ending in ruin.

31, 32. The war of one king with another king may stand for the warfare which the disciple has to wage with Satan and all the forms and powers of evil. Christ has stated, and the Scripture has shown, that a great conflict is to be carried on, great efforts are to be put forth (ch. 13: 24), great sacrifices to be incurred. Happily, he who proposes to follow Jesus is not left to do it in his own strength. But by his own faculties he must intelligently survey the duty, and resolve to avail himself of that aid which shall supplement his own powers in their most strenuous exercise. **Going to make war against.** *Goeth to encounter*, of the Revision; "is pursuing a course likely to bring him into conflict," is preferable. The supposition is, that the former is threatened with an attack.—**Asketh conditions of peace**, desiring to avoid actual battle. This is, of course, not a counsel to shrink from contest with our spiritual adversary, but does imply that we should be careful to have more than the twenty thousand on our side. And if only we be resolved on that which is right, in God's strength, the sure word of prophecy says, "Fear not: for they that be with us are more than they that be with them." (2 Kings 6: 16.)

33. So, likewise (better, *therefore*), **whosoever he be of you that forsaketh** (or, *renounceth*) **not all that he hath, he cannot be my disciple.** This is the conclusion established by both the preceding examples. To *renounce* is the same as to "bid farewell to" in ch. 9: 61, and the phrase is translated by Davidson "bid good-bye to." Well might the Saviour call upon them to count the cost of being his disciples, in any sense worth considering at all. Well, if he should check the fanatical zeal of the worldly multitude.

34. Salt (the Greek adds *therefore*) **is good.** The word *therefore* shows that the metaphor salt is suggested by the preceding account of true discipleship. Its well-known and indispensable dietetic utility, as well as its ceremonial significance, made it eminently suitable to shadow forth various religious truths. (Matt. 5: 13; Mark 9: 50.) Here the Saviour employs it to signify that disposition that moves a man to follow him, and qualifies him to do so worthily. That is an excellent thing, eminently **good**, understanding it to be sincere, deliberate, permanent. The disciple possessing it will not be like the multitude that Jesus sees hanging upon him in mere expectancy of temporal honor and advantage, but will be ready, forsaking all else for him, to endure unto the end. Such a disciple has in him the salt which is the preservative and antiseptic principle of his own life, and becomes a means of preservation to the society in which he lives.—**But if** (*even*) **the salt have lost his** (*its*) **savor.** We hardly need to bring in here the supposition that Christ has in mind an impure salt, mingled with gypsum, and other earthy matters, such as we are told was sometimes used in Palestine. That would, doubtless, be naturally of very different degrees of saltness, and would, on exposure to the weather, lose what it might have had. But the figure presupposes a good quality of salt; and so we more justly understand him to simply suppose the case that it should lose its saltness. But does this assume the possibility that a true disciple may lose the grace which makes him such? Such a *possibility* it does seem to assume, but no more asserts the reality

35 It is neither fit for the land, nor yet for the dunghill; *but* men cast it out. He that hath ears to hear, let him hear.

CHAPTER XV.

THEN *a* drew near unto him all the publicans and sinners for to hear him.
2 And the Pharisees and scribes murmured, saying, This man receiveth sinners, *b* and eateth with them.
3 And he spake this parable unto them, saying,

35 wherewith shall it be seasoned? It is fit neither for the land nor for the dunghill: *men* cast it out. He that hath ears to hear, let him hear.

1 Now all the publicans and sinners were drawing near unto him for to hear him. And both the Pharisees and the scribes murmured, saying, This man receiveth sinners, and eateth with them.
3 And he spake unto them this parable, saying,

a Matt. 9: 10....*b* Acts 11: 3; Gal. 2: 12.

of such a case than it asserts that salt does ever lose its peculiar pungency and power to hinder corruption. But while we confidently conclude, from various passages of the New Testament, and from the nature of the case, that no true subject of regenerating grace ever has or will become utterly void of the new life, yet surely nothing prevents it, in any case, but the continued operation of the renewing Spirit. And, as such continued operation supposes the continued co-operation of the free activities of the soul that is born again, Holy Scripture is plain, pointed and importunate in urging the necessity of care and diligence, that such soul may not fail of the eternal life. (John 15: 5, 6; Matt. 5: 13; Mark 9: 50; Heb. 4: 1; comp. 3: 1; 6: 4-6; 2 Pet. 1: 10, 11.)—**Wherewith shall it be seasoned,** literally, *restored to its proper savor and efficacy?* and, in the application, made capable of doing the work, exerting the influence of a disciple.

35. It is neither fit for the land, nor yet for the dunghill. Some refuse salt might yet be useful as a dressing for the land; or, if not to be so used directly, might improve the manure heap. But the deterioration of which Christ thinks is total, irremediable, destructive. **Men cast it out.** The order of the words in the Greek: *Out they cast it!* marks Christ's sense of the utter worthlessness and vanity of an outward religiousness which is a mere profession, totally void of his own Spirit. That this topic is of great practical importance, is intimated in the solemn formula, **He that hath ears to hear, let him hear.** So let every one that *reads* rouse his faculties of mind and heart to due consideration of the Great Teacher's words.

Ch. 15: 1, 2. CHRIST'S INTERCOURSE WITH PUBLICANS AND SINNERS OFFENDS THE PHARISEES.

1. Then (correctly, *and*) **drew near** (better, *were drawing near*) **unto him all the publicans and sinners for to hear him.**

Neither the time nor the place is definitely indicated; but only the fact that somewhere there was a great concourse of the despised publicans and their associates to him, in the course of which the incident to be related took place. The word **all** emphasizes the freedom with which he allowed any one of that class to approach him and share his teachings. His enemies would say that *any* publicans were good enough to be the friends of Jesus. **For to hear him.** The *for* is, of course, quite superfluous at the present day.

2. And (*both*) **the Pharisees and scribes murmured, saying, This man receiveth sinners, and eateth with them.** This complaint is one with which we are already familiar (5:30; 7:34); but it was new from these hypocrites, and gave occasion to a series of very interesting instructions. That he should receive, in the sense of welcoming sinners, was bad enough to Pharisaic bigotry; but eating with them was shockingly scandalous.

3. And he spake unto them this parable. The word **parable** must have at least a two-fold reference to that of the lost sheep, and to that of the lost drachma, which is connected with the former by the conjunction "or." The two are but phases of one illustration. Perhaps the account of the prodigal son might also be considered a branch of the same discourse, as it obviously carries forward the explanation of his position toward publicans and sinners, and the justification of it against the Pharisees. To it, however, there was a new beginning, **And he spake,** perhaps after noticing the effect of the preceding parables. It is worthy of special remark that all the interesting and precious instruction of this chapter, and almost all that follows to chapter 17: 10, comes to us through Luke's Gospel alone, and may have all hung on the little incident of the murmuring of hypocritical worldlings, because Jesus, on a certain occasion, acted like himself. We might fondly wish, had God not pleased to have it as it is, that still other evangelists

4 *What man of you, having an hundred sheep, if he lose one of them, doth not leave the ninety and nine in the wilderness, and go after that which is lost, until he find it?
5 And when he hath found it, he layeth it on his shoulders, rejoicing.
6 And when he cometh home, he calleth together his friends and neighbours, saying unto them, Rejoice with me: for I have found my sheep *b* which was lost.
7 I say unto you, that likewise joy shall be in heaven over one sinner that repenteth, *c* more than over ninety and nine just persons, which need no repentance.

4 What man of you, having a hundred sheep, and having lost one of them, doth not leave the ninety and nine in the wilderness, and go after that which
5 is lost, until he find it? And when he hath found
6 it, he layeth it on his shoulders, rejoicing. And when he cometh home, he calleth together his friends and his neighbours, saying unto them, Rejoice with me, for I have found my sheep which was
7 lost. I say unto you that even so there shall be joy in heaven over one sinner that repenteth, *more* than over ninety and nine righteous persons, that need no repentance.

a Matt. 18: 12....b 1 Pet. 2: 10, 25....c ch. 5: 32.

had preserved for us still more of the gracious words that proceeded out of his mouth.

4-7. THE LOST SHEEP.

Jesus supposes the case of a shepherd having sheep enough to make the temporary neglect of the vast majority for the sake of one a striking fact, yet not so many that the one should fail of the personal care of the owner, and be constantly recognized or missed. **In the wilderness**—the untilled, treeless, hilly region in various parts of Palestine, whose only use was for the pasturage of stock, and into the ravines of which, and bushy hollows along the scantily fed watercourses, a vagrant animal might stray. That he should **leave the ninety and nine** to go after the lost one, is a feature of the figure not applicable to the work of Christ as the spiritual shepherd. This is here to signalize his concern about the **lost**. Having pursued the search till successful, **he layeth it on his shoulders**, a familiar practice with shepherds when the creature is sick, fatigued, or in any way unable to travel on its own feet. **Rejoicing** alike in the retrieval of his own loss, and in the rescue of his sheep from danger and distress. **And when he cometh home**, evidently bringing the sheep thither, which he will not trust again readily to the risks of the wilderness, **he calleth together his friends and** (*his*) **neighbors**—probably to some rustic entertainment—**saying, Rejoice with me, for,** etc. The Good Shepherd would have all his friends share with him the delight of saving souls. What man would not act thus? Is it then strange that God in Christ should act likewise?

Considering the manifest occasion of this parable, we cannot doubt that the "ninety and nine" represent, primarily, the mass of the Jewish people, as professedly religious, in Christ's time. The lost sheep is the careless, worldly, and ceremonially irreligious element of the population, wretched in this world, as being outcasts from more worthy society, and depraved morally, through exclusive companionship with such. The shepherd's care for the estray shows Christ's pity for the erring and sinful, especially for the neglected and despised of earth. The active pursuit of the lost one until it is found illustrates his yearning desire that they should be saved. And the joy of the owner, with his friends and neighbors, over the recovered wanderer, pictures the **joy in heaven**, *i. e.*, of God and the angels, over one repenting sinner. Thus the defence of Christ's sympathy with the publicans rests on God's interest in the salvation of every sinner that turns to him. The **just** (*righteous*) **persons which** —regarded as such (δίκαιοι)—**need no repentance**, are the more respectable part of the community, and ostensibly religious. They think themselves righteous, and are so, in outward respects, compared with the publicans. Christ does not at all admit that they are so in such sense as to remove them from the need of repentance (see ch. 13: 3, 5), but according to their own view of themselves. He tells them that their life cannot afford him the delight which he takes in the moral renovation of a conscious and acknowledged sinner. However many there may be who are not *such*, they cannot occasion *such* rejoicing. So the joy of parents over the recovery of a child from an apparently mortal disease is greater than that over a whole family that have occasioned no concern for their health. No other language could be better adapted to raise in his hearers the query whether they, too, did not really need repentance. It should not be overlooked that this joy is in heaven, where they *are* familiar with instances in plenty of perfect righteousness, none of which, for their very commonness, can excite such a thrill of delight as the case of one who turns from the way of sin and ruin to holiness and salvation. The joy of God and the angels

8 Either what woman having ten pieces of silver, if she lose one piece, doth not light a candle, and sweep the house, and seek diligently till she find it?
9 And when she hath found it, she calleth her friends and her neighbours together, saying, Rejoice with me; for I have found the piece which I had lost.
10 Likewise, I say unto you, there is joy in the presence of the angels of God over one sinner that repenteth.
11 And he said, A certain man had two sons:

8 Or what woman having ten ¹pieces of silver, if she lose one piece, doth not light a lamp, and sweep the house, and seek diligently until she find it?
9 And when she hath found it, she calleth together her friends and neighbours, saying, Rejoice with me, for I have found the piece which I had lost.
10 Even so, I say unto you, there is joy in the presence of the angels of God over one sinner that repenteth.
11 And he said, A certain man had two sons:

1 Gr. *drachma*, a coin worth about eight pence.

---

over the results of Christ's work among sinners was a reproof to the Pharisees for their morose indifference, and even displeasure at it.

8-10. THE LOST DRACHMA.

This parable has the same general design, is indeed, as we have above noticed, only an alternative statement of the preceding thoughts, introduced by **Either.** As the other exhibited the Saviour's care for abandoned sinners, on account of their pitiable state, this contemplates them as property, the value of which to himself he cannot forego.—(Godet.) It was a custom with Christ thus to duplicate parables illustrative of one main truth (5: 36-39; 13: 19-21), with only incidental differences. Here he may have desired to bring home to the hearts of women the intensity of divine love toward the ruined and wretched, by an illustration drawn from their own sphere. The proportion of the "lost" to the safe, suggested here, is tenfold as great as in the preceding parable—*one piece of money out of ten*, one sheep out of a hundred. The **piece of silver** was the Greek *drachma*, the Roman *denarius*, "penny" of our version. See on ch. 7: 41. This amount would be more, proportionally, to a poor woman, than the one sheep to the shepherd before supposed.—**Light a candle** (better, *lamp*), **and sweep the house.** These are actions parallel to the hard and patient exploration of the shepherd through the wilderness, and are equally natural to our thought, considering that the house would be dark, without glazed windows, and probably with no floor but the trodden earth.—**And when she hath found it.** She exhibits her joy in a manner perfectly analogous to that of the successful shepherd, and strictly appropriate to a woman, since the **friends** here are shown by the Greek word to be women. As this parable says nothing of "leaving" the nine coins, or of a comparison of the joy with any other, we have impressed on us simply the joy of angels, and of all like them, in the conversion of a sinner.

11-32. PARABLE OF THE PRODIGAL SON.

The Saviour's course of condescending, laborious, saving sympathy for the socially banished and morally lost, has thus been doubly justified by a comparison with familiar and rational human proceedings. He has sufficiently explained the divine care in the matter, but has said nothing of the inward experience of the objects of this care. For this purpose, it was necessary that the object of search and rescue should be of the human kind,—a man, not an animal or a thing. He now, therefore, adds a third parable, to clarify and complement his instruction concerning the rescue of a sinner through the gospel, and so, ultimately, though indirectly, to finish his apology for intercourse with publicans and sinners. The bereft shepherd and the impoverished woman become here the compassionate and yearning father; the strayed sheep and the lost coin, a wayward son, whose absence makes the paternal mansion poor; and the finding of whom involves the whole series of experiences in the process of a sinner's repentance and return to God. It has well been held as the chief of the parables, most expressive of God's love, most fully descriptive of the affections of the soul, in its wanderings and its conversion.

11. And he said, A certain man had two sons. The man denotes God, the Father, by creation, of all men. The two sons represent two types of character, two classes of men, everywhere met with, and, in Christ's time, visible in the Pharisee and the publican. The younger son is the publican, and chiefly engages the attention of our Lord, as was to be expected in this connection; the other being presented rather as a background for this picture. It is natural that, as the volume of instruction widens, starting from verse 2, the particular case of the publican and the Pharisee should be less sharply kept in view. It does not, therefore, hinder that case from being still the real text, that this parable puts the acknowledged sinner in contrast with the self-

Q

12 And the younger of them said to *his* father, Father, give me the portion of goods that falleth *to me.* And he divided unto them *a his* living.
13 And not many days after the younger son gathered all together, and took his journey into a far country, and there wasted his substance with riotous living.
14 And when he had spent all, there arose a mighty famine in that land; and he began to be in want.
15 And he went and joined himself to a citizen of that country; and he sent him into his fields to feed swine.

12 and the younger of them said to his father, Father, give me the portion of ¹ *thy* substance that falleth to
13 me. And he divided unto them his living. And not many days after the younger son gathered all together, and took his journey into a far country; and there he wasted his substance with riotous
14 living. And when he had spent all, there arose a mighty famine in that country; and he began to be
15 in want. And he went and joined himself to one of the citizens of that country; and he sent him into

a Mark 12: 44.——¹ Gr. *the.*

righteous professor in so general a way as to describe any wanderer from God who sins and suffers and repents.

12. And the younger of them said, Father, give me the portion of goods—thy property—**that falleth to me,** *i. e.,* which is to fall to me at thy death. This would be, according to the principles of Jewish inheritance, one-third of the substance, leaving twice as much to the older brother. His proposal illustrates the rise of apostasy in the soul. Man is not content to leave the control of his means of enjoyment to his Creator, and receive such allotments as he deems best; but chooses rather to have all in his own hands, and follow his own pleasure.—**And he divided unto them his living**—rather, *the* living—the means of subsistence for the family. **Living** is the same as **goods,** or, *property*, in the previous sentence, only thought of here as the basis of a livelihood. As we see later that the father is still at the head of the place (ver. 22,31), we understand that the partition to the elder brother was only provisional; allowing to him the income, perhaps, above the father's support, until his death. God does not constrain men to what is best for them, at the sacrifice of their freedom.

13. And not many days after—so impatient was he to taste the sweets of uncontrolled self-will—**he gathered all together**—turned his property into such form that he could use it abroad—**and took his journey into a far country.** The Saviour may have imagined him as going to Alexandria, Antioch, or Rome, places which promised rich opportunities of pleasure in the spending of his means. In the interpretation, it pictures a growing alienation from God, leading to forgetfulness and inability to perceive him, as if one had got into a country where God was not.—**And there wasted**—scattered right and left—**his substance with riotous living. Riotous** covers the idea of both luxury and profligacy. He squandered his money on the gratification of his baser appetites. One short sentence tells the whole history of his fortune. It is gone. A bare subsistence by hard labor is all that he can hope for in that country, even with a continuance of general prosperity and abundance. Such is the state of the worldling who, forgetful of God, has tried all forms of earthly pursuit and indulgence that are possible for him, and, without more at any time than the delusive phantom of enjoyment, now sees that his way has been folly, and says of his remaining days, "There is no pleasure in them."

14. And when he had spent all—just when it was specially necessary for him that other people should have plenty—**there arose a mighty famine in**—throughout—**that land** —*country,* as in ver. 13—**and he**—*he himself*—**began to be in want.** No art or talent of his could insure him the means of easy subsistence, when the most virtuous and industrious were in straits. He is a type of the sinner who begins to realize that there is no true satisfaction for his soul in the ways of the world, in leaning to his own understanding, following his own caprice. But he will still try some other resource before turning to the only possible stores of supply.

15. And he went and joined himself to a citizen (lit., *one of the citizens*) **of that country.** The verb for "join," signifies, primarily, "to glue" one thing to another, and implies that he bound himself closely to a foreigner, a Gentile. He who has forsaken the gentle control of a father, is brought at length to subject himself utterly to the power of an alien stranger. Perhaps it was in expectation of sympathy and consideration; but what he has done becomes painfully clear to him when he finds to what a base, unhallowed occupation he is assigned.—**And he sent him** —out of the town—**into his fields, to feed swine.** The dependence of a sinner upon fellow-sinners, in his spiritual emergency, is a delusive trust.

16 And he would fain have filled his belly with the husks that the swine did eat: and no man gave unto him.
17 And when he came to himself, he said, How many hired servants of my father's have bread enough and to spare, and I perish with hunger!
18 I will arise and go to my father, and will say unto him, Father, I have sinned against heaven, and before thee,

16 his fields to feed swine. And he would fain [1] have filled his belly with [2] the husks that the swine did eat: and no man gave unto him. But when he came to himself he said, How many hired servants of my father's have bread enough and to spare, and
18 I perish here with hunger! I will arise and go to my father, and will say unto him, Father, I have

---

[1] Many ancient authorities read, *have been filled*....[2] Gr. *the pods of the carob tree.*

---

16. And he would fain have filled his belly with the husks—*pods*—**that the swine did eat.** Husks gives the effect intended, but does not translate the Greek word; that designates the fruit of a tree common about the eastern end of the Mediterranean, called the carob tree, and St. John's bread, and box-horn. It is closely related to the locust (*acacia*) with us (see the illustration in Smith's *Dictionary of the Bible*, Art. Husks), and the pods of one species of our locust are very similar in appearance to those here spoken of. They contain a slight amount of coarse nutriment, and, in lack of better provender, are sometimes fed to cattle and swine, and are even eaten, in extreme need, by the poorest people. This distressed man, apparently, did not regard them as suited to satisfy the appetite, still less as able to afford real nourishment; but would have crammed his belly with them to assuage the gnawings of hunger. **And no man gave unto him,** even a portion of this wretched fodder. Such is the depth of degradation and misery to which, by so ruinous stages, the wayward son has sunk. And in his case we have a description, true to the life, of the forlorn condition, the misery and helplessness, of the soul, whether in poverty or wealth, which has given itself up to worldly pursuits and pleasures, and has forgotten God. Such a one may not always be aware of his own wretchedness; still less does he understand his guilt; but so does he appear to the angels, to God, to Christ.

17-24. Picture of the Return of that Soul to God.

17. And (or *but*) when he came to himself. His desolate circumstances led him at last to reflection on the causes of his sad condition. This exercise of thoughtfulness is called a coming to, or rather *into*, himself. A somewhat similar expresssion is used of Peter in Acts 12 : 11, where the thought is that he came into a distinct and clear use of his faculties. Here, as if the prodigal had been "beside himself," and a worse nature had had the control of him, he comes to be himself once more, so far as to exercise some natural, unperverted deliberation about his state. Clear consideration at once showed him the reason of all his unhappiness and penury, in the fact that he had forsaken his father. **He said, How many hired servants of my father's have bread enough and to spare.** There is a profusion of all things necessary to health and comfort abounding even to those most remotely connected with my father's house. No special import of the "hired servants" has been satisfactorily suggested, as having been in the Saviour's mind. **And I—a** son, naturally destined to a much happier lot than they—**perish**—am perishing (*here*) **with hunger.** A most pitiful end, and shameful, surely, if it can be avoided, to perish *here*, in this estrangement from my father; in rags, debasement, and the contempt of unclean strangers. Herein is a vivid portrayal of the first steps of repentance of sin. Any man, even the most fortunate outwardly, is liable, in his worldliness, to have it flash across his thought that his course is yielding no real enjoyment to his better nature; is, rather, wrong and unworthy of him. He wonders if there is not something better, something in which all the capacities of his being can rejoice. In some favored hour he goes further. He seeks earnestly for the explanation of his dissatisfaction and unrest. Why has utter failure attended all his plans for the attainment of true welfare? Candid, deliberate inquiry finally discovers the reason why, in his life-long abandonment of God as his father, and refusal to accept his wise and loving control. It is a short step from this to see that the remedy lies in the contrite return of the heart to him.

18. Repentance is complete; that is to say, there is an effectual change of mind, of judgment, affection, and purpose, when the man can say, sincerely and truly, **I will arise and go to my father, and will say unto**

19 And am no more worthy to be called thy son: make me as one of thy hired servants.
20 And he arose, and came to his father. But *a* when he was yet a great way off, his father saw him, and had compassion, and ran, and fell on his neck, and kissed him.
21 And the son said unto him, Father, I have sinned against heaven,*b* and in thy sight, and am no more worthy to be called thy son.

19 sinned against heaven, and in thy sight: I am no more worthy to be called thy son: make me as one 20 of thy hired servants. And he arose, and came to his father. But while he was yet afar off, his father saw him, and was moved with compassion, and ran, 21 and fell on his neck, and ¹kissed him. And the son said unto him, Father, I have sinned against heaven, and in thy sight: I am no more worthy to be called thy son.

a Acts 2:39; Ephes. 2:13, 17....*b* Ps. 51:4.——¹ Gr. *kissed him much.*

him, Father, I have sinned, etc. Here is to the full the sense of guilt and folly, the readiness to confess it, the longing after forgiveness, the humility which is willing to take the lowest place, hoping only that some undeserved favor may yet be shown. This is the rational posture of a soul which is conscious of having sinned against its God. With this the warfare against God is at an end. Faith is not named, but faith operates in every exercise of such a disposition; belief in God's fatherly compassion, and a trust which commits itself unreservedly to him.

20. And he arose and came to his father. This acting out of the better mind that he had adopted is the counterpart of what we theologically distinguish from repentance, as **conversion.** The Scripture constantly calls it "turning," where "to be converted" is the phrase in our familiar version. It is the practical reversal of the course of life, conformably to the new purpose of the soul; conduct tinctured with holiness, expressive of the purer views, emotions, and tendencies of the heart. It fulfills the direction, "Repent and be converted." (Acts 3:19.) A single phrase thus describes the whole process of the wanderer's return, not accomplished with the facility or the gayety of his departure; attended with many turns of thought as to the manner in which he would be received, but cheered with the assurance that he might, at least, share the privilege of the "hired servants." **But when** (*while*) **he was yet a great way off, his father saw him,** etc. As if he had never ceased expecting that the son would become wiser, and return to the father's roof, he was perpetually on the watch. As soon, apparently, as he had come within the range of vision, the father recognized the child. That that child was making his weary way homeward was enough. —**He had** (or, *was moved with*) **compassion**; that indescribable yearning of affection which melts the man arose within him, and, doubtless, affected both looks and gait. **And ran**— notwithstanding his age and paternal dignity— **and fell on his neck** (comp. Gen. 45:14; 46:29), **and kissed him,** tenderly, repeatedly, as at ch. 7:38. The truth to nature of this description reveals a profound acquaintance with the human heart, and with the heart of God. For so God "waits to be gracious," yearns over his distressed children, in their folly, and joyfully meets the first manifestation of a desire to return.

21. And the son said unto him, Father, I have sinned against heaven, and in thy sight. The verb **have sinned** is preterite in the Greek, and so in ver. 18, "*I sinned,*" looking back to the primal, all-comprehending transgression, in breaking away from the father's control. **Against heaven** is rendered by some "unto heaven," as though the magnitude of his iniquity was to be represented as towering even to heaven, and filling all the intervening space. But, rather, heaven, as the abode of God and angels and all that is holy, is personified, and sin is thought of as violation of its will and spirit and example. (Meyer.)—**And I am no more worthy to be called thy son.** Westcott and Hort add, "make me as one of thy hired servants," whether rightly the text-critics must decide. The sentence is found in the three most important MSS. of this passage, B., D., and ℵ., with other uncials, which are supported by various auxiliary authorities. Against it are the greater number of uncials, including A. and L., with many subsidiary authorities. What seems to have contributed largely to its exclusion from most critical texts is the fact that Augustine, not finding it in his copies, has, in his comments on the verse, shown such beautiful reasons for the omission, compared with v. 19, that we feel that the prodigal ought not to have repeated these words to his father. It is easy to see, however, what propriety the Latin Father might have discovered in them, had he been familiar with one of the early texts in which they were found. If we understand that sen-

22 But the father said to his servants, Bring forth the best robe, and put it on him; and put a ring on his hand, and shoes on *his* feet:
23 And bring hither the fatted calf, and kill it; and let us eat, and be merry:
24 ᵃ For this my son was dead, and is alive again; he was lost, and is found. And they began to be merry.
25 Now his elder son was in the field: and as he came and drew nigh to the house, he heard music and dancing.
26 And he called one of the servants, and asked what these things meant.
27 And he said unto him, Thy brother is come; and thy father hath killed the fatted calf, because he hath received him safe and sound.

22 thy son.¹ But the father said to his ²servants, Bring forth quickly the best robe, and put it on him; and put a ring on his hand, and shoes on his 23 feet: and bring the fatted calf, *and* kill it, and let us 24 eat, and make merry: for this my son was dead, and is alive again; he was lost, and is found. And they 25 began to be merry. Now his elder son was in the field: and as he came and drew nigh to the house, 26 he heard music and dancing. And he called to him one of the ²servants, and inquired what these things 27 might be. And he said unto him, Thy brother is come; and thy father hath killed the fatted calf, be-

ᵃ ver. 32; Ephes. 2:1; 5:14; Rev. 3:1.——1 Some ancient authorities add, *make me as one of thy hired servants.* See ver. 19......2 Gr. *bondservants.*

tence not to have been spoken here, the better explanation of the omission is that the father was too eager, in his joy, to hear more of confession.

22. But the father said to his servants, Bring forth the best robe—the one best suited to denote love and honor—**and put it on him.** This and the following acts, putting a signet ring on his hand (see *Dict. of Bib.,* Art. Ring), **and shoes on his feet,** are all tokens of his full restoration to the paternal favor, and a preparation for the further festivities in celebration of his return.

23. And bring (omit, hither) **the fatted calf.** The Greek word is used also for a heifer, or young bullock, of greater age than we mean by "calf." The article points to a definite, well-known animal, kept for a special feast, perhaps in hope of this very occasion. **Kill it, and let us eat, and be** (or, *make*) **merry.** This, according to universal custom, would be the crowning evidence of the joy of the father and family at the restoration of his son. The merriment intended is that joy which manifests itself in the gayety and mirth of a banquet. (Comp. Ruth 3: 7.) The picture is drawn from the country customs of the time. The verb translated *kill* is specifically appropriate to the idea of "sacrifice." We cannot consistently suppose that it was used fully in that sense here, but when the father says "sacrifice it," his feeling reaches after something more interesting and solemn than an ordinary meal.

24. For this my son was dead, and is alive again—came to life—**he was lost, and is found.** An excellent reason for great gladness.—**Was dead.** Dead to me, dead to virtue, dead to happiness. **Was lost;** repents the thought, and, as would seem, in a way designed to bring this recovery into the manifest series of the lost sheep and the lost piece of silver. The being dead typifies the state of sin and exposure to eternal punishment (Rom. 8:6); and the coming to life is the entrance upon that state of freedom from sin and service to God, the end of which is "everlasting life." (Rom. 6: 22, 23; comp. 1 John 3: 14.)—**And they began to be merry.** This is for the present parable the parallel to the rejoicing of the shepherd and the woman (ver. 8, 9), and has also its counterpart in the joy of God and his angels. That the latter reasonably exceeds the joy excited by the case of any number of such as need no repentance, appears from the account—

25-32. OF THE ELDER SON.

This is teaching additional to what could find place in one of the preceding parables concerning the ninety-nine just persons.

25. Now his elder son was in the field: toiling in a spirit which he himself, in ver. 29, calls "service," or, literally, "bond-service," to his father—**and as he came**—at the close of the day—**and drew nigh to the house, he heard music and dancing.** This was a part of the merry-making of the household, significant of the joy of *pardon;* but the tired and joyless soul of the Pharisee, and worker out of his own righteousness, knows nothing of this. Suspicious, jealous, and destitute of true filial confidence, he does not go to his father, in sympathy, or for explanation.

26. He called one of the servants, and asked (or, *inquired*) **what these things meant** (lit., *might be*). Cheerfulness and rejoicing were things so strange in that abode of slavish propriety, that their natural manifestations were a mystery.

27. And he said unto him, Thy brother is come, etc. The servant told him all he knew; the change in the brother's character would not come within his range of notice.

28 And he was angry, and would not go in: therefore came his father out, and entreated him.
29 And he answering said to *his* father, Lo, these many years do I serve thee, neither transgressed I at any time thy commandment: and yet thou never gavest me a kid, that I might make merry with my friends:
30 But as soon as this thy son was come, which hath devoured thy living with harlots, thou hast killed for him the fatted calf.
31 And he said unto him, Son, thou art ever with me, and all that I have is thine.
32 It was meet that we should make merry, and be glad; *a* for this thy brother was dead, and is alive again; and was lost, and is found.

28 cause he hath received him safe and sound. But he was angry, and would not go in: and his father
29 came out, and intreated him. But he answered and said to his father, Lo, these many years do I serve thee, and I never transgressed a commandment of thine: and *yet* thou never gavest me a kid, that I
30 might make merry with my friends: but when this thy son came, who hath devoured thy living with
31 harlots, thou killedst for him the fatted calf. And he said unto him, ¹ Son, thou art ever with me, and
32 all that is mine is thine. But it was meet to make merry and be glad: for this thy brother was dead, and is alive *again*; and *was* lost, and is found.

a ver. 21.—¹ Gr. *Child.*

28. The impulse of a natural fraternal affection would have been to rush in and signify delight at the wanderer's safe return. But this man's conduct was like that of the Pharisees toward the publicans whom Christ won to his kingdom.—**And he was angry, and would not go in.** His base feeling partook of vexation that favor should be shown to an unworthy member of the family, a grudging of joy to others in which he could not sympathize, and grumbling for the consumption of property which would be only a loss to him. He would have nothing to do with it all.—**Therefore came his father out.** He might justly have left him sulking to his own damage, yet he symbolizes God in his universal kindness, desiring the salvation of Pharisee as well as publican.—**And entreated him.** We may imagine the arguments by which he would try to induce the reluctant spirit to join the festive company within.

29. And he answering said to his father. Of course, we are to have a surly refusal; but notice the ground on which it is rested by a hard, pains-taking, self-satisfied unloving, unfraternal, censorious Pharisee. **Lo**—a thing to be particularly noticed; he does not, like his repentant brother (ver. 21), employ the appellation, Father—**these many years**—from my birth to the present hour—**do I serve thee;**—render bond-service—**neither,** etc. (better, *and I never transgressed a commandment of thine*)—I have been always and absolutely perfect in obedience. But observe the lack of *love* in all he says.—**And yet thou never gavest me a kid**—to say nothing of a calf, or heifer. His selfishness and jealousy appear in his emphasis on **me:** to ME, thou never gavest.—**That I might make merry with my friends**—honest and virtuous people, as they are.

30. But as soon as (or, *when*) **this thy son was come** (*came*)**, which hath devoured thy living with harlots, thou hast killed for him the fatted calf.** The loss of the property evidently offends him as much as the vice. And observe that it is a brother's amiable comment which alone informs us, specifically, of this most degraded trait of the prodigal's excess, even if it were true, and necessarily involved in the charge of "riotous living."

31. And he said unto him, Son—the Greek is, *child*, a term of more tender affection. The father's impartial love has regard for both.—**Thou art ever with me, and all that I have is thine.** This is an answer to the objection that no special exhibitions of favor had been made to the elder son. There had been no occasion for them; he had shared in the daily abundance of the father's house. There had been no room for them; he was always there, and the celebration of a return could only be made when there had been a departure. The Saviour does not, in this connection, pass judgment on the question whether the Pharisees, represented by the elder son, were as righteous as they claimed to be (ver. 29). Assuming them to be righteous, legally, they were entitled to the blessings of a legal covenant, and were enjoying them according to their legality. But his kingdom includes only those who feel and distinctly admit their unrighteousness, and so are led to repentance and faith in God's promise of mercy, the result of which is forgiveness on his part, and adoption. The enforcement of this truth was better suited than anything else imaginable to awaken in the hearts of the self-righteous, also, the inquiry whether this would not be the better way for them.

32. (*But*) **it was meet**—morally incumbent—**that we should** (lit., *to*) **make merry**

CHAPTER XVI.

AND he said also unto his disciples, There was a certain rich man, which had a steward; and the same was accused unto him that he had wasted his goods.

1 And he said also unto the disciples, There was a certain rich man, who had a steward; and the same was accused unto him that he was wasting his goods.

and be glad. This emphasizes the duty of joy and gladness, as opposed to the sullen moroseness of the elder son—*to make merry and be glad* standing first in the Greek sentence. Joy and mirth are appropriate and pleasing in the sight of God on fit occasions; and the bringing up of the miserable, the outcast, the lost, to peace and virtue, is eminently a fit occasion.—**For this thy brother**—his brother, and so of the same nature and worth as himself; although he would not call him "brother," but, "thy son" (ver. 30). **Was dead and is alive** (omit **again**). The explanation of the verse is the same as of verses 23, 24. Rejoicing on such an occasion was as proper for the ceremonially just, or righteous, men, as for any; but their spirit was most unjust. Some have interpreted this parable as indicating the Jewish nation by the elder son, and the Gentiles by the younger. Doubtless, we can *apply it*, in several particulars, to the contrast between those two sections of mankind; but its primary reference was, clearly, as pointed out above. And on the principle that every Scripture is applicable to all men, in proportion as they are such as those originally addressed by it, we may find it true of every sin-sick, repenting, believing soul, over against the worldly, hard, impenitent, self-sufficient neighbor, who feels no need of repentance, and sees no sense in it.

Ch. 16. 1-13. Parable of the Dishonest Steward.

1. And he said also unto his (literally, *the*) **disciples.** There is no intimation of any change of scene or time, but only of the persons immediately addressed. Previously it had been the Pharisees (ch. 15:3); now it is the **disciples**, meaning the body of his adherents, not merely the twelve. The particular design of the parable was to teach all his followers the right use of earthly riches in reference to the future and eternal life. Its logical connection with the preceding parables, supposing it to have followed them, in the hearing of substantially the same company (ver. 14, the Pharisees were listening, although he was not talking to them,) has been differently understood. It is barely possible that

the folly of the younger son in "wasting" his inheritance (ch. 15:13), instead of turning it to some profitable use, may have suggested an application to Christ's followers, of the instruction given by another instance of the "wasting" of a pecuniary trust, in the verse before us. To impress the intended lesson, our Saviour supposes the case of a rich landed proprietor, the management of whose estate is committed to a steward, completely trusted, and of respectable social position. This man is found by his employer to be in the habit of wasting, squandering, his property; *i. e.*, the income of the business carried on. When he is notified that he is discharged from the office, and required to furnish his account of the state of the property, he studies what means of living are possible for him, now that this is to be taken away. Promptly he decides to court the favor of his master's tenants, by great remission of claims that lay against them, in return for which they would gratefully afford him a living when he should need it. It is assumed that this procedure, the details of which are dramatically described in a couple of cases, proves successful; and as a specimen of shrewd, though dishonest policy, in the use of riches to promote temporal good, Jesus finds in it a pattern of worthy prudence in the religious employment of money to promote heavenly blessedness. **There was a certain rich man which had a steward.** The rich man represents God; not Satan, nor Mammon. The **steward** is not called a servant, although even slaves often filled positions of exalted trust and responsibility. His office was that of overseer and manager of the affairs of his employer. If we think of the latter as a great Roman or Oriental proprietor, whose slaves might be numbered by the thousand, and his tenants, some of them, large farmers, we see that the post of steward would be one of no mean rank. In the parable he stands for a disciple of Christ, entrusted with earthly possessions to be turned to account for promoting the interests of his proprietor, God. Although not many rich men were attaching themselves to Christ, yet some of the many publicans who flocked to him were likely to be men of

2 And he called him, and said unto him, How is it that I hear this of thee? give an account of thy stewardship; for thou mayest be no longer steward.
3 Then the steward said within himself, What shall I do? for my lord taketh away from me the stewardship: I cannot dig; to beg I am ashamed.
4 I am resolved what to do, that, when I am put out of the stewardship, they may receive me into their houses.
5 So he called every one of his lord's debtors unto *him*, and said unto the first, How much owest thou unto my lord?
6 And he said, An hundred measures of oil. And he

2 And he called him, and said unto him, What is this that I hear of thee? render the account of thy stewardship; for thou canst be no longer steward. And the steward said within himself, What shall I do, 'seeing that my lord taketh away the stewardship
4 from me? I have not strength to dig; to beg I am ashamed. I am resolved what to do, that, when I am put out of the stewardship, they may receive me into
5 their houses. And calling to him each one of his lord's debtors, he said to the first, How much owest
6 thou unto my lord? And he said, A hundred ¹ meas-

---

1 Gr. *baths*, the bath being a Hebrew measure. See Ezek. 45: 10, 11, 14.

---

wealth, and many others had property to make them comparatively rich. All such should think themselves God's servants in the administration of whatever they had. The accusation of the steward, in the parable, was of such a nature, and with such evidence, as to convince the proprietor of the untrustworthiness of his agent. Hence he summons him, not to institute any trial, or even examination, but after a complaint of wounded confidence—

2. **How is it,** etc.—better, *what is this that I hear of thee?*—to announce his dismissal, and to demand a statement of the affairs under his charge. **Give an account** (lit., *render the account*) **of thy stewardship; for thou mayest be no longer steward.** It may seem that, in the wide discretion involved in the management of such a trust, the unfaithfulness and peculations had not been such as would constitute a ground for a criminal prosecution. The master appears ready to let him go upon his presenting the account of the state of the property, which was necessary to conduct it properly thereafter. The minutiæ of the illustration can hardly be applied in the practical lesson. They prepare the way for his discharge from the office, which discharge answers to the disciple's death.

3. The steward's reflections on his case suggest no feeling of repentance for his conduct, and no shade of unfairness on his lord's part. They do betray imperturbable composure, readiness of invention, unscrupulous willingness for whatever seems expedient.—**What shall I do?** etc. His dependence on the continuance of his stewardship for a living, shows that he had not saved, for his own permanent advantage, any part of what he had embezzled from his master. In this, he was a pattern of the rogues and defrauders of our age, the most egregious of whom, while cheating the confidence of others out of enormous sums, and involving many in utter ruin, are

seldom found to have secured any fortune to themselves thereby.—**I cannot** (lit., *have not strength to*) **dig**; yet manual labor was all that honestly lay between him and utter destitution.—**To beg I am ashamed.** The Jewish sentiment is well expressed in Eccles. 40: 28: "My son, lead not a beggar's life; for better it is to die than to beg."

4. **I am resolved what to do.** It is as if, after profound study, the thought had flashed upon him: "I have it; I know now what to do."—Farrar on the passage. **That, when I am put out of the stewardship, they may receive me into their houses.** His cessation from the office is decreed, but is not yet actually effected. This fact gives the basis of his scheme. **They** refers to the persons whom he proposes to lay under such obligations, and so to involve, apparently, at least, in his rascality, that they will, from gratitude, and from fear of exposure, repay him when he needs it.

5. **So he called every one of his lord's debtors.** There is room for difference of opinion as to whether he called them jointly, or in succession. His business was transacted with them separately. Many understand that these debtors were middlemen, shopkeepers, who had bought large quantities of the crops of the estate, for which they were yet holden. But what follows agrees better with the supposition that they were tenants, each cultivating a considerable farm, and following, mainly, a distinct line of production, of whose fruits they were to return the proprietor's share in kind. Two cases are mentioned, merely as specimens of the procedure with an indefinite number. That they are to have unequal abatements favors the view that they came before the agent one at a time.—**How much owest thou?** This question was natural, as addressed to a tenant, whose account would be the basis of a settlement.

6. **And he said, A hundred measures** (βάτος, Heb., *bath*) **of oil.** As the ratio be-

Cʜ. XVI.]   LUKE.   249

said unto him, Take thy bill, and sit down quickly, and write fifty.
7 Then said he to another, And how much owest thou? And he said, A hundred measures of wheat. And he said unto him, Take thy bill, and write fourscore.
8 And the lord commended the unjust steward, because he had done wisely: for the children of this world are in their generation wiser than ᵃ the children of light.

ures of oil. And he said unto him, Take thy ¹ bond,
7 and sit down quickly and write fifty. Then said he to another, And how much owest thou? And he said, A hundred ² measures of wheat. He saith unto
8 him, Take thy ¹ bond, and write fourscore. And his lord commended ³ the unrighteous steward because he had done wisely: for the sons of this ⁴ world are for their own generation wiser than the sons of the

ᵃ John 12:36; Ephes. 5:8; 1 Thess. 5:5.—1 Gr. *writings*....2 Gr. *cors*, the cor being a Hebrew measure. See Ezek. 45:11....3 Gr. *the steward of unrighteousness*....4 Or, *age*.

tween Hebrew measures and our own is hard to make out, estimates of the capacity of the *bath* vary from four and a half to nine gallons. Josephus, our most important authority, in spite of much inconsistency in his several statements, clearly implies, however, its equivalence to the Greek *firkin* (μετρητής), (John 2:6), which we know (Smith's *Class. Antiq.*, Art. Métretes), to have been about nine gallons. (See *Dict. of Bib.*, pp. 3506 f.) **Oil**, of the olive, was one of the staples of life in Palestine, and the olive tree was held in high esteem by the people. The oil stood to them in place of butter, lard, oil, etc., in our culinary uses. Notice, the debtor does not say he is holden *for* so much oil, but that this quantity of that article is what he owes. **Take**—rather, *receive*, as though it was handed back to him—**thy bill**—lit., *writings*, account current, or book account. **Sit down quickly, and write fifty. Quickly**, since time presses; my settlement must be made. **Write fifty**—either making out a new account, according to which you are to pay fifty measures, or simply alter the letter (*qoph*, or *rho*) for one hundred into that (*nun*, or *nu*) for fifty. This man would thus be relieved of obligation for fifty firkins of oil.

7. The next man would, in like manner, be favored to the extent of twenty out of one hundred measures of wheat. The proportion was altered here, for aught we can see, at the caprice of the steward. It was smaller than in the preceding case, the measures being very much larger. The Hebrew *cor* (Greek, κόρος), which is named here, was a dry measure, containing ten times the *bath*, or *firkin*, mentioned above for the oil; hence, ten bushels and upward. There would be a saving to the debtor of one hundred and sixty bushels of wheat. Suppose such reductions to be carried through a long list of tenants, and it is manifest that the steward is warranted in expecting a large compensation from them. We may suppose, with many, that he was only foregoing the premium which he had ordinarily taken for himself on what he actually paid to the lord; but such details must be pure imagination.

8. At all events, the rich man, on learning the trick to which his agent had resorted, was pleased with it as a specimen of true Oriental shrewdness.—**And the lord**—namely, of this steward—**commended the unjust steward** —the Greek, "*steward of injustice*," strongly marks this trait of his character—**because he had done wisely** (*prudently*). It is strange that, with the better example of Wiclif before them, Tyndale, and the chief translators since, including the authors of the Revised Version, should have rendered the Greek, φρονίμως, *prudently*, as if it had been σοφῶς, *wisely*. The latter is used properly in a worthier sense; the former applies properly to what is ingeniously adapted to the accomplishment of any practical ends. Both this adverb and the strong assertion of the injustice of the steward show that his master did not praise him as dishonest, but as quick-witted, and shrewd in the choice of measures fit to help him out of difficulty. He had settled with the tenants in such way that their books would show a great deal less due to the proprietor than they had expected; yet, as he was still the agent, his act was conclusive. His course could be presented as an example, accordingly, of the prudent, well-considered, use of pecuniary means for the promotion of future important designs. **For the children** (*sons*) **of this world** (or, *age*)— meaning the period which precedes the establishment of the Messianic kingdom—"this present evil world"—**are in** (*for*) **their** (*own*) **generation wiser** (*more prudent*) **than the children** (*sons*) **of** (*the*) **light.** This sentence gives a reason (*for*) why the worldling steward should have acted shrewdly. It is just a particular case under a general rule. **Children** (or, *sons*) **of this world** are, according to a Hebrew way of speaking, men who share in the spirit of the time, bear a character appropriate to it. So of "the

9 And I say unto you,*a* Make to yourselves friends of the mammon of unrighteousness; that, when ye fail, they may receive you into everlasting habitations.

9 light. And I say unto you, Make to yourselves friends ¹ by means of the mammon of unrighteousness; that, when it shall fail, they may receive you

a Dan. 4:27; Matt. 6:19; 19:21; ch. 11:41; 1 Tim. 6:17, 18, 19.—1 Gr. *out of.*

children of light" (Eph. 5:8; 1 Thess. 5:5).—**Generation**—sort of people, "kith and kin." The sense of the sentence, then, is that the people of the world are more shrewd and successful in turning to profitable account their relations to other such men, than the true children of the kingdom (comp. Matt. 8:12) are in regard to their brethren in Christ. The tenor of the parable restricts this judgment, in large measure, to the employment of wealth, worldly goods. One "son of this world" is signalized, who so used the property of which he had control, though not his own, as to gain favor from his fellows, of much value to the rest of his life. What he did prudently, but not honestly, the disciples should do, with the means committed to them by God, both prudently *and* honestly, by aid and favor to their brethren, that their heavenly joys might be eternally the richer. Kindness and beneficence to those in need would, in the Christian sphere, be the course analogous, in point of prudence, to that of the unjust steward in the unscrupulous courses of this world.

9. And I say unto you—as that lord praised his agent—**Make to yourselves friends of** (rather, *by means of*) **the mammon of unrighteousness.** Mammon is the Chaldee name for riches, sometimes personified, in thought, as when our Saviour speaks of serving Mammon (ver. 13). Making friends by means of mammon, or, out of mammon, is then, so using wealth as to gain friends, and secure the gratitude and good will of those whom we have helped. Mammon is said to be the **mammon of unrighteousness,** because in many cases its acquisition and use implied so much of iniquity that one who saw this in its profoundest depths and boundless breadth, might well characterize it sweepingly as, in itself, "richesse of wickednesse," Wiclif; or, "wicked mammon," Tyndale. Compare his declarations concerning the difficulty of salvation to a rich man. Among the first manifestations of the distinctive Christian spirit, in the infant church, was the disposition to act according to this precept. (Acts 2:44, 45; 4:34, 35). It was too strongly antagonistic to carnal nature not to decline with the decline of devotion and zeal in the church. But wherever we get a view of the spirit of Christianity, in subsequent ages, something appears of a consciousness of duty to use money Christianly. Even in our own day, with its immoderate eagerness for pecuniary gain, there is, perhaps, more than ever a public sense of the claims of society on wealth, plainly traceable to Christ's teaching, which promises a yet closer compliance with his example and spirit. **That when ye fail** (rather, *it shall fail*), or, "shall have failed," which it will at death, when stewardship must cease—**they may receive you into everlasting habitations** (literally, *the eternal tabernacles*). This is a more picturesque way of saying, "that you may enjoy the fruit of your beneficent use of earthly riches through eternal ages." This figure for the residence in heaven is obviously suggested by the mention of "their houses." (ver. 4). *Eternal tabernacles,* or, *tents,* is an *oxymoron;* which, in applying so incongruous an epithet as *eternal,* emphasizes the contrast between the transient habitations of earth and the everlasting abodes to which we go. (John 14:2; 2 Cor. 5:1). The word **they** points apparently to the friends who shall have been made. There is indeed a difficulty in making plain how the beneficiaries of the prudent rich among the sons of light are to receive them into the places of celestial joy. But the fiction of the intercession of departed saints is not even faintly suggested by the idea that those who have gone before **receive**=welcome—not lend, nor bring, nor introduce, into the heavenly blessedness those who have introduced them into the spiritual life, or greatly enriched it for them, on the earth. And when we see the glorified Jesus himself making the kindness of his followers to those less well off the comprehensive reason for welcoming them to his Father's kingdom (Matt. 25:34 ff.), there seems great propriety in those poor themselves joyfully greeting the arrival of their benefactors among the blessed. The only serious hindrance to the reception of this view as being intended by the language, is that it supposes the objects of loving liberality to have departed first to the reward, while in practice that would be the less common case.

10 a He that is faithful in that which is least is faithful also in much; and he that is unjust in the least is unjust a.so in much.
11 If therefore ye have not been faithful in the unrighteous mammon, who will commit to your trust the true *riches?*
12 And if ye have not been faithful in that which is another man's, who shall give you that which is your own?
13 b No servant can serve two masters: for either he will hate the one, and love the other; or else he will hold to the one, and despise the other. Ye cannot serve God and mammon.

10 into the eternal tabernacles. He that is faithful in a very little is faithful also in much; and he that is unrighteous in a very little is unrighteous also in
11 much. If therefore ye have not been faithful in the unrighteous mammon, who will commit to your trust
12 the true *riches?* And if ye have not been faithful in that which is another's, who will give you that which
13 is 1 your own? No 2 servant can serve two masters; for either he will hate the one, and love the other; or else he will hold to one, and despise the other. Ye cannot serve God and mammon.

a Matt. 25: 21; ch. 19: 17....*b* Matt. 6: 24.——1 Some ancient authorities read, *our own*....2 Gr. *household-servant*.

But this partial incongruity may have been inevitable in the otherwise very expressive figure. The statement of the verse is thus an application of the preceding parable, and sets forth the Christian's duty, as antithetically analogous to the course of the wicked steward. The other possible reference of the word **they** is, to those, indefinitely conceived of, who may be the proper agents of such a service, as the angels. (Ch. 16: 22; Matt. 24: 31).

10-13. THE RIGHT USE OF RICHES.

10. He that is faithful in that which is least (or, *in a very little*—comp. 19: 17), **is faithful also in much**, etc. A maxim of experience in worldly affairs, which imports that the right use of worldly goods is faithfulness in a small thing, and is indispensable to the use and enjoyment of the higher riches of salvation. It thus enforces the precept in verse 9. The benevolent employment of riches is faithfulness to that trust.

11. If therefore ye have not been faithful—read, rather, *If ye did not evince yourselves faithful;* the point of view is at the day of judgment—**in the unrighteous mammon.** The sense was explained in the preceding paragraph. **Who will commit to your trust the true riches? The true riches** are the heavenly blessedness, which is genuine wealth, or welfare, satisfying and inalienable, and so, real; while the earthly riches, being neither satisfying nor permanent, are a sham and mockery. The question implies that no one will give them, and seems to import that heaven itself will be a trust committed to him that receives it, to be used for furthering the purposes of God. What a rebuke to the selfish and luxurious wealth of nominal Christendom! How many candidates for the heavenly riches may be arrested at the door, by the question, How did you employ the unrighteous mammon trusted to you on the earth?

12. That which is another man's—(strictly, *another's*), namely, God's, whose steward, for the administration of God's property, the disciple was, during his earthly life. —**Who shall give you that which is your own?** *i. e.*, an eternal interest in the kingdom, that good part which shall never be taken away from you. The heavenly possession, once obtained, is ours, subject to no revocation, withdrawal, loss, or impairment. There is evidence so strong in favor of the reading "*our own*," instead of **your own**, that Westcott and Hort have substituted the former for the latter. It is not, however, decisive, on external grounds; and anything less than that cannot warrant our supposing that Jesus reckoned himself among the disciples, in an uncertainty like this.

13. No servant—"domestic," Davidson, or house-servant—**can serve**—obey the commands of—**two masters.** A caution to the disciples that they must not let the service of God, in the use of wealth, slide into a service of mammon. The maxim is found in a perfectly appropriate connection at Matt. 6: 24; but its fitness here, also, is so obvious as to warrant the conclusion that it was repeated by Christ. It is here more precisely stated. In a general view, it would be questionable whether no one can serve two masters. It would have to be understood of a simultaneous service to masters whose requirements are incompatible with each other. This is specifically indicated in our passage. No house-servant can render unqualified, absolute service (δουλεύειν) to different masters.—**For either he will hate the one**—A, **and love the other**—B, so as to give the latter the real allegiance—**or he will hold to one**—A, so as to render him the real service—**and despise the other**—B, giving no willing heed to his

14 And the Pharisees also, ª who were covetous, heard all these things: and they derided him.
15 And he said unto them, Ye are they which ᵇ justify yourselves before men; but ᶜ God knoweth your hearts: for ᵈ that which is highly esteemed among men is abomination in the sight of God.
16 ᵉ The law and the prophets *were* until John: since that time the kingdom of God is preached, and every man presseth into it.

14 And the Pharisees, who were lovers of money, 15 heard all these things; and they scoffed at him. And he said unto them, Ye are they that justify yourselves in the sight of men; but God knoweth your hearts: for that which is exalted among men is an 16 abomination in the sight of God. The law and the prophets *were* until John; from that time the gospel of the kingdom of God is preached, and every man

a Matt. 23:14....*b* ch. 10:29....*c* Ps. 7:9....*d* 1 Sam. 16:7....*e* Matt. 4:17; 11:12, 13; ch. 7:29.

commands.—**Ye cannot serve God and mammon.** These are, eminently two masters who demand, each, the full devotion of the man. The service of God must be the supreme care; and all care for mammon must be brought under subordination to this.

14-18. THE PHARISEES CONDEMNED.

14, 15. These verses stand in an equally close relation to the foregoing and to the parable below (ver. 19-31).—**And the Pharisees also** (also doubtful)—the same to whom he had spoken (15:32)—**who were covetous** (or, *lovers of money*), **heard all these things.** Although he had ceased addressing them, they were listening. This character of the class agreed with many representations of our Lord concerning them, and with various other evidence.—**And they derided** (or, *scoffed at*) **him.** The verb expresses great contempt, as well as abusiveness = "turned up their noses at him." We may almost hear their coarse jeers at his teaching about wealth: "That he should talk about the right use of money!" "Stewardship!" "The incompatiblity of the love of riches with salvation!" "Sour grapes!"—**Ye are they which justify yourselves before men.** Pass yourselves off for righteous, with those who see only the outward appearance.—**But God knoweth your hearts,** and knows that this is only an *appearance*, a cloak and pretense. He finds no righteousness there, where it should all be; if there were any.—**For that which is highly esteemed** (*exalted*) **among men is** (*an*) **abomination in the sight of God.** What a condemnation of the ambitions, pursuits, honors, judgments, of this world!

16-18. These verses are hard to bring into a manifest train with the discourse before and after. Yet they here constitute a train of their own, though reported each, in other Gospels, in a different historical connection. There is no reason, however, to conclude with some that they are thrown in here as scattered statements, not supposed to have any original relation to each other. And, on careful consideration, we find the whole to exhibit the joints of an argument (the details not being preserved) to prove the culpability of the Pharisees in their sham righteousness, from their own law, when apprehended in its true spirit. The argument is that the law and the prophets, the Old Testament system, which was in legitimate force until John the Baptist, is, although since replaced, as to its organized polity, by the kingdom of God, not only not abolished, but even sharpened and made more exacting, on the disposition of its subjects. This prepares the way for the sentence (ver. 31) that that law shows the need of repentance, on the part of the Pharisees, of their sin of covetousness, and the misuse of wealth. The strictness of the requirement of the law upon the spirit is then exemplified in the gospel form of the law concerning divorce. We have thus a fresh application of the principles of the kingdom of God as laid down in Matt. 5:16, 20, 31 f.

16. Were until John; *i. e.*, were in force, or (in antithesis to "the gospel is preached," below, comp. Acts 15:21) were preached. No verb is expressed in the Greek. Their full and formal authority continued until John the Baptist came, announcing the proximity of the Messianic reign, and even until the installation by him of Jesus in the Messianic office. John was the boundary line between the Old and the New Economy, yet not so but that he himself stood at the highest stage and culminating point of the former, (ch. 7:28.)—**Since** (rather, *from*) **that time** —(Matt. 11:12; "from the days of John")—**the kingdom of God is preached**—announced in glad tidings (εὐαγγελίζεται). The announcement is effected through John, but especially by Christ himself and his disciples. On the idea of **the kingdom of God,** see on ch. 6:20.—**And every man**—everybody; men of every description, even the publicans, in large numbers—**presseth into it.** The same Greek verb is used in a similar connection, in Matt. 11:12, as a passive, in the sense

17 ᵃ And it is easier for heaven and earth to pass, than one tittle of the law to fail.
18 ᵇ Whosoever putteth away his wife, and marrieth another, committeth adultery: and whosoever marrieth her that is put away from *her* husband committeth adultery.

17 entereth violently into it. But it is easier for heaven and earth to pass away, than for one tittle of the 18 law to fail. Every one that putteth away his wife, and marrieth another, committeth adultery: and he that marrieth one that is put away from a husband committeth adultery.

---

a Ps. 102: 26, 27; Isa. 40: 8; 51: 6; Matt. 5: 18; 1 Pet. 1: 25....b Matt. 5: 32; 19: 9; Mark 10: 11; 1 Cor. 7: 10, 11.

---

of "is the object of eager attempts." "suffereth violence;" here it is in the middle voice, "is forcing his way into," "eagerly strives to enter." This is a vehement statement of the vehement facts then patent to the observation of Christ's hearers. John's mission had produced a great excitement concerning the kingdom of heaven, and Christ's own teaching and works had latterly strengthened it, so that multitudes were eagerly seeking unto him, and were striving, more or less intelligently, to secure the blessings which he offered. This popular zeal had been strongly manifested since the feeding of the five thousand in Galilee. On the present journey toward Jerusalem we catch frequent glimpses of excited, enthusiastic throngs, in spite of the enmity of many leading men, culminating soon afterward in the multitudinous procession of the so-called Palm Sunday before his crucifixion. Jesus had, doubtless, sad reason to note the absence from this following of most of those rulers whose conversion would have done so much to win the adherence to him of the nation. He was also distinctly aware that many of the people who heard him gladly failed to appreciate him in his highest character, as the Saviour of sinners; but this widespread and earnest favor toward him may easily account for the hyperbole, **every man,** etc. The more obviously so, since the present tense (in Greek) of the verb **presseth into** does not express a completed deed, but an effort, a process, an inchoate and tentative act. In Matthew the same meaning is differently conceived, as already intimated in this note.

17. And (or, *but*) **it is easier for heaven and earth to pass,** etc. The form of expression implies that it is impossible for the law, in its spirit as divinely intended, not to reach complete fulfillment. This is affirmed to prevent the mistake that, because now the kingdom of God was superseding the Mosaic Economy, the obligation of the true law was in the least degree weakened. **One tittle** (*keraia*), is one of the minute appendages of Hebrew letters (comparable to the dot of an i with us). The slightest particle of the meaning of no word or letter of the law should relax its hold. Its true fulfillment, the gospel alone, as Christ teaches (Matt. 5: 17-20), is adapted to bring about, and does, according to Paul (Rom. 7: 1-6; 8: 2, 3), actually bring about.

18. In what manner, and to what extent Christ fulfills the law, even while he sets free from the law its outward control, this verse is intended to give a typical example. The marriage relation, which the ancient law aimed to strengthen and subject to divine authority—although leaving, necessarily, for the time (Matt. 19: 8) much room for human caprice, was now made absolutely indissoluble. Neither party to the union can treat it as null, so as to contract another marriage, without forfeiting the character of Christ's disciples. One qualification omitted in this brief and fragmentary declaration, we are bound to supply from the fuller discussion in Matthew—"saving for the cause of fornication" (Matt. 5: 32). That cause, once established, has of itself put asunder those whom God had joined together. No law of the kingdom is more plain than that adultery is chargeable on man or woman who marries again while a former wife or husband lives, not having been found guilty of adultery. This principle was peculiarly suited to show the superior purity and unworldliness of Christ's instructions, as compared with the Jewish law.—The foregoing explanation of these three verses, as an application of the law to condemn the self-justification of the Pharisees, appears to be at least as consistent with itself, and with what went before, as any other which has been proposed. It is at least an unwarranted dictum of Immer (*Hermeneutics*, p. 207 Eng. Trans.), that "it is quite idle elaboration to strive to bring out a connection between these three sentences." They are in his view "only detached apothegms." That each one stands separately in an apparently natural historical connection in Matthew, and even the supposition that they have respectively their true connections there, does not at all hinder their having here a logical relation to each other

19 There was a certain rich man, which was clothed in purple and fine linen, and fared sumptuously every day:
20 And there was a certain beggar named Lazarus, which was laid at his gate, full of sores,

19 Now there was a certain rich man, and he was clothed in purple and fine linen, ¹ faring sumptuously every day · and a certain beggar named Lazarus

¹ Or, *living in mirth and splendour every day.*

and to the whole train of discourse. If we agree that the sentences were spoken under the circumstances indicated in Matthew, we may inquire whether Luke found them combined in one of his documents, with or without an evident design, or whether he himself so combined them, finding them scattered in his sources, without indication of the manner of their origin.

19-31. Parable of the Rich Man (Dives) and Lazarus.

If we give up connection of thought between verses 15-18 and the preceding, this parable stands entirely out of relation to them, and to everything before and after. But in that train of ideas which we have indicated, we may trace the joints of a continuous and reasoned discourse, very much abridged in our report. The instruction concerning the right use of riches had led to the insulting taunts of the Pharisees, whose hypocritical self-righteousness had been shown condemned by the true spirit of their own standard of righteousness, namely, the Old Testament revelation. Now a parable is added to exhibit in concrete form the estimation in which God actually holds men who are rich toward themselves (ver. 15), and have failed to heed the teaching on this subject of Moses and the prophets. Verses 19-26 contain the practical comment on verse 15; verses 27-31, that on verses 16-18.

19. (*Now*) **there was a certain rich man, which** (or, *and he*) **was clothed in purple and fine linen, and fared** (lit., *faring*) **sumptuously every day.** Some have alleged that the Saviour, charging no crime on Dives (the Latin word used in the Vulgate for a "rich man"), condemns wealth absolutely. But when we see the connection, as we have traced it above, it appears at once that we have here a type of those money-loving Pharisees (ver. 14) who made sport of Christ's requirement, that money should be benevolently used to the advantage of fellow-men, in the service of God. His dress was after the most luxurious, even royal, style then known. "Living in mirth and splen-

dor," as in the margin of the Revision, is nearer to the Greek than the familiar text. The participle is of the verb which is translated "to make merry" in 15: 23, 32, and describes a life given wholly to self-indulgence and merry-making. He was a perfect example of the prosperity possible for a man who acts not as a faithful steward for God. God's judgment on such could best be shown by following him into the eternal state. The Pharisees held strongly to the doctrine of future retribution.

20, ff. A certain beggar, named Lazarus. A "poor man"; that is, reduced to such straits of penury, by affliction, as to be dependent on the charity of others for subsistence. Christ had not given any name to his imaginary rich man, although Christendom has made one of the Latin adjective "Dives," as stated above. His character was apparent from his mode of life. But to indicate the character of the poor man, Christ sympathetically applies to him the Greek equivalent of the Hebrew Eleazar, **Lazarus** —God's help. Poor, neglected, and despised, he still has God on his side.—**Was laid**—had been laid, or thrown down, and so was lying—**at his gate, full of sores.** He had been laid down near the entrance to the rich man's house, in the expectation of his friends that, from the superfluity of the latter, he would have, at least, subsistence. Thus was furnished to the rich man, without trouble of search, an opportunity to act as God's steward, and to make one friend by means of his mammon. How complete the contrast between God's favorite and the devotee of mammon! He was poor, even to perishing of need; the other, overflowing in wealth; diseased, while the other was in sound health; **desiring to be fed** with the mere offal of that table at which the other surfeited himself in revelry. That he was not supplied with the mere crumbs that he desired, is implied in **moreover**, or, *yea, even*, of the second member of verse 21. He did not receive even so much attention, *yea, even* **the dogs**—those horrid creatures, the dread and abomination of an

21 And desiring to be fed with the crumbs which fell from the rich man's table: moreover the dogs came and licked his sores.
22 And it came to pass, that the beggar died, and was carried by the angels into Abraham's bosom: the rich man also died, and was buried;

21 was laid at his gate, full of sores, and desiring to be fed with the *crumbs* that fell from the rich man's table; yea, even the dogs came and licked his sores.
22 And it came to pass, that the beggar died, and that he was carried away by the angels into Abraham's bosom: and the rich man also died, and was buried.

Eastern community—**came and licked his sores**—as if ready to devour him altogether. The man was, doubtless, in rags, and nearly naked, over against the "purple and fine linen" in which Dives was clad.

22. And it came to pass that the beggar died, etc. Jesus hastens to the consummation of the two lines of experience. We are not offended with the details of a life of sensuality and luxury on the one hand, or distressed with the lingering account of the pains of Lazarus. He **died,** famished, as it would seem, and exhausted by maladies, aggravated, not remedied, by proximity to overflowing abundance. His end was a gentle release. While death reigns in the world through sin, and is always a dreadful cloud over our earthly relations, yet to how many under the gospel, poor and sick and old, yea, and to young also, lovers of God and united to Christ, does his approach come as the greatest of blessings! **And was carried (***away***) by the angels into Abraham's bosom.** The experience after death of the two subjects is related, to some extent, in terms and under images adopted and adapted from the Pharisaic theology of that day. (See the proofs in Wetstein on the passage, and sources in Smith, *Bib. Dict.*, Art., Abraham's Bosom.) The being carried **by angels** was regarded as a special privilege of favored souls; because the doctrine was that only the *souls* of the just could enter Paradise. Meyer supposes that, from the entire omission of reference to the pauper's burial, he is carried away *body* and soul, adducing an expression from the *Kabbala* (Idra Rabba), in which, speaking of certain ones deceased,. "holy angels are said to have carried them within that outspread vail." The proof is slight to support so unique a view. Much more probably no funeral is spoken of in this case, because there was none worthy of mention, as compared with that of the rich man. In **Abraham's bosom,** was a familiar designation of the happy state of the righteous dead in Paradise (ch. 23: 43), during the interval between death and the resurrection (compare 4 Mac. 13: 16), where the faithful brothers are sustained in death by the prospect of being welcomed by Abraham, Isaac, and Jacob. To be in one's bosom was then to enjoy the highest intimacy with him, since, while reclining at table, the head of the next lower on the couch rested against the breast of the one above him. Abraham, as father of the nation, would occupy the place of honor; and to be in his bosom was to be as eminently distinguished as possible. Yet after this expression of the felicity of Paradise had become once familiar, we need not suppose that it always suggested the notion of a banquet; but rather of association and companionship. (*And*) **the rich man also died, and was buried.** Meyer thinks the latter item is stated in contrast with Lazarus, whom he makes to have needed no burial, being translated bodily. It is rather to show that his earthly history was consistently terminated. His burial was something to speak of. It continued and crowned the vain and extravagant pomp of his life. Lazarus' body had been as little cared for dead as living.

23. And in hell (rather, *hades*) **he lifted up his eyes, being in torment.** On *hades*, see note on ch. 10: 15. It was the Greek designation now familiar to the Hebrews, through the Greek translation of the Old Testament, of the abode and condition of the dead prior to the judgment. Thither went good and bad alike, but each (by an advance on the intimations of the Hebrew *sheol*) to his own place, the righteous to Paradise—Abraham's bosom—the wicked to hell (γέεννα), see on 12: 5. **He lifted up his eyes**—taking a survey of his altered state. Comp. Milton, *Par. Lost*, I, 56 ff. **Being in torment.** This indicates to which section of hades he had gone. It is mentioned as though a matter of course, seeing what he was. There had been no external determination of his case; leaving this life, he simply went to his own place. It was the righteous antithesis to that ungodly and inhuman merry-making in which he had lived splendidly on the earth. **And seeth Abraham afar off**—being himself far away from the father of the nation, and centre of the future

23 And in hell he lifted up his eyes, being in torments, and seeth Abraham afar off, and Lazarus in his bosom.
24 And he cried and said, Father Abraham, have mercy on me, and send Lazarus, that he may dip the tip of his finger in water, and *cool my tongue; for I ᵇam tormented in this flame.
25 But Abraham said, Son, ᶜremember that thou in thy lifetime receivedst thy good things, and likewise Lazarus evil things: but now he is comforted, and thou art tormented.
26 And beside all this, between us and you there is a great gulf fixed: so that they which would pass from hence to you cannot; neither can they pass to us, that would come from thence.

23 And in Hades he lifted up his eyes, being in torments, and seeth Abraham afar off, and Lazarus in his bosom.
24 And he cried and said, Father Abraham, have mercy on me, and send Lazarus, that he may dip the tip of his finger in water, and cool my
25 tongue; for I am in anguish in this flame. But Abraham said, ¹Son, remember that thou in thy lifetime receivedst thy good things, and Lazarus in like manner evil things: but now here he is comforted,
26 and thou art in anguish. And ²beside all this, between us and you there is a great gulf fixed, that they who would pass from hence to you may not be able, and that none may cross over from thence to

---

a Zech. 14:12....b Isa. 66:24; Mark 9:44, etc....c Job 21:13; ch. 6:24.—1 Gr. Child....2 Or, in all these things.

---

blessedness, which he had expected naturally to share. **And Lazarus in his bosom.** How precisely their conditions are reversed! Lazarus, who had often sent a longing desire toward the overplus of his feasts, now rejoices in a perpetual communion with holy souls, while the rich man looks on at a distance, and must beg—in vain—for some slight alleviation of his woe.

24. And he cried—called aloud, as the distance required—**and said, Father Abraham.** The appellation implies a claim for favor on the ground of mere physical relationship, to which John the Baptist had warned them (ch. 3:8) not to trust.—**Have mercy on me.** Self-righteousness vanishes in the light of eternity, and he pleads for relief only on the ground of pity.—**And send Lazarus,** etc.; spoken not at all in the tone of supercilious mastership over the beggar, but, as significant of his own profound misery, he prays that the first one who is in a situation to do it, should be allowed to grant him some little relief; even so much as to let one drop of water fall from the finger-tip on his burning tongue.—**For I am tormented** (better, *in anguish*) **in this flame.** The verb is not the one corresponding to torment, in verse 23, but signifies "to be sorely distressed." That fire was then commonly thought to be a cause of pain to lost souls, seems implied; but we know of no documentary support of such a view. Fire was, at all events, a most appropriate symbol of the remorse and apprehension of God's displeasure natural to the self-condemned soul beyond the grave.

25. Abraham denies the request on account of the moral fitness of the appointment as it now is.—**Son**—(*child*)—pitifully recognizing the relationship which Dives had claimed, only the more poignantly to impress a sense of sin and consequent sorrow without end—**remember**—not consider, or anticipate, or do anything that implies hope; but **remember,** and open ever afresh the sources of remorse to the soul that cannot repent.—**That thou in thy lifetime receivedst thy good things**—all that thou didst choose as thy portion. The Greek verb for "*receivedst*" properly means, "didst completely receive," "receive to the full." Hadst thou employed that wealth—which it was thy pleasure to squander—as God's steward, and made to thyself friends of the unrighteous mammon, it would have yielded thee happiness still, and forever. But now it has not virtue to procure for thee one drop of water.—**And likewise** (*in like manner*) **Lazarus evil things:** not his evil things, but such as in God's providence were allotted to him. They, too, are fully done with.—**But now** (*here*) **he is comforted, and thou art tormented** (*i. e., in anguish*). Here gives pungency to the contrast, in memory, of the former to the present state of being.

26. And besides all this—rather, *in* among *all these things*—showing that thy request cannot be granted, is the impossibility growing out of the local relation of the two classes of souls.—**Between us and you**—you (plural), the class to which you belong—**there is a great gulf**—chasm—**fixed.** This is, doubtless, a part of the poetically figurative representation of the unchangeable separation between the righteous and the wicked after death.—**So that**—*in order that*—**they which would pass from hence to you cannot** (lit., *may*—should—*not be able*). That separation was planned in the very constitution of their abode. There should be no passage either way, to seek relief or render aid.

27-31. At the point now reached the lesson called for by the mammon worship of the Pharisees (ver. 14) had been fully given. It was graphically shown how truly "that which is exalted among men is an abomination in the sight of God." But ᵗʰᵉ connection

27 Then he said, I pray thee therefore, father, that thou wouldest send him to my father's house:
28 For I have five brethren; that he may testify unto them, lest they also come into this place of torment.
29 Abraham saith unto him, ᵃ They have Moses and the prophets; let them hear them.
30 And he said, Nay, father Abraham: but if one went unto them from the dead, they will repent.

27 us. And he said, I pray thee therefore, father, that
28 thou wouldest send him to my father's house; for I have five brethren; that he may testify unto them,
29 lest they also come into this place of torment. But Abraham saith, They have Moses and the prophets;
30 let them hear them. And he said, Nay, father Abraham: but if one go to them from the dead, they will

a Isa. 8: 20; 34: 16; John 5: 39, 45; Acts 15: 21; 17: 11.

between the doom of the rich man and his religious character had not been plainly intimated. What follows at once completes the picture of his posthumous state, and shows it to be the result of a lack of faith and repentance, such as a due regard to the Old Testament would have produced. Want of this pious disposition could alone have led to their mockery of Christ's exposition of duty concerning the use of riches (ver. 15), and it proved his opposers generally liable to the rich man's condemnation.

27. I pray thee, therefore—seeing the hopelessness of my case, and that all who die impenitent and unprepared must come hither to anguish. **That thou wouldest send him to my father's house.** The idea of a messenger from *sheol* to the habitations of men is a part of the rhetorical scheme, to emphasize the wretchedness of an impenitent death.

28. For I have five brethren—*brothers.* It is a case where parents are dead. Remembrance of brothers (and other relatives and friends) still living unprepared, is a part of the distress of a lost soul, and shows that perdition does not of necessity involve the destruction of such natural sentiments. **That he may testify unto them, lest they also come into this place of torment.** What testimony he would have Lazarus bear to his brothers was, as we may confidently infer, that the self-indulgent use of their earthly possessions, the failure to regard themselves as God's stewards, would inevitably result in careless, helpless misery after death. Note, that he supposes it must be a holy soul that can possibly deliver such a message; and that the thought does not occur to him of an effectual repentance for them, or for himself, in that abode of woe. He would have them instructed *in time* to avoid the amazing folly, as well as wickedness, which he must rue through eternity.

29. (*But*) **Abraham saith unto him, They have Moses and the prophets**—the same source of wisdom and rule of life which these Pharisees had before them (ver. 16), and which, in its ideal spirituality, is continued in the new kingdom.—**Let them hear them.** To hear is, in this case, to heed, to believe, and to obey. This they could not do, according to the true intent of that revelation, without welcoming all light on the way of life, as it came also from him. But even apart from this thought, they had knowledge far beyond what was vouchsafed to Abraham in the Old Testament record.

30. And he said, Nay, father Abraham: but if one went unto (better, *go to*) **them from the dead, they will repent.** The view expressed is that on which the necromancy of all ages has subsisted. Testimony from the dead returned to life must, it is supposed, have a greater influence on the belief and practice of men, in reference to the realities of that state, than all the testimony of God himself, through his inspired spokesmen. So it was with Saul, King of Israel, in the attempted evocation of Samuel; and so in a multitude of cases of modern conjuration, called spiritualism, or, more properly, spiritism. Yet we might know beforehand that real messengers from the other world could practically testify only to our need of moral amendment—repentance and faith—and a life of holiness here, in order to happiness there. This we know perfectly well already. It is the depraved reluctance of men's hearts to such a change and course of life which makes anything more seem necessary, and would just as surely break the power of any other testimony as it does that of the revelation God has given. We read of no wonderfully good effect of the return of the other Lazarus from the dead; and we know that when the apostles afterward went abroad, testifying and demonstrating that Jesus himself had risen, and made them his witnesses concerning the secrets of eternity, it was only those "who were ordained unto eternal life" that believed; while everywhere, "when they heard of the resurrection of the dead, some mocked."

31 And he said unto him, If they bear not Moses and the prophets, *neither will they be persuaded, though one rose from the dead.

CHAPTER XVII.

THEN said he unto the disciples, *It is impossible but that offences will come: but woe *unto him*, through whom they come!
2 It were better for him that a millstone were hanged about his neck, and he cast into the sea, than that he should offend one of these little ones.
3 Take heed to yourselves: *If thy brother trespass

31 repent. And he said unto him, If they bear not Moses and the prophets, neither will they be persuaded, if one rise from the dead.

1 And he said unto his disciples, It is imposs'ble but that occasions of stumbling should come; but
2 woe unto him, through whom they come! It were well for him if a millstone were hanged about his neck, and he were thrown into the sea, rather than that he should cause one of these little ones to
3 stumble. Take heed to yourselves: if thy brother

---

a John 12: 10, 11....b Matt. 18: 6, 7; Mark 9: 42; 1 Cor. 11: 19....c Matt. 18: 15, 21.

Observe that Dives here recognizes his failure to repent as the reason of his being in the place of torment.

31. If they hear not Moses and the prophets, etc. The utter hopelessness of the case of the Pharisaic class, is thus attested by Abraham himself. Did the Saviour mean to intimate the future incorrigibility of the people, in the face of his own resurrection? To "hear," in this verse, is synonymous with "be persuaded," which is the same as to yield belief to testimony; and all take the place of "repent," in the preceding verse. [It may be proper to add that, while Dives speaks of one *going to them from the dead*, Abraham substitutes for that expression, *a rising from the dead*. This seems to imply the necessity of resurrection in the case of the dead, if they are to appear among men; and so the fact that the resurrection does not ordinarily take place at death.—A. H.]

Ch. 17. 1-4. WOE TO HIM WHO CAUSES THE DISCIPLES TO STUMBLE. HOW SUCH EVIL IS TO BE AVOIDED.

1. There is some doubt whether these verses are a continuation of the preceding discourse, or a different report of what may have been said on another occasion (Matt. 18: 7, 6, 21 f.). We may say, at least, that they seem to stand in a natural and reasoned connection here also. The murmuring (ch. 15: 2) and the derisive comments (ch. 16: 14) of the most influential classes of the religious community on Christ's acts and teachings, were well suited to shake the faith and devotion to him of his weaker disciples; in other words, to cause them to stumble. **Then** (better, *And*) **said he unto the** (*his*) **disciples**—no longer to the Pharisees—(ch. 16: 15), and not yet to the apostles (ver. 5), but to the body of his followers. **It is impossible but that offences will** (better, *should*) **come. Offences** here (σκάνδαλα) are what are commonly called "stumbling-blocks," occasions of stumbling, or actual fall in the course of discipleship to Christ. The Greek word meant the trigger of a trap, contact with which would cause the trap to spring; then, in the Septuagint, the trap or snare; then anything, stone or what not (Heb. *mikshôl*) with which one comes in contact, so as to stumble or be thrown down. Hence, morally, whatever was adapted to shock the confidence of believers, and cause wavering or apostasy in the life of faith. It may arise among Christians themselves, or in the bearings of the world upon them, and is named here, probably, with reference to the malicious words and deeds of the Pharisees, as calculated to turn the disciples away from him. The impossibility of their not coming lies in the moral antagonism of the world to him and his cause. It would cease should the world become thoroughly converted to his spirit. **But woe unto him,** etc. That necessity, lying in the prevalence of imperfection and sin, only makes more conspicuous the criminality of him who voluntarily causes the offence.

2. It were better (literally, *well*) **for him if a millstone,** etc. The Saviour's earnestness gives an extraordinary character to his style. He conceives of the fate as having already befallen; and a literal translation would be, nearly: "It is profitable for him—he is better off—if a millstone lies about his neck and he has been cast into the sea." In plain prose, to have lost his natural life is a lesser damage than to have committed such a sin, viz., **that he should offend one of these little ones** (rather, *cause one of these little ones to stumble*). These are the recent converts, immature disciples, believers who need encouragement, rather, and strengthening; that one should deliberately aim to turn them back, and lead them to fall away, is a truly diabolical wrong.

3. Take heed to yourselves—lest ye

against thee, *rebuke him; and if he repent, forgive him.

4 And if he trespass against thee seven times in a day, and seven times in a day turn again to thee, saying, I repent; thou shalt forgive him.

5 And the apostles said unto the Lord, Increase our faith.

6 *And the Lord said, If ye had faith as a grain of mustard seed, ye might say unto this sycamine tree, Be thou plucked up by the root, and be thou planted in the sea; and it should obey you.

4 sin, rebuke him; and if he repent, forgive him. And if he sin against thee seven times in the day, and seven times turn again to thee, saying, I repent; thou shalt forgive him.

5 And the apostles said unto the Lord, Increase our 6 faith. And the Lord said, If ye had faith as a grain of mustard seed, ye would say unto this sycamine tree, Be thou rooted up, and be thou planted in the

a Lev. 19: 17; Prov. 17: 10; James 5: 19.... *b* Matt. 17: 20; 21: 21; Mark 9: 23; 11: 23.

also, unawares, and through inconsistency with your principles, practice the same evils as the Pharisees have now practiced. This seems to be the most probable connection, unless we give up the attempt to trace any at all. If thy brother trespass (*sin*) —against thee, is pretty plainly in the thought, considering what follows, although the authorities for the Greek text fully warrant the Revision in leaving the words simply to be understood. In case of a personal wrong suffered by a disciple, he is not by wanton severity of judgment and insistance on punishment, to create "scandals," or cause offence to Christ's little ones. Rebuke him—*i. e.*, point out to him the evil he has done, and so represent its iniquity as to bring him to feel it. This is required for his own amendment. And if he repent—sincerely recognize and confess his fault—forgive him. To forgive is to remit all claim for punishment, and positively to desire the offender's welfare. One is thus to forgive the trespasses of others as one hopes to be forgiven by God. In both cases it is on the ground of manifested repentance.

4. And if he sin against thee seven times in a day, etc. The mention of seven times, like that of "seventy times seven" (Matt. 18: 22), teaches that, no matter how often, as often as occasion may require, the spirit of forgiveness is to be exercised. It is as constant a trait of the true Christian character as is faith, or dependence on God for mercy. And seven times in a day turn again to thee, saying, I repent. "Turning again to" implies that he has by his sin turned away from; and is here, toward man, what elsewhere the verb signifies toward God—a "conversion." It is the outward expression of the inward change signified by I repent; repentance and conversion toward an injured brother. So eminently does this spirit of forgiveness belong to the inmost essence of Christianity, that nothing could be more natural than for the Saviour to treat the lack of it as a dangerous occasion of offence. Whoever fails to exhibit it, egregiously misrepresents the profession of discipleship.

5, f. THE APOSTLES TAUGHT THE POWER OF FAITH.

Even the apostles are made sensible of their insufficiency for such imitation of the Master. This appears to be the sense of their prayer, Increase our faith; literally, "*add to us faith.*" Faith is rightly apprehended by them as the root principle of all holy emotion and acts, love among the rest, in which is included the spirit of forgiveness.

6. This verse should be rendered, And the Lord said, If ye *have* faith as a grain of mustard seed, ye *would* say unto this sycamine tree, Be thou, etc. The sycamine tree was a species of mulberry, probably distinct from "the sycamore" (ch. 19: 4). This was named as an apparently solid and immovable object then before their eyes. The present indicative of the verb following *if* assumes that they have such faith—"if ye have faith, and I know ye have." Thus the sentence implies, by the very irregularity of its form, the surprise of our Lord that they do not act out the faith which they have. "Ye have so much faith,—and exercising it"—ye *would* say, not ye might say. Be thou plucked up (better, *rooted* up), etc.,—"let any work of divine power be performed," in the way of your duty as members and ministers of my kingdom. He could hardly have intended, literally, to promise the power of merely physical prodigies, something which neither Christ nor his apostles ever wrought. And it *would have obeyed* you. This way of speaking supposes the *ye would say* to have been actually done, and the effect to have instantly followed. So certain is it that it would follow, if they should so say. The Saviour thus teaches that, to increase faith, we simply

7 But which of you, having a servant plowing or feeding cattle, will say unto him by and by, when he is come from the field, Go and sit down to meat?
8 And will not rather say unto him, Make ready wherewith I may sup, and gird thyself, ªand serve me, till I have eaten and drunken; and afterward thou shalt eat and drink?
9 Doth he thank that servant because he did the things that were commanded him? I trow not.
10 So likewise ye, when ye shall have done all those things which are commanded you, say, We are ᵇunprofitable servants: we have done that which was our duty to do.
11 And it came to pass, ᶜas he went to Jerusalem, that he passed through the midst of Samaria and Galilee.

7 sea; and it would obey you. But who is there of you, having a ¹servant plowing or keeping sheep, that will say unto him, when he is come in from the
8 field, Come straightway and sit down to meat; and will not rather say unto him, Make ready wherewith I may sup, and gird thyself, and serve me, till I have eaten and drunken; and afterward thou shalt eat
9 and drink? Doth he thank the ¹servant because he
10 did the things that were commanded? Even so ye also, when ye shall have done all the things that are commanded you, say, We are unprofitable ²servants; we have done that which it was our duty to do.
11 And it came to pass, ³as they were on the way to Jerusalem, that he was passing ⁴along the borders

a ch. 12: 37....*b* Job 22: 3: 35: 7; P-, 16: 2; Matt. 25: 30; Rom. 3: 12; 11: 25; 1 Cor. 9: 16, 17; Philemon 11....*c* Luke 9: 51, 52; John 4: 4.—1 Gr. *bondservant*....2 Gr. *bondservants*....3 Or, *as he was*....4 Or, *through the midst of*.

need to exercise what we have, however little, *even* **as a grain of mustard seed.**

7-10. The Absence of Merit in the Works of the Disciples.

The continuity of discourse which we have been able to trace, with a degree of probability hitherto, through this chapter, can hardly be carried further. Meyer finds a link in the implied liability of the disciples to arrogance, on account of the works of faith, of which they were capable. It seems more reasonable to suppose that Luke found this piece of instruction well suited to close up the series of counsels which the Lord had been addressing to them. For this purpose what could be more fit than a lesson of humility? This lesson is delivered in a sort of hypothetical parable. Suppose a master should require his slave, when returning from the day's work out of doors, to prepare and serve for him the supper, before taking his own meal. The slave, in obeying, would have done no more than his recognized task, and no one would think it worthy of special commendation or reward.

10. So likewise ye, when ye shall have done all, etc.—if that time should ever come —it will still be incumbent on you to be humble; say to yourselves, **We are unprofitable servants.** This does not mean "we have been of no use," but "we have no surplus of merit beyond any faithful *servant;*" or, as the Saviour himself explains, "we have simply done that without doing which we should have been culpably unfaithful"— **that which it was our duty to do.** The things commanded were all comprehended in love (John 15: 10, 12), in its various manifestations. If humility became those who should have fulfilled this commandment, how much more those who are perpetually conscious of coming short in this duty. In perfect consistency with this, Christ teaches plainly, elsewhere, that there are, and are to be, ample rewards for fidelity in his service, only as a pure gift of grace, and most ample where there is least thought of merit, or claim for any benefit as earned.

11-19. The Cleansing of Ten Lepers.

The evangelist now turns from the series of discourses beginning with chapter 14, and continued to this point without evident change of place. From the statement in verse 11, it appears that the following incident occurred near the border between Galilee and Samaria. It belongs to the final journey toward Jerusalem, announced ch. 9: 51, and again mentioned ch. 13: 22. But whether it comes in chronological order, so that all reported in ch. 9: 51—17: 10 has taken place in the south of Galilee, or whether a part of the foregoing events have occurred in Perea, so that we now have an earlier transaction, out of its real order, cannot be positively decided. We think it more likely that portions of the preceding narrative belong to a more advanced stage of the journey, and that what is reported in this paragraph had taken place considerably earlier.

11. And it came to pass, as he went (rather, *as they were on the way*) **to Jerusalem**—a general designation of the time—**that he passed**—was passing—**through the midst of Samaria and Galilee.** This designation of locality might, with equal warrant of the Greek, be translated *between* **Samaria and Galilee.** This suits better with the mention of Samaria first, instead of Galilee, and with the statements in Matt. 19: 1; Mark 10: 1, that this journey lay through Perea, and with the fact that the next place definitely named is Jericho (ch. 19: 1). We may thus

12 And as he entered into a certain village, there met him ten men that were lepers, *a* which stood afar off:
13 And they lifted up *their* voices, and said, Jesus, Master, have mercy on us.
14 And when he saw *them,* he said unto them, *b* Go shew yourselves unto the priests. And it came to pass, that, as they went, they were cleansed.
15 And one of them, when he saw that he was healed, turned back, and with a loud voice glorified God,
16 And fell down on *his* face at his feet, giving him thanks: and he was a Samaritan.

12 of Samaria and Galilee. And as he entered into a certain village, there met him ten men that were 13 lepers, who stood afar off: and they lifted up their voices, saying, Jesus, Master, have mercy on us. 14 And when he saw them, he said unto them, Go and shew yourselves unto the priests. And it came to 15 pass, as they went, they were cleansed. And one of them, when he saw that he was healed, turned back, 16 with a loud voice glorifying God; and he fell upon his face at his feet, giving him thanks: and he was

a Lev. 13: 46....*b* Lev. 13: 2; 14: 2; Matt. 8: 4; ch. 5: 14.

see the Saviour now turned eastward toward the Jordan, with Samaria on the right and Galilee on the left hand. The proportion of Galileans among the lepers would lead to the inference that he was on Galilean ground, perhaps soon after the event of ch. 9: 52-55. That this eastward movement was understood by Luke to have crossed the Jordan is uncertain, as he neither mentions such a fact, nor says anything inconsistent with the supposition of it.

12. As he entered into a certain village, there met him ten men that were lepers. On the case of Lepers, see on ch. 5: 12. Of the ten, it appears that nine were Jews, one a Samaritan; mingling without scruple, in their misery. That so many were together makes it probable that they had assembled in anticipation of Christ's arrival. **Which stood afar off,** under a sense of their reputed uncleanness, especially in the presence of a great teacher, like Jesus of Nazareth. Little did they realize his superiority to those ceremonial scruples when good was to be done to needy men. Wetstein, on the passage, gives quotations from the Rabbinic literature to show their aversion to lepers. Two Rabbis disputing the question maintained: one, that it was not fit to come within a hundred cubits of a leper; the other, within four cubits, when he stood between them and the wind. Another would not eat an egg if laid in a courtyard where a leper was. One, when he saw a leper, assailed him with stones, saying: "Off to thy own place, lest thou defile others," etc.

13. And they—of themselves, without waiting to be spoken to, as the Greek shows—**lifted up their voices,** so as to be heard a long way, **saying, Jesus, Master,** using, appropriately here, the term peculiar to Luke, which signifies rulership, authority (ἐπιστάτης). **Have mercy on us.** In what manner, needed no explanation. The plea was obviously equivalent to "Heal us of our dreadful malady."

14. And when he saw them—being roused by their cry—**he said unto them**—without waiting for plea or explanation, calling aloud—**Go and shew yourselves unto the priests.** From the mention of **priests,** more than one, it has been supposed that Christ had in mind one for the Jews and one for the Samaritans, as he would have each go to his own priest. This, if so, would be a curious and peculiar case; and it is more probable that our Lord first had his attention called to the Samaritan, as such, when he came afterward to thank him. Our Lord had probably in mind the class of priests. He gave no explicit answer to their prayer, but his direction to them to fulfill the commandment of the law, touching those who were healed of leprosy (Lev. 14: 2), must have given them confidence that healing was to come to them. And it came. They started promptly for Jerusalem; for the purificatory rites must be performed at the seat of sacrifice (Lev. 14: 13, 23). **And . . . as they went**—apparently without any sudden or striking change—**they were cleansed** of their defilement and most cruel plague. Such an experience might well suspend the ceremonial duty, until they had discharged the moral duty of gratitude and praise to the author of their cure. They had not gone so far away that they did not know Jesus was still where they had left him.

15. And one of them . . . turned back, and with a loud voice glorified God (literally, *with a loud voice glorifying God.*) In him the appropriate sentiment was awakened, and the right conduct followed. He recognized God as the source of the great blessing to him, and made the air resound, as he retraced his steps, with songs and shouts of praise to God. He would have everybody know of the divine mercy illustrated in his case.

16. Jesus also, as the medium through whom the mercy had come to him, seemed to him almost as the real author of it, which indeed

17 And Jesus answering said, Were there not ten cleansed? but where are the nine?
18 There are not found that returned to give glory to God, save this stranger.
19 ᵃ And he said unto him, Arise, go thy way: thy faith hath made thee whole.
20 And when he was demanded of the Pharisees, when the kingdom of God should come, he answered them and said, The kingdom of God cometh not with observation:
21 ᵇ Neither shall they say, Lo here! or, lo there! for, behold, ᶜ the kingdom of God is within you.

17 a Samaritan. And Jesus answering said, Were not the ten cleansed? but where are the nine? ¹ Were there none found that returned to give glory to God,
19 save this ²stranger? And he said unto him, Arise, and go thy way: thy faith hath ³made thee whole.
20 And being asked by the Pharisees, when the kingdom of God cometh, he answered them and said, The kingdom of God cometh not with observation:
21 neither shall they say, Lo, here! or, There! for lo, the kingdom of God is ⁴ within you.

a Matt. 9: 22; Mark 5: 34; 10: 52; ch. 7: 50; 8: 48; 18: 42,...b ver. 23,...c Rom. 11: 17.—1 Or, there were none found . . . save this stranger.... 2 Or, alien,... 3 Or, saved thee.... 4 Or, in the midst of you.

he was. **And fell down on his face at his feet, giving him thanks** — worship and gratitude. **And he was a Samaritan**—implying that the others were Jews, and probably that the fact of this one being a Samaritan now first broke on the attention of Jesus. It seems to have deeply saddened his heart. It afforded, indeed, an omen of the accession of worshipers to his kingdom from among the strangers, but of the thanklessness of his own nation.

17. And Jesus answering said, Were there not ten (literally, *Were not the ten*) **cleansed? But where are the nine?** The point of his question is that the nine were morally bound, as well as the one, to express their gratitude to him. It was a case where "mercy," the spiritual service of God, might properly interrupt, for a sufficient season, the "sacrifice," or ceremonial service, which, according to the law, Christ had enjoined. Their case seems to show, again, that effectual faith in the healing power of Jesus was consistent with great dullness of the moral regard that he prized so much more highly.

18. There are (rather, *were*) **not found that returned to give glory to God except this stranger**—alien, man of another race. The interrogative form (see Revision) is preferred by some, and is consistent with the Greek; but not more so than our familiar rendering. The logical force of the statement has been already indicated.

19. And he said, Arise, go thy way, thy faith hath made thee whole (literally, *saved thee*, as in 7: 50); thou mayest proceed to the priest with the assurance that thou art thoroughly cured; and it is thy faith in me, as the dispenser of supernatural blessings, on account of which thou art rescued from so sad a case. What could more powerfully move him to consider and accept *all* which Jesus had to offer to the faith of men? Might not

he, who had thus made this life a new thing to him, dispense the higher boon of eternal life?

20, 21. Concerning the Coming of the Kingdom.

The appearance of the Pharisees again leads to the supposition of a distinct occasion, whose date and locality are left undetermined.

20. And when he was demanded of (better, *And being asked by*) **the Pharisees when the kingdom of God should come** (literally, *cometh*). They were looking for a reign of the Messiah, under which all the glorious predictions of the prophets would be literally fulfilled, with many circumstances added by their later theology. (See on 6: 20.) They had their views as to what the manner of the Messiah would be, and what events would precede and attend his coming, but hardly assumed to fix a precise date for the event. They could not, being Pharisees, have inquired of Jesus, as being himself the Messiah, around whose throne the kingdom would crystallize; but, as a religious teacher of high repute, they might be curious to have his views on the question. A less charitable, but, perhaps, at this time, a more probable, explanation, would be, that they hoped, by some unreasonable, or unorthodox, expression of his, to disparage his wisdom, or his piety, and perhaps bring him into collision with the authorities. Whatever the motive, our Saviour was, as ever, prepared. He answers their query by showing the impossibility of answering it in their sense. **The kingdom of God cometh not with observation;** *i. e.*, attended by such outward phenomena that, by observing them, one may say, Here it is; it has come!

21. Neither—when it is really come—**shall they say, Lo, here! or, lo, there!** *it is*—so that if you go to such or such a place, you will see it. The coming of the kingdom, being a spiritual thing, is marked by no appearances, or limitations, of which men can say that

22 And he said unto the disciples, *The days will come, when ye shall desire to see one of the days of the Son of man, and ye shall not see it.

22 And he said unto the disciples, The days will come, when ye shall desire to see one of the days of

*See Matt. 9: 15; John 17: 12.

they are here or there. Hence, neither can the instant of its emergence on the field of history be exactly known by signs patent to human observation. — **For, behold, the kingdom of God is within you.** The Greek preposition for **within** (ἐντὸς), is found elsewhere in the New Testament only at Matt. 23: 26, "the inside." Other Greek usage will, doubtless, warrant such a rendering as that of our version. Nor would the sense thus given concerning the kingdom of God, as being a spiritual experience, be in the least unscriptural. It would also be a suitable answer to the Pharisees, that the kingdom was not to be discovered by external scrutiny. Such reasons might suffice to prevent a change of the text in the Revision; but we think, nevertheless, that their marginal alternative reading is to be preferred, *in the midst of you*, among you within your circle, not outside of it. For this the lexical authority is at least equal. (See the use illustrated in Meyer on the passage, and more fully in the later editions of Liddell and Scott's Lexicon, or in Rost und Palm's *Griech. Wörterbuch*). The same sources will supply instances of the other use. But it is less probable that one who wished to say "within you," in the sense of "in your minds," should avoid the very familiar phrase (ἐν ὑμῖν), and employ one nowhere else found in the New Testament. Again, that Christ should speak of the kingdom of God as being an affair of the soul merely, a "psychological kingdom," "an ethical condition," may not be, as Meyer suggests, a *modern* idea, yet it does seem strange to the teaching of the Synoptical Gospels. Once more; since this language is addressed expressly to the Pharisees, it is hard to perceive how the kingdom could be in *their* spirits, at all events. But it might with truth and great propriety be said to be "among them," "in their sphere, circle, neighborhood, society," when he the King was there, with even one faithful believer and subject. See on 6: 20. This fact was equally a confirmation of the statement that the kingdom cometh not with observation, and, as plainly as was likely to be useful, intimated their duty to recognize his Messiahship.

22-37. Concerning the Future Glory of the Kingdom.
22. And he said unto the disciples. They had listened to his declaration of the presence and invisibility to sense of the kingdom, from which they might assume either that they already knew all there was of it, and so think it of little account, or conclude that the fuller measure of its privileges was to be immediately enjoyed, and so be deluded into premature exultation. To forestall either form of mistake, the following discourse was admirably adapted. It shows that a considerable period of waiting was to elapse, bringing some experiences to the disciples; that meanwhile, he himself must suffer and be cast off; that the world would then fall into great forgetfulness of him, and live as though he was never to return; that this would involve peril and temptation to his followers, in the midst of which the Son of man would be revealed. A comparison of this passage with the corresponding portions of Matt. 24, viz., verses 26, 28, 37-41, raises the question, as in one or two cases before, whether we have two reports of the same discourse, referred to different occasions, and if so, which is to be regarded as the true date, or whether our Lord so nearly repeated the same words at different times. Now, it is pretty obvious that our discourse has reference almost entirely to the final advent of the Lord, at the end of the world; while Matthew's embraces many features of the coming at the destruction of Jerusalem and of the Jewish State. The Note of Dr. Fred. Gardiner on the question, at p. 155 of his *Greek Harmony of the Gospels*, is discriminating and helpful: "Another instance in which St. Matthew, having omitted the narrative of this period, preserves some important parts of its discourses, by connecting them with a similar discourse uttered somewhat later. By transposing these passages to this place [into parallelism with the corresponding verses of the passage before us], the twenty-fourth chapter of St. Matthew may become clearer to the student. A single verse of St. Luke (31), on the other hand, requires to be transposed to that discourse by

23 *a* And they shall say to you, See here; or, see there: go not after *them*, nor follow *them*.
24 *b* For as the lightning, that lighteneth out of the one *part* under heaven, shineth unto the other *part* under heaven; so shall also the Son of man be in his day.
25 *c* But first must he suffer many things, and be rejected of this generation.
26 *d* And as it was in the days of Noe, so shall it be also in the days of the Son of man.
27 They did eat, they drank, they married wives, they were given in marriage, until the day that Noe entered into the ark, and the flood came, and destroyed them all.

23 the Son of man, and ye shall not see it. And they shall say to you, Lo, there! Lo, here! go not away,
24 nor follow after *them:* for as the lightning, when it lighteneth out of the one part under the heaven, shineth unto the other part under heaven; so shall
25 the Son of man be ¹ in his day. But first must he suffer many things and be rejected of this genera-
26 tion. And as it came to pass in the days of Noah, even so shall it be also in the days of the Son of man.
27 They ate, they drank, they married, they were given in marriage, until the day that Noah entered into the ark, and the flood came, and destroyed them all.

a Matt. 24: 23; Mark 13: 21; ch. 21: 8....*b* Matt. 24: 27....*c* Mark 8: 31; 9: 31; 10: 33; ch. 9: 22....*d* Gen. 7; Matt. 24: 37.—1 Some ancient authorities omit, *in his day*.

the arrangement of both St. Matthew and St. Mark."—**The days will come**—rather, *days will come.* The Greek has no article. The Saviour would not indicate definite days, but more affectingly, days of a certain quality, days of difficulty, hardship, distress, as shown by what follows. See on 5: 35.—**When ye shall**—*will*—**desire to see one of the days of the Son of man.** Their troubles and trials would be such, at various times before his return, that they would long for the rest and refreshment of even one of those days which he had taught them to anticipate, in the glory and blessedness of the finished kingdom in heaven. The following context shows this to be the meaning, rather than to make the sentence refer backward to the days they were then spending in his earthly society.—**And ye shall**—*will*—**not see it;** *i. e.,* not till many repetitions of such desire. They would still have to wait and toil and suffer.

23. And they shall—*will*—**say to you**—in your fatigue and faint-heartedness—**See here, or see there:** (correctly, *Lo there! or, Lo here!)*—is the Messiah manifested. The rest of the verse should be translated—**Go not** (*away*) from the place in which Providence has placed you—**nor follow after them.** In your forlornness you will be especially liable to delusion; but no one shall know of my coming sooner than you.

24. For as the lightning that (or, better, *when it*) **lighteneth,** etc. The point of comparison is the instantaneousness and universal visibility of the lightning flash, throughout the whole circle of the horizon. **So shall also the Son of man be in his day.** "The brightness of his coming" also will shine equally, in the same moment, over the whole world, and prove, not only that he has come, but that he is as near to one as to another. Without attempting at all to foretell the date of that glorious appearing, our Lord mentions some things which must precede it, the occurrence of which would mark the lapse of the intervening time, and the prediction of which was well calculated to check elation on their part, and to quicken them in diligence to "be found of him in peace." The first thing was the sad and shameful fate soon to overtake their blessed Master himself.

25. First must he suffer many things—all, indeed, that were involved in the unspeakable humiliation, dishonor, and violence that should precede the crucifixion, and in the agonies of that death itself. **And be rejected of this generation.** This rejection may be mentioned as one item of that suffering, or, more probably, as an additional distress, from the refusal of his generation, even after his death and resurrection, to receive him as their Messiah.

26. The state of things to follow these events, the general forgetfulness of him, and indifference to all the interests of eternity, are compared to the unbelief and utter worldliness of men in Noah's times. This will be the case especially in the period within which will fall **the days of the Son of man**—the time when he shall come again for judgment and for redemption.

27. They did eat, they drank, etc. A graphic picture of the absorption of men in merely worldly affairs, made more vivid by the omission of the conjunction. The use of the imperfect tense in the original, "they were eating," etc., helps to conceive the unexpectedness of the great catastrophe when it came. **They married,** is said of the men; **they were given in marriage,** of the women. **And the flood came and destroyed them all.** Carelessness and unbelief of God's word did not arrest his threatened judgment. Compare Gen. 7: 11-23.

Ch. XVII.] LUKE. 265

28 *Likewise also as it was in the days of Lot; they did eat, they drank, they bought, they sold, they planted, they builded;
29 But ᵇthe same day that Lot went out of Sodom it rained fire and brimstone from heaven, and destroyed them all.
30 Even thus shall it be in the day when the Son of man ᶜis revealed.
31 In that day, he ᵈ which shall be upon the housetop, and his stuff in the house, let him not come down to take it away: and he that is in the field, let him likewise not return back.
32 ᵉRemember Lot's wife.
33 ᶠWhosoever shall seek to save his life shall lose it; and whosoever shall lose his life shall preserve it.
34 ᵍI tell you, in that night there shall be two *men* in one bed; the one shall be taken, and the other shall be left.

28 Likewise even as it came to pass in the days of Lot; they ate, they drank, they bought, they sold, they planted, they builded; but in the day that Lot went out from Sodom it rained fire and brimstone from 30 heaven, and destroyed them all: after the same manner shall it be in the day that the Son of man is 31 revealed. In that day, he who shall be on the housetop, and his goods in the house, let him not go down to take them away: and let him that is in the field 32 likewise not return back. Remember Lot's wife. 33 Whosoever shall seek to gain his life shall lose it: but 34 whosoever shall lose *his life* shall ¹preserve it. I say unto you, In that night there shall be two men on one bed; the one shall be taken, and the other

ᵃ Gen. 19....ᵇ Gen. 19; 16, 21....c 2 Thess. 1: 7....d Matt. 24: 17; Mark 13: 15....e Gen. 19: 26....f Matt. 10; 39; 16: 25; Mark 3: 35; ch. 9: 24; John 12: 25....g Matt. 24: 40, 41; 1 Thess. 4: 17.——1 Gr. *save it alive.*

28, 29. The Same Lesson is Repeated from Another Most Impressive Portion of the Sacred History. (See Gen. 19: 15-25.)

30. This verse makes the application of both the parallel cases preceding to the case of the world at the second advent.

31. It was remarked above that this verse appears, by a reference to the corresponding passages of Matthew and Mark, to belong to a prophecy of the destruction of Jerusalem, as typical of the end of the world. It may have been uttered as a part of another discourse, and gathered out of the general store of Christ's recorded sayings by different apostolic men in different combinations. On this hypothesis, the whole remainder of the address now before us naturally points to the final appearance of our Lord; but **in that day,** of this verse, will point to the visitation upon Jerusalem, before the end of that generation. Then, when the Roman forces should be at hand (see ch. 21: 20 f.), there would be no security for Christ's disciples but in immediate flight.—**He which shall be upon the housetop,** etc. A graphic enforcement of the necessity of haste. Any one in the city, at the moment on the flat roof of his house, whither they went for fresh air, or retirement and meditation, must, as soon as he is informed of the impending danger, give all heed to escape from the city. To save property in the house below must not detain him. To descend, if that could be done without detention, or to rescue dependent lives, is not in these terms forbidden; but the losing of time to save goods. One must, of course, leave the roof somehow; but it is probable that, in many cases, time might be gained by passing from one roof to another before coming down. The same direction would apply, with the requisite modification, to all who should be in any city. —**And he that is in the field, let him likewise not return back,** viz.: to his house, to rescue property, or promote any temporal interest. Godet would apply these two verses also to the duties pertaining to the final advent; but this is, in our judgment, rather to extort a sense than to develop the true sense.

32. It is a case like that of the destruction of Sodom, where infinite consequences depend on expedition and even haste.—**Remember Lot's wife.** She stands as a perpetual memento to subsequent generations of the danger of delay in the crisis of salvation. It is always a crisis of salvation to one who has not solidly established peace between himself and God.

33. Whosoever shall seek to save (literally, *gain* = acquire) **his life shall lose it.** This, with what follows, connects itself not inappropriately with verse 31, regarded as referring to the destruction of Jerusalem, as is perfectly natural from the typical character of the latter event. But with the most perfect propriety it continues the train of discourse supposed to be interrupted at ver. 30, as relating to the last judgment. In reference to that, all efforts to secure the natural life, at the sacrifice of fidelity to the Lord, will be thrown away, and result in a loss of the life eternal. On the contrary, **whosoever shall lose his life**—faithfully persevere in obedience to Christ, even unto death, if necessary —**shall preserve it,** by carrying it forward, perfected and blessed, in the heavenly state.

34-36. The world, alas! will not have been all converted to Christ, and sad discriminations of destiny will be made, involving eternal breach of the nearest natural associations.—**In that night there shall be two men in one bed,** etc. The word **night,** so

35 Two *women* shall be grinding together; the one shall be taken, and the other left.
36 Two *men* shall be in the field; the one shall be taken, and the other left.
37 And they answered and said unto him, *a* Where, Lord? And he said unto them, Wheresoever the body *is*, thither will the eagles be gathered together.

35 shall be left. There shall be two women grinding together; the one shall be taken, and the other shall 37 be left.[1] And they answering say unto him, Where, Lord? And he said unto them, Where the body *is*, thither will the [2] eagles also be gathered together.

CHAPTER XVIII.

AND he spake a parable unto them *to this end*, that men ought *b* always to pray, and not to faint;
2 Saying, There was in a city a judge, which feared not God, neither regarded man:

1 And he spake a parable unto them to the end that 2 they ought always to pray, and not to faint; saying,

a Job 39:30; Matt. 24:28....*b* ch. 11:5; 21:36; Rom. 12:12; Ephes. 6:18; Col. 4:2; 1 Thess. 5:17.—1 Some ancient authorities add ver. 36, *There shall be two men in the field; the one shall be taken, and the other shall be left.*...2 Or, *vultures.*

---

used, no more obliges us to believe the Parousia will occur in the night time than the mention, afterward, of grinding at the mill proves that it will take place in the daylight. Indeed, we know that it must take place to some in the day-time, while it is night to others. So one example is taken here from the night and one from the day. —**The one**—who is ready for Christ's coming—**shall be taken**—to the eternal felicity of the glorified kingdom; **the other** —when unprepared—**shall be left**—apart from all that joy, in his own appropriate experience.

35. Women, among their other drudgery, had each morning to grind the quantity of meal for the family uses during the day. This was done with a hand-mill, at which the strength of two women was required. Thus is indicated the interest of women also in the solemn lesson.

Ver. 36 of the Received Greek Testament and of the Common Version is, beyond reasonable question, an interpolation here in Luke, from Matt. 24:40.

37. And they—the disciples (ver. 22)—**answered and said** (or, literally, *answering say*) **unto him, Where, Lord?** Where will these wonderful events take place? Bewildered, perhaps, certainly not intent simply on the practical use of what the Master had communicated, the disciples, as the Pharisees had asked after the precise *time* of the manifestation of the kingdom, seek to know its *place*. But our Lord knew how to turn their minds from outside matters of curiosity to deeper truths, requiring and exercising spiritual penetration.—**Where the body is. Body** = carcass (Matt. 24:28); that is, of a dead animal, is a symbol of the spiritually dead mass of men whom the Advent will overtake.— **Thither will the eagles be gathered together.** Perhaps the more correct word for **eagles** would have been "vultures"; but it matters little, as the vultures were eagle-like, and both sorts familiar in Palestine, were carrion eaters. They represent the ministers of God's justice (comp. Matt. 13:41-42), and will be present wherever the guilty are found. In this view the accomplishment of the kingdom is considered in its bearing on the impenitent and incorrigible; and we are taught that it can as little be located in a particular place as referred to a definite time.

Ch. 18.—1-8. DUTY OF UNREMITTING PRAYER. PARABLE OF THE UNJUST JUDGE.

1. And he spake a parable unto them —the disciples—**to this end, that men** (better, *they*) **ought always to pray, and not to faint.** Not content with foretelling and describing that perilous period (ch. 17:22 ff.), **he spake a parable,** to illustrate their duty in the long waiting for his advent.—**Always to pray**—to be always praying. His object was not so much to teach this duty as, assuming it, to show something of the manner and effect of it. They would be in great danger of losing heart (ch. 17:22) and forsaking their faith, the remedy for which would be unceasing prayer; and in reference to this duty (πρὸς τὸ δεῖν, κ. τ. λ.), he spake the parable.

2. Saying, There was in a city a judge, which (*who*) **feared not God, neither regarded man.** The Greek gives a fictitious character to the narrative by saying *a certain city*, *a certain* judge. That our Saviour should represent his Father by so unworthy a judge is perplexing, till one notices that it is by way of contrast that he so represents him. It is, in this respect, like the parable of the unneighborly friend (ch. 11:5 ff.), and analogous to that of the unjust steward (ch. 16:1 ff.). To give the intended lesson of perseverance in prayer under discouragement, Jesus could not so forcibly have used the image of an earthly judge,

3 And there was a widow in that city; and she came unto him, saying, Avenge me of mine adversary.
4 And he would not for a while: but afterward he said within himself, Though I fear not God, nor regard man;
5 ᵃ Yet because this widow troubleth me, I will avenge her, lest by her continual coming she weary me.
6 And the Lord said, Hear what the unjust judge saith.
7 And ᵇ shall not God avenge his own elect, which cry day and night unto him, though he bear long with them?

3 There was in a city a judge, who feared not God, and regarded not man: and there was a widow in that city; and she came oft unto him, saying, 4 ¹ Avenge me of mine adversary. And he would not for a while: but afterward he said within himself, 5 Though I fear not God, nor regard man; yet because this widow troubleth me, I will avenge her, ² lest she wear me out by her continual coming. And the 7 Lord said, Hear what ³ the unrighteous judge saith.

ᵃ ch. 11: 8....ᵇ Rev. 6: 10.—1 Or, *Do me justice of:* and so in ver. 5, 7, 8.....2 Gr. *bruise;* or, *lest at last by her coming she wear me out*.....3 Gr. *the judge of unrighteousness.*

---

upright, and promptly considerate of the equity of a cause. But when he shows that such perseverance might overcome the sluggishness of one most utterly void of piety, justice, and philanthropy—fearing not God, nor caring for the rights or wrongs and sufferings of men—he had already proved what power it would have with our just and compassionate God.

3. And there was a widow in that city. She represents Christ's disciples, his church. No image could be better suited to express their helplessness and pitiable state in an unfriendly world, and their absolute dependence on the equity of the Supreme Judge.—**And she came** (oft) **unto him,** or, *kept coming* **to him,** showing that her case was urgent, and received little attention, **saying, Avenge me of mine adversary**—do me justice against him, so that I may be free from injuries and annoyance at his hands. The special nature of her wrongs, whether of dues withheld, or unjust claims alleged, is left entirely to imagination.

4. And he would not for a while—and evidently never would, from any disposition to do justice in the case. **But afterward he said within himself, Though,** etc. He owns himself insensible to any unselfish and proper motive, from heaven or earth.

5. Yet because this widow troubleth me—as I have some regard for self, for my own ease and quiet. **I will avenge her**—cause justice to be done her, and defeat her adversary. **Lest by her continual coming**—"her coming forever."—Dr. S. Davidson—**she weary me.** The preferable rendering is, *lest she come at last and beat me.* Greek, "lest at last coming she beat me." For the last clause the Revision substitutes "wear me out," but places "bruise" in the margin as the sense of the Greek. The Greek word is hard to translate faithfully without an appearance of unbecoming levity. But our Lord pictures the unprincipled judge to the life. In the spirit of mingled impatience and jest, he uses a verb which signifies "to give one a black eye"; much like our "to beat one black and blue." In his bantering soliloquy the man supposes she may do him bodily harm; lest she pound me. (Vulg. *sugillet me.*) See, particularly, Farrar on the passage.

6. Hear what the unjust judge—Greek, *judge of injustice*—**saith.** Behold how such a wretch is constrained by incessant petitions against his inclination to help a woman in distress.

7. And shall not God avenge—cause the vindication of—**his own elect** (omit *own*), **which cry day and night unto him?** The argument is what logic calls from the less to the greater. If such a man, from mere selfish annoyance at importunity, will do what is requested, how much more will a holy and righteous God hear the prayers of his chosen people, ascending by day and by night, for deliverance from affliction? **Though he bear long,** etc.; rather, *And he is long-suffering over them.* This reading is better supported than that of the Common Version. The construction and meaning is not clearly obvious, which may have occasioned a change of the text. We might translate interrogatively, "Will he not avenge .... and will he be long-suffering over them?" that is so as to spare their adversaries? The answer to the last question would then be "No." Or, we may regard this sentence as having slipped colloquially from the relative into the direct affirmative form; "which cry unto him and he is long-suffering over them," instead of "which cry, and over whom he is long-suffering," i. e., bears long with their adversaries. The latter we prefer. It supposes that there is to be some delay in God's vindication of

8 I tell you *that he will avenge them speedily. Nevertheless when the Son of man cometh, shall he find faith on the earth?
9 And he spake this parable unto certain ᵇ which trusted in themselves that they were righteous, and despised others:
10 Two men went up into the temple to pray; the one a Pharisee, and the other a publican.

8 And shall not God avenge his elect, who cry to him day and night, ¹ and yet he is longsuffering over them? I say unto you, that he will avenge them speedily. Howbeit when the Son of man cometh, shall he find ² faith on the earth?
9 And he spake also this parable unto certain who trusted in themselves that they were righteous, and
10 set ³ all others at nought: Two men went up into the temple to pray; the one a Pharisee, and the other a

a Heb. 10: 37; 2 Pet. 3: 8, 9....b ch. 10: 29; 16: 15.——1 Or, and is he slow to punish on their behalf?....2 Or, the faith....3 Or. the rest.

his church, even while she calls on him, whether for her own increase of sanctification, or that the time of her enemies may be fulfilled; but the answer will come.

8. I tell you (better, *say unto you*) **that he will avenge them speedily.** The question proposed answers itself in the asking; but this "I say unto you" betrays the depth of the Saviour's earnestness. **Speedily** cannot, in consistency with the design of the parable (ver. 1), mean "very soon," measured from the moment of its utterance; but measured from the point where the vindication begins, after long waiting, it will soon be accomplished.—**Nevertheless, when the Son of man cometh, shall he find faith on the earth?** He had already foretold (ch. 17: 26, 27) that, at his advent, the disciples would find themselves in a world given up to business and pleasure, utterly forgetful of him. At another time, looking forward into the same general state of things, he said (Matt. 24: 12), "and because iniquity shall abound, the love of many shall wax cold." And now the prospect of the trials and temptations to which his followers are to be subjected before his return, is so clearly present to him, so much had he seen already of the possibility of defection, that our Lord appears sadly to question whether he should, at his coming, find faith, manifested in persevering prayer, like that of the widow, still existing on the earth. Shall not his very earnest concern in this matter itself so affect many hearts of his followers, that they will not be found asleep, or intoxicated with the spirit of the world?

9-14. PARABLE OF THE PHARISEE AND PUBLICAN.

It is not so clear that what is now to be related followed immediately upon the preceding events. It may have done so, and Luke probably received the account of it as belonging to this journey and time.

9. And he spake (*also*) **this parable unto certain which trusted,** etc. To what class, sect, or party, they belonged, or whether to any one class, is not told us. It is, considering the commonness of unreasonable self-esteem, well left applicable equally to disciples and unbelievers, Pharisees and publicans, to all who **trusted in themselves**—had confidence resting on themselves—**that they were righteous.** The word righteous is used in its ordinary, Old Testament sense, meaning, "conformed to the will of God," and so entitled to his favor. Whoever thinks he already stands well enough in the sight of God, and needs no repentance and spiritual renewal, belongs to the kind of people here intended. An exact translation gives the sentence a perfectly general reference: "Certain who trust in themselves that they are righteous, and set others at nought."—So Dr. S. Davidson. Our curiosity is naturally excited as to the particular marks by which Jesus at this time recognized such. They seem to have been very clearly differentiated to him.—**And despised others** (lit., *set all others at naught*). The next step to the opinion that one is as good as is necessary, is spiritual pride. Pride is essentially the disparagement of others in comparison with oneself. So this clause is only the other face of the same medal. God's righteousness in a man will lead him, first, to look on whatever he can possibly approve in himself as the fruit of divine grace; and, secondly, to recognize good in every fellow-man; at least, not to think all others of no account.

10, 11. Two men went up into the temple, etc. In prayer, if anywhere, we may expect to discern the true character of men. It was consistent with the whole formal and ritualistic character of the Old Testament religion that the temple should give a special sacredness and value to its exercises. Hence, we find that all who lived at Jerusalem thought it important to offer their prayers, at the hours consecrated to that, in the temple courts. Thus, all classes and qualities of men would come into proximity and comparison there. The Saviour signalizes two, standing at the opposite poles of reputed righteousness,

11 The Pharisee ᵃstood and prayed thus with himself, ᵇGod, I thank thee, that I am not as other men are, extortioners, unjust, adulterers, or even as this publican.
12 I fast twice in the week, I give tithes of all that I possess.
13 And the publican, standing afar off, would not lift up so much as his eyes unto heaven, but smote upon his breast, saying, God be merciful to me a sinner.

11 publican. The Pharisee stood and prayed thus with himself, God, I thank thee, that I am not as the rest of men, extortioners, unjust, adulterers, or even as
12 this publican. I fast twice in the week; I give tithes
13 of all that I get. But the publican, standing afar off, would not lift up so much as his eyes unto heaven, but smote his breast, saying, God, ¹be merciful to me

a Ps. 135: 2....*b* Isa. 1: 15; 58: 2; Rev. 2: 17.——1 Or, *be propitiated.*

a Pharisee and a publican, in regard to whom, he is particular to intimate, that they had one thing in common: they were both men. See the general account of the two classes, on ch. 3: 12; 5: 17.—**The Pharisee stood.** It is not intended to reprehend the standing posture, for that was then common, and the publican also assumed it. But the Greek word implies a certain ostentation and formality in his act, like our "taking his stand" (Hebrew, *yatsabh*, Hithp.).—**And prayed thus with himself.** The authorities leave it not quite certain whether we should connect the words "stood by himself, and prayed thus," or, as just given. The latter is much more probable. **With himself**—including the idea of "by himself," "apart," but, specifically, "to himself"—in his unexpressed thought.—**"God, I thank thee."** The omission of the interjection O, is warranted by the Greek, which uses only the vocative (or nominative) case; but as that is true of a thousand instances in the New (likewise in the Old) Testament, where the feeling of translators has led them to prefix the interjection, we cannot understand this as designed to indicate lack of reverence in the Pharisee. The publican again followed the same way. We may judge him, not by the form, but by the substance, the contents, of his prayer.—**That I am not as other men are** (lit., *as the rest of men*), etc. Here we see nothing properly called *prayer*, as there is not a word of supplication, or even request, in it. There is no confession, no consciousness of sin or moral deficiency, no want of anything. There is an air of thanksgiving to God, but without evidence of reason for it, to assure us of sincerity; as he ascribes nothing of his vaunted excellences to God's help or influence, but enumerates all as if they were a natural growth out of his unaided nature. It is a most graphic self-delineation of one who trusts in himself that he is righteous. The meritorious grounds of his proud thankfulness are, negatively, **that I am not as** *the rest of* **men.** He, in

terms, makes of himself one class, possibly intending to embrace other members of his own sect, over against which he looks down on the other class, embracing all the human race besides. The latter are conceived of as guilty of the sins which pertain not to him—**extortioners, unjust,**—or, *unrighteous*—**adulterers.** A truly sublime display of the setting at naught of other men. We may compare the divine judgment of his class, at least, in ch. 11: 42 ff., with the parallel passages in Matthew and Mark, and John 8: 7-9.—**Or even as this publican.** How, then, does the publican stand towards the rest of mankind? He must be one of them, and the *even* presupposes that he is not necessarily so bad as the criminals who have been named. It is hard to think that a Pharisee would acknowledge anything good in a publican; but, perhaps, the fact that the latter is found in the house of prayer, at the proper hour, is allowed some weight in his favor. That is the more charitable view of the Pharisee's meaning. It may be understood, I thank thee that I am not as bad as even this publican, not to say extortioners, etc. The deficiency of other men goes even to that length.

12. The positive virtues of this paragon are, **I fast twice in the week; I give tithes of all that I possess** (or, *get*, or, *acquire*). Both were extra-legal merits, as no weekly fasting was required by the law, and tithes were due not from **all** gains, but only from the productions of the fields. These are doubtless mentioned as typical of the whole system of traditional performances, which, to the abomination of Jesus, had superseded the weightier matters of the law—judgment, and the love of God. Thus ends the Pharisee's pretence of a prayer.

13. But the publican, standing afar off—as if feeling himself unworthy to mingle with other worshipers, or to come near the sanctuary—**would not lift up so much as his eyes unto heaven**—so far was he from "taking his stand" like the Pharisee—**but

14 I tell you, this man went down to his house justified *rather* than the other: *a* for every one that exalteth himself shall be abased; and he that humbleth himself shall be exalted.
15 *b* And they brought unto him also infants, that he would touch them: but when *his* disciples saw *it*, they rebuked them.
16 But Jesus called them *unto him*, and said, Suffer little children to come unto me, and forbid them not: for *c* of such is the kingdom of God.

14 ¹a sinner. I say unto you, This man went down to his house justified rather than the other: for every one that exalteth himself shall be humbled; but he that humbleth himself shall be exalted.
15 And they were bringing unto him also their babes, that he should touch them: but when the disciples
16 saw it, they rebuked them. But Jesus called them unto him, saying, Suffer the little children to come unto me, and forbid them not: for ²to such belongeth

a Job 22:29; Matt. 23:12; ch. 14:11; James 4:6; 1 Pet. 5:5, 6....*b* Matt. 19:13; Mark 10:13....*c* 1 Cor. 14:20; 1 Pet. 2:2.——1 Or, *the sinner*....2 Or, *of such is*.

smote—kept smiting—**upon his breast**—"the seat of conscience" (Beng.), in token of grief and shame for his sin. **Saying, God be merciful to me a sinner;** properly, *the* sinner. The American Bible Union Version and Dr. S. Davidson give the article conformably to the Greek, and the Revision allows it as the alternative. The verb rendered **be merciful,** found elsewhere in the New Testament only once, signifies "be thou propitiated," and implies the need of expiation, in order to reconciliation with God. We cannot say that the Saviour meant to make the publican distinctly conscious of this meaning, but a word is ascribed to him which carries the feeling of it. He certainly might have thought of the sacrificial significance of the offerings connected with the hour of evening prayer (ch. 1:9-10). And that was all the publican's prayer. Unlike the effusion of the Pharisee, it *was* all *prayer.* And what element of a true prayer, in the light of his time, did it lack? It was a most earnest and humble petition, from the heart, giving utterance to profound repentance, an all absorbing desire for the favor of God, through mercy alone, as the fruit of atonement.

14. The Saviour's vigorous **I say unto you** —repeated (see on ver. 8)—assures us that it had the effect of true prayer.—**This man went down to his house**—which would naturally be lower than the temple—**justified rather than the other.** The Greek verb "justified" is cognate with the adjective for "righteous" (ver. 9). Thus the outcome of the parable is that those who feel and own their sins in prayer to God are recognized by him as righteous (justified), while those who trust in themselves that they are so remain condemned.—**For every one that exalteth himself**—cherishes a high sense of his own goodness—**shall be abased**—rated low in God's esteem; **but he that humbleth himself**—takes a low view of himself, in relation to God and his fellow-men—**shall be exalted** —in the favor of God. God's thoughts of a man are inversely as his own of himself, when he is considering his standing before God.

15-17. CHRIST'S TREATMENT OF LITTLE CHILDREN.

Here our narrative comes into parallel again with the other Synoptical Gospels. (Matt. 19:13 ff.; Mark 10:13 ff.). From this point forward Luke proceeds, for the most part, side by side with one or both the others. Either he has reached the end of his special account of this journey, or has taken from it all that answered to his design. By comparing the order in Mark's Gospel, we see that this incident occurred after an instructive discourse concerning divorce.

15. And they brought unto him—were at the time bringing unto him—**also infants** (*their babes*), **that he should touch them.** Mothers in the company that now followed him, impressed with his holiness and benignity, and finding their own souls helped by his teaching and consolation, desired his blessing on their children. To this end they wished him to **touch them;** put his hands on them, as the gesture of blessing, and pray. (Matt. 19:13.) There is no evidence that they expected any material effect from the laying on of his hands, but they may have supposed that this act would constitute a physical channel for the spiritual benefit from the holy prophet to the child.—**But when his disciples saw it**— that they were actually bringing their infants into contact with the Master—**they rebuked them**—spoke chidingly, to prevent them from carrying out their purpose. The disciples probably thought it wrong that the time of their Lord should be taken up about women and little children. It was beneath his dignity, and likely to diminish the honor in which they would wish him to be held.

16. But Jesus called them unto him— either addressing the little ones directly, in tones of gentle invitation, or bidding the

17 *a* Verily I say unto you, Whosoever shall not receive the kingdom of God as a little child shall in no wise enter therein.
18 *b* And a certain ruler asked him, ¹ saying, Good Master, what shall I do to inherit eternal life?

17 the kingdom of God. Verily I say unto you, Whosoever shall not receive the kingdom of God as a little child, he shall in no wise enter therein.
18 And a certain ruler asked him, saying, Good ¹ Master

a Mark 10: 15....*b* Matt. 19: 16; Mark 10: 17.——1 Or, *Teacher.*

parents to bring them, **and said**—to the disciples—and thus severely rebuking *them*—**suffer** (*the*) **little children to come unto me, and forbid**—hinder—**them not.** Our Lord thus expressed the deep interest which he ever felt in little children, and may well, at the same time, have desired to administer salutary correction to the arrogant mind of his disciples. Indeed, it seems extremely probable that, if the disciples had not interfered, Jesus would have simply granted the request of the mothers, and we should have heard little of it. The following account is rather a lesson to the disciples, than a judgment concerning the state of children. The use of a word appropriate to *babes*, and of another denoting little children, to the same persons, shows that they were of various ages, from earliest infancy up. **For of such is the kingdom of God. Such**—in respect to docility, submissiveness, absence of worldly ambition, and filial love, are the members of my kingdom. Of course it is not meant that all the traits of all children are desired by Christ in his followers; but those which all recognize as appropriate to early childhood, and notice with pleasure in them.

17. Verily I say unto you, Whosoever shall not receive the kingdom of God as a little child, etc. This generalizes the preceding statement, and shows, not that mere child-likeness guarantees membership in Christ's kingdom; but that, without that teachableness, humility, trust, and obedience, no one can have part or lot therein. Thus it explains how multitudes of excellent people, as the world judges, naturally remain aloof from connection with Christ. Yet who can deny or doubt that this childlike attitude toward God and his gracious offers in the gospel, is as much more reasonable for a man than the opposite character, as it is in the case of a child toward its earthly parent? The attempt to draw any direct authority for infant baptism from this passage, has long been given up by scholars. The absolute lack of all proper ground for that practice is indicated, however, in the way even so excellent a commentator as Van Oosterzee still strives to draw some warrant from these verses. "The desire of the mothers to see their children blessed by Jesus sprang from a similar feeling of need [to that] from which afterward the baptism of children proceeded." But the baptism of children is a sacrament, in the view of all Pedobaptist theologians; and does a sacrament proceed from the wish of mothers? Rather, as they (Protestants, at least) tell us, from express divine appointment, recorded in the Scripture. Van Oosterzee proceeds: "The Saviour, who approved the first named wish, would, if asked about it, undoubtedly not stand in the way of the latter." This "undoubtedly" is surely too strong. If it were certain that the Saviour was favorable to infant baptism, why did he not say it, or have it said? If the idea be that he would now consent to it, if asked, it is amazing that one aware of the innumerable and inexpressible evils which have obviously cursed his cause in consequence of it, should dream of such a thing.

18-23. A Ruler Instructed as to the Attainment of Eternal Life.

18. And a certain ruler asked him, saying, Good Master—*teacher*—**what shall I do to inherit eternal life?** As ruler, he was a magistrate of some degree, probably as a head man of the synagogue. Matthew 19: 20, tells us that he was "a young man," and Mark 10: 17, that he was very earnest in his manner, running to meet Jesus, as he was coming out of some house, and "kneeling before him." Everything promised a willing and obedient learner. There is no appearance of a desire to "tempt" Jesus, as in a somewhat similar case (ch. 10: 25), but a sincere wish to know the truth touching a most important question. His address to Jesus shows that he regarded him simply as a Teacher=Rabbi; and the epithet "good" would have as much the air of patronage as of reverence. The question, **What shall I do?** etc., proves him to stand on the platform of outward legality,

19 And Jesus said unto him, Why callest thou me good? none is good, save one, *that is,* God.
20 Thou knowest the commandments, *a* Do not commit adultery, Do not kill, Do not steal, Do not bear false witness, *b* Honour thy father and thy mother.
21 And he said, All these have I kept from my youth up.
22 Now when Jesus heard these things, he said unto him, Yet lackest thou one thing; *c* sell all that thou hast, and distribute unto the poor, and thou shalt have treasure in heaven: and come, follow me.

19 ter, what shall I do to inherit eternal life? And Jesus said unto him, Why callest thou me good?
20 none is good, save one, *even* God. Thou knowest the commandments, Do not commit adultery, Do not kill, Do not steal, Do not bear false witness, Honour
21 thy father and mother. And he said, All these
22 things have I observed from my youth up. And when Jesus heard it, he said unto him, One thing thou lackest yet: sell all that thou hast, and distribute unto the poor, and thou shalt have treasure in

a Ex. 20: 12, 16; Deut. 5: 16-20; Rom. 13: 9....*b* Ephes. 6: 2; Col. 3: 20....*c* Matt. 6: 19, 20; 19: 21; 1 Tim. 6: 19.

assuming that salvation was to be acquired by particular acts, and not otherwise.

19. Jesus finds in the word "good," which he had used, a text for a sermon on that goodness which was necessary to eternal life. —**Why callest thou me good?** As teacher, in which character alone thou dost recognize me, that term does not apply to me, in the eminent sense which thou shouldst comprehend.—**None is good, save one, that is, God.** By that standard, the man might judge what character was needed, on his part, to dwell happily with God in life eternal.

20. Thou knowest the commandments, etc. The statement implied a direction to keep them in the spirit of that goodness, as an answer to his question. Notice, that Jesus refers him only to commandments "of the second table," enjoining duties to fellow-men. Some judge this to have been because he thought reflection on these would suffice to convict him of sin. How much, then. would he be humbled in view of deficiencies of obedience and love toward God? But as it is a common fact that Jesus and his apostles, in summarizing the law, confine themselves to the commandments of this class, we may suppose that it was because men could more easily test themselves by these than by the profounder, more spiritual requirements of Godlike love.

21. And he said, All these have I kept—(*did I keep*)—**from my youth up.** He appears surprised that Jesus should think it necessary to remind him of *these* commandments. He was a virtuous and pious man. Possessed with the Pharisaic idea of keeping the law as being the performance or avoidance of such and such acts, and supposing there was some great thing more, probably, among the added requirements of the Rabbis, on which salvation must clearly hang, he could not see any value in Christ's instruction. Was there nothing more?

22. Now (rather, *And*) **when Jesus heard these things, he said unto him, Yet lackest thou one thing. One thing;** but in that, everything. The external observance of the law, Christ does not dispute with him. He seems even to have been sincerely interested in the young man, as Mark's account expressly shows. The one thing lacking, was that spirit of self-denying love, which is the first commandment of all, and the soul of each commandment. It can exist towards men in Christ's sense, only as it is the redundancy, the overflow, of supreme love to God. To bring this home to his inquirer, Jesus prescribes conduct, by his course concerning which the presence or absence of such a spirit will at once appear.—**Sell all that thou hast and distribute unto the poor, and thou shalt have treasure in heaven; and come, follow me.** A unique requirement, expressly given to this man alone, of all with whom Christ discoursed about salvation, cannot convey the absolute and general condition of salvation. It was given to him as suited to make plain what he lacked in order to moral perfection (Matt., ch. 19: 21) and eternal life. It required him to sacrifice earthly wealth for the good of needy fellow-men, because that would be the most effectual test of *his* love to his neighbor; and, quite probably, because Christ desired him to give himself to the ministry of the gospel, as Peter and Andrew, James and John had done—*leaving all.* We can easily imagine that he would, thus proved, have made a useful laborer in God's harvest. It will be noticed that this consecration of his worldly goods to charity was not itself to be a saving act. It was only preparatory to that course of discipleship to Christ which would lead to eternal life.—**And come, follow me.** Thus, the loss of his property would prove an eternal gain; it would simply have been converted into a fund of divine favor, which would yield him unfailing revenues of bliss, as *treasure in heaven.* Thus had the man been answered on the ground of the law, so as

23 And when he heard this, he was very sorrowful: for he was very rich.
24 And when Jesus saw that he was very sorrowful, he said, *How hardly shall they that have riches enter into the kingdom of God!
25 For it is easier for a camel to go through a needle's eye, than for a rich man to enter into the kingdom of God.
26 And they that heard it said, Who then can be saved?

23 heaven: and come, follow me. But when he heard these things, he became exceeding sorrowful; for he
24 was very rich. And Jesus seeing him said, How hardly shall they that have riches enter into the
25 kingdom of God! For it is easier for a camel to enter in through a needle's eye, than for a rich man to
26 enter into the kingdom of God. And they that

a Prov. 11 : 28; Matt. 19 : 23 ; Mark 10 : 23.

to bring him to salvation in the gospel, if there was in his heart any drawing of the Father toward Christ.

23. And when he heard this, he was—*became*—**very sorrowful: for he was very rich.** That he was **sorrowful** shows that he could not dispute the teaching. These were different things, however, from what he was used to hear concerning the way of life. To do any number of the most difficult works would be a trifle to the renunciation of his darling treasures. "His countenance fell at the saying." (Mark, ch. 10: 22. Revision.) The consecration of his deepest heart to God, to make his whole earthly life subservient to the will of God, and thus to find his own happiness in promoting that of others, was too great a price for him to pay. We can imagine the Saviour disappointed and grieved. The test which he had proposed—essentially the same, though different in phrase—that he had required of several of his followers, instead of developing a germinant faith, had apparently driven him away from salvation. True, as Farrar says on the passage, "nothing forbids us to hope that the words of Jesus, who loved him, sank into his soul, and brought him to a humbler and holier frame of mind. . . . The day came when Saul of Tarsus was, like this youth, 'touching the righteousness which is in the law, blameless;' but *he* had grace to count all things but loss for Christ." The ruler, certainly, never found eternal life on any easier conditions, probably never at all.

24-30. SUGGESTED LESSON CONCERNING WEALTH.

24. And when Jesus saw, etc. According to the best text the verse reads: **And Jesus** (*seeing him*) **said, How hardly shall** (or, *do*) **they that have riches enter into the kingdom of God!** The man's despondency and perturbation reminded Jesus of a fact which he must have often noticed. His converts had been mostly from the poor. The rich also heard him, in numbers; but their greater contentment with their earthly lot; their engrossment in the business, the cares, and the pleasures of life; pride of intellect; and the fetters of fashionable society,—all operated to restrain them from embracing the humiliating, though pure and blessed, tenets of the Teacher of Galilee. The present tense of the verb, which is to be preferred, supposes that some actually become true disciples; which fact it is, in all the circumstances, that seems remarkable to our Lord. What difficulties wealth throws in their way!

25. For it is easier for a camel to go (or, *enter in*) **through a needle's eye,** etc. Perhaps some signs of surprise and incredulity in the hearers led the Saviour thus to confirm and intensify his statement. For a camel to pass through the eye of a needle was a natural impossibility; and for a rich man to be saved he declares is still harder. All attempts to soften this statement, either by supposing the needle's eye to be a figure for a narrow door in a city gate—of which use of the term there is no proof at all—or, that the Greek word for *camel* was changed from one meaning "cable," or "rope" —for which there is no text authority, and which also would be literally impossible, all such attempts are vain and unnecessary. Christ, as often, to more deeply impress a truth, speaks the language of hyperbole, for which his hearers would, and all sensible readers do, make proper allowance.

26. And they that heard it—including some of the disciples (Matt., ch. 19 : 25)—**said, Who then can be saved?** They would perhaps have been less surprised, if he had said, "How hardly do the poor enter in!" And the bearing of their question was, "If the rich, with all their means for giving alms, and time for the performance of religious works, have so great difficulty, what is to become of us?" Or, is it possible that, in the crudeness of their conceptions concerning the Messiah's kingdom, they had included riches as an es-

27 And he said, "The things which are impossible with men are possible with God.
28 ᵇThen Peter said, Lo, we have left all, and followed thee.
29 And he said unto them, Verily I say unto you, ᶜThere is no man that hath left house, or parents, or brethren, or wife, or children, for the kingdom of God's sake,
30 ᵈWho shall not receive manifold more in this present time, and in the world to come life everlasting.
31 ᵉThen he took unto him the twelve, and said unto them, Behold, we go up to Jerusalem, and all things ᶠthat are written by the prophets concerning the Son of man shall be accomplished.

27 heard it said, Then who can be saved? But he said, The things which are impossible with men are possible with God. And Peter said, Lo, we have left
29 ¹our own, and followed thee. And he said unto them, Verily I say unto you, There is no man that hath left house, or wife, or brethren, or parents, or
30 children, for the kingdom of God's sake, who shall not receive manifold more in this time, and in the ²world to come eternal life.
31 And he took unto him the twelve, and said unto them, Behold, we go up to Jerusalem, and all the things that are written through the prophets shall

a Jer. 32 : 17 ; Zech. 8 : 6 ; Matt. 19 : 26 ; ch. 1 : 37.....*b* Matt. 19 : 27.....*c* Deut. 33 : 9.....*d* Job 42 : 10.....*e* Matt. 16 : 21 ; 17 ; 22 ; 20 : 17 ; Mark 10 : 32.....*f* Ps. 22 ; Isa. 53.——1 Or, *our own homes*....2 Or, *age.*

sential endowment of all its members, and could not imagine salvation without it?

27. And (rather, *But*) **he said, The things which are impossible with men**—to their view, and by their power—**are possible with God.** This is the true explanation of the foregoing paradox. The conversion of a rich man, without special divine interposition, was literally impossible. That of any man was a work of God's grace; that of a rich man, from the incident which they had just witnessed, seemed most strikingly so. But God could accomplish even that.

28. And Peter said, Lo, we have left (we *left* when thou didst call us)—**all** (rather, *our own*)—property, or, homes—**and followed thee.** Coleridge, somewhere, sharply reproaches Peter's question (Matt. 19 : 27) as indicating a groveling and mercenary spirit. But surely it requires no great charity to the chief apostle to presume that he was naturally and unselfishly curious, if not anxious, after the exciting case of the ruler, and the startling comments of the Saviour, to understand how he himself and his fellow apostles stood related, in these respects, to the eternal life.

29. Luke does not record the answer of Jesus in special reference to the case of the apostles, given in Matthew, but the more general one applicable to all disciples who had made any sacrifice for him. **Verily**—a statement of importance is to follow—**there is no man that hath left house, or wife,** etc. Christ seems, by his enumeration of objects given up, to represent all types of loss and sacrifice to which his disciples were, and would be, liable. Such things were, of course, to be abandoned when, and in so far as, they stood in the way of a complete devotion of the believer to the service of Christ. **For the kingdom of God's sake**—in order to gain, and worthily to maintain citizenship, in that.

30. Who shall not receive manifold mo. in this present time—age, world. Mark says "an hundred fold," and both he and Matthew refer expressly to the objects which had been specified as forsaken for Christ. This proves that there was no thought intended of material or quantitative recompense; only that much greater satisfaction of the higher nature of every such man would come than he could have enjoyed in a selfish, worldly use of what he has thus sacrificed. **And in the world to come life everlasting** (better, *eternal life.*) This, while begun in the present, mundane state (John 17 : 2), is still enjoyed with so many drawbacks and limitations, that it is natural to our imperfect experience to think of its main blessedness as lying entirely in the world above. The condition of attaining it is here seen to be the renunciation of earthly delights found incompatible with whole-hearted attachment to Christ and his cause. Its essence is peace with God, and the unhampered exercise of all the faculties of the soul in communion with him—partial in time, perfect and complete throughout eternity.

31–34. JESUS AGAIN FORETELLS HIS DEATH AND RESURRECTION.

31. The Saviour takes an occasion, as before (ch. 9 : 22, 44), when the hopes of the disciples had been excited, so that they could better bear, and perhaps needed, a more sobering aspect of their case, to declare what he was to suffer, in order to establish the kingdom of God. The nearness of his passion, too—**we go up to Jerusalem**—made some fresh announcement concerning it appropriate. The prediction here given, as compared with the passages just cited, discloses that his sufferings

32 For *he shall be delivered unto the Gentiles, and shall be mocked, and spitefully entreated, and spitted on:
33 And they shall scourge *him*, and put him to death: and the third day he shall rise again.
34 *b* And they understood none of these things: and this saying was hid from them, neither knew they the things which were spoken.
35 *c* And it came to pass, that as he was come nigh unto Jericho, a certain blind man sat by the wayside begging:
36 And hearing the multitude pass by, he asked what it meant.
37 And they told him, that Jesus of Nazareth passeth by.
38 And he cried, saying, Jesus, *thou* son of David, have mercy on me.
39 And they which went before rebuked him, that he should hold his peace: but he cried so much the more, *Thou* son of David, have mercy on me.

32 be accomplished unto the Son of man. For he shall be delivered up unto the Gentiles, and shall be mocked, and shamefully entreated, and spit upon: and they shall scourge and kill him; and the third day
34 he shall rise again. And they understood none of these things; and this saying was hid from them, and they perceived not the things that were said.
35 And it came to pass, as he drew nigh unto Jericho,
36 a certain blind man sat by the wayside begging: and hearing a multitude going by, he inquired what this
37 meant. And they told him, that Jesus of Nazareth
38 passeth by. And he cried, saying, Jesus, thou Son of
39 David, have mercy on me. And they that went before rebuked him, that he should hold his peace: but he cried out the more a great deal, Thou Son of

a Matt. 27: 2; ch. 23: 1; John 18: 28; Acts 3: 13....*b* Mark 9: 32; ch. 2: 50; 9: 45; John 10: 6; 12: 16....*c* Matt. 20: 29; Mark 10: 46.

were to be in fulfillment of prophecy, at the hands of Gentiles; and adds some details of the abusive treatment which would precede his death. See on those passages.—Then —(*And*) he took unto him the twelve—took them apart from the throng, that he might fully unbosom his heart to them alone.—We go up to Jerusalem, with the understanding (comp. ver. 35), "and shall soon be there."—And all things that are written concerning the Son of man shall be accomplished— better, as in the Revision, *all things that are written through the prophets shall be accomplished unto the Son of man.* That what was to *be accomplished unto the Son of man* would take place in fulfillment of the prophets, was as well suited as any truth could be, to reconcile the disciples to their occurrence, and would eventually have such an effect.

32. They would afterward reflect that almost every detail of the humiliation and suffering of their Lord had been precisely foretold by him.

34. And they—emphatic, or distinctive= "they, on their part"—understood none of these things. The teaching was so contrary to all their previously formed notions concerning the Messiah and his fortunes, that the words, although perfectly intelligible in other connections, conveyed no clear thought to their minds. Yet it is intimated that there was a higher reason for their blindness, so peculiarly dense, in the counsels of God. For it is added, And this saying—the declaration itself, in which Christ had spoken of these things—was hid—had been concealed—from them. Not so much, we may believe, in the way of judicial blindness, as if they had blamefully missed the true sense; but rather through mercy, that they might not be prematurely aware of the trials before them, but first find the import of the prediction, when they should most need its comfort.—Neither knew they, etc. A necessary result of the preceding statement.

35-43. HEALING OF A BLIND MAN NEAR JERICHO.

Luke's account of this event, compared with that of Matt., ch. 20: 29-34, and of Mark, ch. 10: 46-52, suggests two difficulties: First, he mentions one sufferer relieved (agreeing in that with Mark); second, he places the occurrence at their entrance into Jericho; the others, at his departure. The first is easily obviated. Though there were two, many reasons are supposable why some of the reports of the event should have dwelt upon one, to the neglect of the other. Mark indicates one: that one of those healed was son of a man of more or less note, one Timæus. As to the place, one cure may have been effected when the Lord was drawing near to the city; the other, when he was going away from it. It would be consistent with Matthew's practice, to condense the two accounts into one; while Luke mentions the former, Mark, the latter case. It is easy to conjecture what, with more circumstantial knowledge, might be seen to be the fact, and so do away with all appearance of discrepancy. This is sufficient to refute the charge of necessary contradiction.

The narrative is highly graphic. We are made to see the sufferer sitting, as if to rest from his own journey, by the way-side. The great multitudes which have been repeatedly mentioned as following Jesus of late, raise a

40 And Jesus stood, and commanded him to be brought unto him: and when he was come near, he asked him,
41 Saying, What wilt thou that I shall do unto thee? And he said, Lord, that I may receive my sight.
42 And Jesus said unto him, Receive thy sight: ᵃthy faith hath saved thee.
43 And immediately he received his sight, and followed him, ᵇglorifying God: and all the people, when they saw it, gave praise unto God.

40 David, have mercy on me. And Jesus stood, and commanded him to be brought unto him: and when
41 he was come near, he asked him, What wilt thou that I should do unto thee? And he said, Lord, that
42 I may receive my sight. And Jesus said unto him, Receive thy sight: thy faith hath ¹ made thee whole.
43 And immediately he received his sight, and followed him, glorifying God: and all the people, when they saw it, gave praise unto God.

CHAPTER XIX.

AND *Jesus* entered and passed through Jericho.
2 And, behold, *there was* a man named Zaccheus, which was the chief among the publicans, and he was rich.

1 And he entered and was passing through Jericho.
2 And behold, a man called by name Zacchæus; and

a ch. 17: 19....*b* ch. 5: 26; Acts 4: 21; 11: 18.——1 Or, *saved thee.*

din in passing, which excites the curiosity of one who could not see as to what it meant. The answer is given as a cold matter of fact: "Jesus of Nazareth passeth by." The name reminds him of what he has heard of the wonderful deeds of this personage in that part of the country. Instantly, therefore, he calls aloud, **Jesus, thou son of David**—thus proving his persuasion of the Messiahship of our Lord—**have mercy on me**. This speaks his sense of need, and, equally, of unworthiness. He can ask help only for pity's sake, without any claim or allegation of merit.—**And they which went before**—in the van of the procession, leaving Jesus nearer the middle of the line than he generally stood (ch. 19: 28; Mark. ch. 10: 32)—**rebuked him**—thinking it unseemly that so great a personage, on so stately an occasion, should be disturbed by a blind beggar. Surely, they could not have been long in the Master's company. The blind man instinctively appreciated his character more truly.—**But he cried so much the more**—what a trait of natural earnestness!—**Son of David, have mercy on me!** It seems probable that the appellation **Son of David**, from the lips of a few petitioners in the Gospels, recognized Jesus in the most general way as the fulfillment of obvious prophecies concerning the Messiah.

40. The true princeliness of our Saviour now appears in what his would-be guardians thought unworthy of him.—**And Jesus stood** —catching, through the stir, the cry of need; himself on foot, he arrested the attendant throng.—**And commanded that he should be brought**—led—**unto him**, by the hands, very likely, of some who had thought it unbecoming that the wretch should address their Lord.

41. What wilt thou that I shall do unto thee? The question would excite the faith of the sufferer, and draw the attention of all to his wretched case. It itself throws the door of mercy open, implying that whatever was needed should be done.—**And he said, Lord, that I may receive my sight**—is what I desire—but a blessing so great that I dare not plainly ask it.

42. Without the slightest hesitation, the healing word was spoken: **Receive thy sight; thy faith hath saved thee.**

43. With the former word sight came to the blind eyes; **immediately he received his sight.** The latter was added to honor the faith which the man had exercised, and show that there had not been merely an arbitrary exercise of the divine power. For the man not only, but for the whole crowd, this reference to faith was of essential consequence.—**And followed him, glorifying God.** (See on ch. 5: 25.) He thus gave the best evidence possible, at the moment, that the mercy of Christ had reached not only his bodily eyes, but his heart, now filled with joyful gratitude to God, who had wrought through Christ.—**And all the people .... gave praise unto God.** A general enthusiasm of outward praise, at least, animated the throng, which their leaders, just before (ver. 39), would fain have hindered from this glorious view.

Ch. 19. 1-10. CONVERSION OF ZACCHEUS.

1. And Jesus entered and passed (or, *was passing*) **through Jericho.** This city, famous, rich, and strong, before its destruction by Joshua on his entering the land of Canaan, had afterward arisen, in spite of the curse which he pronounced on its site; and, through various fortunes, had become again, under Herod the Great, and later, a flourishing and important city. It lay about seven

3 And he sought to see Jesus who he was; and could not for the press, because he was little of stature.
4 And he ran before, and climbed up into a sycamore tree to see him: for he was to pass that way.
5 And when Jesus came to the place, he looked up, and saw him, and said unto him, Zaccheus, make haste, and come down; for to day I must abide at thy house.

3 he was a chief publican, and he was rich. And he sought to see Jesus who he was; and could not 4 for the crowd, because he was little of stature. And he ran on before, and climbed up into a sycomore 5 tree to see him: for he was to pass that way. And when Jesus came to the place, he looked up, and said unto him, Zacchæus, make haste, and come

miles west of the Jordan, opposite the place where the river parted to allow passage for the Israelites, and the same distance northwest of the Dead Sea, where that river empties into it. Standing in a little oasis of freshness and verdure, it seemed a Paradise to the traveler who came upon it, wearied from the arduous canyons of the western mountain (ch. 10: 30), or parched and thirsty through the arid sands of the Jordan plain. We have rather assumed, in the preceding exposition, that Jesus now came to Jericho through Perea, the country beyond the Jordan, according to the representation of Matthew and Mark (Matt. 19: 1; Mark 10: 1). Luke, indeed, does not say so, nor does he say anything to the contrary. It was possible to come from Galilee to Jericho following the west bank of the Jordan, down through the inhospitable gorge in which the river winds its way (the Arabah, *Ghor*). But as our Saviour evidently desired on this journey to reach as many people as possible, and made provision (ch. 10: 1) for quite extensive proclamation of the gospel, we cannot think Luke supposed that to be the real course, or that the Saviour could have been detained through a long series of discourses at any one place in the sparsely inhabited valley of the Jordan. Nor would he then have needed to pass **through Jericho.** He had now crossed that river by the well-known ford, where Joshua had crossed in the early day.

2. And, behold, there was a man named Zaccheus. The name being Hebrew, from a root meaning *pure*, he was evidently of the Jewish stock. The name (Zaccai) occurs (Ezra 2: 9; Neh. 7; 14); **which was the chief among the publicans**—chief of the tax-gatherers—**and he was rich.** Jericho was celebrated for its production of highly prized balsam, and other articles of commerce; and lying on the only route of trade across Southern Palestine, between the West and the East, must have given much occupation to the exacters of revenue. Such were frequently Jews; and as Zaccheus is called a chief of the tax gatherers, we may suppose he superintended the collection of revenue over a district requiring others, more strictly called "publicans," under him. See on ch. 3: 12. We have seen (on the passage just cited) that those who followed his business were able to make it very profitable. Perhaps no one of them in Palestine would have opportunity for *greater gains*. Hence it is very naturally added—**and he was rich.**

3. And he sought to see Jesus who he was. He wanted to know by his actual looks the man of whom he had heard much in that region, as a great teacher and wonder-worker, and especially as one considerate and sympathizing toward men of his class. His feeling may have partaken of a desire which would prepare him more readily to receive the instructions of Christ; but that we can only conjecture. **And could not for the press, because he was little of stature.** The earnestness of his desire appears in the manner in which he overcame the difficulty.

4. And he ran (*on*) **before**—in front of the advancing procession—**and climbed up into a sycamore tree**—more exactly—*went up on a sycamore*. The sycamore, or figmulberry, was a low-growing, wide-spreading tree, which gave little occasion for "climbing," in the proper sense, and the Common Version may mislead our conception of what Zaccheus really did. **For he was to**—had to, was bound to—**pass that way.**

5. We cannot at all say whether Jesus had known anything of Zaccheus before; he might easily learn his name, and something of his character, from the comments which his conduct would draw from the crowd. We may well suppose that this conduct, interpreted by the look and air of the man, as Jesus drew near, would indicate in him an unusual preparedness for the reception of the gospel. Hence the seemingly abrupt direction, **Make haste, and come down; for to-day I must abide at thy house.** The necessity implied in **I must,** lay in the fitness with his whole plan of saving the lost, of such a tarrying to enlighten and win the chief tax-gatherer. At his house, would he be better able to influence Zaccheus for his spiritual good. There is

278 LUKE. [Ch. XIX.

6 And he made haste, and came down, and received him joyfully.
7 And when they saw *it*, they all murmured, saying, "That he was gone to be guest with a man that is a sinner.
8 And Zaccheus stood, and said unto the Lord; Behold, Lord, the half of my goods I give to the poor; and if I have taken any thing from any man by *a false accusation, c I restore *him* fourfold.
9 And Jesus said unto him, This day is salvation come to this house, forasmuch as d he also is *a son of Abraham.

6 down; for to-day I must abide at thy house. And he made haste, and came down, and received him
7 joyfully. And when they saw it, they all murmured, saying, He is gone in to lodge with a man
8 that is a sinner. And Zacchæus stood, and said unto the Lord, Behold, Lord, the half of my goods I give to the poor; and if I have wrongfully exacted
9 aught of any man, I restore fourfold. And Jesus said unto him, To-day is salvation come to this

a Matt. 9: 11; ch. 5: 30....b ch. 3: 14....c Ex. 22: 1; 1 Sam. 12: 3; 2 Sam. 12: 6....d Rom. 4: 11, 12, 16; Gal. 3: 7....e ch. 13: 16.

nothing to lead us to think that the house of Zaccheus stood outside of the city.

6. And he made haste, and came down, and received him joyfully. Everything bespoke heartfelt and lively gratification at the privilege of entertaining the great teacher, the reputed Messiah.

7. And when they—the accompanying multitude—**saw it, they all murmured.** In the brevity of the narrative, much is left to imagination in filling out the scene. We may, first of all, emphasize the impression which the mere presence of Jesus, the manner of his intercourse, the tones of his voice, and the sentiments of his conversation made on Zaccheus. We can hardly help assuming, also, that there was much discourse exchanged between the host and his guest, during the stay of the latter.—**I must abide**—in the house, whether the stay was of a few hours only, or lasted over night. Much of this may have passed, and the interest of the publican have ripened into an intelligent and deliberate faith, while this murmuring went on.—**Saying that he was**—*is*—**gone**—*in*—**to be guest**—*to lodge*—**with a man that is a sinner.** *To lodge*, would naturally imply that Christ was tarrying over at least one night; but not necessarily so. **He *is* gone *in***=he went in—is spoken after the visit has continued for some time. Their calling Zaccheus **a sinner** does not *prove* that he was more so in their estimation than any publican..

8. And Zaccheus stood—properly, *took his stand*, as at ch. 18: 11. At some point of the time, he, being aware of their opprobrious cries, resolved to meet them before the Saviour, and so stood forth, in calm and unabashed dignity. Was it the dignity of conscious innocence toward their accusations, or of penitent rectification of conscious wrongs? Godet and others take the former view, according to which the publican says: "Lord, I am not so unworthy of thy attention as they allege; I give, habitually, the half of my goods to the poor," etc. This has in its favor the present tense of the verbs—**I give, I restore.** But against it lies the absurdity of habitually giving half one's goods, and remaining rich; that it almost precludes the question of such a man's exacting aught "wrongfully" of any man; and, above all, that it breathes no whisper of repentance. Therefore, we hold to the common view, that Zaccheus now meets his defamers by declaring that he does, here and now, to Jesus vow the gift of half his fortune to the poor, both out of gratitude for the blessing which comes to him through the presence of the Lord, and also as a restitution of what he may have acquired not with that honesty which, in Christ's presence, at least, he feels right. To make this last point sure, he specifically vows to restore fourfold to any individuals from whom it shall appear that he has, in his office, taken what they should not have paid. Thus, the present tense of the verb is fully justified. (Comp. Matt. 24: 40 ff.; 26: 2; Revision; comp. Butt, *N. T. Gram.*, p. 205). The resolution and promise went far beyond anything required in the law in such a case. See the law concerning such a trespass, in Num. 5: 6, 7, where a fine of one-fifth only, besides the principal sum, is imposed. Here was such exercise of the spirit of the law of love as had been required of the rich young man (ch. 18: 22). It was an exhibition of true repentance, and faith in the Lord Jesus, which Zaccheus might more confidently rely on against the reproaches of the crowd, than upon protestations of innocence, even though well founded.

9. And Jesus said unto him, This day—in consequence of my abiding at this house to-day (ver. 5) —**is salvation come to this house**—in the pardon of sins to its proprietor—**forasmuch as he also is a son of Abraham.** The last sentence, while addressed to the publican, is modified in form

Ch. XIX.] LUKE. 279

10 *For the Son of man is come to seek and to save that which was lost.
11 And as they heard these things, he added and spake a parable, because he was nigh to Jerusalem, and *because they thought that the kingdom of God should immediately appear.
12 *He said therefore, A certain nobleman went into a far country to receive for himself a kingdom, and to return.

10 house, forasmuch as he also is a son of Abraham. For the Son of man came to seek and to save that which was lost.
11 And as they heard these things, he added and spake a parable, because he was nigh to Jerusalem, and *because they supposed that the kingdom of God
12 was immediately to appear. He said therefore, A certain nobleman went into a far country, to receive.

a Matt. 18: 11. See Matt. 10: 6; 15: 24.....b Acts 1: 6.....c Matt. 25: 14; Mark 13: 34.

into a justification of the favor shown him as against the reproaches of the people. Christ would say, "in blessing him, I go not beyond the circle of my mission" (Matt. 10: 5, 6; 15: 24). He was one of "the lost sheep of the house of Israel."

10. For the Son of man is come to seek and to save that which was lost. Quite in the spirit of chs. 5: 32; 13: 16; and of the whole of chapter 15. Zaccheus was lost to his neighbors, in the infamy of his occupation; to Jesus, in the estrangement of his heart from the peace of God. Thus we see Christ at the very close of his life, persisting, and now against greater inducements than ever before, through the offered homage of a numberless and friendly throng, in manifesting a special favor toward those whom that throng specially despised and avoided; or—because they specially needed his sympathy and aid.

Part IV. Ch. 19: 11; 24: 53. Approach to Jerusalem, and Fulfillment of the Time that He Should be Received Up. (Ch. 9: 51). We cannot maintain that Luke's narrative expressly indicates a new beginning here, as it has done for the three preceding Parts; but, in common with all the other Gospels, it treats the events of the week now to follow with such fullness, and such concentrated unity of interest, as to show that they had a pre-eminent and unique interest in his plan. Henceforth he is entirely on common ground with one or more of the evangelists, in the principal statements of his Gospel to the end.

11-27. Parable of the Ten Pounds. (Or, *minae*.)

11. And as they heard these things, he added, etc. This is evidently a general designation of the time. Not precisely while they were hearing his discourse with Zaccheus, but while the impression of that was fresh in their minds; the next recorded thing that he spoke, was the following parable. **Added and spoke,** is a Hebraism for "spoke further." **Because he was nigh to Jerusalem**—about fourteen miles only from the objective point of their long pilgrimage, at which the opportunities of instructing them would soon end. **And because they thought** (or, *supposed*) **that the kingdom of God should immediately appear**—show itself, or be displayed. **Immediately** is emphatic. This was the main reason for uttering the parable. Their idea was, that, as soon as they reached Jerusalem, "the glorious appearing" of the Son of man would blaze forth. This statement of reasons why he spoke the parable, proves that its intention was, primarily, to show that the glory of his kingdom would be seen only after a considerable interval; and, secondarily, to teach the chief disciples how that interval should be spent. He accordingly compares himself to a man of noble birth, entitled to exercise kingly dominion, but needing first to be duly invested with this authority by the supreme power, a long way off. Meantime, he leaves with selected bond-slaves of his an important sum of money, an equal amount to each, to be employed for the furtherance of his interests during his absence. On his return he finds that some of these servants have made excellent use of his deposit, and rewards them proportionally; while one, who had done nothing, is disgraced and stripped of his trust. Incidentally we learn that the community at large, over whom he sought the dominion, disliked him, and vainly sought to hinder his receiving it; but, being defeated in their opposition, they were cruelly punished by him in his triumph.

12. A certain nobleman. The figure might be suggested by the frequent cases in which princes of the Herodean family, and others, in that age, had to apply to the Roman Emperor, for monarchical authority in Palestine, and the adjacent provinces. The case of Archelaus, in particular, might, as Meyer and others have noticed, the more naturally be remembered here, at Jericho, because he had left there a splendid palace, and other

13 And he called his ten servants, and delivered them ten pounds, and said unto them, Occupy till I come.
14 ᵃBut his citizens hated him, and sent a message after him, saying, We will not have this man to reign over us.
15 And it came to pass, that when he was returned, having received the kingdom, then he commanded these servants to be called unto him, to whom he had given the money, that he might know how much every man had gained by trading.
16 Then came the first, saying, Lord, thy pound hath gained ten pounds.

13 for himself a kingdom, and to return. And he called ten ¹servants of his, and gave them ten ²pounds, and said unto them, Trade ye *herewith* till I come.
14 But his citizens hated him, and sent an ambassage after him, saying, We will not that this man reign over us.
15 And it came to pass, when he was come back again, having received the kingdom, that he commanded these ¹servants, unto whom he had given the money, to be called to him, that he might
16 know what they had gained by trading. And the first came before him, saying, Lord, thy pound hath

a John 1:11.——1 Gr. *bondservants*....2 *Mina*, here translated a pound, is equal to one hundred drachmas. See ch. 15:8.

memorials of his luxurious reign. (Josephus, *Antiquities*, xvii., 13, 1.) His case, at all events, would furnish a strict parallel to the incidents mentioned in ver. 14, 27.—**A far country** stands for the celestial state, in which the Father dwells in glory. **To receive a kingdom** signifies the sending the Son of man forth again in the glory of his Father and of the holy angels, when every knee shall bow before him, and every tongue confess that he is Lord.

13. And—before he went—**he called ten servants** = slaves—**of his**—*own*. By a colloquial inaccuracy, the commissioning the servants is mentioned after he is said to have departed. The ten servants were only a selection of the whole number that such a personage would possess. Their being bondservants would not hinder their standing high in the confidence and favor of their lord. Why just ten? A smaller number would hardly have been consistent with the dignity of such a nobleman, while twelve would have pointed too palpably to the apostles.—**Of his own**, and, therefore, absolutely subject to his authority.—**And gave to them ten pounds**—one to each servant. What is here called a pound was the Attic *mina*, containing silver equivalent to near seventeen dollars now, but then, practically, far more valuable. At most the sum is so small, compared with the talents, in Matt. 25:14, ff., as to prove that that cannot be a report of this parable. It was sufficient to exercise and test the capacity of these servants with reference to larger responsibility after his return. (Meyer.)—**Occupy**—*trade ye*—**till I come.** The pound symbolized the ability for usefulness in the cause of Christ, and trading therewith would be the turning such ability to the best account for its purpose. In particular, we may perhaps safely say, that the pound committed to each servant was Christ's truth (the gospel), his ordinances, his Spirit. **Occupy** formerly meant nearly the same as "use money for gain" (Plut., in *Richardson's Dictionary*), from the Latin verb *occupare*, one meaning of which was "to invest money," either as a loan at interest, or in purchases for profit. This is the sense of the Greek verb used by Christ. Coverdale, "chaffer ye"; Tyndale, "buy and sell." Compare "by trading" (ver. 15).—**Until I come** is, in the best MSS., "while I am coming," as if the whole interval of absence was one coming.

14. His citizens are his fellow-citizens, while he is yet a candidate merely for the rule over them; his future subjects, should he become king. The Jews are plainly intended, as using every possible means to hinder Jesus from attaining to his destined dominion. There may probably have been an allusion to the well-known case of Archelaus. (Josephus, *Antiquities*, xvii. 11, 1 ff.)

15. This verse is prophetic of Christ's procedure when he shall come in royal authority at the end of the world. **How much every man had gained by trading;** the Greek is, nearly, "Who had accomplished anything by trading, and what." This would determine with what fidelity and success they had *occupied*. In "that day" the Judge will strictly inquire who has turned to account that fund of truth and grace which was lent to each one, and how much more there is of it now for future use.

16. Then came the first, etc., (literally, *And the first came before him*). The reports of three only are given, that being enough to exhibit the whole method and spirit of the trial. The order, first, second, third, is so conceived that the first proves the one who has been most successful in his traffic, the second the next best; then (passing over all who were profitable in less degrees), third, the one who has done nothing. Or, are we to

17 And he said unto him, Well, thou good servant: because thou hast been a faithful in a very little, have thou authority over ten cities.
18 And the second came, saying, Lord, thy pound hath gained five pounds.
19 And he said likewise to him, Be thou also over five cities.
20 And another came, saying, Lord, behold, *here is* thy pound, which I have kept laid up in a napkin:
21 b For I feared thee, because thou art an austere man: thou takest up that thou layedst not down, and reapest that thou didst not sow.
22 And he saith unto him, c Out of thine own mouth will I judge thee, *thou* wicked servant. d Thou knewest that I was an austere man, taking up that I laid not down, and reaping that I did not sow:

17 made ten pounds more. And he said unto him, Well done, thou good 1 servant: because thou wast found faithful in a very little, have thou authority over ten cities. And the second came, saying,
18 over ten cities. And the second came, saying,
19 Thy pound, Lord, hath made five pounds. And he said unto him also, Be thou also over five
20 cities. And 2 another came, saying, Lord, behold, *here is* thy pound, which I kept laid up
21 in a napkin: for I feared thee, because thou art an austere man: thou takest up that thou layedst
22 not down, and reapest that thou didst not sow. He saith unto him, Out of thine own mouth will I judge thee, thou wicked 1 servant. Thou knewest that I am an austere man, taking up that I laid not down,

a Matt. 25: 21; ch. 16: 10....*b* Matt. 25: 24....*c* 2 Sam. 1: 16; Job 15: 6; Matt. 12: 37....*d* Matt. 25: 26.——1 Gr. *bondservant*....2 Gr. *the other*.

understand that out of every three one has turned out useless, and two, more or less profitable servants? **Saying, Lord, thy pound hath gained**—did of itself work out besides—**ten pounds.** He does not take the credit of having done it; the master's pound has wrought with this result. Supposing the capital to have signified, as imagined above, we need not puzzle ourselves as to the form in which the increment appears at the last day. It may be in the enlarged spiritual acquirements and developed gifts and graces of the servant himself, or, also, in the propagation of these powers of usefulness in other converted souls. Enough, that there are now eleven pounds where there was but one. He has invested, traded, well.

17. And he—the Lord—**said**—*unto him*—**Well!**—*bravo*—**thou good servant.** What joy does even this foreshadow, for the disciple who shall behold the smile of his Lord and Saviour, at the last day? **Because thou hast been**—*didst prove*—**faithful in a very little, have thou authority over ten cities.** Comp. ch. 16: 10. Farrar says that Archelaus thus rewarded the chief subjects who had been faithful to him. **In a very little.** All duties and performances in the preliminary dispensation of the Son of man will seem trifling, like the charge of a few dollars, when measured on the scale of eternal affairs. **Have thou authority over ten cities.** The Greek expression strongly marks the continuation of this office, nearly as "be thou having," etc. The government of cities may prefigure oversight and responsibility in behalf of those less well off in the heavenly state. At all events, we may conclude that the Lord will there have a field for the exercise of all the talents and capacities of his servants which he has developed in them here.

18, 19. The second servant called has, according to his ability, done well also with the treasure committed to him, and receives a reward proportional to that of the other, as was the efficiency. The teaching naturally suggests a gradation in the rewards of the blessed, absolutely considered, while that of each one is complete for him. Comp. Matt. 20: 23; Mark 10: 40.

20. The third, instead of being so called, is spoken of simply as **another**—Greek, *the other;* that is of the three. **Lord, behold, here is thy pound, which I have kept** (rather, *I kept*) **laid up in a napkin.** He has effected nothing by trading with, or otherwise investing it; and all his time, which was due to his master, has been simply idle.

21. For I feared thee, etc. His apology mingles equally insult and hypocrisy.—**Thou art an austere man.** Harsh and unjust in thy dealings with inferiors. Every trait of the imaginary nobleman is incompatible with the supposition that this could have been spoken sincerely.—**Takest up that thou layedst not down,** sounds like a proverbial euphemism for "dost commit robbery." The point of this, as an apology, would be, that it was obviously unsafe, with one so inhumane, to venture his money in commercial enterprises, which might miscarry; and so he had simply kept the deposit safely idle.

22. Out of thine own mouth will I judge thee=from thy excuse I will convict thee of unfaithfulness to me—**a wicked servant. Thou knewest that I was**—Greek, *am*—**an austere man,** etc. This sentence is best understood as ironically interrogative: **Thou**

23 Wherefore then gavest not thou my money into the bank, that at my coming I might have required mine own with usury?
24 And he said unto them that stood by, Take from him the pound, and give *it* to him that hath ten pounds.
25 (And they said unto him, Lord, he hath ten pounds.)
26 For I say unto you, [a] That unto every one which hath shall be given; and from him that hath not, even that he hath shall be taken away from him.
27 But those mine enemies, which would not that I should reign over them, bring hither, and slay *them* before me.
28 And when he had thus spoken, [b] he went before, ascending up to Jerusalem.

23 and reaping that I did not sow; then wherefore gavest thou not my money into the bank, and †1 at my coming should have required it with interest?
24 And he said unto them that stood by, Take away from him the pound, and give it unto him that hath the ten pounds.
25 And they said unto him, Lord, he hath ten pounds. I say unto you, that unto every one that hath shall be given; but from him that hath not, even that which he hath shall be taken away from him. Howbeit these mine enemies, who would not that I should reign over them, bring hither, and slay them before me.
28 And when he had thus spoken, he went on before, going up to Jerusalem.

a Matt. 13: 12; 25: 39; Mark 4: 25; ch. 8: 18....b Mark 10: 32.——1 Or, *I should have gone and required.*

knewest, didst thou? and so didst not dare to trade with my money?
23. Wherefore, then—for that very reason—**gavest not thou my money into the bank, that at my coming I might**—rather, *and I, at my coming, would have required it with interest.* It is assumed that there it would have been safe, and drawing interest. **Bank** is, in the Greek, simply *table,* viz., of the brokers, or money-changers (Matt. 21: 12; John 2: 15). These became also lenders; and their business developed, in the course of ages, into that of the bank. The interest on the master's pound, so used, would, doubtless, in that day, have amounted to more than so unenterprising a servant would have made in any other way. No satisfactory explanation of the religious significance of the **bank** has been offered. The words **mine own** are warranted by nothing in the Greek.
24. And he said unto them that stood by—the officers of this king—**Take** (*away*) **from him the pound,** etc. A direction so strange led the attendants to expostulate, apparently interrupting their lord before he had finished his sentence.
25, 26. And they said unto him, Lord, he hath ten pounds—as though that was a reason why he should not have more given him. But in a case like this, it was the very reason why he should. And our Saviour proceeds, without noticing the interruption, **I say unto you, That unto every one that hath shall be given,** etc. Here the meaning might still admit of application to an earthly case; but it is evident that the antitypical truth alone is in the mind of Jesus. The parable showed that the disciple that hath the spiritual gifts and means of Christian usefulness, is he that uses them. Every such man, by the very use, increases their amount, and becomes fit to have more committed to him.

The man who had put them away in a handkerchief, did not *have* them, in any proper sense of the word, and eventually will be stripped of them, in every sense. Nothing is said here, as in regard to the misused talent in Matt., ch. 25, of punishment to the craven servant, beyond the disgraceful deprivation of his trust. This may, perhaps, signify that he has been convicted only of inefficiency in the special and selected function assigned to him, but may still continue in some lower grade of service than that of the ten. Some hint of such an intention is suggested by the conjunction "howbeit" of the next sentence.
27. But (or, *howbeit*)—there is a more serious case than his to be attended to—**those mine enemies which would not,** etc. This sentence, which was primarily aimed at those Jewish foes who so malignantly hated Jesus then, and afterward madly remonstrated, in effect, with the Great King (see 23: 18) against having him as their Messiah, is of dreadful import to all, of every nation and age, who refuse our Saviour's gentle yoke. (Matt. 27: 25; John 19: 15.)
28. Progress Toward Jerusalem.
28. And when he had thus spoken, he went before—in front of the crowd—**ascending up** (better, *going up*) **to Jerusalem.** The solemn journey, which had been interrupted in Jericho, was resumed upon finishing this discourse. Jesus took his customary place, at the head of the line. In what sense they were *going* **up to Jerusalem,** was explained in the note on the reverse movement of the man going down to Jericho. See on ch. 10: 30. Jericho, about fourteen miles distant, was not far from 3,600 feet lower than the summit of Mount Olivet, which they must cross.
29-46. Arrival at Jerusalem.
At least one day must be understood to

CH. XIX.] LUKE. 283

29 ^a And it came to pass, when he was come nigh to Bethphage and Bethany, at the mount called *the mount* of Olives, he sent two of his disciples,

29 And it came to pass, when he drew nigh unto Bethphage and Bethany, at the mount that is called

a Matt. 21: 1; Mark 11: 1.

have passed between the movement just treated of, and the continuation of it, which is now before us. Of that day no notice is taken in either of the Synoptical Gospels. For we have now come where we can, from the Four Gospels, determine, with great probability, the dates of events, relatively to the day of the crucifixion. Our Saviour died on Friday of the week; and, as generally under-

Of our Lord's experience, in the bosom of a well-beloved family, during that last Sabbath of his life, we can form imaginations only. Luke writes as if entirely unaware of that stop at Bethany, as do Matthew and Mark also, though they show afterward that they were cognizant of the supper at Bethany. (Matt. 26: 6; Mark 14: 3.)

29. And it came to pass—on the morn-

BETHANY.

stood, that was the 15th of Nisan, the day of the Passover. Now in John 12: 1, we read that Jesus came to Bethany, which was on the road from Jericho to Jerusalem, "six days before the passover," and was entertained in the house of Simon the leper. In ver. 12 he sets out, the next day, on this journey to Jerusalem, which we are following in Luke. As the Passover began, that year, Thursday evening at sun-down (Friday eve, in the Jewish reckoning), "six days before" carries us to the evening of Friday, 9th Nisan, Sabbath eve, where and when on his passage from Jericho, as spoken of in ver. 28 here, he must have rested over the Sabbath.

ing of the first day of the week—**when he came nigh to Bethphage and Bethany, at the mount that is called the mount of Olives.** This mountain, so named from ample olive orchards on its western slope, stretches from north to south on the east of Jerusalem, and distant, at its summit, from the wall of the city, 2,000 or 2,500 feet. It must be crossed in passing between Jerusalem and Jericho. The village of **Bethany** lay on the eastern slope of the ridge, "fifteen furlongs," or about a mile and three-quarters southeast of the city. **Bethphage** was a place closely connected with Bethany; but whether merely a district in which Bethany

30 Saying, Go ye into the village over against you; in the which at your entering ye shall find a colt tied, whereon yet never man sat: loose him, and bring him hither.
31 And if any man ask you, Why do ye loose him? thus shall ye say unto him, Because the Lord hath need of him.
32 And they that were sent went their way, and found even as he had said unto them.
33 And as they were loosing the colt, the owners thereof said unto them, Why loose ye the colt?
34 And they said, The Lord hath need of him.
35 And they brought him to Jesus: ᵃand they cast their garments upon the colt, and they set Jesus thereon.
36 ᵇAnd as he went, they spread their clothes in the way.
37 And when he was come nigh, even now at the descent of the mount of Olives, the whole multitude of the disciples began to rejoice and praise God with a loud voice for all the mighty works that they had seen;

30 Olivet, he sent two of the disciples, saying, Go your way into the village over against you; in the which as ye enter ye shall find a colt tied, whereon no man ever yet sat: loose him, and bring him. And if any
32 one ask you, Why do ye loose him? thus shall ye say, The Lord hath need of him. And they that were sent went away, and found even as he had said
33 unto them. And as they were loosing the colt, the owners thereof said unto them, Why loose ye the
34 colt? And they said, The Lord hath need of him.
35 And they brought him to Jesus: and they threw their garments upon the colt, and set Jesus thereon.
36 And as he went, they spread their garments in the
37 way. And as he was now drawing nigh, *even* at the descent of the mount of Olives, the whole multitude of the disciples began to rejoice and praise God with a loud voice for all the ¹mighty works

---

a 2 Kings 9: 13; Matt. 21: 7; Mark 11: 7; John 12: 14....*b* Matt. 21: 8.——1 Gr. *powers.*

---

was, or some village otherwise unknown, or the village spoken of in the next verse, is a matter of dispute. The latter is quite probable; in which view it is mentioned before Bethany, as being the point now brought to mind, and defined by the latter as being more generally known. This place must have lain between Bethany and Jerusalem. **He sent two of his disciples.** He had now come so near that it was necessary to make preparations that he might enter the city conformably to the description of the prophets.

30. Saying, Go ye into the village over against you. In the absence of more definite topographical knowledge, it is not clear in what sense the village was **over against** them. Dr. F Gardiner (*Greek Harmony*, p. 172, note) is authority for the statement that "the road from Bethany to Jerusalem, as it passed along the side of the Mount of Olives, encountered a deep valley, and made a long detour around the head of the valley, to avoid the descent and ascent. A short footpath, however, led directly across the valley, and it was, probably, from the point where this parted from the road, that the disciples were sent for the ass to the village on the opposite side, where the path again met the road [at the *winding-road* (Mark 10: 4), not **where two ways met**]—a site still marked by ruins. The owner could have seen the whole procession winding around the valley; and he must have already known, from the multitudes going out of Jerusalem to meet Jesus (John 12: 13), what it meant." The **colt** was an ass's foal (Matt. 21:2, 7). Such were not despised among the Jews, but held honorable (Judg. 5: 10; 10: 4; 12: 14).—**Tied,** as if awaiting the Messiah's use.—**Whereon yet never man sat.** Animals unsubdued to earthly uses seem to have been thought more worthy of the divine use. See Deut. 21 : 3 ; 1 Sam. 6: 7.

31. The Lord would here be understood to mean the Teacher, perhaps the Messiah; and rather implies that the owner of the animal was a disciple, or one interested in Jesus of Nazareth.

32-35. The exact correspondence of the facts, as they found them, with what Christ had foretold, was well adapted to confirm their faith, and that of all who became aware of it.—**And they**—the throng of people—**cast** (or, *threw*) **their garments upon the colt, and** (omit **they**) **set Jesus thereon.** It was the best substitute they could afford for the trappings with which the steeds of monarchs and other dignitaries were caparisoned, when they rode in state. He was now ready to receive their recognition of his Messiahship, and for the first time in his life, so far as we are informed, journeyed otherwise than on foot, or in the boats on the Lake of Gennesaret.

36. And as he went, they spread their clothes in the way. Another touching display of their reverence. Matthew and Mark add, that they cut off branches from the trees and tender herbage, and strewed in the way, as if to carpet the road for their Heavenly King. For similar display, see 2 Kings 9: 13; 2 Macc. 10: 7; Herod. 7: 54, and a multitude of references in Wetstein on Matt. 21: 8.

37. And when he was come (better, *as he was now drawing*) **nigh**—to Jerusalem—**at the descent of the mount of Olives,** having just crossed the summit, when the view of the

38 Saying, *Blessed be* the King that cometh in the name of the Lord: *peace in heaven, and glory in the highest.
39 And some of the Pharisees from among the multitude said unto him, Master, rebuke thy disciples.
40 And he answered and said unto them, I tell you that, if these should hold their peace, *the stones would immediately cry out.
41 And when he was come near, he beheld the city, and *wept over it,

38 which they had seen; saying, Blessed *is* the King that cometh in the name of the Lord: peace in
39 heaven, and glory in the highest. And some of the Pharisees from the multitude said unto him, ¹ Master, rebuke thy disciples. And he answered and
40 said, I tell you that, if these shall hold their peace, the stones will cry out.
41 And when he drew nigh, he saw the city and wept

---

a Ps. 118: 26; ch. 13: 35....b ch. 2: 14; Ephes. 2: 1....c Hab. 2: 11....d John 11: 35.—1 Or, *Teacher*.

---

city first broke upon them—**the whole multitude of the disciples began to rejoice.** The word **disciples** is here used in a comprehensive sense (comp. John 6: 60, 66), as including the mass of the great throng which we can see swayed by the surges of an irresistible enthusiasm. It is, in the main, the same **multitude,** or, *multitudes,* making up the caravan from Galilee, and Perea, who accompanied him through Jericho; many of whom had probably hastened on to Jerusalem, when he paused, on Sabbath eve, with his friends in Bethany. These, with numbers from other quarters, influenced by their report of his coming, were the "much people" (John 12: 12, 13) who, on this Sunday morning, "took branches of palm trees, and went out to meet him." Turning then in the direction of the train, they might constitute those whom Matthew (ch. 21: 9) speaks of as "those that went before"; while the procession from Bethany were those "that followed." When we remember what countless numbers flocked to the holy city, on occasion of the Passover, and how easily such a host is heated to a popular excitement, even without clear understanding of the cause of their zeal, imagination easily combines the scattered hints of the Four Gospels into a scene of gigantic commotion, like what is beheld in some great city in honor of a favorite ruler; on the departure of an army in an agonizing national crisis; or at the return of a victorious commander from the salvation of a people's cause. We may hear their jubilant hallelujahs, as they **began to rejoice and praise God with a loud voice,** etc. **The mighty works that they had seen,** included all those which had recently occurred on their journey; but, particularly, the raising of Lazarus—an event that had lately drawn many of them out to Bethany, to see Jesus and Lazarus; and all the long series of mighty works of mercy, which one and another could recall out of his past life. Their praise was to God, who had sent them the Messiah.

38. One form of their ascription was, **Blessed be the King that cometh in the name of the Lord.** When they style Jesus a king, they distinctly recognize in him the Messiah. (Ps. 118: 26.)—**In the name of the Lord,** as representing the person, wearing the character, and sharing the authority, of Jehovah.—**Peace in heaven.** The cessation of divine anger toward sinners, as the fruit of the Messiah's mission, and consequent salvation. — **Peace,** with the Hebrew, comprehended all welfare, and was equivalent to salvation. This is the effect of it to men.— **And glory in the highest**—that is, places— accrues to God from his mercy in the Anointed One. See the hymn of the angels. (Ch. 2: 14.)

39. And some of the Pharisees from (omit **among) the multitude**—apparently of the milder sort, who were yet uncertain about the character and aims of the Galilean Teacher—**said unto him,** Master=*Teacher* —**rebuke thy disciples.** Finding that the zeal of the people tended actually to make of Jesus the Messiah, they seem to have supposed that, if reminded of it, he would correct their mistake.

40. He rather rebukes *them.* The fact of his Messiahship should no longer be suppressed, or in any degree concealed. It must come forth; and these human voices are God's proclamation of the truth. That **the stones would immediately cry out,** is a hyperbole, similar to that used by John the Baptist. (Matt. 3: 9.)

41. And when he was come near, he beheld the city. This marks a stage of the journey in advance of that intended in ver. 37. There he "was drawing nigh," and the van of the vast procession may have caught sight of the Holy City, and thus been roused to an outburst of adoration. Now the view had fairly arrested the attention of our

42 Saying, If thou hadst known, even thou, at least in this thy day, the things *which belong* unto thy peace! but now they are hid from thine eyes.

42 over it, saying, ¹ If thou hadst known in this ² day, even thou, the things which belong unto ³ peace!

1 Or, *Oh that thou hadst known*....2 Some ancient authorities read, *thy day*....3 Some ancient authorities read, *thy peace*.

Lord himself.—**He saw the city.** By whichever of the three branches of the road from Bethany he might be following—it was probably the southern and more gentle one—he would, on surmounting the crest of the ridge, stand one or two hundred feet higher than the temple area, and still farther above most other parts of Jerusalem. It was then a very strong and splendid city, although narrowly limited in extent by its very site.

few moments, grouped in silence.... The one thought 'This is Jerusalem' absorbs all others. 'Thy servants take pleasure in her stones.' It is like revisiting a father's grave, or the home of one's youth, and no one is disposed to expatiate on the outline or details of the landscape; for over it hover the memories of redemption achieved, and the victory over the grave." (Canon Tristram, *Land of Israel*.) What memories, what historic asso-

JERUSALEM.

Among a number of striking features, the temple would attract the first glance by its grandeur and magnificence. Even in the present dilapidation of the city, this scene awakens profound emotion in every thoughtful and sensitive soul. "It is a glorious burst as the traveler rounds the shoulder of Mount Olivet, and the Haram wall [on the site of the temple] starts up before him from the deep gorge of the Kidron, with its domes and crescents sparkling in the sunlight—a royal city. On that very spot he once paused, and gazed on the same bold cliffs, supporting a more glorious pile.... We gazed for a

ciations, therefore, must it now have awakened in the breast of Jesus! But only to darken and distress his prevision of the fate of the beloved city. **He wept over it.** Broke out into loud and tearful lamentations. The verb used (κλαίειν) properly denotes "*loud* expressions of grief"; see Liddell and Scott. The dreadful contrast between what might have been and what is to be!

42. If thou hadst known, even thou, at least in this thy day, the things which belong unto thy peace! Excess of the Saviour's feelings breaks off the sentence (compare note on ch. 13: 9), "what wouldst

43 For the days shall come upon thee, that thine enemies shall ᵃcast a trench about thee, and compass thee round, and keep thee in on every side,
44 And ᵇ shall lay thee even with the ground, and thy children within thee; and ᶜthey shall not leave in thee one stone upon another; ᵈ because thou knewest not the time of thy visitation.
45 ᵉAnd he went into the temple, and began to cast out them that sold therein, and them that bought;

43 but now they are hid from thine eyes. For the days shall come upon thee when thine enemies shall cast up a bank about thee, and compass thee round, and
44 keep thee in on every side, and shall dash thee to the ground, and thy children within thee; and they shall not leave in thee one stone upon another; because thou knewest not the time of thy visitation.
45 And he entered into the temple, and began to cast

a Isa. 29: 3, 4; Jer. 6: 3, 6; ch. 21: 20....b 1 Kings 9. 7, 8; Micah 3: 12., .c Matt. 21: 2; Mark 13: 2; ch. 21: 6....d Dan. 9: 24; ch. 1: 68, 78; 1 Pet. 2: 12....e Matt. 21: 12; Mark 11: 11, 15; John 2: 14, 15.—1 Gr. palisade.

thou not have escaped?" The shorter and more simple form of the Revision *probably* represents the correct text. **Peace** is, here again, prosperity, welfare, salvation. **The things which belong** to it are repentance, faith in the Messiah, true righteousness, on the ground of which alone it could be enjoyed. To know these is not merely to recognize them as being necessary, but to approve, adopt, and cherish them. **In this thy day**, or, "in thy day," the last opportunity afforded thee. **Even thou**, or, "thou also," as well as others who believe in me; thou especially whose leaders are so alienated from God, and on whose repentance so much depends. **But now they are hid from thine eyes. Now**—as the case stands! **They are hid from thine eyes**, or, more exactly, *were hidden*, viz., by the judicial appointment of God. Thou *wouldst* not see them; hence it was his will that thou shouldst be blind to them. Comp. ch. 9: 45; 18: 34; concealment, but with a merciful design.

43-44. These verses predict so precisely what actually befell Jerusalem forty years afterward, that critics who deny all real prophecy, even on the part of Christ, of course treat them as a prophecy after the event. Not only the general evidence of an earlier date of the Gospel refutes this, but the supernatural character of Christ, in any view of the record, and the unquestionable fact that he did, in some terms, foretell the ruin of the city, give an antecedent probability that he would come thus near to the history. **The days shall come**—should rather be, *days will come*. See on ch. 5: 35; 17: 22. **Cast a trench**—rather, *a bank*—**about thee**. The Revision is to be preferred in these verses, where it differs from the Common Version. **A bank about thee**—is the enclosing rampart, by which the enemy will shut thee in, to prevent escape or succor. **Because thou knewest not**, etc. It is implied that if they had appreciatively known

that the coming to them of Jesus was the crisis of their opportunity to turn unto the Lord, they would have believed, and been saved. Then their city would have stood perpetually illustrious in the kingdom of God. Their failure, however, to apprehend the full purport of the manifestation of Jesus being the result of prejudice and self-interest, was no excuse for their murderous opposition to him. Comp. ch. 23: 23, 24.

45, 46. CHRIST EXERCISES SUPREME AUTHORITY IN THE TEMPLE.

Mark (ch. 11: 11) gives the succession of events with special distinctness, and Matthew (ch. 21: 11, 12) adds some graphic details. It would appear that that "Palm Sunday" ended with a survey of the temple, preliminary to further work there. The driving out of the traffickers, as reported here by Luke, occurred, probably, the next day. Compare Mark 11: 12, "on the morrow." The night was spent, as were all that followed, until the last, at Bethany (Mark 11: 11), or, at least, on the Mount of Olives (ch. 21: 37).

45. And he went into the temple, and began to cast out, etc. The Revision rightly leaves out here, in Luke, the four last words of this verse. That Jesus should have thus purified the temple courts twice in his life (comp. John 2: 13 ff.), is thought by some so improbable, that they take this as only another report of the same occurrence as that in John. Really, however, it is not in the least unnatural that there should be fresh occasion for our Lord's righteous displeasure. The impression made by the former chastisement would soon pass away. The sooner, because a great number, whose pecuniary interests were involved in the unseemly traffic, would combine their influence against the innovation. Officials of the temple, and some of high rank in the Sadducean priesthood, whose great fortunes were at stake, would make a mighty combination. They would, doubtless, insist on the great convenience of having money-

46 Saying unto them, *a* It is written, My house is the house of prayer; but *b* ye have made it a den of thieves.
47 And he taught daily in the temple. But *c* the chief priests and the scribes and the chief of the people sought to destroy him,
48 And could not find what they might do: for all the people *d* were very attentive to hear him.

46 out them that sold, saying unto them, It is written, And my house shall be a house of prayer: but ye have made it a den of robbers.
47 And he was teaching daily in the temple. But the chief priests and the scribes and the principal men of the people sought to destroy him: and they could not find what they might do; for the people all hung upon him, listening.

CHAPTER XX.

AND *it came to pass, that* on one of those days, as he taught the people in the temple, and preached the gospel, the chief priests and the scribes came upon *him* with the elders,

1 And it came to pass, on one of the days, as he was teaching the people in the temple, and preaching the gospel, there came upon him the chief priests

---

a Isa. 56 : 7....*b* Jer. 7 : 11....*c* Mark 11 : 18; John 7 : 19; 8 : 37....*d* Acts 16 : 14....*e* Matt. 2) : 23.

---

changers present at this central spot, to give coin current at Jerusalem to those who came from all parts of the world, in order to meet the demands of the temple, and all their need for other purchases. And what should hinder the animals required for sacrifices from being kept in the same convenient neighborhood? The scruples of some might be obviated by the consideration that it was only the Court of the Gentiles that they used for these purposes. A number of festivals had passed since Jesus taught them the previous lesson, and it would be strange if the old practices had not re-established themselves in full vigor, with all the accompanying fraud, extortion, and practical robbery of the ignorant, poor, helpless worshipers in the sacred precincts. Jesus would at once perceive the vanity of all pleas of convenience, as a justification of such abuses and crimes. Therefore, "**he began to cast**—*drive*—**them out.**" We are not told now of the use of scourges, as before (John 2 : 15). His personal presence, after the demonstration of the day before, was enough to scatter the evil doers; and we see, from the parallel passages, that he made a clean sweep of all their traffic, with its apparatus.

46. Saying unto them, It is written (Isa. 56 : 7), (*And*) **my house is**—*shall be*—**the**—*a*—**house of prayer**—upon which some of his hearers might recall from Isaiah, "for all the nations," those Gentiles whom they did their utmost to cheat and despoil. Jeremiah (7 : 11) had addressed his contemporaries as if they thought the house called by Jehovah's name "a den of robbers," in which very words Jesus tells the people who cowered before him, **but ye have made it a den of thieves**—"a robbers' cave." What could more clearly portend a destruction of the hypocritical place, as complete, and vastly more astounding than that which followed Jeremiah's words!

47, 48. SKETCH OF OUR LORD'S ACTION, AND OF THE MACHINATIONS OF HIS FOES.

47. And he taught (better, *was teaching*) **daily in the temple**—through Monday, Tuesday, and Wednesday. **But the chief priests and the scribes, and the chief** (*men*) **of the people sought**—all this time—**to destroy him.** The favor of the people toward him had risen to such a pitch as to allow no delay. They must destroy him, or a religious revolution, through his influence, would destroy them—destroy their influence and emoluments.

48. And could not find what they might do—what means they could employ to reach their end. Not that scruples of conscience could have restrained them from any measures, however violent or bloody. But prudence hindered. **For all the people were very attentive to hear him.** (Better, as in the Revision, *For the people all hung upon him, listening.*) These were the days of Christ's lordship in his temple. The power of the ordinary rulers was utterly subverted, and they were obliged to resort to underhanded and deceitful ways, lest they should bring upon themselves the fury of their own populace. This was eminently so in the first days of the week.

Ch. 20. 1-8. The chapter presents several instances of the thwarted attempts of the chief priests and scribes to destroy him; and specially graphic is this picture of the failure of the whole body of the rulers to entrap the Lord in his speech.

1. And it came to pass (omit **that**) **on one of those days.** A comparison of Matthew and Mark shows that it was on Tuesday,

2 And spake unto him, saying, Tell us, by what authority doest thou these things? or who is he that gave thee this authority?
3 And he answered and said unto them, I will also ask you one thing; and answer me:
4 The baptism of John, was it from heaven, or of men?
5 And they reasoned with themselves, saying, If we shall say, From heaven; he will say, Why then believed ye him not?

2 and the scribes with the elders; and they spake, saying unto him, Tell us: By what authority doest thou these things? or who is he that gave thee this
3 authority? And he answered and said unto them,
4 I also will ask you a ¹question; and tell me: The baptism of John, was it from heaven, or from men?
5 And they reasoned with themselves, saying, If we shall say, From heaven; he will say, Why did ye not

a Acts 4: 7; 7: 27.—1 Gr. word.

---

after the withering of the fig tree that he had cursed the preceding (Monday) morning, on the way from Bethany to Jerusalem. As he taught (better, *was teaching*) **the people in the temple, and preached** (or, was *preaching*) **the gospel,** according to the custom noted. (Ch. 19: 47.) The *teaching* would be principally an exposition of the Messianic intent of the Old Testament, the application of which to his own character and work would be the **preaching of the gospel.** (Comp. ch. 4: 16-21.) We may well suppose that large numbers were now thronging him, "hanging upon him, listening," so that any interruption would attract great attention. Just at such a moment, an interruption did occur, of the most formidable description; one which, if anything could, might have abashed Jesus himself. **The chief priests** (ch. 9: 22) **and the scribes** (ch. 5: 21) **came upon him, with the elders** (ch. 9: 22). The order of words in the Revision is preferable to that in the Common Version. It looks like a formal delegation from the Sanhedrin, or great religious council of the nation, similar to that which was sent to John the Baptist, in the beginning of the Gospel (John 1: 19 ff.). Selected members, representing all sections of the body, venerable in years and character, and arrayed in their distinctive robes of office, constituted an apparition well adapted to overwhelm the populace with reverence and awe. The statement that they **came upon him,** implies a degree of suddenness, if not surprise, in their appearance. The design was soon manifest.

2. And (*they*) **spake unto him, saying, Tell us, by what authority doest thou these things?** The imperative, **Tell us,** is consistent with the whole air of superiority and command which the visit bespoke. As overseers, in divine providence, of the religious instruction of the people, neither the people nor Jesus himself would question the propriety of their inquiring into the credentials of one who assumed the function of a messenger of God; only let them do it with an honest and earnest desire to know the truth. But their question was rather in regard to things *done*. **These things** would include, primarily, the cleansing of the temple courts, the day before, and all that he had done and allowed on the day of his arrival. The people listening would be likely to associate with these the blasting of the fig-tree, the giving sight to the blind, the raising of Lazarus—all that guaranteed him to be the prophet of Galilee, the Messiah of the nation. With this extent, the question, **by what authority doest thou these things?**—understood, as they intended it, viz., what man, what eldership, what college of rabbins, gave it to thee? (which is the sense of their alternative question)—was likely to seem absurd. The practical sum of it was in their minds, "How, when, where, didst thou receive this authority from us?" As their inquiry was proper in form, the Lord gave a respectful reply.

3. And he answered and said unto them, I will also ask you one thing (better, *a question);* **and answer** (or, *tell,* as in ver. 1) **me.** To answer a question by proposing another has always been allowable, but is often very troublesome. Christ's repetition of their **Tell** me assumes a dignity and dominion equal to theirs.

4. The baptism of John, was it from heaven, or of (literally, *from)* **men?** The **baptism of John** is put briefly for the whole mission of John. Now, John had notoriously testified to the Messiahship of Jesus, and that to the embassy sent from this very body, perhaps including some of these very men. An answer to his question, therefore, would greatly clear the way toward an answer to theirs, and perhaps render further answer unnecessary. Did John do what he did, and say what he said, as a prophet, the spokesman of God?

**5. The tables were at once turned. They,

T

6 But and if we say, Of men; all the people will stone us; *for they be persuaded that John was a prophet.
7 And they answered, that they could not tell whence it was.
8 And Jesus said unto them, Neither tell I you by what authority I do these things.
9 Then began he to speak to the people this parable; *A certain man planted a vineyard, and let it forth to husbandmen, and went into a far country for a long time.

6 believe him? But if we shall say, From men; all the people will stone us: for they are persuaded that John was a prophet. And they answered, that they
7 knew not whence it was. And Jesus said unto them,
8 Neither tell I you by what authority I do these things.
9 And he began to speak unto the people this parable: A man planted a vineyard, and let it out to husbandmen, and went into another country for a season.

a Matt. 14: 5; 21: 26; ch. 7: 29....b Matt. 21: 33; Mark 12: 1.

not he, were perplexed.—**And they reasoned with themselves**—thus betraying to the people their confusion, at once—**saying, If we shall say, From heaven,** etc. It was as plain as day that, if they admitted the prophetic character of John (of which they had convincing evidence), they condemned themselves for not welcoming as the Christ him whom that prophet had declared such. They might, therefore, have denied John this character, evidence or no evidence; but then they would forfeit the confidence, and even incur the hatred, of the people—which, in all their malice and machinations, they were now anxious to avoid.

6. But and—omit and—**if we say, Of men**—acting self-moved, or with only the warrant of other men—**all the people will stone us: for they be** (are) **persuaded that John was a prophet.** So universal was this belief, that the rulers feared a general insurrection if it was challenged. An additional proof of the extent and depth of the impression made on the nation by John's work. Perhaps none of the ancient prophets had been so completely recognized as such. Hence, stones would be the ready weapons of the enraged people against blasphemous impeachment of his authority.

7. And they answered, that they could not tell (rather, *knew not*) **whence it was.** This answer, if truthful, proved, as every one might see, such incapacity to recognize the source of prophetic authority, that they had no claim to question Christ's. If false, as would be the more natural view, it the more decidedly exempted him from their jurisdiction.

8. He could not say, like them, "neither do I know"; but assuming that their answer meant "we will not tell you," he dismissed them, silenced and crest-fallen, with, **Neither tell I you by what authority I do these things.** We may profitably notice the divine calmness of our Saviour; the promptness, propriety, and force with which he met this sudden, unexpected, and most imposing assault from hostile powers, before which an ordinary Hebrew would have quailed.

9-19. PARABLE OF THE WICKED HUSBANDMEN.

Having effectually baffled these dignitaries, Jesus uttered a parable to the people, but for the rulers, who, or a portion of whom, continued to listen. This is sufficiently apparent from verse 16, below, and is confirmed by Matt. 21: 28-33; Mark 12: 1.

9. Then (*And*) **began he to speak to the people this parable: A certain man planted a vineyard, and let it forth** (*out*) **to husbandmen, and went into a far** (rather, *another*) **country for a long time.** The intended reference of the chief features of the allegory is plain. The proprietor is God. The **vineyard** is the Jewish State, the Theocracy, with its responsibilities, privileges, promises, rewards. The planting it, was its establishment in the land of Palestine, with all that inclosure of institutions, rites, and customs which should at once promote its own prosperity, and keep it distinct from the rest of the world. The **husbandmen** to whom it was let out, were the administrators of the government under God—the judges, kings, priests, and all that successively constituted the hierarchy. The "fruits" expected by the proprietor of this vineyard, were obedience to his will, as declared in the law, which was to prepare the way for a universal reign of grace to sinful men, while it meantime fostered a character of humility, uprightness, mercy, piety, among the people who made up the plants of the vineyard. The **servants**, were the prophets, sent in succession, to require this fruit at the hands of the people, represented and moulded by their rulers. Three stages of their mission are mentioned, denoting that they were sent repeatedly; not, necessarily, just thrice. Many of them were ill-treated; some of them, even slain—particularly, John the Baptist. The

Ch. XX.] LUKE. 291

10 And at the season he sent a servant to the husbandmen, that they should give him of the fruit of the vineyard: but the husbandmen beat him, and sent him away empty.
11 And again he sent another servant: and they beat him also, and entreated *him* shamefully, and sent *him* away empty.
12 And again he sent a third: and they wounded him also, and cast *him* out.
13 Then said the lord of the vineyard, What shall I do? I will send my beloved son: it may be they will reverence *him* when they see him.
14 But when the husbandmen saw him, they reasoned among themselves, saying, This is the heir: come, let us kill him, that the inheritance may be ours.
15 So they cast him out of the vineyard, and killed *him*. What therefore shall the lord of the vineyard do unto them?
16 He shall come and destroy these husbandmen, and

10 long time. And at the season he sent unto the husbandmen a ¹servant, that they should give him of the fruit of the vineyard: but the husbandmen
11 beat him, and sent him away empty. And he sent yet another ¹servant: and him also they beat, and handled him shamefully, and sent him away empty.
12 And he sent yet a third: and him also they
13 wounded, and cast him forth. And the lord of the
14 vineyard said, What shall I do? I will send my beloved son: it may be they will reverence him. But when the husbandmen saw him, they reasoned one with another, saying, This is the heir: let us kill
15 him, that the inheritance may be ours. And they cast him forth out of the vineyard, and killed him. What therefore will the lord of the vineyard do
16 unto them? He will come and destroy these husbandmen, and will give the vineyard unto others. And when they heard it, they said, ²God forbid.

1 Gr. bondservant....2 Gr. Be it not so.

son—whom the proprietor decides to send after the last of his servants has failed, is, of course, the Lord Jesus himself; and the plot of the husbandmen against him, is what the chief priests and scribes are now engaged in working out, that they may continue to hold their control over the people, with its honors and emoluments. It is a pathetic picture of the present case of the Son of man, with reference to its historical antecedents, and its impending tragedy. The husbandmen—a more comprehensive term, instead of the more precise, "vine-dressers," "vineyardists." They are the men who would employ the vine-dressers.—For a long time, covers the period from the settlement in Canaan to the coming of Christ.

10. At the season—namely, when the effect of his favor to this people should have shown itself in their gratitude, obedience, and love to him.—Of the fruit of the vineyard, not absolutely all of it. It implies an arrangement with the husbandmen that they were to have some share of the benefit, in improved and happier lives of rulers and people.

12. In no case, at no period, do they meet God's reasonable requirement with fidelity and righteousness. In this, the Saviour simply summarized their recorded history. Throughout that, from the men who "outlived Joshua" (Judg. 2:7), we search in vain for the account of a single generation that served Jehovah with more than a rare, meagre, half-hearted devotion. Scarcely a king that, through his life-time, remained faithful to the national covenant with God. The ascending degrees of their cruelty to his servants, as here set forth, show that they became worse instead of better.

13. Their course had culminated in this harder than brazen-heartedness of these men, who now hear without relenting the pathetic emotion of the Father in heaven, when, as the last expedient, he says, I will send my beloved Son: it may be they will reverence him.

14. It was painting the present state of things to the life, when Jesus represents the rulers as turning this extremity of fatherly affection into an occasion for the supreme exercise of their rebellion and hate.—Let us kill him, that the inheritance may be (*become*) ours. The motive of their murderous wickedness is laid open before them—that, the Messiah being put out of the way, they may sit in his place, as they already sat "in Moses' seat." What was originally and properly a piece of land entrusted to their care, on certain unfulfilled conditions, has become, in their view, an inheritance handed down to them, so that, if the legitimate heir be got rid of, it will fall of right to them.

15. Their plan is put in execution.—They cast him out of the vineyard, and killed him. Christ speaks of that as already accomplished, which is to take place after three days. The casting the son out of the vineyard, means, perhaps, nothing more than that they put him off from the field which he claims, and which they usurp, before they put him to death. Some think it refers to a formal excommunication of Jesus, but without adducing any proof of such a fact. Forsaking now the form of narrative, Christ inquires as to the future consequences of this conduct. —What therefore shall the Lord of the vineyard do unto them?

16. The answer to his question must prob-

shall give the vineyard to others. And when they heard *it*, they said, God forbid.

17 And he beheld them, and said, What is this then that is written, *a* The stone which the builders rejected, the same is become the head of the corner?

18 Whosoever shall fall upon that stone shall be broken; but *b* on whomsoever it shall fall, it will grind him to powder.

19 And the chief priests and the scribes the same hour sought to lay hands on him; and they feared the people: for they perceived that he had spoken this parable against them.

17 But he looked upon them, and said, What then is this that is written,
The stone that the builders rejected,
The same was made the head of the corner?
18 Every one that falleth on that stone shall be broken to pieces; but on whomsoever it shall fall, it will scatter him as dust.
19 And the scribes and the chief priests sought to lay hands on him in that very hour; and they feared the people: for they perceived that he spake

a Ps. 118: 22; Matt. 21: 42....*b* Dan. 2: 34, 35; Matt. 21: 44.

ably be understood in our passage, and so in Mark, as the Lord's own to his own question. Matthew gives substantially the same, as extorted from one of those rulers by the vividness of the narrative.—**He shall** (rather, *will*) **come and destroy these husbandmen, and shall** (*will*) **give the vineyard to others.** The privileges of the kingdom of God will soon be withdrawn from the Jews, as a visible polity, with temporal advantages; its earthly rulers will be superseded, and its intended benefits will become the spiritual prerogative of individuals, Jews or Gentiles, who are ready to receive it.—**And when they**—that is, some of the parties threatened—**heard it, they said, God forbid** (or, rather, *Let it not be*). The familiar form may be more to our taste, but that does not warrant bringing the name of God into such vehement expressions a thousand times, in the Bible, when its authors left it out. From what follows, it would seem that what they would avert was not merely the destruction, but the cause of it, in the murder of the son of the lord of the vineyard. "Let that not be, in order that those natural consequences may not follow!"

17. The Saviour replies, in effect, "That must be, else how shall the Scripture be fulfilled?" **And he beheld them**—*looked on them*—with a glance of searching penetration —**and said, What is this then that is written** (Ps. 118: 22). **The stone**, etc. Do you not see that what my parable portends is deeply suggested in your ancient Scripture? The passage cited celebrates the triumph of some prominent personage typically connected with the typical kingdom of God. Foes would have depressed him; but he is raised to the highest honor. This Jesus applies to himself, making the rulers the builders of the Theocracy, who have rejected him only to be defeated, in seeing him exalted to headship in that structure. **The same**—that very person, he and no other—**is become**—

(or, *was made*) **the head of the corner.** This last phrase is a Hebraism for a stone so fitted and placed as, by forming part of two walls, to bind them together at a corner, and give security to the whole structure. Whether it is conceived of as coping out the main wall at the top (Jer. 51: 26), or the foundation wall, on which the edifice rested (Is. 28: 16; 1 Pet. 2: 6, 7), or, as placed at any desired elevation, admits of question.

18. Whosoever shall fall upon that stone shall be broken, etc. Now the corner stone is imagined lying on the ground, and liable to be stumbled over; then as raised aloft, ready to be precipitated on the heads below. Or the idea of construction may simply have been dropped; the thought having passed to that of a stone capable of doing harm. The teaching is, that those who took offence at Jesus in his earthly manifestation would perish; but still more miserably those who should continue to despise him after his exaltation to the right hand of God. The former will be crushed, the latter scattered as dust—literally, winnowed—with the effect that the wind will blow them away. Comp. Ps. 1: 4.

19. This verse at once closes the account of the parable, and introduces the next attempt of his enemies. **And the chief priests and the scribes the same hour sought to lay hands on him.** The order in the Greek is: *And the scribes and the chief priests sought to lay* (their) *hands on him in that very hour.* We shall see on ch. 22: 3, that they had already contracted with Judas for the betrayal of Jesus, but did not think it expedient to try to carry out their plan until after the feast. But the exasperation of the Sanhedrists had now become so intense that they were almost ready to seize him on the spot. **And they feared the people.** Comp. ver. 6. Another important fact which tempered their rage, and obliged them to try other expedients to

20 *a And they watched *him*, and sent forth spies, which should feign themselves just men, that they might take hold of his words, that so they might deliver him unto the power and authority of the governor.
21 And they asked him, saying, *b* Master, we know that thou sayest and teachest rightly, neither acceptest thou the person *of any*, but teachest the way of God truly:
22 Is it lawful for us to give tribute unto Cæsar, or no?
23 But he perceived their craftiness, and said unto them, Why tempt ye me?
24 Shew me a penny. Whose image and superscription hath it? They answered and said, Cæsar's.

20 this parable against them. And they watched him, and sent forth spies, who feigned themselves to be righteous, that they might take hold of his speech, so as to deliver him up to the ¹ rule and to the
21 authority of the governor. And they asked him, saying, ² Master, we know that thou sayest and teachest rightly, and acceptest not the person *of any*, but of a truth teachest the way of God: Is it
22 lawful for us to give tribute unto Cæsar, or not?
23 But he perceived their craftiness, and said unto them, Shew me a ³ denarius. Whose image and
24 superscription hath it? And they said, Cæsar's.

a Matt. 22: 15....*b* Matt. 22: 16; Mark 12: 14.——1 Or, *ruling power*....2 Or, *Teacher*....3 See marginal note on Matt. xviii. 28.

reach their end without danger to themselves. **For they**—*i. e.*, the scribes and chief priests—**perceived that he had spoken** (literally *spake*) **this parable against them.** This explains the first member of this verse—they **sought to lay hands on him.**

20-26. ANOTHER PLOT OF THEIRS FOILED.

20. And they watched him—looking out for a good opportunity and contrivance—**and sent forth spies**—men suborned, or instigated to practice fraud—**which should feign** (literally, *feigned*) **themselves just** (better, *righteous*) **men.** They hypocritically professed great care to do their duty to God and man, in the hard relation which they stood in toward the existing government. **That they might take hold of his words** (*speech*), **that so they might deliver him,** etc. They had arranged a scheme of such ingenuity that, whatever he might say, seemed certain to make him guilty before the religious or the civil authority. **Unto the power**; *i. e.*, the civil rule or magistracy, however administered—**and authority of the governor**—the Roman Procurator, Pilate. Only the latter could decree the death penalty, nothing less than which would satisfy their malignity. From the other Synoptists we learn that among these lyers-in-wait were some who were disciples of the Pharisees, and some who were Herodians. The former would share the spirit and represent the ability of the Pharisees, although, apparently, not full-fledged members of the sect (Matt. 22: 16); and they could serve as witnesses on the Pharisaic side. The Herodians were such as originally supported the rule of the Herodian family; and, as this depended on the Roman power, they indirectly supported the Roman, as opposed to the patriotic rule. They were thus at the opposite pole of political principle to the Pharisees; but common antagonism to Jesus,

as a revolutionary reformer, made them one for the moment. Their coming to him in company might tend to throw him off his guard; their consentient testimony, at all events, would have the greater weight. It is worthy of note that Luke says nothing of Pharisees here; only of chief priests and scribes. So also in the preceding section, from ver. 1. He does not even mention them again through all these proceedings. And here is, chronologically, the last reference to them by Matthew or Mark, until they come, with others, to Pilate (Matt. 27: 62) about the body of Jesus. John also alludes to them as now active only once. (Ch. 18: 3.) The denunciation of the Pharisees, in Matt. 23, belongs to an earlier date.

21. And they asked him, saying, Master (*Teacher*), **we know that thou sayest and teachest rightly,** etc. Their question is suspended by a very adroit piece of flattery, which they might naturally suppose would be likely to throw Jesus off his guard. —**Neither acceptest thou the person of any.** To accept the person was the same as "to respect persons"—a Hebrew expression for "to pervert justice in favor of any one," to show partiality in pronouncing judgment. They say, in effect, "We desire to know the honest truth, however it may bear on our conduct, and are sure that thou art the teacher who can give it to us."

22. Is it lawful for us to give tribute—pay taxes—**unto Cæsar, or no?** The last two words betray the desire for an explicit and categorical answer. Yes, or no?

23, 24. But he perceived their craftiness. If he said "Yes," the Herodians would be pleased, while the whole Pharisaic zeal, and that of the patriotic populace, would be kindled against him. But if he answered "No," siding with the Pharisees against such political subjection, he would still more

25 And he said unto them, Render therefore unto Cæsar the things which be Cæsar's, and unto God the things which be God's.
26 And they could not take hold of his words before the people: and they marvelled at his answer, and held their peace.
27 *Then came to *him* certain of the Sadducees, *which deny that there is any resurrection; and they asked him,

25 And he said unto them, Then render unto Cæsar the things that are Cæsar's, and unto God the things
26 that are God's. And they were not able to take hold of the saying before the people: and they marvelled at his answer, and held their peace.
27 And there came to him certain of the Sadducees, they that say that there is no resurrection; and they

a Matt. 22: 35; Mark 12: 18. ...*b* A: 23: 6. 8.

directly come into collision with the ruling power of his nation. We should not have been surprised to find it written that he reflected for a moment. But no; instantly, with the same imperturbable serenity which we noticed in ver. 3, ff., he **said unto them, ... Show me a penny**—a *denarius*. This coin would be appropriate, as a unit in the reckoning of the taxes and tolls. **Whose image and superscription hath it? They answered and said, Cæsar's.** The coin current in their country, bearing the likeness of the Emperor for the time being, would be a proof that he was sovereign over them, and prepare the way for the admirable solution of their question which is to follow. The coin produced would probably be one of Tiberius, the reigning Emperor. (Cæsar was the dynastic designation of the Emperors, like Kaiser in Germany, Zar in Russia, and not a personal name. "On one side would be the once beautiful, but now depraved, features of Tiberius; the title *Pontifex Maximus* was probably inscribed on the obverse."—(Farrar.)

25. Render therefore (or, *Then*)—in consideration of what that implies—**unto Cæsar the things which be** (or, *that are*) **Cæsar's, and unto God the things which be** (*that are*) **God's.** The former were the tribute, in various forms of tax levied, necessary to sustain the government under which they lived; the latter, the love and service, constituting piety and true holiness, which were due to the Heavenly Ruler. Christ does not content himself with an answer to their secular question merely, but shows that there is a religious side to secular duties. Fidelity to the state is not only consistent with duty to God, but is included in it.

26. And they could not (or, *were not able to*) **take hold of his words** (lit., *the saying*) —as they had set out to do (ver. 20)—**before the people.** Again, in the presence of the people, they were plainly defeated in their attempt to entrap him.—**And they**—the spies—**marvelled at his answer**—it was the wonder, not of admiration, but of amazement—**and held their peace.** Their efforts against the Saviour were, for the time, entirely silenced. "They left him, and went their way" (Matt. 22: 22). This was the end of an attempt proceeding from the Pharisaic party.

27-39. Sadducees Would Test Him Concerning the Resurrection.

27. Then came—*And then came*—**to him certain of the Sadducees.** These were a sect of the Jews next in prominence to that of the Pharisees, which we have met so often. In Matthew's Gospel they are much more frequently mentioned than in Luke.[1]—**Which**

[1] They appear obscurely, first about the middle of the second century before Christ, as the priestly party of the Asmonæan rulers. Around them gathered a small but powerful number of the worldly rich, and influential officials of the commonwealth. They were in some sense politico-religious liberals. Against the tendency of the Pharisees to multiply traditional precepts, "fencing" the law, and to sharpen the distinctions which should naturally separate the Jews from other nations, they favored freedom from other restrictions than those which were expressly commanded in the law; and although rigid in their interpretation of some of these requirements, were inclined, generally speaking, to let down the barriers between themselves and the heathen, and, at times, to make very little of the Jewish peculiarities. What was at first a practical tendency, the result of inclination and regard for personal interest, would eventually work out principles for itself. What was at first largely political and secular in their course could not fail, in a period of such intense popular religiousness, to take on also a religious character. The rule of their development, in every respect, was antithesis to the principles and movement of the Pharisees. For a considerable period the fortunes of the nation varied with the varying preponderance of the two parties in the government of the state. More particularly, as to their principles, we see both by inevitable inference from what is explicitly told us about them, and from the utter absence of any contrary intimation:

1. That they took no account of a Messiah to come. This would be enough of itself to justify our Saviour's warning to his disciples to beware of their teaching and influence (Matt. 16: 6, 11, 12). They are by him asso-

28 Saying, Master; *Moses wrote unto us, If any man's brother die, having a wife, and he die without children, that his brother should take his wife, and raise up seed unto his brother.
29 There were therefore seven brethren: and the first took a wife, and died without children.
30 And the second took her to wife, and he died childless.
31 And the third took her; and in like manner the seven also: and they left no children, and died.
32 Last of all the woman died also.
33 Therefore in the resurrection whose wife of them is she? for seven had her to wife.
34 And Jesus answering said unto them, The children of this world marry, and are given in marriage:

28 asked him, saying, ¹Master, Moses wrote unto us, that if a man's brother die, having a wife, and he be childless, his brother should take the wife, and 29 raise up seed unto his brother. There were therefore seven brethren; and the first took a wife, 30 and died childless; and the second; and the third 31 took her; and likewise the seven also left no chil-32 dren, and died. Afterward the woman also died. 33 In the resurrection therefore whose wife of them 34 shall she be? for the seven had her to wife. And Jesus said unto them, The sons of this ²world

---

a Deut. 25: 5.——1 Or, *Teacher*....2 Or, *age*.

---

deny that there is any resurrection. Some members of this sect, emulous of a victory over the Great Teacher, by whom the rival party had been baffled, and in a matter where confirmation of their own tenet might be gained, now come forward with a puzzle concerning the doctrine of the resurrection of the dead. They evidently thought they had a *reductio ad absurdum* of that doctrine.

28. Moses wrote unto us, If any man's brother die, having a wife, and he die without children (or, better, *and he be childless*), etc. They refer to the peculiar provision of the Mosaic law (Deut. 25: 5) concerning levirate marriages. According to that, in order apparently to preserve the family estate in the land, as well as the name of each individual proprietor, when a man died childless, his brother (the eldest, probably, by preference, whether already married or not), should take the widow to wife, and the first born son should be reckoned, not as his, but the son of the former husband, and inherit his name. This had probably been an ancient usage of the Hebrews, as of some other nations, and would be less remarkable in a society where polygamy was practiced, and not forbidden in the law.

29-33. On this provision of law they present a case, real or supposed, of a woman who became the wife of seven brothers in succession, who all died childless. How would the doctrine of a resurrection apply to such a case, seeing that—for this is the nerve of their argument—in that supposed other life, she must be the wife of a former husband, and cannot be of more than one? They had very probably found this a graveling question to the orthodox party, judging from verse 39.

34. And Jesus said unto them—as calmly and as promptly as in the preceding cases—**the children (*sons*) of this world** (or, *age*) **marry**—spoken of the men—**and are given in marriage**—spoken of the women. The word *sons* is very frequently used in the Bible to denote the people—sons and daughters, men and women. So here. In a large proportion of the instances in the Common Ver-

---

ciated with the Pharisees, not as similar, but antithetical, and complementary, so that between them they represented all opposition to the gospel.

2. Josephus tells us that they rejected the fiction of the Pharisees concerning a body of unwritten laws, or precepts, handed down from Moses through the elders of the people. Herein they had the full support of Jesus in his condemnation of their "traditions," which so often made void the true law of God. They may probably at first have claimed to be bound only by the plain requirements of their ancient Scriptures; but finding their spontaneous tendency in practice to be hampered by the prophetic teachings, it is exceedingly probable, though not stated, that they shortened their rule of life to the Five Books of Moses.

3. From Luke we learn, in the passage before us, and from Acts 23: 8 (comp., also, 4: 1, 2), that they denied the doctrine of the resurrection. Josephus says the same, and furthermore, that they disbelieved the immortality of the soul. As he belonged to the Pharisaic party, we cannot be certain just what abatement is to be made from his statements on the latter point. We can easily suppose, from their almost certain undervaluation of the other Scriptures, compared with the Pentateuch, that they would maintain that there was no clearly *revealed* proof of any resurrection. That their skepticism should have gone so far as to reject (Acts 23. 8) the existence of "angel" and "spirit", namely, a supermundane, finite spirit, can with difficulty be reconciled with faith, even in the Pentateuch. Indeed, we greatly lack the means of making out completely any article of their doctrinal system.

4. One other thing of some importance we are told by Josephus: that they held to the absolute freedom of a man to will good or evil, unhelped and unhindered by any Divine Providence, or power of fate; the latter meaning, probably, any divine decree. Hence, a man's fortunes were in his own hand. Rewards and punish-

35 But they which shall be accounted worthy to obtain that world, and the resurrection from the dead, neither marry, nor are given in marriage:
36 Neither can they die any more: for *a* they are equal unto the angels; and are the children of God, *b* being the children of the resurrection.
37 Now that the dead are raised, *c* even Moses shewed at the bush, when he calleth the Lord the God of Abraham, and the God of Isaac, and the God of Jacob.

35 marry, and are given in marriage: but they that are accounted worthy to attain to that ¹ world, and the resurrection from the dead, neither marry, nor are
36 given in marriage: for neither can they die any more: for they are equal unto the angels; and are
37 sons of God, being sons of the resurrection. But that the dead are raised, even Moses shewed, in *the place concerning* the Bush, when he calleth the Lord the God of Abraham, and the God of Isaac, and the

a 1 Cor. 15: 42, 49, 52; 1 John 3: 2....*c* Rom. 8: 23....*c* Ex. 3: 6.—¹ Or, *age*.

sion of the Old Testament where "children" occurs, the Hebrew has "sons." From the other Synoptists we learn, in addition, that Jesus referred their question to two mistakes, and very gross mistakes for expounders of Scripture to make, in that they knew not the Scriptures, nor the power of God. Both which mistakes are exposed in his argument; the second one first.

35. But they which be (rather, *that are*) **accounted worthy to obtain that world,** (or, *age*) to which, namely, the resurrection will lead, the age of completed Messianic blessedness—**and the resurrection from the dead**—without which that is not obtained —**neither marry nor are given in marriage.** This, we have reason to think, was then a great theological novelty. They, not knowing the power of God to provide for a different social state in the future life, supposed that there also the family relation must be repeated and continue.

36. Jesus shows them why that would be neither necessary nor appropriate. *For* (this is in the true text) **neither can they die any more.** They are immortal; hence there is no need of procreation to maintain the population of that world; therefore they do not marry. But why can they not die any more? **For they are equal unto the angels**—angel like, in that they are spiritual beings; not, necessarily bodiless, but incapable of dissolution. This again is confirmed by the statement: **and are the children**—*sons*—**of God, being the children**—*sons*—**of the resurrection**—that is to say, owing that life, not to any human or created parentage, but to the power working in their resurrection, which power is God's, they are the *sons* of God, and so as immortal as he. How truly the Sadducees had not known "the power of God"! And the argument which spoiled their *catch* in regard to the resurrection of the pious dead, assumes and teaches also the existence of the angels, in refutation of another tenet of theirs. (Acts 23: 8.)

37. Now he will show that they "knew not the Scriptures," either. **Now** (rather, *But*) whatever you may think of my declaration—**that the dead are raised**—present for future—**even Moses shewed.** This does not prove that the Sadducees held that only the Pentateuch was sacred and authoritative, however this may have been; but it asserts that, without looking further into the Scriptures, even in one of its first books, Moses shewed. The Greek verb means "disclosed," "gave the means of knowing."—**At the bush**=in that part of the Scripture which treats of God's interview with Moses in the Burning Bush

ments must all come in the present life; therefore, the man who prospered proved that he had chosen right; and if he was poor, or otherwise unfortunate, he was, as he ought to be, simply reaping the fruit of his character and acts. It was, accordingly, quite natural that the Sadducees should be charged with harshness toward the poor, and unrelenting severity against those who had broken the laws. This is of interest, when we learn that Annas and Caiaphas, at the time of Christ's trial, were Sadducees, "and all that were with them" in the Sanhedrim" (Acts 5: 17). It was the Pharisees in this Council, if ever any, who inclined to leniency in judgment of the accused (Acts 5: 33 ff.; 23: 9).

There were priests among the Pharisees, also; but not generally those of the highest rank, or wealth, or power. The Sadducees desired the welfare of their country, but through worldly policy, and for temporal advantage; the Pharisees, through the favor of God toward their scrupulous piety, and in the expectation of Messianic rewards.

If we were to guess which is right among the three conjectures that have been put forth in regard to the origin of the name Sadducees, we should side with those who think it to be from the Hebrew root for "righteous."

The chief source of information concerning them is Josephus. His scattered, fragmentary, and sometimes partial notices, are discussed in Whiston's foot-notes; in Prideaux's *Connections*; better, with some estimate of the Rabbinic references, in Ewald's *History*, vol. 5; still better, as regards the Talmudic lore, in Grätz, *Geschichte der Juden*, vol. 3; Derembourg, *Histoire de la Palestine*, etc.; and Edersheim's *Life and Times of Jesus*, B. iii., ch. 2.

38 For he is not a God of the dead, but of the living: for *all live unto him.
39 Then certain of the scribes answering said, Master, thou hast well said.
40 And after that they durst not ask him any *question at all.
41 And he said unto them, *How say they that Christ is David's son?
42 And David himself saith in the book of Psalms, *The LORD said unto my Lord, Sit thou on my right hand,
43 Till I make thine enemies thy footstool.

38 God of Jacob. Now he is not the God of the dead,
39 but of the living; for all live unto him. And certain of the scribes answering said, ¹Master, thou
40 hast well said. For they durst not any more ask him any question.
41 And he said unto them, How say they that the
42 Christ is David's son? For David himself saith in the book of Psalms,
The Lord said unto my Lord, Sit thou on my right hand,
43 Till I make thine enemies the footstool of thy feet.

a Rom. 6: 10, 11.....*b* Matt. 22: 42; Mark 12: 35.....*c* Ps. 110: 1; Acts 2: 34.—1 Or, *Teacher*.

(Ex. 3: 2-6). Before the convenience of division into chapters and verses was known, the Hebrews referred vaguely to a considerable section of their Bible by naming some prominent feature of the record there, as the Bush, in this place; Elijah (Rom. 11: 2), (comp. Meyer's note; the Bow (2 Sam. 1: 18).—**When he calleth the Lord the God of Abraham,** etc. How Moses reveals to us that he had a conception of the great truth of a future life, is explained in the next verse. In that conception was involved that of the resurrection of the dead.

38. The Sadducees might have been ready to dull the edge of his proof by alleging that this language meant that God, in speaking to Moses, was the same God who had been worshiped by Abraham, Isaac, and Jacob, successively, during their lives. Our Saviour, with a divine insight, perceives that such a view stripped the declaration of all reason and value, in relation to those to whom it was addressed. Of what consequence was it to Moses and his people, to be informed that the God who now summoned them to a task of enormous hardship, hazard, and privation, had been the God of men preceding them, whom he had left to death and annihilation? No; they still lived; for **he is not a God of the dead, but of the living.** The article is wanting in the Greek: "*Of dead, of living persons.*"—**For all live unto him**—to his view, in relation to him. Sublime, consoling truth! Gone from their wonted places on the earth, lost in the darkness to those who remain behind, the departed saints, "that are accounted worthy to attain to that world," live unto God, and are more immediately present with him. This being clear, the certainty of a resurrection for them was as much a tenet of Jewish theology at that time as it is of Christian now.

39, 40. IMPRESSION MADE BY THIS DISCOURSE.

39. Then (or, *And*) **certain of the scribes answering said, Master, thou hast well said.** The scribes were Pharisaic in their views and practice, and would sincerely rejoice in the refutation of the heretical Sadducees. Still, it implied unusual frankness and liberality on the part of these few, that they should express their sentiments in Christ's favor now.

40. Well, indeed, had the Teacher spoken.—**And** (*For*) **after that they durst not ask him any question at all;** or, *durst not any man ask him any question.* It is common for the harmonizers to place before this verse the question of a scribe concerning the greatest commandment (Matt. 22: 34 ff.; Mark 12: 28 ff.). If it were certain that this occurred so late, we must suppose Luke to have spoken of those questions which he knew, excluding this; or that he regarded this as substantially identical with what he had before narrated, and not having a different intention from the former questions of this chapter. All parties had now been utterly foiled in their attempts to harm him.

41-44. DAVID'S LORD DAVID'S SON.—How?

41. And he said unto them—the scribes (ver. 39), although the question probably challenged the understanding of all professed teachers present—**How say they**—the rabbis—**that** (*the*) **Christ**—the Anointed, the Messiah of the Old Testament—**is David's son?** The question shows that the Jewish teachers interpreted the prophecies as indicating that the Messiah would be of the offspring of David. But how do they reconcile that with other statements of Scripture?

42. And (*For*) **David himself saith in the book of Psalms** (110: 1), **The LORD said unto my Lord,** etc. Here the **LORD** stands for Jehovah in the Hebrew, and **my Lord** is a different word, used when the Supreme Being

44 David therefore calleth him Lord, how is he then his son?
45 ᵃ Then in the audience of all the people he said unto his disciples,
46 ᵇ Beware of the scribes, which desire to walk in long robes, and ᶜ love greetings in the markets, and the highest seats in the synagogues, and the chief rooms at feasts;
47 ᵈ Which devour widows' houses, and for a shew make long prayers: the same shall receive greater damnation.

44 David therefore calleth him Lord, and how is he his son?
45 And in the hearing of all the people he said unto
46 his disciples, Beware of the scribes, who desire to walk in long robes, and love salutations in the market-places, and chief seats in the synagogues,
47 and chief places at feasts; who devour widows' houses, and for a pretence make long prayers: these shall receive greater condemnation.

a Matt. 23:1; Mark 12:38....*b* Matt. 23:5....*c* ch. 11:43....*d* Matt. 23:14.

was to be named without calling him Jehovah, or simply God (*Elohim*). Thus David, the author of the Psalm, in prophetic vision, hears Jehovah addressing his (David's) Lord = God, as the Messiah, and placing him in the position of divine honor and authority over all the enemies of Jehovah's rule.

44. David therefore calleth him Lord, how is he then his son? How, indeed, except as the bearer of two characters, that of his son by natural descent, that of his Lord, as sharing in the divine nature, by which he is qualified to sit at the right hand of Jehovah and wield the government over his subjects, some of whom are in rebellion against him. (Ps. 110: 5, 6; comp. Ps. 2.) Jesus does not answer the question, but leaves it for them to answer. He had claimed the honor due to the Messiah (ch. 19: 38-40), born in Bethlehem, of the seed of David, and had shown at the same time that they were about to put him to death. Could it be that they would murder him whom David had worshiped as his Lord? Whether the thought of such a thing came into their minds, we cannot say. At all events, they made no answer. Answering as well as questioning, in the way of argument, was done with between them and Christ.

45-47. WARNING AGAINST THE SCRIBES.

45. Then (rather, *And*) **in the audience** (better, *hearing*) **of all the people, he said unto his disciples.** To his disciples; but for the people also who heard. The experience of the last two days might well have given him a fresh and heightened sense of the willing blindness, the self-seeking, and fraudulent hypocrisy, of the ruling classes, and of the peril to the people from their influence. He would fain have received them to his favor, up to the last moment; but without repentance on their part this could not be, and repentance was the furthest in the world from their hearts. They would murder their Lord rather.

46. Beware of the scribes. Be not deceived by their show of piety; catch not their spirit; follow not their example.—**Which desire to walk in long robes**—official gowns, distinctive of office, and calling for special reverence.—**And love greetings** (or, *salutations*) **in the markets** (*market-places*, or public squares)—those profound *salaams*, humble and protracted prostrations, which simulated, even where they did not express, respect; such as may be seen in any Mohammedan city at the present day, especially toward their holy men.—**Chief rooms**—*chief places.* (See on 14: 7, 8.)

47. Which devour widows' houses. They abused the confidence placed in them by reason of their reputed piety, and which secured to them the trusteeship of the estates of widows. These they so far perverted to their own emolument, through commissions and charges, sometimes, probably, by more palpable spoliations, that the widows saw themselves impoverished while their guardians grew fat. It is a pity and shame that similar hypocrisy and fraud has continued ever since, often sheltering itself under the Christian name.—**And for a shew** (*pretence*) **make long prayers.** By spending much time, at the hours of prayer, in forms of devotion, in the temple or the public squares, and openings of the streets (where things were exposed for sale), they disguised their lack of love toward God, and regard for the rights of men.—**The same shall receive greater damnation**—greater, that is, than open and manifest offenders, by as much as their hypocrisy has secured to them a greater facility in wrong. The Greek for *damnation* is "judgment," often, as here, involving condemnation.

Ch. XXI.] LUKE. 299

CHAPTER XXI.

AND he looked up, *and saw the rich men casting their gifts into the treasury.
2 And he saw also a certain poor widow casting in thither two ᵇ mites.
3 And he said, Of a truth I say unto you, ᶜthat this poor widow hath cast in more than they all:
4 For all these have of their abundance cast in unto the offerings of God: but she of her penury hath cast in all the living that she had.

1 And he looked up, ¹and saw the rich men that were casting their gifts into the treasury. And he saw a certain poor widow casting in thither two
3 mites. And he said, Of a truth I say unto you, This
4 poor widow cast in more than they all: for all these did of their superfluity cast in unto the gifts: but she of her want did cast in all the living that she had.

a Mark 12: 41....b See Mark 12: 42....c 2 Cor. 8: 12.—1 Or, and saw them that . . . treasury, and they were rich.

Ch. 21. 1-4. The Widow's Contribution.

1. And he looked up, and saw the rich men—that were—**casting their gifts into the treasury.** This beautiful incident belongs to the series of events and teachings which have filled chapter 20, and might well have terminated that chapter. Compare Mark 13: 1, which shows that after this, Jesus left the temple, at evening, as usual in these days, for the Mount of Olives. That **he looked up,** may mean that he had been bowed in meditation, or that the offerings were made on a place above that on which he sat. The exact position of **the treasury** is not certainly known. Lightfoot, in his *Area Templi* (opera I. 697 ff., also in Ugolino, *Thesaurus,* Vol. 34; translated in his *Works,* IX. 313. ff.), understands the treasury to have been in the Court of the Women, where stood, according to Talmudic testimony, eleven of the thirteen treasure chests, with trumpet-mouth openings, which Jewish tradition declares to have been placed for the reception of donations toward the several needs of the divine service. If it was the cloister surrounding this court, or some part of it, Christ, sitting in the court, would obviously be **over against it.** (Mark 12: 4.) Before this time, Jesus is said (John 8: 20) to have spoken " in the treasury, as he taught in the temple." The gifts of the rich men were voluntary contributions for various religious and charitable uses; and probably the several chests just spoken of were labeled, each to receive the money for a separate purpose. The men were thus performing one of the three great acts of piety, in which their "righteousness" was exercised. (Matt. 6: 1-4.) In the former temples, treasuries are spoken of as though they had been strong "chambers," for the reception and preservation of temple gifts, in which at times wealth of immense value was held.

2. And he saw also a certain poor widow casting in thither two mites—worth, say, two *centimes,* French, or two-fifths of our cent. On the value of the **mite,** see on ch. 12: 59. Schöttgen on Mark 12: 42, cites a Rabbinic rule that a single mite should not be given to the eleemosynary chest, from which he infers that the widow's gift was the very smallest that was allowed. Unless we knew that her gift was not eleemosynary, it does not appear how Meyer can deny that the citation is apposite.

3. And he said, Of a truth, I say unto you, that this poor widow cast (not *hath cast*) **in more than they all.** How truly God looketh at the heart! According to that the gift of one, a woman, very poor, outweighs the donations of " many rich men," who "cast in much." (Mark 12: 41.)

4. For all these have (rather, *did*) of **their abundance** (or, *superfluity*) **cast in unto the offerings** (simply, *gifts*) **of God; but she of her penury**=*want* (omit **hath**) **cast in all the living that she had.** God's estimate of benevolence takes in not only what is given, but what is reserved. The mere pittance of the widow, bestowed out of what was not enough for a living—*her want,* or lack—was of more value in his sight than the great sums out of the *superfluity* of men who, no matter how much they gave, had still left more than they had any need to use.—**Abundance,** or, *superfluity,* is the overplus beyond reasonable needs; **penury,** or, *want,* is deficiency compared with the requirements for life.—**All the living,** etc., means, probably, all that she had for the next day's subsistence.

Thus closes, in Luke's narrative, the public activity of the life which began in a stable, and passed on to the end, zealous, indeed, for the true welfare of all men, but specially concerned that the poor, the outcast, the wretched, should not fail of the riches and blessedness of the life everlasting. The wealth and magnificence of the temple, soon

5 ¶ ᵃAnd as some spake of the temple, how it was adorned with goodly stones and gifts, he said,
6 *As for* these things which ye behold, the days will come, in the which ᵇthere shall not be left one stone upon another, that shall not be thrown down.
7 And they asked him, saying, Master, but when shall these things be? and what sign *will there be* when these things shall come to pass?

5 And as some spake of the temple, how it was adorned with goodly stones and offerings, he said,
6 As for these things which ye behold, the days will come, in which there shall not be left here one stone upon another, that shall not be thrown down.
7 They asked him, saying, ¹Master, when therefore shall these things be? and what *shall be* the sign

a Mark 24 : 1; Mark 13 : 1....*b* ch. 19 : 44.——1 Or. *Teacher.*

---

swallowed up in fire and blood, are to us a tradition and a dream. The benevolence of a poor widow stands forever distinct and conspicuous over its ruin, as a proof that the humble heart, and Christ-like, is God's most precious temple.

5-36. PROPHECY OF THE DESTRUCTION OF THE TEMPLE, AND OF THE LAST DAYS.

It seems not inappropriate that our Great Prophet, who was about to accomplish his function of Great High Priest, should close his utterances connected with the temple by this prophecy in the strictest sense. He looks forward to the destruction of the temple, of the Old Testament polity, and, as closely joined with that, of the whole pre-Messianic constitution of things. We need to bear in mind that he here speaks as a *prophet*, in the manner of other prophets; sometimes, in figurative and metaphorical language, not describing the future with the definiteness of history, leaving much obscure in the interpretation, until the events shall be fully accomplished. These are obvious features of prophecy in the Old, and elsewhere in the New Testament, and hence, to be looked for here. If it be objected that he was divine, and other prophets human, let us not forget that he, also, was human. When we consider that he himself said, concerning this very subject—his own second advent—that he knew not the day nor the hour, we can only speculate, with reverence, as to what difference there was in prophetic activity between him and the earlier prophets, who spoke as they were borne on by the Holy Spirit. See on ch. 17: 22 ff.

5-9. OCCASION OF THE FOLLOWING PROPHECY. PRELIMINARY CAUTION.

5. And as some spake of the temple, how it was adorned with goodly stones and gifts. From Luke's account, we might think of this conversation as arising within the temple courts. Matthew 24: 1, and Mark 13: 1, show us that it was as he went forth from the temple, on Tuesday evening —Wednesday eve, in the Jewish reckoning —and that the subject was proposed by his disciples. Could it be that they remembered what he had said (ch. 19: 43, 44), and **spake** in the way of lamentation over so much beauty and grandeur? The **goodly stones** included splendid pieces of marble; colossal columns, wrought with the highest perfection of architectural skill; mighty masses of shaped stone, that entered into the substructure and main walls of the enclosure. The **gifts** were costly objects, which the piety of ages had dedicated to the God of the temple, until they had become a treasure of incalculable value. Comp. 2 Mac. 3: 6, 11; 5: 16; Josephus, *Antiquities*, xv. 11: 3.

6. As for these things which ye behold, ... there shall not be left one stone upon another, etc. How this must have amazed the disciples, with their ideas of the sanctity, as well as the vastness, of the place, we may conceive from the fact that Titus himself, when he saw the greatness of the rock masses in its walls, ascribed its conquest to the power of God. (Josephus, *Jewish Wars*, vi., 9, 1.) But the demented obstinacy of the Jews had driven him to destroy it against his choice (Josephus, *Jewish Wars*, vi., 4, 5), and thus God had, indeed, through him, wrought out the Saviour's prediction.

7. They had walked on, perhaps in meditative silence, down the steep slope from the temple eastward, and up the side of Olivet, until they were again on a level with, or above, the temple platform, and over against it. Then Jesus sat down, as we learn from Matt. 24: 3, and Mark 13: 3. **And they asked him**—as if nothing else had engaged their thought—**but when** (*when therefore*) **shall these things be?** Familiar with those expressions of the Old Testament which seemed to ascribe eternal perpetuity to the temple and the holy city (1 Kings 9: 3; 2 Chron. 6: 6; 7: 16), and to make it the centre of worship for the universal and perfected kingdom (Isa. 2: 2, ff.; 27: 13; Ps. 68: 15, 16), the disciples might easily conclude

8 And he said, "Take heed that ye be not deceived: for many shall come in my name, saying, I am *Christ*; and the time draweth near: go ye not therefore after them.
9 But when ye shall hear of wars and commotions, be not terrified: for these things must first come to pass; but the end *is* not by and by.
10 ᵇ Then said he unto them, Nation shall rise against nation, and kingdom against kingdom:

8 when these things are about to come to pass? And he said, Take heed that ye be not led astray: for many shall come in my name, saying, I am *he*; and,
9 The time is at hand: go ye not after them. And when ye shall hear of wars and tumults, be not terrified: for these things must needs come to pass first; but the end is not immediately.
10 Then said he unto them, Nation shall rise against

a Matt. 24: 4; Mark 13: 5; Ephes. 5: 6; 2 Thess. 2: 3......*b* Matt. 24: 7.

that this predicted destruction involved, in some way, the end of all earthly things. Having been already roused from the grosser fancies of the Jewish theology, concerning an earthly, sensuous reign of the Messiah, they had also caught from their Master the idea of a celestial, spiritual reign, to begin after that state of things should be broken up. Matthew shows that their question did actually make reference to the "end," consummation, or completion, of the world, or age, as well as to Christ's coming again, when the destruction should take place. Neither Mark nor Luke alludes to that here. Having before (in ch. 17) given a discourse of Jesus concerning the end of the world (see on ver. 22–37), Luke's sources seem to have presented here what principally related to the destruction of Jerusalem, but not without mingling to some extent a view of the final coming. **And what sign will there be** (more correctly, *what shall be the sign*) **when these things shall come to pass** (or, *are about to come to pass*)? Their question is two-fold: When? and preceded by what sign? Jesus may have seen that to answer the former, had it been possible for him, would have been a shock to their preconceptions, as harmful as it would be for him to say that he could not answer it in the sense in which they proposed it. As to the sign, also, it was best that they should think about it in such a way as to stimulate their perseverance in the faith. Accordingly, as in other cases of curious and unpractical questionings, he turns their attention, rather, to such truth as will be important for them in all their future career. And note, that, as indefiniteness of the time to elapse must be maintained, while it is intimated (ver. 32) that in some sense all is to be accomplished within that generation, he must speak throughout as though those whom he addressed were to live till the final consummation.

8. Take heed that ye be not deceived (or, *led astray*). Compare ch. 17: 22. A caution not to be dissuaded from faith in him during the time of waiting for "these things to come to pass." **For many shall come in my name,** *i. e.*, calling themselves the Christ, **Saying, I am Christ; and the time draweth near,** *i. e.*, the time of the enthronement of the Messiah, and the end of the world. The history of the times immediately following is too scanty to allow us to say that this was, or was not, fulfilled of pretended Christs. The analogy of generations before (in Palestine) and since, renders it extremely probable that there were such Christs; and if his words be understood in a more general sense of religious leaders, Simon Magus is a type of common occurrence. The Lord would guard them from supposing prematurely that his return, indissolubly associated in their minds with the destruction of Jerusalem, was near. **Go ye not therefore after them.** Give them no credence. Be not persuaded to leave your posts of patient continuance in my service, where your heavenly Father shall have stationed you.

9. But when ye shall hear of wars and commotions—*tumults*—political disturbances—**be not terrified.** The last verb is appropriately used in classical Greek of a scared animal: "be not scared." The histories of Josephus and Tacitus are sufficient to show that numbers of such events occurred within the next forty years, some of them within, and others bordering on, the Jewish sphere. The general coloring of Old Testament prophecies might lead the disciples to interpret these things as portents of the judgment—"the day of the Lord." **But the end is not by and by** (*i. e.*, *immediately*). Such an announcement of the plan of Providence was well adapted to prevent unnecessary apprehension and disturbance of mind.

10–19. A CURSORY VIEW OF COMMOTIONS, DANGERS, AND DUTIES, TO PRECEDE THE SIEGE OF JERUSALEM.

10, 11. Then said he unto them. This formula denotes a certain solemnity, as though the prophetic forecast took a higher flight, a

11 And great earthquakes shall be in divers places, and famines, and pestilences; and fearful sights and great signs shall there be from heaven.
12 ᵃ But before all these, they shall lay their hands on you, and persecute *you*, delivering *you* up to the synagogues, and ᵇ into prisons, ᶜ being brought before kings and rulers ᵈ for my name's sake.
13 ᵉ And it shall turn to you for a testimony.
14 ᶠ Settle *it* therefore in your hearts, not to meditate before what ye shall answer:
15 For I will give you a mouth and wisdom, ᵍ which all your adversaries shall not be able to gainsay nor resist.
16 ʰ And ye shall be betrayed both by parents, and brethren, and kinsfolks, and friends; and ⁱ *some* of you shall they cause to be put to death.

11 nation, and kingdom against kingdom: and there shall be great earthquakes, and in divers places famines and pestilences; and there shall be terrors
12 and great signs from heaven. But before all these things, they shall lay their hands on you, and shall persecute you, delivering you up to the synagogues and prisons, ¹ bringing you before kings and governors for my name's sake. It shall turn unto you
14 for a testimony. Settle it therefore in your hearts,
15 not to meditate beforehand how to answer; for I will give you a mouth and wisdom, which all your adversaries shall not be able to withstand or to
16 gainsay. But ye shall be delivered up even by parents, and brethren, and kinsfolk, and friends; and *some* of you ² shall they cause to be put to death.

a Mark 13: 9; Rev. 2: 10....*b* Acts 4: 3; 5: 18; 12: 4; 16: 24....*c* Acts 25: 23....*d* 1 Pet. 2: 13....*e* Phil. 1: 28; 2 Thess. 1: 5..../ Matt. 10: 19; Mark 13: 11; ch. 12: 11....*g* Acts 6: 10....*h* Mic. 7: 6; Mark 13: 12....*i* Acts 7: 59; 12: 2.—1 Or. *you being brought*....2 Or. *shall they put to death.*

broader sweep. We need not be particular to show that all these predictions were literally fulfilled before the year seventy, although this has often been done. As our Lord looked into the future, he saw the world full of these convulsions of society, and of nature, and that each generation, including the first, would have its share of them. **Fearful sights**—or, more generally, *terrors*—include all sights, sounds, reported wonders.—**Great signs shall there be from heaven**—meteoric prodigies, comets, boreal lights, falling stars, flaming swords, and conflicts of warriors in the sky, as reported by Josephus and Tacitus. Such things have been often apparent to the imagination, in times of national trouble. Book vi. of Josephus' *Wars of the Jews*, is sufficient to help one to realize what may have been before the mind of Christ.

12. But before all these, they—the people about you, Jews or Gentiles—**shall** (*will*) **lay their hands on you**, etc. If any one feels a lack of harmony between this statement and Matt. 24: 9, or Mark 13: 9, which seem to make the persecutions come after, or in company with these things, he may obviate the difficulty either by laying a special emphasis on *all*—"before *all* these"—which the Greek will warrant, or he may understand "before," not as showing a relation of time, but of importance—above all these things. Excellent scholars have, respectively, adopted both views. But the adverb "then" hardly gives occasion for much difficulty. The persecutions here foretold, were, as a matter of fact, among the first experiences of disciples after the time of this discourse. See the Book of Acts, from ch. 4: 3, throughout. —**Delivering you up to the synagogues**—as in the case of Stephen, and those whom Saul persecuted.—**And into prisons**—as with Peter and John (Acts 4: 3; 5: 18); the apostles (16: 23), Paul and Silas.—**Being brought**—rather, *Bringing you*—**before kings and rulers**—as in the case of Paul. (Acts 23: 24; 25: 13, 23.)

13. It shall turn to you for a testimony; *i. e.*, prove an opportunity for you to testify more widely and effectively to the truth of the gospel. (Compare Acts 5: 41; Phil. 1: 12, ff.) The practice of the apostles, Peter and Paul eminently, as familiar to us from the Acts, interprets the meaning here.

14. Settle it therefore—seeing that it is to be a testimony for me—**not to meditate before what ye shall answer** (literally, *study not beforehand to defend yourselves*). To meditate has in it something of anxious forethought; the parallel word in Mark being that which the Revision translates "be not anxious." In such an emergency they are forbidden to depend on any ability of their own.

15. For I will give you a mouth and wisdom. Utterance and thought, matter and manner, substance and form of discourse. The cause being his, Jesus assumes the whole care of its management through them. —**Which all your adversaries shall not be able to gainsay nor resist** (rather, *to withstand or to gainsay*). That is, so as effectually to arrest their testimony, or to break its evidential force. In another sense they might powerfully resist and silence the disciples, but the testimony of these would prevail, even at the sacrifice of their lives, if need be.

16-19. The darkest aspect of their future is yet to be mentioned, and the best of their consolation.

16. And ye shall be betrayed (*will be delivered up*) **both by parents, and brethren**

17 And ᵃ ye shall be hated of all men for my name's sake.
18 ᵇ But there shall not a hair of your head perish.
19 In your patience possess ye your souls.
20 ᶜ And when ye shall see Jerusalem compassed with armies, then know that the desolation thereof is nigh.
21 Then let them which are in Judæa flee to the mountains; and let them which are in the midst of it depart out; and let not them that are in the countries enter thereinto.
22 For these be the days of vengeance, that ᵈ all things which are written may be fulfilled.

17 death. And ye shall be hated of all men for my
18 name's sake. And not a hair of your head shall
19 perish. In your ¹ patience ye shall win your ² souls.
20 But when ye see Jerusalem compassed with armies, then know that her desolation is at hand.
21 Then let them that are in Judæa flee unto the mountains; and let them that are in the midst of her depart out; and let not them that are in the
22 country enter therein. For these are days of vengeance, that all things which are written may be

ᵃ Matt. 10: 22....ᵇ Matt. 10: 30....ᶜ Matt. 24: 15; Mark 13: 14....ᵈ Dan. 9: 26, 27; Zech. 11: 1.—¹ Or, steadfastness....2 Or. lives.

(*brothers*), **and kinsfolks, and friends.** This, which has often come to pass, in the experience of Christ's followers, has given them a sharper pang than all the distress which other enemies could possibly inflict. — **And some of you shall they cause to be put to death.** Many a martyrdom has been brought about, in the persecutions of the Christian ages, through the murderous zeal of near relatives, and, alas! professed disciples of Jesus.

17. And ye shall (or, *will*) **be hated of all men for my name's sake.** (Acts 28: 22; 1 Cor. 15: 30, 31; 1 Pet. 2: 12.) These passages but indicate the sentiment awakened by the first presentation of the pure principles of Jesus in all countries and times.

18. But (rather, *And*)—at the same time—**there shall not a hair of your head perish.** This is not put as an antithesis to the preceding statements, as "but" would imply; it simply continues the enumeration of particulars, adding to those fearful predictions this pleasant one. Thus, of course, it could not, after ver. 16, mean that no physical harm should befall them; but they should suffer no damage as to the best portion of their true, spiritual welfare, nor fail of the full accomplishment of all which God would work through them. The utmost rage of their adversaries should turn out "rather for the furtherance of the gospel," and for their personal salvation. (Phil. 1: 12, 19.)

19. In your patience possess ye (rather, *ye shall win*) **your souls.** The Revision correctly reads it as a promise, not a command. **Patience,** here, as commonly in the New Testament, is persevering endurance, against obstacles, in the exercise of faith. By this, those who held out faithful till his return would *win*, or *gain*, acquire, "purchase" (McClellan), make sure of, their souls. This is according to Matt. 10: 22; Rom. 2: 7; 2 Tim. 2: 12. The opposite case is that of John

15: 6. The declaration closes the preceding series thus: By faithful endurance of persecutions and trials for my sake, not only will ye not suffer the least real damage, but rather, by this very course make sure of your souls = your eternal life.

20-23. Siege and Subjugation of Jerusalem.

The discourse approaches nearer to an intimation of what the sign of these things should be. (Ver. 7.)

20. Compassed with armies—according to the prediction (ch. 19: 43). The history may be read in Jos. *Wars of the Jews*, V. 6. 7. The sense is equivalent to that of "the abomination of desolation," (Matt. 24: 15). The Greek participle being in the present tense—*becoming surrounded*—there is no ground for Meyer's saying that Luke makes the designation of time *too late* for the escape of Christians in Jerusalem.

21. Then let them which are in Judæa flee to the mountains. The warning is intended for the disciples who may be there; and early Christian writers tell us that by following this instruction when the danger came, those warned did flee to the high lands over the Jordan, and all escaped. Eusebius, *Eccl. Hist.* III. 5. Epiphanius *Cont. Hæres*, Ed. Migne, 1. col. 404 f. The direction is then made more specific, **Judæa** including, 1. the city of Jerusalem, 2. the "countries," the rural spaces, or fields, with their villages. **In the midst of it.** This means of Jerusalem, mentioned (ver. 20). Christians there must leave the place, and those in the country parts of Judæa must not think of entering into the city, as would be natural, considering its apparently impregnable security. That would now be a broken reed to all who should lean upon it.

22. For these be (*are*) **the days of vengeance**—the infliction of righteous retribu-

23 a But woe unto them that are with child, and to them that give suck, in those days! for there shall be great distress in the land, and wrath upon this people. 24 And they shall fall by the edge of the sword, and shall be led away captive into all nations: and Jerusalem shall be trodden down of the Gentiles, b until the times of the Gentiles be fulfilled. 25 ¶ c And there shall be signs in the sun, and in the moon, and in the stars; and upon the earth distress of nations, with perplexity; the sea and the waves roaring; 26 Men's hearts failing them for fear, and for looking after those things which are coming on the earth: d for the powers of heaven shall be shaken.

23 fulfilled. Woe unto them that are with child and to them that give suck in those days! for there shall be great distress upon the ¹ land, and wrath 24 unto this people. And they shall fall by the edge of the sword, and shall be led captive into all the nations: and Jerusalem shall be trodden down of the Gentiles, until the times of the Gentiles be ful- 25 filled. And there shall be signs in sun and moon and stars; and upon the earth distress of nations, in perplexity for the roaring of the sea and the bil- 26 lows; men ² fainting for fear, and for expectation of the things which are coming on ³the world: for the

aMatt. 24: 19....b Dan. 9: 27; 12: 7; Rom. 11: 25....c Matt. 24: 29; Mark 13: 24; 2 Pet. 3: 10; 12....d Matt. 24: 29.—1 Or, *earth*....2 Or, *expiring*....3 Gr. *the inhabited earth*.

tion on the guilty, forewarned, obstinate, blinded capital of the Jews. **That all things which are written may be fulfilled.** (Deut. 28: 49 ff.; 1 Kings 9: 6-9; Isa. 29: 1 ff.; Mic. 3: 12; Dan. 9: 26 f.). "For the wrath is come upon them to the uttermost." (1 Thess. 2: 16).

23. Woe unto them that are with child, and to them that give suck in those days. Their case in particular is bewailed, because they will be peculiarly unable to bear that long and hurried flight, which alone can avert a horrible fate. **For there shall be great distress in** (*upon*) **the land, and wrath upon** (*unto*) **this people.** Josephus, speaking long afterward of the fulfillment of this prophecy, says (*Pref. to Jewish Wars*), "It appears to me that the misfortunes of all men from the beginning of the world, if they be compared to these of the Jews, are not so considerable as they were." (*Jewish Wars*, V. 10, 5). "Neither did any other city suffer such miseries, nor did any age ever breed a generation more fruitful in wickedness than this was, from the foundation of the world." Such, repeated in substance a hundred times, was the testimony of one of themselves, an eye-witness both to the wickedness and the distress.

24. And they shall fall by the edge of the sword, etc. Here again Josephus (*Jewish Wars*, V. 9, 3 f.) is our authority for the statement that in that whole war there were 97,000 of the Jewish people sold as slaves into the various countries, and that 1,100,000 perished—600,000 by famine. "Accordingly, the multitude of those that therein perished, exceeded all the destruction that either God or man ever brought upon the world." **And Jerusalem shall be trodden down of the Gentiles**—a striking representation of the humiliation of the once glorious city! **Until the times—seasons—of the Gentiles be fulfilled. The times of the Gentiles**—their seasons—or opportunities, are to be understood as the antithesis of the season of Jerusalem (ch. 19: 44), the opportunity, that is, which is to be afforded the Gentiles for sharing the blessedness of the gospel. They are even to administer the kingdom of God, the true theocracy, which will be taken away from the wicked husbandmen, and given to others. (ch. 20: 16). That period, as distinguished from the existing one, would be eminently the times of the Gentiles. The plural, **the times,** is freely employed by us, as a larger synonym, for "the time," and so in Scripture. (1 Tim. 4: 1; 2 Tim. 3: 1). The plural may, of course, be used to signify different periods, of the nations successively (Godet), but not so reasonably. **Fulfilled**=ended, brought to a close. That would be naturally at the end of the world, unless some intimation were given of a prior date. There is nothing to indicate that Christ had in mind a restoration of the city, and re-occupation of it by the Jews.

25-28. PRECURSORY INTIMATIONS OF THE SECOND ADVENT.

25. And there shall be signs in the sun, and in the moon, and in the stars. The time intended is that near the close of "the times of the Gentiles." Then the world, including a worldly church (ch. 17: 26, 30), will be admonished by prodigious phenomena, in heaven above, and in the earth beneath. Unwonted and portentous aspects of the heavenly bodies above, eclipses, meteors, comets. These, which had been witnessed before the destruction of Jerusalem, are to be expected prior to the coming of the Lord.—**And upon the earth distress of nations, with** (rather, *in*) **perplexity; the sea and the waves roaring** (rather, *for*—on account of—*the roaring of the sea and of the billows*—as in the Revision). The **distress** or anxiety of the na-

CH. XXI.] LUKE. 305

27 And then shall they see the Son of man *coming in a cloud with power and great glory.
28 And when these things begin to come to pass, then look up, and lift up your heads; for *your redemption draweth nigh.
29 ° And he spake to them a parable: Behold the fig tree, and all the trees;
30 When they now shoot forth, ye see and know of your own selves that summer is now nigh at hand.
31 So likewise ye, when ye see these things come to pass, know ye that the kingdom of God is nigh at hand.
32 Verily I say unto you, This generation shall not pass away, till all be fulfilled.

27 powers of the heavens shall be shaken. And then shall they see the Son of man coming in a cloud with power and great glory.
28 But when these things begin to come to pass, look up, and lift up your heads; because your redemption draweth nigh.
29 And he spake to them a parable: Behold the fig
30 tree, and all the trees: when they now shoot forth, ye see it and know of your own selves that the
31 summer is now nigh. Even so ye also, when ye see these things coming to pass, know ye that the king-
32 dom of God is nigh. Verily I say unto you, This generation shall not pass away, till all things be

a Matt. 24: 30; Rev. 1: 7; 14: 14....*b* Rom. 8: 19, 23....*c* Matt. 24: 32; Mark 13: 28.

tions = Gentiles?—is occasioned by their perplexity, or inability to understand *the roaring of the sea*, etc. These commotions on the earth are the counterpart to the celestial wonders just spoken of.

26. A more particular statement of the nature of that distress, and its cause.—**Men's hearts failing them** (or, *Men fainting*) **for fear**—because of the persuasion raised that some dreadful visitation is portended—**and looking after** (lit., *expectation of*) **those things which are coming on the earth**—*world; i. e., the inhabited world* (οἰκουμένη). *Fainting*, or swooning, is more true to the Greek, which, however, is stronger yet, as the Revision shows in the margin; "expiring," breathing out life. Some great catastrophe is certainly at hand.—**For the powers of heaven** (*of the heavens*) **shall be shaken.** This is given as the ground of all the changes spoken of in these two verses, **the powers of** *the heavens* being those forces and laws which hold the heavenly bodies in their places, and maintain the visible order of the universe. These are so disturbed, to the Saviour's view, that it is as if all nature were falling into ruin. Luke avoids all decided recognition of the popular and poetic view of the heavens, or sky, as a firm canopy, or vault, in which the heavenly bodies are fixed, or under which they move. In the Revelation (ch. 6: 13), the stars fall out of it upon the earth. And in Matthew 14: 29, it is added to what we have here, that "the stars shall fall from heaven." In the light of the more advanced science of modern times, such views may be thought childish, as, doubtless, many of the most advanced scientific views now seem to perfect knowledge; but to the simple conception of earlier days, nothing could be more sublime than these descriptions of general collapse and destruction.

27. And then—in the midst of these agitations, which themselves occur suddenly—while the framework of nature is breaking up—**shall they see the Son of man coming in a cloud.** They are the inhabitants of the earth at the time, saints and sinners.—**In a cloud.** So the Saviour departed from the earth, and so, it is promised, that he shall return (Acts 1: 9-11). Comp. 1 Thess. 4: 16, 17. The cloud is his vehicle—"who maketh the clouds his chariot" (Ps. 104: 3).—**With power and great glory.** Expressive, partly, of the indescribable majesty and splendor of his personal appearance, partly, of the impressiveness of his attendant train. (Matt. 25: 31; 1 Thess. 4: 16.)

28. And when these things begin to come to pass. The emphasis is on **begin.** That state of things will not long continue. It is the omen of an imminent revolution, which will be to the disciples a glad and glorious deliverance. It is a time, therefore, that calls for prompt action. Hence, the Lord says: **Look up, and lift up your heads.** He views them as bowed down under the trials and disappointments of the long waiting for him (ch. 17: 22; 18: 8), and calls to them, literally, "Straighten yourselves up"; behold the happy change! The Lord is at hand!—**For your redemption draweth nigh.** Redemption is, here, deliverance from the infirmity, pains, and various trials of the mortal state, and introduction into the perfect holiness and bliss of heaven.

29-31. A parable. The word is used in its most general sense—an illustrative comparison. The sense is obvious: As surely as you know from the fresh shoots of the trees in spring that summer is at hand, so surely may you understand, when the things of which I have spoken come to pass, **that the kingdom of God is nigh,** in its completed glory and blessedness.

**32. Verily I say unto you, This generation shall not pass away, till all be ful-

U

33 ᵈHeaven and earth shall pass away; but my words shall not pass away.

33 accomplished. Heaven and earth shall pass away; but my words shall not pass away.

a Matt. 24: 35.

filled. **This generation**—the race of men now living. Their term of life was then estimated, as now, at from thirty to forty years. The term might be fairly extended, if there were need, to sixty or seventy years, during which some portion of those then living would continue. But this does not seem to be called for. Doubtless the term **generation,** in itself considered, might apply to the Jewish race, or to the perpetual succession of believers; but the propriety of such reference in this case is not apparent. True, the declaration that *all* which had just been predicted would come to pass within about forty years from that time occasions a serious difficulty, when we look back on it in the cool light of history, and can see that, after many generations, the Son of man has not come in his final glory yet. There are three obvious ways of *diluting* the difficulty:

1. The discourse, as given by Luke, or by either of the other Synoptists, is abridged, and demonstrably not given in the actual order of its delivery. This appears from the fact that each differs, in points, from both the others. And if we suppose some sentence to have been spoken which is not recorded for us, or the present sentence to have been spoken with some unrecorded modification, the knowledge of that might relieve the statement of all appearance of discrepancy with later facts.

2. Christ, as we have said before, is speaking, in all this, as a prophet. Now prophecy, as a rule, takes no precise note of elapsing time. What it foresees, it foresees as passing pictorially before the vision, in its separate acts, or even as simultaneously present, with no standard to measure, or, rather, with no hint of the existence of, definite intervals of time. On this view of prophecy, see Jahn, *Introduction to the Old Testament,* § 81; Fairbairn, *On Prophecy,* ch. v., § 2; Oehler, *Theology of the Old Testament,* §§ 210, 215, f.; Hengstenberg, *Christology of the Old Testament,* iv., App. vi.; and the same, briefly, Smith, *Dictionary of the Bible,* iii., p. 259 a. If, then, we might be allowed reverently to imagine that our Lord now beholds all down to the destruction of Jerusalem as one moving picture, and all after that down to the grand consummation as another, then all (*things*) might express the former, which would take place before that generation should have ceased from the earth. "The times of the Gentiles," the commotions of heaven and earth, and the coming of the Son of man, appear as one event, accomplished in effect when its first hour struck, following the "all things" which shall have been fulfilled.

3. The sentence under consideration may have early become misplaced in the reports of the discourse. We see frequently verses and whole paragraphs, of the same contents, differently situated in the different Gospels. It does not seem improbable that, if another, a verbatim, report had been brought from the very lips of Jesus, we should have found these words somewhat differently connected with the preceding. Such variation would be particularly liable to occur in the discourse before us. The subject was mysterious and abstruse. The two ends, that of Jerusalem and that of the world, were so blended in the prophecy, and according to the custom of prophecy, that, to the apprehension of the disciples, they became almost entirely identified. We, who live after the fulfillment touching the one event, find it difficult to distinguish in the oracle what related to each event. How impossible must it have been for the disciples to do so before either event! They would, naturally, remember the discourse as one, on one theme, and did notoriously cherish the belief that the second coming might take place within the term of their own lives. There would thus be to them no occasion for minute care in the connection of this sentence. It seems, therefore, in no special degree improbable that some change of its position had become fixed in the early reports of the discourse. That it was allowed, in God's providence, to be so handed down to us, might be (known unto God are his own reasons) to give the most effectual proof that our records of the Gospel were written before the year 70 A. D.—a proof which the speculations of these last days have shown to be of exceeding great importance.

33. Heaven and earth shall pass away; but my words shall not pass away. The

34 ¶ And *take heed to yourselves, lest at any time your hearts be overcharged with surfeiting, and drunkenness, and cares of this life, and *so* that day come upon you unawares.
35 For *b* as a snare shall it come on all them that dwell on the face of the whole earth.
36 *c* Watch ye therefore, and *d* pray always, that ye may be accounted worthy to escape all these things that shall come to pass, and *e* to stand before the Son of man.

34 But take heed to yourselves, lest haply your hearts be overcharged with surfeiting, and drunkenness, and cares of this life, and that day come on
35 you suddenly as a snare: for *so* shall it come upon all them that dwell on the face of all the earth.
36 But watch ye at every season, making supplication, that ye may prevail to escape all these things that shall come to pass, and to stand before the Son of man.

a Rom. 13: 13; 1 Thess. 5: 6; 1 Pet. 4: 7....b 1 Thess. 5: 2; 2 Pet. 3: 10; Rev. 3: 3; 16: 15....c Matt. 24: 42; 25: 13; Mark 13: 33....d ch. 18: 1... e Ps. 1: 5; Ephes. 6: 13.

strongest possible assertion of the verity and trustworthiness of his prediction. It was firmer than the solid earth, more enduring than the changeless firmament. They might remove; but his words, never.

Surfeiting, is the effect of yesterday's debauch.—**Cares of this life**—rather, "cares pertaining to life," here viewed as a worldly, self-indulgent life, a luxurious living.—**And so that day come upon you unawares.**

MOUNT OF OLIVES.

34-36. WARNING AGAINST FORGETFULNESS, AND WORLDLY INDULGENCES. NEED OF WATCHFULNESS AND PRAYER.

34. And (*But*) take heed to yourselves, lest at any time (*haply*) your hearts be overcharged, etc. It gives us a fresh sense of the painful apprehension which Christ had of the instability of his disciples, that he should, under these circumstances, intimate the possibility of such a lapse of faith and patience on their part. Comp. 18: 8; 17: 27, 28. How soon his faithful messengers found it necessary to utter like admonitions, may be seen in Rom. 13: 12-14; Heb. 10: 35-39.—

The Greek word for **unawares** is used to denote the suddenness of the day of the Lord (1 Thess. 5: 3). It is properly translated in the Revision *suddenly*, and, according to the best authorities, **as a snare** follows immediately upon it, instead of going into the next verse. It is this suddenness which makes it overtake one "unawares." As the springing of a trap on the game, will be the ruin of those found unprepared.

35. None in all the earth but those who are waiting for their Lord, at his coming, will escape an awful surprise.

36. Watch ye therefore (*But watch ye*)—

37 ᵃAnd in the day time he was teaching in the temple; and ᵇat night he went out, and abode in the mount that is called *the mount* of Olives.
38 And all the people came early in the morning to him in the temple, for to hear him.

37 And every day he was teaching in the temple; and every night he went out, and lodged in the mount that is called Olivet. And all the people came early in the morning to him in the temple, to hear him.

CHAPTER XXII.

NOW ᶜthe feast of unleavened bread drew nigh, which is called the Passover.

1 Now the feast of unleavened bread drew nigh,

a John 8:1, 2....*b* ch. 22:39....*c* Matt. 26:2; Mark 14:1.

be wide awake, having your faculties all in due exercise, and fit for serious service—**always** (*at every season*)—by day and by night, whether he come in the second watch, or in the third. —**And pray**—rather, *Making supplication.* This precept supposes that, beyond all vigilance and fidelity on their part, they needed divine care and help.—**That ye may be accounted worthy** (the more probable reading is, *may prevail*—have strength)—**to escape all these things**—these faults and iniquities (**ver. 34**); probably, also, the calamities and punishments implied in **that day** (**ver. 34**)— **and to stand before the Son of man. Stand**=take your stand, as in ch. 18:11; see note ch. 19:8. It implies a certain stateliness, and consciousness of dignity and right. This is more conformable to usage of the verb form than Meyer's "be placed"; that is, by the angels. So to stand before the Lord, at his coming, requires that one should have watched and prayed, and faithfully done a servant's part.

37, 38. Luke closes his narrative of Christ's labors and teachings during the last three days of his public activity, by a particular statement of how he spent the time. The days in the temple, from the Sunday on which he arrived there; his nights on the Mount of Olives, probably at the house of his friends in Bethany. The first night he spent there; the more general expression here, allows us to think that he may have changed his location, as prudence required. **Abode**=*Lodged*— passed the night. In classic Greek, the verb often signifies "to lodge in the open air"; but probably not so here. **Early in the morning**—strictly, at the dawn, as the custom was to be stirring very early. His nights were without ease, and his days diligently devoted to his Father's business.

Ch. 22. 1-6. JUDAS BARGAINS WITH THE RULERS TO BETRAY JESUS.

The *work* of our Lord on earth was done.

Wednesday (most of Thursday also) appears to have been spent in a seclusion, the experiences of which are completely hidden from us. According to the Jewish custom at that time, of beginning the day at sundown, and reckoning the hours which followed, to the next day, the discourse in chapter 21, belonged to the eve of Wednesday. But except one pathetic sentence in Matthew (26:2) we have no further information concerning him during all that day. When we remember how often, during his previous life, the Master, in great emergencies, retired for special prayer and communion with his Father, we may well suppose that he was thus engaged on this critical day. The tenderness of his address to the disciples (**ver. 14 ff.**), breathes something of the spirit of Gethsemane, and may well imply hours of previous converse with God, concerning his approaching sufferings, and the peril and disconsolateness of his brethren.

1. Now the feast of unleavened bread drew nigh, which is called the Passover. Feast of unleavened bread—so called because all leaven, through the entire week, and part of the preceding day, must be carefully banished from their houses. "The Passover" and "the feast of unleavened bread," were often entirely synonymous expressions, to name the period of seven (or eight) days, set apart in Exodus, (chapters 12, 13), as a perpetual memorial of the deliverance of the people out of captivity in Egypt. It properly began on the eve of the 15th of the first month (now called Nisan), or, as we should say, on the evening of the 14th, and extended through the 21st. But the fourteenth, as a preparation day, was often reckoned with it. From Matthew and Mark, we learn more definitely that the Passover was now two days off. The time is accordingly some point in the 13th of the month. All attempts to identify the day with the precisely corresponding one in the Roman Calen-

2 And ᵃthe chief priests and scribes sought how they might kill him; for they feared the people.
3 ¶ ᵇ Then entered Satan into Judas surnamed Iscariot, being of the number of the twelve.
4 And he went his way, and communed with the chief priests and captains, how he might betray him unto them.
5 And they were glad, and ᶜcovenanted to give him money.

2 which is called the Passover. And the chief priests and the scribes sought how they might put him to death; for they feared the people.
3 And Satan entered into Judas who was called Iscariot, being of the number of the twelve. And he went away, and communed with the chief priests and captains, how he might deliver him unto them.
5 And they were glad, and covenanted to give him

a Ps. 2:2; John 11:47; Acts 4:27....b Matt. 26:14; Mark 14:10; John 13:2, 27....c Zech. 11:12.

dar, and so with our own, are frustrated by the uncertainty as to what year it was of the building of Rome.

2. And the chief priests and scribes sought—more exactly, *were seeking*—**how they might kill him**—in what possible way they might be able to do that which, in some way, they had determined should be done. **For they feared the people.** This is a reason for their having to **seek how they** might do it without harm to themselves.

3. At the nick of time for them, comes Judas with a plan which meets their need. **Then** (*And*) **entered Satan into Judas.** *And*—associates this event with their "seeking how they might destroy him," so as to show that the treachery of Judas relieved their perplexity. That Satan entered into Judas, means that the devil, to accomplish his malignant purposes against our Lord, took advantage of the wickedness of Judas, to direct him as a serviceable tool. Many other psychological explanations of the act of the traitor have been ingeniously attempted; but to carry them through without the supposition of Satanic agency has proved a sea of difficulty in which all have floundered—none swum. John (12:1) informs us that at a feast in Bethany, on the previous Sabbath eve, (ver. 1, "six days before the Passover"), Jesus had rebuked Judas for his complaint on account of the waste of costly ointment by Mary, in testimony of her affection for the Lord. Matthew (26:14) and Mark (14:10) connect the action of Judas here with that same feast, and imply, though they do not state, that he took offence at the Master's remark. In the rebuke which Jesus there administered to the false disciple (John 12:7), they appear to find the motive to the now ripened crime. Luke omits that episode. **Being of the number of the twelve.** This adds a pathetic touch to the description of our Saviour's fate, while it shows how acceptable such co-operation would be to themselves, and fixes a blacker stain on the treachery of Judas.

4. And he went his way (literally, *away*), **and communed with the chief priests and captains**—heads of the Levitical force of temple guards—**how**—on what terms, at what time, in what manner—**he might betray** (literally, *deliver*) **him unto them.**

5. And they were glad—as well they might be, at a proposition to do the very thing they desired, even "during the feast" (comp. Matt. 26:5), and from such a source—**and covenanted to give him money.** The sum mentioned by Matthew was thirty pieces, *shekels*, doubtless, containing each 270 grains of silver. The authorities differ considerably concerning the value of the shekel in the period now before us. Some put it as low as 48 cents, (Gesenius, *Hebrew Wörterbuch*, 8th ed., s. v. *Shekel*; two-thirds of a Prussian thaler, although the data there given lead naturally to a different result); others, as high as 74 cents (Prideaux, *Connexions*, i., 117, Wheeler's ed., three English shillings). The most definite fact in the case is that Josephus (*Antiquities*, iii., 8, 2) states the value of the shekel as equal to the Attic tetradrachmon, which contained 270 grains of silver. This is ascertained partly from theoretical statements, and partly from the weight of existing specimens. Thus it would now be worth somewhat more than 57 cents of coin silver; much more in our nominal silver dollar. See, on the weight of the Attic didrachm, R. S. Poole, in Smith's *Dictionary of the Bible*, p. 3496 a; McClintock and Crook's *Theological Cyclopædia*, article *Money*, p. 644; Madden's *Jewish Coinage*. It must always be understood, however, that a given weight of the precious metals was then several times more valuable, relatively to the necessaries of life, than it is at present. Less than twenty dollars, therefore, in our money, was what they weighed to Judas as the price of his Master's life. Whether he distinctly understoood that he was selling that

6 And he promised, and sought opportunity to betray him unto them in the absence of the multitude.

7 ¶ ª Then came the day of unleavened bread, when the passover must be killed.

6 money. And he consented, and sought opportunity to deliver him unto them ¹ in the absence of the multitude.

7 And the day of unleavened bread came, on which

a Matt. 26: 17; Mark 14: 12.——1 Or, *without tumult.*

life, appears questionable, from the compunction which he manifested when it became clear (Matt. 27: 3, 4) that such was likely to prove the fact. Eighteen or nineteen dollars they offered to give.

6. **And he promised** = agreed to it. To appreciate fully the mental process of the traitor, is, as we before remarked, almost hopelessly difficult. Certain facts are obvious, and certain inferences are natural; but we have still left ample scope for the influence of Satan in the result. He was a hard, avaricious man, with no sentiment that could stand against his greed for gain. "He had the bag, and bare what was put therein," (John 12: 6.)— is best understood to mean "he took for himself from the bag." He even stole contributions that were made to the support of Jesus. At the same time, he may have shared the gross ideas of his generation concerning the temporal advantages that were to come through the Messiah to those who should join themselves to him. As treasurer of the Lord and his company, he would naturally calculate on some corresponding honor in his manifested kingdom. From recent discourses he might have noticed indications that the manifestation was yet remote, and that an interval of want, and trial, and danger, and shame, was to precede it. The course of Jesus in the matter of the three hundred pence worth of spikenard perfume would, of course, reveal to him the profound want of sympathy between the Master and himself. The pomp and enthusiasm of Palm Sunday might well revive his expectation of a speedy assumption by Jesus of royal dominion; but this was soon blasted by the failure to take advantage of the popular favor, and by the explicit predictions of Tuesday evening, on Olivet. Disappointment, vexation, overmastering covetousness, combined to prepare him to fall under the influence of Satan. The latter was said above to have entered into him, possessed him, not so as to relieve him of the guilt of his conduct, but, rather, so as to make it the heavier, in that he voluntarily opened the way to such a possession.—**And sought opportunity to betray** (*deliver*) **him unto them in the absence of the** (*a*) **multitude.** They had not contemplated the possibility (Matt. 26: 5) of putting Jesus out of the way "during the feast," simply because the assembled crowd, largely from Galilee, would endanger insurrection. But Judas' plan of seizing him in the night, when he could guide them, obviated that objection. But he still had to seek opportunity, as not knowing the place, perhaps not even the time, when Christ would observe the Passover.

7-13. PREPARATION FOR THE PASSOVER. (Thursday evening; eve of Friday.)

7. **Then came,** etc.; better, **And the day of unleavened bread came when**—*on which*—**the passover must be**—in compliance with the law—**killed** or, *sacrificed.* Before (ver. 1) it was drawing nigh; now it has come. This day was the 14th of Nisan, before noon of which all leaven must be put away from the houses; and in the afternoon the paschal lamb must be slain. On this account, it appears also to have been called "the preparation of = for, the Passover." (John 19: 14). But with what day of the week did this 14th day of Nisan coincide that year? If we knew certainly what year it was of the Roman era, chronologers could easily determine the question. As it is, we are turned to another question. On what day of the month was Christ crucified? That the day of the week was a Friday, scarcely is or can be disputed. (Ch. 23: 54; John 19: 31). Could we add that it was the 15th of Nisan, then we should know at once that the 14th was Thursday, beginning at about 6 P. M. on Wednesday. If we suppose now that the day mentioned in our verse was Thursday, the natural inference would be that the Passover would be killed in the afternoon, after about three o'clock, and the supper eaten by the disciples that evening, after Friday, the 15th, had begun, when the whole nation were doing the same. The same impression is made by the other Synoptic Evangelists (Matt. 26: 17), especially Mark 14: 12, and from every mention of the meal as a "Passover." Indeed, from the chief indications of date in these Gospels no doubt would probably ever have arisen, that the

8 And he sent Peter and John, saying, Go and prepare us the passover, that we may eat.
9 And they said unto him, Where wilt thou that we prepare?

8 the passover must be sacrificed. And he sent Peter and John, saying, Go and make ready for us the
9 passover, that we may eat. And they said unto

Last Supper of our Lord took place simultaneously with the Passover meal of the Jews generally. But when one goes with unbiased mind to the Gospel of John, he finds the leading indications of time pointing to a different hour. The "supper" spoken of (John 13: 2) is correctly regarded as identical with that of the Passover in our chapter; but it is said (ver. 1) to have taken place "before the Passover." Again in ver. 29, when Judas went out, some thought he had gone to buy the things which they needed for the feast; as if the feast was yet to come, and there was free opportunity to make any purchases. This, many think, could hardly have been supposable on the Passover evening. In John 18: 28, the rulers, on the morning of the crucifixion, were careful against defiling themselves, that "they might eat the Passover." In ch. 19: 31, the Jews, because it was "the preparation," that the bodies should not remain upon the cross on the Sabbath (for the day of that Sabbath was a high day [as it would be if also the day of the Passover supper]) besought Pilate, etc. On the basis of these diverging representations, the judgment of Christian scholars has always been divided as to whether Jesus then celebrated the Passover with his disciples, according to the common usage, and at the regular time, or instituted a new observance, "*this* Passover" = "our Passover," on the evening before, and was himself put to death at the hour when the Jewish lambs were superfluously bleeding, at the temple. Those who are controlled by the obvious sense of John's narrative, suppose that Saturday (the Sabbath) was the proper Passover day, the 15th of Nisan; that the lambs were sacrificed on Friday afternoon, and the supper eaten that evening, after the Sabbath had begun. The early Christian writers generally appear to have taken this view, as have several of the most eminent scholars recently, especially those who have treated John's Gospel by itself. The prevalent view, however, has been that to which the Synoptical narrative would most naturally lead—that Friday was the true Passover day, and Thursday evening the hour of the Passover meal. We do not undertake to decide the question, which would involve too much of the interpretation of John's Gospel. The fact that the most eminent expositors have differed in their judgment in the matter, through all periods of independent exegesis of the New Testament, and never more so than within the past twenty-five years, shows that the probabilities are pretty evenly balanced. Whichever conclusion a man may have reached, he will be more likely, in proportion as he has investigated most thoroughly, to see how another may have come to a different result from the same data. A breath may seem sufficient to have turned the scales. We shall proceed to develop what saliently presents itself as the view of our Evangelist. **The day of unleavened bread** was Thursday, beginning at sundown, or, at that season, about 6 P. M. on Wednesday. **Must be killed**, properly, **sacrificed.** Not merely killed, or slaughtered, but the use was regarded as a sacrifice, commemorative of the birth of the people into a nation at their deliverance from Egypt, the house of bondage, and typical of the "Lamb slain from the foundation of the world." Here, however, we need think only of the day, after the night was past. **Must be**—because the law so required. Many changes in the mode of celebrating the Passover distinguished the now existing practice from that first prescribed, but only as they had been found necessary, or helpful. The usages will be found described in any of the better Bible Dictionaries.

8. **And he sent**—probably from Bethany—**Peter and John, saying, Go and prepare us the passover, that we may eat.** This direction may have been issued in the forenoon of the day, or even early in the afternoon. Luke alone gives the names of the "two of his disciples" (Mark 14: 13) who were to find and suitably furnish the needed room, to select the lamb, and have it slain and roasted, and to provide the other viands required for the meal.

9, 10. The Lord's answer to their question, where they should eat the supper, may have been given designedly in such a way as to keep the knowledge of the place from Judas,

10 And he said unto them, Behold, when ye are entered into the city, there shall a man meet you, bearing a pitcher of water; follow him into the house where he entereth in.
11 And ye shall say unto the goodman of the house, The Master saith unto thee, Where is the guestchamber, where I shall eat the passover with my disciples?
12 And he shall shew you a large upper room furnished: there make ready.
13 And they went, and found as he had said unto them: and they made ready the passover.
14 *a* And when the hour was come, he sat down, and the twelve apostles with him.

10 him, Where wilt thou that we make ready? And he said unto them, Behold, when ye are entered into the city, there shall meet you a man bearing a pitcher of water; follow him into the house whereinto he goeth. And ye shall say unto the goodman
11 of the house, The [1] Master saith unto thee, Where is the guest-chamber, where I shall eat the passover
12 with my disciples? And he will shew you a large
13 upper room furnished; there make ready. And they went, and found as he had said unto them; and they made ready the passover.
14 And when the hour was come, he sat down, and

a Matt. 26: 20; Mark 14: 17.—1 Or, *Teacher*.

---

for the present. That a man should be carrying water in the street, was remarkable, since that was the task of women, and would imply that he was of a servile condition. This is implied also in the Greek word for man applied to him (ἄνθρωπος), and, more plainly, by the distinction between him and the householder, of the next verse. It is said there was a custom that the head of each family should bring water from a certain spring, with which to wet up the unleavened bread for the Passover. But this man was not head of the house; nor does it appear how, among the thousands that would be carrying water at the same time, on that supposition, the incident could have served as a sign.

11. The Master (*Teacher*) saith unto thee, Where is the guest-chamber? etc. The man must probably have been an adherent of Jesus, with whom there had been an understanding that the Teacher should have the use of his chamber, or attic. It was regarded as a duty that householders in Jerusalem, and the suburbs, within which the sacrificial Passover might be eaten, should grant any spare room for the use of visiting worshipers at the feast.

12. A large upper room furnished. It would need to be of a good size to accommodate thirteen men at table. Nothing is certain as to whose house it was. Some have ingeniously fixed on that of the mother of John Mark, author of the Second Gospel, in which the disciples were gathered at Acts 12: 12, as if it were a usual thing. In Acts 1: 13, the disciples had also met in a large "upper-chamber," and this, it is said, may have been understood as connecting the other two instances. The argument is not so strong as a spider's thread. **Furnished**—properly, *spread*—having reference, primarily, to rugs and cushions, but including, doubtless, the table, dishes, and other necessary articles. The simple earthen dishes were usually supplied by the company; and these, with the skin of the sacrificial victim, were left as remuneration to the proprietor of the house.

13. The correspondence of the facts with so unusual an announcement, was calculated to confirm their faith in the divine mission of their Master, at a time when such confirmation was needed.

14-18. THE PASSOVER MEAL.

14. And when the hour was come, he sat down—reclined at table—**and the twelve apostles with him.** The word **twelve** is omitted by the best editors. The hour for commencing the meal was not definitely prescribed. The roasting of the lamb would not begin till after sundown, and at any time after that was finished they might proceed to the table. The posture at the table was the usual one, at that time, of reclining on couches, extended nearly at full length. A figure representing to the eye a formal banquet scene, of the later classical period, may be seen in Smith's *Dict. of the Bib.*, Art. Meal, and in others. We must divest the Last Supper of all the luxury and parade of such pictures, and think only of the recumbent posture about a plain table, possibly so arranged as to form three sides of a square. This may be compared with a family scene in our time; that picture, more to the formality of our public banquets. To the list of Greek verbs signifying this reclining posture, given in Smith's *Dict. of the Bib.*, p. 1843, should have been added the verb used here (ἀναπίπτω). The apostles were all with him, certainly at the paschal meal, at least, yet the word **twelve** was probably added to the text much later. Why no other disciples, men or women, were joined with the twelve, we may conjecture. Evidently, not many could be drawn into one Passover company ("not less than ten, nor more than twenty"—Josephus); and, besides

15 And he said unto them, With desire I have desired to eat this passover with you before I suffer:
16 For I say unto you, I will not any more eat thereof, *a* until it be fulfilled in the kingdom of God.
17 And he took the cup and gave thanks, and said, Take this, and divide *it* among yourselves:

15 the apostles with him. And he said unto them, With desire I have desired to eat this passover with 16 you before I suffer: for I say unto you, I shall not eat it, until it be fulfilled in the kingdom of God.
17 And he received a cup, and when he had given thanks, he said, Take this, and divide it among

a ch. 14: 15; Acts 10: 41; Rev. 19: 9.

---

the need of a strictly private opportunity with the apostles, he could not prudently make selections out of the general body of his followers. Other reasons are obvious why he should not summon a crowd to the *preparatory* rite, which he intended to institute.

15. With desire I have desired to eat this passover with you before I suffer. Compare "blessing I will bless," "hearing ye shall hear, and seeing ye shall see," a Hebrew way of expressing certainty of assertion, or intensity of emotion. It is with the shadow of Calvary already casting its solemnity over his spirit—**before I suffer**—that our Lord opens his tender address. That would be one reason why he should earnestly desire to eat **this Passover**—it was his last. In it were represented the most sacred memories of his nation, some of his own cherished religious associations since he was twelve years of age, and the most affecting truths of the ancestral religion. That he should choose to associate its observance so closely with his last hours on the earth, was most natural. To eat it with the apostles—**with you**—would peculiarly hallow their intercourse, and afford him opportunity to intimate to them, most impressively, the cessation of the old ordinance, by its passing over into the antitypical observance which was to distinguish the new kingdom to the end of the world. Being *his* last, this was to be *the* last Passover of the system of types and shadows, and to merge in that simple rite which would commemorate the origin of the new spiritual society on earth.

16. For I say unto you, I will not any more eat thereof (or, *it*), **until it be fulfilled in the kingdom of God.** This confirms and explains the "desire" of the preceding verse, by showing that this is his last Passover.—**Any more**, which is omitted in the Revision, has respectable evidence in its favor, but was perhaps only a natural supplement to fill out the obvious sense.—**Will not** is a strong negative = "certainly shall not."—**Until it be fulfilled in the kingdom of God.** This meant "never again in our earthly relation to each other"; but that he would join them in celebrating a feast of analogous significance in that glorious relation which he should afterward sustain to them, and to which this was leading. It is not so certain that he did not here look forward to the communion of his saints with himself and with each other in "the breaking of bread," under the Dispensation of the Spirit, as Godet, on the passage, assumes. Comp. ch. 14: 30, 35; Acts 10: 41. But, surely, the full sense of it cannot exclude the heavenly banquet, at which they shall come from the east and west, from the north and south, and shall sit down with Abraham and Isaac and Jacob in the kingdom of heaven, (Ch. 13: 29; 14: 15-25; Matt. 8: 11; Rev. 19: 9.). That ceremony would be **fulfilled** in that which it signified, the blessedness of complete salvation. This blessedness is compared to the joys of a banquet.

17. And he took the cup (better, *received a cup*), **and gave thanks, and said.** Each of the Four Evangelists has his own order of narrating the incidents connected with this meal, although Matthew and Mark nearly coincide, and Luke and John each relate much which the others do not speak of. To make out of the four different, but consistent, accounts the actual order of proceeding, is the task of the harmonist. We may notice that all assume the Jewish meal to have gone on, to a more or less full completion, before the Last Supper was instituted. Thus, here, the cup was one of the drinking cups, filled with diluted wine, which were required in the process of the Passover. Farrar, on the passage, briefly indicates the custom of the Jews, in observing the Passover, as follows: "(1.) Each drinks a cup of wine—'the cup of consecration'—over which the master of the house pronounces a blessing. (2.) Hands are washed, and a table carried in, on which are placed bitter herbs, cakes of unleavened bread, the *charoseth* (a dish made of dates, raisins, and vinegar), the paschal lamb, and the flesh of the *chagigah*, or feast offering. (3.) The father dips a morsel of unleavened bread and bitter herbs, about the size of an olive, in the *charoseth*, with a benediction, and distributes a similar "sop" to

18 For *I say unto you, I will not drink of the fruit of the vine, until the kingdom of God shall come.

19 ¶ ᵇ And he took bread, and gave thanks, and brake it, and gave unto them, saying, This is my body which is given for you: ᶜ this do in remembrance of me.

18 yourselves: for I say unto you, I shall not drink from henceforth of the fruit of the vine, until the

19 kingdom of God shall come. And he took ¹ bread, and when he had given thanks, he brake it, and gave to them, saying, This is my body ² which is

_{a Matt. 26: 29; Mark 14: 25....b Matt. 26: 26; Mark 14: 22....c 1 Cor. 11: 24.—1 Or. a loaf....2 Some ancient authorities omit, which is given for you . . . which is poured out for you.}

all present. (4.) A second cup of wine is poured out, and the youngest present asks the meaning of the service, to which the father replies. (5.) The first part of the Hallel (Psa. 107-114) is sung. (6.) Grace is said, and a benediction again pronounced; after which the father distributes bitter herbs and unleavened bread dipped in the *charoseth*. (7.) The paschal lamb is eaten and a third cup of wine is handed round. (8.) After another thanksgiving, a fourth cup — the cup of joy — is drunk. (9.) The rest of the Hallel (Psa. 115-118) is sung." It will be noticed how often "blessing," "benediction," all being of the nature of thanksgiving to God, is mentioned here, showing the joyful, eucharistic nature of the feast. To which "cup," as mentioned in this series, the **cup** in our text refers, is not certain; but probably the first. It appears to have been handed to the head of the table by some attendant, from whom he *received* it. It should be observed that our minute accounts of Jewish usage, in the celebration of the Passover, are all modern, compared with the time of Christ; and, while we know that some changes have resulted from the cessation of the sacrifices, we cannot be sure how far what is now done resembles the original practice.¹—**Divide it among yourselves.** Share ye the contents of the one cup, either by drinking out of it in turn, or by pouring out a portion into each one's cup. This does not preclude the idea of Christ drinking a portion of the wine also. But this occasion is to be the last.

18. I say unto you—a solemn assertion— **I will not**—as in ver. 16—**drink of the fruit of the vine.** Some have inferred, from this way of speaking, that Jesus, here and in ver. 16, declared that he would not eat this Passover, nor drink of the wine which he offered them. *From henceforth*, as in the Revision, which is, by general consent, the true reading in this verse (whether "any more" stand in ver. 16 or not), forbids that conclusion. Besides, he had just said (ver. 15) that he had longed for that privilege, and not to "eat and drink" would be to treat the solemn ordinance with disrespect, in the absence of known justifying reasons.—**Fruit of the vine**=wine. There is supposed to be an allusion to the formula of praise and blessing just used at the consecration of the cup, which is said to have included the sentence, "Blessed be thou, O Lord, our God, who hast created the fruit of the vine."

19, 20. INSTITUTION OF THE LORD'S SUPPER.

19. And he took bread—a loaf, or flat cake (like our sea-biscuit) of the unleavened bread—**and gave thanks.** This may have come in where, according to the usual practice, the lamb had been eaten, and the requirements of the original law fulfilled. We may suppose the Saviour to have explained to his disciples the abrogation of the ceremony which they had just concluded; how the typical significance of that lamb was to be fulfilled in him; and that the breaking of this loaf, often repeated, would keep them in remembrance of him as the source of their spiritual life, and of the formal establishment of a new spiritual society, founded on faith and love to him. What was essential to be recorded is reported to us; but we cannot suppose that so important an event would take place without much explanation. **And brake it, and gave unto them.** As to the manner of doing it, we are left in the dark; whether he himself distributed a portion to all, or simply broke the loaf in two, and left each one to break off a piece for himself, or effected the object in some other way. Each Christian will be likely to think the mode to which he is used the original one; and happily, it is quite immaterial whether it be so or not. **Saying, This is my body which is given**—not—has been given, but, "is in the act of being given"—**for you.** For the metaphorical use of **is**, in the phrase "**this**

_{¹ We may now refer to the full and specially learned account of Passover customs in Edersheim's *Life and Times of Jesus*. Book v., ch. 10.}

20 Likewise also the cup after supper, saying, ᵃThis cup is the new testament in my blood, which is shed for you.

20 given for you: this do in remembrance of me. And the cup in like manner after supper, saying, This cup is the new covenant in my blood, *even* that

a 1 Cor. 10: 16.

is my body,'' compare John 10: 7; 15: 1; 1 Cor. 10: 4. Recall also how often, in the Old Testament, God is said to *be* a shepherd, fortress, high tower, rock, shield, etc., etc. That the language could ever have been supposed to assert the actual identity of the loaf with the body in which he was then active before them, is one of the greatest marvels of intellectual subtilty and perverseness. But still greater is the fancy that, even if such a thing could have been true in that case, bread, or semblance of bread in the hands of any one of millions of the professed ministers of Christ (Romish or other priests) would become every moment anew, in a thousand places, the veritable body of the Lord. And greatest wonder of all is, that belief in the truth of such delusions, should be pronounced essential to salvation by those assuming to be rational stewards of Christ's household. Probably, **body** is used by *synecdoche* for the person, as in Rom. 2: 1, because it is in relation to the body that his person, *slain* in founding the new economy of salvation, is viewed. **My body which is** (*being*) **given for you,** should be taken in connection with—as represented by the bread. Not his body absolutely, but his body so situated and regarded. Thus the metaphor may be roughly paraphrased: "In this broken loaf you may see me, giving myself to death, through the rending of my body, as your Redeemer from sin and all misery." However little the disciples may have then apprehended the full significance of his words, we may be sure that they swelled in the soul of Jesus into a fullness of meaning which it is our wisdom to ponder rather than discuss, or try in other words to explain. They were spirit and they were life. The disciples must have delighted afterward to reflect how, not in anger or complaint, but with the tenderness of yearning love, he said: **Which is *being* given for you. What a gift! This do in remembrance of me.** Here we have, as in 1 Cor. 11: 24, in the same words, the direction to the disciples to repeat the act which he was performing, after he was gone. From Paul's account (which he had "received of the Lord") (1 Cor. 11: 23), we learn also (ver. 26) that

the usage was to be kept up till the return of the Saviour. **This do,** viz.—break a loaf, and distribute to each other. How often, is left to their judgment, as they should ascertain in their practical need. **In remembrance of me.** Observe that he does not say, In perpetual view of me, as materially present. Not, henceforth, primarily in commemoration of the salvation out of Egypt, but in remembrance of redemption wrought through me. Observe, he does not say "of my death," but **of me,** who, through my earthly life and death have wrought out your salvation from sin and eternal death. [But compare 1 Cor. 11: 26, Revision. *For as often as ye eat this bread, and drink the cup, ye proclaim the Lord's death till he come;* and the language of Christ in John 6: 53, 54. These passages certainly suggest that it is the Saviour as crucified who is to be remembered at the Holy Supper.—A. H.] The Supper was thus, all its circumstances considered, appointed to be a feast commemorative of the Author and Finisher of our faith, who, through death, destroyed him that hath the power of death. (Heb. 2: 14). It would aid them to think of him as he that "liveth and *was dead*"—sad necessity! wonderful condescension!—and behold he is alive, and liveth forevermore. (Rev. 1: 18). We cannot fail to see that through the Acts and Epistles, even in the Revelation, the suffering, humiliation, death, in which, on the part of Christ, redemption began, is prevailingly swallowed up, to the thought of his disciples, in life, exaltation, and glory.

20. Likewise also the cup, etc.—(better, *And the cup in like manner*)—that is, he took, giving thanks, and gave to them—**after** (*the*) **supper.** We may see that after the preceding incident had broken in upon and superseded the progress of the Passover meal, conversation had gone on, as they were wont to prolong the customary feast; and that when the time arrived for closing the service, Jesus completed the new rite by this addition. So is it well where his disciples, in this feast, join with the use of the symbolical emblems of their Lord's body, edifying converse of their

21 ¶ ᵃ But, behold, the hand of him that betrayeth me is with me on the table. | 21 which is poured out for you. But behold, the hand of him that betrayeth me is with me on the table

ᵃ Ps. 41:9; Matt. 26:21, 23; Mark 14:18; John 13:21, 26.

Lord, and of their progress in the divine life. He took **the cup**—that, namely, in which he had them drink the Passover wine. Matthew and Mark make no mention of that; hence they say here, "*a* cup." From this, we may gather that there were several cups on the table, doubtless one for each guest, as there was a loaf for each; but that Jesus chose to have them drink also of one and the same cup, and to eat of one and the same loaf. Luke, indeed, does not expressly mention the eating and drinking—only implies it; but Matthew repeats the injunction to eat and drink, and Mark mentions the fact that they drank. The symbolical significance of this act is fully as important as that of the elements themselves. The likeness of our Redeemer's flesh and blood is not set before us in this ordinance merely for contemplation; not as an object lesson, to present to us through the eye what we have already seen and heard; but as the food of spiritual sustenance, to be appropriated by us, ever anew, with that peculiar exercise of faith and love which we have, through sympathy of brethren and joint participation with them, in the very nature of Christ. This, and nothing less, is to eat that bread and drink that cup.—**Saying, This cup is the new testament** (*covenant*) **in my blood.** Here there would be the same room, as above, with the "bread and body," to assert that the cup *was*, actually and materially, the new covenant. The word **is**, though in the Greek not expressed, is there in effect. There is really a double figure: the cup for its contents, the red wine; and the wine for the blood by which the covenant was ratified and sealed. The word frequently translated testament in the Common Version, meaning, widely, an arrangement or disposition of affairs, specifically by will or testament, is generally used in Scripture in the sense of bargain, league, covenant; and especially of that arrangement entered into between God and the Hebrew nation, at Sinai, according to the conditions of which he was to be their God, and they his people. That covenant was consummated and ratified by the sacrificial use of blood (Ex. 24:8; Lev. 17:11; Heb. 9:19, 20). That having, after long trial, failed to produce its intended results, in a people worthy of God, Jeremiah (31:31) declared that a new covenant should be established in its place. This new covenant, we learn from the Epistle to the Hebrews, was established through the mediation of Christ (ch. 8:6, 8-10; 10:16 ff.). To it the Saviour refers in our verse, saying, in effect, that the cup, by its red wine, showed the establishment, through his blood, of that new relation between God and men, in the gospel, such that, by virtue of the expiation effected by that blood, faith in him would secure pardon, friendship with God, holiness of spirit, and true salvation.—**Which is** (*being*) **shed** =*poured out*—**for you.** The blood has not been shed yet; but, as is said in Matthew and Mark, also, is in the act of being poured out. The atoning work is conceived of as already begun.—**For you**—as individuals who need and are benefited by it, and as representing the whole needy race of men.

21-23. TREACHERY OF JUDAS EXPOSED.

Matthew and Mark mention this incident prior to their account of the Last Supper, but without saying when Judas went out. In John, it is less easy to make out its relation to the other events. The question is interesting simply from its bearing on another, namely: Was Judas present at the Lord's Supper? The narrative before us proceeds as if he was. John, who does not mention the institution of the Lord's Supper, places the departure of Judas at some point of the preliminary meal—"after the sop," or morsel, dipped in that sauce called *charoseth*. See on verse 17. The other Synoptics easily admit the supposition that he left the table before the institution of the Supper.

21. But, behold, the hand of him that betrayeth me—*delivers me up*—**is with me on the table.** The **but** here is, rather, "except," "only," or "nevertheless." "**Is** *being* shed for you; *nevertheless* one of *you* is planning to put me to death." The hand being on the table is simply an incident of the close relation of friendship which it implied. The thought was much in the mind of Jesus through the evening, as we may judge from John's narrative.

[Ch. XXII.] LUKE. 317

22 *a* And truly the Son of man goeth, *b* as it was determined: but woe unto that man by whom he is betrayed!
23 *c* And they began to inquire among themselves, which of them it was that should do this thing.
24 ¶ *d* And there was also a strife among them, which of them should be accounted the greatest.
25 *f* And he said unto them, The kings of the Gentiles exercise lordship over them; and they that exercise authority upon them are called benefactors.
26 *g* But ye *shall* not *be* so: *a* but he that is greatest among you, let him be as the younger; and he that is chief, as he that doth serve.
27 *h* For whether *is* greater, he that sitteth at meat, or he that serveth? *is* not he that sitteth at meat? but *i* I am among you as he that serveth.

22 For the Son of man indeed goeth, as it hath been determined: but woe unto that man through whom
23 he is betrayed. And they began to question among themselves, which of them it was that should do this thing.
24 And there arose also a contention among them,
25 which of them was accounted to be ¹ greatest. And he said unto them, The kings of the Gentiles have lordship over them; and they that have authority
26 over them are called Benefactors. But ye *shall* not *be* so: but he that is the greater among you, let him become as the younger; and he that is chief, as he that doth serve. For whether is greater, he that
27 ² sitteth at meat, or he that serveth? *is* not he that ² sitteth at meat? but I am in the midst of you as he

a Matt. 26: 24....*b* Acts 2: 23; 4: 28....*c* Matt. 26: 22....*d* John 13: 22, 25....*e* Mark 9: 34; ch. 9: 46..../ Matt. 20: 25: Mark 10: 42....Matt. 20: 26; 1 Pet. 5: 3....*g* ch. 9: 48....*h* ch. 12: 37....*i* Matt. 20: 28; John 13: 13, 14; Phil. 2: 7.—1 Gr. *greater*....2 Gr. *reclineth*.

22. **And truly the Son of man goeth, as it was** (or, *hath been*) **determined,** viz., by the eternal counsel of God. The crime of Judas would not of itself necessitate the death of his Master—that was already bound to be.—**But—again—nevertheless—woe unto that man by whom he is betrayed,** or, *delivered up*. The fact that conduct is overruled by God for the furtherance of his plans, does not clear the agent of any particle of his responsibility for the iniquity of his acts. Comp. Acts 2: 23; 4: 27, 28.

23. How earnest and sad their inquiries, may be read in John 13: 22 ff.

24–30. AMBITION OF THE APOSTLES AGAIN CORRECTED.

It is, doubtless, strange to find the apostles, at this point of such an occasion, comparing views as to the estimation in which they were respectively held *as* apostles; but to change the order of the section to an earlier hour of the evening, *on that account*, is very precarious. Here, again, our Gospel appears plainly to look back to what has immediately preceded.

24. And there was (*arose*) **also**—besides the inquiry of the preceding verse, or, more probably, besides the strange incident concerning Judas—**a strife**—emulation, rivalry—**among them, which of them should be** (rather, *is*)—now, after the experience had of them, and when, it seems, great responsibilities are to come upon them—**accounted the greatest** (lit., *greater*). On the Greek use of the comparative where we should expect the superlative adjective, see on 9: 46. **Accounted**—in whose judgment? Perhaps in that of the body; perhaps, in the Master's; or, more generally, in everybody's. If we may suppose the difference to have arisen at their coming together, it might relate to position at the table, to be determined by their Lord's estimation.

25. Such peculiarly untimely ambition must have grieved the heart of Jesus, but did not affect his temper. Calmly and patiently he set himself to quell strife, by recalling to them the true idea of discipleship to him. **The kings of the Gentiles exercise** (or, *have*) **lordship over them.** Their noblest really stand above and control the rest.—**And they that exercise authority upon them are called benefactors.** The same truth stated, with the terms inverted. They that exercise authority—have lordship; benefactors kings. Those who exercise control enjoy the honor of it. The title *benefactor* (Εὐεργέτης), also of Saviour (Σωτήρ), was assumed by several Syrian and Egyptian monarchs as their official designation. The people, in their abjectness, sometimes bestowed the title—once honorable—on rulers neither worthy nor helpful. This fact makes it less strange that the disciples should have made the mistake.

26. But ye shall not be so—as members of my kingdom, where other principles prevail.—**But he that is greatest among you, let him be** (*become*) **as the younger,** etc. Another Hebrew-like parallelism, to impress the thought by repeating it, with slight variation, in carefully balanced phrases. **The greatest** (lit., *the greater*) he that is chief; **the younger** (since old men were rather to be waited on)=he that doth serve. The law here is, that honor accrues to service; he that humbleth himself shall be exalted. Comp. 14: 11; 18: 14.

27. He enforces his lesson by reference to his own example.—**But I am among** (or, *in the midst of*) **you as he that serveth.** Re-

28 Ye are they which have continued with me in my temptations.
29 And ᵇI appoint unto you a kingdom, as my Father hath appointed unto me;
30 That ᶜye may eat and drink at my table in my kingdom, ᵈand sit on thrones judging the twelve tribes of Israel.
31 ¶ And the Lord said, Simon, Simon, behold, ᵉSatan hath desired *to have you*, that he may ᶠsift *you* as wheat:
32 But ᵍI have prayed for thee, that thy faith fail not: ʰand when thou art converted, strengthen thy brethren.

28 that serveth. But ye are they that have continued with me in my trials; and ¹I appoint unto you a kingdom, even as my Father appointed unto me, that ye may eat and drink at my table in my kingdom; and ye shall sit on thrones judging the twelve tribes of Israel. Simon, Simon, behold, Satan ²asked to have you, that he might sift you as wheat; but I made supplication for thee, that thy faith fail not: and do thou, when once thou hast turned again,

a Heb. 4:15....b Matt. 24:47; ch. 12:32; 2 Cor. 1:7; 2 Tim. 2:12....c Matt. 8:11; ch. 14:15; Rev. 19:9....d Ps. 49:14; Matt. 19:28; 1 Cor. 6:2; Rev. 3:21....e 1 Pet. 5:8....f Amos 9:9....g John 17:9, 11, 15....h Ps. 51:13; John 21:15, 16, 17.—1 Or, *I appoint unto you, even as my Father appointed unto me a kingdom, that ye may eat and drink, etc.*...2 Or, *obtained you by asking.*

versing the usage of this world, according to which a master sits at the table and others wait on him, I, who am your master, place myself in relation to you *as a servant*. (Comp. Matt. 20:28.) He refers almost certainly to the fact of his washing their feet that evening. His whole course had been full of the manifestations of the same helpful condescension. "It is enough for the disciple that he be as his master," or, teacher. Matt. 10:25, Revision.

28. (*But*) **Ye are they which have continued with me in my temptations.** The *but* is essential. It marks strongly the passage of the Saviour's thought to a more favorable view of their case. Your present low ambition surprises and grieves me; *but* I remember that, while thousands have come and gone, attracted for the moment by certain aspects of my work, and repelled by the first glimpse of its unworldly spirituality, **ye have continued with me**—remained faithful through all.—**In my temptations.** These were the persecutions, trials, and dangers, which, with still increasing force, appealed to him to turn aside from the arduous and fatal course to which he had been appointed. They were at once afflictions and temptations, trying also to his disciples; but they no more than he had swerved.

29. And I—I, on my part, in return for your fidelity—**appoint unto you a kingdom,** (*even*) **as my Father hath appointed unto me.** Your relation is not to be always one of inferiority, service merely, carrying with it privation and reproach. There is rule, dominion, kingship, for you; but, like mine, a share of mine, not of this world, not in its fruition here.

30. That ye may eat and drink at my table in my kingdom. This is mentioned as the object of appointing to them a kingdom, namely, that they may enjoy closest intimacy and supreme felicity with him. (Ch. 19:17, 19; Rom. 6:17; 2 Tim. 2:12.)—**And sit** (rather, *ye shall sit*) **on thrones judging the twelve tribes of Israel.** (Matt. 19:28; Rev. 3:21.) Not twelve thrones, as in Matthew. Judas is no longer of them, and they know not yet how his place is to be filled. The sitting on thrones and the number twelve are a part of the drapery of his idea, but the essence of it is that in the day of judgment their testimony concerning the truth of the gospel and its indispensable power to save shall condemn the mass of the unbelieving Jews, who now condemn him and them. In this verse is the only instance in which Jesus calls the "kingdom of God" and "of heaven" "my kingdom." He is thinking of that state when he shall appear as the King indeed. (Comp. Matt. 25:34, 40.)

31-34. Peter Warned and Encouraged.

31. Simon, Simon, behold, Satan hath desired (rather, *asked*) **to have you.** The abruptness of the opening suits with a deeply moved mind, as if recalling a peril which had threatened all the disciples (**you,** plural) as well as Judas. The Saviour is aware of a specially vehement temptation to them which the adversary had planned, probably in connection with his own capture and death, which he represents in terms drawn from Satan's appeal against Job. (Job 1:9-11; 2:3-6.) His eagerness is spoken of as a request to God that the disciples might be given into his power. **That he may sift you as wheat.** The force of the comparison is that he may toss and shake you up and down; *i. e.*, alarm and harass you, by threats and afflictions, until you lose your presence of mind, and your hold of the promises, and so fall from the faith, as the chaff and dust fall from the sieve and are blown away. To what danger from Satan may one be exposed unawares!

32. But I have prayed (rather, *I made sup-*

33 And he said unto him, Lord, I am ready to go with thee, both into prison, and to death.
34 *a* And he said, I tell thee, Peter, the cock shall not crow this day, before that thou shalt thrice deny that thou knowest me.
35 *b* And he said unto them, When I sent you without purse, and scrip, and shoes, lacked ye any thing? And they said, Nothing.
36 Then said he unto them, But now, he that hath a purse, let him take *it*, and likewise *his* scrip: and he that hath no sword, let him sell his garment, and buy one.

33 stablish thy brethren. And he said unto him, Lord, with thee I am ready to go both to prison and to
34 death. And he said, I tell thee, Peter, the cock shall not crow this day, until thou shalt thrice deny that thou knowest me.
35 And he said unto them, When I sent you forth without purse, and wallet, and shoes, lacked ye any
36 thing? And they said, Nothing. And he said unto them, But now, he that hath a purse, let him take it, and likewise a wallet: ¹ and he that hath none, let

a Matt. 26: 34; Mark 14: 30; John 13: 38....*b* Matt. 10: 9; ch 9: 3; 10: 4.—1 Or, *and he that hath no sword, let him sell his cloke, and buy one.*

plication) **for thee**—offered earnest, longing prayer—**that thy faith fail not**. This was for Peter specially; **for thee, thy faith**. Why for him in particular of all the disciples? Because he was a leader in influence, whose standing or falling would largely determine that of the rest.—**And when thou art converted** (*when thou once hast turned again*), **strengthen thy brethren**. *Turned;* that is, from that denial of his Lord which Peter was soon to make. This is the general sense of the verb translated "to be converted," "to turn again." On the idea of **strengthen**, see Acts 14: 22.

33. And he said unto him, Lord, I am ready to go with thee, both into prison, and to death. The order of the Revision is, *Lord, with thee*, etc., and indicates the emphasis on **with thee**. Peter felt that the Master's language implied a special peril to his fidelity; and, with characteristic promptness, protests a courage and constancy, which it must have pained the heart that knew him better than he knew himself to hear.

34. And he said, I tell thee, Peter. The honorable name (Matt. 16: 18) is used, for the sentiment is honorable; but with a pathetic intimation that as the name was at first (Matt. 16: 22) followed by "Be it far from thee, Lord," so the present audacity would turn to shameful cowardice.—**The (*a*) cock shall not crow this day**—which began at sundown that evening—**before that thou shalt thrice deny that thou knowest me.** All three Synoptists speak of a three-fold denial, Mark of the cock crowing "twice." Cock-crowing, here, as elsewhere, is a synonym for earliest morning. "Before the morning light fairly dawns thou wilt deny, not once, but three times; not that thou art a disciple of mine, one of my company, a sharer of my aims, but that thou even knowest who I am." This to him who had once said, "Thou art the Christ, the Son of the living God!"

35-38. THE DISCIPLES FOREWARNED OF COMING DANGERS.

35. And he said unto them, When I sent you without purse, and scrip (or *wallet*), **and shoes, lacked ye anything?** Comp. ch. 9: 1, ff.; Matt. 10: 9, 10. He turns their thoughts back to that comparatively peaceful time, that they might the better realize the great change which they are to meet, now that the power of his enemies is about to remove him, and to operate uncontrolled. They were able to answer, **Nothing**. The favor in which Jesus and his work were held in Galilee, secured to them a welcome reception, and hospitable, or, at least sufficient, entertainment.

36. But now, he that hath a purse, let him take it—he may often have to pay his way—**and likewise his scrip** ,or, *a wallet*) ;—a store of provision and clothing will stand him in hand, when other resources are not available—**and he that hath no sword, let him sell his garment** (*cloak*) **and buy one**. The rendering of the Revision, which puts the word **sword**, as in the Greek, at the end, may not necessitate a different meaning. "He that has none"—meaning a "sword"—"let him by all means buy a sword." But more probably, considering the marked correlation of "he that hath" (a purse and wallet) and "he that hath not," we are to supply to the latter also "a purse and wallet." Then the meaning is: if one hath these, let him out of them, with money or extra clothing, buy a sword; but if not, let him sell even the indispensable outer garment for that purpose. Verse 38 shows that this was not to be taken literally, and the whole course of the apostles, subsequently, proves that they did not, on reflection, so understand him. It was an impressive way of saying that they must be careful for their defence and preservation by natural means against opposition and dangers hitherto strange.

37 For I say unto you, that this that is written must yet be accomplished in me, "And he was reckoned among the transgressors: for the things concerning me have an end.
38 And they said, Lord, behold, here are two swords. And he said unto them, It is enough.
39 ¶ *b* And he came out, and *c* went, as he was wont, to the mount of Olives; and his disciples also followed him.
40 *d* And when he was at the place, he said unto them, Pray that ye enter not into temptation.

37 him sell his cloak, and buy a sword. For I say unto you, that this which is written must be fulfilled in me, And he was reckoned with transgressors: for
38 that which concerneth me hath ¹ fulfilment. And they said, Lord, behold, here are two swords. And he said unto them, It is enough.
39 And he came out, and went, as his custom was, unto the mount of Olives; and the disciples also followed him. And when he was at the place, he said
40 unto them, Pray that ye enter not into temptation.

---

a Isa. 53 : 12 , Mark 15 : 28....*b* Matt. 26 : 36 ; Mark 14 : 32 ; John 18 : 1....*c* ch. 21 : 37....*d* Matt. 6 : 13 ; 26 : 41 ; Matt. 14 : 38 ; ver. 46.——¹ Gr. end.

---

37. For—as ye cannot expect more favorable treatment than I, your Lord—**I say unto you, that this that is written must yet be accomplished in me: And he was reckoned among** (*with*) **the transgressors.** The quotation is substantially from Isa. 53: 12. What was there said of the faithful and suffering servant of Jehovah, Jesus declares must, according to the divine intention, be fulfilled in his experience. He should be treated as a transgressor; as such should suffer death. Similar treatment they must expect to receive. (Ch. 21 : 12, 16.) **For the things,** etc.; rather, *that which concerneth me hath an end*=has reached its end. The time for the fulfillment of the prophecy has come. All this goes to emphasize the truth that each one should, metaphorically, have a sword.

38. The disciples had taken him literally. **And they said, Lord, behold, here are two swords.** They had found, on examination, that there were among them two such weapons;—Peter had one of them (ver. 50)—how obtained, or for what use, we can only guess—and probably desired to know whether those would suffice. They must have felt how stupid they had been in supposing that Jesus really advised them to use such carnal weapons against a hostile world, when they perceived the tone of compassionate irony in which he said, **It is enough.**

39-46. THE AGONY IN THE GARDEN.

39. And he came out, and went, as he was wont, to the mount of Olives. The Supper was ended, with its attendant discourses, including some at least of the long series in John 14-17. A part of these may have been spoken while on the way out of the city, across the ravine of Kidron, or even after they had reached the scene of the following incident. From our narrative we might judge that the movement was made simply to reach the usual lodging place of these nights (ch. 21 : 37), the Mount of Olives. On the relation of this mountain to Jerusalem, see again on ch. 19: 37, and the Bible Dictionaries. **And his** (rather, *the*) **disciples also followed him,** as they were wont, probably, although it may be meant that he preceded them, and that they followed in fear, as at Mark 10: 32.

40. And when he was at the place. This may mean, consistently with the preceding verse, the place to which he was wont to go; and thus it would countenance the supposition broached above, on ch. 21 : 37, that he did not go always at night to Bethany, but may have lodged privately at some other place on that mountain. More probably, it means the place for which he had set out that evening. Luke does not name, or even describe it. From John (18 : 1), we learn that it was "a garden= pleasure-ground, park. The particular word translated "place," in Matt. 26: 36; Mark 14: 32, would lead us rather to think of a private property—a place, or country-seat—into which visitors had liberty to enter. It was named Gethsemane=oil-press, as the spot where the olives which grew abundantly, at that time, in the neighborhood, were pressed for their oil. Near the foot of Mount Olivet, as it slopes toward Jerusalem, and about 250 yards from the Golden Gate, stands an ancient church, bearing a name in Arabic, evidently derived from Gethsemane. In close proximity, a walled enclosure shuts in a few (eight) very old olive-trees, which eminent botanists have supposed to be 2,000 years old. (Ritter iv., 169). Tradition affirms that they were there in the fourth century. That this is the veritable scene which heard the prayers and groans of our Saviour, is as likely as any of the unsupported traditions of great antiquity. The most competent modern observers, however, are here, also, much divided in opinion. See Caspari, *Chron. and Geog. Introd. to the Life of Christ*, p. 222.—**He said unto them, Pray that ye enter not into temptation.**

Ch. XXII.] LUKE.

41 *And he was withdrawn from them about a stone's cast, and kneeled down, and prayed,
42 Saying, Father, if thou be willing, remove this cup from me: nevertheless *b* not my will, but thine, be done.

41 And he was parted from them about a stone's cast; 42 and he kneeled down and prayed, saying, Father, if thou be willing, remove this cup from me: never-

a Matt. 26:39; Mark 14:35....*b* John 5:30; 6:38.

Luke is brief in his account of the scene, although he alone mentions the assisting angel (ver. 43), and the bloody sweat (ver. 44). He says nothing of the preliminary selection of the three chief apostles; of Christ's peculiar distress of mind; of his withdrawing from the three selected companions; of the three-fold

41. And he was withdrawn from them about a stone's cast. The passive form, "*was* withdrawn," "separated," is noticeable, as if it was by some influence exerted upon him that he removed. He was not so removed but that he could have the sense of their presence and sympathy, and that they, some of

GETHSEMANE.

repetition of his prayer; of his gradual restoration to serenity of mind, as he prayed; of the somnolence of the disciples, renewed again and again; and of his apology for them. We can only explain this by supposing that our Gospel follows an account of the scene which aimed to give only the substance of the transaction. This it does, in full harmony with the other accounts, with the particulars of which Luke was, possibly, not acquainted. **Pray**—continue in prayer—**that ye enter not into temptation.** This was to be the matter of their constant desire toward God, that they might not, in the trying circumstances before them, be found off their guard so that these should prove sufficient to turn them from their discipleship.

them, could be aware of what he experienced in that dark hour.—**And kneeled down, and prayed.** While Luke, as we have said, does not mention the thrice-repeated petition, he uses a form of the verb which distinctly shows that it was not a single request, but a continued supplication — was engaged in prayer, or, kept praying.

42. Father. In this hour of overwhelming distress through the carrying forward of God's plan concerning him, he still looks up with filial confidence to him as his Father.—**If thou be** (*art*) **willing**—if thou canst consent—find it consistent with thy pleasure—**remove this cup from me.** Cup, by metonymy, for its contents, which, again, is the measured experience of joy or sorrow allotted

V

43 And there appeared ᵃ an angel unto him from heaven, strengthening him.
44 ᵇAnd being in an agony he prayed more earnestly; and his sweat was as it were great drops of blood falling down to the ground.

43 ¹theless not my will, but thine, be done. ¹And there appeared unto him an angel from heaven, strengthening him. And being in an agony he prayed more
44 earnestly; and his sweat became as it were great

a Matt. 4: 11....*b* John 12: 27; Heb. 5: 7.——¹ Many ancient authorities omit ver. 43. 44.

to one as his portion by God. This was a common way, in Hebrew, of naming one's divinely appointed fortune, especially when regarded in the light of a retribution (Ps. 23: 5; 75: 8; Isa. 51: 17; Ezek. 22: 31.). **Remove.** The Greek verb was employed by classical writers to denote the act of a servant in taking dishes off the table. (Grimm, *Clavis*, s. v.). Thus, Christ prays that, if it please God, that experience of pain, and shame, and death with torture, which was now beginning, might be removed from before him. The combined statements of the three Evangelists open to our view a mystery of agony which no other being on earth, not the most exquisitely tortured of martyrs, ever knew. The perfect humanity of Jesus, instead of rendering him less susceptible to pain, and grief, and sorrow, would render him the more capacious of all these, through its identification with the divine nature, which made him properly the Son of God. Beyond the susceptibility to agony arising from the obvious circumstances of our Saviour, natural, as we may say, to such a being, and capable of being imagined by us, there was that infinite volume of experience connected with his propitiatory function, about which we may inquire and wonder, but not dogmatize. If it seem strange to us that he should even conceive the possibility of his now escaping that end, to which his whole earthly mission had pointed, we perhaps do injustice to the unique perfection of his humanity. The sympathy which he himself gave to John the Baptist, in an analogous, but infinitely less trying case, we may well accord to him. For he, too, was a man (1.Tim. 2: 5). Deity lay involved ever in that "form of a servant," not so as to hinder at all that he should act as one "found in fashion as a man." Hence, we need not wonder that a human shrinking from unspeakable distress should, for a moment, have made him quail. Luke beautifully makes this phase of his feeling a transient outburst; as, indeed, the other Gospels also represent it as passing away in a moment. For the sentence of which we are speaking ends with: **Nevertheless**—whether it may be removed or not—**not my will, but thine, be done.** This, which is the essence of all true prayer, repeats with emphasis the "if thou art willing," and, with the previous request, condenses the *Pater Noster* into a single sentence. Who can ever require such faith to say, "Father, thy will be done," as Jesus needed and exercised at that moment? The prayer can never fail of fulfillment, and that the best possible fulfillment, "even thy will, O my Father."

43. In our Saviour's case it was fulfilled, as with the prayer of Paul that his thorn in the flesh should be taken away, by giving the requisite support that God's will might be endured.—**And there appeared an angel unto him from heaven, strengthening him.** It is uncertain whether the angel would have been visible to other eyes, if others had been present. He is not said to have come, but he **appeared unto**=was seen by the Saviour. In some way this proof of the presence and sympathy of celestial beings gave him increased ability to bear what he had taken upon him with the approbation of his Father. We cannot so well comprehend this as the benefit of that earlier angel-ministry, after his temptation (Matt. 4: 11); but the help was, doubtless, equally real to him. And so the terrible conflict might go on.

44. **And being in an agony, he prayed more earnestly.** The participle is of the Greek verb "to become," and means, here, "getting to be in an agony"; so that the thought is that, after he had prayed, and had received angelic succor, the distress was allowed to increase, and, with it, his prayer grew more intense. Even the sympathy of his Father, manifested through his angel, did not prevent his anguish from reaching such a pitch that it forced the sweat through his pores—**and his sweat was** (*i.e.*, *became*) **as it were great drops of blood falling down to the ground.** This phenomenon was neither sweat alone nor blood alone. The latter is forbidden by the **as if**, the former by the fact that there would be little force in comparing sweat to blood, in respect merely

45 And when he rose up from prayer, and was come to his disciples, he found them sleeping for sorrow,
46 And said unto them, Why sleep ye? rise and ᵃ pray, lest ye enter into temptation.
47 ¶ And while he yet spake, ᵇ behold a multitude, and he that was called Judas, one of the twelve, went before them, and drew near unto Jesus to kiss him.

45 drops of blood falling down upon the ground. And when he rose up from his prayer, he came unto the
46 disciples, and found them sleeping for sorrow, and said unto them, Why sleep ye? rise and pray, that ye enter not into temptation.
47 While he yet spake, behold, a multitude, and he that was called Judas, one of the twelve, went before them; and he drew near unto Jesus to kiss

a ver. 40....b Matt. 26: 47; Mark 14: 43; John 18: 3.

to its form as drops, or as to their size. It is the color, also, caused by blood oozing forth through the skin, and coagulating as such, so that the sweat was like blood-clots (θρόμβοι), not mere **drops**, rolling off on the ground. Aristotle (*Hist. Anim.*, iii., 19) is cited as authority for the occurrence of this bloody sweat in abnormal experiences of men. He says that in certain extraordinary states the blood becomes very much liquified—and flows through in such a manner that some have perspired blood. (Other references in Wetstein, Lightfoot, *Exercit. in loci.* Meyer.) Gethsemane thus appears a prelude and epitome of Calvary, wanting only the physical distress and actual death to complete the experience. Alone with God, he faces the final agony, feels it by anticipation overwhelming him,—all that was involved in being made sin for sinners; shrinks from it, receives strength, rather, to endure it still further; then becomes calm and self-possessed, so as to be ready for the public sacrifice of himself, which he goes forth to meet.

45. And when he rose up from prayer —having been bowed down to the ground (Matt. 26: 39)—**and was come** (better, *he came*) **to his disciples, he found them sleeping for sorrow.** We have thus condensed, in Luke, the three-fold return to the three chosen disciples in Matthew and Mark, and their thrice renewed drowsiness. Here, as no mention has been made of the selected three, all the eleven are assumed to have fallen asleep. That any of them should have fallen asleep in such circumstances is naturally, to our thought, monstrous, especially after the injunction in ver. 40. It certainly shows us that they were far, even yet, from comprehending the seriousness of the crisis in which they stood. That the Saviour, deeply grieved as he was, should still find some apology for them, in the weakness of the flesh (Matt. 26: 41), may lead us to judge them leniently. They had begun the previous day early; it was now certainly after midnight. They were in the habit of going early to rest. The Saviour had tarried long in his agony, the night was chilly, and the **sorrow** which they felt, from even their dim apprehension of their Master's trouble, would predispose them to sleep. This effect has been not unfrequently experienced in cases of grief and sorrow, and that it had been noticed in early times is evident from the more or less appropriate citations in Wetstein on this passage.

46. And said unto them—as he waked them—**Why sleep ye?**—"What, could ye not watch with me one hour?" (Matt. 26: 40.) **Rise and pray, lest ye enter into temptation. Rise.**=rouse yourselves. The direction to pray must have painfully reminded them how they had heeded the same given to them an hour or two before. The same, yet not exactly. The Greek allows us at least to question whether the former did not prescribe what they were to pray for, namely, "not to come into temptation"; and this why they should pray, namely, in order that they might not come into temptation. It is not certain that such a difference was intended. **Rise** expresses here, as just said, the notion of "stand promptly up," and implies their urgent need of faith and courage: and keep praying that you may not find your trials a temptation.

47-53. The Arrest.

Everything is now ready for the sacrifice. We see no more reluctance on the part of the Lamb of God. The experience of the garden, while it has shown the inevitableness of the long foreseen issue, has given something of a foretaste of its pains. It has shown, also, that, however appalling, Heaven will give strength to bear them to the end. Calm resignation to the lot which has been appointed to him, explainable only from a clear perception of what is involved in his mediatorial office, is what we notice in him henceforth to the end.

47. While he yet spake, behold, a mul-

48 But Jesus said unto him, Judas, betrayest thou the Son of man with a kiss?
49 When they which were about him saw what would follow, they said unto him, Lord, shall we smite with the sword?
50 ¶ And *a* one of them smote the servant of the high priest, and cut off his right ear.
51 And Jesus answered and said, Suffer ye thus far. And he touched his ear, and healed him.
52 *b* Then Jesus said unto the chief priests, and captains of the temple, and the elders, which were come to him, Be ye come out, as against a thief, with swords and staves?

48 him. But Jesus said unto him, Judas, betrayest
49 thou the Son of man with a kiss? And when they that were about 'him saw what would follow, they
50 said, Lord, shall we smite with the sword? And a certain one of them smote the ¹ servant of the high
51 priest, and struck off his right ear. But Jesus answered and said, Suffer ye thus far. And he touched
52 his ear, and healed him. And Jesus said unto the chief priests, and captains of the temple, and elders, that were come against him, Are ye come out, as

a Matt. 26: 51 ; Mark 14: 47 ; John 18: 10....*b* Matt. 26: 55 ; Mark 14: 48.——1 Gr. *bondservant*.

titude, and he that was called Judas, etc. The composition of the multitude is described in John 18: 3. It included a band of the Roman garrison near the temple enclosure, as well as a number of the Hebrew rulers and their minions. They were guided by Judas, as he had bargained. (ver. 6.) The clear indications at the table (ver. 21) that Jesus was aware of his treachery had decided him, if not already so intending, to take the moment of the feast for carrying out his purpose. Knowing the habit of his Master to resort to this mountain at night, he would, if he found that the company had left the upper room, proceed thither at once.—And he drew near unto Jesus, to kiss him, and did actually kiss him (Matt. 26: 49; Mark 14: 45), and that with a show of affection, as the form of verb there used shows= kissed him tenderly. The kiss was a common expression of greeting among friends, of men toward each other; and Christ submitted to it now, that the will of God might be accomplished.

48. Jesus makes nó resistance, as their formidable array of men, and weapons, and torches, indicated a belief that he would; he interposed no supernatural obstruction, as they probably supposed he might. By his simple question, **Judas, betrayest thou the Son of man with a kiss?** he proves that he is aware of the secret intention of that salute (Matt. 26: 48), and rebukes the traitor for so much superfluous hypocrisy. **With a kiss** betrayest thou me, dishonoring that sacred sign of love, when simply to have pointed a finger would have been enough? **The Son of man,** and, as such, Son of God, and divinely attested Messiah.

49. It might have been what Jesus had said in the upper room about the need of swords, which led his followers now to think of physical resistance. Perhaps Calvin's thought that it was a special temptation of the devil, here, as in their recent sleep, which confused them, is not without probability.

50. Without waiting for Christ's answer, Peter (see John 18: 10) drew one of the two swords which were among them, **and smote the servant**—slave—**of the high priest**—Malchus by name—**and cut off his right ear.** The **right** ear is mentioned simply because the report included that little circumstance. When and where the Synoptic accounts were framed, it might not have been safe to mention the name of him who struck this blow; when and where John wrote, there could be no danger.

51. **And** (rather, *But*) **Jesus answered**—to their question in verse 49—**and said, Suffer ye thus far.** He addresses the disciples, and says in effect, "No, do not smite" (but' the deed was done, even as he spoke); "rather suffer even this, namely, that with wicked hands they should take and slay me." Other expositions—some very far fetched, some trivial—have been given to **thus far.** The Greek—"even unto this," implies that it was a great concession which he asked of them; as indeed it was. To repair the injury done to Malchus, which standing might greatly harm his cause (comp. John 18: 36), he now for the last time—and probably in behalf of one who was most forward against him—put forth that healing touch which had so often carried health to the sick, soundness to the lame, the leprous, the deaf, the blind, and life to the dead. **He touched his ear, and healed him.** Whether by replacing the several pieces, or by causing its equivalent to grow, it is vain to conjecture. It was probably at this time that his disciples all forsook him and fled. (Matt. 26: 56.)

52. One word did our Lord then deign to the heads of the different sets who made up the "multitude" of his pursuers. **Be** (or, *Are*)

Ch. XXII.]   LUKE.   325

53 When I was daily with you in the temple, ye stretched forth no hands against me: *but this is your hour, and the power of darkness.
54 ¶ *Then took they him, and led *him*, and brought him into the high priest's house. *And Peter followed afar off.
55 *And when they had kindled a fire in the midst of the hall, and were set down together, Peter sat down among them.
56 But a certain maid beheld him as he sat by the fire, and earnestly looked upon him, and said, This man was also with him.

53 against a robber, with swords and staves? When I was daily with you in the temple, ye stretched not forth your hands against me: but this is your hour, and the power of darkness.
54 And they seized him, and led him *away*, and brought him into the high priest's house. But
55 Peter followed afar off. And when they had kindled a fire in the midst of the court, and had sat down together, Peter sat in the midst of them.
56 And a certain maid seeing him as he sat in the light *of the fire*, and looking stedfastly upon him, said,

a John 12:27....*b* Matt. 26:57....*c* Matt. 26:58; John 18:15.....*d* Matt. 26:69; Mark 14:66; John 18:17, 18.

ye come out as against a thief—*robber?* This was indeed to be reckoned with the transgressors, and seems to have most keenly stung the pure and holy soul which no man had ever yet convinced of sin.

53. When I was with you daily in the temple, ye stretched forth no hands against me. Had I been a criminal, ye might have apprehended me on any day of my life among you. No, your attack is directed against a man whom ye know to be innocent; and for the capture of such a man ye take upon you, in the night, the task of the lowest constable. **But this is your hour.** So the Saviour explains their conduct: it is the hour appointed in God's counsel, foretold in the prophets (Matt. 26:56), for you to work your unhallowed will. **And the power of darkness**—the power by which you are impelled is that which darkness gives to wicked men to perpetrate evil deeds (Grimm, *Clavis*, s. v. σκότος), a power which you could not have exercised in the light of day, when I was among you. The word **darkness** inevitably suggests also, in this connection, metaphorically, that moral empire whose rulers were "the powers of darkness." (Col. 1:13). But the explanation here does not require that.

54–62. He is Carried a Prisoner to the High Priest's House. Peter's Denial.

54. Then took they (or, *And they seized*) **him, and led him, and brought him into the high priest's house.** The high priest at this time was Caiaphas (Matt. 26:57), according to the appointment of the Roman power. His father-in-law, Annas, however, was an ex-high priest, in the disordered customs of the time, and considered in some sense as invested with the office still (see on chap. 3:1), and from John 18:13, we learn that Jesus was taken first to his house, and there subjected to a preliminary examination (John 18:19-24. Revision, ver. 24). Annas is there (ver. 19) called the high

priest. Of this, neither of the Synoptics takes any account, and, although it actually involved nearly all there was even of a pretended trial, it was of no decisive importance in the result. On the probable succession of the trials, see on verses 66-70.—**And Peter followed afar off.** Interest in his Master struggled in him yet with moral cowardice. He would see what became of him. We are not told here how he got into the court of the high priest's house, but John supplies the information. John himself had gone in with the crowd about Jesus, and then, through some acquaintance with the high priest, was able to induce the woman who kept the entrance gate to let Peter come in also. See John 18:15, 16. But as that was in the court of Annas, while what follows here took place in the court of Caiaphas, it seems necessary to assume that both lived in different parts of a house which surrounded one and the same central court. As they were so closely related, and the house of the wealthy and powerful Annas would be grand and spacious, nothing could be more natural than that it should afford habitation for them both. The sending Jesus, therefore, from Annas to Caiaphas, need be nothing more than having him taken across a spacious interior court to the opposite apartment.

55. Peter joined the company of subordinate officers and servants, who had kindled a fire of charcoal (John 18:18) in the midst of the court, under the open sky. The nights there, at that season, were likely to be quite cold.

56. But (or, *And*) **a certain maid beheld him as he sat by the fire** (rather, *toward the light*). Fire is not in the Greek, though the light is from the fire.—**And earnestly**—*stedfastly*—**looked upon him, and said, This man was also**—as well as John—**with him.** The Revision is more accurate than the Common Version. See it above. The maid-servant was either the portress, whom John mentions as having called forth one de-

57 And he denied him, saying, Woman, I know him not.
58 ªAnd after a little while another saw him, and said, Thou art also of them. And Peter said, Man, I am not.
59 ᵇAnd about the space of one hour after another confidently affirmed, saying, Of a truth this *fellow* also was with him: for he is a Galilean.
60 And Peter said, Man, I know not what thou sayest. And immediately, while he yet spake, the cock crew.
61 And the Lord turned, and looked upon Peter. ᶜAnd Peter remembered the word of the Lord, how he had said unto him, ᵈBefore the cock crow, thou shalt deny me thrice.

57 This man also was with him. But he denied, saying, Woman, I know him not. And after a little while another saw him, and said, Thou also art *one*
59 of them. But Peter said, Man, I am not. And after the space of about one hour another confidently affirmed, saying, Of a truth this man also
60 was with him: for he is a Galilean. But Peter said, Man, I know not what thou sayest. And im-
61 mediately, while he yet spake, the cock crew. And the Lord turned, and looked upon Peter. And Peter remembered the word of the Lord, how that he said unto him, Before the cock crow this day,

a Matt. 26: 71; Mark 14: 69; John 18: 25....*b* Matt. 26: 73; Mark 14: 70; John 18: 26.....*c* Matt. 26: 75; Mark 14: 72....*d* Matt. 26: 34, 75; John 13: 38.

---

nial from Peter, or some one who may have been with her when the company came in.

57. And (or, *But*) **he denied him**—*him* is of doubtful authority—**saying, Woman, I know him not.** The very form of expression which Jesus had predicted. Why should he, more than John, who also was known, and by implication ("this man, *also*"), declared to have been with Jesus, have lied to shun the charge?

58. Another—"man" must be understood, as the word man in Peter's answer shows. Moreover, the pronoun, in the Greek, is masculine.

59. And about the space of one hour after another—man—confidently affirmed, etc. This appears to correspond to the third denial, in Matthew and Mark, inasmuch as they all find the proof in the fact that Peter was a Galilean.

60. Man, I know not what thou sayest: I do not understand whom or what your talk is about. This completely fulfilled what Christ had predicted: "Thou wilt deny that thou knowest me" (ver. 34). The different reports of Peter's denials present the agreements and differences natural to so many independent, truthful accounts of the same series of exciting events, in which numbers have participated. They all speak of three denials, in the courtyard of the high priest's house, or in the space surrounding it, with a fire burning in the midst of it. The persons bringing the charge do not coincide throughout. In the first denial, it is a maid-servant in each account. In the second, Luke has "another," in the masculine; John has "they," the company. In the third, Matthew and Mark have "they that stood by"; Luke, "another" *man*; John, "one of the servants of the high priest." In regard to the time, all make the three to have taken place before a cock crew, except Mark, who informs us, in 14: 30, that Jesus had said, "before the cock crow twice," and who mentions one cock crowing after the first denial. It is hard to see how, under the circumstances, three truly independent narratives could better agree in everything essential to a true report. The subject is fully treated in Andrews' *Life of our Lord*, in Robinson's, and Gardiner's *Harmonies*, and well, succinctly, by Westcott, *Introd. to Gospels*, p. 301, note.—**And immediately, while he yet spake, the cock crew.** We may well suppose that in the state of mind which had racked Peter for the last hour or two, the sound must have struck him as a death knell.

61. And the Lord turned, and looked upon Peter. Luke alone has preserved for us this touching incident—one of the most precious items of knowledge concerning Christ which we owe to his Gospel. In any of the rooms on the lower floor of the house, all opening out through the porch into the court, it would, naturally, be possible for the Saviour to see Peter, anywhere within the light of the fire. Probably, Jesus, absorbed in his own cause, had paid little attention to him before. It is almost certain that Peter could have paid little attention to him. But now, the sound of the cock drew the eyes of both together, and Peter met that look. In it were mingled sorrow, admonition, yearning love, beseeching appeal. But we cannot describe it; its quality must be judged from what we previously knew of the parties, and from its present effect. It had power to prevent the backsliding of Peter from hardening into the apostasy of Judas. It awakened in his breast the clear memory of that love which trembled in the tones of Jesus, when he said, "Before the cock crow, thou shalt deny me thrice."

62 And Peter went out, and wept bitterly.
63 ¶ ᵃ And the men that held Jesus mocked him, and smote him.
64 And when they had blindfolded him, they struck him on the face, and asked him, saying, Prophesy, who is it that smote thee?
65 And many other things blasphemously spake they against him.
66 ¶ ᵇ And as soon as it was day, ᶜ the elders of the people and the chief priests and the scribes came together, and led him into their council, saying,
67 ᵈ Art thou the Christ? tell us. And he said unto them, If I tell you, ye will not believe:

62 thou shalt deny me thrice. And he went out, and wept bitterly.
63 And the men that held ¹ Jesus mocked him, and
64 beat him. And they blindfolded him, and asked him, saying, Prophesy: who is he that struck thee?
65 And many other things spake they against him, reviling him.
66 And as soon as it was day, the assembly of the elders of the people was gathered together, both chief priests and scribes; and they led him away into their council, saying, If thou art the Christ,
67 tell us. But he said unto them, If I tell you, ye

ᵃ Matt. 26: 67, 68; Mark 14: 65.... ᵇ Matt. 27: 1.... ᶜ Acts 4: 26. See Acts 22: 5.... ᵈ Matt. 26: 63; Mark 14: 61.—1 Gr. him.

62. And Peter went out, and wept bitterly. Oh, could he have confessed his sin to his Master! Could he have heard one word of pity and encouragement! But he could only weep in deep repentance, with loud and bitter lamentation.

63-65. MOCKERY OF JESUS BY THE JEWISH CAPTORS.

This is the same abuse of the Saviour which Matthew and Mark report at the ends of their account of the preliminary night trial before Caiaphas. Luke consistently places it here, as he does not notice that trial, only supposes it going on through the time of Peter's second and third denials. The chief men having brought the Lord to a pretended conviction of blasphemy, leave him, while waiting for the morning court, to the contumely of the constables and other Jews. The abuse was to be repeated afterward by the Gentiles. (Matt. 27: 27; Mark 15: 16; John 19: 2.).

63, 64. And the men that held Jesus mocked him—made sport of him—**and smote him.** The original makes the particular injuries to be the mockery, thus: "mocked him, beating him; and blindfolding him, they asked him," etc. Into the hands of what men had he fallen, that this could be sport for them? The "beating" here was such as properly implies the use of rods or scourges. For blindfolding, McClellan has properly "muffling." **Prophesy**—with thy eyes bandaged, tell by thy prophetic power—**who is it that smote** (*struck*) **thee?** It was the peculiarly Jewish manifestation of hatred toward the Prophet whom Moses had foretold for them.

65. And many other things blasphemously spake they—and did—against him. See the parallel passages, and compare Isa. 50: 6.

66-70. THE REGULAR TRIAL BEFORE THE FULL COURT BY DAYLIGHT.

All the Evangelists make much of the case of Peter, from the point when he came into the court yard of Annas and Caiaphas, until the decisive cock crowing. One, two or three hours may have elapsed. Meantime, Jesus, after being sent over from Annas to the proper high priest (John 18: 24), had been questioned by Caiaphas and the other members of the chief court, or Sanhedrin, with such as had been among his captors, or were waiting his arrival, in hope of drawing from him something that might serve as a ground of condemnation. The narrative of their persecution, rather than examination, may be read in Matt. 26: 59-68; Mark 14: 55-65. Neither of the other Gospels mentions this pretence of a trial. It could not claim, on their own principles, to be a regular trial on a capital charge, for they were now forbidden to condemn any man to death in the night. (*Sanhedrin*, 9. 1). But they made it serve to bring him to an utterance of what they, with great pretence of horror, called blasphemy, and so held the case until the full Sanhedrin (a *quasi Sanhedrin*) could be formally assembled. Of the decisive inquest held in the third instance, Luke in the following verses gives the only account.—See note on p. 355.

66. And as soon as it was day—as soon, therefore, as it would be legal, and long before sunrise—**the elders of the people and the chief priests and the scribes came together.** The three constituent elements of their head council are formally narrated, as they were at ch. 20: 1. We have before noticed the absence of all mention of the Pharisees in connection with these last scenes. The fact is considered in Farrar, *L. of C.*, ii., 332.—**And led him into their council.** The place of their meeting was, probably, no longer the office in one front of the high priest's palace. Comp. Matt. 27: 5.

67. Art thou (Revision, *If thou art*) **the**

68 And if I also ask *you*, ye will not answer me, nor let *me* go.
69 *Hereafter shall the Son of man sit on the right hand of the power of God.
70 Then said they all, Art thou then the Son of God? And he said unto them, *Ye say that I am.
71 *And they said, What need we any further witness? for we ourselves have heard of his own mouth.

68 will not believe: and if I ask *you*, ye will not answer. But from henceforth shall the Son of man be seated at the right hand of the power of God.
70 And they all said, Art thou then the Son of God?
71 And he said unto them, *Ye say *it*, for I am. And they said, What further need have we of witness? for we ourselves have heard from his own mouth.

CHAPTER XXIII.

AND *the whole multitude of them arose, and led him unto Pilate.

1 And the whole company of them rose up, and

a Matt. 26: 64; Mark 14: 62; Heb. 1: 3; 8: 1....*b* Matt. 26: 64; Mark 14: 62....*c* Matt. 26: 65; Mark 14: 63....*d* Matt. 27: 2; Mark 15: 1; John 18: 28.——1 Or, *Ye say that I am.*

Christ? tell us. Their object was to draw from him here what he had previously declared (Matt. 26: 64; Mark 14: 62), that they might base formal action upon it. The attempt to convict him of any secular crime appears to have broken down with the failure of the cruel and unprincipled Annas. Perhaps they thought they might use his claim to be the Messiah as threatening to the civil government established. Any evidence of such a purpose might leave the Saviour, while not at all varying from his previous acknowledgment, to repeat it now, by implication, in such a way as to give not the slightest color to a secular complaint.—**If I tell you, ye will not believe.** It was simply to turn his declaration into a weapon against him that they wanted him to speak. Former professions of his Messiahship (John 8: 58; 10: 30) had only sharpened their hatred against him.

68. And if I also ask you—questions touching the Scripture proof of my Messiahship—**ye will not answer me, nor**—when those questions indicate my innocence—**let me go.** The last clause is probably spurious.

69. Hereafter (rather, *from henceforth*) —from now on—**shall the Son of man sit** (or, *be seated*) **on the right hand of the power of God.** The meaning is, although you will not admit my title as Messiah, your action is bringing it to pass that I shall be recognized, from this day, if not on earth, yet in my seat of heavenly majesty, as a sharer of God's power.

70. They saw that this was more than an assertion of Messiahship, even of divinity. **Then said they all, Art thou then the Son of God?**—as thy language plainly implies.—**Ye say that I am.** A Hebrew way of saying, Yes; I am. Comp. Matt 26: 64 with Mark 14: 62. So that the Lord had repeated his confession, but without saying a word calculated to offend the Roman power, or in the slightest degree to violate any law, human or divine.

71. And they said, What need we any further witness? Finding it impossible to obtain more, they must content themselves with what only they could wrest into a ground of accusation. What they had heard from him might be misrepresented as blasphemy; but this would have little weight with a Roman judge.

Ch. 23. 1-25. JESUS BEFORE PILATE.

In the account of the trial before the Roman governor we may recognize in Luke three distinct stages—ver. 1-7, 8-12, 13-25. Of these the second, in which he submits the prisoner to Herod's judgment, is peculiar to our Gospel; the others are distinctly marked in all the rest. The outline of these, as given in the Synoptics, must be filled up from John's report.

1-7. First stage of the trial. Summary acquittal of Jesus by the Roman authority.

1. And the whole multitude of them arose, and led him unto Pilate. The word here is not the one (ὄχλος) usually translated **multitude** in the Gospels; but, as this Greek also (πλῆθος) distinctly denotes a full number, crowd, or throng, **multitude** seems more appropriate than "company." (Revision.) They would of themselves constitute a numerous body; and it is enough to suppose that, in order to command compliance with their desire, they went in a full procession and official array. How many of the "people" (ver. 13) had already joined the "whole council" (Mark 15: 1) we cannot tell. It is a disputed question whether Pilate now lived, when at Jerusalem, in the magnificent palace on Zion, left by King Herod, or in the Castle Antonia, where

2 And they began to accuse him, saying, We found this *fellow* ^a perverting the nation, and ^b forbidding to give tribute to Cæsar, saying, ^c that he himself is Christ a King.
3 ^d And Pilate asked him, saying, Art thou the King of the Jews? And he answered him and said, Thou sayest *it.*
4 Then said Pilate to the chief priests and *to* the people, ^e I find no fault in this man.

2 brought him before Pilate. And they began to accuse him, saying, We found this man perverting our nation, and forbidding to give tribute to Cæsar, 3 and saying that he himself is Christ a king. And Pilate asked him, saying, Art thou the King of the Jews? And he answered him and said, Thou sayest 4 *it.* And Pilate said unto the chief priests and the

a Acts 17: 7....*b* See Matt. 17: 27; 22: 21; Mark 12: 17....*c* John 19: 12....*d* Matt. 27: 11; 1 Tim. 6: 13....*e* 1 Pet. 2: 22.

the Roman garrison was quartered, just off the northwest corner of the temple. The latter supposition is more probable, at this time, since Herod Antipas being in the city, would more likely be allowed the use of the palace. There was, however, another palace, west of the temple and above it (Josephus, *Antiquities,* xx., 8, 11), which Herod might have occupied. A proper conception of Pilate himself, and of his relation to the distribution of justice at Jerusalem, is necessary to a right appreciation of this narrative. After the dethronement of Archelaus, son of Herod the Great, Judea and Samaria were put under the control of imperial procurators, who governed the district in behalf of the Emperor. Their primary function was the collection of the r. venues; but they also had, while interfering as little as possible with the local laws and customs, to superintend the administration of justice. The Roman policy was careful, in particular, that the lives of the provincials should not be unjustly sacrificed under a pretence of justice. In Palestine, on what occasion is not definitely known, the authority of carrying into execution a sentence of death had been taken away from the Jewish magistrates. (John 18: 31.) Pontius Pilate was the fifth of this series of Roman governors of Palestine. (Derenbourg, *Histoire de la Palestine,* p. 197, f.) He had been appointed by Tiberius, at the instance of his favorite, the crafty and cruel Sejanus, whose creature Pilate was. He was an unprincipled and haughty Roman knight, who, for his own ease, would have liked to rule over Palestine quietly; but who had already blundered, perhaps, rather than pushed himself, into two serious conflicts with the Jewish authorities and people. Out of these he had come, not without peril to himself. He now thoroughly hated and despised that people, and they repaid him with like sentiments. To this man, standing in this superior, and to them galling, relation, the proud and arrogant Jewish magnates led

Jesus on that early morning of the Passover day. **They led him unto Pilate.** Compare the particulars in John.

2. And they began to accuse him, saying, We found this fellow (better, *man*) **perverting the** (better reading, *our*) **nation,** etc. This was probably after they had attempted, as in John, to have Pilate condemn him on the ground simply that they called him a malefactor. The present charge brought out the fact, not previously apparent, that they wished him sentenced to death. Even he could not think of that without some proper proof. For proof, they now substitute clamorous and vague accusations that he was ruining the nation by teaching the people political heresies. The forbidding to pay taxes we have seen (ch. 20: 25) to be precisely the opposite to what he had solemnly taught within the week. Pilate may have had some general knowledge of the Jewish expectation of a Christ. That could only be of interest to him if it threatened the civil welfare

3. When, therefore, he heard the idea king associated with him, he simply asked him, **Art thou the King of the Jews?** strongly emphasizing the pronoun thou, so incredible, not to say absurd, did the notion seem. Christ's calm and frank affirmative, **Thou sayest it,** would be the best proof possible to the world-worn Roman that his prisoner used the word **king** in some unworldly sense (see this fully in John), and would rather awaken awe in himself than apprehension of guilt on the part of Jesus. The skepticism of that day was, as it generally is, compatible with the profoundest superstition.

4. This process of accusation and investigation, though the account is doubtless greatly abridged, took but a short time; and, as the result, **Pilate said**—to the excited throng of accusers—**I find no fault in this man.** This is the first declaration of his innocence, from the only competent — even approximately competent—and impartial tribunal. It car-

5 And they were the more fierce, saying, He stirreth up the people, teaching throughout all Jewry, beginning from Galilee to this place.
6 When Pilate heard of Galilee, he asked whether the man were a Galilæan.
7 And as soon as he knew that he belonged unto *a* Herod's jurisdiction, he sent him to Herod, who himself also was at Jerusalem at that time.
8 ¶ And when Herod saw Jesus, he was exceeding glad: for *b* he was desirous to see him of a long *season*, because *c* he had heard many things of him; and he hoped to have seen some miracle done by him.
9 Then he questioned with him in many words; but he answered him nothing.

5 multitudes, I find no fault in this man. But they were the more urgent, saying, He stirreth up the people, teaching throughout all Judæa, and beginning from Galilee even unto this place. But when Pilate heard it, he asked whether the man were a
7 Galilæan. And when he knew that he was of Herod's jurisdiction, he sent him unto Herod, who himself also was at Jerusalem in these days.
8 Now when Herod saw Jesus, he was exceeding glad: for he was of a long time desirous to see him, because he had heard concerning him; and he
9 hoped to see some ² miracle done by him. And he questioned him in many words; but he answered

a ch. 3:1....*b* ch. 9:9....*c* Matt. 14:1; Mark 6:14.——1 Gr. *sign.*

ried with it, of course, that he would not consent to the harmless man being put to death.

5. And they were the more fierce (or, *urgent*). Was their so nearly won success to prove a failure, after all? We may imagine what the *urgency* of an Oriental mob would be, in the fear of such a disappointment. Still, they have nothing to add to their complaint, except to substitute **stirreth up** for "perverting," (ver. 2), and to state the extent to which his agitation had reached—**from Galilee to** (rather, *even unto*) **this place**—*i.e.*, over the whole land. They may have intended to remind Pilate of the immense excitement of the preceding first day of the week, when the host which had been gathering, from Galilee thitherward, had thrown the whole city and environs into commotion.

6, 7. In the perplexity of Pilate, balancing between unwillingness to commit a great judicial outrage, and fear to provoke the hostility of the Jewish leaders, the word Galilee struck his ear as a signal of relief. **And as soon as** (or, *when*) **he knew that he belonged unto** (or, *was of*) **Herod's jurisdiction**—Galilee and Perea—**he sent him to Herod**, etc., (lit., *sent him up unto*). To *send up* was the technical term for "submit to a superior tribunal." The vileness of Herod's character and life did not at all hinder scrupulous attention on his part to the ceremonial observances of the Jewish religion.—**Who himself also was at Jerusalem.** He had come to the Passover with the rest. He had no authority here, where he did not stand fully on a par with a Roman knight, with whom he had before quarreled. It would be good policy, however, for Pilate to stand well with him, and he now had an opportunity to show him harmless respect. He might, also, probably, get help toward a better understanding of what was becoming to him a terribly embarrassing question: What to do about this Jesus? Herod would be likely to know if he were a criminal; and, if not, his decision would countervail the demand of the priests. The first stage of the trial had resulted in a clear declaration of the innocence of Jesus.

8-12. SECOND STAGE OF THE TRIAL. JESUS BEFORE HEROD.

8. And when Herod saw Jesus, he was exceeding glad. His joy was in the gratification of a curiosity like that which he had once cherished concerning John the Baptist (Mark 6:20), before he understood him.—**For he was**—had been—**desirous to see him of a long season** (*time*)—ever since the time of ch. 9:9, ff.—**because he had heard many things of him**—*i. e., concerning him.* **Many things is**, probably, not part of the text. This was enough to give him a wish to see the man of whom so much was said. When he used to hear that talk, at least, at one period (9:9), he was in a very different state of mind from the present. He was then conscience-smitten, and afraid that Jesus was John, risen from the dead. Now all is changed. His conscience no longer disturbs him, and to his earthly soul, a man in chains was very different from the same man filling all Galilee with the rumor of his mighty works. Still, we read that he **hoped to have seen some miracle done by him**. It was in the spirit which had led the Jews, again and again, to demand of the Lord a sign, which, from the time of Satan's call, that he should throw himself down from the pinnacle, he would never give. Had it been the request of some poor, blind one for sight, or of some leper for healing, doubtless the miracle would still have been wrought. But not for heartless and caviling curiosity.

9. Then (or, *And*) **he questioned with him** (omit *with*) **in many words**—put many forms of questions, and renewed his effort

10 And the chief priests and scribes stood and vehemently accused him.
11 *And Herod with his men of war set him at nought, and mocked *him*, and arrayed him in a gorgeous robe, and sent him again to Pilate.
12 ¶ And the same day ᵇPilate and Herod were made friends together: for before they were at enmity between themselves.
13 ᶜAnd Pilate, when he had called together the chief priests and the rulers and the people,
14 Said unto them, ᵈ Ye have brought this man unto me, as one that perverteth the people: and, behold, ᵉI, having examined *him* before you, have found no fault in this man touching those things whereof ye accuse him:
15 No, nor yet Herod: for I sent you to him; and, lo, nothing worthy of death is done unto him.

a Isa. 53 : 3....b Acts 4 : 27....c Matt. 27 : 23; Mark 15 : 14; John 18 : 38; 19 : 4....d ver. 1 : 2....e ver. 4.—¹ Many ancient authorities read, *I sent you to him.*

again and again. His questions aimed probably at the satisfaction of his personal and standing desire to solve the mystery of his popular influence, more than at a determination of the criminality or innocence of Jesus—the point now at issue. **But he answered him nothing.** He saw the utter frivolity of the attempt of Herod, before whom he must have felt a human mortification more oppressive than in anything else connected with his passion. And while against his persecutors no words could avail aught, his own dignity was best preserved by silence. Recall the Lord's indignant designation of him as "that fox."

10. Meanwhile, impatient for the condemnation which alone they desired, **the chief priests and scribes stood and vehemently accused him.** They thought it necessary to rouse Herod to do the business for which they visited him.

11. And Herod with his men of war—*i. e., soldiers*—who were only a body guard there in Jerusalem—**set him at nought**—treated him as if of no account—**and mocked him**—treated him with ridicule; nothing here is said of bodily injury—**and arrayed him in a gorgeous robe** (rather, *in gorgeous apparel*), **and sent him again to Pilate.** In this burlesquing of the dress of royalty consisted the mockery. As to the color of the robe we can determine nothing, though it was probably purple, the imperial color, although the Greek marks only its splendor (Λαμπράν). We are not told that he sent any word with Jesus, as indeed he could have little to tell; little that he had discovered. But he either said, or his act implied, that Pilate must take the responsibility of deciding his case, and that he found no fault in him (ver. 15) worthy of punishment.

12. And the same day Pilate and Herod were made friends together: for before, etc. Herod was won by the respect that Pilate had shown in submitting so important a prisoner to his jurisdiction, and Pilate was glad to be at peace with Herod, whose ill-will might be dangerous to him at Rome. We can hardly say that the mutual estrangement melted away in common opposition to Jesus, for Pilate has shown no personal enmity to him. He evidently desired to find ground for setting him free, without peril to himself. This second stage of the trial has resulted in a second admission of our Lord's innocence.

13-25. THIRD STAGE. FRESH EXPEDIENTS OF PILATE TO AVOID A CONDEMNATION.

13. The chief priests and the rulers and the people. Notice that now, for the first time, Pilate formally calls **the people** into the consultation. We had once (ver. 4) mention of the "people" as an accidental thing. Now they are to play an important part in the transaction. He had not failed to perceive that these accusations had slight backing from the respectable masses, and probably knew what remarkable zeal for this teacher they had manifested within the last few days. By their co-operation he might resist the demand of the rulers that Jesus should be slain.

14, 15. Ye have brought (*here* is to be omitted) **this man unto me,** etc. The effect of the whole declaration is, that the case stands just where it did when he pronounced judgment at an earlier hour (ver. 4). Nay, it

16 a I will therefore chastise him, and release *him*.
17 b (For of necessity he must release one unto them at the feast.)
18 And c they cried out all at once, saying, Away with this *man*, and release unto us Barabbas:
19 (Who for a certain sedition made in the city, and for murder, was cast into prison.)

16 nothing worthy of death hath been done by him. I
18 will therefore chastise him, and release him.¹ But they cried out all together, saying, Away with this
19 man, and release unto us Barabbas: one who for a certain insurrection made in the city, and for mur-

a Matt. 27 : 26 ; John 19 : 1....*b* Matt. 27 : 15 ; Mark 15 : 6 ; John 18 : 39.....*c* Acts 3 : 14.——1 Many ancient authorities insert ver. 17, *Now he must needs release unto them at the feast one prisoner. Others add the same words after ver. 19.*

was stronger now; for Herod's judgment supported his own. Whichever of the two readings in verse 15 we follow—**I sent you to him** (or, *he sent him up unto us*)—the main sense is the same. Herod has examined him, and finds no fault in him, touching those things of which ye accuse him. In the Common Version, **unto him** applies to Herod : it is decided that Jesus has committed no capital crime against Herod, under whose jurisdiction he has lived. The Greek might mean "in his (Herod's) estimation." In the Revision, **by him**, of course. refers to Christ.

16. I will therefore chastise him, and release him. Notice the **therefore**. What an inference! I have examined him and found him innocent. Pilate, who is most competent to judge, has examined him, and found him innocent. The charge of a capital crime is not sustained; no other crime is even alleged. **Therefore I will chastise him.** If he could only have had the manhood, the decision, of an honorable judge, and have said firmly and finally, "therefore he is acquitted," he would not have stained his hands with the blood of " that just man " (Matt. 27 : 19) and his own name with eternal infamy. But how, then, would the Scripture have been fulfilled, and the eternal counsel that the Christ must suffer? The chastisement here referred to was that awful scourging at the hands of Roman soldiers which often preceded crucifixion, and did so here. (Matt. 27 : 26.) Pilate now wished to substitute this for a proper death sentence. He might well suppose that this ought to satisfy even the Jewish malice; for this scourging sometimes ended in death. See, once for all, the tragic description in Cicero, *Against Verres*, and others. They are quoted in Wetstein on Matt. 27 : 26. The details are too horrible to recite.

17. The sentence (in the Common Version) here put in parentheses as ver. 17 lacks support of the most decisive documents, and seems to have been a gloss from Matt. 27 : 15,

which crept into the text. [It is wanting A, B, K, L, J, H.—A. H.] It was intended to explain by it the mention of Barabbas in the next verse. The custom alluded to, of releasing a prisoner at the Passover Feast, is spoken of by Matthew and John as obligatory on the governor. Of the reason for such a custom, and of the time of its origin, nothing is known.

18. The people had abundant evidence of the wavering state of Pilate's mind, and, finding that he had begun to yield, had all encouragement to persevere. They knew, indeed, that they had no basis of argument, but they knew also the virtue of uproar.— **And they cried out all at once, saying, Away with this man, and release unto us Barabbas.** We may imagine a clamor (like that at Ephesus, Acts 19 : 28-34) in which nothing was heard, for a length of time, but "Away with him! Give us Barabbas!" They had once before extorted a great concession from Pilate in this manner. Josephus tells us (*Antiquities*, xviii., 3, 1), that when Pilate had offended the people, by placing the effigies of the Emperor on the military ensigns in the city of Jerusalem, they went to Cesarea and surrounded his palace with their importunities day and night, holding out against threats of instant death, which were backed up by the presence of Roman troops, until the procurator was obliged to yield, and order the images removed.

19. The verse explains the mention of Barabbas in the preceding verse. **Barabbas** —*Bar-Aba*, signifies, probably, son of a father, or Rabbi. (Comp. Bartimæus, Bar-Jonah.) Nothing at all is known concerning him except what is told in the Gospels at this place. The Greek pronoun **who** (ὅστις)="a man of such sort that " indicates the feeling of the writer. It appears that he had been concerned, probably as a leader, in one of those tumultuary outbreaks which marked that time—in the course of which he had committed murder. He was thus in prison,

20 Pilate therefore, willing to release Jesus, spake again to them.
21 But they cried, saying, Crucify *him*, crucify him.
22 And he said unto them the third time, Why, what evil hath he done? I have found no cause of death in him: I will therefore chastise him, and let *him* go.
23 And they were instant with loud voices, requiring that he might be crucified. And the voices of them and of the chief priests prevailed.
24 And *a* Pilate gave sentence that it should be as they required.
25 And he released unto them him that for sedition and murder was cast into prison, whom they had desired; but he delivered Jesus to their will.

a Matt. 27: 25; Mark 15: 15; John 19: 16.

---

ready to be punished with death. Being of better parentage, his guilt would be the greater; and it was probably because Pilate supposed him to be thought so very bad that he suggested to them (Matthew and Mark) that he would let loose upon them Barabbas, if he condemned Christ. Luke simply assumes that Pilate had proposed to release Jesus and keep Barabbas. The others tell us that his suggestion was encouraged by his knowing that the persecution of Jesus arose not from ill-will of the people, but from the envy of the chief priests, lest the influence of Jesus should supersede theirs. Not only did he not find the people falling in with that, but the influence of the leaders was effectually used (Matt. 27: 20) to enlist an obstreperous demand of the multitude that the insurgent murderer should be released, and Jesus put out of the way. There may well have been many among them who kept aloof from any such demonstration. They were silent; and that so large a proportion of a crowd which, in great part, unquestionably, joined in the applause and adoration of Jesus as the Messiah on the preceding Sunday, now joined in the cry, is a sad illustration of the proverbial fickleness of popular favor.

20. Pilate (omit **therefore**), **willing** (*desirous*) **to release Jesus, spake again** (*called aloud*) **to them.** This was in the midst of their shouting, when it would be hard to make himself heard. What he wanted to say was in the strain of further protestation against wrong to an innocent man.

21. It was of no use. **But they**—instigated by the priests, and many of them now rid of their transient and superficial faith in Jesus—**cried** (*shouted*), ... **Crucify him, crucify him.** It was the first mention of *this* awful mode of execution, and showed how their fury rose as they gave it breath, and how their demand of Pilate increased as they saw more clearly that they could get what they would have.

22. The judge who had lost the opportunity of *deciding* the case, by parleying with the perverters of justice, wastes his breath in repeating assertions of the innocence of their victim, and proposes anew the already rejected substitute for death.

23. And (or, *But*) **they were instant** — urgently insisted — **with loud voices, requiring** (*asking*) **that he might be crucified. Requiring,** in the sense of demanding, would seem the appropriate designation of their act, but is not the natural sense of the Greek verb. —**And the voices of them and of the chief priests prevailed. And of the chief priests** is left out by the best authorities. Against reason and justice, noise carried the day. They got, by sheer pressure of **voices,** what they had neither argument for nor any particle of proof.

24. And Pilate gave sentence that it should be as they required (lit., *that what they asked for should be done*). A sad and shameful verdict. It seemed to our Evangelist so perverse a decision, that we plainly discover the melancholy interest with which he viewed it, in the comment of the next verse.

25. And he released unto them him that for sedition (or, *insurrection*) **and murder was cast into prison, whom they had desired; but he delivered Jesus to their will.** The Revision gives the emphatic arrangement of the Greek: *But Jesus he delivered to their will.* And their will was *the cross.* Monstrous preference! to keep a murderer and destroyer of the public peace, while sending to torture and death the Saviour of human souls—even theirs—the Lord of life and glory. At an early period, as early as

26 ᵃ And as they led him away, they laid hold upon one Simon, a Cyrenian, coming out of the country, and on him they laid the cross, that he might bear it after Jesus.
27 And there followed him a great company of people, and of women, which also bewailed and lamented him.

26 And when they led him away, they laid hold upon one Simon of Cyrene, coming from the country, and laid on him the cross, to bear it after Jesus.
27 And there followed him a great multitude of the people, and of women who bewailed and lamented

ᵃ Matt. 27 : 32; Mark 15 : 21. See John 19 : 17.

Origen's time, there were copies of Matthew's Gospel, which had, in 27: 17, the word "Jesus" before Barabbas: "Jesus Barabbas, or Jesus which is called the Christ." It was a curious mistake, which, having once crept into the text, presented the alternative so forcibly: Will ye have Jesus (the Saviour) Barabbas, or Jesus (the Saviour) that is called the Christ? and would be so rich in homiletical suggestions that it naturally became quite common. Meyer, following Fritsche, and some other respectable critics, supposes that to have been the original reading; but see Westcott and Hort (Appendix, p. 20), and Tregelles on the passage, who give ample reasons for regarding it as an interpolation. The events of this chapter, hitherto, must have busily occupied the time from 5 A. M., or earlier, until about 8 A. M. During a considerable part of it, amid all the movements to and fro, the ribaldry and violence, the clamor and uproar, of which he was the subject, the Divine Sufferer has not uttered one recorded word. "As a sheep before her shearers is dumb, so he openeth not his mouth." But what thoughts must have passed through his mind! What feelings must have torn his heart! He had not closed his eyes in sleep during the preceding night. His experience, from the moment he entered the garden, had been of a kind most exhausting to body and soul, closing with that terrible scourging which Luke alone, of all the Evangelists, has left under the veil of silence.

26-32. THE WAY TO THE CROSS.

26. And as they led him away—from the scene of the trial to the place of crucifixion. That place was doubtless the usual one for the execution of criminals, in which character, merely, these who now had to deal with Jesus would regard him. **They laid hold upon one Simon, a Cyrenian, coming out of the country, and on him they laid the cross, that he might** (or *to*) **bear it after Jesus.** They started with Jesus bearing his cross himself (John 19: 17), according to the custom usual with those who were on the way to crucifixion. We need not think of the cross as being so large and heavy a structure as it is often represented in the pictures. The scarcity of timber in the neighborhood of Jerusalem would hardly allow that, at least for the numbers of Jews that were crucified there sometimes by the Romans. (Jos. *Ant.*, xvii. 10, 10; *Wars* ii. 14, 9). It would contain no more material than enough, when set in the earth, to raise a man clear of the ground, and to support his weight. It is not unlikely that the perpendicular posts may have remained permanently fixed in the place of death, and only the rude cross timber have to be carried thither. (Farrar, *L. of C.*, ii., 393). But in the state of weakness to which we have just seen the Saviour reduced, even this may naturally have overpowered him before he had gone far. At the point where he was ready to sink, they meet **Simon, a Cyrenian**—from Cyrene, a country stretching along the northern coast of Africa. That he was **coming out of the country,** proves nothing as to whether he was first coming into the city, or was resident there for a shorter time (as for the Passover), or for a longer period. Whether he was then a disciple we know not, but from the familiar way in which Mark (15: 21) speaks of him as the father of Alexander and Rufus (compare for the latter, Rom. 16: 13), we judge that he was afterward known as such; possibly as converted at this time. The names were too common, however, to afford any certainty that Alexander and Rufus, occurring later in the New Testament, designate the same men. Him the centurion, sparing the citizens of Jerusalem, impressed into service for relieving Jesus of the burden of the cross.

27. The great multitude which followed probably included, besides those men who gloated over his sufferings, and would feast their eyes with his death, many also that shared only in the popular curiosity that always attends an execution, modified in this case by wonder as to what might happen with one who had so lately received the general

28 But Jesus turning to them said, Daughters of Jerusalem, weep not for me, but weep for yourselves, and for your children.
29 ᵃ For, behold, the days are coming, in the which they shall say, Blessed *are* the barren, and the wombs that never bare, and the paps which never gave suck.
30 ᵇ Then shall they begin to say to the mountains, Fall on us; and to the hills, Cover us.
31 ᶜ For if they do these things in a green tree, what shall be done in the dry?
32 ᵈ And there were also two others, malefactors, led with him to be put to death.
33 And ᵉ when they were come to the place, which is called Calvary, there they crucified him, and the malefactors, one on the right hand, and the other on the left.

28 him. But Jesus turning unto them said, Daughters of Jerusalem, weep not for me, but weep for yourselves, and for your children.
29 For behold, the days are coming, in which they shall say, Blessed are the barren, and the wombs that never bare, and the
30 breasts that never gave suck. Then shall they begin to say to the mountains, Fall on us; and to the
31 hills, Cover us. For if they do these things in the green tree, what shall be done in the dry?
32 And there were also two others, malefactors, led with him to be put to death.
33 And when they came unto the place which is called ᶠ The skull, there they crucified him, and the malefactors, one on the right hand and the other on

a Matt. 24:19; ch. 21:23....b Isa. 2:19; Hosea 10:8; Rev. 6:16; 9:6....c Prov. 11:31; Jer. 25:29; Ezek. 20:47; 21:3, 4; 1 Pet. 4:17....d Isa. 53:12; Matt. 27:38....e Matt. 27:33; Mark 15:22; John 19:17, 18.—ᶠ According to the Latin, *Calvary*, which has the same meaning.

---

worship. Some at least must have felt sympathy and amazement at the strange fortune through which their beloved and trusted leader was now passing. But what was remembered as worthy of record was the outspoken grief of women in the company, who **bewailed** — with vehement gestures of woe—**and lamented him.** They are addressed afterward as daughters of Jerusalem; but this does not, from Old Testament usage, hinder our supposing there were among them some of those who came with him from Perea and Galilee.

28. This manifestation of interest in his suffering, bold even in its weakness, had power to unseal the closed lips of Jesus, and draw forth a response, which Luke alone has preserved for us, from the incidents of that hour. **Weep not for me, but weep for yourselves, and for your children.** I am not to be pitied. Great as are my appointed pains, they have a great end in view; they are transient also, and will end in glory and joy. (Heb. 12: 2.) But woeful, indeed, is the experience which I foresee for you and the next generation of this people.

29. **Blessed are the barren,** etc. Those tenderest relations of parentage, which should naturally be an occasion of the richest blessing, will, in the times of starvation and slaughter that are coming, fill life with anxiety, and mourning, and horror, and inflict a sharper pang on mothers, famished, or dying of violence, as they think of the woes of their children left behind.

30. An application of the prophecy in Hosea 10: 8. Comp. Isa. 2: 19; Rev. 6: 16; 9: 6. It was originally intended to picture the helplessness and despair of God's enemies, when they find the threats of punishment which they have despised now receiving fulfillment, perhaps in the caves and recesses of the mountains, to which they have fled for unavailing shelter. All this would be eminently fulfilled in the near history of the Jewish nation; and the more dreadfully, by reason of this crowning crime of crucifying their Messiah.

31. The aim of this obscure verse is evidently—**for**—to confirm the prediction just uttered. The **green tree** represents the innocent and holy Saviour in the spirituality and vigor of his life; **the dry** tree, the morally dead and sapless people, typified by the fig-tree, blasted by his word, four days ago. The figure involved in the verse, lies in the comparative facility with which fire, the symbol of wrath, kindles upon a dry tree and a green. If **they,** these wicked rulers, so easily vent their wrath on me, what will be done to them by God!

32. It is probable that Pilate, having two criminals awaiting execution, took this opportunity to put them to death, as much to signify his contempt for the Jews and their solemn feast-day, as for the convenience of disposing of three cases at once. He was, unconsciously, fulfilling the prophecy: "And he made his grave with the wicked," "And he was numbered with the transgressors." (Isa. 53: 9-12). It has, not without some force, been urged by those who hold this Friday to have been only the preparation for the Passover, that the scribes, however ready to allow the death of Jesus to be perpetrated, would not, without remonstrance, have suffered the great Paschal Sabbath to be defiled by ordinary executions.

33-38. JESUS RAISED UPON THE CROSS, AND AGAIN MOCKED.

33. And when they were come to the

place, which is called Calvary (or, *The skull*). The local and vernacular name was Golgotha, as given in the other Gospels. This signified, in the Aramæan tongue, *a skull*, the Greek word for which was naturally used by Luke. That was the meaning of the Latin word *Calvaria*, also, which served to translate the Greek in the early Latin versions, and so came into the early English versions from the Latin. The name was *probably* applied to the place before us from some resemblance of form to that of the crown of the skull. If so, that is the only intimation of any "hill" there—("hill of Calvary")—even of the slightest elevation. We can say nothing further concerning the locality than what the Scripture itself affords us, with any certainty whatever. From Hebrews 13: 12, we infer that it was "without the gate," and John 19: 20 tells us that "the place where Jesus was crucified was nigh to the city." That is all we can know as to its distance from, or its relations to, the city. In that locality, there was a garden, and in the garden, a tomb (John 19: 41). Accordingly, we find in the present city of Jerusalem a Church of the Holy Sepulchre, which conveniently shows under its one roof the cave of the entombment, and the place where the cross stood. The evidence in favor of that being the place is as trustworthy as that which abounds in Roman Catholic churches in favor of the genuineness of pieces of the "true cross," or of a bone of John the Baptist. The arguments *pro* and *con* may be seen balanced in Smith, *Dict. of Bib.*, Art. Palestine; Robinson's *Bib. Geography;* and Ritter's *Geog. of Pal.*, Gage's Translation.—**There they crucified him**—meaning here, precisely, raised him upon the cross. It is well, once for all, to consult a full description of the punishment by the cross, in any good Bible Dictionary, or in a work on Jewish Antiquities, as Jahn's *Archæology.* It was not, properly, a Jewish practice, but, derived from the East, and from the Semites of Northern Africa, it had become common through the Macedonian and Roman Empires. It was employed only in the case of the most desperate criminals, and of slaves. The cross was, as we have described it on verse 26; yet some report that, instead of the single cross-piece, on which the arms were stretched, two pieces were sometimes used, so fitted to the post that the arms extended obliquely forward. See Geikie, *Life of Christ,* ii., 558. In the middle of the upright stick was fixed a stout peg, astride of which the sufferer was relieved of a part of the excruciating burden upon his hands. Sometimes, as it appears, he was attached to the cross before that was set in the ground; but, usually, not till afterward. The hands were nailed to the cross bar, the feet (whether separately?) to the upright below. Winer, *Realwörterbuch,* Art. Kreuzzigung, strongly maintains, however, that the feet were not, *ordinarily*, pinned, but only bound. His citations should be critically compared with those of John. In the case of strong men, in full vitality, death might not follow from this infliction for several days; not, indeed, until hunger produced it. From the first moment, however, the pain of the lacerated limbs; the impeded circulation through the whole distorted frame; the fever, and naked exposure to the weather,—were trials such as to make death seem a blessing, and to insure its arrival, in most cases, in two or three days. It is a truly horrible fate to think of, in the case even of malefactors, such as those who were to suffer on either side of Jesus, and supposing them to have been the worst wretches that ever ravaged human society. When we would mention it in connection with our gracious Lord, whose whole life was one of stainless innocence, of perfect righteousness, of self-sacrificing kindness toward all men, the pen refuses to complete the description. Yet it is well, sometimes, to dwell upon the facts which are intimated in the trite phrase, "the sufferings of Christ," and when we say we believe that "he suffered under Pontius Pilate." Suffered—what? Happily, we need not and cannot comprehend it all; but we may profitably remember that, with all that infinite physical anguish, the holy soul of our Saviour grieved at a fate so contrary to his proper desert—almost forsaken by friends, the laughing stock of his foes, and under that unimaginable consciousness that he was enduring it all as the representative of a sinful race, even of those who were putting him to death—dying thus himself, that they might not eternally die. One touch of mercy seems to have been given to the Crucifixion by the Romans, or, possibly, by Jewish compassion, but of which Jesus chose not to share the intended advantage. They were accustomed to give to the condemned person a stupefying potion before he was nailed to the cross, that

[Ch. XXIII.] LUKE. 337

34 Then said Jesus, Father, *a* forgive them; for they know not what they do. And *b* they parted his raiment, and cast lots.
35 And *c* the people stood beholding. And the *d* rulers also with them derided *him*, saying, "He saved others; let him save himself, if he be Christ, the chosen of God.
36 And the soldiers also mocked him, coming to him, and offering him vinegar,

34 the left. [And Jesus said, Father, forgive them; for they know not what they do. And parting his garments among them, they cast lots. And the people stood beholding. And the rulers also scoffed at him, saying, He saved others; let him save himself, if this is the Christ of God, his chosen. And the soldiers also mocked him, coming to him, offering him

a Matt. 5: 44; Acts 7: 60; 1 Cor. 4: 12....*b* Acts 3: 17....*c* Matt. 27: 35; Mark 15: 24; John 19: 23....*d* Ps. 22: 17; Zech. 12: 10....*e* Matt. 27: 39; Mark 15: 29.——1 Some ancient authorities omit, And Jesus said, Father, forgive them; for they know not what they do.

his susceptibility to pain might be diminished. It was a mixture of the juice or extract of some bitter herb with myrrh, in wine; and this, according to Matthew and Mark, was offered to Jesus the first thing, but refused by him. He would pass through his appointed trial with faculties clear, and all his powers in full exercise.

34. Then said Jesus, Father, forgive them; for they know not what they do. This was probably spoken at the moment when they began their horrid task of torture. He must have had reference, not to the Roman soldiers, who were actually inflicting the pain, but to those Jewish scribes and priests who were virtually doing it, as they were actually gloating over it. That Jesus should, even in that extreme agony, pray for those who were persecuting him unto the death, is a sublime, but not amazing, exhibition of the spirit which he ever inculcated on his followers (Matt. 5: 44; compare Isa. 53: 12); but it has in all ages seemed strange to many that he could say they knew not what they were doing. Yet Peter, addressing a part of this same company (Acts 3. 17), said, "I wot that through ignorance ye did it, as did also your rulers." In neither case was the statement intended to clear them from blame. It purported only that, blinded by prejudice and self-interest, or, naturally influenced by leaders who were so, they understood not clearly that they were murdering their Messiah, the Son of God. This was the first of the seven "words" or utterances of Jesus on the cross. Of these Luke gives three (add ver. 43, 46), all additional to what are preserved in the other Gospels. The other four are—John 19: 26: "Woman, behold thy son"; Matthew 27: 46; Mark 15: 34, "Eloi, Eloi, lama sabachthani?" John 19: 28, "I thirst"; and 19: 30, "It is finished." **And they parted his raiment, and cast lots.** Compare Revision. The person crucified was usually stripped naked; and the four soldiers that carried out the execution of each victim regarded his clothes as their perquisite.

John (19: 23, 24) gives the detail of their proceedings. Luke summarily says that they distributed all by lot.

35. And the people stood beholding. They are not said to have derided him. More humane and sympathetic, apparently, than the class above them, this class looked on with wonder, and many, we may be assured, with grief; contrasting this end with what their crude hopes had promised five days before. **And the rulers also** (omit **with them**) **derided him**—as well as looked with the people. **Derided**—jeered; the Greek denotes the most intense mockery. See on ch. 16: 14. They added to derisive looks and gestures, taunting words; saying, **He saved others; let him save himself, if he be Christ, the chosen of God.** The Revision reads properly, "The Christ of God, his chosen." The **he** was ironically emphatic. **Saved**—in the mouths of these people—meant no more than deliverance from pains and bodily evils. In that view there was a certain point in their ridicule. Little did they imagine that only by thus suffering unto death could their innocent victim become, in the highest sense, a Saviour, "the author of eternal salvation" to those who should be willing to suffer with him. Their taunt became very familiar to his disciples, as it was repeated wherever they went, in the first ages—the absurdity of presenting as a Saviour, one who had died on the cross.

36. And the soldiers also—Romans and heathen, as well as Jews—**mocked him**—made sport of him—**coming to him, and offering him vinegar.** There may probably have been three quaternions of the soldiers, one for each cross. To their hardened souls, yet not harder than the Jewish priests, no dignity was sacred, all suffering was simply food for laughter. They, accordingly, had their own brutal way of making amusement out of the most exquisite agony that was ever known. Being aware that Jesus was suffering as one called King, they came with mock

W

37 And saying, If thou be the King of the Jews, save thyself.
38 *a* And a superscription also was written over him in letters of Greek, and Latin, and Hebrew, THIS IS THE KING OF THE JEWS.
39 *b* And one of the malefactors which were hanged railed on him, saying, If thou be Christ, save thyself and us.
40 But the other answering rebuked him, saying, Dost not thou fear God, seeing thou art in the same condemnation?
41 And we indeed justly; for we receive the due

37 vinegar, and saying, If thou art the King of the
38 Jews, save thyself. And there was also a superscription over him, THIS IS THE KING OF THE JEWS.
39 And one of the malefactors that were hanged railed on him, saying, Art not thou the Christ? save
40 thyself and us. But the other answered, and rebuking him said, Dost thou not even fear God, seeing thou art in the same condemnation? And we
41 indeed justly; for we receive the due reward of our

a Matt. 27: 37; Mark 15: 26; John 19: 19....*b* Matt. 27: 44; Mark 15: 32.

reverence, offering him vinegar, *i. e.*, the soured wine of their own drink, mingled with water. At a later hour (Matt. 27: 48), some one, moved with real compassion, reached to his mouth a sponge filled with vinegar, that he might taste it, if he would; but now they brought it before him, tantalizing him, if possible, with the sight of what he could not touch. It was a savage jest.

37. They here took up the gibe of the Jews (ver. 35), and handed it down in the Gentile line—a stumbling-block to Jews, and to Greeks foolishness. (1 Cor. 1: 23.)

38. And a superscription also was written over him. . . . This is the King of the Jews. This had probably been attached to the upper extremity of the cross, over his head, immediately when Jesus was raised upon it. It had been written by Pilate himself, or by his order (John 19: 19). Mark (15: 26) speaks of it as a customary thing; and it is known to have been usual to carry a sign before the condemned, stating his offence, or (perhaps, also) to have it proclaimed by a crier. Luke mentions the inscription here, either to show why the soldiers addressed Christ as King of the Jews, or, more probably, as an additional feature of the mockery. The different forms of the "title" in the Four Evangelists, may be accounted for, largely, by the variations of expression for the one thought in the three languages (John 19: 20) in which it had been written. Luke might have rendered literally into Greek an Aramæan sentence, KING OF THE JEWS, *he* (the IS is not expressed in the Greek). "He," thus used, would be likely to convey a shade of contempt (often given in our Gospels as "this *fellow*"). This was intended by Pilate as an insult to the Jews, who, when they saw the aim of his sentence, would realize that in yielding to them he had given them again a dagger stab. See Josephus, *Antiq.*, xviii. 3, 2. Hence their vain petition to Pilate (John 19: 21, 22) that it might be changed.

39-43. THE PENITENT MALEFACTOR.

39. And one of the malefactors which were hanged railed on him. Were hanged intimates simply the suspended position of one on the cross. Matthew and Mark speak in the plural, of "the thieves also which were crucified with him," "they that were crucified with him," as having reproached him. From this, it is probable that, at first, both taunted him. It was evidently brought into the early and commonly diffused account as another instance, and an eminent one, of the obloquy vented on Jesus by passers by, by priests and scribes, by soldiers, and now by fellow-sufferers. With that aspect of the case, the first two Gospels stop, especially as these were both only malefactors, while Luke, in his researches, found the additional fact here following, for which the world must ever remain indebted to his truly catholic Gospel.—**If thou be Christ** (or, in the true text, *Art not thou the Christ*), **save thyself and us.** This might, in itself, be understood as no worse than an impatient and faithless appeal to Jesus, on the ground of his Messiahship, to save them from their wretched condition. But the **thou** has, in the Greek, a sarcastic tone, and the statement of the narrator, as well as the comment of the other felon, shows that it was spoken (comp. ver. 35, 37) in ridicule.

40. But the other—now, at least, fully convinced of the Messiahship of his companion in distress—**answering, rebuked him, saying.** The rebuke consisted in what follows: **Dost not thou**—an echo of "thou" in the other's question to Jesus—(*even*) **fear God**—not even fear him, to say nothing of repentance and prayer to him—**seeing thou art in the same condemnation**—under a sentence of death, and therefore about to stand before God.

41. And we indeed justly—stand in this condemnation—**for we receive the due reward of our deeds.** It has been, not un-

reward of our deeds: but this man hath done nothing amiss.
42 And he said unto Jesus, Lord, remember me when thou comest into thy kingdom.
43 And Jesus said unto him, Verily I say unto thee, To-day shalt thou be with me in paradise.
44 ᵃ And it was about the sixth hour, and there was a darkness over all the earth until the ninth hour.

42 deeds: but this man hath done nothing amiss. And he said, Jesus, remember me when thou comest ¹ in
43 thy kingdom. And he said unto him, Verily I say unto thee, To-day shalt thou be with me in Paradise.
44 And it was now about the sixth hour, and a darkness came over the whole ²land until the ninth

ᵃ Matt. 27: 45; Mark 15: 33.——¹ Some ancient authorities read, into thy kingdom....² Or, earth.

reasonably, conjectured that these "robbers" had been concerned in the affair with Barabbas, which involved "insurrection and murder." **But this man hath done nothing amiss.** Not only has committed no crime, done no wrong, as against any human law, but has done nothing **amiss**, bad, improper. This defence of Jesus supposes much more knowledge of him than what the speaker could have gathered on this scene, as still more evidently does his prayer which follows. From the wide publicity of Christ's travels and teaching, through the country as well as the city and towns, nothing is more supposable than that the man had heard him speak, and got some idea of his principles, claims, and promises.

42. And he said unto Jesus, Lord, remember me when thou comest into (in) thy kingdom. Into is unwarranted by the text used by the translators of 1611. They should have written *in*. Westcott and Hort have now adopted "into," but on hardly convincing authority. It is not possible to overestimate the clearness and strength of faith which could lead the man with such earnestness to recognize in his fellow-sufferer a king, who was afterward to reappear in royal majesty. He even commits his eternal interests into that king's hands. The thought of his prayer was, probably, "in the gathering together of thy subjects, when thou comest again in royal power, do not condemn and to save, do not forget to call me from the grave, and place me among thy redeemed." It was, in his mind, a distant blessing for which he thus humbly prayed. As given in the Common Version, supported by Westcott and Hort, the sense of the prayer might, in consistency with the circumstances, probably be, "When thou comest back into thy promised reign as Messiah on the earth, forget not to let me share in its blessings."

43. In granting his prayer, Jesus assures him, not of a far distant, but an immediate, blessing. **Verily I say unto thee, To-day shalt thou be with me in paradise. To-day** has the place of emphasis. The sum of the promise is, "I will remember thee then; and, as the earnest of it, thou shalt at once be with me in the region of the blessed dead."—**Paradise**—a word of Persian, or Armenian, origin, meant, probably, a pleasure-garden, or beautiful park. Transferred into the later Hebrew, it is translated "orchard" (Cant. 4: 13), "garden" (Eccl. 2: 5), "forest" (Neh. 2: 8), and, spelled in Greek letters, as here, it is used in the Septuagint to translate the Hebrew for "garden," as the "Garden of Eden." Thus it was freely adopted to denote a place of delight; and we find it in the later portions of the New Testament as a synonym for heaven, or at least some part of the immediate home of God (2 Cor. 12: 4; Rev. 2: 7)—"paradise of God." Some think that to be the reference here; but, as Acts 2: 31 (comp. Acts 2: 27; 1 Pet. 3: 18, 19) seems plainly to teach that Jesus spent the interval between his death and resurrection in the world of the dead, or at least went directly thither, it is generally thought more likely that in our passage Paradise is, rather, that sphere of Hades—the general receptacle of the dead—in which the saints are happy in "Abraham's bosom." See note on ch. 16: 23. Certain early church Fathers, following Jewish speculations, supposed the Garden of Eden still to exist as a scene of extra-mundane felicity, neither in heaven nor on earth. (Grimm, *Clavis*, s. v.) The penitent on the cross would understand it in the sense common among his countrymen at that time. Indeed, if Christ had spoken directly in Greek, the language used here would naturally have reached the allegorical meaning, consciously, through the literal and primary: To-day wilt thou be with me in the pleasure-garden (ἐν τῷ παραδείσῳ).

44–49. THE LAST SCENE. MID-DAY DARKNESS. A SILENCE OF THREE HOURS, BROKEN ONLY BY AN EXPIRING WORD.

44. And it was (*now*) about the sixth hour—12 M. Our Lord had been three hours

45 And the sun was darkened, and *the veil of the temple was rent in the midst.
46 And when Jesus had cried with a loud voice, he said, *Father, into thy hands I commend my spirit: *and having said thus, he gave up the ghost.

45 hour, ¹the sun's light failing: and the veil of the
46 ²temple was rent in the midst. ³And Jesus, crying with a loud voice, said, Father, into thy hands I commend my spirit: and having said this, he gave

a Matt. 27: 51; Mark 15: 38....b Ps. 31: 5; 1 Pet. 2: 23....c Matt. 27: 50; Mark 15: 37; John 19: 30.——1 Gr. *the sun failing*----2 Or, *sanctuary*....3 Or, *And when Jesus had cried with a loud voice, he said.*

on the cross (Mark 15: 25), and the agony from his wounds, and the distorted posture in which he hung, might have made further speech impossible. **And there was a darkness over all the earth** (better, *the whole land*) **until the ninth hour.** How must all mockery and jeering have been turned into amazement and fear! The secondary cause of it, if there was any, cannot be known. The efficient cause was God's power, exerted so as to veil from human eyes the closing pains of his own dear Son.

45. And the sun was darkened (rather, *the sun's light failing*). This adds to the preceding statement of the fact of darkness, simply that it was due to a darkening of the sun, by which light was cut off everywhere. Or, is the thought of the writer that darkness spread over the face of the earth so dense and broad that the sun itself was hidden from view? The text followed by the Revision is clear of ambiguity, and assigns a true cause of the darkness. "The sun's light"—or, more directly, "the sun failing." The terms used are those appropriate in Greek to signify an eclipse; but might be used to mark an effect like that of an eclipse, without asserting that the moon then shut out the light. That, of course, would be an imposibility at the Passover season, when the moon was full. It is difficult to decide between the texts; but the authority for the latter seems at least fully equal to that against it. No explanation of the fact, however, which attempted to do away with its miraculous character, would be consistent with the earthquake, the torn veil of the temple, the rending of the rocks, and bursting of tombs (Matt. 27: 51, ff.)—all in sympathy with the Divine Sufferer on the cross. **And the veil of the temple was rent in the midst.** This veil was the great and splendid curtain which served in part as the partition, in the temple, between the inner shrine, "holy of holies," and the outer sanctuary, in which some priest must visit the altar of incense every day. Beyond that dividing veil had been the ark, in the tabernacle, and in the first temple, and the cherubim over the ark,

the seat of the Shechinah, whither only the high priest could ever penetrate, and he only once in the year, to make atonement for the sins of the people. The tearing of that veil from the top to the bottom, in connection with the death of Christ, was suited better than anything else imaginable to shadow forth the end of the office of the earthly high priest, and the opening of a new and living way, by which every one, through Christ's all sufficient sacrifice, may approach the very throne of God for himself. This event took place near the end of the three hours of darkness. Luke mentions no word spoken during this awful interval, and we can only dimly imagine what thoughts and feelings occupied the mind of our Lord. From the first two Gospels we may gather something of the intensity of his distress, by their one recorded utterance: "My God, my God, why hast thou forsaken me!" Such was his sense of abandonment and solitariness in that dreadful gloom; so intolerable and overwhelming were his pains of body and mind; that for the moment, while we must believe that his Father had never been more well pleased in him, it was to him as if God had utterly forsaken him, and left him without sympathy or aid. See the valuable notes on that passage in Doctor W. N. Clarke's *Commentary* on Mark, in this series. It might have been about that time that there was extorted from him the one only expression of natural infirmity—"I thirst" (John 19: 28). Somewhat later the darkness echoed the words "It is finished," and the scene closes with a sentence which Luke alone records.

46. And when Jesus had cried with a loud voice, he said—rather, *And crying with a loud voice, Jesus said.* It was the last effort of dissolving nature. Not as if he were yet in full strength; we have seen reasons above why, physically, Jesus could not be expected long to survive that accumulation of sufferings; but as is often seen that, just before a lingering death, the remnant of life blazes forth in one supreme effort, so Jesus, with a full and distinct voice, uttered these

CH. XXIII.] LUKE. 341

47 *Now when the centurion saw what was done, he glorified God, saying, Certainly this was a righteous man.
48 And all the people that came together to that sight, beholding the things which were done, smote their breasts, and returned.
49 *And all his acquaintance, and the women that followed him from Galilee, stood afar off, beholding these things.

47 up the ghost. And when the centurion saw what was done, he glorified God, saying, Certainly this
48 was a righteous man. And all the multitudes that came together to this sight, when they beheld the things that were done, returned smiting their
49 breasts. And all his acquaintance, and the women that followed with him from Galilee, stood afar off, seeing these things.

a Matt. 27: 54; Mark 15: 39....b Ps. 38: 11; Matt. 27: 55; Mark 15: 40. See John 19: 38.

---

last words: **Father, into thy hands I commend my spirit.** It is the language now of calm and filial trust in a Father consciously present. "I intrust to thy charge and disposition that life which I received of thee, and which has accomplished thy appointed work, borne all thy holy will." **Spirit** is, here, the principle of life. Comp. ch. 8: 55; James 2: 26.—**And having said thus** (rather, *this*), **he gave up the ghost** (or, *he expired*). That, of course, is what the verb here, translated strictly, means; but the translators and revisers have, perhaps, been moved to retain it in this passage, and in Mark 15: 37, 39, instead of giving its direct sense, to favor the idea that Jesus gave up his life in some other sense than that in which Stephen, or Paul, or John yielded his. It is, indeed, noticeable that both the expressions for Christ's decease ("gave up the ghost," Matthew and John) avoid the usual word, "died." This, we suppose, is not so much because they thought of what he had said in John 10: 18, but because they thought of him, in an altogether peculiar way, as alive even in death; he was dead, and is alive, and liveth forevermore. In the death of our Lord, moreover, it is involved, necessarily, that there was a unique consent of his will to the will of his Father, known beforehand, that he should thus die. But this must be so thought of as to distinguish it from everything like the voluntary shortening of his stay in life. How terrible, even to our apprehension, was that misery, in view of which, prolonged through those hours of agony, we breathe more freely, knowing that the Son of man is dead! His pains are ended, and he has entered into "the joy that was set before him." By this one sacrifice of himself, all other sacrifices are forever superseded, as a condition of the forgiveness of sin, and of full salvation.

47-49. IMPRESSION MADE UPON BEHOLDERS.

47. On the centurion. Now when the centurion—who had charge of the soldiers that wrought the crucifixion—**saw what was done**—the death of Christ in that manner, and all the wonderful phenomena attending it—**he glorified God**—by rendering due honor, though late, to God's Servant and Messiah—**saying, Certainly this was a righteous man.** Both his own manifestations of character and God's remarkable interposition in his case proved it.—**Righteous man** is only an interpretation of the sentiment which in the other Synoptics took the form, "a (not *the*) Son of God."

48. The multitude. And all the people (literally, *multitudes*) **that came together to that** (rather, *this*) **sight.** This describes the mass of the people whom we have seen attracted to the vicinity of the cross, as to any popular spectacle (θεωρία, a sight), and who "stood beholding" (ver. 35), not reviling. Even the rabble that mocked may also have been referred to now, as changed in their views and feelings, by **beholding the things which were done**—a more comprehensive expression than that in the preceding verse.—**Smote their breasts, and returned.** They felt that great cruelty and a horrible wrong had been committed on an innocent person, and may have feared the vengeance of that God who had so exhibited his displeasure in the heavens above them and the solid earth beneath.

49. The nearer circle. And all his acquaintance—those who had some interest in him from personal knowledge, including even some disciples, probably, that lingered in amazement—**and the women that followed** (*with*) **him from Galilee.** See 8: 1-3. They neither skulked, nor were so lost in the crowd as to be undistinguishable. Their names are several of them given in the parallel narratives. The word **stood** is emphatic in this place, as if, while others were breaking up, or had left the ground, they remained, unwilling to abandon the spot. Thus we

50 *a* And, behold, *there was* a man named Joseph, a counsellor; *and he was* a good man, and a just:
51 (The same had not consented to the counsel and deed of them;) *he was* of Arimathea, a city of the Jews: *b* who also himself waited for the kingdom of God.
52 This *man* went unto Pilate, and begged the body of Jesus.

50 And behold, a man named Joseph, who was a
51 councillor, a good man and a righteous (he had not consented to their counsel and deed), *a man* of Arimathea, a city of the Jews, who was looking for
52 the kingdom of God: this man went unto Pilate, and

a Matt. 27 : 57 ; Mark 15 : 42 ; John 19 : 38....*b* Mark 15 : 43 ; ch. 2 : 25, 38.

notice a three-fold rendering of homage to Jesus after his death: of the centurion; of the Jewish multitude; of Christ's acquaintances and disciples. And the attentive reader will have seen, in these last chapters, that there were three forms of trial before the Jewish authorities, and as many sentences to death for blasphemy; three accusations before the secular magistrates, Pilate and Herod, and as many declarations of innocence.

50-56. THE BURIAL.

Of course, no friends of Jesus could have previously made any preparations for the burial of their Master, and no known friend was in a situation that he could do it now, when the necessity appeared. Yet how much depended on his being buried in some way like that which God had planned. To men it might indeed seem that no necessity for burial had arisen, since the bodies of those crucified were commonly left on the cross until burial was no longer possible. But here that difficulty was obviated by the ceremonial sanctity of those Jews who had slain Jesus, but could not bear that his unburied corpse should remain into the next day, which was a day of a great Sabbath. That would defile their city, and hinder the worthy celebration of their feast. This led them to ask and obtain of Pilate (John 19: 31) that the body should be taken down that night. So it was, not a bone having been broken, after his side had been pierced with a spear, so that there flowed from it mingled blood and water, which the bursted arteries had allowed to collect about his heart. And now the providence of God calls forth out of the darkness two men, able and willing, with the faithful women, to do the rest.

50. **And, behold**—a divine interposition!—(Omit the words **there was**) **a man named Joseph** (*who was*) **a counsellor**—a member of the Sanhedrin, and so of eminent respectability—**a good man, and a just**=*righteous*—excellent in general character, and scrupulously upright and just. He would neither as a private man do wrong, nor, as a counsellor, sanction injustice. This is proved by the parenthetic sentence:

51. **The same** (or, *He*) **had not consented to the counsel and deed of them**—(better, *their counsel*, etc.), namely, in condemning Jesus. Matthew adds that he was rich, which made his intervention here the more effectual. His residence—**Arimathea**—was, apparently, the city of Samuel's parents (1 Sam. 1 : 1), Ramathaim; called, also (1 Sam. 1 : 19), Ramah, which is supposed to have lain a few miles north of Jerusalem.—**Who also himself waited** (or, *was looking*) **for the kingdom of God**. This is a proper description of most of that class who had, during the life of Jesus, shown a readiness to receive him. That one so prominent, before unheard of, should appear at this dark hour, may help to explain the instances of seeming friendliness toward Jesus which we have more than once had to notice, on the part of Pharisees. Such were anticipating the near advent of the Messiah, and were more free to consider his claims. Joseph, indeed, had before this become a disciple of Jesus (Matt. 27 : 57), so far as to believe in his Messianic character and claims, but had concealed this fact (John 19 : 38) until now. Strange revelation! to be made at such an hour, of a brotherhood with the band of scattered and dismayed disciples, in attachment to the Saviour slain, on the part of one of the members of the great Council of the nation.

52. **This man went unto Pilate, and begged** (simply, *asked for*) **the body of Jesus**. The act was a strange one, as seldom did any person concern himself about the body of one who had been gibbeted on a cross. It even required a considerable boldness, at the time, to show an interest in that man's body. But the character and social position of Joseph would now stand him in hand; and Pilate, after making himself sure that Jesus was really dead so soon, freely granted his request. Cicero states that the Roman procurators sometimes exacted money of those who desired the bodies of their friends. Meantime, another secret disciple, Nicodemus,

Ch. XXIII.] LUKE. 343

53 *And he took it down, and wrapped it in linen, and laid it in a sepulchre that was hewn in stone, wherein never man before was laid.
54 And that day was *the preparation, and the sabbath drew on.
55 And the women also, *which came with him from Galilee, followed after, and *beheld the sepulchre, and how his body was laid.
56 And they returned, and *prepared spices and ointments; and rested the sabbath day *according to the commandment.

53 asked for the body of Jesus. And he took it down, and wrapped it in a linen cloth, and laid him in a tomb that was hewn in stone, where never man had yet lain. And it was the day of the Preparation,
54 55 and the sabbath ¹drew on. And the women, that had come with him out of Galilee, followed after, and beheld the tomb, and how his body was laid.
56 And they returned, and prepared spices and ointments.

---

a Matt. 27 : 59; Mark 15 : 46....b Matt. 27 : 62....c ch. 8 : 2....d Mark 15 : 47....e Mark 16 : 1..../ Ex. 20 : 10.—1 Gr. *began to dawn*.

---

of similar standing among the Jews, although we are not told expressly that he was a member of the Council, came to take part in this pious care for the remains of the Teacher sent from God (John 19 : 39, 40). There had, probably, been concert between him and Joseph.

53. And he took it down—with the help of Nicodemus (John 19 : 38-40)—**and wrapped it in linen**—*in a linen cloth*. The deceitful imagination of painters has depicted this simple transaction in a hundred phases of falsehood, to which the simple sentence given to it in each of the Four Evangelists, lends not a shadow of warrant. There is not a hint that any disciple, save Joseph and Nicodemus, had anything to do with it; as, indeed, the women could not properly have. The linen was at once a covering, and a temporary winding-sheet.—**And laid it** (rather, *him*) **in a sepulchre** (better, *tomb*) **that was hewn in stone.** We have already seen that, in the vicinity of the place of crucifixion, was a garden, in the sense in which Gethsemane was a garden; "and in the garden a new sepulchre" (John 19 : 41). From Matthew (27 : 60), we learn further, that Joseph had caused this tomb to be hewn, proving that the property was his. The tomb having been carved out of the rock, would make it a secure receptacle.—**Wherein never man before was laid.** Entirely undefiled, therefore, and more suited, in the estimation of our Lord's followers, to be the resting-place of one so holy as he. Comp. ch. 19 : 30.

54. And that day was the preparation. Although the Scripture had required no such thing, the tradition of the elders had made Friday, after the ninth hour, a preparation for the Sabbath, beginning at sunset. Jos. *Ant.* xvi., 6, 2. This day was not only a preparation for the Sabbath, but for the Passover, in some sense of the word. (John 19 : 14). **And the sabbath drew on**—literally, *the Sabbath was dawning*—a curious transfer of ideas appropriate to the opening light of the natural day, to the deepening twilight of the day beginning with night. There was need of haste, therefore, in disposing of the body before the sacred time should begin. This made the nearness of the new tomb a more manifest favor of Providence.

55. And the women, etc., followed after, and beheld the sepulchre. Although they could take no part in the lowering or draping of the naked body, they had noted, at a distance, what was done, and would not leave the precious relic out of sight, until they had marked the place where it was to rest. As far as appears, if they had not done so, none of the eleven would have known where to look for the Master's body, when the question should arise whether he had risen. Two other Gospels name two in particular, "Mary Magdalene, and the other Mary," "Mary of Joses," who were among these women. The statement that they followed—to see where the tomb was to be—almost of itself refutes the tradition that the cross and tomb were in close proximity, so as to be both included within the compass of the Church in Jerusalem.

56. And they returned—into the city—**and prepared spices and ointments.** These were the aromatic and fragrant substances necessary for anointing the body. They might procure them that evening before business was suspended. Mark expressly says (ch. 16 : 1) that the two Marys bought spices after the Sabbath was past—*i. e.*, after sundown Saturday, and although the tense of his verb there may rarely be used where a pluperfect might have been (as Luke 24 : 1), this ought never to be presumed, where the writing does not intrinsically require it. It would be better to assume, as Luke makes no mention of the hour, that he had put that item of his narrative out of its proper order; or, better still, that the women of whom he speaks were

CHAPTER XXIV.

NOW *upon the first *day* of the week, very early in the morning, they came unto the sepulchre, *bringing the spices which they had prepared, and certain *others* with them.

1 And on the sabbath they rested according to the commandment. But on the first day of the week, at early dawn, they came unto the tomb, bringing

a Matt. 28: 1; Mark 16: 1; John 20: 1....*b* ch. 23: 56.

other than the two Marys, and made their purchases at a different time. **And rested the sabbath day according to the commandment.** This really belongs with the first sentence of the next chapter, as together making one verse, as the rendering and arrangement in the Revision shows. They could not, according to the received views of their time, proceed with even so sacred a labor as the proper laying out of the remains of their revered Master, until the Sabbath was past, and the light of the first day of the week had come. As there was nothing to tell of the word or work or fortune of Christ during the interval, we hear not a syllable out of those thirty-six hours. Yet how much must have passed in the experience of the disciples! A merely human narrative would surely have entertained us with an account of the individual reflections, and the mutual conferences, during that day of memories and anticipations on the part of the disciples of the Lord.

Ch. 24. The chapter is occupied with a summary account of two great events—the Resurrection, and the Ascension—in some of their circumstances and effects.

1-49. THE RESURRECTION.

This is represented to us by Luke in the four stages following: (1.) The tomb is discovered to be empty by certain of the believing women (1-11). (2.) Jesus manifests himself alive to two disciples, on the way to Emmaus (13-32). (3.) He was meantime seen by Simon in Jerusalem (33-35). (4.) He appears to the whole company, as they were comparing accounts, proves to them that he is really risen, and that this is according to the Old Testament Scriptures (36-46.) (5.) Solemnly commissions them to bear witness through the world of these truths (47-49).

The other Gospels mention a number of other appearances of the Saviour to his disciples prior to the ascension. The arranging of them all into a clearly consistent history is, confessedly, a perplexing task, as would be the same in the case of any exciting fact, presenting many phases to many interested persons, all whose accounts might influence the various reports concerning it, that were preserved some time after. Such perplexity is, notoriously, often experienced in reconciling the various proofs of crime committed, which proofs, nevertheless, completely establish the fact of the wrongful deed. All that can be required in such a case is, that on some natural supposition all these reports might be true; and even this would not, ordinarily, be indispensable to their credibility. On such hypotheses, harmonizers of the Gospels have, more or less satisfactorily, arranged the various incidents connected with the resurrection of our Lord.

In all thinking on the subject, it is to be borne in mind that the facts pertaining to the great event of that day, and within the knowledge of some, were practically innumerable; that of these, each writer consciously limits himself to a selection, alluding to some which he does not relate (Matt. 28: 16; Luke 24: 34); that each is determined by his own character, and the specific design of his writing, in the choice which he makes; and that all have a practical, not a philosophical or dialectic end in view, namely: to show that Jesus was alive after his death and burial, so that we, believing in him, may have eternal life. Comp. John 20: 31. More particularly on this last point, it may be important to remark that none of the Synoptics, if even John, writes to *prove* that Jesus rose from death. This was a cardinal fact, not questioned, as would appear, by the Jews of Jerusalem, on the basis of which believers, for whom the Gospel memoirs were written, were believers (1 Cor. 15: 1-8). All that these memoirs did, was to *narrate* such facts connected with the resurrection as their authorities severally furnished them, and as it comported with their respective objects in writing to mention. Quite different might have been their dealing with the facts which they relate, had they proposed them to

Ch. XXIV.] LUKE. 345

2 *And they found the stone rolled away from the sepulchre.
3 *And they entered in, and found not the body of the Lord Jesus.
4 And it came to pass, as they were much perplexed thereabout, *behold, two men stood by them in shining garments:

2 the spices which they had prepared. And they
3 found the stone rolled away from the tomb. And they entered in, and found not the body ¹ of the
4 Lord Jesus. And it came to pass, while they were perplexed thereabout, behold, two men stood by

a Matt. 28:2; Mark 16:4....b ver. 23; Mark 16:5....c John 20:12; Acts 1:10.——1 Some ancient authorities omit. *of the Lord Jesus.*

be traversed by coldly critical unbelievers, not to say that they might have added others, for the simple purpose of averting or silencing skepticism. As it is, there is no trace of any such purpose. Thus, we have not a treatise, an argument, a polemic, but a Gospel, an announcement of glad tidings.

An excellent Essay on this subject is that of Dr. Edward Robinson, in the *Bibliotheca*

STONE AT A JEWISH SEPULCHRE.

Sacra, February, 1845. See also his brief statement in the *Greek Harmony of the Gospels*, p. 258, ff.; Gardiner's note, *Greek Harmony*, p. 253, f. ; and, on the principles of comparison of the Gospels, especially Westcott, *Introduction to the Study of the Gospels*, ch. vi., p. 325, ff.

1-12. THE TOMB FOUND VACANT.

1. Now upon the first day of the week, etc. This, as we saw at the close of the preceding chapter, is but the complement of the sentence there begun: "The preparations for anointing the Lord's body were interrupted,

indeed, by the rest of the Sabbath, but were resumed at the first light of the next day." **Very early in the morning:** literally, *at deep dawn.* This shows their diligence to complete the delayed duty of suitably disposing of the beloved relic. The subject of the sentence, **they came,** etc., is "the women" of 23 : 55.—**Bringing the spices.** Powdered aromatic substances and fluid perfumes appear to have been used in laying out the dead body for burial. Nothing is said of embalming—a practice not in any strict sense employed by the Hebrews: but we are told (Mark 16: 1) that their design was to "anoint" the body.

2. And they found the stone rolled away from the sepulchre—*tomb.* This was at once a surprising and a welcome fact; because the stone used to close the entrance to the tomb was so large as to have given the women anxiety about removing it (Mark 16: 3). The rolling it away somewhat favors the idea that the entrance was from the horizontal surface of the ground ; yet the same term might have been employed if the door opened into the perpendicular face of a hill or rock. The latter supposition is the more probable., John uses a more general word—"taken away." See cut of stone at a Jewish sepulchre.

3. And they entered in. This could hardly have included Mary Magdalene, who, when she saw the stone removed, "runs and comes to Simon Peter." (John 20: 2.) **And found not the body.** The Lord had arisen before their arrival, at the earliest dawn. More particularly we are not informed as to the time.

4. Even after the proof of their obtuseness concerning the Saviour's promise, displayed in their plan for anointing the body, one would think that the vacant tomb would have brought it to their mind that he was to rise the third day, so as to leave no room for "*perplexity.*" They may have thought something about those predictions in a blind way, but needed an aid to their faith. And, **behold**

5 And as they were afraid, and bowed down *their* faces to the earth, they said unto them, Why seek ye the living among the dead?
6 He is not here, but is risen: "remember how he spake unto you when he was yet in Galilee,
7 Saying, The Son of man must be delivered into the hands of sinful men, and be crucified, and the third day rise again.
8 And ᵇ they remembered his words,
9 ᶜ And returned from the sepulchre, and told all these things unto the eleven, and to all the rest.
10 It was Mary Magdalene, and ᵈ Joanna, and Mary *the mother* of James, and other *women that were* with them, which told these things unto the apostles.
11 ᵉ And their words seemed to them as idle tales, and they believed them not.

5 them in dazzling apparel: and as they were affrighted, and bowed down their faces to the earth, they said unto them, Why seek ye ¹ the living
6 among the dead? ² He is not here, but is risen: remember how he spake unto you when he was yet
7 in Galilee, saying that the Son of man must be delivered up into the hands of sinful men, and be
8 crucified, and the third day rise again. And they
9 remembered his words, and returned ³ from the tomb, and told all these things to the eleven, and to
10 all the rest. Now they were Mary Magdalene, and Joanna, and Mary the *mother* of James: and the other women with them told these things unto the
11 apostles. And these words appeared in their sight

a Matt. 16:21; 17:23; Mark 8:31; 9:31; ch. 9:22....b John 2:22....c Matt. 28:8; Mark 16:10....d ch. 8:3....e Mark 16:11; ver. 25.——1 Gr. *him that liveth.*...2 Some ancient authorities omit, *He is not here, but is risen*....3 Some ancient authorities omit, *from the tomb.*

two men stood by them in shining garments. It was the form of men which they saw; but the lustre of their apparel was that peculiar to angelic epiphanies (John 20:12; Acts 1:10), although the appearance of Moses and Elijah on the Mount of Transfiguration had probably been similar, as the raiment of Jesus himself certainly was at that time (ch. 9:29,30). 'It was the earthly parallel to the unspeakable brilliance and glory of heaven.

5. Afraid—*affrighted*—**and bowed down their faces to the earth**—the posture of awe and reverence. **Why seek ye the living** (properly, *him who is living*) **among the dead?**—in a tomb, where the dead alone are ordinarily found. There were no dead really in that tomb.

6, 7, He is not here, but is risen. This simple and obvious explanation has now to be confirmed to them (it could not be more plainly proved) by the very language which Jesus himself had repeatedly spoken to them, not long before—**Remember how he spake unto you when he was yet in Galilee.** (Ch. 9:22; comp. ch. 18; 32 f). The fulfillment so exact of the former part of his prediction might well have prepared them to believe the whole of it.

8. And they remembered his words, and understood them now; and, doubtless, began to wonder whether the word concerning resurrection might not have come true. How much trouble would they have spared themselves, had they sooner taken his explicit language to heart! But then *we* should have lacked one proof of the reality of the resurrection, which comes to us from the perfect absence, on their part, of all suspicion that any such thing had taken place, until the evidence thrust upon them from many sources became overwhelming.

9. And returned from the sepulchre, etc. It is reasonably supposed that they may have done this by different routes, and that the various experiences of two (or more) parties of them may have occasioned differences in the several narratives.—**Unto the eleven.** This is now the designation of the remaining body of the disciples, and might be employed where the number was not complete.—**And all the rest.** Not only **the eleven,** had regained courage and faith; but other adherents of Jesus, of whom we afterward find one hundred and twenty assembled, had begun to associate again with the apostles.

10. All the Evangelists mention Mary Magdalene as one who was first at the tomb, and the first two include other two Marys; all these stating this fact at the beginning. Luke writes as if it had now occurred to him that he had omitted this statement, and needed to supply the lack. He also adds, what the other Gospels presuppose, that there were others with the Marys.—**Mary Magdalene** (see ch. 8:2), **Joanna** (ch. 8:3).—**Mary the mother of James,** viz.: James the Less, as he is called, to distinguish him from James the son of Zebedee. We thus identify her with "Mary the wife of *Clopas,*" John 19:25, Revision, but not with the sister of our Lord's mother, there mentioned. The latter half of the verse reads, in the best text, as represented by the Revision, omitting **which.**

11. And their words seemed to them (*appeared in their sight*) **as idle tales.** The apostles, we might almost say, were kept from believing in the resurrection of Jesus until all, in succession, had the evidence of personal demonstration, that they might the more convincingly testify of this fact to the world.

12 ᵃThen arose Peter, and ran unto the sepulchre; and stooping down, he beheld the linen clothes laid by themselves, and departed, wondering in himself at that which was come to pass.
13 ᵇ And, behold, two of them went that same day to a village called Emmaus, which was from Jerusalem *about* threescore furlongs.

12 as idle talk; and they disbelieved them. ¹ But Peter arose, and ran unto the tomb; and stooping and looking in, he seeth the linen cloths by themselves; and he ᵃdeparted to his home, wondering at that which was come to pass.
13 And behold, two of them were going that very day to a village named Emmaus, which was three-

a John 20: 3, 6.....*b* Mark 16: 12.——1 Some ancient authorities omit ver. 12... ᵃ Or, *departed wondering with himself.*

12. Then (or, *But*) **arose Peter, and ran unto the sepulchre,** etc. This movement seems likely to have been the same as that recorded in John (20: 3-10); and if it was, it had taken place earlier in the day, when Mary Magdalene first reported that the Lord was gone from the tomb. **Stooping down**—may indicate that the entrance to the tomb was of slight elevation in the hill-side, or that it ran sloping into a subterranean chamber.—**He beheld the linen clothes laid** (rather, *lying*) **by themselves**—literally, *alone; i. e.,* apart from any corpse. This was evidence that the body had not been snatched away, but that care had been taken in leaving the place. This idea is, however, much more fully expressed in the parallel passage of John, who gives the account which had possibly served as a source of this statement in Luke.—**In himself.** This is more probably to be referred to the verb **departed,** signifying, *departed to himself; i. e.,* to his own house=went home. We seem rather to need information whither he went, than as to the sphere of his wonder. The expression "to himself," in this sense, suggests at once the French, (*chez soi*) *to his home;* and Kypke, on the passage, gives many examples of a similar use of the Greek phrase. Peter was yet in that state of wonder which involves study and leads to knowledge. Tischendorf omits this verse; Tregelles brackets it; Westcott and Hort enclose it in double brackets; but the Revision rightly retains it as probably authentic.

13-32. Jesus manifests himself to two disciples at Emmaus.

13. Two of them went (rather, *were going*) **that same day to a village called Emmaus,** etc. These two were, apparently, of "the rest." (**Ver. 9;** comp. **ver. 33.**) The site of this village is still a matter of search, as no place bearing the name has been discovered at a distance of about seven miles from Jerusalem. The place called Culonieh, N. N. W. of Jerusalem, is by many thought to be the spot. That seems like the Latin *Colonia,* which might not unnaturally be applied to that Ammaus where Josephus says (*Jewish Wars,* vii., 6. 6) that Titus Cesar settled eight hundred veteran soldiers. The distance of this place, however, from Jerusalem, is dubious, from the various texts of Josephus. [It seems very probable, if not perfectly certain, that the site of Emmaus has at last been ascertained, through the enterprise of Mrs. Finn, widow of the late James Finn, British Consul for Jerusalem and Palestine from 1845 till 1863. In a paper contributed by her to the "Quarterly Statement of the Palestine Exploration Fund," for January, 1883, is an account of the steps by which she was led to the discovery of this site. "The etymology of the name Emmaus led us to the conclusion that, wherever the Emmaus of St. Luke might be, there must also have existed hot baths; and the modern Arabic use of the term Hammâm, as applied to baths generally, whether of natural hot springs or of water artificially heated, led us further to the idea that St. Luke's Emmaus need not be a place of hot springs, but that it might be a place where abundance of water had caused the establishment of artificial baths of some importance. We convinced ourselves, before long, that there is but one place, within the circuit of sixty furlongs from Jerusalem, where there is a sufficiently copious spring of water for the supply of baths. *That place is the pretty valley of Urtas, which is about seven and one-half Roman miles, or sixty furlongs, from Jerusalem, south of Bethlehem.* The valley descends from the ancient Etham (the fountain of which still bears that name), and passes round the base of the Herodium (or Frank Mountain), on its way to the Dead Sea. These two places, Etham and Herodium, are among those whose distance from Jerusalem is specified by Josephus. He tells us that Etham was fifty furlongs off (*Antiquities,* viii., 7, 3), and that Herodium was sixty furlongs off (*Antiquities,* xiv., 13, 9). Urtas, village and spring, lies between the two." See the article referred

14 And they talked together of all these things which had happened.
15 And it came to pass, that, while they communed *together* and reasoned, *a* Jesus himself drew near, and went with them.
16 But *b* their eyes were holden that they should not know him.
17 And he said unto them, What manner of communications *are* these that ye have one to another, as ye walk, and are sad?
18 And the one of them, *c* whose name was Cleopas, answering said, unto him, Art thou only a stranger in Jerusalem, and hast not known the things which are come to pass there in these days?
19 And he said unto them, What things? And they said unto him, Concerning Jesus of Nazareth, *d* which was a prophet, *e* mighty in deed and word before God and all the people:
20 *f* And how the chief priests and our rulers delivered him to be condemned to death, and have crucified him.
21 But we trusted *g* that it had been he which should have redeemed Israel: and beside all this, to day is the third day since these things were done.
22 Yea, and *h* certain women also of our company made us astonished, which were early at the sepulchre;
23 And when they found not his body, they came, saying, that they had also seen a vision of angels, which said that he was alive.
24 And *i* certain of them which were with us went to the sepulchre, and found *it* even so as the women had said: but him they saw not.

14 score furlongs from Jerusalem. And they communed with each other of all these things which
15 had happened. And it came to pass, while they communed and questioned together, that Jesus him-
16 self drew near, and went with them. But their eyes
17 were holden that they should not know him. And he said unto them, ¹What communications are these that ye have one with another, as ye walk? And
18 they stood still, looking sad. And one of them, named Cleopas, answering said unto him, ²Dost thou alone sojourn in Jerusalem and not know the things
19 which are come to pass there in these days? And he said unto them, What things? And they said unto him, The things concerning Jesus of Nazareth, who was a prophet mighty in deed and word before
20 God and all the people: and how the chief priests and our rulers delivered him up to be condemned to
21 death, and crucified him. But we hoped that it was he that should redeem Israel. Yea and beside all this, it is now the third day since these things came
22 to pass. Moreover certain women of our company
23 amazed us, having been early at the tomb; and when they found not his body, they came, saying, that they had also seen a vision of angels, who said
24 that he was alive. And certain of them that were with us went to the tomb, and found it even so as

a Matt. 18: 20; ver. 36....*b* John 20: 14; 21: 4....*c* John 19: 25....*d* Matt. 21: 11; ch. 7: 16; John 3: 2; 4: 19; 6: 14; Acts 2: 22....*e* Acts 7: 22....*f* ch. 21: 1; Acts 13: 27, 28....*g* ch. 1: 68; 2: 38; Acts 1: 6....*h* Matt. 28: 8; Mark 16: 10; ver. 9, 10; John 20: 18....*i* ver. 12.——
1 Gr. *What words are these that ye exchange one with another*....2 Or. *Dost thou sojourn alone in Jerusalem, and knowest thou not the things.*

---

to for the full evidence, which appears to be satisfactory.—A. H.] The men, probably, started early in the forenoon.

14. Talked together (better, *communed one with another*), as in the next verse.

15. Communed together and reasoned —(more exactly, *questioned*, or *debated together*). The subject engaged their deepest interest, and they were discussing with each other the possible reconciliation of difficulties and clearing up of their perplexity. This absorption in the theme of their discourse might itself have hindered their noticing particularly the man who **drew near and went**=was journeying—**with them.**

16. But their eyes were holden, etc. This was an additional, and, apparently, a divinely ordered impediment to their recognizing him. Their vision was supernaturally restrained. Comp. verse 31. Mark (16: 12) simply represents Jesus as being manifested "in another form."

17. What (omit **manner of**) **communications are these?** etc. The literal translation is, *What words are these which ye throw back and forth to each other?* As though their discourse was of the nature of an inconclusive discussion. See the Revision for the last part of the verse, though the text is doubtful. .

18. And the one of them, whose name was Cleopas, answering said. Omit the before **one**. The mention of the name would guide some of the first readers of the Gospel to a definite person; to us, it is only a name. **Art thou only a stranger,** etc., (or, *Dost thou alone sojourn in Jerusalem, and not know?* etc.) The sense is, "Art thou the only one sojourning in Jerusalem without becoming aware of these all-important events"? The men are themselves so full of the fate of Jesus, that they see not how even a stranger, as they judge him to be, there only for the feast, can fail to be thinking of the same subject as themselves. If he is not, he must be the only such man.

19-24. The Saviour, in order that he may the more precisely adapt himself to their state of mind, chooses to draw out their sentiment in their own words. Accordingly, in answer to his question, **What things?** they intimate that they have viewed Jesus as a mighty prophet, whom the rulers have had unjustly condemned and crucified. Would Peter and the other ten, at this time, have failed to speak of Jesus as the Messiah? Even the confession of these two implies such a conception of him; for they had **trusted** (rather, *hoped*) **that it had been** (or, *was*) **he**—he, and none other—

25 Then he said unto them, O fools, and slow of heart to believe all that the prophets have spoken:
26 ^aOught not Christ to have suffered these things, and to enter into his glory?
27 ^bAnd beginning at ^cMoses and ^dall the prophets, he expounded unto them in all the scriptures the things concerning himself.
28 And they drew nigh unto the village, whither they went: and ^ehe made as though he would have gone further.
29 But ^fthey constrained him, saying, Abide with us: for it is toward evening, and the day is far spent. And he went in to tarry with them.

25 the women had said: but him they saw not. And he said unto them, O foolish men, and slow of heart to believe ¹in all that the prophets have spoken!
26 Behoved it not the Christ to suffer these things, and
27 to enter into his glory? And beginning from Moses and from all the prophets, he interpreted to them in all the scriptures the things concerning himself.
28 And they drew nigh unto the village, whither they were going: and he made as though he would go
29 further. And they constrained him, saying, Abide with us: for it is toward evening, and the day is now

<small>a ver. 46; Acts 17: 3; 1 Pet. 1: 11....b ver. 45....c Gen. 3: 15; 22: 18; 26: 4; 49: 10; Num. 21: 9; Deut. 18: 15....d Ps. 16: 9, 10; 22; 142: 11; Isa. 7: 14; 9: 6; 40: 10, 11; 50: 6; 53; Jer. 23: 5; 33: 14, 15; Ezek. 34; 23: 37: 25; Dan. 9: 24; Micah 7: 20; Mal. 3: 1; 4: 2.
See on John 1: 44.....e See Gen. 32: 26; 32: 7; Mark 6: 48..../Gen. 19: 3; Acts 16: 15.—1 Or. after.</small>

which should have redeemed (*would redeem*) **Israel.** Yet their hope has been disappointed. Their emphasis on the fact that **to day is the third day,** shows that they recall his prediction about rising on that day; but this may, quite probably, have been brought to them by the women's report of what the angels had said on that subject. They relate the mission of the women to the tomb, that morning, and, probably, that of Peter (ver. 12); whether of John, also (John 20: 3)? —**Certain of them which were with us.** There had two or more gone to the tomb, within the knowledge of these men, and so within that of Luke. As he had not related the event, it shows that he was not aiming to tell all he knew. These last had **found it even so as the women had said**—in respect, namely, to the absence of the body, and perhaps, to the presence of the angels. The result of it all was, that they find themselves intellectually perplexed; while their sentiment of attachment to the Great Teacher is affectionate and strong.

25. Then he said unto them, O fools—(better, *foolish men*). It is not the strong term, "fools," but, rather, "unintelligent," "without due understanding."—**And slow of heart**—sluggish and backward in disposition—**to believe**(*in*) **all that the prophets have spoken.** The Saviour recognizes a state of the heart and readiness of the will as entering, equally with clearness of understanding, into the conditions of faith. A strong emphasis lies on the word **all.** They had overlooked the prophecies of suffering and death.

26. Ought not Christ to have suffered, etc. The Revision is better: *Behoved it not the Christ to suffer these things?*—rejection at the hands of men, humiliation, pain, and death. Did not God's purpose concerning the Messiah, as indicated in the Scriptures, involve all this? **And to enter into his glory.** Was not this also a part of that purpose, which could be accomplished only through the Messiah's death? "Thus St. Luke mainly dwells on the resurrection as a spiritual necessity; St. Mark as a great fact; St. Matthew as a glorious and majestic manifestation; and St. John in its effects on the minds of the members of the church." Farrar, epitomizing Westcott.

27. And beginning at (strictly *from*) **Moses**—touching on all the Messianic intimations in the Pentateuch—**and** (*from*) **all the prophets**—and going through with the prophecies in them pertaining to himself—**he expounded unto them in all the Scriptures the things concerning himself.** Of course it was only a selection out of all the Scriptures, that the time would allow him to expound. Besides Moses=the law, and the prophets, there was that third section, as the Jews classified the books, the Hagiographa, or "holy writings," including particularly the Psalms and other poetical books. (See ver. 44). If Luke could have imparted to us the instruction communicated in that discourse, developing the true sense of the prophecies, from the opening Gospel of Genesis 3: 15, to the Sun of Righteousness, Mal. 4: 2, what volumes of groping discussion in later ages might we well have spared!

28. And he made as though he would have gone (rather *go*) **further**—*i. e.,* he carried forward the part still, in which he had acted, of one traveling in the same direction with them, and would have gone on if they had not besought him to tarry. It was his general course to bestow his blessings upon faith, in answer to prayer.

29. And they constrained him—practiced a sort of gentle violence upon him—**saying, Abide with us; for it is toward**

30 And it came to pass, as he sat at meat with them, he took bread, and blessed it, and brake, and gave to them.
31 And their eyes were opened, and they knew him; and he vanished out of their sight.
32 And they said one to another, Did not our heart burn within us, while he talked with us by the way, and while he opened to us the scriptures?

30 far spent. And he went in to abide with them. And it came to pass, when he had sat down with them to meat, he took the ¹ bread, and blessed; and breaking
31 it, he gave to them. And their eyes were opened, and they knew him; and he vanished out of their sight.
32 And they said one to another, Was not our heart burning within us, while he spake to us in the

a Matt. 14:19.——1 Or, *loaf.*

---

evening, and the day is (*already*) far spent. His conversation may have whiled away some hours, between walking and rest. They would have had him spend the night with them. And he went in to tarry—*i. e., abide*—with them. It was apparently their own house, or that of one of them. He simply granted their prayer; the word "abide," in this sentence, being from the same Greek as that in the preceding sentence. It is applicable to a longer or shorter stay.

30. And it came to pass, as he sat at (better, *when he had sat down to*) meat—reclined at table—with them, he took (*the*) bread—Greek, *the loaf*—and blessed it, and brake, and gave to them. *Offered praise*—would be a better rendering than blessed it. The Saviour's assumption of the headship of the table must have seemed strange to the two disciples, even if, as some suppose, they were tarrying at an inn; still more so, if it was at their own house. An old Jewish rule, reported in later books, makes it obligatory to say grace where there are three at the table. Had these disciples been of the eleven, we might naturally think the meal intended as the repetition of the Supper three nights before. Still we should feel that there was much lacking to the proper description of such a meal. And as these two disciples had not been present at the institution of the Lord's Supper, they could not be reminded of that. It was rather in the way of his usual custom of praising God for his goodness, at the beginning of a meal, that the Saviour now proceeded. This disposes at once of various dogmatic inferences of Roman Catholics and others.

31. And their eyes were opened, and they knew—*recognized*—him. Here was a divine act performed upon them, at the moment of his distributing the bread, which did away with the restraining influence spoken of (ver. 16); their eyes were no longer "holden," and in the peculiar spirit and manner of his opening their meal, they perceived that it was he. And he vanished out of their sight. As suddenly and mysteriously as he had drawn near (ver. 16), he now disappeared. He did not go—but was gone. Already we discern that air of mystery, materiality spiritualized, which hangs around the whole manifestation of our Lord, during the forty days of his resurrection life. To some he was visible at certain times, but not at all times; and to others not at any time. Now his organic frame appears in the solidity of a human body, and subject to ordinary human conditions; and again, it moves as unrestrictedly as if it were a bodiless soul.

32. Now they realized what they had lost. Did not our heart burn within us, while he talked with us by the way, and while he opened to us the Scriptures? Better, as in the Revision. The omission of and by the best texts, makes the opening the Scriptures more manifestly the same thing as the talking to them in the way. The heart *burning within* them denotes that indescribable fervor of religious interest awakened in their hearts by the clear apprehension of truth concerning God, and his plan of redemption through Christ. Opening the Scriptures to one is, plainly, causing one rightly to appreciate the truth there written, in its appropriateness to the seeking soul. It was an unspeakable privilege to have Christ humanly near, to aid in this; and, thanks to his name! he is equally present to the prayerful, trusting heart, through the Comforter whom he sends at all times. Very appropriately, Farrar, on the passage, cites, upon this account of Christ's interview with the brethren at Emmaus, Cowper's beautiful application of the narrative, in his poem *Conversation*, at the passage beginning:

> It happened on a solemn eventide,
> Soon after he that was our surety died.

Cowper piously moralizes upon the incident:

> Now theirs was converse such as it behooves
> Man to maintain, and such as God approves.

33 And they rose up the same hour, and returned to Jerusalem, and found the eleven gathered together, and them that were with them,
34 Saying, The Lord is risen indeed, and *a* hath appeared to Simon.
35 And they told what things *were done* in the way, and how he was known of them in breaking of bread.
36 *b* And as they thus spake, Jesus himself stood in the midst of them, and saith unto them, Peace *be* unto you.
37 But they were terrified and affrighted, and supposed that they had seen *c* a spirit.
38 And he said unto them, Why are ye troubled? and why do thoughts arise in your hearts?
39 Behold my hands and my feet, that it is I myself: *d* handle me, and see; for a spirit hath not flesh and bones, as ye see me have.
40 And when he had thus spoken, he shewed them *his* hands and *his* feet.
41 And while they yet believed not *e* for joy, and wondered, he said unto them, *f* Have ye here any meat?
42 And they gave him a piece of a broiled fish, and of an honeycomb.
43 *g* And he took *it*, and did eat before them.

33 way, while he opened to us the scriptures? And they rose up that very hour, and returned to Jerusalem, and found the eleven gathered together, and
34 them that were with them, saying, The Lord hath
35 risen indeed, and hath appeared to Simon. And they rehearsed the things *that happened* in the way, and how he was known of them in the breaking of the bread.
36 And as they spake these things, he himself stood in the midst of them, *1* and saith unto them, Peace
37 *be* unto you. But they were terrified and affrighted,
38 and supposed that they beheld a spirit. And he said unto them, Why are ye troubled? and wherefore
39 do questionings arise in your heart? See my hands and my feet, that it is I myself: handle me, and see; for a spirit hath not flesh and bones, as ye behold me
40 having. *2* And when he had said this, he shewed
41 them his hands and his feet. And while they still disbelieved for joy, and wondered, he said unto
42 them, Have ye here anything to eat? And they
43 gave him a piece of a broiled fish. *3* And he took it, and did eat before them.

a 1 Cor. 15 : 5....*b* Mark 16 : 14; John 20 : 19; 1 Cor. 15 : 5....*c* Mark 6 : 49....*d* John 20 : 20, 27....*e* Gen. 45 : 26..../ John 21 : 5....*g* Acts 10 : 41.—*1* Some ancient authorities omit, *and saith unto them, Peace be unto you*....*2* Some ancient authorities omit ver. 40....*3* Many ancient authorities add, *and a honeycomb*.

33-35. Return of the two disciples to Jerusalem. Exchange of reports with the eleven and others.

33. And they rose up the same hour, etc. Joy would lend speed to their steps, and whether a return that night had been in their plan or not, they were back in Jerusalem before the evening had passed. With haste, we may suppose that less than two hours would suffice.

34. The eleven anticipate them in announcing an appearance of the Lord to Peter. It was the eleven who said, **The Lord is risen,** etc. The fact that Luke has not mentioned that in his narrative, shows that he selects his facts out of an ample store. Comp. on verse 34.

35. And they told, etc.—namely, Cleopas and his companion. **They** is emphatic; "they, on their part." The disbelief ascribed to the eleven, in Mark 16: 13, 14, had reference to this particular appearance, and might rest on the supposed improbability that Christ should be in widely separated places at or near the same time.

36-49. Christ surprises the company, convinces them, gives them their commission.

36. And as they thus spake (lit., *spoke these things*)—in the very warmth of their agitated conference concerning him—**Jesus** (rather, *he*) **himself stood in the midst of them.** Here, again, no coming on his part is reported; but while their discourse went on, there he stood! The effect of such an apparition might well be to excite timidity and fear, in spite of what they had heard of his being alive—nay, indeed, specially on that account. He therefore adds, **Peace be unto you.** It was the familiar salutation which they had a hundred times received at his lips. Even thus, it is not surprising that his presence, in that manner, as of one from the invisible world, filled them with a joyful but wondering awe.

37. But they were terrified and affrighted, and supposed that they had seen (better, *saw*) **a spirit.** The perturbation of mind is mentioned as a reason for their mistake; literally, *becoming terrified and affrighted, they supposed*, etc. The same popular delusion, that the disembodied spirits appear in the semblance of a body, led the apostles once before to imagine that Christ, walking on the water in the night, was a ghost. (Matt. 14: 26; Mark 6: 49.) The word they used then was "phantasm," or "spectre," but meaning, as here, "a ghost." Luke makes no mention of reproach to them (comp. Mark 16 : 14), which was even more called for here, when they not only disbelieved the testimony of those who had seen him risen, but that of their own eyes; but he shows us the forbearance of the Lord in reasoning with them, and giving them demonstrative proof.

38. Why are ye troubled? and why do thoughts arise in your hearts (*wherefore do reasonings*) **arise in your hearts?** Their feelings were abnormally disturbed, and there were intellectual struggles against the legitimate conclusion, from the sight of him, that he was really alive.

39-43. He gave them three "infallible proofs" that it was indeed he, the Jesus whom

44 And he said unto them, *These are* the words which I spake unto you, while I was yet with you, that all things must be fulfilled, which were written in the law of Moses, and in the prophets, and in the psalms, concerning me.
45 Then *b* opened he their understanding, that they might understand the scriptures,
46 And said unto them, *c* Thus it is written, and thus

44 And he said unto them, These are my words which I spake unto you, while I was yet with you, how that all things must needs be fulfilled, which are written in the law of Moses, and the prophets, 45 and the psalms, concerning me. Then opened he their mind, that they might understand the scriptures; 46 tures; and he said unto them, Thus it is written, that the Christ should suffer, and rise again from the

a Matt. 16: 21; 17: 22; 20: 18; Mark 8: 31; ch. 9: 22; 18: 31; ver. 6....*b* Acts 16: 14....*c* ver. 26; Ps. 22; Isa. 50: 6; 53: 2, etc.; Acts 17: 3.

they had known, in his proper person, and no spectre; first, by causing them to see his scarred hands and feet (ver. 39, 40), from which we learn that the feet of Jesus had been *nailed* to the cross; secondly, by letting them feel him that he was not a mere semblance of Jesus, but himself bodily. In regard to this, as bearing on the relation of his person to the glorified, spiritual body (comp. 1 Cor. 15: 50), we can only speculate, and that to little use. We are, perhaps, warranted, from what the chapter tells us, in concluding that our Saviour was in an absolutely unique condition, belonging of right to the future life, but called by his office to maintain a recognizable relation to his disciples here a little longer. Thirdly, he **did eat before them a piece of a broiled fish,** which they gave him. The clause **and of a honeycomb** is a late addition, being absent from all the four earliest manuscripts which contain the passage. Nothing further, surely, could be needed to scatter all their doubts.

44-47. Harmony of all that has occurred in his case with the Scriptures.

44. And he said unto them, These are the (correct reading. *my*) **words which I spake unto you,** etc. Some harmonists make the following discourse parallel to what is related in Acts 1: 4 ff., as if an interval of near forty days had passed. But there is no hint of any such separation in the record; on the contrary, Luke connects this to the preceding precisely as if Christ went on naturally from verse 43. The section is to be regarded as a provisional and private instruction, followed by a commission, different from the public and more formal declarations in Matt. 28: 18-20; Mark 16: 15-18; and Acts 1: 4-8. **These are** *my* **words.** These events, pertaining to my death and resurrection, are the fulfillment of my words, **which I spake unto you.** See the references at verse 6. **While I was yet with you.** He looks back on the relations existing before his death, as now ended; he is no longer with them, except transiently and at intervals, and not at all to continue work like that in which he was then engaged. **That all things must be fulfilled.** This, namely, was the purport of the words which I spake unto you. Jesus often referred his disciples to prophecies in their Scriptures which must be fulfilled by action or suffering on his part; and John represents him (ch. 19: 28) as declaring his thirst on the cross, in order that a typical prophecy in Ps. 69: 21 might be fulfilled by his drinking of the vinegar. Then all had been fulfilled. **Which were** (*are*) **written in the law of Moses,** etc. This is the fullest description that we have of the contents of the Old Testament, as arranged in his day (see above on ver. 27). There were, and are now, in the Hebrew Bibles, three Divisions: (1) the Law (five books of Moses); (2) the Prophets, including the historical books from Joshua to II. Kings, except Ruth (called the Former Prophets), and what we call the Prophets, except Daniel (the Later Prophets); (3) the Writings in Latin, named *Hagiographa* (including all the other books of the Old Testament). As the Psalms are the first, and, in a prophetic aspect, the most important portion of this Division, the Saviour here calls the whole, by *synecdoche*, the Psalms. Generally he is content to speak of the whole as the Law and the Prophets; but here would indicate the necessity of fulfilling everything in the whole Bible.

45. Then opened he their understanding that they might understand the Scriptures. This seems to describe an effect produced in them such that they were thenceforward to be capable of discerning the true sense of any prophecy of the Old Testament. Blessed power! What could it be but a larger measure of the Spirit by which the prophets were borne on, when they uttered their messages from God? (Comp. ver. 32; Ps. 119: 18; 1 Cor. 2: 10 ff.; Matt. 11: 27; 16: 17; John 16: 13.). The lack of this power was shown in ch. 18: 34.

46. And said unto them, Thus it is

it behooved Christ to suffer, and to rise from the dead the third day:
47 And that repentance and ^a remission of sins should be preached in his name ^b among all nations, beginning at Jerusalem.
48 And ^c ye are witnesses of these things.
49 ^d And, behold, I send the promise of my Father upon you: but tarry ye in the city of Jerusalem, until ye be endued with power from on high.
50 And he led them out ^e as far as to Bethany, and he lifted up his hands, and blessed them.

47 dead the third day; and that repentance ¹ and remission of sins should be preached in his name unto 48 all the ² nations, beginning from Jerusalem. Ye are 49 witnesses of these things. And behold, I send forth the promise of my Father upon you: but tarry ye in the city, until ye be clothed with power from on high.
50 And he led them out until *they were* over against Bethany: and he lifted up his hands, and blessed

a Dan. 9: 24; Acts 13. 38, 46; 1 John 2: 12....b Gen. 12: 3; Ps. 22: 27; Isa. 49: 6, 22; Jer. 31: 34; Hosea 2: 23; Micah 4: 2; Mal. 1: 11'....c John 15: 27; Acts 1: 8, 22; 2: 32; 3: 15....d Isa. 41: 3; Joel 2: 28; John 14: 16, 26; 15: 26; 16: 7; Acts 1: 4: 2: 1. etc...e Acts 1: 12.—1 Some ancient authorities read, *unto*....2 Or, *nations*. *Beginning from Jerusalem, ye are witnesses.*

written, and thus it behooved Christ to suffer. Better, as in the Revision. See Psa. 22; Isa. 50: 5-9; 53; comp. Acts 17: 3. The words, **and thus it behooved,** are wanting in all the more important MSS.—**And to rise from the dead the third day.** See Psa. 16: 10, 11; comp. Acts 2: 25-32; 13: 33-35. The absence of passages in the Old Testament clearly applicable to the clause **on the third day** (our Saviour found this typically foreshadowed in the restoration of Jonah, after three days), may have caused the words **and thus it behooved** to be added as an explanatory gloss. But our Saviour passes freely from the things expressly spoken beforehand about him, to those which were logically or historically involved in them. This remark applies especially to the next verse, which also comes in here as a part of the things which were written, because, to the Saviour's mind, they are a mere extension of that.

47. And that repentance and (or, *for*) **remission of sins should be preached,** etc. The Greek order of the words implies some emphasis on **preached;** "and that proclamation should be made in his name of repentance and remission of sins unto all the nations," etc. This indicates prominently the next step that was to be taken, now that the provision for universal pardon has been made through his death and resurrection. It leads, also, to the announcement of their function in the matter, in the next verse.—**Beginning at Jerusalem.** "To the Jew first, and also to the Greek" (Rom. 1: 16). Although the nation had sold its birthright to primacy in the kingdom of God, as proposed to them by the Messiah personally, the offer should be still extended to them, under the Dispensation of the Spirit, through the witness to his resurrection. Comp. Acts 3: 19-26.

48. And ye are witnesses of these things. And is no part of the text, and should be omitted. This verse describes the primary function of the apostles, and eye-witnesses generally, of the risen Jesus. **These things** are the same that he has been so designating in verses 26, 44; namely, those pertaining to his resurrection from the grave, implying the fact of his death and burial, as it occurred. Of course, these naturally drew after them the account of his whole public life. Comp. Acts 1: 8, 21 ff. Here is no formal consecration to an office; that had already been done, so far as was necessary; but it was a statement of the first and most important duty involved in the office of the apostles, and which every disciple could discharge, in his measure, who had seen Christ alive from the dead. How clearly the apostles recognized this as their duty; see the last reference above, and Acts 2: 32; 3: 15; as well as the tenor of their whole proclamation throughout the Acts.

49. And, behold, I send the promise of my Father upon you. The compound verb used means *send forth*. **The promise** means the special influence of the Spirit of God, promised Joel 2: 28. Comp. Isa. 44: 3; John 14: 16, 17, 26; 15: 26; 16: 7; Acts 1: 5, 8. This would be the indispensable prerequisite to the discharge of their office. Comp. 1 Cor. 2: 12-16. Not yet fully understanding this, they might be inclined to go forth on their mission prematurely.—**But tarry ye**—sit ye down—**in the city of Jerusalem, until ye be endued** (*i. e., clothed*) **with power from on high**—that power which only the reception of the Spirit could impart. See, again, Acts 1: 8.

50-53. THE ASCENSION.
50. And he led them out as far as to Bethany. This also (comp. on ver 44) is added as though no space of time came between it and the preceding discourse; but all followed on the evening of the resurrection day. Yet we find, in Acts 1: 3-10, that Luke was distinctly aware that Jesus had continued

354 LUKE. [Ch. XXIV.

51 *a* And it came to pass, while he blessed them, he was parted from them, and carried up into heaven.
52 *b* And they worshipped him, and returned to Jerusalem with great joy:
53 And were continually *c* in the temple, praising and blessing God. Amen.

51 them. And it came to pass, while he blessed them, he parted from them, ¹and was carried up into
52 heaven. And they ²worshipped him, and returned
53 to Jerusalem with great joy: and were continually in the temple, blessing God.

---

a 2 Kings 2 : 11 ; Mark 16 : 19 ; John 20 : 17 ; Acts 1 : 9 ; Ephes. 4 : 8....*b* Matt. 28 : 9, 17....*c* Acts 2 : 46 ; 5 : 42.——1 Some ancient authorities omit, *and was carried up into heaven*....2 Some ancient authorities omit, *worshipped him, and*.

---

on the earth forty days longer. During that time took place the meeting with the eleven (John 20: 26-29), when Thomas was present, and the last disbeliever was convinced; his appearance to seven of the apostles, in the familiar scene by the Sea of Tiberias (John 21: 1-24); and again to the eleven, in the mountain in Galilee (Matt. 28: 16-20; Mark 16: 15-18), where he formally renewed and expanded their apostolic commission. Some have supposed that at the time of writing his Gospel, Luke had not learned clearly this succession of events, but was informed of it before he composed the Acts. As Paul, however, with whom Luke was so intimately associated, had shown before this (1Cor. 15: 4-7) that he knew well of a considerable interval between the resurrection and the ascension, it is hard to believe that Luke did not understand it before he wrote first. It is more probable that Luke, knowing well that some time elapsed before the ascension, but expecting to speak of that more fully in his later treatise, now threw into one view, "a perspective view," as it has been called, all which he thought it necessary to communicate now concerning the interval before the ascension, and the ascension itself. Some think that an intimation of successive stages of the history is given, in the repetition took place, is not precisely indicated. Tradition fixed the scene as at the highest summit of the ridge. It is as likely to have been in some retired nook near his beloved Bethany. The phrase **as far as to Bethany** marks the *terminus ad quem* of his movement without obliging us to think that he entered the village.—**And he lifted up his hands**—the attitude of invocation—**and blessed them**—besought, with thanksgiving and praise, God's blessing on them. We may imagine what intensity and fullness of desire breathed through his prayer.

51. The verse paints his departure. While he was in the act and attitude of blessing them, **he was** (omit **was**) **parted from them**. This is expressed in the Greek, naturally, as an instantaneous act; while the next verb causes the mind to dwell on the movement—**and carried up into heaven**—borne on a cloud, as we see in the Acts, slowly and visibly, before their eyes. The upward direction accorded with the popular conception of the celestial locality, as above the firmament—a conception almost inevitable for everyone, since the traditions of language have identified the blessed abodes with the sky. This sentence is omitted from the text by Tischendorf, and is admitted by other high authorities to be doubtful; but three of the five chief ancient manuscripts have it, and it is rightly retained in the Revision.

52. The same remark applies to the text of the first clause here. **And they worshipped him**—not as if now first seen to be worthy of divine honor (comp. Matt. 28: 9, 19), but now, doubtless, with a special reverence and adoration. **And returned to Jerusalem with great joy.** Their Saviour had entered into his glory, and they were sure of sharing the same when he should return to take them to himself. What strength and zeal, to do and bear, would this manifest demonstration of the triumph of their Leader and Head impart to these favored witnesses, and, through their testimony, to the first generations of those who believed on him through their word!

53. And were continually in the temple, praising and blessing God. The best MSS. omit **praising**. The temple, which has been the scene for so many ages of all authorized public worship of the true God, and which Jesus has consecrated to their hearts by his participation with them there, will not readily be forsaken by the disciples. The Master has taught them to tarry about it for the present, and great changes in their assembling to themselves. (vers. 43.). **Blessing God.** All their view of him would now be brightened by the light from the Sun of Righteousness; the types and shadows of their ceremonies would gradually become clear and significant, through their acquaintance with the antitype and substance of them all. views of what is involved in the gospel will be required, before they can willingly desert it. The Acts will show the history of that change. **Continually**—that is, whenever the appointed services called them thither; but not so as to prevent their having a place of

NOTE.
See verses 66-71, page 327.

Was our Saviour subjected to one, two, or three examinations before Jewish authorities at this time? The prima facie impression made as we read severally and compare the four records is, unquestionably, that there were three. On that view, the interpretation given above proceeds. In John xviii. 13-24, as the Revision correctly reads and renders ver. 24, we have a simple, interesting, and thoroughly self-consistent scene, in the house of Annas. He is called "high priest," as in Luke iii. 2; Acts iv. 6, although Caiaphas is stated to be formally such that year, and is particularly so named, as if to make the proper distinction, when Jesus is finally sent over to the house of Caiaphas. For when the cruel and haughty Annas makes nothing by his impertinent questions to his prisoner; but brings on himself implied rebuke for his permission of illegal violence toward him—"Annas *therefore* sent him [not to be *translated* 'had sent,' even if there were much probability that it should be so interpreted] bound unto Caiaphas, the high-priest." (John 18: 24.)

Matthew xxvi. 57, 59-68; Mark xiv. 53, 55-65, give an account of another pretence of inquest in the house of Caiaphas, before a considerable body of chief priests and other councillors, for the assembling of whom time may have been given by the delay with Annas. In the court of this house goes forward the same testing of Peter which had begun in the court of Annas' house. Nothing is reported by these writers of such questions as had been put to Jesus by Annas; but the result is a mock judgment that he is worthy of death. All this took place deep in the night. The first two Evangelists allude also to a session of the formal and complete council after daybreak.

Of this session, Luke, in the passage above considered, furnishes the only detailed report. Of this alone does he give any report, indeed; perhaps, because it alone could pretend to a legal, or even reasonable formality, or give a shape to their indictment of Jesus which they would dare to lay before the Governor.

Here are thus three distinct, important, complementary accounts of the so-called trial, with quite intelligible reasons why they should all be given. Probably thousands, in the beginning of the written Gospel, having each only one of the four records, lived and died in the belief that each had a veritable narrative of the transaction. Were they misled? We, having all the four, and minutely comparing them, may desiderate fuller information to harmonize them perfectly. But surely they present no extraordinary perplexities. We have noticed all that occur in the exposition of Luke. The simple and long-familiar hypothesis of a domicile for Annas, such that its large inner court was the court also of that of Caiaphas, clears away the chief difficulty.

A word further on this topic seemed called for since Edersheim just now, in his very valuable *Life and Times of Jesus*, also supposes John to bring Jesus before Annas for nothing; and that what seems to be an interview with the latter, was really with Caiaphas. Not so Weiss, nor Westcott, in his *Commentary on John*. But Mr. H. C. Vedder, in a learned and able monograph on the Trial of Jesus, in the *Bibliotheca Sacra* for October, 1882, maintains the identity of the examination of Annas with that before the assembly of notables with Caiaphas. Confining attention to his ingenious and suggestive diatessaron, one will hardly escape his conclusion. But, as we have stated, the impression made by the respective narratives seems to us different. The important thing is, that we should not, for the sake of a form of harmony, introduce into the testimony of John, an inconsistency more serious than any seeming discrepancy between him and the other Gospels.

www.ingramcontent.com/pod-product-compliance
Lightning Source LLC
Chambersburg PA
CBHW030256240426
43673CB00040B/987